LUDWIG WITTGENSTEIN: CRITICAL ASSESSMENTS

LUDWIG WITTGENSTEIN
Cambridge, 1946

By kind permission of Timothy Moore

LUDWIG WITTGENSTEIN

Critical Assessments

Edited by Stuart Shanker

Volume Three

From the *Tractatus* to *Remarks on the Foundations of Mathematics*:
Wittgenstein on the Philosophy of Mathematics

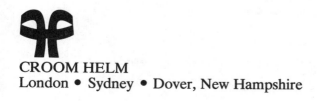

CROOM HELM
London • Sydney • Dover, New Hampshire

Introduction and editorial matter © 1986 Stuart Shanker
Collection © 1986 Croom Helm

Croom Helm Ltd, Provident House, Burrell Row,
Beckenham, Kent BR3 1AT
Croom Helm Australia Pty Ltd, Suite 4, 6th Floor,
64-76 Kippax Street, Surry Hills, NSW 2010, Australia

British Library Cataloguing in Publication Data

Ludwig Wittgenstein: critical assessments.
   1. Wittgenstein, Ludwig
   I. Shanker, Stuart
   192   B3376.W564

     ISBN 0-7099-2384-8

Croom Helm Ltd, Washington Street,
Dover, New Hampshire 03820, USA

Library of Congress Cataloging in Publication Data

Main entry under title:

Ludwig Wittgenstein: Critical assessments
  Bibliography: p.
  Includes index.
    Contents: V.1. From the Notebooks to Philosophical Grammar — V.2. From
Philosophical Investigations to On Certainty — V.3. From the Tractatus to Remarks on the
Foundations of Mathematics — (etc.)
    1. Wittgenstein, Ludwig, 1899-1951 — addresses, essays, lectures. I. Shanker, S. G.
(Stuart G.) II.Shanker, V. A.
B3376. W564L77 1986   192   85-29886
ISBN 0-7099-2384-8

Typeset in 10pt Times Roman by Leaper & Gard Ltd, Bristol, England
Printed and bound in Great Britain by
Biddles Ltd, Guildford and King's Lynn

Contents

Acknowledgements

The following articles in this volume are reproduced by kind permission of the authors and/or their publishers:

Steven Savitt, 'Wittgenstein's Early Philosophy of Mathematics', *Philosophy Research Archives*, vol. 5 (1979).

T.F. Baxley, 'Wittgenstein's Theory of Quantification', *International Logic Review*, vol. XI, no. 1 (1980), pp. 46-55.

Intisar-ul-Haque, 'Wittgenstein on Number', *International Philosophical Quarterly*, vol. 18 (1978).

Friedrich Waismann, 'The Nature of Mathematics: Wittgenstein's Standpoint' in *Lectures on the Philosophy of Mathematics* (ed. Wolfgang Grassl), Amsterdam, Rodopi, 1982.

Max Black, 'Verificationism and Wittgenstein's Reflections on Mathematics', *Revue Internationale de Philosophie*, vol. 23 (1965) pp. 284-94.

John V. Canfield, 'Critical Notice: *Lectures on the Foundations of Mathematics*', *Canadian Journal of Philosophy*, vol. 11 (1981), pp. 337-56.

Georg Kreisel, 'Book Review: *Wittgenstein's Lectures on the Foundations of Mathematics*', *Bulletin of the American Mathematical Society*, vol. 1 (1969), pp. 79-90. Reprinted by permission of the American Mathematical Society.

Michael Dummett, 'Reckonings: Wittgenstein on Mathematics', *Encounter*, vol. L, no. 3 (March 1978), pp. 63-8.

Michael Dummett, 'Wittgenstein's Philosophy of Mathematics', *The Philosophical Review*, vol. 68 (1959), pp. 324-48.

Gilbert Ryle, 'The Work of an Influential but Little-known Philosopher of Science: Ludwig Wittgenstein'. Copyright © (September 1957) by Scientific American, Inc. All rights reserved.

S. Morris Engel, 'Wittgenstein's "Foundations" and its Reception', *American Philosophical Quarterly*, vol. 4 (1967), pp. 257-68.

Paul Bernays, 'Comments on Ludwig Wittgenstein's *Remarks on the Foundations of Mathematics*', *Ratio*, vol. 2 (1959) and in *Philosophy of*

Mathematics (eds. Paul Benacerraf and Hilary Putnam), Oxford, Basil Blackwell, 1964.

Michael Wrigley, 'Wittgenstein's Philosophy of Mathematics', *Philosophical Quarterly*, vol. 27, no. 106 (1977), pp. 50-9, Basil Blackwell.

Alice Ambrose, 'Wittgenstein on Some Questions in Foundations of Mathematics', *Journal of Philosophy*, vol. 52 (1955), pp. 197-213.

Emily Grosholz, 'Wittgenstein and the Correlation of Logic and Arithmetic', *Ratio*, vol. 23 (1981), Basil Blackwell.

Robert J. Fogelin, 'Wittgenstein and Intuitionism', *American Philosophical Quarterly*, 5 (1968), pp. 267-74.

Pasquale Frascolla, 'The Constructivist Model in Wittgenstein's Philosophy of Mathematics', *Revista Filosofia*, vol. 71 (1980), pp. 297-306.

Alice Ambrose, 'Wittgenstein on Mathematical Proof', *Mind*, 91, no. 362 (1982), pp. 264-372, Basil Blackwell.

Donald W. Harward, 'Wittgenstein and the Character of Mathematical Propositions', *International Logic Review*, 3 (1972), pp. 246-51.

Charles S. Chihara, 'Mathematical Discovery and Concept Formation', *Philosophical Review*, vol. 72 (1963), pp. 17-34.

C.G. Luckhardt, 'Beyond Knowledge: Paradigms in Wittgenstein's Later Philosophy', *Philosophy and Phenomenological Research*, vol. 39, no. 2 (1978), pp. 240-52.

Barry Stroud, 'Wittgenstein and Logical Necessity', *Philosophical Review*, vol. 74 (1965), pp. 504-18.

Charles F. Kielkopf, 'Wittgenstein, *Aposteriori* Necessity and Logic for Entailment', *Philosophia*, vol. 19, no. 1 (1979), pp. 63-74.

Anton Dumitriu, 'Wittgenstein's Solution of the Paradoxes and the Conception of the Scholastic Logician Petrus de Allyaco'. Copyright 1974 by the *History of Philosophy*, vol. X, pp. 229-37 by permission of the Editor.

Charles S. Chihara, 'Wittgenstein's Analysis of the Paradoxes in his *Lectures on the Foundations of Mathematics*', *Philosophical Review*, vol. 86 (1977), pp. 365-81.

Robert L. Arrington, 'Wittgenstein on Contradiction', *The Southern Journal of Philosophy*, vol. 7, no. 1 (1969), pp. 37-43.

Michael Wrigley, 'Wittgenstein on Inconsistency', *Philosophy*, vol. 55 (1980), pp. 471-84, Cambridge University Press.

Cora Diamond, 'Critical Study: Wright's Wittgenstein', *Philosophical Quarterly*, vol. 31 (1981), pp. 352-66, Basil Blackwell.

David Bloor, 'Wittgenstein and Mannheim on the Sociology of Mathematics', *Studies in the History and Philosophy of Science*, vol. 2. Copyright (1973), Pergamon Press.

Introduction: The Portals of Discovery

S.G. Shanker

It would be an understatement to describe Wittgenstein's writings on the philosophy of mathematics as 'revolutionary'; mystifying would, perhaps, be far nearer the mark. For if there is one area of Wittgenstein's work which has provoked widespread consternation, it is his remarks on the foundations of mathematics. It would have taken a brave soul indeed to stand up against the storm of calumny that raged when *Remarks on the Foundations of Mathematics* and *Lectures on the Foundations of Mathematics* were first published and seek to defend what were originally hailed in the 'Vienna Circle Manifesto' as 'the far-reaching ideas of Wittgenstein' through which the 'essential features' of intuitionism, formalism and logicism would be 'united in the ultimate solution' of the foundations crisis.[1] The Logical Positivists themselves, however, were the first to be bewildered by Wittgenstein's approach to the philosophy of mathematics. When the members of the Circle were given their first substantial opportunity to hear the outlines of Wittgenstein's progress (in the paper which Waismann read at the 1930 Königsberg conference entitled 'Über Das Wesen der Mathematik: Der Standpunkt Wittgensteins', reprinted below as 'The Nature of Mathematics: Wittgenstein's Standpoint') they curtly dismissed Wittgenstein's argument as a muddled version of their own logicist position, and of far less interest and significance than the shattering announcement (made at the same conference) of Gödel's theorem.[2]

Unfortunately, the critical reactions to the publication of *Remarks on the Foundations of Mathematics* have tended to be no less dismissive. For Wittgenstein has been accused, not simply of subversive — even anarchic — tendencies, but even worse, he has repeatedly been charged with that most heinous of mathematical crimes: technical incompetence. The very fact that Wittgenstein decided to confine his remarks almost entirely to the realm of elementary arithmetic has struck some critics as incontrovertible evidence of his pronounced inability to deal with the intricacies of higher mathematics, and hence indicates the limited importance of his excursions into the foundations of mathematics. Moreover, Wittgenstein's failure to complete a manuscript on the philosophy of mathematics to his own satisfaction, and the fact that *Remarks on the Foundations of Mathematics*

1

represents a selection of Wittgenstein's writings culled from various different sources, has encouraged those critics already hostile to the general tone of Wittgenstein's approach to condemn *Remarks on the Foundations of Mathematics* as in far too unfinished a state to be regarded as a significant contribution to the philosophy of mathematics.

Thus we have been told that many of Wittgenstein's thoughts 'are expressed in a manner which the author recognised as inaccurate or obscure; some passages contradict others; some are quite inconclusive; some raise objections to ideas which Wittgenstein held or had held which are not themselves stated clearly in the volume; other passages again, particularly those on consistency and on Gödel's theorem, are of poor quality or contain definite errors.'[3] Although many of the book's detractors have guardedly accepted that *Remarks on the Foundations of Mathematics* should none the less be respected as 'a selection from the jottings of a great philosopher', it has seemed indisputable to a large number of mathematical philosophers that Wittgenstein's highly original and often penetrating insights are seriously marred by his repeated failure to grasp either the point or the mechanics of the subject which he was addressing. But then, as Joyce pointedly remarked in *Ulysses*, 'A man of genius makes no mistakes. His errors are volitional and are the portals of discovery.'

The manner in which the editors have assembled *Remarks on the Foundations of Mathematics* clearly renders it totally impractical to argue that, as in the case of *Philosophical Investigations*, the book follows a carefully plotted overall design. Nevertheless, that is not to say that each of the individual chapters which have been included are not in their own right tightly organised investigations into some fundamental area. Nor is there any reason why the various sections cannot be seen as all contributing — albeit from widely different perspectives — to the same central theme. For that matter, the most likely explanation for Wittgenstein's abandonment of the philosophy of mathematics in the middle 1940s is not that he had run out of fresh inspiration, but rather, that he felt he had accomplished the primary goal which he had set for himself, and hence had moved on to other areas of philosophical confusion which struck him as far more pressing than the onerous task of extracting a cohesive book from his extensive writings on the philosophy of mathematics.

Clearly, then, if we can but identify the overriding goal which Wittgenstein had in mind, we shall at least have acquired an instrumental tool for approaching Wittgenstein's writings on the philosophy of mathematics. And here we are fortunate in that Wittgenstein was constantly stressing that his desire to resolve the foundations crisis remained paramount. But far from treating this as a localised problem — of sole interest, as one constantly hears from working mathematicians, to philosophers intrigued by jejune matters of no practical importance — Wittgenstein saw the foundations problem as resting on our very understanding of the nature of mathematics: of the logical character of mathematical propositions and proofs. Hence, the implications of Wittgenstein's proposed resolution of the 'foundations crisis' are extraordinarily far-reaching, not only for the philosophy of mathematics, but indeed, for the ongoing interpretation of mathematical constructions and thence for the very pursuit of mathematics itself.

Whatever his attitude to the radical positions which Wittgenstein explores in *Lectures on the Foundations of Mathematics* and *Remarks on the Foundations of Mathematics*, there are several reasons why the newcomer to Wittgenstein's work in the philosophy of mathematics should be extremely wary of being unduly influenced by the overt hostility with which the community of mathematical philosophers received these works. To begin with, there is the simple fact that Wittgenstein's background suggests far more than just a rudimentary familiarity with the basic problems of elementary arithmetic. Indeed, that Wittgenstein was deeply interested and proficient in higher mathematical issues is borne out in his manuscripts of the 1930s, where he explored in meticulous detail problems ranging from Cantorean transfinite number theory and the Continuum problem to Skolem's recursion proof or Hilbert's various attempts to construct a consistency proof.

Of course, that in itself does not suffice to clear Wittgenstein of the charge of technical incompetence. But if one looks carefully at the initial disparaging reviews of *Remarks on the Foundations of Mathematics*, one will quickly notice that the actual mistakes which Wittgenstein was supposedly guilty of were never identified as such, although constantly alluded to. Rather, the consensus which seems to have rapidly emerged was that, simply by describing e.g. the consistency problem as an imaginary bogy or Gödel's theorem as philosophically insignificant, Wittgenstein had amply demonstrated his failure to grasp the purport of Hilbert's attempts to construct a consistency proof or the significance and mechanics of Gödel's theorem. Certainly, the objections which Wittgenstein presented to support these radical claims have struck several commentators as, in the words of one critic, 'thin and unconvincing'. Yet Wittgenstein's arguments have stubbornly resisted all of the attempts that have been made to dismiss them on the grounds of incompetency, precisely because the discussions which they have prompted are philosophical, not technical. This alone must give us pause to reconsider our attitude to *Remarks on the Foundations of Mathematics*.

It goes without saying that the proper answer to make to a mathematical error is itself *mathematical*, not philosophical. But the counter-arguments which have hitherto been produced to expose the confusions buried in Wittgenstein's remarks have invariably been *philosophical* — not technical — criticisms! Time and again we see the same pattern emerge: what are presented as corrections are in fact philosophical objections, which in turn are vitiated by the fact that no sustained effort has been made to come to terms with the conceptual background or depth of Wittgenstein's arguments. Whether or not Wittgenstein's criticisms hit their mark — forcing us, as Wittgenstein supposed, to reassess our attitudes to e.g. the consistency problem or Gödel's theorem — is obviously a question which we cannot even hope to consider until we have established the precise philosophical basis for the points which Wittgenstein developed. At any rate, the significance of this blurring of the lines demarcating a mathematical from a philosophical critique should be manifest. For it is much easier to dismiss an argument on technical grounds than to refute it philosophically. But the very fact that the issues which Wittgenstein raised have not died down — despite the strident efforts of his more vitriolic critics to extirpate Wittgenstein's alarming heresies — must in itself make the reader deeply suspicious of those attacks on the *Remarks* which have sought to impale Wittgenstein on the stake of mathematical ineptitude.

Likewise, the repeated suggestion that Wittgenstein's technical limitations in the philosophy of mathematics are demonstrated by his need to confine his discussions to the realm of elementary arithmetic demands equally careful reconsideration. The feeling here is that Wittgenstein constantly shifted from talking about elementary to higher mathematical topics without recognising the vastly different types of technical problems involved. In one sense, perhaps, mathematical philosophers cannot be entirely faulted for having taken this attitude. For it was one of the drawbacks of the manner in which Wittgenstein's *Nachlass* was published that *Remarks on the Foundations of Mathematics* appeared before any of the material from the 1930s. Thus, philosophers found themselves confronted with highly opaque attacks on their work which were the end-result of Wittgenstein's sustained arguments of the 1930s. But without the *Nachlass* to guide them in their assessment of the nature and target of Wittgenstein's criticisms, it would have been exceptionally difficult to grasp the subtleties of Wittgenstein's assault. That is not to say that we should not approach *Remarks on the Foundations of Mathematics* until we have worked our way through *Philosophical Remarks* and the second part of *Philosophical Grammar*, but only, that we cannot hope to glean the full significance of Wittgenstein's mature thoughts without reading them in the light of his rapid development during the 1930s.

Moreover, it is only when we read through Wittgenstein's work in the philosophy of mathematics during the 1930s that we can see the highly important stylistic and thematic process occurring in the presentation of his ideas which shapes *Remarks on the Foundations of Mathematics*. For Wittgenstein came to see that the philosophical problems which occur in the various realms of higher mathematics are fundamentally similar to those which occur in elementary arithmetic. That is, that the type of problem which concerns us in e.g. Cantorean transfinite number theory is, in a key philosophical respect, essentially the same as that which occurs in the construction of a new number system in elementary arithmetic. Hence, Wittgenstein gained in perspicuity what he lost in detailed exegesis by deliberately basing his criticisms of questions which occur in higher mathematics on the philosophical issues which proliferate in elementary arithmetic.

Thus Wittgenstein consciously decided in the late 1930s to simplify in order to clarify his discussion by concentrating on the problems as they occur in elementary arithmetic. But that is not to say that higher mathematics is totally ignored in *Lectures on the Foundations of Mathematics* or *Remarks on the Foundations of Mathematics*; on the contrary, the essential conclusions which Wittgenstein had reached in his initial detailed studies are still present, only now they are developed without the technical apparatus which was present in the earlier manuscripts. Rather, Wittgenstein made his points about higher mathematics in relation to the discussions he had just carried out on problems primarily concerned with elementary arithmetic. For what Wittgenstein was endeavouring to show us is that the problems themselves are borne from the same fundamental confusions; hence, what holds for the integers *vis-à-vis* the natural numbers holds *mutatis mutander* for the relationship of the finite/transfinite cardinals *vis-à-vis* the natural numbers.

That is certainly not to say, however, that when Wittgenstein did discuss Cantor's interpretation of transfinite number theory he attempted to treat it as an elementary arithmetical problem. Nor was Wittgenstein particularly interested in the theological or quasi-mystical aspects of Cantor's response to the Kroneckerian attacks that had been launched against the transfinite cardinals which he had constructed. Cantor's own attitude can best be summed up as erring on the side of zeal. Determined to eliminate any and every feasible objection which might be raised against his creation, he produced a battery of arguments with little regard for their mutual compatibility. On the one hand he wanted to argue that 'inner intuition' alone establishes the reality of the transfinite numbers beyond all shadow of a reasonable doubt; on the other hand, that the reality of the transfinite numbers is irrefutably manifested by physical aggregates. Still later he argued that all that was needed to establish their existence was mathematical consistency. Above all else, however, Cantor believed that in order to show conclusively that the transfinite numbers are as 'real' as the natural numbers, he would have to demonstrate that they are literally an 'extension' of the natural numbers. And it is precisely this last theme which has dominated philosophical discussions of transfinite number theory. For, as far as these former issues are concerned, one might quite rightly feel that they are completely tangential to the central problem which troubles philosophers of mathematics: viz. Cantor's claim that the transfinite cardinals are every bit as 'real' as the finite cardinals. But while the philosophical problem that Wittgenstein was interested in was far more closely bound up with this last issue and not the former muddles, the question which Wittgenstein examined is not the standard dispute over the 'existence' of transfinite cardinals, but rather, whether Cantor's elucidation of these numbers — which, as far as Wittgenstein was concerned, Cantor had successfully constructed — can be intelligibly elucidated in Cantor's terms. (To be more precise, Wittgenstein insisted that the question whether Cantor had successfully constructed transfinite numbers was purely a mathematical affair. Wittgenstein saw his task *qua* philosopher as limited to the problem of clarifying the confusions involved in Cantor's attempt to interpret the significance of his proof.)

As has already been touched on, the transfinite cardinals constituted, according to Cantor, 'an extension of the concept of number'.[4] Significantly, this remark can be interpreted in either of two widely different ways. Wittgenstein would not have disputed the accuracy of this claim provided that it is intended to suggest that the transfinite cardinals represent an extension of the concept of number *per se*. For in this case the remark expresses a philosophically important insight. 'Number', Wittgenstein explained, is a family-resemblance concept; hence, Cantor's construction of the transfinite cardinals represents an important addition to the family of number-systems. (The substantial conceptual problem which this creates is then to clarify precisely in what manner this is the case.) However, should the statement be interpreted to represent the claim that the introduction of the transfinite numbers extends the *domain* of the natural numbers, then it will lead to the very confusion which underlies the so-called proof of the existence of the 'actual infinite'. It was Cantor's great achievement in his *Grundlagen* to recognise the significance of the former theme. Unfortunately, this important insight was immediately undermined by Cantor's further belief in the latter interpretation — which is contained in the 'prose' of his theory — ; a confusion which Cantor bequeathed to subsequent transfinite number theory.

Wittgenstein's attack on the 'actual infinite' rests on the principle that this confusion merely undermines the Cantorean *interpretation*, not the actual *existence* of transfinite numbers. The issue thus calls for philosophical clarification, not mathematical reconstruction. We can see Wittgenstein moving carefully through the various steps of this argument in *Philosophical Remarks* and *Philosophical Grammar*, subjecting the Cantorean interpretation of transfinite number theory to the searching philosophical question of whether it has committed a violation of the basic grammatical distinction between 'finite totalities' versus 'infinite processes'. And, of course, as far as Cantor's interpretation of the transfinite cardinals as concrete proof of the existence of the 'actual infinite' is concerned, there is no way of reducing this issue to the level of elementary arithmetic. The only way of dealing with this aspect of Cantor's argument is to scrutinise each stage of his interpretation of his proof for *Satzsysteme* transgressions of the grammatical boundary demarcating the concept of a 'finite totality' (i.e. of a set) from the concept of an 'infinite process' (i.e. of the indefinite application of a rule).

In this respect, therefore, we cannot hope to expose the confusions which underlie Cantor's interpretation without entering into the intricate details of his complicated proofs; for we must examine the precise manner in which Cantor attempted to apply the same 'larger than' relation which governs the order of the natural numbers to the transfinite cardinal number series. That is, Cantor believed that he could define the transfinite numbers in such a way that the 'larger than' relation would hold both for 'the set of transfinite numbers' in relation to 'the set of natural numbers', and would also govern the relations of the transfinite numbers amongst themselves. Hence, the finite/infinite number system would be governed and unified under the sway of the identical 'larger than' relation: the infinite series of transfinite numbers and the extended system of the finite and infinite number series would be internally ordered by the same relation.

This is not the place to investigate the actual steps in Cantor's complicated attempt to implement this argument. What essentially concerns us is simply the fact that, in order to generate the appearance that he had satisfied the demands of his theory, Cantor in effect employed a myriad of *different* relations which he confusedly regarded as the same in every case, and accordingly introduced the same 'larger than' symbol ('>') in each of the widely different contexts involved. But if it does make sense to describe $2^{\aleph_0}$ as '>' $\aleph_0$, it is certainly not in the same sense that $2 > 1$; and $\aleph_0$ is clearly not '>' the largest natural number in precisely the same sense that $2 > 1$. To suppose otherwise is, in fact, to build in as an assumption the very point which Cantor believed he had proved as a result of his discovery of the transfinite numbers: namely, that the transfinite cardinals extend the domain of the finite cardinals.

From here it was but a relatively short step to Cantor's putative proof that the 'actual infinite' exists. But once Cantor's confusion over the various uses of '>' is removed, we shall be in a position to see, not only the incoherence present in the Cantorean interpretation of the nature of the relationship between the transfinite and finite cardinal number systems, but equally important, that the two issues of the existence of the 'actual infinite' and the existence of transfinite numbers are, in fact, entirely separate matters. The fact that the former notion is unintelligible does not in the least affect the effectiveness of the latter mathematical construction. What it does force on us, however, is the pressing need for a philosophical clarification of Cantor's interpretation of transfinite number theory. By his own light, therefore, Wittgenstein was certainly not engaged in a 'revisionist' or 'finitist' critique of transfinite number theory; he was simply intent on undermining a fundamental misconception by clarifying the grammatical confusion which is buried deep in Cantor's prose interpretation of his theory.

In order to appreciate the full significance of this part of Wittgenstein's argument we obviously must work through the various steps whereby Cantor attempted, first, to distinguish between two different categorial types of number (ordinal and natural), and subsequently, to define the 'larger than' and 'lesser than' relations for cardinals in terms of the comparability of their corresponding powers. But there is another level at which Cantor's argument can, in fact, be seen as committing very much the same form of confusion as that which frequently arises in regard to the construction of new number-systems in elementary arithmetic. For the philosophical question of the nature of the conceptual relationship between transfinite and finite cardinals involves a basic point which is precisely the same as that which occurs in the case of the relationship between e.g. the natural numbers and the integers. Thus, as far as this crucial matter is concerned, the philosophical confusions which occur in the rarefied atmosphere of transfinite number theory mirror those which occur in the familiar domain of elementary arithmetic. Five hundred years of application may have enabled us to become totally blasé today about the presence of negative numbers, but for centuries their introduction caused every bit as much mystification as di i the creation of transfinite numbers, and indeed, elicited far more derision than anything like that which Cantor was forced to endure. As Bell explained, 'When negative numbers first appeared in experience, as in debits instead of credits, they, *as numbers*, were held in the same abhorrence as "unnatural" monstrosities as were later the "imaginary" numbers $\sqrt{-1}$, $\sqrt{-2}$, etc., arising from the *formal* solution of equations such as $x^2+1=0$, $x^2+2=0$, etc.'[5] Indeed, the aim of Wittgenstein's remarks on this theme was to clarify precisely why the very same conceptual problem is involved in each of such apparently diverse cases.

The reason why Wittgenstein chose to dwell on the elementary as opposed to the higher forms of this issue was simply that the philosophical dimensions of the problem are comparatively perspicuous when we are dealing with the relationship of the integers to the natural numbers; for when we consider the relation of the transfinite to the finite cardinals, the matter becomes far more clouded simply because we now find ourselves immersed in an abstract realm where the bulk of our energies are consumed in comprehending the complex technical arguments involved. Thus, by clarifying the nature of the conceptual relation which subsists between the elementary arithmetical systems, Wittgenstein was in effect laying the foundation for his later remarks on Cantor's theory. Hence, we cannot hope to understand the full implications of Wittgenstein's critique of transfinite number theory without first grasping the basis for his oft-repeated claim that 'there are no gaps in mathematics'; and this is a matter which can be fully elucidated by considering the relationship between e.g. the integers and the natural numbers. It is only with this argument — which turns on what Wittgenstein described as the 'autonomy of arithmetical constructions' — firmly in place that we can then move on to the actual details of the conceptual violations of this fundamental theme as they occur in higher mathematics.

In his discussions of the autonomy of mathematical constructions Wittgenstein explained why, although the construction of a new number system marks an extension of the general concept of 'number', it is misleading to speak of the new system as an expansion of an old number system. As Waismann put this at the conclusion of 'Wittgenstein's Standpoint': 'where it looks as if one had extended a system, one has, in fact, climbed to a system of higher multiplicity.' [cf. p. 60ff. below] That is, when we create a new numerical series we are in fact constructing a new grammatical system in which analogues of questions which were *unintelligible* in a previous system are bestowed with a meaning and thence a solution. In the natural number system, for example, '5 − 7 = ?' is not just unsolvable: it is unintelligible. Obviously there are striking parallels between '5', '+5', '7' and '+7' (viz. they behave in the exact same manner as far as addition is concerned). But the claim that the members of the two number-systems are grammatically distinct — that we cannot look at the integers as in some sense 'filling in a gap' in the natural number system, or treat the members of the two series as interchangeable — is based on the fact that it simply *makes no sense* to subtract a larger from a smaller number in the natural number system. Hence, by constructing the integers we have not, strictly speaking, enabled ourselves to resolve what was an unanswerable question in the natural number system. For to be a significant question it must, Wittgenstein repeatedly emphasised, be in principle possible to answer what has been asked. Rather, we have constructed an analogue of the original 'question', which in the context of the integers is both significant and answerable.

The crucial point to grasp here, therefore, is that a new number system does not expand the domain of an old number system: it extends the family of systems gathered under the concept of 'number'. The integers do not provide a 'completion' of the natural numbers; the two types of number are grammatically distinct. As Waismann explained in *Introduction to Mathematical Thinking*, '"3" and "+3" have, so to speak, a different logical grammar ... The negative numbers are not a later complement of the natural numbers. In reality they are two entirely separate number systems ... on two different levels.'[6] We must be extremely careful, therefore, to distinguish between the various number systems. '3', '+3' and '3/1' are by no means one and the same number: 'they only correspond to one another, which means that they play a different role in their calculi.'[7] Hence, just as it makes no sense to say that '+2 > 1', so too it makes no sense to say that '$\aleph_o$ > n' (let alone that '$2^{\aleph_o}$ > $\aleph_o$' in precisely the same manner that '2 > 1'). For in each case we have incoherently tried to apply a relation which is only properly intelligible when both terms are drawn from the same system. The primary consequence of this illicit attempt to mix the terms of two different systems just is to induce us to disregard the fact that arithmetical systems are autonomous: to treat the construction of new systems as in some sense extending the domain of the previous system.

Far from being a consequence of his failure to grasp the complex issues involved in higher mathematics, therefore, Wittgenstein's decision to provide the background for his forays into higher mathematics in the philosophical problems which occur in elementary arithmetic is a basic theme which lies at the heart of *Remarks on the Foundation of Mathematics*, rendering it, not a disordered arrangement of fragmentary remarks on the philosophy of mathematics, but rather, a carefully planned presentation and application of this fundamental point. Moreover, it is precisely this thematic structure which establishes *Remarks on the Foundations of Mathematics* as a work of such extraordinary depth and power. Indeed, had Wittgenstein been guilty of the technical incompetence which his more implacable critics have accused him of, then discussions of *Remarks on the Foundations of Mathematics* and *Lectures on the Foundations of Mathematics* would quickly have ceased. Yet, as the articles gathered in this volume attest, these books have continued to fascinate and stimulate even their most unsympathetic readers, and issues which were brusquely dismissed on the grounds of their supposed inanity have stoutly refused to succumb to the obscurity which many had otherwise expected.

An excellent example of the unexpected intractability of the questions which Wittgenstein raised is provided by his notorious remarks on the problem of consistency. 'Why', he asked at one point, 'should a certain configuration of signs not be allowed to arise? Why this dread? Why the tabu?' (*WWK* 119) At face value comments such as this have struck many commentators as so patently absurd that they have been roundly dismissed as the posturings of an amateur. It made no difference that some found themselves arguing — with no awareness, it should be stressed, of the incongruity in their position — first, that finitistic consistency proofs are obviously essential to the successful manufacture of bridges, and then in the next breath, that Gödel's theorems had established the impossibility of constructing a finitistic absolute proof of consistency for arithmetic (which can be represented within arithmetic). It is no wonder that, with such a tension suffusing the argument, Wittgenstein's remarks have continued to exercise the imagination (or niggle at the conscience) of contemporary philosophers of mathematics. Clearly, they are aware, there is some peculiarity in the problem. Thus the more adventuresome wonder whether, despite its apparent weaknesses, there might not after all be some important insight buried in Wittgenstein's seemingly bizarre comments on the innocuousness of contradictions; while the more desperate ponder whether Wittgenstein may not have exposed us to a totally novel — and perhaps irrefutable — form of scepticism in the philosophy of mathematics.

The first prejudice that we must rid ourselves of is the idea that Wittgenstein was unaware of the technical implications of the counter-arguments which Turing presented in *Lectures on the Foundations of Mathematics.* For one thing, the objections which Turing voiced were by no means unfamiliar to Wittgenstein; Waismann had raised essentially the same points nine years before, as we can see in the discussions recorded in *Wittgenstein and the Vienna Circle.* The essence of Wittgenstein's rejoinders to both Waismann and Turing is that their objections are completely beside the point, simply because they have failed to grasp the grammatical nature of the axioms of a system, or of a contradiction derived within a mathematical system. In other words, Wittgenstein never responded that Waismann's and Turing's arguments are themselves technically flawed; it is rather that they are unrelated to the philosophical point with which Wittgenstein was concerned. Indeed, Waismann's and Turing's arguments are merely a recapitulation of the standard themes in the original discussions of the problem of consistency: the very themes that Wittgenstein had originally formulated his argument to combat. Or rather, to circumvent and hence subvert.

This last remark holds the key to the strategy which Wittgenstein pursued. The main question which the problem of consistency poses is: how can we be certain that the inferences in a proof-system are truth-preserving? How, that is, can we be certain that the axioms of a system do not contain a 'hidden' contradiction which might one day manifest itself when we seek to apply the rules of the calculus in some novel application? The brunt of Wittgenstein's response to this apparent dilemma was, of course, that it is idle to seek to, as it were, categorically establish that no such possibility could ever arise. For even if such a feat were technically feasible, it is, in fact, irrelevant; the discovery of such a contradiction would in no way impair any of the previous calculations that had been performed with that calculus, nor need it *ipso facto* spell the demise of any future applications of that calculus, given that the manner in which we respond to such a contingency remains a perfectly open matter. Among the options open to us we might simply choose to ignore the contradiction and continue to employ that calculus (despite our awareness that in such-and-such a situation a contradiction will result); or we might seek to circumvent the occurrence of that contradiction with certain *ad hoc* arrangements; or we might even decide — in those cases where the presence of a contradiction at such a juncture is deemed to be intolerable — to either abandon the calculus entirely, or else construct a new calculus to supersede the existing one, similar in all respects to the previous system apart from the fact that we have rendered it impossible to derive any consequences from the contradiction in question (i.e. by introducing a new postulate explicitly prohibiting any inferences from that contradiction).

This last argument has struck many philosophers of mathematics as particularly feeble. For the trouble with an inconsistent system, so we are constantly being reminded, is simply that anything would follow from a contradiction. Thus Waismann, Turing, and still later Chihara, have all wanted to insist that Wittgenstein simply misunderstood the nature of the dilemma. Wittgenstein, they have all objected, merely fixed his attention on one of the consequences of the problem, when the crisis which we are really concerned with lies in the axioms of the system, which are capable of generating (as Chihara put it) 'infinitely many' such contradictions. The inescapable dilemma which an inconsistent system thrusts upon us, therefore, is simply that every well-formed formula would be derivable in an inconsistent system; that is, it would be possible to infer the negations of theorems as well as the theorems themselves in such a system.

The possibility that Wittgenstein could have failed to grasp the significance of this point seems, however, extremely remote. For not only was he repeatedly forced to listen to this standard objection, but even more importantly, it could justly be said that Wittgenstein's exposition of the problem was primarily directed against precisely this argument. In order to grasp the subtleties of Wittgenstein's position, however, we must first try to place ourselves in a position where we shall at least be able to discern the general theme of Wittgenstein's approach. For once again it is crucial that we clarify what Wittgenstein was objecting to in philosophical terms in the traditional perceptions of the problem before we accuse him of mathematical myopia. Thus, in order to appreciate the thrust of Wittgenstein's arguments it is essential that we consider, not so much the technical details of the various 'consistency proofs' that have been offered, as the *point* of Hilbert's programme: the philosophical assumptions and objectives which lie at the heart of Hilbert's original conception of the problem of consistency. For Wittgenstein deliberately sought to bypass the various mathematical and 'meta-mathematical' issues that have predominated in discussions of 'proof theory' and focus instead on the cogency of the *premises* underlying the formulation of Hilbert's problem. Indeed, as we shall see, the essence of Wittgenstein's approach is that he undertook, not to *refute* the doubts which Hilbert had raised, but rather to *exclude* them by demonstrating that the anxieties on which they rest arise from a misguided conception of a mathematical system.

According to Hilbert the discovery of the paradoxes in set theory had rendered the situation in contemporary mathematics 'intolerable'. To this Wittgenstein responded that, far from being intolerable, the paradoxes are harmless and the crisis is non-existent. In order to establish this he carefully examined the logical grammar of such concepts as *justification* and *reliability* in respect to mathematics; concepts which, again, can be far more readily elucidated in elementary as opposed to higher mathematical topics. Indeed, where Hilbert had insisted that the key to a solution lies in 'completely clarifying the nature of the infinite',[8] Wittgenstein's solution of the problem completely disregards transfinite number theory. Thus, whereas Hilbert argued that the notion of consistency is perspicuous in elementary number theory and that our basic problem is to discover how to deploy this paradigm for transfinite number theory, Wittgenstein countered that, on the contrary, neither elementary nor higher mathematics is 'reliable' in the manner in which Hilbert repeatedly suggested.

It is precisely here where the sceptical chorus begins to swell. For whereas Hilbert had at least sought to render elementary arithmetic immune from the sceptical doubts which reputedly plague transfinite number theory, Wittgenstein attempted, according to the 'sceptical' interpretation, to generalise Hilbert's problem so that it applies to all of mathematics. But, far from this being Wittgenstein's intention, the basic theme in Wittgenstein's writings on the philosophy of mathematics — indeed, throughout his writings on philosophy *simpliciter* — is that 'Scepticism is *not* irrefutable, but *obvious nonsense* if it tries to doubt where no question can be asked. For doubt can only exist where a question exists; a question can only exist where an answer exists, and this can only exist where something *can* be *said.*' (NB 44) The point is thus, not that mathematical calculi are irretrievably unreliable, but quite the reverse, that it is nonsense to speak of the epistemological reliability or otherwise of elementary and higher mathematics. Hence, the reason why Wittgenstein's own argument concentrated on elementary number theory is simply that he intended to attack the problem at its root. For the real goal of Wittgenstein's argument was to undermine the very notion of a 'consistency proof' in the mathematical or 'meta-mathematical' sense in which Hilbert — and those following him who continue to regard this as a pressing matter — wish to employ the concept. Ultimately, Wittgenstein demonstrated that there is no 'consistency problem' simply because the sceptical issues which are purportedly involved here are, in fact, unintelligible: a product of misguided grammatical confusions.

The epistemological framework of Hilbert's approach is absolutely fundamental to his programme. He began his argument by recording his complete agreement with the intuitionists that there is a body of mathematical truths which are grasped intuitively. Like the intuitionists, Hilbert adopted this as his starting-point in order to erect the foundations of mathematics on a species of epistemologically basic mathematical truths: mathematical truths that are intuitively self-evident. An epistemologically basic set of mathematical objects exists, he argued, and the propositions about these objects are 'grasped intuitively', and 'not subject to verification'. The trouble occurs, however, when we shift from the level of these finitary mathematical propositions to higher mathematics (just as the sceptical problems so worrisome to reductionists arise when we shift from e.g. sensation to material-object language). In 'Neubegründung' Hilbert explained that 'of course, all of mathematics cannot be comprehended within this sort' of intuitively-grasped finitary propositions: 'The transition to the standpoint of higher arithmetic and algebra ... already denies these intuitive procedures.'[9] As far as non-finitary mathematical propositions are concerned, therefore, we cannot know whether these are true independently of having a proof for them. Furthermore, we cannot have any faith in the truth of such a proof until we have constructed a 'meta-mathematical' proof which establishes that our formal proof is itself reliable. Thus, to know that a non-finitary formula is true we need to possess both a proof of the theorem and a consistency proof of the system.

The basic problem that remains, however, is to explain how we are to make sense of a consistency proof in finitary terms. It was here that Hilbert turned to the inspiration provided by Weierstrass' revolutionary work in the foundations of analysis. The secret was to reduce transfinite problems to finitary terms. Hilbert's own solution was to argue that it is possible to do this in the construction of a consistency proof simply because a consistency proof is a 'meta-mathematical' proof *about* the system in question, not a proof *within* the formal system. And since the formal system under 'meta-mathematical' scrutiny is itself comprised of intuitively given symbols (when 'drained of all their meaning'), the epistemological status of a consistency proof is thus the same as that of the intuitively evident propositions about finitary elementary propositions. (I.e. a consistency proof will not involve unbounded quantification over the symbols of a formal system.)

The most notable features of this argument are first, that Hilbert assumed that we are concerned with a problem of justification, and second, that the general strategy which he consequently formulated was based entirely on classical epistemological lines. Indeed, at one point Hilbert went so far as to argue that 'Where we had propositions concerning numerals, we now have formulas which themselves are concrete objects that in their turn are considered by our perceptual intuition.'[10] Hilbert's original argument was phrased, therefore, in terms which deliberately mirrored the standard reductionist approach to the refutation of epistemological scepticism. And it was precisely this theme which Wittgenstein set out to demonstrate is unintelligible in the context of the grammatical nature of mathematical systems, and hence which led to such confusions as Hilbert's conviction that mathematical calculi stand in need of a 'consistency proof' before they can be deemed trustworthy. The core of Wittgenstein's criticisms were therefore directed almost entirely at this level of Hilbert's argument.

The basic issue which Hilbert's programme raises is whether mathematical truth stands in need of justification. It is not just a question of whether what Hilbert called 'ideal' propositions are reliable (i.e. whether the truths of transfinitary mathematics can be justified). For Hilbert assumed that *all* mathematical truth must be justified. In the case of elementary mathematics this is ultimately provided by intuition. But since intuition is the only mechanism which we possess for eliminating sceptical objections, we must discover some method of reducing the justification of higher mathematical propositions to intuitively evident propositions. Thus, the point of a consistency proof, Hilbert argued, is quite simply that it 'provides us with a justification for the introduction of our ideal propositions' (i.e. non-finitary propositions about 'ideal elements' such as 'points at infinity' and 'a line at infinity').

There are several different elements in Wittgenstein's response to this argument. At the most fundamental level, Wittgenstein set out to establish that mathematical truths stand in no need of justification: they are necessarily true in virtue of their logical grammar. Of course, the problem of mathematical necessity remains one of the central issues in the philosophy of mathematics. But while philosophers have vainly struggled to come to terms with the nature of mathematical necessity by investigating the manner in which we recognise mathematical truths or by identifying the source of mathematical necessity, Wittgenstein focused on the logical grammar of necessary propositions, thereby demonstrating that even before we can make sense of the so-called 'epistemological' or 'ontological' dimensions of the problem we must first clarify what it is for a proposition to be necessary: which is entirely a question of logical grammar. But then, once we have answered this logical question, no so-called 'two-fold problem of necessity' remains to trouble us: we have already said all that can or need be said about what constitutes a necessary truth. Furthermore, once we have grasped that mathematical propositions are *rules of grammar* — norms of representation (rather than descriptions of the world) which fix the use of mathematical concepts which are themselves used to state truths about the world — we shall then be in a position to see that Hilbert's worries about the reliability of mathematical truths are entirely spurious: a confusion borne from the failure to distinguish between the type of certainty which characterises a normative system from that which occurs in empirical contexts. (*infra*)

From the various complex themes which are contained in Wittgenstein's remarks on consistency, there is only space here to comment briefly on what are perhaps the two central strands in his argument: the claim that the concept of a 'hidden' contradiction is unintelligible, and the insistence that contradictions *per se* are harmless. Throughout his discussions of this topic Wittgenstein continually stressed that contradictions do exist in mathematics, and indeed, that we make extensive use of their presence (e.g. in indirect proofs). But the prior question which Wittgenstein concentrated on is, what exactly does it mean to speak of a *hidden* contradiction: a contradiction which we cannot discern now, but which we might encounter some time in the future? The first basic point that Wittgenstein developed is that it simply *makes no sense* to ask whether a 'hidden' contradiction exists, given that 'it only makes sense to ask a question when we possess a method for answering it'. And this, he told Waismann and Schlick, 'is the essential thing on which everything to do with the question of consistency depends'. (*WWK* 127-8)

The assumption that it makes sense to speak of a 'hidden' contradiction is similar to the confusion underlying the so-called 'sceptical interpretation' of Wittgenstein's remarks on rule-following. For it confuses 'overlooked' with a distinctively sceptical interpretation of 'hidden'. Wittgenstein acknowledged that it makes sense to say that I have overlooked a contradiction, but only in so far as I can scrutinise my rules to discover such an oversight. But I cannot then suppose that I have scrutinised my rules yet have still overlooked the contradiction. The grammar of 'scrutinise' is such that it rules out the possibility of merely overlooking a contradiction. That is to say, we must distinguish carefully between *carelessness* and *unsurveyability*. But in order to generate his sceptical hypothesis Hilbert conflated these two logically distinct notions; as for example, when he argued that 'It is necessary to make inferences everywhere as reliable as they are in ordinary elementary number theory, which no one questions and in which contradictions and paradoxes arise only through our carelessness.'[11]

Wittgenstein seized on this theme when he argued that the difference between an 'overlooked' and a 'hidden' contradiction amounts to the difference between *surveyability* and *unsurveyability*. (*WWK* 195) We cannot speak of 'overlooking a contradiction' unless a method exists for definitively excluding the possibility that a contradiction has been overlooked. And it is precisely this step which Hilbert transgressed. In order to generate his sceptical thesis he assumed that it is possible to survey the rules of a system and *still* overlook a contradiction. Such a misguided assumption rests on the premise that surveyability relates to 'perceptual recognition', and hence exposes us to the same sorts of sceptical problems which plague classical epistemology. The answer to this argument is thus to show how 'surveyability' is a term of grammar: of the logical possibility of answering a question. (Cf. 'Approaching the *Investigations*', Volume Two and 'The Appel-Haken Solution of the Four Colour Problem' in this volume.) To say that a question is surveyable is to say that a method for answering it exists. Likewise, the proper answer to give to the mathematician's anxiety that a 'hidden' contradiction might exist in a system is that 'I am given a contradiction only by a method for discovering it!' (*WWK* 195)

The assumption that it makes sense to speak of a 'hidden' contradiction in a system rests, therefore, on the basic epistemological premise that we are compelled to answer the sceptical objection that we can never be certain, when we have surveyed our rules, that we have not overlooked some contradiction. Just as Wittgenstein's discussion of rule-following sets out, not to *refute*, but rather to undermine the 'sceptical' argument,[12] so too his reaction to the consistency problem is to demonstrate that the proper response to Hilbert's worry is to dissolve it: to *exclude* the possibility of doubt here. Thus, whereas Hilbert's putative 'consistency proof' was an attempt to refute the sceptic, Wittgenstein's answer is that the real solution must be to undermine the 'sceptical' challenge by demonstrating that the 'doubt' being raised here is unintelligible.

There are several distinct elements in Wittgenstein's consequent argument that contradictions *per se* are perfectly innocuous. One point is to re-examine the traditional proof that every well-formed formula is derivable in an inconsistent system. As was mentioned above, the crux of Wittgenstein's response to this issue is that we need only 'make it a rule then not to draw any inferences from a contradiction', an answer which has struck many critics as a blatant evasion of the issue at stake. For the problem, they feel, lies in the axioms, not in one of the consequences which we derive from them. The standard proof of this proceeds as follows: in a system S in the propositional calculus with the following three axioms

(1) $(p \rightarrow (q \rightarrow p))$
(2) $((p \rightarrow (q \rightarrow r)) \rightarrow ((p \rightarrow q) \rightarrow (p \rightarrow r)))$
(3) $((-q \rightarrow -p) \rightarrow ((-q \rightarrow p) \rightarrow q))$

with Modus Ponens as the only rule of inference, we can derive the following lemma:

$$-p \rightarrow (p \rightarrow q)$$

I.e. if S is inconsistent — so that we can prove both p and $-p$ — then any wff q would be provable.

The proof of the lemma proceeds as follows:

1.	$-p$	By Hypothesis
2.	p	By Hypothesis
3.	$p \rightarrow (-q \rightarrow p)$	Axiom 1
4.	$-p \rightarrow (-q \rightarrow -p)$	Axiom 1
5.	$-q \rightarrow p$	2,3 MP
6.	$-q \rightarrow -p$	1,4 MP
7.	$((-q \rightarrow -p) \rightarrow ((-q \rightarrow p) \rightarrow q))$	Axiom 3
8.	$(-q \rightarrow p) \rightarrow q$	6,7 MP
9.	q	5,8 MP[13]

It is clear what is supposed to be going on here. The lemma is an instantiation of axiom 3; hence, it is one of the rules of the system that from a contradiction any wff is derivable. But whereas such a rule is only contained implicitly in the axioms, the lemma is supposed to make the point explicitly. But then, just as axiom 3 does not mention a contradiction, neither does the lemma. How, then, does it accomplish its appointed task? The key is that we are meant to see the lemma as running on two separate tracks — #'s 1,4,6 versus #'s 2,3,5 — which come together in the final three steps of the proof. The lemma thus does not *state* that any wff is derivable from a contradiction but rather it *shows* this. All that the lemma actually states is that, from the negation of a theorem it follows that anything can be derived from the subsequent affirmation of that theorem. The purpose of the proof of the lemma is then to show how our definition of an absolute system follows from the consequence of the axioms.

Wittgenstein continually maintained that the straightforward answer to this argument is simply to make it a rule that '"(p & $-p$)" is prohibited'. The trouble with this answer is that 'p & $-p$' never occurs explicitly in the proof of the lemma. The key to Wittgenstein's argument, however, is that it does occur *implicitly*: indeed, that the proof of the lemma turns on this covert use. The two-track nature of the proof of the lemma only serves to obscure the fact that we have actually begun the argument with the premise 'p & −p'. Thus, the point of Wittgenstein's objection is not to attack the *conclusion* of the lemma: it is to address the very *premise*, and thus stop the proof of the lemma before it can even begin. For when removed of this deceptive two-track structure what the proof of the lemma really states is:

1. −p & p	By Hypothesis
2. (−p → (−q →−p)) & (p →(−q →p))	Axiom 1
3. (−q → −p) & (−q → p)	1,2 MP
4. ((−q → −p) → ((−q → p) → q))	Axiom 3
5. (−q → p) & (−q → p) →q	3,4 MP
6. q	3,5 MP

Thus, the key to Wittgenstein's argument is that it is *only* by assuming that you can draw inferences from a contradiction that you can generate the proof of the lemma. And it is for this reason that we need only make it a rule that you can draw no inferences from a contradiction. In other words, the answer to Turing is that you cannot get any conclusion you like *without* actually going through the contradiction, and this is something we need not do. 'The only thing is to show him which way not to proceed from a contradiction.' (*LFM* 222)

In order to lay Turing's anxieties completely to rest, however, Wittgenstein had also to establish why Turing's worries about the disastrous effect which a 'hidden' contradiction would supposedly have upon the application of a system are themselves unfounded. Here the point turns entirely on what we understand by a 'contradiction'. For the essence of a contradiction is that it represents a 'stalled move' in a calculus; when we are told to do two opposite things in a game, for example, the result is that we can do nothing: we have reached the 'edge of the chess-board'. (*WWK* 120) 'In arithmetic, too, we reach the "edge of the chess-board", for example when we have the problem 0/0. (If I wanted to say that 0/0 = 1, then I could prove that 3 = 5, and thus I would come into conflict with the other rules of the game.)' (*WWK* 125) It is not Wittgenstein's elucidation of the nature of a contradiction that critics have objected to, however, but rather the consequences which he drew from this grammatical point. The crux of the issue lies, therefore, in the force of Turing's objection in the light of the logical grammar of 'contradiction'.

Thus, the argument is not concerned with the Wright–Wrigley claim that Wittgenstein's objection turns on the theme that 'logic is antecedent to truth'; that, as Wright puts it, 'our rules of inference are antecedent to truth. (That is, they are among the criteria of truth for the statements to which they are applied.)'[14] Whereas the idea behind the Turing/Chihara objection is that an 'inconsistent' system will lead us from true premises to false conclusions, the point of the Wright–Wrigley defence is that there is 'no Olympian standpoint from which it may be discerned who is giving the right account of the matter'.[15] Both positions rest on the very assumption which Wittgenstein had sought to rule out on strictly logical grounds. A contradiction cannot lead us from a true to a false proposition, nor from a true to a 'true-as-considered-in-this-system' proposition; for a contradiction cannot *qua* 'stalled move in the calculus' lead anywhere. And it is for this very reason that the idea that an application could have proceeded unaware that it harboured a concealed contradiction is absurd. For had there been a contradiction in the application of the calculus we could never have built the bridge in the first place which is supposedly in imminent danger of collapsing from our unnoticed contradiction. We could not *not* notice a contradiction, because in the face of a contradiction an application must grind to a halt: we simply cannot proceed until this blockage has been removed.

It was for this reason, therefore, that Wittgenstein repeatedly stressed that you could not suddenly discover a hidden *mathematical* flaw in a calculus which has already been applied. Of course, it is always possible to discover mistakes in the calculations that were performed, but then, that does not represent any flaw in the calculus. Nor is it a point in which the advocates of the 'consistency problem' are interested. Nevertheless, a large part of Wittgenstein's discussion is devoted to clarifying the manner in which the champions of the 'consistency problem' trade on the confusion between contradictions and mathematical errors, often treating the former as if they were a species of the latter. Likewise, it is always possible that we have committed an engineering error in the manner in which we applied the calculus, but then, that is clearly an empirical, not a mathematical matter. Again, the defenders of the cogency of the 'consistency problem' are loath to confuse such an important distinction, yet here too Wittgenstein exposed the equivocations in their arguments. But the chief point in all this is to demonstrate that it makes no sense to treat the 'consistency problem' as a *mathematical* issue: a structural defect which can undermine the soundness of a calculus. For, as all of the above arguments confirm, the notion of a 'hidden' contradiction is unintelligible, while the presence of a contradiction is both a familiar and utterly innocuous feature of mathematical calculi.

Wittgenstein did not suggest or assume that the foregoing resolution of the problem of consistency disposes of the foundations problem. On Hilbert's conception such would indeed be the case, but Wittgenstein proceeded on the understanding that the two issues are distinct albeit related areas of philosophical confusion which demand independent investigation. In the former issue we are concerned with the reliability of the calculi we employ. It is not the concept of mathematical truth *per se* that is under consideration, but rather, the problem is one of guaranteeing that some future mathematical discovery will not undermine our pre-existing faith in the theorems yielded by a calculus. In other words, the problem is one of elucidating what is meant by regarding a calculus as sound. But the heart of the foundations problem lies, as Frege pointed out in *Foundations of Arithmetic*, at a deeper philosophical level. (cf. *FA* §3) The problem here is ultimately that of clarifying the logical status of mathematical truth in order to establish the basis for our conviction that mathematics is, as Hilbert described it, 'a paragon of certitude'. Thus, the foundations crisis does not simply amount to the anxiety that mathematical systems might unbeknownst to us contain 'hidden' contradictions. More importantly, it is based on the fundamental philosophical dilemma that it is not at all clear what it means to describe a mathematical proposition as a 'necessary truth'.

When it was finally borne in (by the startling developments during the nineteenth century in number theory and geometry) that nature could be described in myriad ways, philosophers concluded, not that they had mis-construed the character of the necessity and strict universality of mathe-matical truth, but rather, that mathematical truths might not be necessary and universal after all. In his *Personal Memoirs* Russell recalled how he turned to the philosophy of mathematics because he 'wanted certainty in the kind of way in which people want religious faith. I thought that certainty is more likely to be found in mathematics than elsewhere. But I discovered that many mathematical demonstrations, which my teachers expected me to accept, were full of fallacies, and that, if certainty were indeed discoverable in mathematics, it would be in a new field of mathe-matics, with more solid foundations than those that had hitherto been thought secure.' But his effort, he admitted, proved to be in vain, for 'after some twenty years of very arduous toil, I came to the conclusion that there was nothing more that I could do in the way of making mathematical knowledge indubitable'.[16] The very fact that Russell felt that certainty was 'more likely' to be found in mathematics than in any other field already betrays, however, a profound misunderstanding of the grammatical nature of mathematical propositions and proofs.

What Russell ultimately failed to realise was that his disappointment was due, not to the enormous difficulty of the task which he had undertaken, but rather, to the presuppositions with which he had approached it. The fact that Russell concluded that his search for the indubitability of mathematical knowledge was ultimately fruitless indicates his complete obliviousness of the possibility that there was any problem in his conception of mathe-matical truth, or indeed, in his conception of the *indubitability* of mathe-matical knowledge. One of the primary features of Wittgenstein's resolution of the foundations problem is his demonstration that both of these themes are mistaken, and collapse together. Once we understand the grammatical nature of the necessity which characterises mathematical truth we shall understand the nature of the 'indubitability' — the logical *exclusion* of doubt — which characterises mathematical knowledge. We will then be in a position to see how the belief in the 'withering of mathe-matical truth' and the resigned acceptance of the fallibility of mathematical knowledge rest firmly on a misunderstanding of the nature of this distinction, and hence of mathematical truth. Indeed, of mathematics *simpliciter*.

The key to Wittgenstein's resolution of the 'foundations crisis' rests, therefore, on the insight that 'in mathematics we are convinced of *grammatical* propositions; so the expression, the result, of our being con-vinced is that we *accept a rule*.' (*RFM* III §27) That is, we treat mathe-matical propositions as 'rules of grammar': grammatical conventions which fix the use of mathematical concepts. Hence, the necessity of mathematical propositions derives solely from the fact that we use them as norms of representation which determine the bounds of sense. The 'foundations crisis' was the direct result of the failure to grasp the significance of this logical grammatical point, which resulted in the muddled attempt to seek for an epistemological justification of the certainty of normative expressions when their necessity is entirely a consequence of the manner in which they are employed: 'To accept a proposition as unshakably certain means to use it as a grammatical rule: this removes uncertainty from it.' (*RFM* III §39) Thus, Wittgenstein demonstrated that the resolution of the 'foundations crisis' lies, not in the *refutation*, but rather, in the *logical exclusion* of the sceptical doubts which inspire it. Far from commending any sort of scepticism about mathematical certainty therefore, what Wittgenstein actually demonstrated was the absurdity involved in the supposition that such a possibility is intelligible.

That is certainly not to say that Wittgenstein's 'conventionalist' account of mathematical necessity does not bring with it a host of problems of a different order. In particular, it has been hotly disputed in recent years whether Wittgenstein was offering a 'full-blooded' or a 'modified' conventionalist account of logical necessity. In fact, Wittgenstein was offering neither, and the problems which this framework introduces threaten to undermine the powerful insights contained in Wittgenstein's normative conception of mathematics. Wittgenstein was not just repudiating the details of the logical positivist account of mathematical truth (the putative paradigm of the 'modified' account): he was pursuing an explanation which is *toto caelo* different from their version of conventionalism. The key to the logical positivist conception of conventionalism is the premise that a mathematical proposition is a *tautology*: a compound proposition of no factual content which is true in virtue of the meanings of its constituent words together with the syntactic rules governing their combination. But this approach does not in the least apply to Wittgenstein's conception of mathematical propositions as rules of grammar. For there is no compositional picture of sentential meaning operating in the latter; whether or not a sentence expresses a rule depends solely on the manner in which it is used. Moreover, whereas Wittgenstein argued that mathematical propositions are rules of grammar *as opposed* to tautologies, the Logical Positivists argued that mathematical propositions are tautologies *because of* the pre-existing syntactic and semantic conventions governing the meanings and combinations of words in a language. Yet tautologies themselves, according to the Logical Positivists, are not conventions, but rather, the direct consequence of the arbitrary conventions governing the use of signs and the meaning of words. It is all too easy to overlook the significance of these differences, however, in the general haste to classify both Wittgenstein's and the Logical Positivists' accounts as species of essentially the same form of mathematical conventionalism. (That is, as different positions within the same framework.) But if it is legitimate to describe Wittgenstein's argument as 'conventionalist', this certainly cannot be in the logical positivist sense.

The full import of the divergence between Wittgenstein's and the

Logical Positivists' conceptions of conventionalism is borne out when we consider how Wittgenstein's argument enabled him to resolve Poincaré's objection that logicism fails to explain how mathematics can be an inventive and constantly growing discipline. If mathematics reduces in principle to an 'immense tautology' Poincaré asked, then 'how can we ever discover something new in mathematics?'[17]

It was a problem which reduced the Vienna Circle to a confused psychological argument with uncharacteristically metaphysical undertones. Thus Ayer, for example, argued in *Language Truth & Logic* that 'The power of logic and mathematics to surprise us depends, like their usefulness, on the limitations of our reason', but that 'A being whose intellect was infinitely powerful would take no interest in logic and mathematics. For he would be able to see at a glance everything that his definitions implied, and, accordingly, could never learn anything from logical inference which he was not fully conscious of already.'[18] Wittgenstein's argument, however, completely sidestepped this dilemma: mathematical propositions are 'rules of grammar' which we *freely construct*, and it is precisely this autonomy which accounts for the constant growth of mathematics.

It has been widely argued, however, that the real problem with this last conventionalist argument is that you cannot base the necessity of a mathematical truth on an arbitrary linguistic practice. The most common criticism levelled against conventionalism is that mathematical truth must be sempiternal and universal: properties that outstrip the reach of conventions, which are rooted to the decisions of a speaker or a community. In a single sentence Donald Harward dismisses the entire conventionalist approach for failing to see that '"2 + 2 = 4" does not mean that "here and now, 2 + 2 = 4" or "in general contexts 2 + 2 = 4"'. Hence the conventionalist simply 'misconstru[es]' what the mathematician is most interested in: the necessity of mathematical propositions'.[19]

It is indeed part of Wittgenstein's ultimate objective to drive out the metaphysical concept of necessity from the normative domain of mathematics, but only in order to make room for the logical certainty which characterises mathematical propositions *qua* rules of grammar. But Wittgenstein certainly did not think that the rule '2 + 2 = 4' means 'here and now, 2 + 2 = 4' or 'in general contexts, 2 + 2 = 4'. The former reading would be like saying that the rule only applies at this instant, while the latter treats mathematical propositions as statistical generalisations. Yet neither did he think that '2 + 2 = 4' means 'in all possible worlds at all possible times 2 + 2 = 4'. Both this and its denial are equally absurd; just as it would be to argue that 'here and now it is true that the bishop moves diagonally in chess', or to turn to possible world semantics in order to specify *when* and *where* it is true that the bishop moves diagonally. Clearly it is the question itself which is the source of this confusion. These misconceptions are caused by the failure to grasp that to describe a mathematical proposition as a rule is simply to recognise that we could not describe anyone who denied that '2 + 2 = 4' as operating with our mathematical rules; to say that 2 + 2 *must* equal 4 is merely to recognise that we use this rule as a standard of correct representation.

The point of describing mathematical propositions as grammatical conventions is that it focuses attention on the general theme that meaning is determined by intra-linguistic rules rather than a connection between language and reality, while at the same time retaining the basic premise underlying the metaphysical conception of mathematical necessity that the negation of a mathematical truth results in a contradiction. But this argument has failed to soothe the anti-conventionalist's qualms for the very reason that what principally disturbs him is the worry that it cannot just be a matter of our arbitrary whim that we say that $2 + 2 = 4$; we must, he feels, in some sense be compelled to say that $2 + 2 = 4$. He might very well appreciate that when Wittgenstein described a mathematical proposition as a 'grammatical convention' his principal concern was to undermine the platonist assumption that a mathematical proposition is a necessary truth because it corresponds to or describes some supervenient mathematical reality, yet still feel that there must be some non-metaphysical sense in which we are *compelled* to construct the proposition '$2 + 2 = 4$'.

We must be careful in our response to this objection that we do not over-extend Wittgenstein's conventionalist argument (in the manner of the 'radical conventionalist' interpretation) by overlooking the distinction between what Wittgenstein said about the creation of new connections within a proof-system or the construction of an entirely new proof-system, as opposed to the application of the established rules of a proof-schema. This distinction obviously bears strongly on how we deal with such elementary examples as the proposition '$2 + 2 = 4$'. This could hardly be regarded as the 'direct expression' of a linguistic convention. Rather, it is a consequence of the rules governing the addition of the natural numbers, and we would have no choice but to say of someone who insisted that '$2 + 2 \neq 4$' that he did not know how to add (or at any rate, that what he meant by 'addition' was not at all the same as what we understand by the term). It is thus extremely misguided to fasten onto this type of example when approaching what Wittgenstein said about the construction of new connections within a proof-system or of a new proof-system. For it totally confuses what Wittgenstein said about the *application* of established mathematical rules with the *construction* of new mathematical rules, and thus it undermines Wittgenstein's point about what Lakatos called 'the logic of mathematical discovery'; i.e. the genesis of mathematical knowledge.[20] The weakness in the Logical Positivists' argument was, as we have just seen, thoroughly demonstrated by their profound inability to deal with the problem of the discovery of mathematical truths. Lakatos seized on this point when he argued that you cannot account for the 'logic of mathematical discovery' in deductivist terms.[21] But Lakatos' argument does not apply to Wittgenstein's conception, which threads a way between the logicist model and Lakatos' own 'heuristic' approach. For, on Wittgenstein's argument, the genesis of mathematical knowledge lies in our freedom to construct *new* mathematical rules.

That is not to say that, although mathematicians construct their new rules freely, they do so blindly or capriciously. Wittgenstein emphasised in *Remarks on the Foundations of Mathematics* that 'a mathematician is always inventing new forms of description. Some, stimulated by practical needs, others, from aesthetic needs, — and yet others in a variety of ways.' (*RFM* I § 167) Thus, Wittgenstein continually stressed that there are a host of important factors which guide the mathematician in his construction of new mathematical rules. The crucial point to grasp here, however, is that none of these factors *compels* him to construct these rules, but rather that he constructs whichever rules he chooses because of his interest in the results which are thus obtained. The problem is to distinguish between the platonist picture, which assumes that the mathematician is constrained to construct certain rules, and Wittgenstein's conventionalist account, which argues that the considerations which guide mathematicians' constructions are drawn from the uses to which they wish to put their mathematical systems or the aesthetic qualities which excite their admiration and pleasure.

Even more to the point, perhaps, Wittgenstein did not abandon the 'interrelatedness of mathematical truths' by adopting a conventionalist account of mathematical propositions. The fact that the rules which mathematicians construct are 'autonomous' does not mean that mathematical truths, once they have been constructed, cannot be rendered interdependent. The point is that these interconnections are not somehow there, waiting for us to discover them. In other words, the interdependency between mathematical truths are only there once the mathematician has created them, and the considerations which guide his decisions may appertain to certain aesthetic features or to the uses to which he wishes to put these new rules, but in any event, he guides himself by appealing to such criteria. The fact remains that mathematics is indeed a 'free-floating structure', but one which operates on certain regulative principles. To be sure, Wittgenstein insisted that 'a mathematician is an inventor, not a discoverer'. (*RFM* I § 168) Yet that does not mean that Wittgenstein's aim was to banish the process of discovery altogether from the province of mathematics; rather, his chief desire was to locate the act of mathematical discovery where it properly belongs: in the normative construction of rules of grammar. For the 'portals of mathematical discovery' are the possibilities created by *grammatical innovation*: by the introduction of new conceptual links between pre-existing mathematical concepts or the creation of entirely new conceptual systems.

This may be the argument of an iconoclast, but it is certainly not that of a subversive. For Wittgenstein was definitely not trying to convince us that 'philosophy and mathematics have nothing to say to one another'; that 'no mathematical discovery can have any bearing on the philosophy of mathematics'.[22] On the contrary, Wittgenstein constantly emphasised that it is the basic task of philosophy to interpret mathematical discoveries: that is, that mathematical innovations provide *material* for philosophical reflection by throwing up new conceptual problems. Thus, the actual result of Wittgenstein's argument turns out to be that there is indeed an intimate link binding mathematics and philosophy; just as there is between e.g. philosophy and psychology. But whereas the problem in psychology is that 'there are experimental methods and *conceptual confusion*' (*PI* p. 232), in

mathematics there are grammatical constructions and confused interpretations. (It is because of this shared liability to conceptual confusion that
'an investigation is possible in connexion with mathematics which is
entirely analogous to our investigation of psychology'. (*PI* p. 232)) The
point is that the direction of this relationship is the very opposite from that
commonly supposed by philosophers of mathematics. It is not philosophy
that should be influenced by mathematics: it is mathematics that should be
vitally influenced by philosophy. In so far as mathematicians must constantly engage in the interpretation of their concepts and calculi in the
course of their constructive work, they must continually engage in a
philosophical consideration of the meaning of these terms. Thus, from a
position which steadfastly avoids any hint of mathematical revisionism,
Wittgenstein presents us with a conception of the philosophy of mathematics that has extraordinarily far-reaching implications for our understanding and pursuit of mathematics.

Notes

1. *Wissenschaftliche Weltauffassung: Der Wiener Kreis*, in Otto Neurath, *Empiricism and Sociology* (eds. M. Neurath and R.S. Cohen), Dordrecht, D. Reidel Publishing Co., 1973, p. 311.

2. Cf. Hans Hahn's closing remarks in the 'Discussion about the Foundations of Mathematics' in *Empiricism, Logic and Mathematics* (ed. Brian McGuinness), Dordrecht, D. Reidel Publishing Co., 1980, pp. 37-8. John W. Dawson Jr, 'Discussion of the Foundation of Mathematics', *History and Philosophy of Logic* (1984); John W. Dawson Jr, 'The Reception of Gödel's Incompleteness Theorems', *Philosophy of Science Association*, 2 (1984).

3. Michael Dummett, 'Wittgenstein's Philosophy of Mathematics' in *Truth and Other Enigmas*, London, Duckworth, 1978, p. 166, pp. 121-37 below.

4. Cf. Joseph Warren Dauben, *Georg Cantor: His Mathematics and Philosophy of the Infinite*, Cambridge, Harvard University Press, 1979, p. 96.

5. E.T. Bell, *Men Of Mathematics*, New York, Simon and Schuster, 1965, p. 356.

6. F. Waismann, *Introduction to Mathematical Thinking*, New York, Harper & Row, 1959, pp. 41-2.

7. Ibid., p. 61.

8. David Hilbert, 'On the Infinite' in *From Frege to Gödel: A Source Book in Mathematical Logic* (ed. J. van Heijenoort), Cambridge, Harvard University Press, 1977, p. 376.

9. David Hilbert, 'Neubegründung der Mathematik' in *Gessammelte Abhandlungen*, Berlin, Springer, 1935, p. 165.

10. Hilbert, 'On the Infinite', p. 379.

11. Ibid., p. 376.

12. Cf. 'Sceptical Confusions About Rule-Following' in Volume Two.

13. Cf. Elliott Mendelson, *Introduction to Mathematical Logic*, New York, D. Van Nostrand Co., 1979, pp. 31ff.

14. Crispin Wright, *Wittgenstein on the Foundations of Mathematics*, London, Duckworth, 1980, p. 376.

15. Ibid., p. 311.

16. Quoted in Morris Kline's *Mathematics: The Loss of Certainty*, Oxford, Oxford University Press, 1980, p.229.

17. Cf. Henri Poincaré, *Science and Hypothesis* (trans. W.J. Greenstreet), London, 1905, Chapter One.

18. A.J. Ayer, *Language Truth & Logic*, London, Victor Gollanca Ltd, 1970, pp. 85, 86.

19. D. Harward, 'Wittgenstein and the Character of Mathematical Propositions', pp. 259-63 below.

20. Imre Lakatos, 'The Deductivist Versus the Heurisitic Approach', in *Proofs and Refutations: The Logic of Mathematical Discovery*, Cambridge, Cambridge University Press, 1976.

21. Ibid., pp. 142ff.

22. Dummett, 'Wittgenstein's Philosophy of Mathematics', pp. 121-3, below.

49

Wittgenstein's Early Philosophy of Mathematics

Steven Savitt

1. Introductory

Wittgenstein's remarks in the *Tractatus*[1] on mathematics are very obscure both in detail and in general import. Paul Benacerraf and Hilary Putnam wrote, 'In his *Tractatus Logico-Philosophicus*, Wittgenstein maintained, following Russell and Frege, that mathematics was reducible to logic.'[2] On the other hand, Max Black claims, 'Wittgenstein does not regard mathematics as reducible to logic, in the manner of Whitehead and Russell.'[3] Since such authorities are at loggerheads, I shall in this paper have to spend much time simply indicating how I read the text. This discussion will fall into two parts, corresponding to the traditional way of splitting up the thesis of logicism: (1) The *concepts* of mathematics can be explicitly defined in terms of logical concepts. (2) The *theorems* of mathematics can be derived from logical axioms through purely logical deduction.[4]

My own general view, which I shall defend below, is that Wittgenstein was not a logicist in the Frege-Russell sense but that he held the propositions of mathematics to be very like those of logic. To present my view in detail, however, I must start with a discussion of operations.

2. Operations

The main discussion of operations in the *Tractatus* is in the 5.2's. Starting from the assertion that the 'structures of propositions stand in internal relations to one another' (5.2), which is the linguistic reflection of the fact that possible situations stand in internal relations to one another (4.125), Wittgenstein says, 'In order to give prominence to these internal relations we can adopt the following mode of expression: we can represent a proposition as the result of an operation that produces it out of other propositions (which are the bases of the operation).' (5.21) Then, in what seems to be the closest to a definition of 'operation' in the *Tractatus*, Wittgenstein adds, 'The operation is what has to be done to the one proposition in order to make the other out of it.' (5.23)

26

Two comments are necessary. First, although Wittgenstein seems to be at pains in some of his remarks to emphasise that operations connect propositions (in addition to those quoted above, see 5.233), he also writes, 'The internal relation by which a series is ordered is equivalent to the operation that produces one term from another.' (5.232) An example of such a series (a series of forms, as he also calls it) is the number series (4.1252), and signs for numbers are *not* propositions. Secondly, since N, the operation of joint negation, is the paradigm instance of an operation (5.5, 5.502) and since N operates on an arbitrary number of propositions (5.503), one must overlook the implication in 5.23 (and 6.01) that an operation has only a single proposition as its basis.

Since the number series is a formal series, it is important to introduce Wittgenstein's notation for an arbitrary term in such a series; he calls it a notation for the general term of a series of forms (5.2522). If 0 is an operation then the general terms of the series of forms, a 0'a, 0'0'a, ... is indicated by '[a, x, 0'x]', in which: (i) 'a' represents the initial term of the series, (ii) 'x' indicates any term selected arbitrarily from the series and (iii) '0'x' is the term that immediately follows x in the series. Wittgenstein called the bracketed expression a variable.

3. The Concepts of Mathematics

The main discussion of the concepts of mathematics in the *Tractatus* is in the 6.0's. Wittgenstein has already claimed that all propositions can be generated by applying the operation N to the elementary propositions. This is what all propositions have in common; hence the general form of a proposition can be represented in the notation introduced in the last section as

$$[\bar{P}, \bar{\xi}, N(\bar{\xi})]$$

where P must be the set of all elementary propositions (6; 3.341. 5.471-5. 4.72).[5]

Once we are given the general form of a proposition, then also we are given 'the general form according to which one proposition can be generated out of another by means of an operation' (6.002), and so Wittgenstein introduced 'the general form of an operation 0'( )' as follows:[6]

$$[\bar{\xi}, N(\bar{\xi})]' (\bar{\eta}) (=[\bar{\eta}, \bar{\xi}, N(\bar{\xi})]).$$

It is difficult, however, to see just what is being generalised here. 0 seems to be no more than N, the operation of joint negation. But *this*, claims Wittgenstein, is how we arrive at numbers.

An operation may be applied to its own results, which Wittgenstein termed 'successive applications' of that operation (5.2521). In 6.02, he considered the formal series generated by applying the general form of an operation successively, starting from an arbitrary base. That would be written:

(1) $x, 0'x, 0'0'x, 0'0'0'x, \ldots$

He presented the following definitions:

(2) $\qquad\qquad\qquad x = 0^{0'}x$ $\qquad\qquad$ Def.,
$\qquad\qquad 0'0^{n'}x = 0^{n+1'}x$ $\qquad\qquad$ Def.,

and then re-wrote (1) as:

(1') $0^{0'}x, 0^{0+1'}x, 0^{0+1+1'}x, 0^{0+1+1+1'}x, \ldots$

Then he presented a final set of definitions:

(3) $\qquad\qquad\qquad 0+1 = 1$ $\qquad\qquad$ Def.,
$\qquad\qquad\quad 0+1+1 = 2$ $\qquad\qquad$ Def.,
$\qquad\qquad 0+1+1+1 = 3$ $\qquad\qquad$ Def., (and so on).

Presumably, then, (1') could be re-written as:

(1'') $0^{0'}x, 0^{1'}x, 0^{2'}x, 0^{3'}x, \ldots,$

but Wittgenstein did not explicitly draw this conclusion. From these definitions, Wittgenstein did conclude, 'A number is the exponent of an operation.' (6.021)

One preliminary comment on the above is in order before proceeding to the rest of the 6.0's. From the realistic standpoint of Frege, all Wittgenstein has done so far is to introduce *numerals*. Did Wittgenstein identify numbers with numerals? If he did, why did he not mention and try to dispose of the formidable barrage of criticism that Frege aimed at that position?[7] If he did not, what then are the numbers? Since there are no remarks in the *Tractatus* addressed directly to these questions, I shall have to try to answer them, later in this paper, on the basis of whatever indirect evidence I can muster.

The remaining remarks of the 6.0's are very obscure — obscure in intent if not in meaning. Wittgenstein wrote, 'The concept of number is the variable number.' (6.022) This is so because the concept of number is identified with 'what is common to all numbers' (6.022), which is identified with 'the general form of a number' (6.022), which in turn is given as

$[0, \xi, \xi+1]$ (6.03);[8]

and he has already called this notation a variable (see section 2).

The first difficulty with these remarks is how to reconcile them with 6.021. If a number is really the exponent of an operation, then surely the general form of a number is that which is given in 6.02:

$[0^{0'}x, 0^{n'}x, 0^{n+1'}x].$

In this light, 6.03 seems just wrong. The second difficulty is simply that, since Wittgenstein made minimal use of the concept of number and the general form of a number, it is unclear why he introduced them at all.

The final remark of the 6.0's is 6.031: 'The theory of classes is completely superfluous in mathematics. This is connected with the fact that the generality required in mathematics is not *accidental* generality.' The first assertion presumably reflects Wittgenstein's belief that he had just exhibited a way to introduce numbers without relying on set theory, as Whitehead-Russell and Zermelo had done. The second remark must be connected with Wittgenstein's criticisms of Whitehead and Russell's Axiom of Infinity (5.535) and Axiom of Reducibility (6.1232-6.1233), especially the latter. He claimed that these axioms, essential to the derivation of the propositions of mathematics in *Principia Mathematica*, could be more than accidentally true. I am not able even to hazard a guess, however, as to the connection Wittgenstein saw between the first and second of these remarks.

4. A Criticism Considered

'Russell,' writes Black, '... bore the applications of arithmetic to counting in mind. Wittgenstein seems to have made no provision for such application.'[9] Although there is much yet to be said about the Tractarian view of mathematics, I believe that Black's criticism, which pertains solely to Wittgenstein's numbers, can profitably be discussed now.

What conditions must be met in order that one's numbers, in some reconstruction of number theory, be applicable to counting? Quine, fortunately, has given a clear account of the matter:

> The conditions upon all acceptable explications of number (that is, of the natural numbers 0, 1, 2, ...) can be put ... succinctly ...: any *progression* — i.e., any infinite series each of whose members has only finitely many precursors — will do nicely. Russell once held[10] that a further condition had to be met, to the effect that there be a way of applying one's would-be numbers to the measurement of multiplicity: a way of saying that (1) There are *n* objects *x* such that F*x*. This, however, was a mistake; any progression can be fitted to that further condition. For, (1) can be paraphrased as saying that the numbers less than *n* admit of correlation with the objects *x* such that F*x*. This requires that our apparatus include enough of the elementary theory of relations for talk of correlation, or one-one relation; but it requires nothing special about numbers, except that they form a progression.[11]

The series of numbers (or numerals) introduced above by Wittgenstein is a progression in Quine's sense and so would be an 'acceptable explication of number' *if* a way can be found to express Quine's (1). Wittgenstein, however, has dismissed set theory from his 'apparatus', so he can have no theory of extensional relations; and while it might well be argued that a theory of intensional relations would be *compatible* with all that Wittgenstein has written in the *Tractatus*, it is clear that no such theory is presented there. How, then, can Wittgenstein express (1)?

The answer, I believe, is provided by 5.5321. Back at 5.53 Wittgenstein introduced the following convention: 'Identity of object I express by identity of sign, and not by using a sign for identity. Difference of objects I express by difference of signs.' Using this convention, he then remarks at 5.5321, 'And the proposition "*Only one x* satisfies f( )", will read "(Ex).fx:~(Ex,y).fx.fy".' Following this lead (and modernising the notation slightly), Quine's (1) can be expressed in Wittgenstein's correct conceptual notation as

(1^*) $(Ex_1, x_2, \ldots, x_n) (Fx_1 \& Fx_2 \& \ldots \& Fx_n) \& \sim (Ex_1, x_2, \ldots, x_{n+1})$ $(Fx_1 \& Fx_2 \& \ldots Fx_{n+1})$,

where the subscripts on the variables may be in the expanded form $0+1$, $0+1+1$, etc. Thus I believe that Wittgenstein can meet all Quine's requirements and hence escape Black's criticism.

5. The Propositions of Mathematics

The main discussion of the propositions of mathematics in the *Tractatus* is in the 6.2's. The parallels between the points made there about the propositions of mathematics and those made in the 6.1's about the propositions of logic are quite striking. Here is a summary of the 6.1's: (1) The propositions of logic are tautologies; they *say* nothing. (2) The propositions of logic *show* the formal (or logical) properties of language and of the world. (3) A logical truth can be recognised by calculation from the symbol alone. Proof *in logic* is superfluous. (4) The tautologies are, in fact, not needed, since what they show could (in a proper notation) be seen from the constituent propositions themselves. Now the 6.2's: (1') The propositions of mathematics are equations; they do not express thoughts. (2') The propositions of mathematics, like the tautologies of logic, show the logic of the world. (3') The 'correctness' of a mathematical proposition can be perceived without comparing it to the facts. (4') Mathematical equations are not needed, since what they show must be evident from the expressions themselves. These similarities are what I had in mind when I wrote above that in Wittgenstein's view mathematics was quite like logic. Let us examine them now in detail.

As for (1) and (1'), a tautology says nothing, even though it is genuinely part of the logically correct language, because it agrees with all the truth-possibilities of its elementary propositions; it excludes nothing. An equation says nothing because it is not part of the logically correct language at all (see 5.533). Black's remarks that equations are 'part of the symbolism' are wrong.[12]

Wittgenstein throws some light on (2) in 6.124, in which he claims that the propositions of logic presuppose that there are objects and atomic facts.

No such illumination is provided for (2′). He does say that equations show that 'the two expressions connected by the sign of equality have the same meaning' (6.232), but surely this is a poor candidate for the logic of the world. Moreover, if Wittgenstein did provide some convincing illustration of (2′), he would then have to reconcile it with 6.232. I find this remark of Wittgenstein's (6.22) very mysterious.

Concerning (3) it is important to emphasise that it was supposed by Wittgenstein to state 'the peculiar mark of logical propositions' (6.113). 'The whole philosophy of logic' is contained in the fact that a logical truth can be recognised as such without having to compare it to reality (6.113). That he supposed equations to have this property too seems sufficient grounds for asserting that on Wittgenstein's views the similarities between the propositions of logic and mathematics are far more significant than their differences.

That equations *do* have this property is the point of 6.2321: 'And the possibility of proving the propositions of mathematics means simply that their correctness can be perceived without its being necessary that what they express should itself be compared with the facts in order to determine its correctness.' So *this* is what proof of an equation comes to — its correctness can be seen by an examination of the signs which comprise it.[13] But how is this correctness perceived? On Wittgenstein's *general* view of identity statements, the truth of 'a=b' is found by examining the elementary propositions of the correct conceptual notation or perspicuous language to see whether for each such proposition containing 'a' there is another proposition containing 'b' in the corresponding position (and *vice versa*).[14] This observation, I would conjecture, explains at least part of what Wittgenstein meant in 6.233: 'The question whether intuition is needed for the solution of mathematical problems must be given the answer that in this case language itself provides the necessary intuition.'

I must comment here on some remarks in the *Tractatus* — those remarks on proof in mathematics in 6.24 and 6.241 — which might seem to contradict what I have just said. Wittgenstein writes in 6.2341: 'It is the essential characteristic of mathematical method that it employs equations. Indeed it is a consequence of this method that every proposition of mathematics must be obviously true.' 'Obviously true' cannot, as Black correctly points out,[15] mean self-evident, a notion which Wittgenstein scorns (6.1271). It must mean something like: not in need of any appeal to facts in order to determine their truth or falsity. Thus while all the propositions of mathematics must be 'obvious' in this sense, they need not be obvious in the ordinary sense of easily recognisable; and I take 6.24 and 6.241 to be saying that by 'the method of substitution' one can start with obvious (in the ordinary sense) equations and proceed to generate unobvious ones, thus facilitating *recognition* of these less evident ones, but *all* these equations are none the less obvious in Wittgenstein's special sense. This interpretation provides yet another parallel between the 6.2's and the 6.1's.[16]

As for (4), Wittgenstein writes that 'in a suitable notation' tautologies would be superfluous, for we could 'recognise the formal properties of

propositions by mere inspection of the propositions themselves'. (6.122)
For example, that

$$((p \supset q) \& p) \supset q$$

is a tautology shows that 'q' follows from '$(p \supset q)$ & p', but we could see
this from the propositions themselves (6.1221). To parallel this,
Wittgenstein wrote: 'But the essential point about an equation is that it is
not necessary in order to show that the two expressions connected by the
sign of equality have the same meaning, since this can be seen from the two
expressions themselves.' (6.232)

There is one important observation to be made about (4) and (4′). What
tautologies show (at least, *part* of what they show; see 6.1201 for another
example) and what equations show is that a certain sort of inference is
permissible. The former shows (sometimes) that a certain proposition
follows from certain others, and the latter shows that a certain substitution
can be made. This similarity seems to be what Wittgenstein had in mind in
6.2: 'Mathematics is a logical method.' (See also 6.234.) But this *similarity*
does not provide sufficient grounds for rendering 6.2 and 6.234 as 'Mathematics is a *part* of logic' as B.F. McGuinness did.[17]

6. A Criticism

The great logicists, Frege and the authors of *Principia Mathematica*, did
not merely provide explications of the natural numbers, an accomplishment
which the quote from Quine in Section 3 should convince us is relatively
slight; they also showed what assumptions or axioms were necessary in
order to derive the propositions of mathematics by purely logical inference
rules and how these derivations would be constructed. It is well known that
they failed to establish the second half of the thesis of logicism — in Frege's
case because his system was inconsistent, in Whitehead and Russell's
because the Axiom of Reducibility was not a purely logical axiom. It is time
now to see how solid a foundation Wittgenstein gives to the propositions of
mathematics.

The crucial doctrine of Wittgenstein's is the one I have labelled (3′), the
view that the 'correctness' of a mathematical proposition can be perceived
without comparing it to the facts. In place of the formally precise notion of
proof of Frege and Russell, Wittgenstein substituted his nebulous doctrine
of *showing* by a correct notation. Of course, there are deep obscurities
about the idea of a correct notation, especially since Wittgenstein gives no
clear description of the process of analysis which leads one to it; but let us
put this problem aside and return to one I introduced in Section 3. In the
6.0's is Wittgenstein introducing numbers or numerals?

Although Wittgenstein writes that 'A number is the exponent of an
operation' (6.021), I claim that his exponents of operations (i.e. his
numbers) are symbols; hence, from a Fregean point of view, they are
merely numerals or names of numbers — not the numbers themselves. An

example of a mathematical proposition is '2 x 2 = 4' (6.241). This implies that the '1', '2', '3', etc. introduced in 6.02 are among the symbols that flank '=' in the equations — a claim which is hardly surprising. But these expressions are spoken of as having meaning (*Bedeutung*) in 6.232 and 4.241; and this is *absolutely necessary* for maintaining (3'), since it is the identity *of meaning* of two expressions that is supposed to show itself in the symbols themselves and that obviates any investigation of reality.

But what are the meanings of these numerals? Are they objects, which are spoken of as the meanings of names (3.203)? If they are, then it would be clear — clear for the *Tractatus*, at least — how language could show the truth of the propositions of mathematics. There is much reason, however, to hold that they are not. First of all in the 4.12's, Wittgenstein introduced the notion of a formal concept. He wrote that 'object', 'complex', 'fact', 'function' and 'number' signify formal concepts (4.1272) and that it can not be said but only shown that something falls under a formal concept. Since Wittgenstein spoke of 'object' and 'number' as signs for different formal concepts and since the implication of that whole section is that not merely different entities, but entities of different types or categories, fall under the various formal concepts mentioned there, one must conclude that numbers are not objects.

Secondly, if Wittgenstein believed that the meanings of numerals were objects, then he would either have to admit the possibility that his arithmetic might have only a finite number of numerals, which is absurd, or he would have to hold it to be evident that there were an infinite number of objects. Wittgenstein wrote, however: 'Elementary propositions consist of names. Since, however, *we are unable to give the numbers of names with different meanings*, we are also unable to give the composition of elementary propositions.' (5.55; emphasis added.) 'Give' in this context clearly means give *a priori*; and since the meaning of a name is an object (3.203), Wittgenstein implies that it is not possible to determine *a priori* the number of objects. (See also 5.557.)

One must conclude from this, that the meaning of the numerals introduced in the 6.0's are not objects but (simply) numbers, but there seems to be no discussion of these numbers in the *Tractatus* at all! And even more important, there is barely a hint in the *Tractatus* as to how two expressions could be seen (as in 6.232) to mean the same number, and so (3') would be left largely unsupported. Perhaps it is plausible that one just could see that $1 + 2 = 3$ (i.e. that $(0+1) + (0+1+1) = 0+1+1+1$, when the numerals are written out fully), but to handle equations involving large numbers some procedure must be given for comparing one side of the equation with the other. Transformation of one side into the other through substitutions licensed by simpler equations possibly — but this begins to look like proof.

Perhaps 6.232 should be construed in this broad fashion. One could then read Wittgenstein as introducing a set of axioms in 6.02 and describing a method of proof in 6.241; and then 6.2321 may be read as saying that since equations *can* be proved, they need not be compared with facts. This interpretation of Wittgenstein is closer to Frege and to Whitehead and Russell than any of the others discussed above, giving it at least a familiar feel; but it does not merely modify, it *flatly contradicts,* 6.232 because it is now the proof of an equation rather than 'the two expressions themselves' that shows that the two expressions connected by the sign of equality have the same meaning. To interpret the text in such a way that the primary commentary to a proposition (6.2321) contradicts the proposition on which it comments (6.232) seems to me indefensible. Moreover, since the propositions of mathematics play an important role (6.211) and since on this interpretation they must be proved rather than seen, Wittgenstein can no longer say that the identity sign is 'not an essential constituent of conceptual notation'. (5.533) Thus Wittgenstein's account of the equations of mathematics, on this interpretation, would be incompatible with his general account of identities.

7. Conclusion

None of these alternatives is very satisfying. From the standpoint of philosophy of mathematics, ignoring the rest of Wittgenstein's system, the last is the most plausible, but perhaps that plausibility ultimately rests on its similarity to more familiar views. If this is Wittgenstein's view, then the method of proof is left so vague that it is scarcely possible to evaluate it; and even if all the details could be filled in, one should be under no illusion about what is accomplished. Hilbert wrote that 'the science of mathematics is by no means exhausted by numerical equations and it cannot be reduced to these alone'.[18] Ramsey said that Wittgenstein's view of the propositions of mathematics as equations 'is obviously a ridiculously narrow view of mathematics, and confines it to simple arithmetic ...'[19] Wittgenstein's view, could some way be found to make it work, could not even account for the principle of mathematical induction, much less the real numbers. At best, it is scarcely the beginning of a philosophy of mathematics.

It should not be surprising, then, that so sketchy a position should evoke the contradictory comments quoted at the beginning of this chapter. Since I basically side with Black on this matter, though I disagree with him about important details, I shall give him the last word: 'So, Wittgenstein does not regard mathematics as reducible to logic, in the manner of Whitehead and Russell. On the other hand, what Wittgenstein has already called "the peculiar mark of logical propositions" (6.113*a*), the possibility of perceiving their validity by inspection of the signs that express them, without reference to facts or any other external source of evidence, is equally characteristic of mathematical equations (6.2321). In view of this, the distinction between mathematics and logic must seem somewhat arbitrary.'[20]

Notes

1. Ludwig Wittgenstein, *Tractatus Logico-Philosophicus,* trans. D.F. Pears and B.F. McGuinness (London, 1961). Further references to the *Tractatus* will be by proposition

number and will appear in the text.

2. *Philosophy of Mathematics* (Englewood Cliffs, New Jersey; 1964), p. 14.

3. *A Companion to Wittgenstein's Tractatus* (Ithaca, New York; 1966), p. 340.

4. From Rudolf Carnap's 'The Logicist Foundations of Mathematics' in the *Philosophy of Mathematics*, p. 31. These two parts of the logicist thesis are not independent; (2) could not be true if (1) were false.

5. As Black points out (*Companion*, p. 312), Wittgenstein has introduced the bar notation only in connection with variables (5.501).

6. I use '0' where Wittgenstein uses 'Ω'.

7. See *Translations from the Philosophical Writings of Gottlob Frege*, eds. Peter Geach and Max Black (Oxford, 1960), pp. 182-223.

8. Wittgenstein actually wrote in 6.03 that $[0,\xi, \xi+1]$ is the form of a *whole* number (*ganzen Zahl*) or integer, but he had no systematic distinction.

9. *Companion*, p. 314.

10. *Introduction to Mathematical Philosophy*, p. 10.

11. *Word and Object* (Cambridge, Mass.; 1964), pp. 262-3.

12. *Companion*, pp. 341, 380. I have argued this at length in Chapter III of my unpubl. diss. (Brandeis, 1972) 'Frege and Wittgenstein on Identity, Logic and Number'.

13. I discuss another interpretation of 6.2321 in the next section.

14. This point I have discussed more fully in my dissertation (in Chapter III, Section 5), which is cited in note 12.

15. *Companion*, p. 343.

16. One would expect the 'method of substitution' (6.24) to consist of terms in equations being replaced by other terms with which they had previously been equated, but the sample 'proof' of 6.241 depends on various manipulations of the operation-sign, for which no provision has been made.

17. In 'Pictures and Form in Wittgenstein's "Tractatus"', *Filosofia e Simbolismo*, Archivo di Filosofia, Fratelli Bocca, editori (Roma, 1956), pp. 207-28. Reprinted in Irving M. Copi and Robert W. Beard, *Essays on Wittgenstein's Tractatus* (London, Routledge & Kegan Paul, 1966), pp. 137-56. Reference is to p. 138 of the reprinted version.

18. David Hilbert, 'Über das Unendliche', *Mathematische Annalen*, 95 (1926), pp. 161-90. Reprinted in van Heijenoort's *From Frege to Gödel*, pp. 367-92 as 'On the Infinite'. Quote is from p. 376 of the reprinted version.

19. Frank Ramsey, *The Foundations of Mathematics* (London: Rpt., 1965), p. 17.

20. *Companion*, p. 340. I am indebted to Jonathan Bennett and to the referees of *Philosophy Research Archives* for several helpful comments and corrections.

50

Wittgenstein's Theory of Quantification

Thomas F. Baxley

Hughes Leblanc states in a recent article that "the substitution interpretation of 'all' is *at least* fifty years old: you find it, for example, in Wittgenstein's *Tractatus* and in Ramsey" [8]. The statement appears without reference to textual grounds, since Leblanc's intent in this context is simply to allude to historical antecedents of the deviant theory he is discussing and not to provide an exegesis of either the relevant passages of the *Tractatus* [16] or those of *The Foundations of Mathematics* [13]. This is certainly understandable. Yet this lack provides the occasion for the reflective reader to pause and raise the question of the appropriateness of the claim. For in the reader's mind, if he is at all familiar with contemporary logical theory, the term 'all' in conjunction with the terms 'substitution interpretation' immediately calls to mind the debates between Quine [11], Marcus [19] and others regarding the proper interpretation of the quantifiers. Certainly Leblanc's choice of idiom indicates an allusion to this debate and the concepts upon which it focuses. In the case of the *Tractatus* this characterization is particularly perplexing. For there seems to be general agreement that Wittgenstein defends a truth-functional interpretation of quantification [1, 2, 4, 10], and it is not immediately obvious that the substitutional interpretation and the truth-functional view amount to the same thing. It is not even clear whether or not the two theories are compatible. This is certainly a confusing state of affairs, and one which it is important to clarify. This is true, not only for historical reasons, but for conceptual ones as well. In the following I intend to provide some initial clarification of the issue as to whether or not Wittgenstein held a substitutional interpretation of 'all'. I will argue that a proper account of Wittgenstein's views on this matter necessitates the realization that he advances both a theory of quantification and a theory of generality. These are distinct views and, although they may be accidentally related, they do not essentially involve one another. The first is properly logical and the second involves the theory of symbolism. It must also be recognized that those who articulate either the substitutional or the objectual view of quantification generally do so without advancing *two* theories. That is, the theory of generality and the theory of quantification are combined into one. Once these two points are appreciated it becomes apparent that Wittgenstein's theory of quantification is not the substitutional view. It is truth functional. But it differs from what is normally referred to under that rubric, since the mode of presentation of the arguments of the truth function is general. This, however, is only a manner of *expression,* and accordingly is not logically essential to the author of the *Tractatus.* The realization of this difference, and the further awareness that generality involves the variable, enables one to see more clearly how confusion might arise between sub-stitution and quantification. It will also be briefly shown that the *Tractarian* theory of general propositions is specifically constituted so as to be comple-mentary to and consistent with the theses of truth, truth functionality, generality, and meaning found within.

In order to accomplish the above I partition the paper in the following manner. First, the substitutional interpretation of the quantifiers is pre-sented and it is briefly contrasted with the standard objectual view. An analysis of Wittgenstein's view in the *Tractatus* follows with a comparison of them with the substitutional interpretation. Finally, a brief attempt is made to locate the theory within the general *Tractarian* framework.

Beginning logic students are soon taught that the logic of truth functions is in certain ways inadequate (apparently a lesson which Wittgenstein never mastered). It is pointed out to them that there are arguments which are intuitively valid, yet their validity cannot be demonstrated simply through employment of concepts from the logic of propositions. Such arguments employ general terms, such as 'all', 'some', 'every', etc., in logically essential ways. That is, for the first time generality and the internal structure of propositions is of logical consequence. The logical theory which results from attempts to systematically assess such arguments is ordinarily referred to as quantification theory.

The rudiments of the idea date back at least to Aristotle, but their syste-matic development is perhaps first found in Frege [5]. Russell and Whitehead [14] developed a version which Quine and others find inade-quate for a number of reasons, not the least of which is the apparent failure to observe the use-mention distinction [12]. Quine handled many of the difficulties and contributed to the development of a clear and consistent view of quantification which has now become standard [11]. Although there are those who would take exception to certain implications which he draws from his *objectual* view, few would question the legitimacy of his semantic characterization of it. Quine's view, therefore, or any view essen-tially like his, is standard. It is the one against which any deviant view must be matched. In the following I will present a standard view which is not Quine's, but is similar in relevant respects to it.

There are two complementary ways of providing a semantic characteri-zation of a concept. The semantics can be presented informally — offering for the expression an expression or expressions in a natural language as its meaning — or the semantics can be presented formally by setting up pre-cise truth conditions for the expression in a meta-language. The virtues of each are obvious. The former permits us to "understand" the concept, in the sense that we become *familiar* with it — at least to the degree that we are acquainted with the natural language. The latter provides "understand-ing" since through it one becomes cognizant of its *exact* truth conditions. Not wishing to offend either formalist or informalist, and believing that both formal and informal comparisons are helpful in the matters under dis-cussion I will present each.

First, speaking informally, the so-called existential quantifier '$(\exists x)$' is understood under the standard theory of quantification as asserting that 'there is something x such that' and the universal quantifier '(x)' is under-stood as 'each thing x (in the universe) is such that'. Under this interpretation quantifiers are symbols which function in a referring way and in the case of first order predicate logic they are *about* objects. The mode of reference is indefinite, but it is clear that quantifiers are denoting expressions. These facts point to the appropriateness of Quine's characteri-zation of this view as the objectual view of quantification and they indicate in part why the quantifiers so interpreted are the key to ontological ques-tions.

Viewed formally, the most important semantical aspect of the standard interpretation of the quantifiers is that it employs domains and values. In this model-theoretic or denotational semantic account a domain is con-ceived of as a set of objects each of which is a member of the domain. The variables, 'x', 'y', 'z', etc., which occur in the quantifiers are said to take members of the domain as values. The value of a variable is an object in the domain, and the variables are thought to have the domain as their range.

Normally, the letters 'x', 'y', 'z', etc., perform a double function in quantificational languages. They serve as "real" variables (taking members of the domain as values) and they serve as pronouns for the purpose of cross reference. By employing domain and value semantics, the truth con-ditions, and consequently the meaning, in some sense of the term, of a quantified sentence can be given in a rigorous fashion. First, the Q.L. (quantifier language) is interpreted. An interpretation I(D) is an assign-ment of objects in D (the domain) to the individual constants (if any) in the Q.L. The assignment is such that for each individual constant exactly one individual is given to it. For each n'ary predicate in Q.L. a subset of D^n of ordered sequences of n'ary members of D is assigned. A *valuation* over D, $V_{(D)}$, of the individual variables of the Q.L. is normally understood as any assignment of members of D to the variables. The truth conditions of a sentence of the Q.L. relative to the valuation V can be defined as follows: If F is an n'ary relation and c_1, c_2, c_3, ..., c_n are individual terms, either con-stants or variables, then $F \langle c_1, c_2, c_3, ..., c_n \rangle$ is true on $V_{(D)}$ when the ordered sequence $\langle a^1, a_2, a_3, ..., a_n \rangle$ — where $a_1, a_2, a_3, ..., a_n$ are elements in D assigned to $c_1, c_2, c_3, ..., c_n$ by I_D or $V_{(D)}$ — is one of the n'tuples assigned to F by I_D. $\sim A$ (negation of A) is true if A is not true on $V_{(D)}$. $(A \cdot B)$ (conjunction of A with B) is true if both A and B are true on $V_{(D)}$. Finally, and most importantly for the present purpose, '$(x)Fx$' is true on $V_{(D)}$, if it is true on every valuation $V'_{(D)}$ which differs from $V_{(D)}$ possibly only by assigning to 'x' some other individual in the domain. Any sentence (here I mean closed sentence) is true, if it is true on all valuations over D of the individual variables of Q.L.

The above illustrates in painful detail what is meant by saying that the standard interpretation of the quantifiers employs domain and value semantics, and that the quantifiers are to be understood as making general assertions about objects in a domain.

Although this view of quantification is quite natural, and possesses other virtues as well, contemporary logicians have developed a surprisingly large number of semantical alternatives. Perhaps the best known is the substitutional interpretation advanced by Ruth Barcan Marcus [9]. Informally, the substitution interpretation of quantification can be seen to differ from the objectual view, since under it '$(x)Fx$' is read 'every substitution instance of 'Fx' is true' and '$(\exists x)Fx$' as 'some substitution instance of 'Fx' is true'. Perhaps, a more natural way of expressing this is to say that '$(x)Fx$' means that 'whatever is chosen it is F' and '$(\exists x) Fx$' means 'at lease one of the things chosen is F'. Under this view quantification is concerned with truth and substitution and is *not about objects at all.* Here it is not the case that to be is to be the value of a bound variable, for the variables of quantification neither range over domains of objects nor take individuals in those domains as values. This view places a premium on names and sentence matrices, since names are the substituends of the variables in the sentence forms.

The truth conditions for sentences in a quantified language Q.L. under the substitutional interpretation can be given in as precise a manner as that of the objectual view simply by eliminating reference to the value assignments of individual variables of the Q.L. Consider any n'ary predicate F ($c_1, c_2, c_3, \ldots c_n$) to be true, if the ordered sequence $\langle a_1, a_2, a_3, \ldots, a_n \rangle$ — those elements of D assigned by $I_{(D)}$ to the individual constants $C_1, C_2, C_3, \ldots, C_n$ — is one of the n'tuples assigned to F by $I_{(D)}$. Negation and conjunction are defined as in the objectual case and '$(x)Fx$' is true if every result of replacing 'x' by any individual constant of the Q.L. is true. '$(\exists x)Fx$' is true if some result of replacing 'x' by an individual constant of Q.L. is true. What is worthy of note in the above account is that, while the interpretations of quantifiers is not in terms of values of variables, the truth conditions of the sentences of the Q.L. are nevertheless still determined through reference to a domain of objects and an interpretation. The semantics for a quantificational language need not be of the denotational or model-theoretic form as Hintikka has shown [6]. Nevertheless, the above characterization is markedly suited for the purposes at hand, since the semantical theory implicit in the *Tractatus* determines the truth values of atomic propositions by reference to names of objects which collectively may be conceived of as domain. The choice of this particular brand of the substitutional interpretation functions to maximise the probability of disconfirming the main claim in this paper, if it is false. Keeping the main concepts discussed above in mind, attention is turned to the doctrine of quantification found in the *Tractatus.*

A proposition, according to Tractarian orthodoxy, is the expression of the agreement or disagreement with the possibilities of the existence and non-existence of atomic facts (2.201).[1] Atomic facts are functions of objects and atomic propositions are functions of names (4.24). The sense of a proposition is completely determined when the conditions under which it is true or false — its truth conditions — are specified (4.024). All propositions are truth functions of elementary propositions (5) and the sense of any proposition is the same as its truth possibilities (4.41). Any proposition determines all of logical space (3.42), and the number of forms of truth functions for any number of atomic propositions can be determined a priori. For, if there are n atomic propositions, then the number of truth possibilities is 2n, since each of the n propositions can be either true or false. In addition, since any of the 2n different possibilities can be selected and each either affirmed or denied, the number of different truth functions is 2 2n (4.27-4.42). Wittgenstein advances a procedure for generating all of the 2 2n truth functions. He expresses the formula for generation as '[$\bar{P}$, $\bar{\varepsilon}$, $N(\bar{\varepsilon})$]' and refers to it as the general form of a proposition (6). All propositions are *really* of this form, though apparent forms may be many. What the general form *shows* is that any proposition '$\bar{\varepsilon}$' is the result of successive applications of $N(\bar{\varepsilon})$ to the atomic propositions $\bar{P}$. Certainly there are difficulties with this notion, in that unlike the recursive characterization of natural number, which he also discusses (6.03), there is no simple way to follow the formula interpreted as a rule.[2]

Although general propositions, those containing 'all', 'some', 'every', etc., made it difficult for others to maintain the thesis of truth-functionality, they did not deter Wittgenstein. These propositions were simply truth functions of atomic propositions like any other truth functional expression. The only difference, and it is not a logical one, is the *mode* of presentation of the atomic propositions which serve as arguments of the function.

According to Wittgenstein, the arguments of a function, like the members of a set, can be enumerated or they can be given as the values of another function (5.501). What makes general propositions appear to be logically different from recognized truth functions, is that the arguments of these truth-functions are not enumerated, but they are given generally as values of functions of names. But, the manner of presentation of the arguments of a function is of no *logical* consequence. For the mode of symbolizing is accidental not essential (5.501). Just as '~p' is a symbolic expression of Np different from 'p | p', so too is '~($\exists x$)Fx' a different symbolic expression of $N(\bar{\varepsilon})$. The truth conditions for each are seen to be the same, for when the values of ε are the total values of a function fx for each argument for 'x', then $N(\bar{\varepsilon}) = $ ~ ($\exists x$)Fx (5.52).

We can be a bit more precise about the matter. Suppose that the values of the function fx are enumerated as follows: fa, fb, fc. In such a situation $N(\bar{\varepsilon}) = \{$~ fa, ~ fb, ~ $fc\}$, since $N(\bar{\varepsilon})$ is the result of taking each of the values of the function ε and negating them. It easily follows from a well known metatheorem of functional logic that $\{$~ fa, ~ fb, ~ $fc\}$ is satisfiable if and only if $\{$~ $fa \cdot $ ~ $fb \cdot$ ~ $fc\}$ is. That is, the truth conditions, and accordingly the sense, of the two expressions is the same. Herein lies the reason for the *analogy* between $N(\bar{fx})$ and standard truth functional conjunction. In the case in which there are a finite number of values of a function the analogy is close to complete. It is important to notice, however, that even in the finite case there is a *difference* between a conjunction and a universally quantified statement. The difference is in the manner of *presentation* of the arguments. Quantified expressions are presented *generally,* while conjunctions are enumerated. In the infinite case the mode of presentation becomes critical, since the values of the function can *only* be given generally. As Wittgenstein says himself, "I dissociate the concept *all* from truth functions", since a fusion of the two makes "... it difficult to understand the propositions '$(\exists x)Fx$' and '$(x)Fx$' in which both are embedded" (5.521). The above comments were made in criticism of both Frege and Russell. Their analysis of general statements combined the two notions, consequently confusing the issue making what was logically inessential, essential. As has been shown, according to Wittgenstein, the *logic* of quantification is truth-functional and the fact that it involved generality is a mere accident. For "What is peculiar to the generality sign is first, that it indicates a logical prototype, and secondly, that it gives prominence to constants" (5.522). Neither of the above is a matter of concern for logic in the eyes of the author of the *Tractatus.*

It is noteworthy that Wittgenstein's theory of generality is similar in some respects to the substitutional theory of quantification. Recall that the substitutional theory *essentially* involved substitution and truth, and gave prominence to names and to sentence matrices. However, do such similarities provide sufficient grounds for claims, such as Leblanc's, that Wittgenstein held a substitutional interpretation of the quantifiers? Is the substitutional interpretation in essence a truth functional one, or have the commentators, in characterizing Wittgenstein's theory as truth functional, simply misinterpreted the relevant passages of the *Tractatus*? These questions require attention, and it is time to deal with them explicitly.

Perhaps the most important point to keep in mind is that modern logical theorists, both objectual and substitutional, speak of quantification, but Wittgenstein speaks of quantification and generality — two quite distinct notions. This fact cannot be overemphasized, since it provided the basis of Wittgenstein's criticisms of Russell's theory. This theory involved both notions, and Marcus has characterized it as substitutional [9]. In addition this distinction provides the clue to the puzzle generated by Leblanc's statement. It may simplify matters in what follows, if Wittgenstein's sense of quantification is referred to as Q_1, and the theories involving both Q_1 and generality as Q_2. Once this distinction is made clear Leblanc's claim can be interpreted in one of seven ways.

First, when he claims that Wittgenstein holds a substitutional view of quantification Leblanc could be asserting that Wittgenstein's views regarding Q_1 are substitutional. While this claim has a clear sense, it is not very likely that he intended his statement to be taken in this way, because so viewed it is in all probability false. Wittgenstein's theory of Q_1 is truth-functional. General propositions are, from a logical point of view, no different from any others. They are all of the form $[P, (\bar{\varepsilon}), N(\bar{\varepsilon})]$. Those who hold substitutional theories do not, contrary to certain popular misconceptions, reduce quantified logic to truth functions.[3]

Second, it is possible that the intent of Leblanc's assertion is that Q_2 is equivalent to Wittgenstein's theory of generality. While this too is a clear claim, and perhaps more probable than the first, it is nevertheless still not very likely. As has been noted above, there are semantic similarities between the theory of generality and substitutional quantification. There are also essential differences that are understood only through a literal interpretation of Wittgenstein's *functional* language. He employs argument and value semantics, while the substitutional view employs the concepts of open sentences and names. It is recalled that general propositions are *functions*, but they are not truth functions; they are functions of names. The symbol '*fx*' does not indicate an open sentence, rather it *presents* a function of *x*. Individual constants are arguments of this function and propositions are its values. But all of this is of no logical consequence to the author of the *Tractatus*. At best these matters are preliminary to logic. They are concerned with accidental matters due to the nature of our symbolism. Put bluntly, the theory of generality cannot be equivalent to substitutional quantification, unless the latter does not deal with logic. For what is properly logical are functions of propositions, or functions of functions — truth functions of name functions. And it is Q_1 logic which is concerned with functions of functions.

What has occurred is obvious. Leblanc uses Q_2 when he claims that Wittgenstein holds a substitutional view of quantification. That is, he inadvertently commits the Frege-Russell fallacy.[4] While it is literally false that Q_1 is equivalent to Q_2, it may not be too misleading to claim that there are certain similarities between substitutional quantification and a view of Q_2 which can be gleaned from combining the views of generality and Q_1 in the *Tractatus*. I believe this is what Leblanc's claim amounts to.

Certainly Wittgenstein's "view" is more in accord with the substitutional one than with the objectual one, since he held 'object' to be a pseudo-concept (4.1272). Further, this appears to be true, especially if it is realized that the objectual view is generally conceived of as the sole alternative to the substitutional one. However, there are dangers in characterizing his view as substitutional, as have been shown. One positive point derived from this characterization which deserves mention is that it is misleading to think of Wittgenstein's theory of truth-functions in the standard way. This is especially obvious when a universally quantified statement is rendered as a conjunction and problems arise concerning an illegitimate use of "etc." in the case of non-finite numbers of statements. Wittgenstein's theory of truth functions is not the standard one and neither is his theory of quantification. Finally, as promised above, a very brief attempt to locate the "theory" of quantification within the Tractarian framework.

Certainly it is no exaggeration to say that Wittgenstein's theory of quantification is neither simply truth-functional (at least not so that it could easily be recognized as such by the contemporary reader), nor is it simply substitutional, although there are similarities between the two. It is a unique view particularly shaped by fundamental doctrines of the *Tractatus*. It possesses exactly those characteristics which are required of it in this conceptual setting. Consider first the thesis of truth functionality. General propositions appeared to many, not the least of whom was Russell, to violate this principle. Wittgenstein's theory of quantification coupled with his views on generality showed that the principle was not violated in this case. That is, his analysis of general propositions showed them to be consistent with the thesis of truth functionality. Next, consider the picture theory of meaning, another basic doctrine. Wittgenstein shows through his analysis of general propositions that they *picture* nothing more than do the *set* of atomic propositions to which they are truth-functionally equivalent. Unquestionably there are many difficulties with the picture theory, but the logic of general propositions does not increase the number, when properly understood. Finally, consider the doctrine of truth in the *Tractatus*. An atomic proposition is true if it represents a fact. Since all other propositions are truth functions of atomic propositions they are true just in case the appropriate atomic propositions *represent* facts. Many philosophers held that general propositions were not only meaningful, but many were in fact true. Wittgenstein's analysis of general propositions shows how this could be the case.

Notes

1. As is customary, any reference to the *Tractatus* will be followed by its proposition number, written in parentheses.
2. Anscombe and Hochberg have pointed this out in [1] and [7] respectively. However, this is of little concern here, since I am concerned only to point out that Wittgenstein was quite serious in maintaining that there were no other forms of propositions than $[\bar{P}, \bar{\varepsilon}, N(\bar{\varepsilon})]$. I am not attempting to show that this characterization is recursive.
3. Dunn and Belnap pointed this out in [3] along with other misconceptions or misapprehensions about the substitution interpretation.
4. This is the confusion alluded to above resulting from fusing generality with quantification.

References

[1] G.E.M. Anscombe, *An Introduction to Wittgenstein's Tractatus*, London, Hutchinson and Co., Ltd., 1967.
[2] M. Black, *A Companion to Wittgenstein's 'Tractatus'*, Ithaca, N.Y., Cornell University Press, 1964.
[3] M.J. Dunn and N.D. Belnap Jr., 'The Substitution Interpretation of the Quantifiers', *Nous*, 2 (1968), pp. 177-85.
[4] D. Favrholdt, *An Interpretation and Critique of Wittgenstein's Tractatus*, Copenhagen, Munksgaard, 1964.
[5] J. Van Heijenoort ed., *From Frege to Gödel: A Source Book in Mathematical Logic, 1879-1931*, Cambridge, Mass., 1967. Trans. of Begriffsschrift, eine der arithetischen nachgebildete Formlesprache des reinen Denkens, 1879.
[6] J. Hintikka, 'Two Papers on Symbolic Logic', *Acta Philosophica Fennica*, 8 (1955).
[7] H. Hochberg, "Negation and Generality", *Essays on Wittgenstein*, ed. by E.D. Klemke, Urbana and Chicago, University of Illinois Press, 1971, pp. 464-85.
[8] H. Leblanc, 'Semantic Deviations', *Truth, Syntax and Modality*, ed. by H. Leblanc. Amsterdam, North Holland Publishing Co., 1973, pp. 1-15.
[9] R.B. Marcus, 'Modal Logics I: Modalities and Intentional Languages', *Boston Studies in the Philosophy of Science*, ed. by M.W. Wartofsky, Dordrecht-Holland, D. Reidel Pub. Co., 1963, pp. 77-96.
[10] A. Maslow, *A Study in Wittgenstein's Tractatus*, London, Hutchinson, 1963.

[11] W.V. Quine, 'Existence and Quantification', *Ontological Relativity and Other Essays*, ed. by Dept. of Philosophy, Columbia University, New York, Columbia University Press, 1969, pp.91-113.

[12] W.V. Quine, 'Three Grades of Modal Involvement', *The Ways of Paradox and Other Essays*, New York, Random House, 1966, pp. 158-76.

[13] F. Ramsey, *The Foundations of Mathematics and Other Logical Essays*, London, Routledge and Kegan Paul, 1931.

[14] B. Russell and A.N. Whitehead, *Principia Mathematica*, 2nd ed., Cambridge, University Press, 1935.

[15] E. Stenius, *Wittgenstein's Tractatus: A Critical Exposition of Its Main Lines of Thought*, Ithaca, N.Y., Cornell University Press, 1960.

[16] L. Wittgenstein, *Tractatus Logico-Philosophicus*, trans. D.F. Pears and B.F. McGuinness, New York, Humanitas Press, 1963.

51

Wittgenstein on Number

Intisar-ul-Haque

Arithmetic has always been a source of fascination, so much so that people have attached supernatural and astrological beliefs to certain numbers. Some numbers were regarded as unlucky and others as propitious. Why and how numbers necessitate events remained unexplained. Pythagoreans even went so far as to declare that numbers are the very stuff of the world. Thus, physical units, geometrical points, and arithmetical numbers were equated with one another. Roughly speaking, numbers may be thought of as ideal objects, Platonic forms, to which this world should and must conform. A great setback to this conception of arithmetic and its relation to the world came through the discovery of irrational numbers, which were first discovered by the Pythagoreans themselves. The Pythagoreans tried to conceal this discovery, as it was destructive to their theory. If the diagonal and the side of a square cannot both be described by units — a unit to be arbitarily chosen in terms of size — it means that they cannot both be described or measured completely in terms of units or integral numbers. Zeno's paradoxes further bring to prominence the fact that arithmetical numbers and physical units cannot be identified with each other. Still the belief in the objectivity, existence, or subsistence of numbers persisted. What could numbers be, if not objects?

Nature of Numbers

Our ordinary speech contains natural numbers as if they were proper names. Calculation and manipulation with numbers is easily picturable and surveyable, if they are thought to be objects. If numbers are thought to be only names or numerals, as for example Berkeley as an empiricist and nominalist would have us believe, then it is difficult to account for the necessity and universality involved in arithmetical statements. It was thought that thinking of numbers in terms of immutable and eternal objects may satisfactorily explain the immutability and necessary connections among numbers, and that the difficulties in explaining the connection between the 'ideal' nature of numbers as Platonic Forms and the existing practical objects may not be insurmountable.

In the effort to explain the nature of numbers, viz. what sort of objects the natural numbers are and what sort of necessity is involved in arithmetical statements as formulae, philosophers tried to construct theories in the 19th and 20th centuries, which may broadly be termed logicism, conventionalism, intuitionism, and formalism. Formalism in fact dissolves the problem, because it reduces arithmetic to 'meaningless' or uninterpreted symbols. We may select any signs as uninterpreted symbols and hence they can hardly be regarded as objects. The conventional use of symbols to form formulae and to derive formulae simply explains away the necessity involved in arithmetical statements. Wittgenstein would not accept formalism for its obvious failure to account adequately for the concept of necessity and universality. Intuitionism tries to construct mathematics on the basis of natural numbers, which in turn are constructed from our intuitive perception of 'units'. Wittgenstein is one with Frege in avoiding any psychologism in his account of logic and mathematics. He wants, like Frege, to have an objective analysis of numbers and not one which smacks of psychologism. Hence he rejects intuitionism, although his approach to mathematics almost coincides with that of intuitionism. Both the earlier and the later Wittgenstein criticize logicism at length, which attempts to reduce mathematics to logic. Now, if mathematics is logic, it should have the same truth as logic; and if numbers are objects then they would be logical objects. Wittgenstein denies both: he denies that mathematics is reducible to logic and he denies that numbers are certain objects. He denies the existence or subsistence of any logical or mathematical objects.

Wittgenstein declares in the *Tractatus* that number is a formal or pseudo-concept.[1] He emphasizes that formal concepts must be differentiated from real concepts. Formal concepts, unlike real concepts, can be expressed by variables and by functions. Every variable has a form, which its values must possess. The words like 'complex', 'fact' (*Tatsache*), 'function', 'object', 'number' are formal concepts and hence he says:

> They all signify formal concepts and are represented in the logical symbolism through variables, and not through functions or classes (as Frege and Russell thought).

> Expressions like '1 is a number', 'there is only one zero' and all alike are non-sensical.

He points out that we cannot sensibly say: "There are objects," or "There are 100 objects," or "There are x objects," as we may say "There are books." 'Book' is a real concept, and hence we may express it by a function. We may assert that there are certain things which possess "bookish" properties. Number, on the other hand, is a formal or psuedo-concept for which there cannot be any corresponding object. How can we say that one is a number, when there cannot be any object which may be called number, as there may be an object which may be called book or golden mountain? How can we say that there is only one zero, when zero cannot be the real characteristic of anything? Formal properties and formal relations are structural properties and relations, which Wittgenstein also refers to as internal properties and internal relations in contradistinction to external properties and relations. These formal properties and relations are necessary and their existence cannot be described: as they are necessary and immanent any description of them would involve them and hence they are indescribable. They can only be shown by the sentences which concern the objects in question and which present the states-of-affairs in question.[2] This is the general feature of Wittgenstein's theory of showing and saying: "What can be shown *cannot* be said."[3] Necessity cannot be described but can only be shown. In the existence of real objects and relations there is no question of necessity. Concepts of real objects do not involve the concept of necessity. The general form or structure of numbers gives us the concept of number and this general form can only be given by variables. Wittgenstein gives the general form of the whole numbers as $[0, \xi, \xi + 1]$.[4] Thus he defines '$0 + 1 = 1$ Def., $0 + 1 + 1 = 2$ Def., $0 + 1 + 1 + 1 = 3$ Def. (and so on)'.[5] It is the form which informs us about the nature of number and not any corresponding object.

Formal Immanence

Wittgenstein uses the expression 'Logik' also in the broader sense to include the necessary structure of the world. This structure is only shown and not said, when we describe the world. No description is possible without this formal limitation. This form or structure is immanent and *a priori*, hence there exists no corresponding state-of-affairs. An *a priori* idea would be such whose possibility determines its truth and which would be known true by the very idea itself without any comparable object.[6] A picture pictures or presents the object truly or falsely, but the form of copying is a logical form. Thus every picture is logical and the logic is the reflected image of the world, although there cannot be any true *a priori* picture.[7] This means that there cannot be any state-of-affairs, any model without logical form, which is shown but not said. Two kinds of such logical forms are logical and mathematical. Thus he says that "the logic of the world, which the propositions of logic show in the tautologies, mathematics shows in equations."[8] Thus he declares that the propositions of logic are tautologies; they say nothing as they do not copy any state-of-affairs; they are analytic. Mathematical propositions, on the other hand, though as much *a priori* and formal, are not tautologies but equations. Thus, he later recalled,[9]

> What I said earlier about the nature of arithmetical equations and about an equation's not being replaceable by a tautology explains — I believe — what Kant means when he insists that $7 + 5 = 12$ is not an analytic proposition, but synthetic *a priori*.

The numbers, or in other words number-series (*Zahlenreihe*), is a formal or internal series bounded necessarily by internal or formal relations.[10] We make successive use of operations to obtain numbers. Thus he remarks:

> The general term of the formal series *a, 0'a, 0'0a* ... I write thus: "(*a, x, 0'x*)". This expression in brackets is variable. The first term of the expression is the beginning of the formal series, the second the form of an arbitrary term *x* of the series, and the third the form of that term of the series which immediately follows *x*.[11]

For example, as already mentioned, 3 would be $0 + 1 + 1 + 1$, that is, by applying the successive operation "+1" to the first term 0. Now, there are objects corresponding to any term in the series. The meaning of the term is determined by the formal properties which it has in the series. The same idea is expressed by Wittgenstein in his later writings. For example, in the *Philosophische Grammatik* he says: "... The meaning (*Bedeutung*) of numerals; and the investigation of this meaning is the investigation of the grammar of numerals."[12] In the *Philosophische Bemerkungen*, while remarking that numbers are represented by number schemata, he repeats: "Instead of a question of the definition of number, it is only a question of the grammar of numerals."[13] And again further he reminds us that "arithmetic is the grammar of numbers. Kinds of number can only be distinguished by the arithmetical rules relating to them."

So the terms of the formal series are the numbers, which do not represent any supra-sensible "Platonic" objects or forms. These terms or numbers are only symbols in order to symbolize or show the logical forms of the world; they are the medium to represent arithmetical rules or forms. The grammar of terms betrays structural properties or arithmetical logic of the world. The words like 'grammar of numerals' should not mislead us. These numerals are not like ordinary symbols or words like 'bachelor', 'triangle' to which we assign meanings and which may be avoided. We may imagine a world without bachelors or triangles and we may have languages without these words. But in the same vein we cannot think of a world without some numerical interlinks and correspondingly a language without some counting device. It is for this reason that Wittgenstein reminds us that numbers cannot be represented through classes or functions but through variables. In Wittgenstein's terminology, we would say that numbers display the logical forms of the world and hence they are indispensable and ineluctable, whereas words like 'bachelor' and 'triangle' do not display such logical forms of the world. Hence, when Wittgenstein says that numbers mean the grammar of the numerals in question, this obviously does not mean that numerals are arbitrary symbols which are governed by rules determined by us. He clearly denies that mathematics is a game like chess or patience.[14] In the *Bemerkungen über die Grundlagen der Mathematik* he remarks:

> The numbers (I don't mean the numerals) are shapes, and arithmetic tells us the properties of these shapes. But the difficulty here is that these properties of the shapes are *possibilities*, not the properties in respect to

shape of the things in this shape. And these possibilities in turn emerge as physical, or psychological possibilities (of separation, arrangement, etc.). But the role of the shapes is merely that of pictures which are used in such-and-such a way ...[15]

Thus, the rules exhibited by numbers are necessary. If I count some things as two and count some others as three, then it is necessary that the total would be five when counted together. It is necessary as a logical law like $p \supset [p \vee q]$ viz. if p is true then it follows that either p is true or q is true. Both arithmetical and logical laws are necessary and *a priori* and display logical forms of the world, though in different ways.

The *Tractatus* emphasizes that numbers are given to us with the calculus. The same is repeated later on. For example he reminds us:

... numbers are what I represent in my language by number schemata ...

This is what I once meant when I said, it is with the calculus (system of calculation) that numbers enter into logic.[16]

Our counting procedure is the source of numbers. In counting there is a sort of necessity. Therefore, he points out that "the calculus itself exists in space and time," and questions: "Aren't the numbers a logical peculiarity of space and time?"[17] He goes on to remark that arithmetic or calculus is a more general kind of geometry bringing out the general forms of space and time. And he elaborates his point in saying that "the calculation is only a study of logical forms, of structures, and of itself can't yield anything new."[18] Thus we observe that arithmetic does not consist in arbitrary symbols and arbitrary chosen rules for the association and dissociation of these symbols. Arithmetic shows the necessary structure of space and duration, the logical form of the world. So numbers are not fictitious but are embedded in the very numerical structure of reality. At one place, accordingly, he remarks:

The natural numbers are a form given in reality through things, as the rational numbers are through extensions etc. I mean, by actual forms. In the same way, the complex numbers are given by actual manifolds. (The *symbols* are actual.)[19]

In this quotation Wittgenstein has succinctly described the genesis, nature, and essence of numbers. It is his genius to perceive that numbers are not some super-sensible objects, rather they are the very structure or logical form of the world.

We had observed that according to Wittgenstein the meanings of numbers are given by the very grammar of numerals. This concept is quite in consonance with his concept of numbers as logical form. The logical form of numerals and their grammar are one and the same thing. A numeral is just a symbol to bring out the grammar or logical form of the world. A number-schema shows a schema of logical form of the reality in question. Suppose we have the following two geometrical structures.[20] If we start counting the dots in the

A-Series	B-Series
[ ]	x
[·]	xx
[··]	xxx
[···]	xxxx

·
·
·

·
·
·

blocks of the A-Series, we start with 0, thus our counting schema would be: 0, 1, 2, ... But if we start counting x's in the B-Series, we have to start with 1, and thus our counting-schema would be: 1, 2, 3, ... Whether we should start with 0 or with 1 depends upon the context, the reality in question. Both series show the logical form. This, by the way, disposes of the question of whether or not 0 is a natural number.

Logicism

Both the earlier and the later Wittgenstein vehemently criticize logicism. Among other things he regards logistic definitions of number as illegitimate and misleading. In the *Tractatus*, for example, he accuses Frege and Russell of committing the fallacy of the vicious circle.[21] In order to appreciate the problem in question let us see how Frege and Russell try to reduce arithmetic to logic.

The Italian mathematician, Peano, had systematically presented the basis of natural numbers. He took three primitive notions, viz. 'number', '0' and 'successor' and stipulated five basic assertions about them. These axioms are:

(i)   0 is a number.
(ii)   The successor of any number is a number.
(iii) Two different numbers cannot have the same successor.
(iv)   0 is not a successor of any number.
(v)   Suppose, if 0 has a certain property P and further if a number *n* has the property P then the successor of *n* has also the property P, then every number has the property P. This axiom is called the Principle of Mathematical Induction.[22]

These axioms are even satisfied if we start with any number other than 0, say 50, and assume that it is not the successor of any number. Further, succession may be determined by adding 2 and equating the numbers with even numbers.[23] Thus we need to have an intuitive or explicit meaning of 0 and other terms. If Frege and Russell could show that all the primitive notions and axioms of Peano's system could be reduced satisfactorily to logic, logicism would be justified at least in dealing with natural numbers. If so, arithmetical statements would be shown to be analytic and (if Wittgenstein were right in holding that logical propositions are tautologies) to be tautologies.

Let us see how Frege and Russell attempt to define number. Russell follows the lead given by Frege, and both have almost the same definition of number. Russell is comparatively more explicit and unambiguous. Whereas Russell defines any number as the class of all classes that are similar to the class having so-many members, Frege would define number as the range or class of all concepts similar to the concept of so-many members. Russell exploits the notion of similarity as Frege has already done. A class or concept is similar to another, if and only if their members have one-one correlation. This concept of similarity can be explained solely in logical symbolism, involving second-level quantification over relations. This notion of similarity contains the idea of 'as many as' and is logically prior to and presupposed by the idea of 'how many'. The number x or 'how many' of x is answered by making a correlation with the subset of natural numbers. Hence to define number in terms of similarity is quite justifiable. The next idea, which occurs to us in the above defintion of number, is that it involves a correlation of classes with a class having so many members. Having so many members means having a definite x number of members. This may appear to mean that we are using the concept of number in defining the concept of number. But this is false, because the concept of number in the definitions has already been defined in logical terms. For example, we define the number 'two' in the Russellian way as the class of all similar classes having two members. Now 'two of class A' may logically be defined as follows: There is an x and there is a y such that x is not identical with y and both x and y are members of A, and for any z if z is a member of A then $z = x$ or $z = y$. Symbolically expressed: $[x] [y] [z] [(x\varepsilon A . y\varepsilon A . x \neq y). (z\varepsilon A \supset z = x \text{ v } z = y)]$. Likewise one may say of a class having zero or one member: $(x) (\sim x\varepsilon A)$ or $\sim (\varepsilon x) (x\varepsilon A)$; $(\varepsilon x) (y) (x\varepsilon A . y\varepsilon A \supset y = x)$. Hence classes of any number of members may be expressed in purely logical terms.

But this way of talking merely about the numbers of members would not satisfy Frege and Russell. This way of expression would no doubt satisfy the application of number-concepts in a practical situation, for example in the sentence such as: 'There are nine chairs in this room'. But Frege and Russell would like to conceive numbers which may be dealt with like objects, about which they could say, for example, whether or not such a number is prime. This conception of viewing number is quite different from that of Wittgenstein, who declares that "arithmetic does not talk about numbers, it works with numbers."[24] Frege observed that numbers are used

in singulars and may be used with the definite article, e.g. the number 2 ...,
and that arithmetical statements are essentially identity statements in which
numbers are not used predicatively. Hence he argued for the individuality
and objectivity of numbers. But he forgot to take notice in this connection
that the properties and the quantifiers, i.e. second-level concepts, are also
used in the singular and this in no way guarantees that numbers are
individual objects. The use of the definite article in no way warrants our
saying that the expression in question is a proper name. In the sentence
'The whale is a mammal', 'The whale' is not used as a proper name. From
the fact that the arithmetical statements are equations, it does not follow
that numbers are objects. Wittgenstein also asserts that arithmetical statements are equations, but he arrives at a different conclusion, viz. that they
are not objects but logical forms to be expressed by variables. There can be
equations of quantifiers, e.g. some + some = some or all; all − some =
some; some − some = some or none. Why then should numbers not be
regarded as quantifiers, which may ultimately be reduced to universal or
existential quantifiers as shown above? It appears that it is their realistic
Weltanschauung which compels Frege and Russell to regard numbers as
objects. According to them, to say that such and such a number is a prime
or to say that there are so many prime numbers between 10 and 20 would
be to talk about objects. But for Wittgenstein that is just drawing attention
to "internal states of affairs" (*internen Sachverhalt*), showing the formal
structure or logical form of the world.[25]

It is for this reason that Wittgenstein has no problem about the
applicability of arithmetic. For him "the possibility of application is the real
criterion for arithmetical reality," and "every mathematical calculation is
an application of itself and only as such does it have a sense."[26] This is so
because numbers exhibit the logical form of the world; numbers of calculus
exist in space and time. Hence for Wittgenstein the same concept of
number which is used for practical problems is also used to state characteristics of numbers or series of numbers. For Frege and Russell there is a
genuine problem in expressing numbers as such in logical terms, as they
want a reduction of numbers as straightforwardly expressed in numerals
into logical symbolism, and the expression of numbers as used in their
practical application as already discussed would not do. Let us now resume
our explanation of their attempt to reduce mathematics to logic.

One thing is clear, however, from the above argumentation, that as far
as the Russellian definition of number in terms of sets of sets is concerned,
it does not commit a vicious circle. For example, 'two' would be defined as
the class of all similar classes, each of which has only two members. 'Two'
occurring in the definition is used in the practical application of arithmetic
and has already been used in logical terms; but the number 'two' as such
would be a class, a singular object, though not of a physical nature. In fact,
according to Russell, a propostion about a class is reducible "to a statement
about a function which defines the class, i.e. about a function which is satisfied by the members of the class and by no other arguments. Thus a class is
an object derived from a function and presupposing a function, just as, for
example, $(x).\phi x$ presupposes the function $\phi \hat{x}$."[27] Let us see how the

Russellian attempt fits into Peano's system. The successor relation can also be defined without any vicious circle, for given any number (i.e. a class of all similar classes having, say, x members) we may obtain its successor number by making a logical sum of a unit class (defined as a class having one member only) with all the similar classes already mentioned. Thus, a successor number in question would be a class of all similar classes having $x + 1$ members. Natural numbers are numbers which satisfy the principle of mathematical induction, i.e. axiom (v). This is achieved by saying that numbers inherit all the properties of zero with respect to the successor relation, i.e. properties which the successor of x has, provided x has them. Natural numbers are shown to emerge out of the successor relation, hence axiom (v), viz. mathematical induction, does not need special proof. Peano's first axiom, that 0 is a number, follows immediately as well. Looking closely at the definition of number and axiom (v) it can easily be proved that the successor of any number is also a number (viz. axiom (ii)). Again 0 cannot be the successor of any number (viz. axiom (iv)) because by the very definition of number it follows that a successor number of any class must have at least one member.

One axiom, the third one, viz. that two different numbers cannot have the same successor, does not follow from the Russellian definitions of number and successor relation. According to the Russellian realistic definition of a number, say ten, there should exist or subsist a corresponding class of ten members, for the definition of the number 10 would run: the class of all similar classes having 10 members. If there were no ten objects in the world, then there would not be a class of 10 objects, and consequently there cannot be the number 10. This leads to an objectionable conclusion. Suppose the total number of objects in the world is finite, say x. Then there is a class with x members but no class with $x + 1$ members for the purpose of defining numbers. Rather a class with $x + 1$ members would be an empty class! In the same way the classes with $x + 2$, $x + 3$, ... members would be empty classes, and thus there would be the same corresponding number, viz. 0, the class of similar classes having no member. This means that, if we were to take successors of the number x to be defined in terms of classes with $x + 1$, $x + 2$, ... members, then there would be so many successors of x — all successors being in terms of empty sets, hence by the number 0 — thus contradicting the axiom (iv) and the axiom (iii). In order to avoid this paradoxical situation Russell had to assume the Axiom of Infinity, viz. that there are an infinite number of individuals in the world. But the axiom of infinity is just an empirical assumption and not a logical or self-evident truth. In order to justify his logical definitions of number and successor relation he banks upon non-logical empirical assumptions. But this amounts to undermining the logical character of his definition of number. Thus Wittgenstein asserts:

> The axiom of infinity is nonsense if only because the possibility of expressing it would presuppose infinitely many things, i.e. what it is trying to assert. You can say of logical concepts such as that of infinity that their essence implies their existence.[28]

It seems that in the *Tractatus* Wittgenstein criticizes Frege and Russell on the above discussed ground.[29] He maintains that for the expression of the general thesis, that b is a successor of a, we need a general expression in terms of variables. When we try to express the concept of 'successor of' in terms of the Frege-Russellian definition of numbers as objects we run into difficulty and commit the vicious circle fallacy. He clearly denies that the talk of the existence of a formal concept can be meaningful.[30] A number, being a formal concept, cannot be an object whose existence is to be maintained. In the Russellian definition of a number we need to maintain the existence of a class (or, in the Fregean expression, the existence of a concept) having so-many members. This realistic approach to numbers, according to Wittgenstein, is nonsensical and leads to the vicious circle fallacy. The situation is hardly improved if we define a number in terms of attributes, rather than in terms of classes. For example, the number 'two' would be an attitude of a class having two members. Two or more attributes may have the same extension without being identical. Thus, it may be claimed that numbers defined as an attribute of a class of $x + 1$ members and as an attribute of a class of $x + 2$ are different numbers though both the classes are empty as discussed above. Hence, $x + 1$ and $x + 2$ cannot both be regarded as successors of x. But what about the concept of successor? Can we still successively apply it in order to evolve an infinite series of numbers? We noticed earlier that a successor number was arrived at by making a logical sum of a class with k members and a unit class, thus making a class with $k + 1$ members. How could we actually perform the operation of logical sum, if the classes in question do not have k members and one member respectively. Again, how can we define a null class attributively, so as to exclude such classes as having $x + 1$, $x + 2$, ... but which actually have no members, keeping in view the axiom (iv) that 0 cannot be the successor of any number? Simply by the idea of the attributes of the class with k members and the class with one member we cannot perform addition, unless we already posit these members (in terms of objects) in some way. A unit class, for example was defined as: $(\exists x)\,(y)(x \varepsilon A \,.\; y \varepsilon A \supset y = x)$, that is, we posit a certain member (or an object) in defining the unit class. Defining numbers in terms of attributes as above leaves the problem of positing members (or more exactly positing a certain number of members as the case demands) unresolved. Thus this approach does not lead us out of the vicious circle. The flaw, in fact, lies in the realistic and empirical approach in defining numbers, whether it be in terms of classes or in terms of attributes of classes.

Set-theoretical Approach

This does not mean that there is no way out and that defining numbers in terms of classes is doomed to failure. In fact there are set-theories, other than that of Russell, which attempt to define numbers differently. These theories try to posit members in a class in a different way. For example, we may define 0 as the null class having no member, one as a unit class which has the null class as its only member, the next higher number, i.e. 2, as the class having the previous unit class of number 1 as its only member, and so on ad infinitum. Symbolically expressed, this process would yield the series of numbers in the following way:

$$[\,] = 0; \, [[\,]] = 1; \, [[[\,]]] = 2; \, [[[[\,]]]] = 3; \ldots$$

Thus all numbers, except 0, are defined as unit classes though the sole member of each unit class is different. Or we may adopt another different method of positing members in the classes: 0 is defined as a null class having no member; 1 as a unit class having the null class as its one member; 2 as a class having two members, viz. the null class and the unit class as already defined; the next number as being the next higher class (evolved by the same process) having three members, viz. the null class, unit class, dual class as already defined; the next number 4 being the next higher class having four members, the four members being all the four previously defined classes; and so on ad infinitum. Symbolically expressed this process would yield the series of numbers in the following way:

$$0 = [\,]; \, 1 = [[\,]]; \, 2 = [[\,], [[\,]]]; \, 3 = [[\,], [[\,]], [[\,], [[\,]]]]; \ldots$$

This way of defining numbers would not be acceptable to Russell, because it goes against his theory of types. According to Russell a class must be of the next higher type than its own members. Hence, for example, it is senseless to say that a class is a member of or is not a member of itself. But in the above definitions the members of different classes are of different types in one case and the members of the same class are of different types in the other case, thus making the logical operations impossible. But the theory of types is not an intuitively unassailable or logically provable principle. It is better to do away with it, if we could otherwise resolve the problems. The above definitions of numbers provide us with progressive series as demanded by Peano's system and the axiom of infinity is not needed, as the existence or subsistence of an infinite number of classes in a progressive series is shown to emerge out of the concept of class and null class. This would satisfy Wittgenstein's demand that in the logical concept of infinity its essence should imply its existence. Both definitions in the context of respective set-theories are legitimate and explicate the formal structure of numbers.

We can also construct some other different definitions in terms of classes, which may bring out the same formal structure — in the Tractarian sense of formal internal conditions of the world. If all these diverse, rather conflicting definitions are equally good then it is obvious that the definition of numbers is neither important nor obligatory. What is important is to map out the structure, or, in Wittgenstein's terminology, to show the logical form. These definitions rather support Wittgenstein's assertion that we search not for the definitions of numbers but for the grammar of numbers and numerals and that "arithmetic does not talk about numbers, it works with numbers."[31] The concept of class and the arrangement of classes to express numbers are just media to bring out the logical form of the reality. Different sorts of numerals are also media to show the same logical forms of "arithmetical" reality. In fact Wittgenstein admits the utility of the concept in bringing out the arithmetical type of logical form. Accordingly he says that "numbers are pictures of the extensions of concepts."[32] And he immediately adds: "Now we could regard the extension of a concept as an object, whose name, like any other, has sense only in the context of a proposition ..." Again, he puts a question, "whether it makes sense to ascribe a number to objects that haven't been brought under a concept" and he answers categorically in the negative.[33] But he reminds us:

> The concept is only a method for determining an extension, but the extension is autonomous and, in its essence, independent of the concept; for it's quite immaterial which concept we have used to determine the extension ...

> If I have two objects, then I can of course, at least hypothetically, bring them under one umbrella, but what characterizes the extension is still the class, and the concept encompassing it still only a makeshift, a pretext.

Thus the concept of classes and numbers are media to bring out the logical form. Without some conceptual framework we cannot show arithmetical structure. Arithmetical structure or logical form shows itself through concepts. "A concept is something like a picture with which one compares objects."[34] Wittgenstein further declares that the whole of mathematical activity lies in concept-formation. Thus he says:

> The mathematical MUST is only another expression of the fact that mathematics forms concepts.

> And concepts help us to comprehend things. They correspond to a particular way of dealing with a situation.[35]

Wittgenstein's Attack on Set-theory

It may be remarked that although the shift from the Tractarian view of arithmetic in terms of logical form to the later Wittgenstein's view of mathematical activity in terms of concept-formation is conspicuous, the discussion here on this difference for the purpose at hand, in connection with Wittgenstein's onslaught against set-theory, is not important. It follows from the above that Wittgenstein, in principle, should have no objection against a set-theory which could show adequately the logical form of arithmetical type. We need not assume that numbers are objects in the form of classes. It rather follows from the conflicting definitions of number as sketched above that numbers (or classes) should not be taken as objects; but simply as expressions to depict the grammatical structure of arithmetic. Nevertheless he is vehemently opposed to reducing arithmetic to classes. One reason for this is that he is a steadfast opponent of Frege-Russellian logicism and, like the intuitionists, he thinks that their defects in paradoxes and in definitions are signs that all such reductions are fallacious attempts. Most of his objections to Russell's *Principia Mathematica* may also be applied *mutatis mutandis* to any logical or set-theoretical system.

His objections to logicism and axiomatic set-system are scattered throughout both in his earlier and later works, but we may find a more or less systematic onslaught in Part II of his work *Bemerkungen über die Grundlagen der Mathematik.*[36] One objection we find here is that such an axiomatic set-system is superfluous and cumbersome. For example, in II-3, II-49 he rightly impresses upon us that in the ordinary sense we cannot multiply 234, for instance, by 537. We may construct a corresponding formula in the wearisome logical set-theoretical system. For this correspondence we have to look to our ordinary number-system, thus showing the supremacy of our ordinary arithmetic. We may here support Wittgenstein by remarking that logistic or set-theoretical notation is hardly like binary notation, which could be usefully exploited in scientific techniques (computers). Neither do proofs in the system become more convincing, nor can they replace our ordinary mathematical proofs. Wittgenstein rightly points out that if we had the logistic system, the mathematical invention of differential calculus (II-47), for example, would not have come forth. Even granted that all arithmetical statements are expressible in the system, e.g. in Russell's *Principia Mathematica*, it does not prove by itself that the mathematics so expressed still remains mathematics. Obviously, Russell's *Principia Mathematica* cannot do what our ordinary mathematics does. It follows that mathematics so expressed in *Principia Mathematica* no longer remains mathematics. Hence Wittgenstein criticizes this sort of reduction of mathematics to logic or axiomatic class system as giving a distorted view of mathematics.

One more reason for Wittgenstein's rejection of any reduction to a logical system may also be mentioned. Wittgenstein regarded arithmetical propositions as synthetic *a priori*, but logical propositions are tautologous and analytic; hence the reduction of one sort of proposition to the other is impossible. He takes the distribution of prime numbers as an obvious manifestation that mathematics is synthetic *a priori*, since no analysis of the concept of prime number can provide us with this information.[37] This may be regarded as a general objection to any sort of axiomatization. But it strengthens others of Wittgenstein's objections to logicism by pointing out that, however we may reduce mathematics into logical or class symbolism, we cannot work it in order to evolve such propositions as those concerning the distribution of prime numbers. We have to bank upon ordinary mathematics for this purpose.

But all this critical disparagement does not show that the construction of class-systems is a useless or illegitimate activity. It no doubt shows that mathematics cannot be reduced to a class-system and that we cannot do our ordinary mathematics with, say, Russell's *Principia Mathematica*. But it cannot be ruled out that what a class-system can do, our ordinary mathematics cannot do; and that what a class-system can do may also be quite "logical," useful and illuminating. Following the *Tractatus* we may say that a class-system also shows the logical form of the world but in a different way. Hence, if Wittgenstein wishes to attack the class-system, he should attack it by showing its internal weakness. For example, he should show that no concept of necessity is involved in the class-system such as we find in logic and mathematics, or that certain arguments or inferences of the class-system are not valid. But this sort of approach to class-system he does not consider to be worthwhile. He himself says that he attacks *Principia Mathematica* (or for that matter any class-system) from without. But philosophically this is not enough. Why are logic and mathematics philosophically illuminating? Following the *Tractatus* we may say that they are illuminating because they are the logical forms of the world. It may be that the class-system is also illuminating in the same sense though in a different way. To the question as to why the propositions of logic are "laws of thought" he replies as follows:

'because they bring out the essence of human thinking' — to put it more correctly: because they bring out, or show, the essence, the technique, of thinking. They show what thinking is and also show kinds of thinking.[38]

It may be that the class-system on its own brings out certain features of human thinking which our ordinary logic and mathematics have missed. Hardly anyone now holds that mathematics is reducible to logic or that ordinary arithmetic can be performed with the help of the class-system. Still logicians are constructing class-systems and holding that they are bringing out some necessary features of thinking and not just bringing out formal symbolic structure. We already know the change of the numeral system from Roman numerals to Arabic ones brought about a revolution in our calculation and how further by erecting symbolic systems we have revolutionized our mathematics; how the introduction of quantifiers and other mathematical sorts of devices has broadened Aristotelian logic to the present form. We also know how usefully we are introducing "logical" quantifiers and other logical tools into our mathematics. In fact mathematics and logic are helping each other's progress. We also know that we are usefully exploiting naive (restricted) set-theory. We can test certain logical arguments in set-formulae and we are applying it in electronics. If we broaden the scope of restricted set-theory by legitimately adding more axioms, where does the fault lie? This fits well with Wittgenstein's basic Tractarian view of logical form. He himself says that "logical forms are number*less* (zahl*los*)" and that "therefore there is no philosophical monism or dualism, etc."[39] Thus to limit logical forms only to ordinary logical and mathematical propositions is in fact non-Wittgensteinian. This, accordingly, leads us to investigate further his concept of logical form and his later views on the nature and validity of mathematics and logic. Such issues must be left to later articles.

(This article was written in 1975, during my Senior Fellowship in West Germany granted by the Alexander von Humboldt Foundation.)

Notes

1. *Tractatus Logico-Philosophicus*, 1922 trans. Pears and McGuinness (London: Routledge & Kegan Paul, 1961), 4.1272, 4.126, 4.1271. Cited hereafter as *TLP*.
2. *TLP*: 4.122, 4.123.
3. *TLP*: 4.1212.
4. *TLP*: 6.03.
5. *TLP*: 6.02.
6. *TLP*: 3.04-3.05.
7. For example, *TLP*: 2.225, 6.13.
8. *TLP*: 6.22, also see, for example, 6.1, 6.11.
9. *Philosophische Bemerkungen*, 1930, ed. Rush Rhees (Oxford: Blackwell, 1946), trans. *Philosophical Remarks* (Oxford: Blackwell, 1975), 108. Cited hereafter as *PR*.
10. *TLP*: 4.1252.
11. *TLP*: 5.2522.
12. *Philosophische Grammatik*, 1932, ed. Rush Rhees (Oxford: Blackwell, 1969), Part II, 18. Cited hereafter as *PG*.
13. *PR*: 107, 108.
14. For example, see *PG*: Part II, Sec. III, 11.
15. *Bemerkungen über die Grundlagen der Mathematik*, 1937-44, ed. & trans. G. von Wright, R. Rhees, G.E.M. Anscombe (Oxford: Blackwell, 1967). Part III, 11. Cited hereafter as *RFM*.
16. *PR*: 107.
17. *PR*: 109.
18. *PR*: 111.
19. *PR*: 113.
20. *PG*: e.g., Part II, Sec. IV, 18.
21. *TLP*: 4.1273.
22. Symbolically expressed: (i) Na
(ii) $(x)\,(y)\,(Sxy\,.\,Ny \supset Nx)$
(iii) $(x)\,(y)\,Nx\,.\,Ny\,.\,x \neq y \supset (z)\,(v)\,(Szx\,.\,Svy \supset z \neq v)$
(iv) $(x)\,(Nx \supset\, \sim Sax)$
(v) $(P)\,([Pa\,.\,(n)\,(m)\,(Pn\,.\,Smn \supset Pm] \supset (z)\,Pz)$
23. See *Introduction to Mathematical Philosophy* by Bertrand Russell, Chapters 1 & 2 (2nd ed., London, 1920).
24. *PR*: 109.
25. See, for example, *PR*: 114.
26. See *PR*: 186, 109, 111.
27. *Principia Mathematica* (Cambridge, 1910), I, 62-63.
28. *PR*: 100.
29. *TLP*: 4.1278.
30. *TLP*: 4.1274.
31. See for example: *PG*: Part II, Sec. IV. 18 and *PR*: 109.
32. *PR*: 100.
33. *PR*: 99.
34. *RFM*: Part V, 50.
35. *RFM*: Part V, 46.
36. Consult also C.F. Kielkopf, *Strict Finitism* (The Hague, 1970), Chap. IV.
37. *RFM*: III, 42.
38. *RFM*: I, 133.
39. *TLP*: 4.128.

The Nature of Mathematics: Wittgenstein's Standpoint[1]

Friedrich Waismann
Translated by S.G. Shanker

What I am presenting here is a sketch. The ideas are still developing. Yet those who are familiar with these ideas believe that they contain a promising start, and perhaps my sketch will stimulate further thoughts on the topic.

The goal of these efforts is quite generally a clarification of our understanding of mathematics.[2] The foundations of these efforts go far back to the general logical considerations developed by Wittgenstein in his *Tractatus Logico-Philosophicus*, and I must first of all say a few words about this book. This book deals with the logical foundation of our language. Herein lies an affinity with Russell's approach. But the results are fundamentally different from Russell's.

The first difference concerns the nature of logic. According to Wittgenstein, logic consists of *tautologies*. A tautology is a sentence (of logic) which is true solely on the basis of its inner structure. A tautology does not, therefore, describe any state-of-affairs, for only a proposition which can also be false can communicate a state-of-affairs. Thus the sentences of logic say nothing. |That is the reason why logic by itself can neither be confirmed nor refuted.| As far as I know, this result is generally acknowledged and can be ranked as one of the most significant contributions to logic in the last generation.

A second of Wittgenstein's principles is: what a symbol *shows* cannot be *said* by means of that symbol. If we use a particular type of notation — e.g. the schema of truth-functions — and if the mere appearance of a symbol shows that it is a tautology, then we cannot use the very same symbolism to express that it is a tautology. Thus, there is something unspeakable in every symbol.[3]

If one nevertheless tries to convey this unspeakable then this creates nonsense.

The intention of this book, therefore, is a critique of language; that is to say, a critique of those most general properties of symbolism which is the basis for all our methods of expressing thoughts. One can thus formulate the fundamental idea roughly like this: only facts can be described, and they can be described distinctly. If one tries to describe something other than facts then one misuses the symbolism; that is to say, one offends against the deep internal rules of syntax which lie in the essence of our methods of communication.

A perfectly correct sign-language which meets the demands of logic must protect itself against nonsense. Philosophical discussions only have the object of making us clear about the use of our symbolism. Once this goal is achieved these discussions become superfluous. [These are roughly the thoughts which are depicted in this book. One throws away the ladder after one has climbed up it.]

Now, these thoughts lead to a definite starting-point with respect to mathematics; or to put this more precisely: they lead to a method — a manner of thinking — with which to look at related questions in the foundations of mathematics.

This method — which should always be obeyed in investigations of this kind — consists of two elements:

The first is: in order to ascertain the meaning of a mathematical concept, one must pay attention to the *use* that is made of it; that is to say, one must pay attention to what the mathematician really does in his work.

The second is: in order to visualise the significance of a mathematical proposition one must make clear how it is *verified.* In short: the meaning of a mathematical concept is the manner of its use, and the significance of a mathematical proposition is the method of its verification. [From this it follows that mathematical propositions and their proofs cannot be separated from one another.]

In order to discuss mathematical matters one must always be aware of these two principles. Nothing serves to remove more quickly and thoroughly the confusions and errors which the use of ordinary word-language [with its grammatical categories] brings about.[4]

In this lecture I will discuss the four following points:

(1) The nature of numbers
(2) The idea of infinity
(3) The concept of set
(4) The principle of complete induction.

1

I will speak first of all about our conception of the natural numbers.[5] But before that I want to consider briefly two different positions.

One is the formalist. The nature of this position is well known, and it would be useless to discuss it here. Numerals are regarded as meaningless marks for which certain game-rules are fixed. For some purposes this interpretation is convenient; but it does not suffice for the grounding of arithmetic. Let us take, for example, the proposition 'There are five platonic bodies'. This is undoubtedly a proposition of geometry which is absolutely true. It is impossible, however, to attach a meaning to this proposition if '5' is understood as a meaningless sign; that is to say, as a sign about which we know only that it obeys certain game-rules. On this reading we have no way of distinguishing between the meaning of the assertion 'there are five platonic bodies' and that of the assertion 'there are one hundred and five platonic bodies', since, as is well known, the Peano axioms of arithmetic could just as well be satisfied if one takes the numbers 100, 101, ... instead of the series of natural numbers.

Thus, consideration of the simplest of examples clearly shows that it is hopeless to try to found arithmetic on an implicit definition of numbers; for our numbers must possess a definite meaning, and hence are not[6] something which can be construed in different ways. This shortcoming is the result of the fact that the formalists only considered one aspect of the structure of mathematical forms, thereby neglecting the equally important analysis of mathematical concepts.

The logicist school has concentrated its attention on this second point, and has established a definition of number in purely logical terms. This definition rests on the so-called abstraction-principle: the number two is what all pairs have in common. According to the abstraction-principle the number 2 is thus *defined* as the class of all pairs. Hence, the class of all pairs *is* the number two. That is the logicist definition.

I will not speak here of a difficulty which, although significant, is still not of quite so fundamental a nature; I mean the use that this theory makes of identity. I want to emphasise another point here, which is best illuminated by an argument of Russell's. Suppose, Russell says, that there were exactly nine individuals in the world. Then we could construct the cardinal numbers from 0-9, but 10, which is defined as $9 + 1$, would be the null class. Consequently, 10 — and all of the following natural numbers — would be identical with one another; viz. they would all be 0. In order to avert such an arithmetical catastrophe a special axiom must be introduced; the so-called axiom of infinity. This states that there is one type to which $\aleph_0$ many individuals belong. This axiom thus represents a statement about the world, and the whole of arithmetic now depends essentially on the truth of this axiom. (For example, the introduction of real numbers.) Everyone will therefore be eager to find out whether this axiom is true. But we must reply to this that we do not know — we do not have the least clue — whether or not to believe in the truth of this axiom. And even worse, we *could* never establish the truth of this axiom, for its nature is such that it could never be verified. There is thus no [method] of convincing us of its truth. But in that case, this assumption is absolutely senseless, for the sense of a proposition[7] |lies in the manner| of its verification. Thus, the very possibility of arithmetic will have been based on an unverifiable assumption about the world; on a senseless hypothesis.

If we were to present this idea to an unbiased audience, who could we possibly still hope to convince? Who would still believe that the teaching of the natural numbers is thereby more deeply grounded? If, however, the simple and clear concept of number becomes in this manner so unclear and problematic, we can with good reason conclude that something is definitely wrong with this theory, and that it cannot be considered for the foundation and the clarification of the concept of number.

To summarise briefly these objections, we must say that, as far as formalism is concerned, the interpretation of numbers as meaningless signs is incompatible, so it seems to us, with the application which these signs already have in mathematics. On the other hand, we can acknowledge that the Frege-Russell theory endeavours to give a meaning to numbers. But in linking up this meaning with actual classes, their interpretation introduces a fortuitous, empirical element into arithmetic, thus destroying the *a prioricity* and necessity which is the hallmark of mathematics.

Now that I have spoken about these two interpretations, I will return to the sketch of my own point of view.

We also believe that the number-signs are connected with a meaning. But we do not define this meaning, as Russell does, as the class of classes. According to our basic attitude, we ask ourselves: how do we use numbers? How do they appear in the meaningful propositions of language? If I want to convey by signs to someone else the fact that there are three books on the table, then I can do this in a variety of ways. E.g. I can draw the table with the three books. But whatever form of communication I decide on, all must agree in the fact that three signs must also occur in the communication. The communication yields a picture of the state-of-affairs. Our language is also such a picture. 'There are three books on the table' can be expressed x,y,z are books; x,y,z are on the table. The number-sign 3 no longer occurs explicitly in this formulation, but it appears in the construction of the sentence; namely, in the appearance of the variables x,y,z. Thus, one can remove a number-sign from every assertion in which it occurs by using the corresponding number of variables in that assertion.

What I want to say is: *number is a logical form.* That means, a number is something which a proposition and a fact can have in common. Now, this is very important: a logical form cannot be described; one can only represent it. If I represent five men by five strokes, then I have replaced the men by the strokes. However, the five-number of the men is not replaced, but is represented by the five-number of the strokes. Here we understand the number-sign as a picture. Instead of saying: number is a form, we can also say: number is a representational feature of the symbolism.[8]

The usual kind of presentation of the numbers with the help of the digit-system is based on the exact same principle. At first glance the number 387 does not seem to be a picture of the quantity which it signifies. We must not forget, however, that the rules of syntax which tell us how the signs are to be used must still be added. The numbers 3, 8, 7 are defined. If we go back to the definition — i.e. if we break these signs down step by step — they will indeed assume *the* multiplicity which they signify; for example, 3 = 1 + 1 + 1. Furthermore, the position of the digits also expresses something. Our number-sign contains, therefore, the possibility of changing into other signs which are a direct picture. That is to say, our number signs, together with the rules of syntax, are instructions for the construction of a pictorial symbol.[9]

To define a number, therefore, means: to give an instruction for the construction of a pictorial symbol.[10] The definition of a concept points the way to the verification; the definition of a number-word points the way to the construction. We have thus left the basics of the Russellian position [and now drawn a comparison between our view and the Russellian]. The difference between both positions is the following:

|For Russell, numbers are not originally given. For Russell, numbers are made. We come across the material for this in experience; namely, in the extension of empirical properties. How many numbers we are able to generate and whether we do not run out of material — that is an empirical question. Thus, if we do not exhaust all of the numbers which we need in arithmetic, this is then not an inner necessity, but rather the gift of a fortunate coincidence.

Now, is it not clear that the creation of numbers cannot rest on empirical contingencies in the world? [Is it also not clear that, if there were in fact no properties in the world under which 9^9 things fall, that it would still make *sense* to consider such a class?] Since numbers must be able to represent every conceivable experience they cannot, therefore, be inferred from actual experience.[11]

For us, on the other hand, numbers are logical forms. There can never be a question as to whether or not a form exists, for, of course, we ourselves construct it. In this case we do not have a description and an object of description here, but rather, both fall together. [The possibility of representing a number already guarantees its existence.]

We are now in a position to introduce the crucial distinction which is necessary in this context: namely, the distinction between '*totality*' and '*system*'.|

Natural numbers, space and time-points, etc. form a 'set' in a completely different way than, for example, the benches in this hall. We all sense an essential difference here, and this difference must be capable of a clear formulation.

I distinguish between '[empirical] *totality*' and '*system*'.

How many benches there are in this hall depends on experience. I cannot know it beforehand.

Numbers, space and time-points, logical particles, etc., form a system. It is inconceivable that one should discover a new number, a new point of space or time or a new logical particle. We have the feeling here that everything springs from *one* root. If we know the principle on which the system is based, then we know the whole system. On what, now, does this difference rest?

An empirical totality goes back to a *property* (a propositional function); a system to an *operation*.

I must first explain what I understand by an operation.

An operation occurs when we are concerned with logical forms which are ordered according to some law. Thus the statements

a R b
($\exists$x) . a R x . x R b
($\exists$x,y) . a R x . x R y . y R b

are ordered according to a law. An operation is the transition from one sentence form to another. An operation is what has to be done to the one form in order to turn it into another one. An operation characterises, therefore, not the form, but rather, the difference in form. We are able to generate forms by means of the repeated application of the operation.

Therein lies the great difference between a system and a totality: it is we alone who generate the elements of a system. This is why a system is completely transparent to us. The objects of an empirical totality, however, are something which we come across.

In mathematics we are always confronted with systems, and not with totalities. The fundamental mistake of the prevailing interpretations does not consist in the fact that the essence of a system has not been recognised, but rather, that totalities and systems have been treated in the same manner; i.e. without distinguishing between them. |Let us pursue this difference somewhat further.|

This difference links up with the difference between the words 'meaningful' and 'true'. The set of benches in this hall is given by a property (propositional function). If we are acquainted with a property we do not yet thereby know whether something falls under that property, and if so, how many things fall under it. Only experience can teach us that. A class of true sentences corresponds here to the extension of the property.

What is a point in space? We realise what a point in space is if we pay attention to the meaningful use of the signs which designate points in space. A point in space occurs in a completely different way in our propositions than an object of reality; namely, always as just a part of a description which deals with the objects of reality. I can describe the location of a body if I state how far it is from certain other bodies. This description corresponds to a possible state-of-affairs, regardless of whether the description is true or false. A point in space thus represents a possibility: namely, the possibility of the location of a body relative to different bodies. The expression of this possibility is that the sentence which describes the location is meaningful. The totality of points of space corresponds to a totality of possibilities; i.e. a class of meaningful sentences.

A class of true sentences will be bounded in a completely different way than a class of meaningful sentences. In the first case the boundary will be drawn by experience, in the second case by the syntax of language. Experience bounds sentences from outside, syntax from inside. The range of a function (that is to say, the totality of x-values for which fx is meaningful) is bounded from within, by the nature of the function. And in the same way the class of points in space is bounded from within by means of the syntax of spatial statements. Natural numbers do not form a totality, but rather a system.

We can now see clearly before us the faults of the Russellian theory.

One can divide concepts into two large categories:

meaningful	true
possible	actual
rule of syntax	statement

operation	function
system	totality
a priori	a posteriori

[This classification is connected to the difference between the sayable and the unsayable.] The confusion of these two fundamentally different types of concepts runs through the whole Russellian interpretation like a red thread. Thus, numbers — which are the expression of a possibility — are introduced as the class of classes, and points in space are linked up with factual events.

For Mill the propositions and concepts of mathematics were empirical. For Russell the propositions of mathematics are, to be sure, a priori — they are tautologies — but the concepts are empirical. [Millian empiricism thus continues in part in Russell.] This is a half-way measure, an impossible construction in itself. If one pursues this line, one ends up with Wittgenstein. It is a straight path which leads from Mill via Russell to Wittgenstein. Wittgenstein's point of view is the consequence of thinking through the Russellian interpretation to the end, where it has been purified of the remains of a false empiricism. Certainly this result could only be achieved by descending deep down to the fundamentals of logic. It is just this pioneering work which is accomplished in the *Tractatus Logico-Philosophicus.*

This difference between a totality and a system ties up with a second fundamental remark. Given a totality I can regard those objects which have the property in question and those which do not (e.g. the benches which are in this room).[12]

Given a system one can no longer proceed in this way. A system has no complement. There is nothing lying outside of a system. I want to say: a system is bounded '*from within*'. A set is bounded from outside and the specification of the property is the boundary. What is bounded from within is no totality. Natural numbers, logical particles, space and time-points, the construction of geometry — these are all systems and not totalities.

A system has, therefore, two distinguishing characteristics: it is generated by an operation, and it is bounded from within. (That is to say, it has no complement.)

From this it follows that a system cannot be extended. The negative numbers, for example, are not an amendment to the natural numbers. Natural numbers, rational numbers — these are not different subclasses of the range of numbers, but rather, one can best describe their essence if one says: they are *different chapter-headings of grammar.* The different kinds of number are, so to speak, different categories of words; that is, word-categories that obey a different syntax. Between these different syntactical rules there exist similarities, and for that reason, we characterise them all as numbers.

|The result is thus: one cannot apply the concept of a class in the sense of Russellian logic to the natural numbers, the rational numbers, etc. Where it looks as if one had extended a system, one has, in fact, risen to a system of higher multiplicity.|

Notes

1. This is a translation of the surviving text of Waismann's 1930 Königsberg lecture, 'Über das Wesen der Mathematik: Der Standpunkt Wittgensteins', which was published in Waismann's *Lectures on the Philosophy of Mathematics* (ed. Wolfgang Grassl), Amsterdam, Rodopi, 1982. I am grateful to Dr Grassl and Professor Rudolf Haller for their kind permission to use this version as the basis for my translation. I am also grateful to Sir Isaiah Berlin and Sir Stuart Hampshire, Waismann's literary executors, for their kind permission to publish this English translation. Finally, I am deeply indebted to Dr Rainer Born and Ilse Lechleitner-Born, who very kindly worked over my original draft translations. The following translation is as much a product of their efforts as my own.

2. [The results of this clarification are not statements about mathematics, but rather, a proper understanding of mathematics.]

3. [This unspeakable contains, according to Wittgenstein, the whole of philosophy.]

4. [This yields in particular the following important point of view: a proposition and a proof must be regarded and treated as one and the same thing in mathematics. One must not believe that mathematical propositions possess a meaning of their own. Only a proof gives sense to a mathematical proposition, however, and as long as one does not have a proof one does not know what the expression means.]

|[That is the general logical attitude from which I will proceed. But we have to consider yet another point of view. Namely, it appears that these logical considerations touch deeply on the nature of the infinite. In fact the following explanations aim at nothing less than the definitive elimination of the infinite from mathematics, given that the infinite has been interpreted as a *totality*; and to remove the transfinite means of inference which are connected with it. What I would like to show is how this goal is to be achieved on the basis of Wittgensteinian logic. But I will only indicate the solution of this task for elementary arithmetic, where all of the essential thoughts already emerge. For the construction of analysis there exist attempts which are not yet developed well enough for me to want to speak about them.]|

5. [And I want to show how the idea of the calculus comes off well here.]

6. [are merely signs which occur in a sign-game.]

7. [is the method.]

8. [Russell himself had to make use of this principle of representation in the introduction of certain numbers, for in order to define the number two he had to employ a symbolism that itself possesses the multiplicity which he was supposed to be explaining, which exhibits this multiplicity.]

9. [For all arithmetical symbols, abbreviations, operation-signs, etc. the way back to the pictorial representation of numbers must always remain open. The symbolism of the number-representation is a system of rules for the translation into the pictorial. This is the reason why we are able to understand the significance of an arbitrarily written number-sign without having it explained to us.]

10. [A number-word symbolises, therefore, in a completely different way than a concept.]

11. Insertion: [possible → real. Basic mistake.]

12. Similarly, I can speak about the benches outside of this hall in the same way as I can speak about those inside.

53

Verificationism and Wittgenstein's Reflections on Mathematics

Max Black

"Near the beginning ... he made the famous statement: 'The sense of a proposition is the way in which it is verified'; but [later] he said this only meant 'You can determine the meaning of a proposition by asking how it is verified' and went on to say, 'This is necessarily a mere rule of thumb, because "verification" means different things, and because in some cases the question "How is it verified?" makes no sense'" (Moore, *Papers*, p. 266).

"The sense of a question is the method for answering it ... Tell me *how* you seek and I will tell you *what* you seek" (*Phil. Bem.*, sect. 27, translated).

"To understand the sense of a proposition means to know how to arrive at the decision whether it is true or false" (*Phil. Bem.*, sect. 43, translated).

"Asking whether and how a proposition can be verified is only a particular way of asking 'How do you mean that?' The answer is a contribution to the grammar of the proposition" (*Phil. Inv.*, sect. 353).

Why was Wittgenstein so much interested in mathematics, and for so long? (His *Nachlass* contains hundreds of pages of reflections upon mathematics.) Was he a rationalist metaphysician *manqué*? Did mathematics seem to him, as to his great predecessors, the supreme source of that "sublime" conception of the "essence of reality" that he painfully began to overcome in the *Tractatus* and repeatedly attacked in his later investigations?

The power of mathematics to fascinate and seduce is a prime source of what Wittgenstein called the "sickness of philosophical problems" (*die Krankheit der philosophischen Probleme*) (*Remarks on Fndn. Maths.*, II, sect. 4).

How misleading it is to label Wittgenstein as a finitist, conventionalist or any other kind of -ist (the lazy course followed by some mathematical reviewers of the *Remarks*). He was attempting something very different from "tentatively offering" another set of "foundations". A critic of the game is not another player.

It will be long before we have the "perspicuous" view of Wittgenstein's meditations upon mathematics that we shall need in order to separate what he ultimately rejected from what still remains alive. His attention to verification is only one strand in a complex pattern.

These notes might have been written as questions — "In philosophy it is always good to put a *question* instead of an answer to a question" (*Remarks*, II, sect. 5).

Let 'verificationism' stand for any view implying that the meaning of a proposition is uniquely determined by its verification-procedure(s). Then 'radical verificationism' might be used for a view that *identifies* a proposition's meaning with its verification-procedure(s). A proposition can be taken to be a "significant", meaningful, declarative sentence, or some symbolic equivalent of such a sentence. Alternatively: such a sentence *together with* its meaning. What a "verification-procedure" is will become clearer later.

In the 30's Wittgenstein sometimes sounded like a radical verificationist: "The sense of a proposition is the method of its verification" (*Der Sinn eines Satzes ist die Methode seiner Verifikation*) (*Ludwig Wittgenstein und der Wiener Kreis*, p. 79).

At first sight, something looks grammatically wrong about radical verificationism. If Wittgenstein's 1930 formula were taken literally, we would end up with absurdities like "'X is acid' means the same as 'to dip blue litmus paper in X in order to see whether it turns pink.'" For a "method", a "procedure", is characteristically given by means of an infinitive *clause*. Is this a petty objection? Could we try "'X is acid' means the same as 'If blue litmus paper is dipped into X it turns pink'"? Would this answer to Wittgenstein's intention?

A corollary of verificationism is that in the absence of a determinate verification-procedure there is *no* meaning. "If I can never completely verify a proposition then I could have meant nothing by the proposition" (*L.W.u.d.W.K.*, p. 47, translated). Appeals to the absence of verification-procedures in order to unmask apparent sense as nonsense (as in the earlier fighting days of the Vienna Circle) are very plausible. But positive determination of sense *via* the description of a relevant verification-procedure is a more dubious project.

In a straightforward case of verification, several components of the total process can be distinguished. Take the case where the proposition to be tested, p say, is 'In the Sea of Tranquility, there is now a shoe that matches *this* one'. Specification of the "method of verification" of p will need to include (i) instructions for getting to the test-situation, i.e. for getting to the region of the moon where p's truth-value can be determined; (ii) description of what might be called the testing apparatus — the shoe transported to the spot or, in other cases a ruler, a spectrometer, — or simply a question "in mind"; (iii) specification of the relevant features of the test-situation, i.e. of those facts that will settle the question (the presence or absence of a matching shoe); (iv) statement of the manner in which application of the "testing-apparatus" to the "relevant features" determines the truth or falsity of *p*.

The four parts of the verification instructions answer the following questions: How do we get to the test-situation? What do we need in order to make the test? What are we to look for? Having found this, and "applied" the instrument, by what rule do we pronounce the verified proposition to be true (false)?

We might speak of the verification-*path*, the verification-*apparatus*, the verification-*datum*, and *the truth-allocation rule.*

In simpler cases, some of the four stages are absent, or collapse into one another. I go to the book-case with a question in mind, see the *Tractatus* on the shelf, and say "There it is!" Here, it sounds pedantic to talk about "applying a test-apparatus (the proposition)" and using a "truth-allocation rule". But the distinctions still fit.

The "verification-datum" for a proposition *p* (in our simple model) must be expressible by a (true or false) proposition that is logically equivalent to *p*. Otherwise, something less than *p* would be needed to show that *p* was true; or, else, something more than *p* would be needed to show that *p* was true. So, a fully explicit specification of the "method of verification" of *p* must include *p* or something logically equivalent to *p*.

More simply: '*p* is verified in such-and-such a way' must include *p* or something equivalent to it: the complex proposition cannot be understood without understanding its kernel. So, whenever it is proper to speak of verification, the sense of *p* will partly determine the sense of '*p* is verified'. The converse is obvious: you cannot understand '*p* is verified' without understanding *p*. Does this reduce verificationism to a triviality?

Surely '*p* is verified in such-and-such a way' says *more* than *P*, on any interpretation that does not trivialise verificationism. And '*p*' cannot be logically equivalent to 'If *q* were the case, then *p*'. But then *radical* verificationism must be false: a proposition is *not* logically equivalent to the proposition that the verification procedure would have been successfully followed.

When *p* is a "material-object proposition", identification of the "method of verification" with the "path" *cum* "apparatus" *cum* "allocation-rule" (everything that the verifier has to do) leads to operationalism; while restriction of the "method" to the "verification-datum" leads to phenomenalism.

Three dogmas of classical verificationism: (1) A verification act must settle *p*'s truth-value (verification, not merely confirmation); (2) Such an act must be definitive, so that no subsequent act of verification can challenge, upset or modify it; (3) Differences in verification-procedures entail differences of sense: if *p* can be verified in two different ways, it must have two different meanings, and if *q* and *r* differ in any way in their verifications, they have different meanings. In the 30's, Wittgenstein took all three for granted. Later, he abandoned the dogmas of outright and definitive verification, but remained in the grip of the dogma of plurality of senses.

Do 'I have a toothache' and 'He (Black) has a toothache' have different meanings? Certainly they are not verified in the same way (the first isn't verified at all, in the sense of being tested for truth-value). There are no firm individuating conditions for meanings, no set rules for counting them. In his undogmatic moments, Wittgenstein might have said that it was unimportant whether you counted the propositions as identical or different, provided you remembered the *differences* in their uses.

Verificationism unduly stresses the importance of settling questions (getting knowledge). But not every utterance is an incitement to a truth-value-hunt.

There is little to suggest any principled verificationism in the *Tractatus*. To be sure, there is the one remark, Wittgenstein's closest approach to a principle of verifiability: "To understand a proposition means to know what is the case if it is true" (4.024). But, since "'*p*' is true says nothing else but *p*" (*Notebooks*, p. 9), this remark reduces to the triviality that to understand *p* is to understand '*p* *is true*, i.e. to understand *p*.

One might also cite the remark: "If a question can even be put, it can also be answered" ("*Wenn sich eine Frage überhaupt stellen lässt, so kann sie auch beantwortet werden*", *Tractatus*, 6.45) — which at least smacks of verificationism.

It would be hard, perhaps impossible, to fit verificationism into the ground-plan of the *Tractatus*. With regard to elementary propositions, Wittgenstein had what might be called a *correspondence conception of meaning*. The significant elements of the sentence–fact (its morphemes) severally designate the logical simples, the "objects" (*Gegenstände*), and the concatenation of those morphemes *shows* that the designated objects are thought of as concatenated. The morphemes "hang in one another", but whether the objects they severally stand for do the same is a question of fact, not of meaning (see my *Companion*, p. 119 and *passim* for this interpretation).

But this picture of the "picture theory" defies coherent elaboration. Think of a picturing fact *per impossibile* as itself a *Sachverhalt* whose sense is the obtaining of another *Sachverhalt*. Then the complex picture-fact (the *significant* proposition), *P*, seems analysable at first sight as $a\,b\,c\,.\,a\,D\,p\,.\,b\,D\,q\,.\,c\,D\,r$, where *a, b, c, p, q, r* are "objects" and *D* is the naming or designating relation. But this won't do. *P* cannot be a mere logical conjunction: I cannot, on *Tractatus* principles, produce the sentence-fact *a b c* and *only* refer to *p* (so that *a D p* is a fact, but not *b D q* or *c D r*). Still harder is it to conceive of *a D p, b D q*, and *c D r* being facts while *a b c* is not. For this would be tantamount to naming *p, q* and *r* "outside the context of a proposition". And surely a fact of the form *x D y* cannot be atomic; but if so what kind of structure does it have? Perhaps such difficulties can be overcome with sufficient ingenuity. It is odd that they did not worry the author of the *Tractatus*.

The fiction of a picturing-fact as elementary is in any case untenable.

Authentic sentences must be reproducible, cannot be one-shot affairs in anything that we could call a language. So even the simplest picture-fact must be general and its significant elements (morphemes) must be significant by convention. But then the conventional association of the picture-elements (one is almost inclined to call it their apparent or pseudo-concatenation) cannot be identical with the imputed concatenation of the objects they represent: we have at best parallelism (isomorphism) of logical form between the picture and what is depicted — not the identity of logical form that is the essence of the "picture theory".

A simple model: suppose *per impossible* that a picture-fact in some genuine language consisted of two complexes a-b and c-d, respectively standing for p and q (where a, b, c, d, p, q, are all simple objects, *Gegenstände*) and suppose that some atomic facts involving two objects consist of one "standing next to" the other. The picturing fact, a-b, c-d is intended to be read, by convention, as the fact that a-b, and nothing less, adjoins c-d and nothing less. And this picture-fact means that p stands next to q. But the picture-fact breaks down into the three atomic facts: $a\ b$, $b\ c$, $c\ d$. (There are no complex objects in the ontology of the *Tractatus*.) Hence, the concatenation of p and q is *not* shown by genuine concatenation in the picturing fact. And so in general.

As if all this were not sufficiently troublesome, consider the difficulties of conceiving of the verification of an elementary proposition. Wittgenstein said: "In order to recognize whether a picture is true or false, we must compare (*vergleichen*) it with reality" (2.223) and "Reality is compared with a proposition" (4.05). But how is this is to be done? Set aside the perplexities induced by the conception of comparison as a kind of double-vision: looking simultaneously *at* the proposition and *at* the world. There remains the vexing problem of the verification *approach*. The instructions for testing an elementary proposition $a\ b$ would need to fake the form, so far as I can see, of "Keep looking at the atomic facts until you find $a\ b$ — or else you don't!" But then, verifying the elementary proposition would be a happy accident, if it were true — and such a proposition could never be falsified. For it makes no sense to speak of having scrutinized *all* the atomic facts. The consequent asymmetry between verification and falsification is one of the most disconcerting consequences of the *Tractatus* conception.

It almost begins to look as if it ought to be irredeemable nonsense to speak of the verification of an elementary proposition.

Such troubles, and worse ones, must be expected if we try to impose verificationism on the *Tractatus*. What takes the place of verificationism there, and is easily confused with it, is a postulate of propositional atomism: that *all* propositions must be definite functions of *elementary* propositions. ("It is obvious that in analysing propositions we must arrive at elementary propositions ..." 4.221.) This idea, that all propositions, molecular or complex, are linked to the world *via* elementary propositions that *directly* refer to logical simples is extremely attractive. (It persists, in the later work, radically transformed, as the *leitmotif* that verbal explanations must "come to an end". But the non-verbal link between language and what is outside language is no longer the mythical one of the name-object tie.)

Strip the *Tractatus* of its ontology, as Wittgenstein later did, and much remains that is important. Wittgenstein did not discard the *Tractatus* as one colossal blunder: its main themes, however transformed, can still be discerned in the later work.

The "postulate of propositional atomism" does not entail the "thesis of extensionality". All propositions might be linked to reality *via* elementary propositions without always being truth-functions of them. Suppose it were to make sense, as it does not in the *Tractatus*, for atomic *facts* to "hang together", to concatenate. Let $F = (p\ q\,|\,r\ s)$ be a non-elementary fact resulting from the concatenation of two atomic facts (*Sachverhalte*); let P express the obtaining of F, and $e_1 = (a\ b)$, $e_2 = (c\ d)$ express the obtaining of $(p\ q)$ and $(r\ s)$ respectively. Then F could not be a fact unless both $(p\ q)$ and $(r\ s)$ were facts, but the latter might be facts, through F was not a fact. P would then be a function, but not a truth-function, of e_1 and e_2: the truth of the elementary propositions would be a necessary, but not sufficient, condition for P's truth. (Cf. the combination of chemical *molecules* to produce more complex molecules.)

If this idea worked, we would have to recognize as a logical constant, "concatenation" between *facts*. Perhaps also higher-order "concatenations", or other ways of binding facts together or generating higher-order facts by rearranging their components. Is concatenation of facts any less intelligible than the concatenation of objects? Would not a richer ontology of this sort seem closer on the face of it to the structures suggested by the intensional functions that we seem to recognize in "the only language that we know"?

Logical and mathematical formulas arise through the distance of ordinary language from the minimal language of elementary propositions. (The whole truth about the world could be expressed by a conjunction of true elementary propositions.) We see the world as through a blurred screen. Our (logical?) inability to formulate elementary propositions — or to recognize them if, *per impossible*, we could utter them, is a fundamental reason for needing logical and mathematical operators.

Our language is that of men who are necessarily myopic — and there are no metaphysical lenses to show us the *Sachverhalte*. God needs no logical operators, though even he, presumably, is bound by the ontological rules expressing constraints upon the combinations of objects: he cannot violate the logical syntax of the "minimal language". (Logical space has a grain that is *not* arbitrary.) But, seeing everything as it is, he has no use for mathematics or operative logic (the logic of the received treatises and textbooks). God does not reason.

A striking feature of the logical and mathematical co-ordinate systems that we impose upon reality is their redundancy or intertranslatability. (This is connected with the arbitrariness involved in the choice of an origin and axes and a conventional method of relation to these axes.) We put into our logic and mathematics too much, as it were. So that we seem to "discover" that formulas apparently different in construction "say the same". Hence, the need for logic and mathematics as systems of *calculation*.

Wittgenstein said that the (pseudo-) propositions of mathematics are equations (6.2). He might have said that the pseudo-propositions of logic are equivalences — and so, also, equations of a sort, equations of truth-values. (Every tautology of the kind Wittgenstein had in mind can be brought into the form of an equivalence. For instance $A \supset B$ can be taken as $A \ B \equiv A$.) In logic and mathematics alike we balance formulas against one another.

When the "verification-datum" is expunged, because a priori propositions "say nothing about the world", verification has nothing to work on but the "verification-*path*". Hence, "In logic process and result are equivalent" (6.1262). And "In logic every proposition is the form of a proof" (6.1264). One is inclined to say that the distinction between the logical/mathematical formula and the proof (or calculation) supposed to "establish" it disappears.

Verificationism arose as a refinement of empiricism. In order to adapt it to mathematics one needs to etherealize the doctrine into a *general* theory of meaning.

Logic and mathematics are *activities* of calculation, according to the *Tractatus*. (Later on, Wittgenstein liked to call them "techniques".)

Nothing in the *Tractatus* excludes the possibility of discursive calculation. To be "shown" something does not necessarily involve an Aha experience, a "flash" of insight: "The process of *calculating* mediates (*vermittelt*) this intuition" (6.2331). (But here the use of "intuition (*Anschauung*)" is ironic, I think. If we can perform the calculation, we don't need an "intuition" as well.)

Wittgenstein's conception of mathematics and logic in the *Tractatus* is a highly original, highly suggestive picture, whose influence persists strongly in the later work.

This reading of the *Tractatus* conception of logic and mathematics might be criticised as over-stressing the arbitrary side of the calculating activity. What are we to make of passages like: "The logic of the world, which logical propositions show in tautologies, mathematics shows in equations" (6.22)? And what about: "Logic takes care of itself; all we have to do is to look and see how it does it" (*Notebooks*, p. 11)? Should one say of logic, in Gertrude Stein's phrase, that "it is not real but is really there" (*Paris, France*, p. 2)?

One might make a shift of trying to explain how the apparently arbitrary choice of logical and mathematical coordinate-systems is still indirectly constrained by the "logical grain" of "the World". We arbitrarily select regions of logical space, but the resulting relations of inclusion and exclusion are no longer subject to choice. "Operative" logic is still indirectly controlled by "ontological" logic. If there is a "connection" between logic (or mathematics) and the world, that connection must be "global", not point-to-point.

In the *Tractatus*, logic and mathematics are semi-determined by-products of ontology and its symbolic representations.

There is a striking shift from "Logic permeates (*erfüllt*) the world: the limits of the world are also its limits" (5.61) to such later remarks as: "It would be queer to say that we discover that 13 follows 12. That's our technique — we *make* it this way!" (*Math. Notes*, p. 19) and (of a man who has received a proof): "He indicates his acceptance of a convention" (p. 15). (Of the *Tractatus* symbolism of truth-tables): "Have I explained by this symbolism why logic is true? I have substituted one symbolism for another" (p. 38). (And of the new approach): "I may produce new interpretations, but not in order to say that they are right, but in order to show that the old interpretations and the new are equally arbitrary. I will say, 'Here, choose, take your pick'" (p. 5).

The ontological substructure has gone, and the global logical realism of the *Tractatus* has been finally exorcised.

In the post-*Tractatus* writings, Wittgenstein repeatedly uses something like a principle of verifiability. "In order to learn to understand a proposition's grammar, one will ask: How is this proposition used? What is regarded as a criterion of its truth? What is its verification"? (*Grundlagen der Mathematik*, p. 728).

Linking meaning with "use" might be regarded as a natural development of verificationism. With the terminal verification *situation*, originally conceived as containing the proposition's objective correlate (the "verification datum") now discarded, nothing remains but the verification's *path*. From "path" to "place in a system" to "use" is a very natural transition.

The meaning-as-use conception treats *all* words as syncategorematic. But doesn't this tend to trivialize the conception, by removing the contrast between relatively independent and relatively dependent sentence-constituents? (If the "use" of a name turns out to be to *name* something, nothing has been achieved by substituting "use" for "reference".)

Wittgenstein nearly always appeals to verification-procedures to exhibit *differences* of sense. (This was so even in the *Tractatus*.) Thus, in the *Grundlagen*, this technique is applied to uncover distinctions of meaning (use) that go with 'question', 'problem', 'proof', 'series', 'irrational', 'equation', 'correspondence', 'number', 'sine' and many other mathematical words.

He is like Breughel, whom every detail interests: "My standpoint differs from that of the people who write about the foundations of arithmetic today, in my having no need to belittle (*verachten*) a given calculus, e.g. the decimal system. For me, one calculus is as good as another ... And when one game is after all distinct from another, the one game is as good, *i.e. as interesting*, as the other" (*Grundlagen*, pp. 584-85, italics in original).

Wittgenstein might be called a connoisseur of conceptual distinctions. "For us, in a certain sense — that is to say in grammar — there are no 'slight differences' (*geringe Unterschiede*)" (*Grundlagen*, p. 643).

Wittgenstein's pointillist technique, his intense interests in grammatical details, in what makes the "exceptional case" exceptional, conflicts with the ethos of the creative mathematician. A dedicated mathematician dislikes exceptions, loves formal analogies, enjoys the fictions and dodges by which one mathematical domain is projected on another: he delights in brevity, in "elegance". His maxim might be: Grasp the essential idea and let the journeymen worry about the calculations. Now Wittgenstein is notably unsympathetic to mathematical elegance: he speaks of "stupid (*stumpfsinnig*) striving for elegance" as a chief reason for mathematicians misunderstanding their own operations (*Grundlagen,* p. 740). He wants to raise again the fundamental difficulties that worry an intelligent child on first learning mathematics; and he knows that mathematicians will find this infantile or even repulsive (*Grundlagen,* p. 644). The moral of which is that philosophical clarity is quite a different thing from mathematical insight.

Yet Wittgenstein's approach has its own dangers of distortion, one-sidedness. Mathematical analogies are of the essence of mathematics; and analogies of use are as important as the disanalogies. It is no *accident* that a mathematician uses one sign in so many different ways: mathematics is not willfully ambiguous.

Wittgenstein's insistence that differences of calculation-procedures (proofs) always generate differences of sense (the third dogma of verificationism) generates paradoxes that do not sit well with the program of "drawing attention only to what everybody would accept". (For instance, the multiplication sign in '3 × 1' must have a different "use" from that in '17 × 349').

But why not treat arithmetical equations as nodes in a network of calculations, from and to which *many* paths lead? (Some of these paths, say those that lead to "stroke figures", might be given a privileged status). So far as I can see, this ought to be acceptable to Wittgenstein. For he himself said: "The mathematical proof persuades us by making certain connections. It gives us the place of (236 × 161) in a huge system" (*Math. Notes,* p. 30). Such a modification would have the great advantage of permitting a distinction between calculation *within* a given system and the analogical *extension* of a system. If we are as "free" to get a "wrong" answer to 17 × 349 as we are "free" to invent an arithmetic of infinite numbers, the word 'free' is being used in radically different ways in the two cases.

In spite of Wittgenstein's heroic efforts, nobody has yet looked hard enough at what mathematicians really do. It remains a task of great importance.

References

Math. Notes: Notes by Norman Malcolm of lectures by L.W., spring 1939. Quotations are from an unauthorized edition (San Francisco, 1954, no publisher indicated).

Grundlagen der Mathematik: Unpublished manuscript of 250 pages with this title, part of the so-called 'Big Typescript,' circa 1933 (Cornell University Library, B3376 W83 89d).

Critical Notice: *Lectures on the Foundations of Mathematics*

John V. Canfield

Cora Diamond, ed., *Wittgenstein's Lectures on the Foundations of Mathematics, Cambridge, 1939.* From the Notes of R.G. Bosanquet, Norman Malcolm, Rush Rhees, and Yorick Smythies (Ithaca N.Y.: Cornell U.P. 1976). 300 pp.

It was quite a course. A great philosopher, in command of a profound system of thought, speaking with energy and clarity on a topic that had long occupied him. Cora Diamond's book lives up to the occasion. As far as I can judge, it reconstructs the lectures skillfully and accurately. Dummett remarked that the book contains much gold. It has a good deal to teach any philosopher.

It takes up a series of problems that center on concepts related to mathematics, and offers intriguing and illuminating remarks about them. Some of the topics dealt with are: proof, formalism, pure versus applied mathematics, definitions, identity, logicism, Platonism, negation, and consistency. The book also has helpful things to say on themes of general philosophical interest, such as meaning, criteria, rules, truth and necessity.

No technical apparatus is deployed. The problems in the philosophy of mathematics that Wittgenstein is interested in are not solvable by such means. Contrary to what some have thought, he does not, here or elsewhere, take sides on any issues internal to mathematics. (That and why this is so will become clear below.)

The problems he deals with are made to show themselves in very simple guise, sometimes in examples drawn from games or puzzles. There are also imagined language games, for instance that of a tribe that gives the appearance of calculating precisely, but that uses 'calculations' only as wallpaper decoration. The mathematics he refers to is usually of an elementary kind. In fact he is, characteristically, interested in a childhood level of comprehension in mathematics. There is something magical in the way that he can draw together a child's puzzlement about the proper result of multiplying by zero, and the philosopher's worry about whether mathematics is discovery or invention.

These lectures have one main advantage over Wittgenstein's published works in this area, namely their relative discursiveness. Parts of the contexts for discussions in the *Investigations* and the *Remarks on the Foundations of Mathematics* are sometimes supplied, so that some of the things involved in those discussions become clear for the first time. The *Lectures* particularly illuminates the sections of the *Investigations* that deal with rules, with the relationship between rule and practice, with going on, agreement, intuition, and the like; and these sections, it seems to me, occupy the very center of the later philosophy.

Despite the discursiveness of these *Lectures*, someone who has not puzzled over Wittgenstein's philosophy will likely find the book mysterious both in its main themes and in detail. In this critical notice I try to provide a general orientation to the discussions that fill roughly the first third of the book, and that touch on points mentioned just above. My interpretation is close to Dummett's in his paper, 'Wittgenstein's Philosophy of Mathematics,'[1] but there are some differences as well.

I have tried here to accept Wittgenstein's invitation to bring common-sense into the lecture room, and not leave it in the hall like an umbrella. This has resulted in a review that consists in some part of objections and replies. Only by entering on both sides of such a dialogue can we hope to get at Wittgenstein's thought.

Mathematics and 'Logic'

In the *Begriffschrift*, Frege marked stipulated definitions with a special sign, the doubled judgment stroke '‖—'. A rough and ready way to render a central thesis of Wittgenstein's *Lectures* is to say that for him statements of mathematics are to be understood as prefixed by Frege's doubled judgment stroke. Thus not '7+5=12' but '‖— 7+5=12'; not 'a+b=b+a'; but '‖— a+b=b+a'; not 'A quadratic equation has two roots' but '‖— A quadratic equation has two roots.'

I use Frege's symbol here only as a way of providing a visually emphatic rendering of Wittgenstein's view. Wittgenstein understands definitions quite differently from Frege. The above 'definitions' marked by the doubled judgment stroke are to be read, with Wittgenstein, as rule statements that are linked inseparably to some 'practice' or technique.

If we take '‖—' in this way, the interpretation given above is quite clearly supported by the text of the *Lectures*, for example by this passage: 'If I wanted to give the roughest hint to someone of the difference between an experiential proposition and a mathematical proposition which looks exactly like it, I'd say that we can always affix to the mathematical proposition a formula like "by definition"' (111).

For Frege definition statements are certainly not the whole of mathematics and logic. But for Wittgenstein, as the quote just given indicates, all statements of mathematics (and of logic, in both the traditional sense and in the broadened sense that he employed) are to be marked 'by definition'. These will include not only all mathematical axioms, but all theorems as well, including geometrical ones.

For Frege, the axioms of geometry are synthetic, because one can consistently deny any of them.[2] Not so for Wittgenstein. The parallel axiom, say, and its several non-Euclidean alternatives are all true — true by definition. But each of these various definitional truths holds in its own system. Geometrical axioms and theorems are a priori, and necessary, but necessary relative to a certain system. The true-by-definition statements of Euclidean geometry make up one system and the true-by definition statements of an alternative geometry make up another. It is wrong to say that an alternative to the parallel postulate in any way denies its Euclidean counterpart, anymore than some rule of 'fairy chess' denies a corresponding but different role of chess proper. Unlike Frege, the Wittgenstein of these lectures does not see mathematics as one system, itself part of an all embracing system of truths; rather truths in mathematics, and in general, fall into self-contained, independent systems. Mathematics is a 'motley'.

We know of course that Wittgenstein atomizes language into language games. The expressions in each language game are governed by rules of that game. For example a language game with the color term 'red' might be governed, in part, by the rule that red is the color of this patch. Statements made in the language game, for example, that this book is red, have a different modal status from statements setting out, or reminding someone of, rules of the language game. The latter are atemporal, a priori and necessary, the former temporal and contingent. Wittgenstein's view of mathematics is an extension of this general position. Statements of mathematics are looked at as rules of language. In setting out a mathematical truth one is, in effect, stipulating a 'grammatical rule'. Statements of mathematics are true by definition in just the way that, say, the criterial rule 'Red is the color of this patch' is.

We are not to think of mathematics as stating objective truths, as being, as it were, the physics of numbers. Nor are we to think of a mathematical theorem, say, as following from an axiom due to some objective connection which we discern between the two. Nor are we to think even of meta-mathematics as stating objective truths about its subject matter. A mathematical system, including a 'meta-mathematical' one, is really a list of stipulated rules. At any point we can add this or that new rule to the list; the prior statements on the list do not prohibit our accepting this rather than that new rule. Only pragmatic constraints bind us in deciding on new rules.

If mathematical statements are 'grammatical truths' in the sense just indicated, then in a strange way, and despite his strong and many-sided attack on the logicism of Frege and Russell, Wittgenstein can be seen as giving a version of the logicist thesis that mathematics is a branch of logic. The version is that statements of pure mathematics are statements belonging to 'logic' in his extended sense of 'logic,' on which not only modus ponens and other logical truths in the strict sense belong to logic, but all rules governing language games, such as the above criterion for red, and such a rule governing talk about height as, 'If he is six foot three then he is not six foot seven'.

Wittgenstein retains, from the *Tractatus*, and from Frege, the idea that statements of logic and mathematics have a special status that separates them off from empirical statements. There is no sharp division between the two; there are borderline cases. But the division is there and prominently a part of Wittgenstein's conception of language. Statements of 'logic' in this broad sense are stipulations about the use of terms.

What does '⊩ A quadratic equation has two roots' signify for Wittgenstein? It serves to rule out certain statements as non-moves in the language game in which 'roots' is used as per the stipulation in question. Thus it rules out as 'senseless' — as a non-move in this language game, or as disallowed in this system of 'notation' — the claim, say, that 'This quadratic equation has three roots'.

As noted, Wittgenstein does not think of the statement as reflecting a truth about mathematics in the way that 'The earth has one moon' reflects a truth about the world. Rather he compares it to this example. In some grammars we *distinguish* four cases: nominative, genitive, dative, accusative. 'We could have two or six. We distinguish four cases. This is something quite different from *counting* four cases. We could also distinguish four roots — always two and two alike' (151).

To accept the idea that in school grammar there are four cases would be, on this understanding, to accept a convention. One agrees to mark off four cases when doing grammar, as by saying 'Yes, I see, the knight moves that way' one might agree to move the knight a certain way when playing chess. If mathematics is as Wittgenstein claims, then the acceptance of a mathematical proposition is also an act of acquiescing to a convention. Wittgenstein says: 'Mathematical conviction might be put in the form "I recognize this as analogous to that." But here "recognize" is used not as in "I recognize him as Lewy" but as in "I recognize him as superior to myself" [as one might say this in a ceremony wherein one gives fealty to someone]. He indicates his acceptance of a convention.'(63).

Rules of a language game govern the use of certain expressions; the mere words become symbols in so far as they are bound by the rules-cum-practice of that language game (or another, in which case they become different symbols). So too in mathematics. Pure mathematics, including axioms and theorems are stipulated rules of a language game. The terms governed by these rules are used in statements of applied mathematics. Thus '⊩ 2+2=4' states a convention, and 'She gave him two apples' is a statement made in a language game bound by that convention. Wittgenstein writes: 'One might put it crudely by saying that mathematical propositions containing a certain symbol are rules for the use of that symbol, and that these symbols can then be used in non-mathematical statements'(33).

Mathematics without its application would be a very different thing; the fact that it has widespread application in everyday life and science is essential to it.

To understand more fully the views just sketched it is useful to look at the idea of mathematical proof, which I shall approach by considering an objection to Wittgenstein's general position.

Pap's Argument

Arthur Pap states the following objection against what he called the 'theory that the laws of logic are not propositions but rules of symbolism':

> ... Whatever rules one may have initially stipulated and however arbitrary such stipulations may be, one will thereafter have to *find out* what these rules entail, and the statement that such and such is entailed by the rules could hardly be characterized as itself a rule (p. 184).[3]

If the axioms, say, of a geometry are held true by definition, and conceived of as rules that have been stipulated, it will yet hardly seem a further stipulated rule of the system that such and such a theorem follows from the axioms, because we have to find out whether or not it does. In general if we give a proof of a mathematical statement it will certainly not seem correct to say that it is a stipulated rule of mathematics that the premises of the proof imply the conclusion.

Wittgenstein's contrary idea is that by laying it down that the conclusion follows from the premises we thereby stipulate part of the meaning of the terms involved in premises and conclusion. If one introduced a new word in the language, say 's/he-alor' and went on to stipulate that from the fact the Jones is a s/he-alor it follows that he or she is unmarried, this further stipulation would help determine the meaning of the new term. Mathematical proofs are to be understood on this model. In stipulating that this follows from that we thereby further determine or extend the meaning of the terms involved in the proof. Against this one wants to say that we do not *lay down* that the conclusion follows: rather we *deduce* it. The terms in the premises have their meanings already fixed; and in inferring the conclusion we merely avail ourselves of the meaning of the terms (perhaps of some of the logical terms in the premise or conclusion). Thus against Wittgenstein, it seems a question of objective fact of some sort whether the proposition is a theorem, or whether the allegedly proven proposition really follows. Mathematical proof is not hidden stipulation.

Or is it? I will try to make as favourable a case as I can for Wittgenstein. The place to begin is with an example that seems extremely unfavourable to his position. If he can be defended there, then perhaps he can be defended in all the other cases.

I will prove a simple theorem of the theory of chess, that it is impossible to mate with a king and knight against a king. The most favourable case for getting mate is when the lone king (K) is in the corner, where its freedom of movements is most restricted. The mate must be delivered by the knight (N) and the white king (K) must block the opponent's escape squares. Consider the position indicated in the diagram:

The white king guards two of the three escape squares; but square 6 is open, so it is not mate. Inspection shows that there is no square from which the white king can guard all the escape squares; if the king moves to 9, for example, this will leave 2 as an escape square. The only other square from which the knight can deliver check is 4; but the resulting position is

1	2	3 $\overline{\text{K}}$
4 K	5	6
7	8 N	9

symmetrical to the one shown. Moving $\overline{\text{K}}$ from the corner (e.g. to 6, and N to 7) will obviously just increase the number of escape squares. There will always be at least one escape square.

Thus it has been shown, if informally, that the rules of chess entail that a king and knight by themselves cannot deliver mate. Thus Wittgenstein seems clearly to be wrong.

What options are open to Wittgenstein here? First, he cannot deny that the statement about mate has been proven. But it is important that he would not deny this. Informal as the proof was, he would doubtless count it a proof. What he must say, rather, is that it is consistent to say (1) that the statement has been proven from the rules of chess, and (2) both the statement itself and that the statement follows from the rules of chess are true by definition or stipulation. To see how he can hold (1) and (2) consistent we must examine his remarks in the *Lectures* on proof and on the concept 'analogous'.

Proof and Analogy

Central to that discussion is his difficult but crucial distinction between two senses of 'analogous' and certain related words. It is important to be clear that he is dealing with a family of words, including besides 'analogous,' 'the same,' 'similar' and, to add to the list he gives: 'in accordance with the rule.' In the *Lectures* he discusses 'analogous' in detail, but says that corresponding things may be said about the other words or phrases (see p. 58). His idea is that when someone develops a proof or works out a calculation — say a simple calculation in arithmetic that 25 times 25 equals 625 — each line in the proof or calculation may be said to be derived from the others in accordance with a rule. In writing out the new line we are doing the same in this case as was done by a teacher (say) who showed us how to work out such calculations. Suppose the line in question is the one which is the result of multiplying 25 by 2. We write '50' on that line, and are justified in doing so because we are doing the same here as we were taught to do when we were shown how to multiply numbers by 2. We may never have multiplied 25 by 2 before; and for that reason someone might not want to say that we do the *same* here as there. Instead, then, we might say that we do something analogous to the earlier cases. Or we might say that we do something similar. These later expressions in turn might worry someone, who might think they imply that the new multiplication by 2 departs somehow, and essentially, from the earlier cases and is so to speak, *only* analogous. But 'analogous' here and throughout means something like 'in accordance with the rule or pattern', so that the worry just sounded is misplaced.

Let us then take up the distinction between the two senses of 'analogous'. It will be in line both with Wittgenstein's sometimes confusing terminology, and with his intentions here if we use the terms 'internal' and 'external' to mark the parts of his distinction. These terms are a reminder that the distinction is a close cousin to the one so important in the *Tractatus*.

Suppose someone says that he 'saw on Watson's wall 59 multiplied by 61, analogously to those multiplication sums you showed me.' This conveys to us the information that a certain array of numbers was written on Watson's wall, namely those that would be produced by a school boy correctly carrying out the multiplication according to the usual pattern. This claim about what is on Watson's wall can be either true or false; there exists a criterion for deciding its truth value. It will be false if those two numbers are not multiplied on Watson's wall, or if they are multiplied there but in a different pattern from the usual one, so that the multiplication does not proceed analogously to the ones we have in mind. Here we will say that 'analogously' has an external sense, to mark the fact that claims using it are open to evaluation and may prove true or false, according as they meet or fail to meet the agreed upon criterion, that something is an analogous case if it looks like this or this or this, where one gives paradigms, and where the users of the language are in agreement about whether a given instance matches the paradigms or not. Here Wittgenstein says, the 'use of the word "analogous" is to describe something, to give information about something' (60).

Wittgenstein emphasises that in the example the speakers are not presented explicitly with the two items said to stand in the relationship of being analogous or of being constructed analogously. One of the items, for example, the 'multiplication sums you showed me' might be present, being perhaps visible on a blackboard, but the other term, the multiplication sum on Watson's wall, is not before the speakers. The point of the speaker's utterance is to convey to his hearer what it is that is written on Watson's wall.

By contrast, in 'internal' uses of 'analogous' or 'analogously' both the terms of the relationship are present and the speaker and hearer are fully cognizant of what they are. Wittgenstein says: 'But now we have quite a different language game. I point to two things in turn and say to you, "Surely this is analogous to this." The difference now is that we point to two things instead of to one. Hence this game is not to describe what is here or what is there; for we have both things in front of us and can see them." (60) What we are doing in such a case is something like training someone in the use of 'analogous.'

Here we may note the important connections to the case of training someone to carry on the series +2 (*PI* Sects. 185, 186). If we say to the pupil who carries on the +2 series correctly up to 1000, but then goes on '1004, 1008, 1012 . . .' and so on, that he hasn't gone on in the same way, or — what comes to the same thing — that he hasn't carried out the series after 1000 in a way that is analogous to the way he developed the series before 1000, what are we saying, according to Wittgenstein? Is '1004, 1008, 1012, etc.' the analogous development to '. . . 996, 998, 1000'? To say it is not, Wittgenstein says, is to convey to someone how we wish him to use the term 'analogous' — what we wish to count here as an analogous case. If I say, 'Surely this, and not that is analogous' then I am using 'surely' here as 'a way of buttonholing him, trying to make him do something.' And what I am trying to make him do is to use 'analogous' the way I or we do, and so to mark off the '1004, etc.' continuation as disanalogous.

How, then, does this second use of 'analogous' differ from the first? One way to mark the use would be to return to Frege's double judgment stroke. On the internal, or buttonholing use, 'This is analogous to that' gets marked '||—'; whereas 'The pattern on Watson's wall is analogous to this one' gets marked simply '|—'. (Not of course that Wittgenstein would employ Frege's assertion sign.) The second statement is an empirical one; it might or might not be true. The first states or reiterates a stipulation: 'This is what we call the analogous case.' Or, more closely mirroring Frege's own phraseology in the *Begriffschrift*: 'These are to be counted analogous.'

The application to the notion of proof is as follows.

In constructing a proof the mathematician proceeds, at each new line, by finding the analogous case. But the sense of 'analogous' here is the internal one. The claim that this is analogous to that is internal; we fix it that these cases are analogous. In this way we extend the meaning of 'analogous.' Wittgenstein puts this view of proof as follows:

A proof goes in fact step by step by means of analogy — by the help of a paradigm . . . [In] all proofs you're leading a man step by step, up to saying at each step, "Yes, this is the analogue here." Mathematical conviction might be put in the form, "I recognize this as analogous to that." But here "recognize" indicates his acceptance of a convention (62,63).

I can now indicate how Wittgenstein would answer a part of the objection by Pap given earlier. He would deny a premise of the objection, that 'The statement that such and such is entailed by the rules could hardly be characterized as itself a rule.' For example, for Wittgenstein

> It follows from the rules of chess that the position in the diagram is not checkmate

itself gets marked with the double judgment stroke. It is stipulated and in this sense is a rule. But that does not mean that the rules do not entail the statement about checkmate. Rather Wittgenstein claims to tell us what entailment is. In a proof we move step by step by means of analogy, but analogy in the internal sense. This internal connection is entailment.

But here, and earlier, many objections crowd in; answering some of them will be a way of partially clarifying what is yet a very obscure view.

Chihara's Objections

Chihara has a criticism to enter here:

> What is remarkable about the position taken in this lecture is this: Wittgenstein was not claiming that as a result of seeing the proof, a person is made to change his use of such words as "heptagon" and "can construct": it is the use of the word "analogous" that supposedly is changed (367)![4]

Obviously one of the points being made here is that in the *Lectures* Wittgenstein's view differs from the one commonly attributed to him. That familiar view was bad enough, but the new one is preposterous; or so Chihara seems to imply. The question of whether Wittgenstein really has two different views, or whether, on the contrary, they come to the same thing, will be dealt with below. In the meantime I will try to deal with two arguments that may seem to support the claim, connoted by Chihara's exclamation mark, that the new view is at the very least obviously false.

Someone might argue as follows. Wittgenstein claims both (i) that in constructing proofs, mathematicians (always, or usually) say things like 'This is analogous to that'; and (ii) that when they say these things, 'analogous' has an internal sense. Since (i) is obviously wrong, the whole view is crazy.

There is some textual excuse for the interpretation in (i) above. Wittgenstein says, for example, 'Similarly with proofs: you're leading a man step by step, up to saying at each step, "Yes, this is the analogue here"' (63). In countless cases the person actually says nothing of the sort. But of course Wittgenstein knew that. The question is, what was he claiming, if not something about what people actually say. Simply, I think, that to understand and accept the proof the person must in fact judge at each step that this follows, and that this judgment comes to no more and no less than the corresponding judgment framed in terms of 'analogous' or other of the words he talks about, the judgment, for example, that this is the analogous move to make. His point about this judgment (and not necessarily about something the person actually said) then is, that if we express it by using the word 'analogous' the word will have its internal sense.

Alternative Logical Systems

A second point that may lie behind Chihara's remark has more substance. He explicitly supports a criticism made by Turing during the lecture:

> *Turing*: It certainly isn't a question of inventing what the word "analogous" means; for we all know what "analogous" means (66).

If the use of 'analogous' in question is internal, then we are fixing what is to count as analogous here, according to Wittgenstein; and thereby we extend or change the meaning of 'analogous'. Hence the relevance of Turing's objection that we do not need to invent what we all already know full well.

To deal with this objection we must go to what I think is the core of Wittgenstein's position. This is something we may call the doctrine of alternative logical worlds. In the remainder of this section I will attempt to state this doctrine, and will return in the next section to Turing.

Wittgenstein's espousal of the doctrine comes out in some remarks he makes about Frege's Platonism.

> ... In the mathematical realm 25 × 25 is *already* 625. — The immediate [objection] is: then it's also 624, or 626, or any damn thing — for any mathematical system you like ...
>
> You never get beyond what you've decided yourself; you can always go on in innumerable different ways ... You want to make an investigation, but no investigation will do, because there is always freedom to go into another world (145).

Wittgenstein is not opposing Frege's Platonism with an expanded Platonism, where there is not one kingdom of logical and mathematical truths but infinitely many such kingdoms. But he is pointing out the existence of many different systems of mathematics. That there are such systems (that the statement 'there are such systems' is true) does not commit us to including these or their occupants in our 'ontology', any more than the fact that there is a variation on chess in which the queen moves like a combined bishop and knight entails that this game, or this strangely moving piece, has a place in anyone's ontology, Quine perhaps to the contrary notwithstanding.

The possibility of alternative systems is exactly the same possibility discussed in the case of '+2'. Someone is taught a system for generating from any given number the number two greater than it, where the starting point of the series is zero and the only numbers in the series are those that result from zero by successive applications of the rule '+2.' In the example, of course, a pupil seemingly masters the system up to a certain point, but then goes on in a way that is at odds with the system. He says '1000, 1004, 1008,' etc., instead of '1000, 1002, 1004 ...' etc. What he says is not correct.

Wittgenstein will certainly agree that what the errant pupil says here is not correct. But this means: not correct, in our system. And our system is defined in part by the rule that the correct result of adding 2 to 1000 is 1002, and not 1004. While our system is in part defined by the rule that 1000 plus 2 is 1002, other systems are possible. In one of these the correct result of adding 2 to 1000 is, by definition, 1004.

The pupil went part of the way with us in our system and then departed from it. It turns out that he accepts a different system. Perhaps for someone of his makeup, it is natural to accept such a definition or rule as: 'The correct result of adding 2 to 1000 is 1004.'

But is there nothing in the part of the system that he accepted that will compel him to go in our way? The question cannot be whether there is something that will causally compel him, for that is irrelevant. Everyone may be causally compelled to go on in our way even though there is another system different from ours. Perhaps the sense of the terms he has been taught determine him to go on our way? If by 'sense' is meant Fregean sense, then of course Wittgenstein will deny this. We may well say — and correctly — that the pupil didn't understand the meaning of '+2'. But our criterion for this judgment is that he did not go on in our way. Part of the meaning of '+2' is given by the fact that it is incorrect to say that 1000 + 2 is 1004 (but see the discussion in the next section). Still, there is a system in which the result of the operation they call '+2' on '1000' is 1004. We can easily imagine that the people who have that system teach it to their students in exactly the way that the teacher taught it to the pupil in Wittgenstein's example. That is, the two systems can coincide exactly not only in their initial segments but also in every detail of the teaching or training given any pupil up to the point where the systems diverge. There will not necessarily be any difference between the thoughts and images of a pupil of their system and those of a successful pupil of our system.

What makes the difference between the two systems Wittgenstein believes is simply that in the one it is a rule that 1000 + 2 is 1002 and in the other that it is 1004, etc.

Wittgenstein thought that such divergencies of systems were possible at any point. In the chess example introduced above Wittgenstein would say that it is possible to have a people who are taught to play chess exactly as we are, and who play like us, up to a point, but then diverge. They accept the same verbal or notational formulations of the rules of chess as we do and play it exactly as we do, with one exception: they say that the black king in the position diagrammed, and all similar positions, is in checkmate.

This may seem at first, and maybe a bit later as well, to be ridiculous. Can anyone who knows chess really say, sincerely, looking at the diagrammed position, that the king is in checkmate? There is clearly an escape square, a square that the king can move to and that is guarded by neither white king nor knight. How could anyone purport to understand and accept the rules for moving knights and kings, and the rule for checkmate, and claim that this is checkmate? Yet one can imagine a whole people who find that this is indeed the natural thing to say. They do say it in this case, and they all agree with one another. Here there is no escape square, they say; not when the opposing king and knight are so placed. Hence it is checkmate.

What this comes to is that they have a different game — different at least in the correct (correct in this game) judgment about checkmate in certain cases.

What people will find hard to accept is that someone could agree with the usual statements of rules about how the pieces move, and about what checkmate is, and still call this checkmate. They will say that these people haven't understood what checkmate is, or what a knight or king move is. Indeed they haven't understood, if the criterion for understanding is that one refuses to call the position in the diagram checkmate. But what one cannot deny, as far as I can see, is that: (a) there is a game in which it is checkmate, but which is like our game everywhere else; (b) a person might be taught, and learn, this second game through exactly the training that someone might receive in learning our game, including the same statements of rules and the training in applying those rules; and (c) there will not necessarily by any phenomenological differences between pupils of the different systems; that is, their mind states may be qualitatively the same at all points prior to the divergence.[5]

The 'there is' in (a) is, again, the 'there is' of 'There is a variant of chess in which ...' or 'There is a form of poker in which ...' or 'There is a system in which *not-p or not-q* cannot be inferred from *not-(p and q)*,' and so on. The modal terms in (b) and (c) are to be eliminated along lines Wittgenstein has stressed in a number of places in his writings. 'It is possible that so and so' is to be read as, 'It makes sense to say "so and so"'. This notion of making sense is to be read as something like 'is an allowed move in the language game'. This notion itself is I believe bedrock for Wittgenstein and is to be communicated by examples.

Wittgenstein's doctrine of what I have called alternative logical worlds can be viewed as just a generalization of the chess case just discussed and the '+2' example. The branching we see in these examples is always possible. The branching is not possible within one system, of course; rather at any point there are branching systems.

Stroud has argued that Wittgenstein thinks that in the case of any branching we are locked into our system because any of the alternative systems are incomprehensible to us.[6] I can find no textual warrant for saying that this is Wittgenstein's view and I am sure that Wittgenstein does not think of all the alternatives as unintelligible. What locks us into our system is the fact that we accept the convention according to which our way of proceeding at the branching point is counted as the correct way, and the others incorrect. There may and typically will be pragmatic reasons also for our having the system we have, and for our accepting the definitions we do;

but the discussion of this important and obscure point is beyond the scope of this essay.

The Meaning of 'Analogous'

Turing's objection was that since the mathematician, like the rest of us, already knows the meaning of 'analogous' it is nonsense to say that he is establishing the meaning of this term when he presents a proof. This may seem conclusive, but it is based on a misunderstanding. It fails to understand how Wittgenstein uses the term 'analogous' and like expressions. It is consistent to say that on one use — the use of the term presupposed in the objection — we already know the meaning of 'analogous' while in another — Wittgenstein's — in giving a proof we implicitly fix the meaning of 'analogous'.

We may distinguish a rule-specific from a genus use of 'analogous', parallel to a distinction Wittgenstein drew between what may be called a rule-specific and genus use of terms like 'chess'.[7] In the genus use, chess is a game played according to one or another of a certain open ended set of rules that form a family. Chess was played in the middle ages, for example, although their game differs significantly in some of its rules from ours. On the other hand we might see children playing a chess-like game but with rules that differ in places from ours, and say, 'That's not chess.' Their game might be as close to ours as medieval chess is. The point of our saying it is not chess is to indicate that they are following different rules from ours. In this case we shall say that we use 'chess' in a rule-specific way. If a game differs in even one rule from our present game, then on this rule-specific use it is not chess.

If I ask, 'Is the game they are playing chess?' I may mean my question in a rule-specific or genus use of 'chess.' If I ask 'Is to say it is not checkmate to proceed in a way analogous to the way we were trained in?' then I am suggesting that there are also two uses this question might have. Wittgenstein is interested in the question on its rule-specific use. That use can be clarified further by developing the analogy with the rule-specific sense of chess.

We know chess can be played according to various different sets of rules. To get a particular rule-specific use of 'chess' we simply pick out one of these sets of rules and say that, by definition, something is chess (in this rule-specific use) if and only if it is governed by these rules.

To say what corresponds to such a definition in the case of 'analogous' we must first divide uses of 'analogous' into systems. The systems correspond to certain mathematical systems. Thus consider some axiomatized geometry. At each point where a deduction is made in the system, we could say that the step corresponding to the deduction is the analogous step to take. I will consider the set of such judgments with 'analogous,' tied in this way to a particular mathematical system, as themselves forming one system. Next consider some Wittgenstein variant geometry, an 'alternative logical system' where we begin with the same statements of axioms and of transformation rules, but where at some point we go on in a different way from the original. In this second system too the users of the geometry may say that this particular step, deviant from the point of view of the first system, is the analogous step to take. I shall consider this use of 'analogous' as following within a second system, one that corresponds to the deviant geometry in the way that the first system for the use of 'analogous' corresponds to the first geometrical system. By a rule-specific use of 'analogous' then I will mean one bound by some such definition as: 'Such and such is analogous if it is what is counted as analogous in the following system ...' Here one will identify the system by identifying each of the system's judgments about 'analogous'. A judgment will fail to be analogous in the corresponding rule-specific sense if it departs at any point at all from the judgments in the particular system referred to. If the mathematical system in question allows infinitely many deductions within it (as for example does the system defined by the operation $+2$) then we will not be able to specify completely and in advance the corresponding rule-specific sense of 'analogous'.

It is the existence of the alternative logical systems discussed in the previous section that makes possible this treatment of 'analogous.' The different systems correspond to different rule-specific senses of 'analogous' in exactly the way that each of the variations on chess corresponds to a different rule-specific sense of chess.

When Wittgenstein says that in a proof we determine the meaning of 'analogous' he means that we determine part of some rule-specific use of 'analogous.' The fact that the mathematician has, prior to any proof, already an understanding of the meaning of 'analogous' is irrelevant to Wittgenstein's claim. A general understanding of the meaning of 'analogous,' based presumably on examples, does not by itself allow us to say whether a certain step is analogous in a given rule-specific sense of 'analogous.' If the step is one that has not been taken before, then there will be different possible judgments about 'analogous' and these will each partially determine a particular rule-specific sense of 'analogous.' In the chess diagram case, for example, some people, we imagined, would judge the analogous step to be one that calls the position checkmate. Others judge differently. The first rival judgment determines an essential part of a corresponding system for the use of 'analogous,' and this system differs essentially from that determined by the second judgment. These are alternative systems, and they branch from exactly the same history of teaching or training in the use of 'analogous.'

In saying that we fix the meaning of 'analogous' Wittgenstein is saying that that part of the meaning of the rule-specific sense of analogous that comes out in the judgment about whether this move is analogous or not is fixed when the proof is accepted.

It is, again, consistent with this to say that we already knew the meaning of 'analogous,' provided this only means that we were already all taught how to use it in general. While we knew how to use in it in general, it was still necessary to fix its meaning in so far as this judgment is concerned; for there are many different rule-specific judgments about 'analogous' that are consisent with that general understanding, and with our prior training in the use of 'analogous.'

Wittgenstein and Intuitionism

We can see from the foregoing that Wittgenstein's philosophy of mathematics is deeply committed to having no views on questions internal to mathematics. For example, Wittgenstein will not take sides on the issue of the acceptability of a proof that relies on a principle that an intuitionist, say, would reject. To accept a classical proof is to accept a certain system for the use of terms; in this system the proof is valid, by stipulation. If an alternative school of mathematics rejects the proof, for example on the grounds that it employs the law of excluded middle, then even if the mathematicians of that school employ the same terms as the classical proof employed, it uses them as bound by different rules. As it uses the terms, the 'proof' in question is invalid. We have here simply another case of alternative logical systems. Therefore, as a philosopher of mathematics, Wittgenstein is as indifferent to the mathematical differences between classical mathematics and intuitionism as he is to mathematical differences between two 'rival' geometries. His quarrel is never with statements in mathematics, for example with this or that proof, but only with the patter in English or some natural language that some mathematician, logician or philosopher may use to accompany the strictly mathematical development of this or that school or branch of mathematics. Even then his quarrel is not direct. There is to be no direct challenge and refutation, but only a scrutiny of features of the system in question. In line with this general approach, Wittgenstein denied wishing to drive anyone out of Cantor's paradise, but thought that when people learned to look at this 'paradise' in the way that he did, they might well leave voluntarily.

One Position or Two?

I now take up the question of whether Wittgenstein's position here on the nature of proof differs from that in the *Remarks on the Foundations of Mathematics.* There a proof institutes or marks a change in the meanings of the terms involved in the proof. In the *Lectures*, however, the proof is said to institute or mark a change in the meaning of 'analogous.' I believe, contrary to Chihara, that these are just two ways of stating the same position.

It was noted above that Wittgenstein deals with a family of related terms besides 'analogous.' What he says about 'analogous' is meant to apply to these, and what he would have said, given his general position, about any of these applies to 'analogous.' My reply to the claim that Wittgenstein has changed his position is put most easily in terms of one of the other terms in the family, namely 'follows from.' Admittedly this is not a term that he explicitly lists as one of those he is talking about; but reflection will show that it is a bona fide member of that family. I will omit a detailed application of my remarks to the case of 'analogous.'

Consider from Wittgenstein's viewpoint, the step in a proof where '50' is derived from the lines '25' and '×2.' In fixing that 50 follows from 25 × 2 we thereby fix, in part, the meaning of the terms '2', 'x' and '25.' And in fixing, in part, the meaning of these terms we thereby fix in part what follows from them. For Wittgenstein, part of the meaning of 'fix the meaning of the terms' is 'fix what follows from them;' and vice versa. Logic, on Wittgenstein's broadened understanding of it, concerns inferences that are sanctioned by rules of language. In knowing what follows from a term, in a certain context, we know an important part of the meaning of the term; and vice versa.

Similarly, in the informal proof given, we stipulate that it follows from the rules of chess that the position diagrammed is not checkmate. In so doing we in part fix the meaning of 'checkmate' and the other terms involved in the proof. On the other hand if we say here that we have in part fixed the meanings of these terms, in declaring the position not to be checkmate, then we have automatically thereby fixed, in part, the meaning of 'follows from.' To fix the meanings of a group of terms and to fix what follows from statements using the terms would come to the same thing, on Wittgenstein's understanding of the matter. Of course it would be a rule-specific sense of 'follows from' that would be fixed.

The same general point holds for 'analogous.' To say of writing down '50' that it is the analogous thing to do is to say no more and no less than that '50' is what follows by the rules we are attempting to apply, in this case a rule of multiplication. Hence the above equivalence between fixing the meaning of the terms and fixing what follows holds in the case of 'analogous' too. The appearance of Wittgenstein's having two substantively different views of proof, one in terms of the meaning of words in the proof and the other in terms of the meaning of 'analogous,' is only an illusion.

Another Objection

Surely, contrary to what has been claimed, we do not, in the chess proof and in other proofs, actually stipulate anything. We don't stipulate or lay down or fix or define that it is not checkmate, for example; rather we prove that it is not. To put the point in what Carnap called the formal mode, we would not say that here we have made a stipulation; and to put the point in the material mode, we have not made one. In fact the chess proof and like cases might be used as negative paradigms in teaching someone to use 'stipulate.' We could say, in teaching this term, that one stipulates the original rules, but that one does not stipulate what follows from those rules. For example one does not stipulate that the conclusion of our informal proof follows; one derives it from the rules of chess. Wittgenstein in saying the contrary is apparently claiming something patently false.

There may be a sense, and we can certainly define a sense, in which we do not stipulate that the position is not checkmate, but deduce it. However,

Wittgenstein's use of a term like 'stipulate' or 'define' is justified if there is a legitimate sense of 'stipulate' or 'define' on which his views are correct. There is such a legitimate sense if there are significant family resemblances between cases like the chess proof and cases that are paradigmatic of stipulation or truth by definition.

The *point* of Wittgenstein's using the word 'stipulation' here is to draw our attention to a family of cases; to get us to see this case as a member of a certain sequence, and to get us to see the similarities he has pointed to, and differences between the examples in the series and those examples that our language inclines us to look at, when we are thinking about proof.

It seems that there are such resemblances or similarities and that Wittgenstein's use of the term is therefore justified. The family resemblances are of two kinds. The first has to do with the identical modal status of, on the one hand, explicitly stipulated rules or axioms, and, on the other, the implicit stipulations that Wittgenstein believes are involved in proofs. Neither statements of rules nor of implicit stipulations are made inside a language game; neither has a significant negation; neither is contingent; both are a priori and necessary. Of course these claims are controversial; for example, Kripke thinks that even in the case of an explicit rule or definition, for example, the definition that one meter is the length of this stick, the rule statement is contingent; and others have argued that it is not a priori. But even granting the claim about modality, one would not be justified in speaking of 'stipulation' unless there were resemblances of a second kind. These have to do with the element of freedom required if one is to speak of a stipulation. If one stipulates this rule rather than that, then (a) there are alternatives to the rule, and (b) it is in some way open to one to choose one of these alternatives. We have already discussed Wittgenstein's espousal of the doctrine of alternative logical systems, and we noted two important ways in which one is free to choose one of the alternative systems. One is not bound into a system by one's initial training, nor by one's past mind states, in that it is consistent with either that one go on in the way definitive of one of the alternatives to the system one was trained in. Thus in the case of the implicit definitions constitutive of mathematical proofs, there are alternatives, and one is not bound into a given system. These resemblances to everyday stipulations or definitions lie behind and justify Wittgenstein's claims.

Reply to Pap

In saying that in our informal proof, in the chess case, we implicitly stipulate that the knight and king cannot checkmate the black king, we are not thereby denying that the premises of the proof entail that conclusion; we are rather saying what entailment amounts to, in such a case. Thus one of Pap's points is answered.

A second point Pap made is that in certain cases we do not lay down what is to follow from the rules; we have to *find this out*. Wittgenstein does not have to — and would not — say that in a case like our proof we do not find out whether knight and king can mate. Rather he can say that he is calling attention to what finding out comes to, in such cases. In particular, by saying that we stipulate the answer, he is leading us to see certain differences between finding out in this and similar examples, and finding out in the cases where what is discovered is straightforwardly empirical, as in finding out if rhubarb leaves are poisonous.

An objection very like Pap's is made in several places by Dummett in 'Wittgenstein's Philosophy of Mathematics.' His objection is that when a valid proof is given we have 'no choice but to follow it' (420). Earlier Dummett noted that if a proof proceeds in accordance with an explicitly formulated rule, then we could construct a machine to follow the rule. He asks, rhetorically, 'whence does a human being gain a freedom of choice in this matter which the machine does not possess?' (428). The implication is that in following a proof that proceeds according to an explicitly formulated rule we are not free to choose whether the conclusion follows or not, so that Wittgenstein, who thinks we are, is mistaken.

There is obviously a close connection between this objection about choice and Pap's objection about finding out and not stipulating what follows from our rules. But in what sense does Wittgenstein deny that the conclusion is determined by the premises, and is not a matter open to our choice? In Sect. 189 of the *Investigations* he distinguishes two senses of 'the step is determined by the formula.' In one sense, the criterion for the truth of, say, the step being determined by the formula $y = x^2$ is that the people who use the formula are trained in such a way that they 'all work out the same value for y when they substitute the same number for x.' In this sense of 'determined' a person's saying that the position in the diagram is not checkmate is determined by the rule for checkmate, since he is one of a people so trained that the answer 'no' is unequivocally and unanimously given by all who have been taught chess (let us assume). In a second sense the criterion for the statement about the step being determined by the formula has to do not with what people say, or how they have been trained, but with the type of formula it is. We separate formulae into those that do and those that do not 'determine a value of y for a given value of x.' To use Wittgenstein's examples: '$y = x^2$' is a rule that determines a particular number as value, given another number as value for x, whereas '$y \neq x^2$' does not. We can make corresponding distinctions for 'the rule determines whether the conclusion follows.' The question, then, of whether we are free to choose whether the conclusion follows would be answered 'No' in case either the first criterion or the second yielded the answer no for this case. There are perfectly good senses in which, as Wittgenstein would agree, we are not free to choose whether the conclusion follows; rather, whether it does or not may be determined, in at least two possible senses, as indicated. This does not show that Wittgenstein is wrong in saying that in a proof we implicitly stipulate that the conclusion is to follow from these premises. That we do so is consistent with the conclusions being determined in the two ways in question.

Modus Ponens

It may be objected that there are instances of proof for which Wittgenstein's views become absurd. In particular this is so when the proof is given in an explicitly laid out system and proceeds solely by means of a simple transformation rule such as modus ponens. Suppose then we have such a system, and that we wish to prove a theorem that follows from the axioms simply by an application of modus ponens. Can Wittgenstein possibly say that there are alternative systems here also?

It seems implausible indeed to say so, if the person giving the proof has understood modus ponens, and hence understood that it applies universally. From any two statements of the proper form we are entitled, by the rule, to infer a third. Someone who has been taught the rule and given the two premises must draw the intended conclusion.

But this case is really no different in principle from the '+2' example. We can imagine a people who are taught what is to us an expression of modus ponens, and taught it in exactly the way we are. But when given two premises, for example that 'The Queen is human' and 'If the Queen is human she should be subject to the laws of the land' they count the conclusion 'The Queen should be subject to the laws of the land' as not following from the premises by modus ponens, and insist also that there has been no violation of universality. 'We can imagine' this means that it is logically possible; that a description of the case as given is not ruled out by rules of our language.

'If there were such a people, this would only show that they did not understand modus ponens correctly.' Granted. They accepted a verbal formulation of a rule we took to be modus ponens. In fact it later turned out that the rule they accepted was not modus ponens; for if it were, then, contrary to them, the correct thing to say would be that in the above case the statement about the Queen being subject, etc., follows by modus ponens. We can respond in one of two ways to their claims. (1) They just do not understand modus ponens; (2) What they call 'modus ponens' is in reality a different rule — let us call it 'modus sponens' with different implications in the case in question.

In either case, there exists an alternative system, one in which the rule expressed by the sentence 'Deduce Q from (P and P implies Q)' is different from our rule, even though those who learn the rule are identical in so far as the initial training and practice segments of their lives go, and in so far as the content of their minds during these training and practice sessions goes. And as we have seen, it is the existence of such alternative systems that lies behind the claim that the proof of the statement about the Queen constitutes an implicit stipulation on the meaning of certain terms, for example of 'if ... then ...' and thereby of the rule for 'if ... then ...,' modus ponens.

Final Remarks

I have tried to explore some aspects of Wittgenstein's view of mathematical statements as belonging to 'logic' and as being therefore rules for the use of signs, which rules are laid down in response to certain pragmatic constraints, but which exist, as it were, in a space of alternative systems of rules. Of course a great many aspects of this view have gone unnoticed here. Also, I have only been able to touch lightly on a few objections to Wittgenstein's position. One criticism not discussed concerns consistency. It is well known that he has some strange thesis about it. I think it is much less known what exactly that thesis is. Chihara criticized the *Lectures'* position on consistency, but there is a great deal more to be said on the issue, as he admits. Dummett raises a number of interesting criticisms in the article cited above (although the criticism he gives the most space to, and that seems most convincing when presented, he answers himself some pages later on in the article). Those criticisms deserve extended discussions. So does a criticism he raised recently concerning the fact that mathematicians sometimes come to recognize that a 'proof' that was accepted for years is in fact faulty.[8] It is perhaps not too hard to get a line on how Wittgenstein would deal with this objection; but of course a full discussion is needed. One could also call in question whether the distinction outlined above between internal and external senses of 'analogous' is a valid distinction, clearly made. In particular, making the distinction hinge on whether or not the two terms are present to the speakers, as Wittgenstein *seems* to do, is dubious. Many more objections wait round every corner of the above discussions. I hope that I have done enough to spell out with some clarity what Wittgenstein's view is, and to answer, or make steps toward answering some of the objections that arise, so that the view's aura of strangeness and absurdity is somewhat dispelled.

While of course I do not know whether the position will hold up under scrutiny, I believe that it has not yet been refuted, and that it will richly repay study. So too will many other remarks of Wittgenstein's in these *Lectures*, on topics I have not looked at here.

Notes

1. Michael Dummett, 'Wittgenstein's Philosophy of Mathematics' pp. 121-37 below.
2. Gottlob Frege, *The Foundations of Arithmetic*, trans. J.L. Austin (Oxford: Blackwell 1959) 20e, 21e.
3. Arthur Pap, *Semantics and Necessary Truth* (New Haven: Yale U.P. 1958).
4. Charles S. Chihara, 'Wittgenstein's Analysis of the Paradoxes in His Lectures on the Foundations of Mathematics' pp. 325-37 below.
5. Here someone may raise the strange objection that, after all, Wittgenstein's claims, as I have interpreted them, are quite humdrum and unexciting. If someone says that gold is free at the local bank, that might be interesting, but if it turns out that in his 'language game' gold is defined as 'air' then what he says is stupid and humdrum. Similarly, it may be felt, all that occurs in the puzzling cases Wittgenstein wrote about is that the people who deviate from our practice, for example about the proper result of adding two, have adopted a special way of speaking, which mirrors ours in outward form but which obeys different rules. They seem to contradict and surprise us, but if we understand them properly, they do not, any more than we would be contradicted in our claim that gold is not free at the bank by the above odd speaker. Just as he's just adopted a silly way of talking about air, the '1004, 1008 ...' person has

adopted a strange system for using the sign '+2', and the people who say that the position in the diagram is checkmate simply have a different game than we do, and are not talking about our checkmate.

The premises of this objection, I think, are more or less correct. We are dealing, according to Wittgenstein, with alternative systems for using signs. But this fact does not make Wittgenstein's position humdrum or uninteresting. I think what lies behind this charge is the following inference: The 'gold is free' person's claims and the deviant claim about +2, and the like, are humdrum and uninteresting when correctly understood; therefore so are Wittgenstein's claims about mathematics. This non sequitur confuses the nature of the claims made in mathematics, or the theory of chess, and so on, with Wittgenstein's views of the nature of those claims. If the claims are implicit stipulations, then, one may want to say, they are humdrum. After all, they can hardly be false, if stipulated, and, since they are true in their own system, they do not really contradict seemingly conflicting statements that belong to another system. But it is hardly humdrum or uncontroversial to say that the statements are implicit stipulations, and have those features.

6. Barry Stroud, 'Wittgenstein and Logical Necessity', pp. 289-301 below.

7. *Philosophical Grammar*, ed. R. Rhees, trans. by A. Kenny (Oxford: Blackwell 1974) 476, 477.

8. 'Wittgenstein on Mathematics' pp. 98-110 below.

55

Critical Notice: *Lectures on the Foundations of Mathematics*

Georg Kreisel

W, the favorite pupil of Bertrand Russell, became famous after World War I for a slim volume *Tractatus Logico-Philosophicus*. Apart from the obviously impressive flair and vigor of the style the book remains an outstanding example of the heroic tradition of Western philosophy, with its questions about the general structure of knowledge or the correct analysis of (all meaningful) propositions. Since the questions certainly occur, to anyone, prior to any detailed intellectual experience, more or less the same is expected of the answers. *Tractatus* is quite remarkable in this respect: no appeal to anything that would ordinarily be called a discovery, about physical or mental phenomena, barely any use of new intellectual let alone material tools except — of all things — truth tables for propositional logic. Offstage there was a discovery, chemical atomism: the correct analysis of substances in terms of atoms and the chemical bonds between them. The general idea of *Tractatus* is that there is a (tacitly:finite) supply of simples corresponding to atoms, and so-called elementary propositions about them, independent of each other, as in elementary probability theory, but in contrast to chemical bonding. Arbitrary propositions are then to be analyzed in terms of elementary ones. Sense corresponds to chemically possible combinations of atoms. Actually there was very little about mathematics in *Tractatus* except for a brief reference to an operational analysis — in contrast to the set-theoretic analysis in *Principia*, which is also in the heroic tradition, but a less pure example.

In the decade after *Tractatus* was completed, W turned away from academic life, renounced an immense fortune, and did other romantic things. (He also retained, to the end of his life, a freshness of mind quite unusual even among those not desiccated by an academic atmosphere nor preoccupied with finance.) During that period he became disillusioned with *Tractatus*; so much so that a perfectly trivial objection by a friend triggered his decision to spell out his misgivings, not so much about his personal contribution as about the whole heroic tradition. (The objection concerned the inadequacy of *Tractatus* for a correct analysis of some expressive Italian gesture — as if this were a principal weakness of *Tractatus*.) W found that quite elementary mathematics provided excellent illustrations of weaknesses of traditional foundations, t.f. for short.

Trivially, W's revised views are 'revolutionary' for t.f.; but they are quite close to those of many thoughful mathematicians, for example in Bourbaki's most interesting (and no longer well-known) manifesto: *L'architecture des mathematiques* [1].* A principal problem was to put those views into words convincingly, and W was aware of this fact; thus the last sentence of the book under review stresses [*The seed I am most likely to sow is*] *a certain jargon*; cf. [2]. The main aim of this review is to restate the complaints of W and Bourbaki about t.f., with due regard for the discoveries of mathematical logic (which those authors neglected [3]). By and large, at least in the reviewer's view, the discoveries of logic support the principal complaints. For balance, some local virtues of t.f. will be mentioned at the end. To get generalities out of the way, it is best to begin with a couple of obvious distinctions.

Strategy and tactics (of W and Bourbaki). Naturally, their principal, though not their only target is the best-known branch or 'school' of t.f., familiar from the *formal-deductive presentation* of mathematics in a *universal system*, of the kind often found in the first chapter of a mathematical text (but barely referred to later). W was most familiar with so-called logistic foundations going back to Frege-Russell, Bourbaki with its (set-theoretic) variant going back to Cantor-Zermelo. Usually the universal system has a single 'primitive' symbol, $\in$, besides the logical operations; in logistic interpretations, $P \in Q$ is read as: P has (the property or 'structure') Q, and as: P belongs to (the set) Q in set-theoretic ones. It is then claimed that this sort of presentation provides the 'fundamental' analysis of mathematical notions (and proofs), and, at least occasionally, for example, by Russell, that the use of a single primitive reflects the 'unity' of mathematics.

Probably the most obvious difference between W's and Bourbaki's tactics in discussing such traditional claims is this: Bourbaki refer to wide experience in mathematics, while W uses very elementary examples. The latter are elegant (and popular because most foundational issues present themselves when we know little), but leave open to what extent they are representative of wider experience too.

A more basic difference is strategic. Bourbaki simply record their impression (of set-theoretic foundations) on p. 37: 'This is only one side of the matter, and the least interesting at that', and then go on to describe a better alternative with the same *general* aim: to exhibit, in terms of Bourbaki's basic structures, what is vaguely called the nature of mathematics (Bourbaki speak of 'unity' too though there are several such structures). Bourbaki's strategy leaves professional philosophers cold who *assume* that the proper way to achieve that aim must use the notions prominent in t.f., and dismiss Bourbaki as mere mathematicians lacking the higher sensibility needed for a true interest in t.f.! In contrast, W attempts to convert the

---

*[n] means the *n*th note at the end of this essay, containing historical and bibliographical details.

fundamentalists by 'deflating' the notions and thus the so-called fundamental problems of t.f., stated in terms of those notions. In W's words, he wants to *show the fly the way out of the fly bottle.* He does this with much ingenuity and patience, and some overkill, while Bourbaki ignore the fly which does not see the way out by itself (by the light of the basic structures).

Even granted W's pedagogic aim above, his style does not seem efficient. In the reviewer's opinion, current mathematical logic, which has developed several notions of t.f. (has, so to speak, given them rope), seems much better, and some of those developments have positive interest to boot; cf. [4].

General complaint: deceptive abstractions of t.f. When we know little (but want to make general, 'big' statements), we necessarily use superficial generalities, so-called abstractions. As an example Bourbaki cite, on p. 37, general talk about the 'experimental method' being the link between physics and biology, in contrast, as we know now, to the general laws of molecular biology, which, quite literally, are not superficial at all. Being unquestionably venerable, all branches of t.f. concern principally early generalities; for example, they all agree in regarding such superficial '*defining*' properties as *validity* (of proofs) or *existence* (of mathematical objects) as principal subjects of study, refined by almost equally obvious (and early) subdivisions into broad categories: (i) constructive and nonconstructive validity or (ii) concrete and abstract, in particular, infinite objects. Different branches of t.f. usually differ in picking on one category or the other as comprising all (justified) mathematics, or in the exact boundary they draw; cf. logicist and set-theoretic foundations mentioned above, or finitist and intuitionist (constructive) foundations.

Debates over t.f. generate much heat, an occupational hazard (or attraction) for philosophers, who trade in justifications and similar hot commodities. More importantly, those debates obscure what, on general scientific experience is most suspect: the assumption that those broad categories which are certainly on the surface, should serve for a 'fundamental' theory of (mathematical) phenomena which, on the surface, strike us by their diversity. This suspicion is further obscured, in effect if not by intention, by, so to speak, the opposite assumption, that (most of) those early ideas are not only unrewarding, but simply incoherent or, at least, very difficult to make precise. This is simply false. Quite a number of traditional so-called informal notions have been analyzed precisely and convincingly; both 'grand' and 'modest' ones; of course, not only in t.f., but also in traditional physics (rigid body, ideal fluid, perfect gas, etc.): it just so happens that most of these often very appealing concepts have turned out not to serve very well for a fundamental theory (and others less easy to develop, like chemical composition, were more essential); cf. [5]. Of course, precision by itself is rarely enough to inspire universal confidence; *astrology* is a good (extreme) example, as venerable as t.f., and a model of precision and clarity. And thorough or even brilliant justifications of definitions can be quite sterile: thus analyses of the *area of a triangle* in

Hilbert's *Foundations of Geometry* have not helped with the (genuine) problems of defining the area of a *surface*.

In short, the general complaint (of W and Bourbaki) is that t.f. may be *poor philosophy*, in the broader popular sense of 'philosophy', specifically, if in practice the general aims of foundations are better served by alternatives, for example, by ordinary careful scientific research and exposition. In the reviewer's opinion this alternative is particularly superior to t.f. with regard to reliability, at least, in the bulk of mathematical practice. This conclusion is of course quite consistent with [3] and [5] which show that some developments of t.f. have occasional use (and appeal; being easy to handle, like other developments of simple-minded notions).

Principal complaint: better current ideas than t.f. (not, of course, for the specific problems most prominent in t.f., but for the broad general aims behind t.f.). For all branches of t.f. the matter of *explicit definitions* is utterly trivial: for validity because such defintions can be systematically eliminated from proofs, and for so-called ontology because no existential assumptions are involved. Both Bourbaki and W emphasize — of course in accordance with ordinary mathematical experience — the *choice of explicit definitions*, as incomparably more significant than the glamorous pre-occupations of t.f., not only for discovery, a 'mathematical' affair, but also for intelligibility, a principal factor in reliability, and hence a more strictly 'foundational' business. (In brutal terms: an idealization of reliability, for which this factor is trivial, is a poor idealization.)

Bourbaki treat explicit definitions at length on pp. 42-3, at least, implicitly, in connection with the use of basic structures for solving 'concrete' problems. The scheme is this: (i) A structure S is explicitly defined in 'concrete' (say, number-theoretic) terms. (ii) S is shown to be a basic structure, for example, (shown to satisfy the axioms for) a group or a unitary group. (iii) Known properties of the basic structure are used to yield number theoretic information. Without exaggeration: experience shows that the conscious use of the scheme literally alters our view of mathematics, and so, in the popular sense: our philosophy of mathematics. — N.B. The scheme *would* be significant for t.f. *if* in striking applications the means used to establish (ii) and (iii) were foundationally problematic, not 'reducible-in-principle' to the usual methods of number theory. Not only logicians but, occasionally, also mathematicians *assume* that this must be so. They are wrong. The scheme above is unquestionably effective in existing practice also where the assumption is demonstrably false, as shown up to the hilt by the work referred to in [4], for a wide range of precise formulations of the notions involved.

W stresses the importance of explicit definitions in so many words, specifically, in connection with logistic foundations of numerical arithmetic (a principal topic of his own, limited study of logic). Here structures are explicitly defined in logical terms, and shown to satisfy familiar arithmetic laws. (This kind of thing calmed Frege's indignation at the 'logical scandal' of being left speechless by: What is the number 1?) W stresses the following aspect of logistic foundations (which Frege and Russell, and of course W in his youth, had ignored as being trivial 'in principle'). If the logical formula F_A expresses the arithmetic theorem A, knowledge of A is needed not only to recognize this fact, which goes without saying, but simply to prove F_A *convincingly.* An analogue to this is used frequently in current algebra; if A is a theorem about ordered fields, and F_A the corresponding logical formula, then F_A is in fact proved by using set-theoretic or algebraic operations on ordered fields. Sure, by the completeness theorem, F_A has a proof using only the rules of ordinary predicate calculus, too: but this fact, which is certainly fundamental *if* the assumptions of t.f. are granted, has turned out to be quite marginal in practice. In short, as a matter of empirical fact, arithmetic does more for logic than logic for arithmetic; cf. [6]

Specific complaints about some glamor issues of t.f. W's pet aversions will be illustrated here by just two examples; references to mathematical developments of his complaints are given in [7].

W had a particularly strong aversion to one of the more dramatic topics of t.f.: the matter of *contradictions* as in the paradoxes, or their absence, *consistency*, as in Hilbert's program. Incidentally, at least by implication, Bourbaki too are unimpressed; treating consistency (or the existence of some model) as a by-product; for example, the model of the — theory for the field C of — complex numbers furnished by the Euclidean plane, which was originally hailed for 'legitimizing' $\sqrt{-1}$, is reinterpreted on top of p. 43 as a useful property of the plane. Be that as it may, the familiar dramatics about consistency, etc. are unconvincing. For one thing, one is accustomed to oversights or blindspots which result in straight errors and possible contradictions; cf. Hilbert's recipe for proving Fermat's conjecture (finitistically!): *so lange herumrechnen, bis man sich endlich verrechnet.* Also there are confusions between motions: when P is true for one of them, and — P for another, it is simply futile to ask for a precise location of 'the' error. On the other hand, generally speaking, consistency alone is not too reassuring (from experience with skillful liars). W had a pet complaint: Why not ensure consistency trivially, by modifying the rules in the obvious way? Though he asks, in effect, what would be lost by this, he doesn't really stop for an answer. Actually, his point is well illustrated in a paper by Rosser on mathematical logic, well before 1939 (without having been recognized explicitly by its author): cf. (i) of [7].

Another matter which had long been prominent in t.f., and especially in the writings of W's teacher, Bertrand Russell, is the topic of *higher (infinite) cardinals.* W was particularly offended by the use of the harmless diagonal construction to support heavy infinities: 'harmless' inasmuch as — to W — the point of the construction was perfectly well illustrated by proving that the set of (ordinary) polynomials in one variable cannot be enumerated by a polynomial in 2 variables. W preferred to use the construction in the context of rules (for partial functions), specifically for proving Gödel's incompleteness theorem, incidentally without appeal to the liar paradox. W considered rules $p_1, p_2, \ldots$ for sequences of 0 and 1, where some p_n says: put 0 to 1 at the mth place iff p_m tells you to put 1, resp. 0 at the mth place. (So p_n says: put nothing at the nth place — and the value of $p_n (n)$ is undecided; cf. also (ii) in [7].) Bourbaki's manifesto does not seem to commit itself on the matter of higher cardinals. But it seems fair to say that they would study problems about the natural numbers by means of (suitable generalizations to) finite fields rather than, say, by means of infinite ordinals (which Sierpinski attempted to do, for example, in his counterexample to an analog of Fermat's conjecture).

While the substance of W's complaints is certainly eminently reasonable, the ordinary style of mathematical logic is more efficient (as mentioned on p. 80): one reformulates the theorems involved (as in [7](i) for the case of Gödel's second incompleteness theorem, and in [4] for debunking the 'logical strength' of languages of higher type). In the reviewer's opinion, W is too tolerant of t.f., for example, far too soft on *formalization* as a (necessary) condition for mathematical rigor. Thus, in an exchange with Turing on the subject of making ordinary proofs 'more' formal, W does not question this aim but merely assumes (p. 127, l. 13) that it would be 'easy' to do, incidentally, contrary to an almost universal opinion. The business of formalization is at least as prominent in t.f. as W's pet aversions (and perhaps not so easy to put into perspective: cf. [8]).

W's complaints live up to one of his quotable quotes (on p. 68): Don't treat your common sense like an umbrella. When you come into a room to philosophize, don't leave it outside ... Of course, 'philosophy' (of mathematics) is not meant here in its academic sense, of t.f., but rather in its popular sense as on p. 81. We shall return to possible inadequacies of common sense at the end of the review.

W's advice in place of the kind of analyses proposed in t.f. When confronted — or, in W's terms, 'puzzled', as on p. 266 — by a philosophical problem about (mathematical) notions or proofs, we should see what we *do* with them, how we *use* them (in the lectures under review W concentrated on uses outside mathematics but no longer in conversations in the forties mentioned in [2]). This is like the familiar advice in ordinary mathematics to try and see what makes a proof *work* or, more formally, *dégager les hypothèses utiles*. Fair enough, compared to other elastic advice on conduct (*ad majorem gloriam dei* or its 'enlightened' up-date: *pour l'honneur de l'esprit humain*). But in really doubtful cases, usually more imagination is needed to find the concepts, the *cadre*, for stating a satisfactory answer than to think of the troublesome notion or proof in the first place. As to 'puzzles', many solve themselves in the ordinary course of nature, for example, by means of memorable counter-examples, in particular, ($\mathcal{F}_R$ in [7]) for W's complaint about consistency. As to his other specific complaint, what was there to see in 1939 *à propos* of higher cardinals? Work that has been attributed to W's or related advice is pretty varied, and of uneven interest [9].

Balancing the account on the positive side of t.f. In the reviewer's opinion the weaknesses of t.f., inherent and compared to available alternatives, mattered less to W than the style of t.f.: (i) the almost staggering banality of 'fundamental' notions and problems compared to the ambitious general aims, and (ii) the — basically pretentious — simple-minded language used to formulate the results of t.f. For obvious reasons, elaborated at the end of [9], it is far beyond the scope of any review — and certainly of this reviewer — to try and assess the pedagogic or heuristic value of the stylistic feature of t.f. just mentioned. But it is worth remembering the *possibility* of such a value; perhaps best by reference to related aims, notions and problems which are of about the same vintage as those of t.f., but have made much more progress; specifically, the ideas of the Greeks about physics, in particular, space, time, matter. ([10] contains some documentation concerning the rest of this review.)

The first example one thinks of are, of course, spectacular, such as Einstein's most artistic presentation of the special theory of relativity in traditional philosophical terms, in particular, of the *skeptical*, so-called positivist or operational tradition. As a result of relativity theory there are now masses of data which would admit a 'purer', purely mechanical presentation (without bringing in light, that is, electromagnetic phenomena at all). But Einstein's presentation seems to have a kind of permanent pedagogic appeal even to those of us who, like Einstein, have grown weary of positivism (which tells us to begin with operational definitions, as in [9](ii)a, when in fact theory is needed for their choice). As far as mathematics is concerned, the switch from (i) the nineteenth century's version of the axiomatic method, used by Frege, Dedekind and others to set up categorical axioms (cf. [1]) to (ii) its current first-order version (including most of Bourbaki's basic, in particular, algebraic structures) continues to be introduced in so-called formalist terms, formalism being intended as the specialization of positivism to mathematics. In short, the particular features of knowledge on which positivism concentrates, seem to be occasionally central, at least for pedagogy. Evidently, spectacular successes are few and far between.

For the present (by [9]: necessarily statistical) purpose it is more interesting to look at modest, but appealing uses of t.f. (and their counterparts in physics). For balance, two illustrations from the *speculative* tradition will be given. Both are due to Gödel (who has shown more discretion and above all more flair than most exponents of that tradition). In physics the search for ghosts has so far not proved generally rewarding. But it can lead (one) smoothly to cosmological solutions of Einstein's field equations in general relativity theory with cyclic time: cf. [10] for possible alternatives. In mathematics, the search for open problems, say about the natural numbers, which are settled by means of (axioms about) large cardinals, has not been very rewarding either. In fact — and this is of course the principal conclusion of [4] — the superficial impression that anything like nondenumerable cardinals is used in existing analytic number theory, is simply false. But there is certainly a pedagogic interest in the *possibility* of any effective use of higher set theory for number theory, discovered and stressed by Gödel. What is more, the possibility is 'revolutionary' in the sense that it does not seem to be even remotely suggested by the bulk of mathematical practice.

It seems to the reviewer that, used with much discretion and a little flair, the ideas of t.f. provide *occasional* checks and balances on the strategy of relying on the 'needs' of current practice (Bourbaki) or on current uses (W), presumably, most often when the matters considered are far removed from current scientific study and uses. (By [9](i), mathematicians tend to avoid such matters, like free choice sequences and large cardinals, to mention minor topics from the constructive, resp. nonconstructive branch of t.f.) When musing about the virtues and limitations of t.f., readers may wish to recall the memorable successes of natural science in this century (which we can, perhaps, view with more detachment than our own subject). Some of the early ones in the first quarter, say on atomic and cosmological matters, have a distinct flavor of t.f. Others which have, literally, changed our view of the world even more (like Rutherford's on the structure of the atom), and the extraordinary advances of the last 25 years, which have changed our view of ourselves too, do not. Naturally, the faithful either disregard those advances as not 'fundamental', or assume that things would have gone even better if the early preoccupations had persisted.

Notes

[1] Bourbaki's manifesto appears on pp. 35-47 of *Les Grands Courants de la Pensée Mathématique*, edited by F. Le Lionnais (Cahiers du Sud, Paris, 1948; MR 10. 239). Despite the title, by p. 42, Bourbaki are also concerned with mathematical activity, our 'intuitive resonances' to the 'architecture', that is, to Bourbaki's basic structures — at least within mathematics: by p. 46, Bourbaki regard such 'resonances' to structures occurring outside mathematics as problematic, in line with what is nowadays called the 'unreasonable effectiveness' of mathematics for physical theory. (Would it be *obviously* more 'reasonable' if we were not effective in thinking about the external world in which we have evolved?) Occasionally, one has to read between the lines. Thus the negative remarks on pp. 45-6 about categorical axioms (in contrast to the axioms for basic structures which are realized in many structures) are naturally interpreted in opposition to a preoccupation of t.f., the analysis of so-called informal notions, discussed further in [5]. Some of the best-known analyses of this sort have been of little use: Would Gauss' *Disquisitiones* have been better if he had started with Peano's axioms? Less trivially, in practice, both in pure and in applied mathematics, the particular informal notions we start with often turn out to be unmanageable or otherwise unrewarding, and it is simply better to axiomatize which properties of such notions have been used (for some striking conclusion). What Bourbaki actually say, about the 'sterility' of categorical axioms, is a bit glib. By neglecting such axioms altogether, one loses (pedagogically) useful explanations of the choice of familiar axioms in algebra and of so-called formal independence results; cf. Proc. Sympos. Pure Math. *28* (1976) on Hilbert's problems [HP] for short. (For specialists: pp. 101-2, resp. top of p. 103 are meant.)

[2] The matter of jargon, or style, came up quite often in my conversations with W (from 1942 to his death in 1951). For example, once after W had invited F.J. Dyson, who at the time had rooms in College next to W's, to discuss foundations, Dyson had said he did not wish to 'discuss' anything because *what* W had to say was not different from anything everybody was saying anyway, but he wanted to hear *how* W put it. W spoke to me of the occasion, agreeing very much with what Dyson had said, but finding Dyson's jargon a bit 'odd'. On another occasion W said: Science is O.K.; if only it weren't so grey. Incidentally, 'style' was not a dirty word in the Cambridge of those days, though its significance was not as forcefully analyzed as nowadays, for example, in (the first part of) Solzhenitsyn's Nobel Prize lecture or Bellow's. At least in my own experience the style of W's conversations on foundations (not on everyday matters!) was very different from his public performances, which were always tense and often incoherent. More detail will be given at a lecture to the Forum Philosophicum Austriacum

(September 1977). Without exaggeration: What W actually said in the seminars I attended, did not express at all well his views at the time. This seems very much to the point in connection with the present book, which does not even record what W said in the lectures, but what a bunch of students thought he had said.

[3] W makes passing references to some kind of (mathematical) interest of mathematical logic which had grown out of t.f., but without any hint of what that interest might be. Though this is easier to state now, by 1939 (and especially by 1948, the year of Bourbaki's manifesto), some people with their wits about them had a pretty good idea: for details, see Vaught's story of model theory up to 1945 in Proc. Sympos. Pure Math. *25* (1974), especially about Malcev and Tarski. The principal uses of logic divide into (i) solutions of previously stated problems, and (ii) adequate formulations of natural questions, the latter being, perhaps, of greater interest to philosophers of mathematics. As to (i), the best-known use of logic applies model theory to prove (an asymptotic version of) Artin's conjecture on *p*-adic fields. To be precise, the proof combined a little logic with a good deal of algebra; but the fact remains that though some kind of relation between *p*-adic fields and fields of formal power series had been recognized by algebraists, model-theoretic notions were needed to formulate the relation precisely enough to finish the job. (ii) A good example of using logical, in fact, recursion-theoretic notions for stating a theorem (not only for its proof) is in Higman's work on finitely generated groups [Proc. Roy. Soc. Ser. A *262* (1961), 445-75]. This is a good answer to the (natural) question: 'Which finitely generated groups can be embedded in finitely presented ones? A similar question, with logical answers, is this: What makes algebraically closed or real closed, so-called maximal, ordered fields 'special?' These fields are singled out, among all, resp. all ordered fields (by A. Macintyre) by reference to the elimination of quantifiers ([Fund. Math. *71* (1971), 1-25], resp. in the abstract, jointly with K. McKenna [Notices Amer. Math. Soc. *24* (1977), A28, Abstract = 742-02-4]). Unquestionably, this type of work, especially in (ii), is *satisfaisant pour l'esprit*; but it is hardly central. *Though results from logic are of course applied to many areas, within any one area the successes are strictly local*: (if a choice had to be made) one would lose more by neglecting Bourbaki's basic structures than even the most respectable parts of logic such as model theory or recursion theory.

Apart from local uses of logic as in (i) and (ii) above, there is an almost endless list of applications to intimate pedagogy, to answer contemplative, 'useless' questions which thoughtful mathematicians often ask (themselves): What do we know from what we have done so far? (which is 'useless' if we know that later we shall go much farther); cf. [4].

[4] Good examples of a fly in a fly bottle (or a 'useless' question in the sense of [3]) come from the debates about the axiom of choice or about so-called nonelementary proofs in number theory of purely number-theoretic theorems. (In the twenties such proofs were distinguished by the use of function-theoretic methods; more recently, by the use of *l*-adic cohomology, as in Manin's problem I(a) on p. 36 of [HP]. Of course, some proofs which happen to be elementary are of interest; the issue is whether this 'raw' interest derives from their elementary character.) Practically speaking, except to doctrinaires, knowing how to use the axiom of choice and other nonelementary (civilized) methods is obviously a good thing. But even a nondoctrinaire reflective mathematician may simply want to know if these methods are eliminable from the proofs considered, as in Serre's question whether 'such' uses of the axiom of choice as in his study of homotopy groups are logically necessary. (Though asked in the thrifty fifties, the question was not intended to be useful; for example, it was not expected that a general answer to this question would help in, say, the actual computation of homotopy groups. In short, no illusions were involved.) Inspection of Gödel's work on — what he called — the relative consistency of the axiom of choice gives an easy negative answer to Serre's question, and, of course, a precise formulation of a whole class of 'such' uses; cf. p. 165 of [British J. Philos. Sci. *7* (1956)]. (Consistency was not the main issue because the axiom of choice is true for the (only) notion which, at present, serves to make the consistency of the remaining axioms evident.) Concerning the business of nonelementary proofs, logicians have spent a good deal of time showing that those occurring in *current* number-theoretic practice can be eliminated. In the process we have dotted the *i*'s and crossed the *t*'s by making distinctions between 'direct' and other elementary proofs, introducing suitable definitions of 'logical strength', and finding formal languages progressively closer (than that of set theory) to those used in the branches of mathematical practice concerned. In this way it became

progressively easier to verify that the usual nonelementary proofs can be mechanically converted into — obviously — elementary ones (although, of course, there are purely arithmetic theorems in current metamathematics for which the analogue is not true; cf. pp. 112-13 of [HP]). Put differently, the set-theoretic principles used (implicitly) in actual practice are of low 'logical strength' inasmuch as the replacement schema and other schemata are applied only to formulae of low logical complexity, cf. pp. 108-9 of [HP] or the more detailed exposition by Friedman [Ann. of Math. *105* (1977), 1-28]. But since the instances of those schemata which happen not to be used are not in doubt either, we have little more than a modest discovery of a temporary feature of contemporary practice; we have not yet learned to use other instances efficiently, just as it took time to learn to use efficiently the law of the excluded middle applied to, say, the Riemann hypothesis. In fact, with the elimination before our eyes we see how little is gained by it. As a consequence, and as an example of how mathematical logic actually supports the doubts of W and Bourbaki about t.f., mentioned on p. 81, the issue of nonelementary proofs or, more formally, of 'logical strength' is discredited, and thus the claims of those branches of t.f. for which the issue is central, are refuted: cf. a similar use in [HP], top of p. 116 for consistency proofs of obviously consistent systems. Admittedly, the effort involved recalls Bertrand Russell's description of *Principia* as 'a parenthesis in the refutation of Kant' (on p. 75 in *My Philosophical Development*, New York, 1959). But we have not stopped at such refutations. We have gone on to look for factors which, unlike logical strength, do distinguish between elementary and prima facie nonelementary proofs, and above all measure what is *gained* by the latter; cf. p. 127 of [HP] concerning the reduction of the *genus* of proof figures as a possible measure of the difference.

[5] In this century mathematical logic has provided analyses of traditional concepts (logical language, formal rule, etc.) by means of definitions which are at least as convincing as famous definitions in 'old fashioned' mathematics, for example, of the notion of *length of curves* or, at the other end of the scale, (planar flow of) *ideal fluids*, by use of calculus, resp. function theory. — NB. Both definitions express correctly the notions intended: this is not the issue at all. Both notions are of course so-called theoretical idealizations: only, length does, and the other one does not isolate a dominant factor in (the bulk of) geometry, resp. hydrodynamics; cf. p. 81 about *correct* definitions of the particular notions prominent in t.f. and (lack of) *interest* of anything like those notions for the general aims of foundations. Incidentally, it is now generally recognized that the notion of formal or, equivalently, (idealized) mechanical rule in the sense of recursion theory is a poor idealization for the study of computers; but, for example, by [3](ii) it is a good tool in algebra (and number theory) — to be compared to those parts of function theory which were originally developed for the analysis of ideal fluids, and have found impeccable uses elsewhere; cf. also the end of this review.

[6] In connection with logistic foundations, W overreacts to, admittedly, exaggerated claims; he speaks of 'the disastrous invasion of mathematics by logic'; cf. [Acta Phil. Fennica *28* (1976). 166-87]. Bourbaki observe the academic proprieties; on p. 37 they are respectful about the language (of set-theoretic if not logistic foundations). But when, in footnote 2 on p.40, they come to the importance of their basic structures, they do not even mention that such structures can be defined in the language of sets (and membership, $\exists$). Thus by implication they dismiss the familiar claim, mentioned on p. 80 above, that this definability constitutes the 'unity' of mathematics.

[7] W's 'specific complaints' have been developed into mathematical theorems in the literature. (i) W's idea of modifying any system $\mathfrak{F}$ into an obviously consistent one, $\mathfrak{F}_R$ is treated systematically on pp. 46-48 of [Dissertationes Math.Rozprawy Mat. *118* (1974)], the subscript 'R' standing for Rosser who used a similar idea in [J. Symbolic Logic *1* (1936). 89-91]. If $\mathfrak{F}$ itself is consistent, $\mathfrak{F}_R$ has not only the same theorems as $\mathfrak{F}$, but even the same proofs. What is 'lost' by the passage from F to F_R becomes clear by stating the hypotheses of Gödel's second incompleteness theorem properly. In the usual systems $\mathfrak{F}$ the consistency of $\mathfrak{F}$ cannot be proved. In $\mathfrak{F}_R$ (the consistency of $\mathfrak{F}_R$ can, but) the adequacy of $\mathfrak{F}_R$ for *numerical* arithmetic cannot be proved even when $\mathfrak{F}_R$ is adequate. (ii) W's use of a variant of the diagonal construction to establish incompleteness (in conversation in the forties, not in his writings) was reported in footnote 4 on p. 281 of [Fund. Math. *37*(1950)]. To test his (rough) idea, one also considers a rule, p_p, which says, so to speak, the opposite: put at the mth place what the mth rule tells you to put there. One would expect to be able to write anything at the pth place. But this is not altogether adequate as seen by considering a problem of Henkin's [J. Symbolic

Logic *17* (1952), 160]. The upshot is that the general character of the inferences by means of which p_p 'tells' you what to do, is critical; for so-called cut-free systems we have one answer, for the usual systems another; for a precise exposition, cf. 1.7, 2.7 and pp. 45-6 of [Dissertationes Math. Rozprawy Mat. *118* (1974)].

[8] For perspective on formalization: First of all, there is the empirical fact that the compactness theorem (which has turned out to be very useful, cf. [3]) was first stated by Gödel as a consequence of his completeness proof for Frege's rules. (A separate step is needed to *recognize* just where that theorem is effective; cf. Vaught's article cited in [3].) In short, one has by-products of formalization, of the kind familiar from [5] *in fine*. But the detour via formal rules is not necessary, and not used in modern (model-theoretic) proofs of the compactness theorem. Not unexpectedly, problems about formal rules are *of permanent interest*, not when mere existence is in question, but detail, for example, in a choice among complete sets of rules (and its effect on the geometric structure of the corresponding formal derivations of given theorems). By the nature of the case the choice of relevant *detail* requires more than the kind of general, superficial impressions on which the notions and problems of t.f. are based, for example, notions of (formal) rigor. The most obvious nondoctrinaire need for formalization comes from the application of computers to proofs: trivially, computers operate only on formal data (here: formalized proofs). And computers are certainly needed when measures of proofs are relevant which are hard to calculate by hand, for example, the *genus*, mentioned at the end of [4].

Remarks. (i) The use of computers for operating on, or, as one says, for unwinding 'given' proofs is of course less glamorous than the better-known business of automatic theorem proving (which many of us do better than computers), where one starts with a formula, a conjecture, not with a proof. (ii) The passage from a 'given' proof, say, in a mathematical text, to a formalization should be compared to other processing of 'raw' data for theoretical treatment; for example, to apply physical theory, (physically) significant data are needed, including the correction for artifacts. Correspondingly, the drill or ritual involved in mathematical texts is a likely source of artifacts (like a stylized description of a physical situation by someone not familiar with the relevant theory). (iii) W's obviously offhand comment mentioned on p. 83, to the effect that the passage in (ii) is 'easy', overlooks not only the general problems mentioned, but even the distinction between (absolute) effort and the ratio: effort/reward, familiar from economics (utility and marginal utility). As far as effort is concerned, W may be right, simply because one's subjective judgment tends to be bad! Specifically, at least this reviewer's estimates of the number of lines in a formalization tend to be unreliable even *after* it has been carried out. On one occasion writing down formalizations of 1 and 2 pages felt like 10 resp. 50 pages.

[9] Here are two examples of work attributed to W's advice about 'uses'. Both are extreme, the first in banality, the second in literalmindedness. (i) When proving results about a wrongheaded project, one may stumble over something of interest, as in work on Hilbert's consistency program or, more specifically, the elimination of nonelementary methods in number theory discussed in [4]. Then one tries to formulate that interest. This is familiar enough from the study of false hypotheses in the sciences, less so in the mainstream of pure mathematics which tends to be very conservative (confining itself to obviously relevant or well-tested notions). (ii) Probably the most literalminded interpretation of W's advice, and hence very much more 'philosophical' in the sense of t.f., is elaborated in so-called *operational semantics*, for example, of logical particles. Here the meaning of a word is determined by its 'use'; in mathematics, (tacitly) by formal rules for the use of the word. (The matter was very much in the air in the thirties; most logicians are familiar with it not from W's advice, but from a passing remark by Gentzen, on p. 80 of his collected papers). Lorenz has given two versions of operational semantics, one in his book *Operative Logik*, the other in his *Dialogspiele*, terminology which goes well with W's 'language games'. *Dialogspiele* are 2-person games associated with (many of) the usual logical systems in which the players choose formulas alternately; a formula F is said to be valid, if the proponent of F has a winning strategy; for a detailed exposition, see Kuno Lorenz [Arch. Math. Logik Grundlagenforsch *11* (1968), 32-55, 73-100]. Evidently, as the name suggests, a rather special side of reasoning, scoring debating points, is emphasized here (where, incidentally, the rules of the games are heavily biased in favor of the proponent — as if intended for people who like to talk a lot). Nothing is said about (a) the original choice of the usual logical systems, nor (b) the fact that even after formal rules have been formulated we continue to reason logically without

remembering them; (a) has its parallel in the case of many definitions in mathematics, but not (b). In short, operational semantics goes against (empirical facts about) Bourbaki's intuitive resonances.

Remark. There is a quite separate question whether the work in (i) or (ii) was not only 'attributed' to, but whether, realistically speaking, it was influenced by W's advice. (W was clearly interested in the question, specifically in the *heuristic* and *pedagogic* value of what he had to say — as in his talk about 'disaster' in [6], or about 'tenacious misunderstanding difficult to get rid of' on top of p. 15.) Dramatics aside, these matters are sociological and hence severely statistical, difficult to judge not only because of the hackneyed business about interpreting statistical data, but because of the various skills needed to compile and process them. Abstractly, W was very sympathetic to an 'impersonal', statistical view of sociological matters. But in practice, he did not even try to see whether his particular views could be examined with existing resources; instead he expressed feelings, like ordinary mortals; cf. strong language about 'paradoxes' at the beginning of Bishop's review in AMSB (March 1977) when recording the failures of some starry-eyed projects for mass education (or unsuccessful investors complaining about the 'paradoxes' of the market).

[10] This note contains background material assumed in the last section of this review (pp. 84-5). (i) Concerning the (natural) philosophy of the Greeks, its most obvious actual or potential value has been to make posterity familiar with imaginative, so-called revolutionary ideas in a *general* way, for example, the idea of a *few* elements or of *cyclic* time (Aristotle's *Physics.* Book 8, 265a. 15 or 265b. 10 on 'primary' time and motion). But, as so often with — obviously — premature enterprises, most attempts at more precise or explicit formulations were hopelessly off the mark; for example, Aristotle was unhappy with Anaximander's 'elements': earth, water, air, fire, but didn't even connect them with: solids, liquids, gases, energy as in a course on physics: instead he had the business of: dry, wet, cold, hot (things). (ii) Concerning lack of discretion in the use of t.f., Cantor speculated about higher infinite cardinals bringing us closer to the Almighty, with inconsistent manifolds keeping us at a respectful distance. Perhaps, it should be added that Brouwer's pious doubts, in the skeptical tradition, of our ordinary conceptions are, realistically, hardly any less dubious than Cantor's beliefs; doubts which led to Brouwer's equally pious trust in what he thought he saw in (his) deepest consciousness. Incidentally, in the reviewer's view, Gödel's own proposals for the use of higher cardinals are, at present, *under*valued for an apparently quite accidental reason. He happened to propose them for settling (number-theoretic problems and, above all) the generalized continuum hypothesis, which, demonstrably, is not decided by anything remotely like the cardinals presently considered. (Earlier he had proposed to use the continuum hypothesis itself to settle number-theoretic problems; his own work could be used to refute this proposal; as in [4].) But on the borderline of game theory, in the subject of so-called Borel games, the use of uncountably many iterations of the power set operation has turned out to be demonstrably essential for solving problems about R (at least if 'subsystems' of set theory are to be used, as in Martin's proof of the determinateness of all Borel games [Ann. of Math. (2) *102* (1975), 363-71]). Of course, this is a far cry from number theory and from those 'extravagantly' large cardinals which Gödel had in mind. (iii) To supplement the text where (a) spectacular uses of the skeptical, and (b) modest uses of the speculative tradition are given: (a') in physics, the atomic theory is the standard example of a success fitting into the speculative tradition (atoms being hardly much more plausible than ghosts, from ordinary experience); in mathematics, nonconstructive methods. (b') Modes: uses abound of course: cf., for example, my review of Brouwer's work in *83* (1977) of AMSB (around p. 88).

Remark. It cannot have escaped the reader's notice that there is no counterpart in current foundations to what is surely the most glaring difference between natural science and the early speculations referred to in (i): the skillful use of a massive amount of empirical data. Certainly the history of mathematics — not, of course, mere snippets as in (i)-(iii) above — would seem to provide, at present, the most obvious source of empirical data for the general questions behind t.f., and, in particular, for a scientific study of Bourbaki's 'intuitive resonances' (in [1]). Of course, precautions are needed against overliteral interpretations of the data (cf. end of [2] about misplaced textural criticism) and artifacts (cf. *Remark* (ii) in [8]); as in all sciences, only more so because here the influence of the observer on the observation is particularly strong. The use of statistical data, as in [9] over long periods provides *one* way of taking precautions. It may well be that this historical perspective would be bad for mathematical practice (with busybodies drawing premature 'practical' conclusions from ill-digested data). But in the reviewer's opinion it is certainly good for foundational research, specifically, for *opening up this subject to* (genuine) *problems raised by recent computer-assisted proofs*: (a) Historically — and scientifically, if not artistically — speaking, such proofs, for example, of the 4-color conjecture, involve incomparably more progress than say, the use of large cardinals in (ii) above. Compare the effort which would be needed to explain large cardinals to Archimedes with getting him to understand, let alone put together the largish computer used by Haken and Appel (and compare the general interest of the four color conjecture with that of Borel determinacy). (b) There are genuine doubts about the reliability of computer-aided proofs not resolved by the particular idealizations of reliability, that is the doctrines of rigor in various branches of t.f. Inasmuch as reliability is a principal topic of foundations, these new proofs present novel data for foundations. It would seem premature (to put it mildly) to *assume* that these new data are less fundamental than the matters of 'principle' stressed in t.f.

56

Reckonings: Wittgenstein on Mathematics

Michael Dummett

It was early in 1950 that philosophers of my generation in Oxford, those, that is to say, who were undergraduates or graduate students in the immediately post-War years, first saw any of Wittgenstein's work other than the *Tractatus* and "Some Remarks on Logical Form." In that year, three of Wittgenstein's later works suddenly arrived in Oxford in the form of typescripts: they were the Blue Book, the Brown Book and the Notes on the Mathematics Lectures, the latter in what has turned out to be Bosanquet's version, one of the four from which the present volume[1] has been edited. The first two had been dictated by Wittgenstein for circulation among a select group; the third was merely one person's record of a set of lectures Wittgenstein had given. All three circulated in Oxford with extreme rapidity: there being no xerox machines, the system was for everyone who obtained a set to find five other people who wanted one, engage a typist to type out the entire work with four carbons, and then sell them at cost price.

It is difficult to convey the excitement of reading these works for the first time. Wittgenstein was a distant presence of which we were all intensely aware, but an utterly enigmatic presence. I came up to Oxford, out of the army, just one term after the celebrated meeting of the Jowett Society, in the summer of 1947, which Wittgenstein attended and at which he talked at great length, and so had never even seen him. We were all vividly conscious of his being there in Cambridge, giving classes to selected audiences, and conscious also of the atmosphere of secrecy that surrounded him; we believed that he was probably a great genius, revealing to those fortunate enough to be admitted to his lectures a dazzling and completely original treatment of philosophical questions: but we did not know what it was that he said. There were, indeed, disciples of his, like Wisdom, whose writings we read, and Miss Anscombe, whose lectures we heard; but we could not be sure how faithfully they represented their teacher. And then suddenly, by what channel I never knew, these works arrived, smuggled into Oxford from that city that had been as closed to us as Lhasa.

On me, at least, their impact was tremendous. The force of the personality came through even the pages of blurred typescript: for weeks after I first read them, all that would come out, whenever I attempted to write any philosophy, was a ridiculous pastiche of Wittgenstein, the stylistic mannerisms if not the substance. Later, when, after Wittgenstein's death and the publication of the *Philosophical Investigations*, the secrecy had been dissolved, I remained extremely grateful, not only to whoever had circulated the Blue and Brown Books, but also to the person who had pirated the Notes on Mathematics; to the extent that, when it was published, I understood the *Remarks on the Foundations of Mathematics*, textually quite distinct from the Notes but frequently overlapping in philosophical content, I did so because I had previously read and re-read the Notes.

Bosanquet's Notes, which were written in the third person, had a peculiar charm, due in part to that convention. They opened with the words,

> How is it that Wittgenstein, who is a philosopher and knows little about mathematics, has a right to talk about the foundations of mathematics?

In Miss Diamond's version, conflated from four sets of notes, this appears as:

> I am proposing to talk about the foundations of mathematics. An important problem arises from the subject itself: How can I — or anyone who is not a mathematician — talk about this? What right has a philosopher to talk about mathematics?

No doubt her version is much closer to the words actually uttered on 23rd January 1939; but I do not think it is just sentimental attachment to something that had a great effect on me that leads me to think that some of the charm has gone. It appears, too, that Bosanquet's version was incomplete: there were four further lectures. All the same, it finished marvellously:

> This is most important. It has puzzled Wittgenstein more than he can say, how there can be a short-cut through logic. For the moment he will leave us puzzled.

The end in Miss Diamond's version — the end of a lecture not included in Bosanquet's — sounds authentic, but is less delightful; an abrupt sentence reading:

> The seed I'm most likely to sow is a certain jargon.

Miss Diamond has cobbled together this version of Wittgenstein's lectures from four sets of notes, all of them incomplete, although it is amazing to me that anyone was able to take such copious notes as to make the exercise possible at all. There are some thirty-odd passages where she reports that the versions differed substantially and that she has therefore had to guess at the original form of the remarks. Some might protest that they should have been given the texts of the divergent notes in these cases, so as to estimate the original intention for themselves, but I think she was right not to inflate the length and price of the book in this way: perhaps, however, for the sake of the scholarly, transcripts of all the notes ought to be deposited in some university library.

On the whole, I should judge that Miss Diamond has done an excellent job. Nevertheless, we should not be deluded into thinking that we are reading Wittgenstein, not even, as Miss Diamond warns us, unrevised Wittgenstein. The process of transmission has been too indirect to justify any such idea. Rather, it is as if we were standing outside the closed door of a lecture room, occasionally unable to catch what is being said inside, most of the time hearing a muffled voice which we can largely follow, sometimes sure that we must have misheard, never able to be quite certain that we have heard aright.

Frank Ramsey (who was so enormously influenced by Wittgenstein's earlier work, the *Tractatus*) accused the intuitionists, Brouwer and Weyl, of introducing Bolshevism into mathematics; and he meant the accusation quite seriously — for him, their work was as subversive of cherished traditional practices as was Bolshevist propaganda to Western capitalists. Hilbert, similarly, in a famous cry of defiance to the intuitionists, declared, "No one is going to turn us out of the paradise Cantor has created." Wittgenstein's comment is characteristic:

> I wouldn't dream of trying to drive anyone out of this paradise. I would try to do something quite different: I would try to show you that it is not a paradise — so that you'll leave of your own accord.

He nevertheless feels it necessary to protest that *he* is not introducing Bolshevism into mathematics. Ramsey, no doubt, would have agreed with this; if Brouwer and Weyl were Bolsheviks, then Wittgenstein, in his later phase, was an anarchist.

Consider an arithmetic predicate like "is the sum of two primes." In the view both of a classical mathematician and of an intuitionist, for each natural number, such a predicate either applies to it or does not apply to it: for the classical mathematician, this holds simply because the predicate is well defined; for the intuitionist, it holds because the predicate is decidable — we have an effective means, in principle, for deciding whether or not it applies to any given number. There is disagreement between them, however, over the way we give meaning to a statement involving generalisation over infinitely many natural numbers — for instance Goldbach's conjecture that every even number greater than 2 is the sum of two primes.

The classical mathematician conceives of the matter essentially as follows. Suppose that we assign 1 to every number to which the predicate applies, and 0 to every number to which it does not. Then, if we multiply together all the numbers so assigned to even numbers greater than 2, we shall arrive either at the number 1, in which case Goldbach's conjecture will be true, or at the number 0, in which case it will be false; the conjecture is therefore determinately either true or false.

For the intuitionist, this conception embodies a barbaric mistake about the nature of an infinite process: we cannot specify a determinate number as the final outcome of an infinite process, because an infinite process is by definition one which can never be completed. Hence we can have no conception of the truth of Goldbach's conjecture save as consisting in the existence of a proof of it, a procedure for showing, of each even number greater than 2, that it satisfies the predicate, nor of its falsity save as consisting in a means of deriving a contradiction from the supposition that we could prove it. Since we have no guarantee that we can either prove or disprove the conjecture, we cannot assume that it is either true or false.

Wittgenstein agrees with the intuitionists both about infinity and about mathematical truth ("What is the criterion for its being so — if not the proof?"); but he has an independent reason for denying that Goldbach's conjecture is a proposition having a determinate truth-value independently of our having a proof or disproof of it. He supposes that, when we multiply very large numbers, we find that we simply cannot attain agreement over the result; and he argues that, in such a case, there simply would not be a right result, a result that God would know, even though we could never be sure of it, since "to say that something is the right result is to say that we acknowledge it ... There is nothing for a higher intelligence to know ... we know as much as God does in mathematics."

Now this is not a mere hypothetical case, it is the actual case: there is a bound on the complexity of computations we can in practice carry out at all, and a bound on the complexity of those we carry out with certainty of reaching agreement. It follows that such a predicate as "is the sum of two primes" cannot be regarded as definitely applying or failing to apply to every number, however large. There will be numbers too large for us to be able to decide whether or not the predicate applies to them; and it is useless to say that the predicate is true of such a number provided that, if we *were* able to perform the computation, we *should* decide that it was, or to say that God must know what the correct outcome of such a computation would be. There is, according to Wittgenstein, nothing for God to know; there *is* no right answer.

From such a standpoint, there is an objection to the classical conception of generalisation over an infinite domain even more direct and telling than the intuitionists' considerations about infinite processes, namely that there is not really a definite truth-value attaching to each statement of the form "n is the sum of two primes." We have not really succeeded in associating either the number 1 or the number 0 to each number n, according as the predicate does or does not apply to it; and so, of course, it is nonsense to talk about the product of all the infinitely many numbers, each equal to 1 or to 0, which we have in this way associated with the even numbers greater than 2.

This is not to say that Wittgenstein draws the conclusion so boldly and assertively drawn by the intuitionists, that classical mathematicians reason incorrectly. He says from the outset that it is "most important not to interfere with the mathematicians"; he is very reluctant to say of anyone, "They reasoned wrongly." He is not going to drive anybody out of a paradise; he will simply point out that it is not a paradise, and then they will leave of their own accord. But it does not in practice seem to me to make a great deal of difference; a mathematician who really believed what Wittgenstein says could hardly continue to employ classical reasoning.

Wittgenstein's idea that God does not know any more mathematics than we do (except in so far as He can foresee what we are going to do — since, apart from that, there is nothing to be known; that is, since truth attaches to a mathematical statement only in virtue of our acknowledging it as true) is, for him, a consequence of his general reflections concerning rules. Those reflections figure prominently in the *Investigations,* and the present lectures start from them. The existence of a rule — in particular, a rule of computation or one governing the use of a word or symbol — rests ultimately upon the fact of agreement in practice, amongst human beings who have been taught the rule, over its application, a fact not susceptible of further explanation.

Our natural reaction to such a thesis is to protest that one who has genuinely mastered the rule grasps the general principle underlying its applications. Wittgenstein of course allows that, very often, the mastery of a rule is attained by getting to know a formula or general formulation, and, in other cases, is manifested by the ability to frame such a general formulation. But every formula, every general statement of the rule, could still be misapplied, and we should not say that someone able to give the formula knew the rule unless he applied it as we all do; and we cannot without circularity or an infinite regress suppose that, in each case, someone's knowledge of how to apply a formula consists in his knowing another formula.

Faced with this, we are inclined grudgingly to admit that, in the last resort, Wittgenstein is right, but to suppose that that concession does not make much difference. Wittgenstein's example of the large multiplication sums shows, however, that he took it as making an enormous difference: even multiplication is well defined only for numbers which we can in practice multiply with confidence, because only in that case is there the agreement in practice which is needed to supply an application for "correct" and "incorrect."

Why are we inclined to think that conceding Wittgenstein to be right in the last resort does not make much difference to anything? I think that this is probably because we are impressed by the fact that any computation is a sequence of operations, each of one of a restricted number of kinds. A multiplication sum, for instance, consists in repeated multiplications and additions of single-digit numbers. Suppose that we grant Wittgenstein's thesis for the rules governing the basic constituent operations of a computation-procedure: we concede that, for each instance of any such operation, we might have regarded something quite different as the analogue of what we have done in other cases, and that nothing makes it the true analogue save the fact that we in practice concur in so regarding it.

All the same, what entitles us to speak of a rule governing the operation is the fact, repeatedly emphasised by Wittgenstein, that we do not in practice disagree over how it is to be applied; and this holds good just as much for an instance of such an operation embedded in an enormous computation as for any other. Suppose that we are concerned with a vast multiplication sum, which it takes the most skilled human calculator a month to do by hand; and suppose that we find that, however many individuals perform the same calculation, and however many times each checks and re-checks his working, they just cannot reach agreement on the correct answer. It is the nub of Wittgenstein's position to infer that there is then no such thing as *the* correct answer (and hence no correct answer either to the question whether a number of the order of magnitude of the product is prime or composite).

But we are inclined to reason as follows. Consider any one attempt at the multiplication sum. It consists of an immensely long sequence of operations of a kind familiar to a child at primary school. If we isolated any one such operation, we should have no difficulty in obtaining agreement over whether it had been performed correctly or incorrectly; the difficulty arises only because of the length of the computation as a whole. It is therefore an objective matter whether or not each of the constituent operations has been performed correctly, even though the criterion for its correctness rests solely upon our propensity to acknowledge it as correct. But the sum as a whole is correct just in case each of its constituent operations is correct. Hence God must know, even though we cannot, whether the sum has been done correctly or not; God must know what the right answer is.

Wittgenstein's constant admonition appears to be, "Do not etherealise; do not hypothesise general principles to which we are striving to conform, or imagine an external reality which, by various indirect means, we are trying to uncover: but look at what actually happens, at what we actually do." No one should doubt that this is often good advice to give; the question is whether it is not sometimes the wrong advice. I did not cite the foregoing objection to Wittgenstein's thesis about multiplication as a knock-down argument, but only as a diagnosis of our inclination to suppose that we can concede his fundamental point concerning rules and then carry on much as before. We are disposed to think that there may be some basic rules, out of which all other rules are compounded, and to which Wittgenstein's thesis may apply, but that, given those basic rules, what we normally believe about the complex rules compounded out of them remains unaffected.

I do not think that this simple way of protecting ourselves from the anarchy that Wittgenstein's views appear to threaten is satisfactory; for of course the rules governing, e.g. multiplication do not reduce without residue to those governing the basic operations of multiplying and adding single-digit numbers, but inescapably involve also those determining the order in which these basic operations are performed. It would be the same for any procedure which we should be unable to carry out accurately, or at all — counting a football crowd, for example. It is possible to break the procedure down into sub-operations so simple that no doubt could arise over the execution of any one of them; but the complexity then reappears in the rules determining which operation has to be performed at any point.

To say that Wittgenstein's arguments cannot be swiftly dismissed or restricted in application to a harmless range of basic operations is not to grant that his conclusions carry conviction. He is, of course, well aware that, when simple methods cease to be reliable, more sophisticated ones are invoked. No one can stand on a football ground and count the crowd in the stadium, but it can be counted mechanically by turnstiles at the exits; even the population of London can be counted in a census. Multiplications that we cannot perform can be carried out, if required, by an electronic calculator or computer. We are not inhibited from measuring the distance from the Earth to the Sun by the fact that we cannot place footrules between them.

The question is not the practical one of whether we can find ways of giving answers, but the theoretical one of whether the primitive methods that we use to give answers in simple cases already determine what constitutes the correct answer in every case. Our overwhelming inclination is to believe that they do: that anyone who knows how to count already understands what would be meant by using a 20-digit number to give the number of stars in the universe; that anyone who knows how to show that 103 is prime already knows what would be meant by saying that that 20-digit number is prime; that distance is distance, whether it is a micron, a mile or a million light-years.

We think this, not merely because of the empirical fact that different methods give the same answers in overlapping areas of applicability, but because we see them as governed by the same underlying principles. Whether a human being counts or the turnstiles click, a one-to-one correlation is being established with an initial segment of the numerals; the computer simulates our own procedures of calculation. Wittgenstein is unimpressed by the conception of guiding principles. For him, what gives sense to the question is that it has a correct answer, and what makes an answer correct is that we are able to agree in acknowledging it as correct. Since any method of obtaining an answer is applicable only over a certain range, the meaning of the question can never be fully determined for every possible case.

I do not believe that Wittgenstein's arguments can be easily rebutted; but I also do not believe that he does justice to the strength of the objections to them. This is odd, because, in other connections, he frequently insists on the necessity of attending, not merely to what is said or done, but to the *point* of what is said or done; he might, therefore, be expected to sympathise with the idea of a guiding principle to the extent of distinguishing between the details of a procedure and its point, which it could share with other procedures differing in detail. I shall not here further attempt to reconcile what is sound in Wittgenstein's arguments with what is sound in the objections to them, and indeed, I am unsure how to do so; but such a reconciliation is required if this matter is to be resolved. At present, philosophers largely ignore this cluster of Wittgenstein's ideas, because they perceive that they cannot be wholly correct, and because they run counter to the prejudices that philosophers have in common with everyone else; but, even if, as I think, there is something wrong with the conclusions Wittgenstein drew from those ideas, justice should be done to them.

More generally, it is plain that Wittgenstein did not handle satisfactorily the notion of a mistake in applying a procedure or a rule. In the early lectures, much use is made, as an example, of Gauss's proof of the impossibility of constructing the regular heptagon with ruler and compass. Wittgenstein says that this proof does not show that one might not, in practice, by fiddling about with a ruler and compass, produce a regular heptagon. The mathematician A.M. Turing, who was present at the lectures, and whose comments are about five times as numerous as those of any other member of the audience, remarks correctly that what it shows is that we cannot give instructions for constructing a regular heptagon. But Wittgenstein denies this too: "I might give instructions to someone and he might go on constructing heptagon after heptagon." What the proof does is to persuade us to exclude the expression "construction of the regular heptagon" from our notation: it does not assure us, of some conceivable event, that it will never occur; it imposes a certain restriction on how we shall be prepared to describe whatever occurs.

This is in line with the whole thrust of much of Wittgenstein's discussion: he wants to persuade us to adopt a view of mathematics, not as demonstrating substantial results about what is and is not possible, but as creating paradigms in terms of which we describe things, an ever more systematic framework of description. In spite of his several disclaimers ("I have no right to want you to say anything"; "I have no point"), it is plain that, in this, Wittgenstein had a vision of what he took mathematics to be, a vision that he tries again and again to communicate to his audience.

But, in the heptagon example, it is clear that Wittgenstein does not succeed in making out his case. It is true that the existence of the proof of non-constructibility does not render it inconceivable that we should hit on a set of instructions apparently enabling us to construct regular heptagons: but that is because there might be a mistake in the proof. It has happened that theorems have for many years been accepted to which there subsequently turned out to be counter-examples; we can seldom rule out the possibility that there is a mistake in what has been acknowledged as a proof. If such a set of instructions were to be devised, we should have an apparent counter-example to Gauss's theorem about which regular polygons are constructible; we should know that there must be a mistake either in the proof of the theorem or in the identification of the alleged counter-example, and should set about to discover which.

It thus seems that Wittgenstein confuses the *a priori* character of mathematics — the necessity of its results whenever they are genuine — with certainty, which is not a general characteristic of it; because we are in principle capable of recognising a proof as correct or incorrect, he assumes that we never accept a proof unless we are not merely assured but *certain* of its validity, and hence are prepared to "put it in the archives" and maintain it against all counter-evidence. Turing rightly insists on the possibility of error, but Wittgenstein fails to take his point: on one occasion, when the immediate topic was the multiplication of three-digit numbers (in which it is easy to make mistakes, though also easy to spot them), he responds to Turing's observation by shifting the example and asking what it would be to find that we had always been mistaken in saying that $12 \times 12 = 144$.

It has been commonplace to express the conclusive character of mathematical proof by saying that only in mathematics do we attain certainty; and it seems that Wittgenstein allowed himself to fall into the trap of offering a new explanation of this alleged certainty of mathematical results, instead of exposing it as spurious. We cannot but contrast unfavourably his imaginary accounts of the cavalier manner in which mathematicians would treat hypothetical apparent counter-examples with the careful descriptions by Imre Lakatos in his *Proofs and Refutations*[2] of how they have in fact treated actual ones. I am not recommending Lakatos's philosophical conclusions any more than Wittgenstein's; but they have the merit of really having been based on seeing what we actually do, as, despite his advocacy of that way of proceeding, Wittgenstein's do not.

Wittgenstein's vision of mathematics cannot, I believe, be sustained; it was a radically faulty vision. Nevertheless, although this book is necessarily an imperfect reconstruction of Wittgenstein's words, and although those words were impromptu and unrevised, they were words spoken by a profound philosopher who devoted a great part of his time throughout his life to thinking about mathematics. It therefore contains much more gold than I have been able here to indicate, gold which it will take much intellectual labour fully to extract. The English into which Miss Diamond has rendered the four sets of notes she was using is undistinguished and surely does not bear the stamp of Wittgenstein's personality, as all his writing does; but at least we are spared split infinitives and similar inappropriate Americanisms, save for the inescapable 'I would/will" for "I should/shall", a solecism which, for all I know, Wittgenstein himself may have committed. There are many irritating features, not least Wittgenstein's inability to acknowledge that anyone else is right; it happens several times to Casimir Lewy, in particular, to say things that Wittgenstein himself is going to say a page or two later, only to have as Wittgenstein's immediate reaction a change of subject (see, *e.g.* p. 41, or pp. 45 and 47). But, with all these defects, the book is one that must absorb anyone interested in the philosophy of mathematics, particularly since the expression of Wittgenstein's thought is far more direct and unguarded than in the *Re-*

120   *Wittgenstein on Mathematics*

marks; and we owe much gratitude to Miss Diamond for her labour in producing it.

Notes

1. *Wittgenstein's Lectures on the Foundations of Mathematics, Cambridge, 1939.* Edited by Cora Diamond from the notes of R.G. Bosanquet, Norman Malcolm, Rush Rhees and Yorick Smythies, Cornell University Press; Harvester Press.
2. Imre Lakatos, *Proofs and Refutations: The Logic of Mathematical Discovery* (Cambridge University Press, 1976).

57

Wittgenstein's Philosophy of Mathematics

Michael Dummett

From time to time Wittgenstein recorded in separate notebooks thoughts that occurred to him about the philosophy of mathematics. His recently published *Remarks on the Foundations of Mathematics* consists of extracts made by the editors from five of these. Neither it nor any of these note-books were intended by its author as a book. That it cannot be considered, and ought not to be criticised, as such is therefore unsurprising, though disappointing. Many of the thoughts are expressed in a manner which the author recognised as inaccurate or obscure; some passages contradict others; some are quite inconclusive; some raise objections to ideas which Wittgenstein held or had held which are not themselves stated clearly in the volume; other passages again, particularly those on consistency and on Gödel's theorem, are of poor quality or contain definite errors. This being so, the book has to be treated as what it is — a selection from the jottings of a great philosopher. As Frege said of his unpublished writings, they are not all gold but there is gold in them. One of the tasks of the reader is therefore to extract the gold.

I encounter frequently in conversation the impression that this is typical of Wittgenstein's work in general; I have often heard the *Investigations* characterised as evasive and inconclusive. This seems to me a travesty of the truth; the book expresses with great clarity many forceful, profound, and quite definite ideas — though it is true that a hasty reader may some-times be bewildered by the complexity of some of the thoughts. The contrast with the present volume is marked, and is due entirely to the different origins of the two books.

In the philosophy of mathematics, platonism stands opposed to various degrees of constructivism. According to platonism, mathematical objects are there and stand in certain relations to one another, independently of us, and what we do is to discover these objects and their relations to one another. The constructivist usually opposes to this the picture of our making, constructing, the mathematical entities as we go along. For the Pla-tonist, the meaning of a mathematical statement is to be explained in terms of its truth-conditions; for each statement, there is something in mathematical reality in virtue of which it is either true or false. An example of the explanation of meaning in terms of truth and falsity is the truth-table explanation of the sentential connectives. For the constructivist, the general form of an explanation of meaning must be in terms of the conditions under which we regard ourselves as justified in asserting a statement, that is, the circumstances in which we are in possession of a proof. For instance, a statement made up of two statements joined by a connective is to be explained by explaining a claim to have proved the complex statement in terms of what a claim to have proved the constituent statements consists in; thus a claim to have proved ⌜*A* or *B*⌝ will be a claim to have a method leading either to a proof of *A* or to a proof of *B*. What in practice this will lead to will depend upon the degree of constructivism adopted; for example, if we confine ourselves to decidable statements, then the truth-tables will receive an acceptable interpretation and the whole classical logic will be applicable; if, on the other hand, we allow with the intuitionists a much wider range of mathematical statements to be considered as intelligible, then the law of excluded middle and many other classically valid laws will cease to hold generally. But in either case it is the notion of proof and not the notions of truth and falsity which is for the constructivist central to the account of the meaning of mathematical statements.

We may regard platonism and the various varieties of constructivism not as rivals but merely as means of demarcating different areas of mathematics with respect not to subject-matter but to methods of proof. In this case there are only the essentially mathematical problems of formulating clearly the different conceptions and investigating in detail the mathematical consequences of each. If, on the other hand, one regards the different schools as rivals, there remains the philosophical problem of deciding which of the various accounts is correct. Wittgenstein's book is intended as a contribution to the latter task only. It seems natural to suppose that the philosophical task and the mathematical go hand in hand, for the precise formulation of a conception is not irrelevant to deciding on its correctness, and unexpected consequences of adopting it may lead one to revise one's opinion as to its value. Wittgenstein will have none of this: for him philosophy and mathematics have nothing to say to one another; no mathematical discovery can have any bearing on the philosophy of mathematics.[1] It would seem that he is theoretically committed also to the converse, that no philosophical opinion could, or at least ought to, affect the procedure of the mathematician. This comes out to some extent in his discussion of the law of excluded middle in mathematics. Against one who insists that either the sequence '77777' occurs in the development of π or it does not, he employs arguments similar to those of the intuitionists; and yet it appears that he is not wishing to question the validity in a mathematical proof of, for example, argument by cases, but only to reprove someone who in the course of philosophical reflection wishes to insist on the law of excluded middle.[2] Yet this is not to be taken seriously, for Wittgenstein would always be able to claim that, while he had not shown that certain mathematical procedures were *wrong*, still he had shown them not to have the interest we were inclined to attach to them. Certainly in his discussion of Cantor he displays no timidity about 'interfering with the mathematicians'.[3] I think that there is no ground for Wittgenstein's segregation of philosophy from mathematics but that this springs only from a general tendency of his to regard discourse as split up into a number of distinct islands with no communication between them (statements of natural science, of philosophy, of mathematics, of religion).

As Frege showed, the nominalist objection to platonism — that talk about 'abstract entities' is unintelligible — is ill-taken; if we believe in the objectivity of mathematics, then there is no objection to our thinking in terms of mathematical objects, nor to the picture of them as already there waiting to be discovered that goes with it. Nor is formalism a real alternative. The formalist insists that the content of a mathematical theorem is simply that *if* there is any domain for which the axioms hold good, then the theorem will also hold good for that domain; and he will add that so long as we do not know the axioms to be categorical, a statement of the theory need not be either true or false. But he will not reject the classical logic, since he will agree that in any particular domain for which the axioms hold, the statement will be either true or false; and furthermore, he will allow that any given statement either does or does not follow from the axioms. Since the statement that there exists a proof of a given statement from given axioms is in exactly the same position as, say, an existence-statement in number theory for which we have neither proof nor disproof, the formalist has gained no advantage; he has merely switched from one kind of mathematical object — numbers — to another — formal proofs.

Wittgenstein adopts a version (as we shall see, an extreme version) of constructivism; for him it is of the essence of a mathematical statement that it is asserted as the conclusion of a *proof*, whereas I suppose that for a platonist a being who had *direct* apprehension of mathematical truth, not mediated by inferences, would not be a complete absurdity. There are many different lines of thought converging upon Wittgenstein's constructivism; I shall deal first with his conception of logical necessity.

A great many philosophers nowadays subscribe to some form of conventionalist account of logical necessity, and it is perhaps difficult to realise what a liberation was effected by this theory. The philosophical problem of necessity is twofold: what is its source, and how do we recognise it? God can ordain that something shall hold good of the actual world; but how can even God ordain that something is to hold good in all possible worlds? We know what it is to set about finding out if something *is* true; but what account can we give of the process of discovering whether it *must* be true? According to conventionalism, all necessity is imposed by us not on reality, but upon our language; a statement is necessary by virtue of our having chosen not to count anything as falsifying it. Our recognition of logical necessity thus becomes a particular case of our knowledge of our own intentions.

The conventionalism that is so widespread is, however, a modified conventionalism. On this view, although all necessity derives from linguistic conventions that we have adopted, the derivation is not always direct. Some necessary statements are straightforwardly registers of conventions we have laid down; others are more or less remote *consequences* of conventions. Thus 'Nothing can at the same time be green and blue all over' is a direct register of a convention, since there is nothing in the ostensive training we give in the use of colour-words which shows that we are not to call something on the borderline between green and blue 'both green and blue'. 'Nothing can be both green and red', on the other hand, is necessary in consequence of the meanings of 'green' and 'red' as shown in the ostensive training. We did not need to adopt a special convention excluding the expression 'both green and red' from our language, since the use by someone of this expression would already show that he had not learned what he was supposed to have learned from the ostensive training.

When applied to mathematics, this modified conventionalism results in the sort of account of mathematical truth with which we are so familiar from logical positivist writings. The axioms of a mathematical theory are necessary in virtue of their being direct registers of certain conventions we have adopted about the use of the terms of the theory; it is the job of the mathematician to discover the more or less remote consquences of our having adopted these conventions, which consequences are epitomized in the theorems. If it is enquired what is the status of the logical principles in accordance with which we pass from axioms to theorems, the reply is that to subscribe to these principles is again the expression of the adoption of linguistic conventions, in this case conventions about the use of 'if', 'all', and so forth. This account is entirely superficial and throws away all the advantages of conventionalism, since it leaves unexplained the status of the assertion that certain conventions have certain consequences. It appears that if we adopt the conventions registered by the axioms, together with those registered by the principles of inference, then we *must* adhere to the way of talking embodied in the theorem; and *this* necessity must be one imposed upon us, one that we meet with. It cannot itself express the adoption of a convention; the account leaves no room for any further such convention.

Wittgenstein goes in for a full-blooded conventionalism; for him the logical necessity of any statement is always the *direct* expression of a linguistic convention. That a given statement is necessary consists always in our having expressly decided to treat that very statement as unassailable; it cannot rest on our having adopted certain other conventions which are found to involve our treating it so. This account is applied alike to deep theorems and to elementary computations. To give an example of the latter, the criterion which we adopt in the first place for saying that there are n things of a certain kind is to be explained by describing the procedure of counting. But when we find that there are five boys and seven girls in a room, we say that there are twelve children altogether, without counting them all together. The fact that we are justified in doing this is not, as it were, implicit in the procedure of counting itself; rather, we have chosen to adopt a *new* criterion for saying that there are twelve children, different from the criterion of counting up all the children together. It would seem that, if we have genuinely distinct criteria for the same statement, they may clash. But the necessity of '$5 + 7 = 12$' consists just in this, that we do not count anything as a clash; if we count the children all together and get eleven, we say, 'We must have miscounted'.

This account is very difficult to accept, since it appears that the mathematical proof drives us along willy-nilly until we arrive at the theorem. (Of course, we learned '5 + 7 = 12' by rote; but we could produce an argument to prove it if the need arose.) But here Wittgenstein brings in the considerations about rules presented in the *Investigations* and elsewhere. A proof proceeds according to certain logical principles or rules of inference. We are inclined to suppose that once we have accepted the axioms from which the proof starts, we have, as it were, no further active part to play; when the proof is shown us, we are mere passive spectators. But in order to follow the proof, we have to recognise various transitions as applications of the general rules of inference. Now even if these rules had been explicitly formulated at the start, and we had given our assent to them, our doing so would not in itself constitute recognition of each transition as a correct application of the rules. Once we have the proof, we shall indeed say that anyone who does not accept it either cannot really have understood or cannot really have accepted the rules of inference; but it does not have to be the case that there was anything in what he said or did before he rejected the proof which revealed such a misunderstanding or rejection of the rules of inference. Hence, at each step we are free to choose to accept or reject the proof; there is nothing in our formulation of the axioms and of the rules of inference, and nothing in our minds when we accepted these before the proof was given, which of itself shows whether we shall accept the proof or not; and hence there is nothing which *forces* us to accept the proof. If we accept the proof, we confer necessity on the theorem proved; we 'put it in the archives' and will count nothing as telling against it. In doing this we are making a new decision, and not merely making explicit a decision we had already made implicitly.

A natural reaction to this is to say that it is true enough when we have not formulated our principles of inference, or have formulated them only in an imprecise form, but that it does not apply at all when we have achieved a strict formalisation. Wittgenstein's hostility to mathematical logic is great; he says that it has completely distorted the thinking of philosophers.[4] Because this remark as it stands is so plainly silly, it is difficult to get a clear view of the matter. Consider a favourite example of Wittgenstein's: you train someone to obey orders of the form 'Add *n*' with examples taken from fairly small numbers, then give him the order 'Add one' and find that he adds two for numbers from 100 to 199, three for numbers from 200 to 299, and so forth. Wittgenstein says that there need have been nothing either in what you said to him during the training or in what 'went on in your mind' then which of itself showed that this was not what you intended. This is certainly true, and shows something important about the concept of intention (it is a very striking case of what Wittgenstein means when he says in the *Investigations* that if God had looked into my mind, he would not have been able to see there whom I meant). But suppose the training was not given only by example, but made use also of an explicit formulation of the rule for forming from an Arabic numeral its successor. A machine can follow this rule; whence does a human being gain a freedom of choice in this matter which the machine does not possess?

It would of course be possible to argue that someone might appear to understand a rule of inference in a formal system — a substitution rule, say — and yet later reject a correct application of it; but it remains that we can see *in* the precise wording of the rule that the application was warranted. It might be replied that this is to take for granted the ordinary understanding of the words or symbols in terms of which the rule is framed; an explanation of these words or symbols would be something like Wittgenstein's idea of a rule for interpreting the rule. It is undoubtedly true and important that, while in using a word or symbol we are in some sense following a rule, this rule cannot in its turn be formulated in such a way as to leave no latitude in its interpretation, or if it can, the rules for using the words in terms of which this rule is formulated cannot in their turn be so formulated. But such considerations seem to belong to the theory of meaning in general, rather than having any particular relevance to the philosophy of mathematics. Rather, it seems that, to someone who suggests that Wittgenstein's point about the scope left in deciding on the correctness of an application of a rule of inference is to be countered by concentrating on rules of inference in formal systems, we ought to reply by referring to what Wittgenstein calls the 'motley' of mathematics.[5] He wishes, like the intuitionists, to insist that we cannot draw a line in advance round the possible forms of argument that may be used in mathematical proofs. Furthermore, it might be pointed out that a formal system does not *replace* the intuitive proofs as, frequently, a precise concept replaces a vague intuitive one; the formal system remains, as it were, answerable to the intuitive conception, and is of interest to us only in so far as it does not reveal undesirable features which the intuitive idea does not possess. An example would be Gödel's theorem, which shows that provability in a single formal system cannot do duty as a complete substitute for the intuitive idea of arithmetical truth.

Suppose we are considering a statement of some mathematical theory. To avoid complications, assume that the theory is complete, that is, that it can be completely formalised, but that we are not thinking of any particular formal system. Then a platonist will say that there exists either a proof or a disproof of the statement; the fact that the statement is true, if it is true, consists in the existence of such a proof even though we have not yet discovered it. Now if there exists a proof, we may suppose that there is somewhere an actual document, as yet unseen by human eyes, on which is written what purports to be a proof of the statement. Then Wittgenstein will reply that all the same there does not yet exist a proof, since when we discover the document it is still up to us to decide whether or not we wish to count it as a proof. It is evident that, if this is correct, then all motive for saying with the platonist that there either *is* or *is not* a proof, that the statement must be either true or false, and so forth, has gone. What is not clear is that rejecting the platonist's conception involves adopting this line about proofs; a man might hold that, once the proof was discovered, we had no choice but to follow it, without allowing the correctness of saying, before the proof was discovered, that either there is a proof or there is not. I will return to this later.

Wittgenstein's conception is extremely hard to swallow, even though it is not clear what one wishes to oppose to it. The proof is supposed to have the effect of persuading us, inducing us to count such-and-such a form of words as unassailably true, or to exclude such-and-such a form of words from our language. It seems quite unclear how the proof accomplishes this remarkable feat. Another difficulty is the scarcity of examples. We naturally think that, face to face with a proof, we have no alternative but to accept the proof if we are to remain faithful to the understanding we already had of the expressions contained in it. For Wittgenstein, accepting the theorem is adopting a new rule of language, and hence our concepts cannot remain unchanged at the end of the proof. But we could have rejected the proof without doing any more violence to our concepts than is done by accepting it; in rejecting it we could have remained equally faithful to the concepts with which we started out. It seems extraordinarily difficult to take this idea seriously when we think of some particular actual proof. It may of course be said that this is because we have already accepted the proof and thereby subjected our concepts to the modification which acceptance of the proof involved; but the difficulty of believing Wittgenstein's account of the matter while reading the proof of some theorem with which one was not previously familiar is just as great. We want to say that we do not know what it would be like for someone who, by ordinary criteria, already understood the concepts employed, to reject this proof. Of course we are familiar with someone's simply not following a proof, but we are also familiar with the remedy, namely to interpolate simpler steps between each line of the proof. The examples given in Wittgenstein's book are — amazingly for him — thin and unconvincing. I think that this is a fairly sure sign that there is something wrong with Wittgenstein's account.

Consider the case of an elementary computation, for example '5 + 7 = 12'. There might be people who counted as we do but did not have the concept of addition. If such a person had found out by counting that there were five boys and seven girls in a classroom, and were then asked how many children were present, he would proceed to count all the children together to discover the answer. Thus he would be quite prepared to say that on one occasion there were five boys, seven girls, and twelve children altogether, but on another occasion five boys, seven girls, and thirteen children altogether. Now if we came across such a person, we should know what kind of arguments to bring to show him that in such circumstances he must have miscounted on one occasion, and that whenever there are five boys and seven girls there are twelve children. If he accepts these arguments it will be quite true that he will have adopted a new criterion for saying that there are twelve children present, and again a new criterion for saying, 'I must have miscounted'. Before, he would say, 'I miscounted', only when he noticed that he had, for example, counted one of the children twice over; now he will say, 'I miscounted', when he has not observed anything of this kind, simply on the ground that he got the result that there were five boys, seven girls, and thirteen children. But we wish to say that even before we met this person and taught him the principles of addition, it would have been true that if he had counted five boys, seven girls, and thirteen children, he would have been wrong even according to the criteria he himself then acknowledged. That is, he must have made a mistake in counting; and if he made a mistake, then there must have been something that he did which, if he had noticed it, he himself would then have allowed as showing that he had miscounted.

If we say that if he counted five boys, seven girls, and thirteen children, then there must have been something which, if he had noticed it, he would have regarded as a criterion for having miscounted, then the effect of introducing him to the concept of addition is not to be simply described as persuading him to adopt a new criterion for having miscounted; rather, he has been induced to recognise getting additively discordant results as a *symptom* of the presence of something he already accepted as a criterion for having miscounted. That is, learning about addition leads him to say, 'I miscounted', in circumstances where he would not before have said it; but if, before he had learned, he had said, 'I miscounted', in those circumstances, he would have been right by the criteria he then possessed. Hence the necessity for his having miscounted when he gets additively discordant results does not, as it were, get its whole being from his now recognising such results as a criterion for having miscounted.

If on the other hand we say that it is possible to count five boys, seven girls, and thirteen children without there being anything other than the fact of getting these results such that, if we had noticed it, we should have regarded it as a ground for saying that we had miscounted, then it appears to follow that one can make a mistake in counting (according to the criteria *we* recognise for having miscounted) without having made any particular mistake; that is, one cannot say that if one has miscounted, then either one counted this boy twice, or one counted that girl twice, or ... But this is absurd; one cannot make some mistake without there having been some particular mistake which one has made. It might be replied that we can choose to say that if one has miscounted, then either ..., and that that is in fact what we do choose to say. But if a disjunction is true, then at least one of its limbs must be true; and if a statement is true, there must be something such that if we knew of it, we should regard it as a criterion for the truth of the statement. Yet the assumption from which we started is that someone counts five boys, seven girls, and thirteen children (and hence says that he must have miscounted) and that there is nevertheless nothing apart from his having got these results which (if he knew of it) he would regard as showing that he had miscounted; and hence there can be nothing which (if he knew of if) would show the truth of any one of the disjuncts of the form 'He counted that boy twice', and so forth. One might put it by saying that if a disjunction is true, God must know which of the disjuncts is true; hence it cannot be right to count something as a criterion for the truth of the disjunction whose presence does not guarantee the existence of something which would show the truth of some one particular disjunct. For example, it would be wrong to regard ⌐Either if it had been the case that P, it would have been the case that Q, or if it had been the case that P, it would have been the case that not Q⌐ as a logical law, since it is perfectly possible to suppose that however much we knew about the kind of fact which we should regard as bearing on the truth of the disjunct counter-factuals, we should still know nothing which we should count as a reason for accepting either the one or the other.

It is certainly part of the meaning of the word 'true' that if a statement is true, there must be something in virtue of which it is true. 'There is some-thing in virtue of which it is true' means: there is something such that if we knew of it we should regard it as a criterion (or at least as a ground) for asserting the statement. The essence of realism is this: for any statement which has a definite sense, there must be something in virtue of which either it or its negation is true. (Realism about the realm of mathematics is what we call platonism.) Intuitionists do not at all deny the first thesis; for them one is justified in asserting a disjunction only when one has a method for arriving at something which would justify the assertion of some one particular limb of the disjunction. Rather, they deny the second thesis: there is no reason for supposing in general that, just because a statement has a quite definite use, there must be something in virtue of which either it is true or it is false. One must beware of saying that logical truths are an exception, that there is nothing in virtue of which they are true; on the con-trary, for the realist we are justified in asserting ⌜P or not P⌝ because there must be something in virtue of which either P or ⌜Not P⌝ is true, and hence in any case there must be something in virtue of which ⌜P or not P⌝ is true.

Now there seems here to be one of the big differences between Wittgenstein and the intuitionists. He appears to hold that it is up to us to decide to regard any statement we happen to pick on as holding necessarily, if we choose to do so.[6] The idea behind this appears to be that, by laying down that something is to be regarded as holding necessarily, we thereby in part determine the sense of the words it contains; since we have the right to attach what sense we choose to the words we employ, we have the right to lay down as necessary any statement we choose to regard as such. Against this one would like to say that the senses of the words in the statement may have already been fully determined, so that there is no room for any further determination. Thus, if one takes a classical (realist) view, the general form of explanation of the sense of a statement consists in the stipulation of its truth-conditions (this is the view taken by Wittgenstein in the *Tractatus* and also the view of Frege). Thus the sense of the sentential operators is to be explained by means of truth-tables; it is by reference to the truth-tables that one justifies taking certain forms as logically true.

Since the intuitionist rejects the conception according to which there must be for every statement something in virtue of which either it is true or it is false (and does not regard it as possible to remedy the situation by the introduction of further truth-values), for him the fundamental form of an explanation of a statement's meaning consists in stating the criteria we recognise as justifying the assertion of the statement (in mathematics, this is in general the possession of a proof). We thus specify the sense of the sentential operators, of 'or', for example, by explaining the criteria for asserting the complex statement in terms of the criteria for asserting the constituents; hence, roughly speaking, we are justified in asserting ⌜P or Q⌝

only when we are justified either in asserting *P* or in asserting *Q*. A logical law holds in virtue of these explanations; by reference to them we see that we shall *always* be justified in asserting a statement of a certain form.

Wittgenstein's quite different idea, that one has the right simply to *lay down* that the assertion of a statement of a given form is to be regarded as always justified, without regard to the use that has already been given to the words contained in the statement, seems to me mistaken. If Wittgenstein were right, it appears to me that communication would be in constant danger of simply breaking down. The decision to count a particular form of statement as logically true does not affect only the sense of statements of that form; the senses of all sorts of other statements will be infected, and in a way that we shall be unable to give a direct account of, without reference to our taking the form of statement in question as logically true. Thus it will become impossible to give an account of the sense of any statement without giving an account of the sense of every statement, and since it is of the essence of language that we understand *new* statements, this means that it will be impossible to give an account of the use of our language at all. To give an example: suppose someone were to choose to regard as a logical law the counterfactual disjunction I mentioned above. We try to object to his claim that this is logically valid by observing that either he must admit that a disjunction may be true when neither limb is true, or that a counterfactual may be true when there is nothing in virtue of which it is true, that is, nothing such that if we knew of it we should regard it as a ground for asserting the counterfactual. But he may respond by denying that these consequences follow; rather, he adduces it as a consequence of the validity of the law that there must be something such that if we knew of it we should count it as a ground either for asserting ⌜If it had been the case that *P*, then it would have been the case that *Q*⌝ or for asserting ⌜If it had been the case that *P*, then it would have been the case that not *Q*⌝. For example, he will say that there must be something in which either the bravery or the cowardice of a man consisted, even if that man had never encountered danger and hence had never had an opportunity to display either courage or cowardice. If we hold that he is entitled to regard anything as a logical law which he chooses so to regard, then we cannot deny him the right to draw this conclusion. The conclusion follows from the disjunction of counterfactuals which he elected to regard as logically true in the first place, together with statements we should all regard as logically true; and in any case, he must have the right to regard the conclusion itself as logically true if he so chooses. He will thus conclude that either a man must reveal in his behaviour how he would behave in all possible circumstances, or else that there is inside him a sort of spiritual mechanism determining how he behaves in each situation.

Now we know from the rest of Wittgenstein's philosophy how repugnant such a conclusion would be to him; but what right would he have, on his own account of the matter, to object to this man's reaching this conclusion? It is all very well to say, 'Say what you like once you know what the facts are': how are we to be sure that we can tell anyone what the facts are if it may be that the form of words we use to tell him the facts has for him a different sense as a result of his having adopted some logical law which we do not accept? It might be said that once we discover this difference in the understanding of a certain form of words, we must select another form of words which he does understand as we do and which expresses what we wanted to say; but how are we to know that there is a form of words which does the trick? If we ask him how he understands a certain statement, and he gives the same explanation of it that we should give, this is no guarantee that he in fact understands it as we do; for the mere fact that he recognises certain forms as logically true which we do not recognise means that he may be able to construct arguments leading to the given statement as a conclusion and with premisses that we accept, although we should not accept the argument; that is, he will regard himself as entitled to assert the statement in circumstances in which we should not regard ourselves as entitled to assert it. (An analogy, *not* strictly parallel, is this: we might imagine a classicist and an intuitionist giving explanations of the meaning of the existential quantifier which sounded exactly the same. Yet for all that the classicist will make existential assertions in cases in which the intuitionist will not, since he has been able to arrive at them by means of arguments which the intuitionist will not accept.) Now, in the case we are imagining, it is essential to suppose that our man is not capable of giving any general kind of explanation of the words he uses such that we can, from this explanation, derive directly the meaning he attaches to any sentence composed of these words. For if he could give such an explanation, we could see from the explanation why the logical law which he accepts but we do not *is* necessary if the words in it are understood as he understands them. We should thus have a justification for taking statements of that form to be logical laws parallel to the justification of the laws of classical logic in terms of an explanation of meaning by reference to truth-conditions and to the justification of intuitionist logic in terms of the explanation by reference to assertibility-conditions. But the whole point of the example was that this was a case of simply laying down a certain form of statement as logically true without the requirement of a justification of this kind.

This attitude of Wittgenstein's to logical necessity may in part explain his ambivalence about the law of excluded middle in mathematics. If a philosopher insists on the law of excluded middle, this is probably the expression of a realist (platonist) conception of mathematics which Wittgenstein rejects : he insists that ⌜P or not P⌝ is true because he thinks that the general form of explanation of meaning is in terms of truth-conditions, and that for any mathematical statement possessing a definite sense there must be something in virtue of which either it is true or it is false. On the other hand, if a mathematician wishes to use a form of argument depending upon the law of excluded middle (for example, ⌜If P, then Q⌝; ⌜If not P, then Q⌝; therefore, Q), Wittgenstein will not object, since the mathematician has the right to regard the form of words ⌜P or not P⌝ as holding necessarily if he chooses to do so.

To return to the example of the people who counted but did not have addition, it seems likely that someone who accepted Wittgenstein's viewpoint would wish to reject the alternative: either when one of these people counted five boys, seven girls, and thirteen children there must have been something which, if he had noticed it, would have been for him evidence of his having miscounted, or else he could have done so when there was nothing which would have shown him he had miscounted. He would reject it on the ground that it is unclear whether the alternative is being posed in *our* language or in the language of the people in question. *We* say that he must have miscounted, and hence that he must either have counted this boy twice, or ..., and hence that there was something which if he had noticed it would have shown him that he had miscounted, and we say this just on the ground that his figures do not add up. But he would have no reason for saying it, and would assert that he had probably counted correctly. Now we must not ask whether what we say or what he says is *true*, as if we could stand outside both languages; we just *say* this, that is, we count his having got discordant results as a criterion for saying it, and he does not. Against this I wish, for the reasons I have stated, to set the conventional view that in deciding to regard a form of words as necessary, or to count such-and-such as a criterion for making a statement of a certain kind, we have a responsibility to the sense we have already given to the words of which the statement is composed.

It is easy to see from this why Wittgenstein is so obsessed in this book with an empiricist philosophy of mathematics. He does not wish to accept the empiricist account, but it has a strong allure for him; again and again he comes back to the question, 'What is the difference between a calculation and an experiment?'. The fact is that even if we decide to *say* that we must have made a mistake in counting when we count five boys, seven girls, and thirteen children, our mere decision to treat this result as a criterion for having made a mistake cannot of itself make it probable that in such circumstances we shall be able to find a mistake; that is, if Wittgenstein's account of the matter is correct. Nevertheless, getting such a discrepancy in counting is a very sure sign in practice that we shall be able to find a mistake, or that if we count again we shall get results that agree. It is because it is such a sure sign in practice that it is possible — or useful — for us to put '5 + 7 = 12' in the archives. Thus for Wittgenstein an empirical regularity lies behind a mathematical law.[7] The mathematical law does not *assert* that the regularity obtains, because we do not treat it as we treat an assertion of empirical fact, but as a necessary statement; all the same, what leads us to treat it in this way is the empirical regularity, since it is only because the regularity obtains that the law has a useful application.[8] What the relation is between the regularity and the proof which induces us to put the law in the archives Wittgenstein does not succeed in explaining.

To avoid misunderstanding, I must emphasise that I am not proposing an alternative account of the necessity of mathematical theorems, and I do not know what account should be given. I have merely attempted to give reasons for the natural resistance one feels to Wittgenstein's account, reasons for thinking that it must be wrong. But I believe that whether one accepts Wittgenstein's account or rejects it, one could not after reflecting on it remain content with the standard view which I have called modified conventionalism.

Wittgenstein's constructivism is of a much more extreme kind than that of the intuitionists. For an intuitionist, we may say that every natural number is either prime or composite because we have a method for deciding, for each natural number, whether it is prime or not. Wittgenstein would deny that we have such a method. Normally one would say that the sieve of Eratosthenes was such a method; but with a large number one would not — *could* not — use the sieve, but would resort to some more powerful criterion. It will be said that this is a mere practical, not a theoretical matter, due to the comparative shortness of our lives. But if some fanatic devoted his life to computing, by means of the sieve, the primality of some very large number proved to be prime by more powerful means, and arrived at the conclusion that it was composite, we should not abandon our proof but say that there must be some error in his computations. This shows that we are taking the 'advanced' test, and not the sieve, as the *criterion* for primality here: we use the theorem as the standard whereby we judge the computation, and not conversely. The computation is of no use to us because it is not *surveyable.* A mathematical proof, of which computations are a special case, is a proof in virtue of our using it to serve a certain purpose; namely, we put the conclusion or result in the archives, that is, treat it as unassailable and use it as a standard whereby to judge other results. Now something cannot serve this purpose, and hence is not a mathematical proof, unless we are able to exclude the possibility of a mistake's having occurred in it. We must be able to 'take in' a proof, and this means that we must be certain of being able to reproduce the *same* proof. We cannot in general *guarantee* that we shall be able to repeat an experiment and get the same result as before. Admittedly, if we get a different result, we shall look for a relevant difference in the conditions of the experiment; but we did not have in advance a clear conception of just what was to count as a relevant difference. (It is not quite clear whether in saying that we must be able to reproduce a proof Wittgenstein means that one must be able to copy from the written proof before one and be certain that one has copied without error, or that one must be able to read the proof and understand it so that one could write it down without referring to the original written proof, so that the possibility of a misprint becomes more or less irrelevant. It does not seem to affect the argument which interpretation is adopted.)

Thus the computation, for a very large number proved prime by other means, of its primality by means of Eratosthenes's sieve would not be a mathematical proof but an experiment to see whether one could do such enormous computations correctly; for the computation would be unsurveyable in the sense explained. Now what the word 'prime' means as applied to large numbers is shown by what we accept as the *criterion* for primality, what we take as the standard whereby to assess claims that a number is prime or is composite. The sense of the word 'prime' is not therefore given once for all by the sieve of Eratosthenes. Hence we should have no right to assert that every number is either prime or composite, since for any criterion we may adopt there will be a number so large that the application of the criterion to it will not be surveyable. This throws light on Wittgenstein's insistence that the sense of a mathematical statement is determined by its proof (or disproof),[9] that finding a proof alters the concept. One is inclined to think that such a statement as 'There is an odd perfect number' is fixed quite definitely in advance, and that our finding a proof or a disproof cannot alter that already determinate sense. We think this on the ground that we are in possession of a method for determining, for *any* number, whether or not it is odd and whether or not it is perfect. But suppose that the statement were to be proved, say by exhibiting a particular odd perfect number. This number would have to be very large, and it is unthinkable that it should be proved to be perfect by the simple method of computing its factors by means of the sieve and adding them all up. The proof would probably proceed by giving a new method for determining perfection, and this method would then have been adopted as our *criterion* for saying of numbers within this range whether or not they are perfect. Thus the proof determines, for numbers of this size, what the *sense* of the predicate 'perfect' is to be.

This constructivism, more severe than any version yet proposed, has been called 'strict finitism' by Kreisel and 'anthropologism' by Hao Wang. It was adumbrated by Bernays in his 'Sur le platonisme dans les mathématiques'.[10] As presented by Bernays, it would consist in concentrating on practical rather than on theoretical possibility. I have tried to explain how for Wittgenstein this is not the correct way in which to draw the contrast.

It is a matter of some difficulty to consider just what our mathematics would look like if we adopted this 'anthropologistic' standpoint. Would the Peano axioms survive unaltered? 'Every number has a successor' would mean, in this mathematics, that if a number is accessible (that is, if we have a notation in which it can be surveyably represented) then its successor is accessible, and this at first seems reasonable. On the other hand, it seems to lead to the conclusion that *every* number is accessible, and it is clear that, whatever notation we have, there will be numbers for which there will not be a surveyable symbol in that notation. The problem seems similar to the Greek problem of the heap: if I have something that is not a heap of sand, I cannot turn it into a heap by adding one grain of sand to it. One might solve the present difficulty by arguing as follows. Let us say that we 'get to' a number if we actually write down a surveyable symbol for it. Then we may say: if I get to a number, I can get to its successor. From this it follows that if I *can* get to a number, then it is possible that I can get to its successor; that is, if a number is accessible, than its successor is possibly accessible. Unless we think that 'possibly possibly *p*' implies 'possibly *p*' it does not follow that if a number is accessible, its successor is accessible. We should thus have to adopt a modal logic like S2 or M which does not contain the law (in Polish notation) '*CMMpMp*'. Another consideration pointing in the same direction is the following. 'Surveyable', 'accessible', and so forth, are *vague* concepts. It is often profitable to substitute for a vague concept a precise one, but that would be quite out of place here; we do not want to fix on some definite number as the last accessible number, all bigger numbers being definitely inaccessible. Now the vagueness of a vague predicate is ineradicable. Thus 'hill' is a vague predicate, in that there is no definite line between hills and mountains. But we could not eliminate this vagueness by introducing a new predicate, say 'eminence', to apply to those things which are neither definitely hills nor definitely mountains, since there would still remain things which were neither definitely hills nor definitely eminences, and so *ad infinitum*. Hence if we are looking for a logical theory suitable for sentences containing vague predicates, it would be natural to select a modal logic like S2 or M with infinitely many modalities (interpreting the necessity-operator as meaning 'definitely'). Thus a suggestion for a propositional calculus appropriate to an anthropologistic mathematics would be one bearing to the model system M the same relation as intuitionistic propositional calculus bears to S4. (This system would probably have to have axioms of a similar form to those originally given by Heyting, namely, they would frequently be implications whose antecedent was a conjunction, and would have a rule of adjunction as primitive; for, as has been pointed out to me by E.J. Lemmon, under Tarski's or Gödel's translation an implication whose consequent contains implication reiterated more often than does the antecedent does not usually go over into a valid formula of M, precisely because we do not have in M '*CLpLLp*'.) Another suggestion, made by Dr Wang, is that anthropologistic logic would coincide with intuitionist, but that the number theory would be weaker.

Wittgenstein uses these ideas to cast doubt upon the significance attached by some philosophers to the reductionist programmes of Frege and Russell. We may think that the real meaning of and justification for such an equation as '5 + 7 = 12' has been attained if we interpret it as a statement in set theory or in a higher-order predicate calculus; but the fact is that not only the proof but the statement of the proposition in the primitive notation of these theories would be so enormously long as to be quite unsurveyable. It might be replied that we can shorten both the proof and the statement by using defined symbols; but then the definitions play an essential rôle, whereas for Russell definitions are *mere* abbreviations, so that the real formal statement and formal proof are those in primitive notation. For Wittgenstein notation is not a mere outward covering for a thought which is in itself indifferent to the notation adopted. The proof in primitive notation is not what 'really' justifies us in asserting '5 + 7 = 12' since we never do write down this proof; if someone were to write it down and obtain the result '5 + 7 = 11', we should — appealing to schoolroom addition as a standard — say that he must have made a mistake; we do not even write down the proof with defined symbols; what, if anything, could be called the justification of '5 + 7 = 12' would be the proof that we actually do carry out that every addition sum 'could' be formulated and proved within our formal logical system, and this proof uses methods far more powerful than the rules for ordinary schoolroom addition.

I now revert to the opposing *pictures* used by platonists and constructivists — the picture of our making discoveries within an already existing mathematical reality and the picture of our constructing mathematics as we go along. Sometimes people — including intuitionists — argue as though it were a matter of first deciding which of these pictures is correct and then drawing conclusions from this decision. But it is clear that these are only pictures, that is, that the dispute as to which is correct must find its substance elsewhere — that such a dispute ought to be capable of being expressed without reference to these pictures. On the other hand, such pictures have an enormous influence over us, and the desire to be able to form an appropriate picture is almost irresistible. If one does not believe in the objectivity of mathematical truth, one cannot accept the platonist picture. Wittgenstein's main reason for denying the objectivity of mathematical truth is his denial of the objectivity of *proof* in mathematics, his idea that a proof does not *compel* acceptance; and what fits this conception is obviously the picture of our constructing mathematics as we go along. Now suppose that someone disagrees with Wittgenstein over this and holds that a good proof is precisely one which imposes itself upon us, not only in the sense that once we have accepted the proof we use rejection of it as a criterion for not having understood the terms in which it is expressed, but in the sense that it can be put in such a form that no one could reject it without saying something which would have been recognised before the proof was given as going back on what he had previously agreed to. Is such a person bound to adopt the platonist picture of mathematics? Clearly not; he can accept the objectivity of mathematical proof without having to believe also in the objectivity of mathematical truth. The intuitionists, for example, usually speak as though they believed in the former without believing in the latter. It is true that A. Heyting, for instance, writes, 'As the meaning of a word can never be fixed precisely enough to exclude every possibility of misunderstanding, we can never be mathematically sure that [a] formal system expresses correctly our mathematical thoughts'.[11] But intuitionists incline to write as though, while we cannot delimit in advance the realm of all possible intuitionistically valid proofs, still we can be certain for particular proofs given, and particular principles of proof enunciated, that they are intuitionistically correct. That is to say, the point involved here concerns what Wittgenstein calls the motley of mathematics; the question whether a certain statement is provable cannot be given a mathematically definite formulation since we cannot foresee in advance all possible forms of argument that might be used in mathematics. Still, I suppose that someone might deny even this, in the sense that he claimed for some particular logical framework that every theorem that could be proved intuitionistically could be proved within this framework (though perhaps the proof given might not be reproducible within the framework), and yet remain essentially an intuitionist. For the strongest arguments for intuitionism seem to be quite independent of the question of the objectivity of mathematical proof — whether the proof once given compels acceptance, and whether the concept of valid proof can be made precise. The strongest arguments come from the insistence that the general form of explanation of meaning, and hence of the logical operators in particular, is a statement not of the truth-conditions but of the assertibility-conditions. We learn the meaning of the logical operators by being *trained* in their use, and this means being trained to assert complex statements in certain kinds of situation. We cannot, as it were, extract from this training more than was put into it, and, unless we are concerned with a class of decidable statements, the notions of truth and falsity cannot be used to give a description of the training we receive. Hence a general account of meaning which makes essential use of the notions of truth and falsity (or of any other number of truth-values) is not of the right form for an explanation of meaning.

It is clear that considerations of this kind have nothing to do with mathematics in particular, but are of quite general application. They also have a close connection with Wittgestein's doctrine that the meaning is the use; and I believe that the *Investigations* contains implicitly a rejection of the classical (realist) Frege-*Tractatus* view that the general form of explanation of meaning is a statement of the truth-conditions.[12] This provides a motive for the rejection by Wittgenstein and the intuitionists of the platonist picture quite independent of any considerations about the non-objective character of mathematical proof and the motley of mathematics. On the other hand, it is not clear that someone such as I have described, who accepted the considerations about meaning but rejected the considerations about proof, would be happy with the usual constructivist picture of our making up our mathematics. After all, the considerations about meaning do not apply only to mathematics but to all discourse; and while they certainly show something mistaken in the realist conception of thought and reality, they surely do not imply outside mathematics the extreme of subjective idealism — that we *create* the world. But it seems that we ought to interpose between the platonist and the constructivist picture an intermediate picture, say of objects springing into being in response to our probing. We do not *make* the objects but must accept them as we find them (this corresponds to the proof imposing itself on us); but they were not already there for our statements to be true or false of before we carried out the investigations which brought them into being. (This is of course intended only as a picture; but its point is to break what seems to me the false dichotomy between the platonist and the constructivist pictures which surreptitiously dominates our thinking about the philosophy of mathematics.)

Notes

1. Cf. V, 13, 19; IV, 52; also *Investigations*, II, xiv; I, 124.
2. IV, 10.
3. I, App. II.
4. IV, 48.
5. II, 46, 48.
6. Cf. V, 23, last par. on p. 179.
7. III, 44.
8. E.g., II, 73, 75.
9. But cf., e.g., V, 7.
10. *L'enseignement mathématique*, XXXIV (1935), 52-69.
11. *Intuitionism, an Introduction* (Amsterdam, 1956), p. 4.
12. Cf., also *Remarks*, I, App. I, 6.

58

The Work of an Influential but Little-known Philosopher of Science: Ludwig Wittgenstein

Gilbert Ryle

The late Ludwig Wittgenstein was a deep and influential philosopher of science, yet outside the circle of professional philosophers little is known of the man and his work. This book is the second collection of his papers to be published since his death. The editors of *Scientific American* have asked me to take this occasion, not to review the book, which in any case is too specialized for the general reader, but briefly to describe who Wittgenstein was and what he did.

First for the man.

He was born in 1889 in Austria and died in 1951 in England. He was of Jewish origin, though he was brought up a Roman Catholic. He, with the rest of his family, was intensely musical. His father was a wealthy steel magnate. He himself was trained as an engineer, and was engaged in aerodynamical researches in England when in 1911 and 1912 he became perplexed about the logical and philosophical foundations of mathematics. Advised, apparently, by the German mathematician Gottlob Frege, he went to Cambridge to study under the author of *Principles of Mathematics*, Bertrand Russell.

During the First World War he served in the Austrian army, and ended up a prisoner-of-war in Italy. His rucksack contained the manuscript of the only book of his that was published during his lifetime, the *Tractatus Logico-Philosophicus*. This was published in 1922, with the German text faced by an unreliable English translation. It contains an introduction by Russell, but Wittgenstein disapproved of this. A revision of the translation should appear fairly soon. Wittgenstein became professor at Cambridge in 1939, succeeding G.E. Moore, and he resigned in 1947.

He was a spellbinding and somewhat terrifying person. He had unnervingly piercing eyes. He never used hackneyed expressions — not that he strove after originality of diction, but he just could not think in clichés. To his own regret, he could not help dominating his associates. He remorselessly excommunicated persons of whom he disapproved.

He loathed being connected with academic philosophers, and he avoided academic chores. After 1929 he attended no conferences; he did no reviewing for journals; only once did he attend a philosophical meeting in Oxford; he was inaccessible to visiting philosophers; he read few, if any, of the philosophical books and articles that came out during his last 25 years.

He was like Socrates in rigidly separating the philosopher from the sophist; unlike Socrates in shunning the market place; like Socrates in striving to convert his pupils; unlike Socrates in feeling the need to conserve his genius by insulation. He was hermit, ascetic, guru and *Führer*.

What of the philosopher?

He had no formal training in philosophy. His ferments came from his own insides. I do not know just what shape his initial perplexities about mathematics took. Anyhow he consulted Frege and Russell, and studied their logico-mathematical writings; the central problems of his *Tractatus*, though not the same as theirs, were clearly reactions to their doctrines.

Frege and Russell tried to show that all pure mathematics derives from the completely general truths of formal logic, *i.e.*, that these truths stand to arithmetical truths as Euclid's axioms to his theorems. But what was the point of trying to demonstrate this continuity between logic and arithmetic? Surely the truths of mathematics are as well established as anyone could demand, so what is gained, except for tidiness, by underpinning them with an ulterior foundation?

At that time reflective mathematicians were in trouble. Their science seemed all limbs and no body. The very vigor of these branches was generating cross-purposes between them. The notion of number itself seemed to take as many shapes as there were branches of the science of number. Mathematics felt like a caravanserai, not a house.

Its external relations with other sciences also were precarious. John Stuart Mill had likened the truths of mathematics to those of the natural sciences: they are generalizations from experience susceptible of overthrow by unexpected exceptions. It would be much more surprising to find an exception to $7 + 5 = 12$ than to find a black swan, but only much more. Which is absurd. For another thing, many thinkers, when asked, "Of what entities is mathematics the science?", were giving a psychological answer. The physical world contains countless sorts of things, but it does not contain numbers. There are nine planets, and the earth has one moon. But you cannot see 9 or 1. So, if numbers are not physical things, what else is there for them to be, save ideas in our minds or thoughts or something of the sort? But then arithmetic ought to make allowances for the differences between what goes on in lunatic and in sane minds; in visualizers' and in nonvisualizers' minds, and so on. Which is absurd.

Because mathematics needed, internally, coordination between its members and, externally, autonomy from the inductive sciences, especially psychology, its affiliation to logic felt like a rescue operation. Mathematics could be saved from internal discord and from external pressures by becoming part of the unchallengeable science of logic.

But what sort of science is this? What sort of truths are the truths of logic? What sorts of information does logic give us about what sorts of entities? That is, I think, the central problem of Wittgenstein's *Tractatus Logico-Philosophicus*.

The truths and falsehoods of the natural sciences are truths and false-hoods about what exists and happens in the world. Their truth or falsehood depends upon what is the case with things in the world. But the truths of logic give us no information about the world. "Either it is raining or it is not raining" exemplifies a logical truism, but it tells us nothing about the weather. It is true whatever the weather. "Socrates is mortal" gives us important information or misinformation about Socrates, but "*If* all men are mortal and Socrates is a man, *then* he is mortal" gives us an applied logical truth, which is true whether or not he is mortal.

The truths of the natural sciences are factual truths, while those of logic are purely formal. Their truth is neutral between the world as it is and as it might have been. This formal nature of logical truths shows itself in another way. The truism "Either it is raining or it is not" remains true if for "raining" we substitute "snowing," "freezing" or anything you please. For any proposition whatsoever, either it or its negative is true. The force of "either ..., or not ..." is indifferent to the material fillings of the clauses that it links, so long as the clauses are the same. Hence truths of logic can be expressed most clearly if we algebraize away all material elements like "Socrates," "mortal," and "it is raining." This leaves, for example, "For any *p*, either *p* or not-*p*."

Thus logic is unconcerned with the actual truth or falsity of the factual statements which can be draped on its skeletons. Nonetheless logic is essentially concerned with the truth-or-falsity of these statements, since it has to work out how the truth or falsity of one *would* follow, if another *were* true or *were* false. That Jack went up the hill would have to be true *if* Jack and Jill went up the hill; and from the falsity of "Jack went up the hill" would follow the falsity of "Jack and Jill went up the hill."

Well then, why should we not answer the original problem by saying that the subject matter of logic consists of truths-or-falsehoods, and that it has to discover in them their formal properties which secure that one would be true if another were true? But then what sorts of entities are truths-or-falsehoods, and what sorts of properties are those formal properties?

When I say "It is raining," my words convey something to you. You understand them even though you do not know that it is raining. They make sense, even if it is not raining. So the actual state of the weather is one thing; the truth-or-falsehood that it is raining is something else. In getting the meaning of my words, you are getting not what the state of the weather is, but what-it-is-being-represented-as-being. But what enables expressions to represent things as they are, or as they are not? What enables a complex of symbols to mean something *vis à vis* some actual matter of fact? Consider a simple map representing, truly or falsely, the rel-ative positions and distances of three towns: A, B and C. The dot "A" is one inch higher on the page than the dot "B," and this is two inches higher than the dot "C." This map might tell you that the town A is north of B, which is north of C, and that B is 20 miles from C and 10 from A. How does it do this? By an understood code by which lettered dots stand for towns, the top of the page for north and an inch for 10 miles. It is the way in which the dots are situated on the page that says how the towns are related to one another on the ground. In this case the map, if true, is in certain respects photographically like the corresponding stretch of ground. But with a different code the same dot might represent or misrepresent the heights of three peaks, or the degrees below boiling point of three saucepans. Representation can, but need not, be photographic. The notes played by the musician are not *like* the black marks on his score, yet the arrangement of the latter, by a complex code, may faithfully represent the arrangement of the former.

The "codes" which enable different arrangements of words to represent different states of affairs are enormously complicated, and they vary among different tongues. In English, if you wish to say that Brutus killed Caesar you must put "Brutus" before the verb and "Caesar" after it. Not so in Latin, which achieves the same result by different word terminations. But without applying some syntactical rule or other you cannot say anything, not even anything false. Symbol-structures can represent and misrepresent the structures of actual states of affairs because, though the representing structure is not usually *like* the represented structure, they are still structurally analogous to one another. A sentence has a meaning if its syntax *could* be the structural analogue of an actual state of affairs, even though, when false, it actually has no such factual counterpart. Caesar did not kill Brutus but "Caesar killed Brutus" makes sense since there is, so to speak, room in reality, though unfilled room, for this uncommitted murder.

Not all complexes of words or dots or gestures convey truths or falsehoods. An unorganized jumble of words or dots makes no sense. Even a sequence of words with an orthodox grammar can make nonsense. Lewis Carroll concocted many such sentences; for example, "The Cheshire cat vanished leaving only her grin behind her." Sometimes serious thinkers inadvertently construct senseless sentences. Early geometricians seriously held that Euclidean points are round. A truth-or-falsehood, then, is an organized complex of symbols representing, by analogy of structure, a counterpart actual-or-possible state of affairs. It is, for example, a sentence "in its projective relation to the world." To find out whether it is actually true or actually false we have to match it against its should-be counterpart state of affairs in the world.

Already we can see how Wittgenstein's account of what it is to make sense, that is, to be true-or-false, led to the famous principle of verifiability, by which the logical positivists ostracized as nonsensical the pronouncements of metaphysicians, theologians and moralists. Observation and experiment are our ways of matching the propositions of, say, astronomy against the stellar facts. Where observation and experiment are excluded, our pretended truths-or-falsehoods have no anchorage in facts and so say nothing. They are nothing but disguised gibberish.

What of the truths of logic, the status of which it had been Wittgenstein's main task to fix? Are these also disguised gibberish? Or are they salved by being classed with the most general truths of natural science? Wittgenstein steers between this Scylla and this Charybdis.

An everyday "either-or" statement, like "Either Jack climbed the hill or Jill did," leaves it open which climbed the hill; but it still rules out something that might have been the case, namely, the climbing of the hill by neither of them. But if we ask of an "either-or" truism of logic, like " 'Either Jack climbed the hill or he did not'; what is ruled out by *this* assertion?", we see that the only thing ruled out is Jack's neither climbing nor not climbing the hill. And this is not something which might have been but just happens not to be the case. An ordinary factual assertion gives the "yes" or the "no" answer to a question; it invites us to select the one and to forswear the other. But a truth of logic gives us nothing forswearable to forswear, and so nothing selectable to select. It is factually empty, or "tautological."

It does not, however, follow that the truths of logic are of no use simply because they are uninformative. They serve to show up, by contrast with their own absolute hospitality, the ways in which ordinary statements convey, by their relative shut-doored-ness, positive information or misinformation.

The truths of logic, then, are not nonsensical, though they are empty of information or misinformation. Their business is to *show* us, by evaporation of content, how our ordinary thoughts and assertions are organized.

I pass over Wittgenstein's accounts of the connections and differences between logic and mathematics and between logic and mechanics, important though these are for showing up, by contrast, the positive nature of logic. But I must not pass over his account of the relations between logic and philosophy. For, as his title *Tractatus Logico-Philosophicus* hints, his book was secondarily concerned to fix the status of philosophy. What sorts of things can philosophers tell us — philosophers as distinct from logicians and from scientists? Are the truths of philosophy factual or formal truths?

Earlier philosophers, if they tried at all to place philosophy, had tended to treat it either as psychology or as non-empirical cosmology. But Russell and others realized that philosophy was neither a natural science nor yet a supernatural science. Russell had emphasized the close connection between logic and philosophy by treating all seriously philosophical questions as problems for "logical analysis," as if logic supplied the lines of latitude and longitude, while philosophy had to fill in the geographical detail.

In partly the same way Wittgenstein, having separated off all philosophical from any scientific questions, describes the positive function of philosophy as "elucidatory." Its function is to disclose that logical architecture of our ordinary and scientific thoughts which our vernaculars conceal but which the designed symbolism of logic would expose. But now there breaks out a seemingly disastrous difference between logic and philosophy. The formulae of logic, though they tell us nothing, still show us, so to speak, at their limit the positive force of the "ors," "ands," "alls" and so forth on which our ordinary truths and falsehoods are built. But philosophical pronouncements are in a worse state, since their elucidatory mission is to *tell* us what sort of sense or nonsense belongs to the propositions of the sciences and of daily life; and this is not the sort of thing that can conceivably be told. The meanings, that is, the truths or falsehoods that we express, cannot then be lifted out of their expressions. We can talk sense, but we cannot talk sense about the sense that we talk.

Consider again my map in which the situations of three dots on the page told you, truly or falsely, the situations of three towns. Now I ask you to draw another map which is to tell me not about things on the ground, but about the information or misinformation conveyed by the first map. It is to tell me whether the first map is accurate or inaccurate, and especially it is to tell me the cartographical code by which the three original dots represent the compass bearings and distances of the towns. You will promptly protest that you cannot make a map of what another map says or of how it says it. What an ordinary map alleges about the earth's surface is not another bit of that surface and so a second map could not map it. The significance-conditions which an ordinary map exemplifies are not *stated* by these or any other maps.

Similarly, we normally know when a sentence expresses a truth-or-falsehood, and when it is nonsensical. We read the composition of an actual-or-possible state of affairs out of the composition of the sentence. But we are debarred from *stating* this correlation. Attempts to state it would be attempts to stand outside the significance-conditions of statements. They would therefore break these conditions, and so be nonsense.

Philosophical elucidation advances only over the ruins of its attempted articulations. The sort of clarity that we seek we achieve in becoming conscious of what makes us stammer. Critics quickly pointed out that Wittgenstein managed to say many important and understandable things. So perhaps the language of maps has limitations from which the language of words is exempt; and perhaps the notion of sense is wider than the notion of truth-or-falsehood to empirical fact.

Wittgenstein left many manuscripts which are now in process of being published. The first book to be so published was his *Philosophical Investigations*. This has the German text faced by a quite good English translation.

Philosophical Investigations differs from the *Tractatus* in presentation, subject and direction. The *Tractatus* consists of a chain of sentences or short paragraphs, prefaced by numerical and decimal index-numbers signaling both the train of the argument and the relative weights in it of the successive items. Each sentence seems to be the product of an almost Chinese process of pruning and recasting. Many of them mystify, but the reader cannot get them out of his head. In many stretches the *Tractatus* presupposes familiarity with mathematical logic. The *Philosophical Investigations* is more like a conversation. It is a dialogue between the author and his own refractory self, and it presupposes no technical sophistication. It is split up into relatively long paragraph-sections, the continuities between which are often hard to see. Indeed, they are not always there. Unfortunately the book contains no aids to the reader in the shape of table of contents, index or cross references.

Notoriously the *Philosophical Investigations* throws overboard some of the cardinal positions of the *Tractatus*. Some people assume that this exempts them from trying to understand the *Tractatus*. This is a mistake, since a philosopher jettisons what he has taught himself to do without, and we need just the same teaching.

Moreover, a great deal of the *Tractatus* survives, both in the later Wittgenstein and in us too. It comes natural to us now — as it did not 30 years ago — to differentiate logic from science much as Wittgenstein did; it comes natural to us not to class philosophers as scientists or *a fortiori* as super-scientists; it comes natural to us to think of both logic and philosophy as concerned not with any ordinary or extraordinary kinds of *things*, but with the meanings of the expressions of our thoughts and knowledge; and it is beginning to come natural to us, when we reflect about sense *v.* nonsense, to take as the units of sense what is conveyed by full sentences, and not what is meant by isolated words, that is, with what is *said*, and not with what is, for example, *named.*

How does the later differ from the earlier Wittgenstein? First, his central problem is different. He is no longer exercised about the status of logic. It is philosophy now that is pestering him for justice. Next he had in the *Tractatus* been scanning the notions of sense and nonsense through the perforated screen of logic. Through its apertures he could see only elementary atoms of truth and falsehood being combined into molecular truths and falsehoods by the operations of "and," "or" and "not." The only discernible differences between sayables were in their degrees and patterns of compositeness. All their other differences had been algebraized away. But now he forsakes this screen. He examines those differences between sayables which will not reduce to degrees of compositeness. Where he had examined the algebraized skeletons of statements in which only the logical constants were left functioning, now he watches the functioning of the live expressions with which we say real things. One thing that he quickly remarks is this. Not all sayables are truths or falsehoods. The logician attends only to assertable premises and conclusions. But not all saying is asserting. There is questioning, advising, entreating, ordering, reassuring, rebuking, joking, warning, commiserating, promising, deploring, praising, parodying. We talk a lot to infants and dogs, but we do not make statements to them.

In the *Tractatus* we were told, in effect, that only those sentences made positive sense which could be the premises or conclusions of a bit of natural science. In the *Philosophical Investigations* the door is opened to anything that anyone might say. We are home, again, in the country of real discourse.

The central notion of sense or meaning has correspondingly thawed. In the *Tractatus* truths-or-falsehoods seemed to be icicles of printer's ink; and their coordination with states of affairs in the real world resembled the congruence between the structures of two crystals. But sentences are normally things said, not written, by one person to another. So now Wittgenstein constantly discusses such questions as "How do children, in real life, actually learn to understand this or that expression?" and "How would we teach a savage to count, or tell the time?". Talking sense and following the sense talked by others are things that we have learned how to do; so the notion of sense comes out of the fog if we constantly ask just what we must have learned, and just how we must have learned it in order to be able to communicate. Most of Part I of the *Philosophical Investigations* is concerned with questions about sense, understanding, grasping, mastering, interpreting, etc.

One device that Wittgenstein constantly uses is that of exploring imaginary situations in which people have to think up and teach ways of communicating. A builder, for example, wants his inarticulate assistant to pass him bricks and slabs. How would he teach him to distinguish between the orders "Brick" and "Slab"? How would he teach him to bring *two* or *five* bricks, that is, to understand number-words? Wittgenstein calls these imaginary lingo-creations "language-games." This is unfortunate because many readers think he implies that talking is a sort of *playing*. In fact the central idea behind the label "language-game" is the notion of *rules*. Learning to communicate is like learning to play chess or tennis in this respect, that in both we have to master written or unwritten rules — and there are many different, but interlocking, sorts of rules to be learned in both. The chess player has had to learn what moves are allowed, what moves in what situations would be tactical mistakes, and even what moves in what situations would be unsporting. A crude generalization of Wittgenstein's new account of sense or meaning is that the meaning of an expression is the rules for the employment of that expression; that is, the rules licensing or banning its coemployment with other expressions, those governing its effective employment in normal and abnormal communication-situations, and so on. The dynamic notion of rules to be mastered has replaced the notion of an imposed structural congruence.

With his new notion of meaning, Wittgenstein is in a position to say new things about the philosopher's task of meaning-elucidation. But in the main he avoids trying to give any general account of what sort of task this is, or why and when it needs to be done, though there are passages in which he does enigmatically give such an account. Rather, especially in Part II of *Philosophical Investigations*, he tries to demonstrate in examples what philosophical quandaries are like, how to get out of them and what sideslips of thought get us into them. He is trying to teach us methods of operation, rather than give us the answer to a question in an examination.

I do not think that anybody could read the *Philosophical Investigations* without feeling that its author had his finger on the pulse of the activity of philosophizing. We can doubt whether his hinted diagnosis will do; not that he has located, by touch, that peculiar and important intellectual commotion — philosophical puzzlement.

59

Wittgenstein's *"Foundations"* and Its Reception

S. Morris Engel

I

No one who has been following the reviews of Wittgenstein's posthumously published *Remarks on the Foundations of Mathematics* will have failed to be struck by the almost unanimous sense of disappointment and disapproval expressed by their writers. This unanimity is itself a remarkable phenomenon. It raises, however, a number of questions, foremost among them, whether perhaps the sense of the book has not somehow been mistaken.

It would be tedious and an imposition on the reader to try to discuss here all or nearly all of the reviews which have appeared to date. Fortunately, only quite recently three of the major ones (together with long selections from the *Foundations* itself) have been collected in a volume designed as a textbook for courses in the philosophy of mathematics[1] and I shall use it as my point of reference. Since, however, to select is in a way to interpret, it will not be possible to avoid commenting also on the choice of selections and the questions which such choices tend to raise.

Instead of trying to attack the selections and reviews on several different fronts or issues, I shall perhaps be able to make my point best if I concentrate my attention on merely one. The issue I have chosen has to do neither with mathematics itself, nor even with what we might properly call "the philosophy of mathematics." It might perhaps best be described as dealing with the *psychology* of mathematics. This is not to say that it is therefore unrelated to philosophy, for running throughout all Wittgenstein's works are reflections which, although not in themselves philosophical, have, however, intimate and serious implications for philosophy. This is especially true, I believe, of his contributions here. Certainly they are not contributions to mathematics as such. He himself is careful to point this out. Whether they should be regarded as contributions to philosophy or psychology, and what is to be gained from distinguishing them in this way, is what I wish to explore here. It is the failure to recognize and acknowledge this distinction which, it seems to me, lies behind the unrepresentative character of the selections and the essentially unilluminating nature of the reviews which accompany them.

II

Before turning directly to these questions there are one or two other points which students of Wittgenstein are likely to find disturbing. For some years now many editors and prospective editors have been unable to persuade Wittgenstein's literary executors to permit them to reproduce selections from his works. Partly, the difficulty has been in complying with Wittgenstein's wish that any translation always be accompanied by the original; and partly in accommodating his desire to keep the text intact. (For with a philosophy which, at least in appearance, seems so new and unfamiliar, who can be certain that he has achieved such a familiarity with it as confidently to be able to take such liberties with it.) The present selections thus represent a departure on two counts, for not only are they excerpts from a larger work but are here given only in translation. Although this will no doubt be cheered and welcomed by all prospective editors, others will regard it as a disturbing development.

Lest this may seem rather harsh on the present editors, it should be added that these remarks apply with equal force to the work from which these excerpts are taken. That work is itself a collection of selections from a larger body of jottings. How well the editors did their job not even they can, of course, know and will not be known until such time as the whole work is made available to the public, as it inevitably will be. Unfortunately this is unlikely to happen in the lifetime of present readers. That is why it is unfortunate that the editors decided to offer the public a selection and not the entire mass of material. In such matters it is always better to have either nothing or everything. As things stand, what is available can only detract from Wittgenstein's stature, for the reader may be led to apply inappropriate criteria to it, being misled by the finished quality which a selection inevitably tends to give a work. In its original state no such impression is created to give rise to false expectations and feelings of disappointment.

I do not wish to suggest that the three reviewers whose papers are here reprinted were so misled. That they are disappointed with the work is obvious. "It is hard to avoid the conclusion," Alan Ross Anderson writes in his review, "that Wittgenstein failed to understand clearly the problems with which workers in the foundations have been concerned."[2] A page later he writes: "It is very doubtful whether this application of his method to questions in the foundations of mathematics will contribute substantially to his reputation as a philosopher."[3] Michael Dummett is careful to point out in his opening paragraphs that the present work "has to be treated as what it is — a selection from the jottings of a great philosopher."[4] He notes that the striking contrast between it and the *Philosophical Investigations* (which "expresses with great clarity many forceful, profound, and quite definite ideas"[5]) "is due entirely to the different origins of the two books."[6] Dummett cannot, however, also resist saying of some of Wittgenstein's remarks that they are "plainly silly,"[7] "extremely hard to swallow,"[8] "extraordinarily difficult to take ... seriously,"[9] "thin and unconvincing,"[10] etc. And finally, Paul Bernays is led to say (almost contemptuously) that "Wittgenstein argues as though mathematics existed almost solely for the purpose of housekeeping."[11] Or again: "Wittgenstein's method aims at eliminating a very great deal. He sees himself in the part of the free-thinker combating superstition. The latter's goal, however, is freedom of the mind; whereas it is this very mind which Wittgenstein in many ways restricts, through a mental asceticism for the benefit of an irrationality whose goal is quite undetermined."[12]

In the light of such evaluations one may wonder what led the editors to devote almost a fourth of their text to Wittgenstein. Perhaps anticipating this uneasiness on the part of the reader, they say that what led them to do this was not because "Wittgenstein is more important in the philosophy of mathematics, or even, necessarily, as important as such seminal thinkers as Brouwer, Hilbert, or Frege. Rather it is in view of the great influence that Wittgenstein had on Russell and on the positivists, the great influence that he is currently having on 'analytic philosophers,' and the great difficulty of interpreting his often cryptic remarks on the subjects with which we are concerned" that led them to do so.[13] Concerning the selection of the reviews, they state: "Our purpose in including the reviews of his book is to facilitate discussion of Wittgenstein's later ideas in the philosophy of mathematics by providing possible starting points; we certainly do not wish to give the impression that we regard these criticisims as definitive."[14]

Now although this may be all very well, it is hardly a very forceful justification for including either the selections or the reviews. It might have been very well had the editors chosen reviews of a different sort, but since the present reviews tend to throw the value of the excerpts into doubt, what justification remains for including them in the first place? With such "starting points," in other words, the reader may not think it worthwhile to go on. There remains, of course, Wittgenstein's "great influence" on positivists, analytic philosophers, etc., but that is hardly a proper justification for devoting over a hundred pages to him in a text attempting to deal with the philosophy of mathematics in a systematic way.

Is there any justification at all then for attaching this kind of importance to this last work of Wittgenstein? Are there perhaps certain themes in the work which have somehow escaped notice but which might make a profound difference to our understanding of it? I believe there are. These are, however, as we shall see in a moment, more in the nature of certain psychological rather than philosophical observations. Perhaps that is why they have generally been overlooked.

III

If we are to make room for them we have now to work, I believe, with a threefold division of the subject. There are, first of all, the observations or contributions of a strictly mathematical sort. There are obviously many such remarks in Wittgenstein's book. But we have, of course, Wittgenstein's own word that this is not his main interest. On the contrary, what he seems ostensibly to be doing is the *philosophy* of mathematics.

This is a second-order philosophical discipline and just as legitimate as such other, related second-order philosophical investigations as the *philosophy of art*, the *philosophy of science*, the *philosophy of morals*, etc. Such disciplines are not designed to improve one's *knowledge* of art, or science, or morals (and much less so, of course, to make one more moral, or a better artist, etc.) but rather, by making explicit the foundations, goals, limits, and presuppositions of such studies, are designed to improve one's *understanding* of them. In view of this almost obvious and natural distinction, it is difficult to understand Michael Dummett's criticism that "there is no ground for Wittgenstein's segregation of philosophy from mathematics but that this springs only from a general tendency of his to regard discourse as split up into a number of distinct islands with no communication between them (statements of natural science, of philosophy, of mathematics, of religion)."[15] Furthermore, Wittgenstein himself, he says, occasionally "displays no timidity about 'interfering with the mathematicians'."[16]

These remarks of Dummett's are prefaced by the observation that Wittgenstein's contribution consists in mediating between rival schools of mathematicians regarding such things as their different conceptions of proof, their formulation, consequences, etc. "It seems natural to suppose," he therefore argues, "that the philosophical task and the mathematical go hand in hand, for the precise formulation of a conception is not irrelevant to deciding on its correctness, and unexpected consequences of adopting it may lead one to revise one's opinion as to its value."[17] But we might reply on Wittgenstein's behalf that, of course, this is only "natural" from the mathematician's point of view — and in certain areas not even from his. For he may indeed learn a great deal from the philosopher of mathematics that may be of immediate interest to him. But the philosopher of mathematics has a much wider task; for there are, after all, further matters to explore. (For example, the point — touched on in passing by Dummett himself — that although certain mathematical procedures are not perhaps *wrong*, they may still not possess the *interest* we are inclined to attach to them.[18]) It is not certain Dummett has grasped all the implications of this point. Certainly, as we shall see in a moment, Wittgenstein is doubtlessly right on such points, and Dummett is wrong in insisting that "philosophy and mathematics have nothing to say to one another" and that "no mathematical discovery can have any bearing on the philosophy of mathematics."[19] What is perhaps remarkable is that towards the end of his review Dummett himself seems to recognize that such matters may indeed "have nothing to do with mathematics in particular."[20] But such points, as we shall see in a moment, have to do more with the psychology of mathematics than with its philosophy.

Now if we are right in distinguishing mathematics from the philosophy of mathematics by saying that the latter is a second-order discipline devoted to improving our understanding of what mathematics ideally is or ought to be, then we can say that whereas the philosophy of mathematics is a normative study, the psychology of mathematics is a purely descriptive, empirical discipline dealing not with what mathematics ideally is, but with what our ordinary common understanding takes it to be and the consequences which issue from so understanding it. The distinction here is not unlike that generally drawn between logic and psychology. Although both, as we now tend to regard them, may be said to be studies of the "laws of thought," logic we regard as being concerned with the laws governing the relations among concepts or propositons, psychology with the laws governing mental processes of thinking (the one is regarded by us as being a descriptive discipline devoted to studying how thinking actually takes place, the other as a normative or prescriptive discipline devoted to studying the standards to which our thinking ought to conform).

Assuming this distinction is appropriate, the question is: Is there much of any importance that can be said about the ways in which mathematics is regarded by our ordinary common understanding? If one approaches Wittgenstein's writings from this point of view he will be surprised how much space and thought he devoted to this topic. From this point of view both the present selections and the book from which they are taken are misleading — the selections because they tend to bypass most of Wittgenstein's comments on this matter, the book because it leaves out a good deal that is necessary and which can be gotten (at the moment) only from other sources. Although I have mainly in mind here such further sources of information regarding Wittgenstein's thought as notes taken down at this time by other students (Norman Malcolm's *Math Notes*, for example),[21] I have in mind also such further works as the *Philosophical Investigations*. (Many portions of this work originate from the same period of reflection.)[22] Whether the mass of material from which the *Foundations* was edited contains these further and necessary reflections, only the editors can tell us. They do inform us in their Preface that an Appendix dealing with surprise in mathematics was omitted. As we shall see in a moment, this would certainly be relevant.

IV

One of the themes which is almost indispensable for a proper understanding of Wittgenstein's remarks here has to do with his view regarding the way in which our minds are held captive by "pictures." A certain form of this theme goes back as far as his early work, the *Tractatus*, in which, as everyone knows, a picture-theory figures prominently. The interesting thing here is that although it is true that Wittgenstein gave up *that* picture-theory later on, he never really gave up trying to develop *a* picture theory or explore it in other directions. This is one of those threads in Wittgenstein's thought which has a tendency to break off at certain points but which somehow never completely vanishes from sight.

Now what is it for the mind to be misled or held captive by pictures? A rather striking example of what Wittgenstein had in mind here is to be found in Norman Malcolm's *Memoir* of Wittgenstein. Malcolm recounts how "at one of the at-homes, Wittgenstein related a riddle for the purpose of throwing some light on the nature of philosophy. It went as follows:

Suppose that a cord was stretched tightly around the earth at the equator. Now suppose that a piece one yard long was added to the cord. If the cord was kept taut and circular in form, how much above the surface of the earth would it be? Without stopping to work it out, everyone present was inclined to say that the distance of the cord from the surface of the earth would be so *minute* that it would be imperceptible. But this is wrong. The actual distance would be nearly six inches. Wittgenstein declared that this is the *kind* of mistake that occurs in philosophy. It consists in being *misled by a picture*. In the riddle the picture that misleads us is the comparison of the length of the additional piece with the length of the whole cord. The picture itself is correct enough: for a piece one yard long would be an insignificant fraction of the length of the whole cord. But we are misled by it to draw a wrong conclusion. A similar thing happens in philosophy: we are constantly deceived by mental pictures which are in themselves correct."[23]

I should like to suggest now that when Wittgenstein came to look at the sort of things which people or philosophers were saying about mathematics it struck him that the same thing was true of them too.

In one of his lectures[24] he points out that although certain mathematical expressions lend themselves to misunderstanding, it is not the mathematicians who are misled by them. It is different, however, with the philosopher of mathematics, or the man in the street. Their interest in these matters initially arises not from anything internal or directly relevant to these investigations, but rather from the associations these expressions tend to arouse in their minds. What fascinates them are the pictures which the mathematician's talk about his work tends to conjure up. And these pictures are misleading. For one thing, they tend to make his work seem more important and more glamorous than it would otherwise seem to be. Moreover, although this may not be a bad thing (for without such glamor no one might have become interested in these problems to begin with), such pictures are not what the problems, once begun, are really about. In his own words now:

Certain verbal forms are misleading for a time and then cease to be misleading. The idea of Imaginary Numbers, e.g. There may have been something misleading in this when it was first introduced, but now it is utterly harmless; it just does not mislead anyone, while to say that the appellation "infinite development" is misleading is correct, though of course it does not mislead anyone in his calculations. It misleads in the idea of what they have done and the consequent interest which people have in certain calculations. The idea of the infinite as something huge does fascinate some people and their interest is due solely to that association, though they probably would not admit it. But that has nothing to do with their calculations. We could, e.g., play chess without the board or chessman, by description of the moves, etc. I might say chess would never have been invented apart from the board, figures, etc., and perhaps the connection with the movement of troops in battle. No one would have dreamed of inventing the game as played with pencil and paper. That would be right, but still the game (as played either way) would not be wrong. It is the same with mathematics. There is nothing right or wrong in a calculus, but it is its associations which make it seem worth while. But they are quite different from the calculus. Sometimes the associations are connected with practical applications; sometimes they are not. The association of the infinite is with something huge. Without this association no one would care a damn about the infinite.[25]

Now of course there is nothing wrong with words arousing pictures in our minds or with our tendency to associate the meaning of a word with the picture it arouses. It is different however with certain other words whose pictures tend to be highly misleading — the word "particle" for example. The pictures which such words tend to arouse in our minds lead us to expect the wrong things. Thus, for example, thinking of the formula "the cardinal number of all cardinal numbers" in terms of, say, "chairs" has a kind of dizzying effect on the mind, for the number involved is truly staggering. It conjures up, he says in *Math Notes*, "a picture of an *enormous colossal* number. And this picture has a charm." But the imagery here, although a natural and understandable consequence of our tendency to assimilate and correlate various expressions in our language, is entirely inappropriate. For, in fact, we have as yet, as he puts it, "no right to have an image. The imagery is connected with a different calculus: $30 \times 30 = 900$." The sense of amazement and puzzlement experienced at such occasions is simply a product of a misapplied image.

Wittgenstein goes further than that in fact. If something about a certain subject or problem "charms or astounds" us, he says, we may conclude from this that it is because we have been captivated by the wrong imagery. Imagery of that sort is a function of metaphors and such metaphors remain "fishy" as long as they are "exciting." When we begin to see these things in their true light, the amazement and excitement simply vanishes.

Thus, for example, certain parts of mathematics are regarded as "deep." "But the apparent depth comes from a wrong imagery. It is pedestrian as any calculus." Yet that is precisely the way people were misled about the infinitesimal calculus, when they mistakenly believed that it treated of infinitely small quantities. People said later, "If you look into it, there's nothing infinitely small there." But what did they expect to find; what would it be like for something to be infinitely small? Why are they disappointed? And what do they mean by saying it doesn't treat of the infinitely small? This might be contradicted. First, "infinitely small" hasn't a very familiar use. Second, instead of saying it doesn't treat of something infinitely small, we should say it doesn't treat of *small* things at all.[26] But it is because we think of such things in terms of such misleading images (in terms, for example, of sizes, as here) that we go so wrong. The amazement and excitement which such things inspire in us should be taken as a sign that we have simply been misled.

Wittgenstein speaks in these lectures of "charm," "excitement," "interest," etc., and it is easy to see how these expressions give way later on to such more familiar expressions from his published writings as, for example, "puzzlement," "wonder," "confusion," etc. The transition can be found even in these lecture notes themselves. For example, we find him remarking at one point:

> There is one kind of misunderstanding which has a kind of charm ... we say that the line intersects at an imaginary point. This sets the mind in a whirl, and gives a pleasant feeling of paradox, e.g. saying that there are numbers bigger than infinity ... He has employed a sensational way of expressing what he has discovered, so that it looks like a different *kind* of discovery ... He describes a new state of affairs in old words, and so we don't understand him. The picture he makes does not lead us on. By the words of ordinary language we conjure up a familiar picture — but we need more than the right picture, we need to know the correct use.[27]

And that is precisely where such new notations, he goes on to emphasize here, fail us so badly. The fact is that "in an overwhelming number of cases people do have the same sort of images suggested by words. This is a mere matter of fact about what happens in our minds, but a fact of enormous importance."[28] In view of this, it is not difficult to see why and how confusions arise. For all that is really necessary for this to happen is for us to use familiar words in unfamiliar ways. The pictures aroused will be correct enough but, of course, they will be misleading. And it is in such misleading pictures, he concludes here, "that most of the problems of philosophy arise."[29]

In the *Blue Book* he puts this point in this way: "The new expression misleads us," he says, "by calling up pictures and analogies which make it difficult for us to go through with our conventions. And it is extremely difficult to discard these pictures unless we are constantly watchful."[30] We can be so watchful, he goes on to tell us there, by asking ourselves at such times, "*How far does the analogy between these uses go?*" We can also try to construct, he says, "new notations, in order to break the spell of those which we are accustomed to." These new notations, of course, later become his famous language-games. "The scrutiny of the grammar of a word," he says again further on, "weakens the position of certain fixed standards of our expression which had prevented us from seeing facts with unbiased eyes. Our investigation tried to remove this bias, which forces us to think that the facts *must* conform to certain pictures embedded in our language."[31]

We now turn, however, to the *Philosophical Investigations.* Difficulty lies, he explains it there, in our inability "to get away from the idea that using a sentence involves imagining something for every word." We fail to realize that we do all sorts of things with words — turning "them sometimes into one picture, sometimes into another."[32] Unfortunately, such pictures are often "only like an illustration to a story" and from it alone it is mostly impossible "to conclude anything at all" — for only "when one knows the story does one know the significance of the picture."[33] Mainly, however, the trouble with such pictures is that they seem "to fix the sense *unambiguously*" when this is not at all the case. On the contrary, "the actual use, compared with that suggested by the picture" is "muddied."[34]

Now certainly language has this effect on us — "the picture is there"; nor need we necessarily dispute its "validity in any particular case." But we do "want to understand the application of the picture."[35] And not only is this often lacking, but other pernicious effects result as well. Or, as he puts it later: "What this language primarily describes is a picture. What is to be done with the picture, how it is to be used, is still obscure. Quite clearly, however, it must be explored if we want to understand the sense of what we are saying. But the picture seems to spare us this work: it already points to a particular use. This is how it takes us in."[36]

In order to prevent ourselves from being taken in in this way we ought always to ask: does reality accord with such pictures?[37] These pictures *seem* "to determine what we have to do, what to look for, and how" — but they really do not do so. They *seem* "to make the sense of the expressions unmistakable" but in fact prove to be utterly misleading.[38] For example, "What am I believing in, when I believe that this substance contains two carbon rings? ... there is a picture in the foreground, but the sense lies far in the background; this is, the application of the picture is not easy to survey."[39] In ordinary circumstances such words and the pictures which they generate "have an application with which we are familiar — But if we suppose a case in which this application is absent we become as it were conscious for the first time of the nakedness of the words and the picture,"[40] of how "idle" such pictures are.[41] In the end we must simply regard them as "illustrated turns of speech,"[42] which stand "in the way of our seeing the use of the word as it is."[43] Philosophy, he concludes, "is a battle against the bewitchment of our intelligence by means of language";[44] "a simile that has been absorbed into the forms of our language produces a false appearance";[45] "a picture [holds] us captive."[46]

V

I should not wish to suggest that one can open the *Foundations* and derive from it in some straightforward and immediate way the theory just expounded. This cannot be done even with the *Philosophical Investigations*. To derive a theory from any of Wittgenstein's writings one must pick and choose, order and rearrange, compress and expand. However, once a theory of this kind emerges the work does tend to fall into place. In connection with the *Foundations* some interesting statistics emerge. As it stands the book contains five parts and two appendices. These parts and appendices are divided into separate remarks of varying lengths, totalling 461 in all. Using as one's guide such key terms as "picture," "surprise," "interest," etc., one finds that more than a quarter of Wittgenstein's remarks are somehow connected with this theme. Although this should not be taken to mean that a fourth of Wittgenstein's book is devoted to this theme, it does mean that it is in the foreground of his thought and very much, obviously, permeated by it.

The textbook reproduces liberal portions from all the parts except the second Appendix. Although it does not therefore miss picking up some of the remarks connected with this theme, it picks up only about a fourth of them. This may not seem bad at all. But, unfortunately, it tends to miss the more helpful and illuminating remarks and, ironically, the single portion from which it fails to excerpt (the second Appendix) contains the most important material of all. Although this may have been intentional, the result of it is that the student who reads only the excerpts in this textbook finds himself at a disadvantage when confronted with the reviews, for the remarks which the textbook does pick up do not provide him with a sufficiently clear statement of this theme for him to be able to meet the challenge of the reviews. This is not to say that all the attacks upon Wittgenstein made by the reviewers can be met by appealing to this picture theory. Unfortunately that is not at all so. But as we shall see in a moment, some of the severe misunderstandings can be so clarified.

The theory which Wittgenstein expounds in these *Remarks* is essentially similar to the one which I have tried to reproduce above from other sources. Some of the points are even expressed in almost identical terms, although not always so explicitly as there. Remark number 17 in Appendix II, for example, is a case in point and should be compared with the similar observation (also dealing with the use of the word "infinite") reproduced earlier from *Math Notes*. It runs as follows:

> Ought the word "infinite" to be avoided in mathematics? Yes; where it appears to confer a meaning upon the calculus; instead of getting one from it. This way of talking: "But when one examines the calculus there is nothing infinite there" is of course clumsy — but it means: is it really necessary here to conjure up the picture of the infinite (of the enormously big)? And how is this picture connected with the *calculus*? For its connexion is not that of the picture / / / / with 4. To act as if one were disappointed to have found nothing infinite in the calculus is of course funny; but not to ask: what is the everyday employment of the word "infinite," which gives it its meaning for us; and what is its connexion with these mathematical calculi?

And in his next and final remark in this Appendix, he summarizes his results in these words:

> What I am doing is, not to shew that calculations are wrong, but to subject the *interest* of calculations to a test. I test e.g. the justification for still using the word ... here. Or really, I keep on urging such an investigation. I shew that there is such an investigation and what there is to investigate there. Thus, I must say, not: "We must not express ourselves like this", or "That is absurd", or "That is uninteresting", but: "Test the justification of this expression in this way". You cannot survey the justification of an expression unless you survey its employment; which you cannot do by looking at some facet of its employment, say a picture attaching to it.

This remark is, of course, reminiscent of several other remarks quoted earlier from other sources dealing with this same theme. Throughout many of these remarks Wittgenstein is anxious to put us on our guard against our tendency to be bewitched by pictures which strike our fancy but which on closer inspection have no or extremely weak justification. As he puts it in remark number 16 here:

> If the interest here attaches to the proposition that has been proved, then it attaches to a picture which has an extremely weak justification, but which fascinates us by its queerness, like e.g. the picture of the "direction" of time. It makes one's thoughts reel mildly. Here I can only say: depart as quickly as possible from this picture, and see the interest of this calculation in its application.

That there may be nothing at all trivial in the point Wittgenstein is here urging may perhaps be gathered from a rather recent example — the recent attempts to make a landing on the moon. Scientists feared that such a landing would prove to be either difficult or impossible because of the thick layer of dust with which they believed the moon was covered. But the belief proved to be a myth. As one scientist connected with the project later remarked: it was an idea, he said, which people simply became fascinated with and would not give up, but there was really never any reason to entertain it at all. Wittgenstein has here obviously put his finger on some very deep and pervasive human tendencies which have far-reaching consequences.

In remarks 10, 11 and 12 he offers an extended example of the mechanics of such deceptions. Since his remarks here introduce us again to most of the key terms of the theory ("interest," "mystery," "picture," "excitement," etc.) I shall quote them in full before going on to summarize the main issues in my own words:

> 10. "Fractions cannot be arranged in an order of magnitude." — First and foremost, this sounds extremely interesting and remarkable. It sounds interesting in a quite different way from, say, a proposition of the differential calculus. The difference, I think, resides in the fact that *such* a proposition is easily associated with an application to physics, whereas *this* proposition belongs simply and solely to mathematics, seems to concern as it were the natural history of mathematical objects themselves. One would like to say of it e.g.: it introduces us to the mysteries of the mathematical world. *This* is the aspect against which I want to give a warning. When it looks as if ..., we should look out.
> 11. When, on hearing the proposition that the fraction cannot be arranged in a series in order of magnitude, I form the picture of an unending row of things, and between each thing and its neighbour new things appear, and more new ones again between each of these things and its neighbour, and so on without end, then certainly there is something here to make one dizzy. But once we see that this picture, though very exciting, is all the same not appropriate; that we ought not to let

ourselves be trapped by the words "series", "order", "exist", and others, we shall fall back on the *technique* of calculating fractions, about which there is no longer anything *queer*. The fact that in a technique of calculating fractions the expression "the next greatest fraction" has no sense, that we have not given it any sense, is nothing to marvel at. If we apply a technique of continuous interpolation of fractions, we shall not be willing to call any fraction the "next biggest".

12. To say that a technique is unlimited does *not* mean that it goes on without ever stopping — that it increases immeasurably; but that it lacks the institution of the end, that it is not finished off. As one can say of a sentence that it is not finished off if it has no period. Or of a playing-field that it is unlimited, when the rules of the game do not prescribe any boundaries — say by means of a line. For the point of a new technique is to supply us with a *new* picture, *a new form of expression*; and there is nothing so absurd as to try and describe this new schema, this new kind of scaffolding, by means of the old expressions.

I have been concentrating here entirely on the second Appendix but these relevant points and issues and their further elaboration are to be found scattered throughout the *Foundations*.[47]

Wittgenstein's doctrine of pictures, as some of these remarks show, has important and wide-reaching implications for the logic of discovery. Contained in them as well, however, is something that is of even wider significance. It has to do in a way, I believe, with the point long ago expressed by Bishop Butler that everything is what it is and not another thing. Part of the meaning of this remark is, I believe, that everything should be or ought to be evaluated in terms of the categories which it itself brings along. If we are looking at a work of art, for example, we should resist responding or evaluating it in terms of any external interests that it may have for us. A painting may be interesting to us because of the memories of our childhood it may awaken in us, or because an enormous amount of money was spent in purchasing it, or because it is a painting of the artist's son or mistress, but obviously none of these are what makes the painting a good painting — assuming it is a good painting. If these, then, are the reasons we find ourselves aroused, interested, and fascinated by the work, we can be certain that it is not to the painting as such that we are responding and that in a sense, therefore, we are misled by our *interest* in it.

The same may be said about our experience in connection with other matters as well. If, for example, we find ourselves responding with greater interest and enthusiasm to, say, literature than to mathematics, the chances are that our response to the former is of an external sort. For what may make the work of literature more interesting to us are perhaps the characters with which it deals and with whom we have a certain affinity, or their life stories which seem to shed some light on our own, or the generally large doses of sex which we find pleasurably arousing. But these in themselves are not what makes a great work of literature great and worthy of our attention. What makes it great is not its ability to give expression to these diverse, external needs but rather that it is able to exploit to the full its own peculiar medium and to give expression to itself. And in this sense both literature and mathematics — in fact all the arts and sciences — are as one. Each has its own goals and if they succeed in achieving them are as worthy and internally as interesting as any other. If therefore in view of this we find ourselves responding with greater interest to one as opposed to some other art or object, it is not because of anything that particular art or object (say, literature) possesses that the other does not. More likely, it is rather because we are responding to something that is not at all intimately connected with the thing as it is in itself. For from the point of view of the things themselves, they are simply what they are. If, then, one still tends to arouse more interest than some other object — or even, we might say, if one simply does arouse our *interest* — Wittgenstein is perhaps not wrong in urging us to become suspicious and enquire whether perhaps we are not looking at the thing through some misleading picture. Does infinitesimal calculus strike you as being "deep"? It is as "pedestrian" as any calculus, he would reply.

VI

Now that we have seen something of the wider background in terms of which Wittgenstein's remarks on mathematics must be read, we are perhaps in a better position to evaluate some of the criticisms contained in the three reviews before us. In looking at these reviews we shall not be interested here in evaluating their objections to Wittgenstein's handling of this or that particular mathematical doctrine — for that must be left to mathematicians to decide — but rather in seeing how far they have succeeded in grasping what we might call the intent and spirit of Wittgenstein's thought, particularly as that is revealed in his theory of pictures described above.

From this point of view, Michael Dummett's review is perhaps the least objectionable of the three. What seems to trouble him mainly is Wittgenstein's severe segregation of philosophy from mathematics. This is a pity, for it is precisely this failure on his part to realize fully Wittgenstein's reasons for doing so that has been responsible for Dummett's inability to appreciate the true scope of Wittgenstein's achievement here and from presenting a more balanced and fairer account of it.

Part of that achievement consists, as I tried to suggest a moment ago, in providing us with a way of talking about these matters which enables us to gain a firmer grasp of them. Dummett is not unaware of the power of this new way of talking. He points out, for example, that the opposing pictures used by Platonists and constructivists — the picture of our making discoveries within an already existing mathematical reality and the picture of our constructing mathematics as we go along — often lead their advocates to believe that everything else can be justified in these terms. They sometimes argue, he says, "as though it were a matter of first deciding which of these pictures is correct and then drawing conclusions from this decision" when "it is clear that these are only pictures," and "the dispute as to which is correct must find its substance elsewhere."[48]

This is, of course, good Wittgensteinian doctrine. Surprisingly, however, Dummett goes on to suggest that in his discussion of proof Wittgenstein himself has apparently fallen victim to this error. Although it is certainly not inconceivable that Wittgenstein should commit the very error which he is so anxious to warn others against, the fact that Dummett must resort to Wittgenstein's own terms to point this out, is of course a tribute to their value and power. For that is a kind of criticism which, after all, Wittgenstein himself was the first to make possible. If Dummett does not quite acknowledge this, the other reviewers are even less gracious about it, as we shall see in a moment.

Alan Ross Anderson's review although briefer than the other two is no less severe. Noting that "these fragments were written concurrently with Part I of the *Philosophical Investigations,* perhaps for inclusion in the latter work, had Wittgenstein lived to complete it," he finds it unsurprising "that there is little here that is fundamentally new." "Many of the problems discussed," he points out further, "have already been treated in the earlier volume, and though the remarks here are different in detail, they are the same in spirit." "What *is* new here," he notes however, "is the detailed discussion of several important results in the classical foundations of mathematics ... and of the relation of logic to mathematics."[49] But these discussions too, he says, are merely further illustrations of Wittgenstein's general thesis, and whatever is substantive about them is unfortunately "directed to the battles of twenty-five to fifty years ago" — battle lines that are no longer drawn where they once were.[50] It is very doubtful, he therefore concludes, "whether this application of his method to questions in the foundations of mathematics will contribute substantially to his reputation as a philosopher."[51]

To support these doubts, Anderson proceeds to examine Wittgenstein's treatment of Gödel's theorem. But Anderson's treatment of this discussion is very curious. He realizes, for example, that a good deal of the point of Wittgenstein's discussion here is designed to change our *attitude* toward contradiction. But rather than concentrating on that, as he therefore ought to, he tries to show instead that Wittgenstein misunderstood the *facts* of the case under discussion. I shall not pause here to question whether it is possible to substantiate or sustain the kind of sweeping condemnation expressed in his concluding remarks by merely examining, as he does, one single, abstruse example. Anderson himself is uneasy about this and apologizes to the reader for it. Although his defence is that examples play an important role in Wittgenstein's method, he no doubt suspects that in view of the kind of method it is, no single example can really be considered decisive, one way or the other. Nor will I pause to question the facts of the case. It may be that Anderson's understanding and description of them are completely correct. But what is puzzling about his treatment is that when he does come to deal with these matters on the level on which they were designed to be dealt with, he comes, like Dummett, to charge Wittgenstein with offences which Wittgenstein himself was the first to make intelligible, and there is certainly something ironic about this — if indeed nothing worse.

Anderson grants, for example, that "it may be true that some writers, on the basis of a superficial familiarity with Gödel's result, tried to make something of a mystery of it," and that "it is no doubt in part against such writers that Wittgenstein is aiming his remarks." But, he goes on to declare, "the way to dispel the mystery is *not* to belittle the result, or to argue that it doesn't show what it seems to show." On the contrary, "the way to dispel the mystery *is* to see the result as a straightforward unprovability theorem" — a theorem that "is not even particularly surprising, once one gets over the initial shock."[52]

There are two questions which these comments raise in one's mind: one, Anderson uses here the language of mystery, surprise, and shock, obviously believing it to have a certain point. But the only point that such language has is the one given it by Wittgenstein, for although the concept of surprise has been present in mathematics since the Pythagoreans, the particular emphasis given to it here (and the one apparently accepted by Anderson) is Wittgenstein's own. Anderson must also therefore believe that this language is appropriate and illuminating, although perhaps inappropriately applied in this particular case. But even that is perhaps doubtful, for (and here I come to my second point) if Anderson agrees, as again he seems to, that Wittgenstein's argument is not necessarily directed against mathematics or mathematicians but rather against those who have made a mystery of it (and therefore that it is the "results" as so understood that is at issue here) then he must also agree that the best way to dispel the mystery is indeed to try to belittle these "results" and to point out that they do not show what they seem to show. For how else are we to succeed in showing that the results are really "straightforward" (or "pedestrian" as Wittgenstein would put it)? There is a question here, of course, regarding whose "results" are at stake. But even if we were to grant in this case that it is Gödel's or Russell's results that Wittgenstein is talking about (and not the interpretation placed upon them by others), it is still obvious, as has been shown above, that certainly in a vast majority of cases it is not mathematical inventions as such but their understanding and interpretation (their "office") which is Wittgenstein's theme in this book. On Wittgenstein's behalf, therefore, we might very well wonder whether Anderson himself has not somehow missed the point here.

From the point of view of this paper, Bernays' review is perhaps the most objectionable of the three. Bernays begins by quoting two remarks from Wittgenstein as evidence that, as he puts it, "jocularity of expression is not lacking with Wittgenstein."[53] These are: "... What I am doing is, not to show that calculations are wrong, but to subject the *interest* of calculations to a test" (p. 63, no. 18); and "My task is not to attack Russell's logic from *within*, but from without. That is to say, not to attack it mathematically — otherwise I should be doing mathematics — but to attack its position, its office. My task is not to talk about Gödel's proof, for example, but to by-pass it" (p. 174, no. 16).[54] It may be that Bernays does not mean to be critical when he characterizes these remarks as "jocular." In a sense they are of course that; but from what has been said above, it is clear, I think, that there is dead seriousness in them as well, for we now know what this "interest" is, and what this "within-without" business entails here.

Later on, Bernays says of Wittgenstein that although he tries to maintain a nominalist position, yet, oddly, we find him frequently appealing to facts of "our actual mental attitude." Bernays supports this charge of contradiction in Wittgenstein by the following sample passage:

"In a certain sense it is not possible, therefore, to appeal to the meaning of signs in mathematics, because it is mathematics itself which first gives them their meaning. What is typical for the phenomenon about which I am speaking is that the *mysteriousness* about any mathematical concept is not *straight away* interpreted as a misconception, as a fallacy, but as something which is at all events not to be despised, which should perhaps even be respected. All that I can do is to show an easy escape from this obscurity and this glitter of concepts. It can be said, strangely enough, that there is so to speak a solid core in all these glistening concept-formations. And I should like to say that it is this which makes them into mathematical products."[55]

It is difficult to see where Wittgenstein has contradicted himself here, for although he is indeed referring here to two quite different conceptions of mathematics, he regards one of these conceptions as completely mistaken. That Bernays is not fully aware of the meaning of this passage and especially of such terms in it as "mysteriousness," "glitter," etc., seems to be indicated by the comment he makes upon it. "One may doubt," he says, "whether Wittgenstein has succeeded here in showing 'an easy escape from this obscurity'; one may be more inclined to suspect that here the obscurity and the 'mysteriousness' actually have their origin in the philosophical concept-formation, i.e., in the philosophical language used by Wittgenstein."[56] But how, one might ask, could Wittgenstein be accused here of falling victim to the 'mysterious' when the whole point of the passage is that we should be on our guard against falling prey to this very thing. It is doubtful whether Bernays and Wittgenstein are speaking about the same thing here.

A page later, Bernays says that "Wittgenstein's method aims at eliminating a very great deal. He sees himself in the part of the free-thinker combating superstition. The latter's goal, however, is freedom of the mind; whereas it is this very mind which Wittgenstein in many ways restricts through a mental asceticism for the benefit of an irrationality whose goal is quite undetermined."[57] Although sweeping in its condemnation, this charge is completely unfounded, for although Wittgenstein's method is designed to eliminate a great deal, there is nothing indeterminate about what it desires to eliminate. On the contrary, as we have seen he is very clear and specific about what this is. Had Bernays been more clear himself as to the kind of fictions and superstitions which the method was designed to eliminate, he would hardly have regarded the attempt as either irrational or confining in its effects. For after all, to eliminate such things as are involved here is not to diminish but to expand the human mind.

Bernays ends his first section with an even more sweeping denunciation, involving now not only Wittgenstein but also all those who have fallen under his spell. He writes:

> In contrast to the assertive form of philosophical statement throughout the *Tractatus*, a mainly aporetical attitude prevails in the present book. There lies here, it is true, a danger for philosophical pedagogics, especially as Wittgenstein's philosophy exerts a strong attraction on the younger minds. The old Greek observation that philosophical contemplation frequently begins in philosophical astonishment today misleads many philosophers into holding the view that the cultivation of astonishment is in itself a philosophical achievement. One may certainly have one's doubts about the soundness of a method which requires young philosophers to be trained as it were in wondering.[58]

In terms of the role which such words as "shock," "surprise," and "astonishment" play, as we have seen, in Wittgenstein's work, this remark represents a gross misunderstanding of the whole motive of Wittgenstein's philosophy.[59] For far from being designed to nurture astonishment, the whole point of that philosophy is to understand its source and nature, and, if possible, to dispel it.

VII

To summarize: Wittgenstein's *Remarks on the Foundations of Mathematics* has been received with mixed feelings. Certainly the reason for this is the unfinished and incomplete nature of the material out of which it is composed. Since this publication is merely an incomplete selection from a larger body of unfinished jottings, we are neither in a position to determine in what state Wittgenstein himself might have published them had he had the desire and opportunity to do so, nor whether anything essential to our understanding of the selections published is to be found among the remaining jottings. Although nothing of interest can be said about what Wittgenstein might have done with these remarks had he been able to do so, a number of reasons lead one to believe that one or two things of importance which might have had an effect on our understanding of the work as a whole might indeed have been omitted. A discussion of one such theme — the interest, surprise, and shock which certain mental pictures generate in mathematics — shows this to be indeed the case.

Notes

1. *Philosophy of Mathematics: Selected Readings*, edited with an Introduction by Paul Benacerraf and Hilary Putnam (Englewood Cliffs, New Jersey; Prentice-Hall, Inc., 1964). The

three reviews reprinted in this text are, in order of their appearance in the text: Alan Ross Anderson 'Mathematics and the Language Game,' *The Review of Metaphysics*, vol. 11 (1958), pp. 446-58; Michael Dummett, 'Wittgenstein's Philosophy of Mathematics,' *The Philosophical Review*, vol. 68 (1959), pp. 324-48 see pp. 121-37 above; Paul Bernays, 'Comments on Ludwig Wittgenstein's *'Remarks on the Foundations of Mathematics,' Ratio*, vol. 2 (1959), pp. 1-22 see pp. 165-82 below.

2. *The Review of Metaphysics, op. cit.*, p. 457.
3. Ibid., p. 458.
4. *The Philosophical Review, op. cit.*, p. 324.
5. Ibid.
6. Ibid.
7. Ibid., p. 330.
8. Ibid., p. 332.
9. Ibid., p. 333.
10. Ibid.
11. *Ratio, op. cit.*, p. 14.
12. Ibid., p. 6.
13. Ibid., p. 25.
14. Ibid.
15. *The Philosophical Review, op. cit.*, p. 326.
16. Ibid.
17. Ibid.
18. Ibid.
19. Ibid.
20. Ibid., p. 348.
21. This book consists of notes by Norman Malcolm of Wittgenstein's lectures in the spring of 1939. Unauthorized copies of these notes were made and put on sale in San Francisco in 1954. (The *Remarks on the Foundations of Mathematics* dates from 1937-1944.)
22. Part I of the *Philosophical Investigations* was completed by 1945; Part II was written between 1947 and 1949.
23. *Memoir of Wittgenstein* (London, Oxford University Press, 1958), pp. 53-4.
24. Recorded in an unsigned mimeographed copy of the *Blue Book* in the Hoose Library of Philosophy at the University of Southern California.
25. Lecture Thirteen, dated 5.6.35.
26. *Math Notes*, pp. 62-63.
27. Ibid,, p. 6.
28. Ibid., p. 39.
29. Ibid., p. 41. Cf. here *Philosophical Investigations*, I, 141.
30. *Math Notes*, p. 23.
31. Ibid., p. 43.
32. I, 449.
33. I, 663.
34. I, 426.
35. I, 423.
36. II, vii.
37. I, 352.
38. Ibid.
39. I, 422.
40. I, 349.
41. I, 291.
42. I, 295.
43. I, 305.
44. I, 109.
45. I, 112.
46. I, 115.
47. In addition to remark number i in this Appendix, the reader may find it valuable to examine the following remarks as well: *Part I*: Nos. 6, 14, 74, 118, and 125. *Part II*: No. 29. *Part III*: Nos 12 and 21. *Part IV*: Nos. 6, 9, 16, 25, 29, and 37. *Part V*: Nos 3 and 16.

48. *The Philosophical Review, op. cit.*, p. 346.
49. *The Review of Metaphysics, op. cit.*, p. 446.
50. Ibid., p. 457.
51. Ibid., p. 458.
52. Ibid., p. 456.
53. *Ratio, op. cit.*, p. 2.
54. Ibid.
55. Ibid., p. 4.
56. Ibid.
57. Ibid., p. 6.
58. Ibid.
59. And is on a par with his earlier comment that Wittgenstein must be mistaken about language being a game and therefore about 'language-games' because 'our natural language has in no way the character of a game' (p. 19).

60

Comments on Ludwig Wittgenstein's *Remarks on the Foundations of Mathematics*[1]

Paul Bernays

I

The book with which the following observations are concerned is the second part of the posthumous publications of selected fragments from Wittgenstein in which he sets forth his later philosophy.[2] The necessity of making a selection and the fragmentary character which is noticeable in places are not unduly disconcerting since Wittgenstein in his publications in any case refrains from a systematic treatment and expresses his thoughts paragraph-wise — springing frequently from one theme to another. On the other hand we must admit in fairness to the author that he would doubtless have made extensive changes in the arrangement and selection of the material had he been able to complete the work himself. Besides, the editors of the book have greatly facilitated a survey of the contents by providing a very detailed table of contents and an index. The preface gives information on the origin of the different parts I-V.

Compared with the standpoint of the *Tractatus,* which indeed considerably influenced the originally very extreme doctrine of the Vienna Circle, Wittgenstein's later philosophy represents a rectification and clarification in essential respects. In particular it is the very schematic conception of the structure of the language of science — especially the view on the composition of statements out of atomic propositions — which is here dropped. What remains is the negative attitude towards speculative thinking and the permanent tendency to disillusionize.

Thus Wittgenstein says himself, evidently with his own philosophy in mind (p. 63, No. 18): 'Finitism and behaviorism are quite similar trends. Both say: all we have here is merely ... Both deny the existence of something, both with a view to escaping from a confusion. What I am doing is, not to show that calculations are wrong, but to subject the *interest* of calculations to a test.' And further on he explains (p. 174, No. 16): 'My task is not to attack Russell's logic from *within,* but from without. That is to say, not to attack it mathematically — otherwise I should be doing mathematics — but to attack its position, its office. My task is not to talk about Gödel's proof, for example, but to by-pass it.'

As we see, jocularity of expression is not lacking with Wittgenstein; and in the numerous parts written in dialogue form he often enjoys acting the rogue.

On the other hand he does not lack *esprit de finesse*, and his formulations contain, in addition to what is explicitly stated, many implicit suggestions.

Two problematic tendencies, however, appear throughout. The one is to dispute away the proper rôle of thinking — reflective intending — in a behavioristic manner. David Pole, it is true, in his interesting account and exposition of Wittgenstein's later philosophy,[3] denies that Wittgenstein is a supporter of behaviorism. This contention is justified inasmuch as Wittgenstein certainly does not deny the existence of the mental experiences of feeling, perceiving and imagining; but with regard to thinking his attitude is distinctly behavioristic. Here he tends everywhere towards a short circuit. Images and perceptions are supposed in every case to be followed immediately by behavior. 'We do it like this', that is usually the last word of understanding — or else he relies upon a need as an anthropological fact. Thought, as such, is left out. It is characteristic in this connection that a 'proof' is conceived as a 'picture' or 'paradigm'; and although Wittgenstein is critical of the method of formalizing proofs, he continually takes the formal method of proof in the Russellian system as an example. Instances of proper mathematical proofs, which are not mere calculations, which neither result merely from showing a figure nor proceed formalistically, do not occur at all in this book on the foundations of mathematics, a major part of which treats of the question as to what proofs really are — although the author has evidently concerned himself with many mathematical proofs.

One passage may be mentioned as characterizing Wittgenstein's behavioristic attitude and as an illustration of what is meant here by a short circuit. Having rejected as unsatisfactory various attempts to characterize inference, he continues (p. 8, No. 17): 'Thus it is necessary to see how we perform inferences in the practice of language; what kind of operation inferring is in the language-game. For example, a regulation says: "All who are taller than six foot are to join the ... section." A clerk reads out the names of the men, and their heights. Another allots them to such and such sections. "X six foot four." "So X to the ... section." That is inference.' Here it can be seen that Wittgenstein is satisfied only with a characterization of inferring in which one passes directly from a linguistic establishment of the premises to an action, in which, therefore, the specifically reflective element is eliminated. Language, too, appears under the aspect of behavior ('language-game').

The other problematic tendency springs from the program — already present in Wittgenstein's earlier philosophy — of strict division between the linguistic and the factual, a division also present in Carnap's *Syntax of Language.* That this division should have been retained in the new form of Wittgenstein's doctrine does not go without saying, because here the approach, compared with the earlier one, is in many respects less rigid. Signs of a certain change can in fact be observed, as, for instance, on p.

119, No. 18: 'It is clear that mathematics as a technique of transforming signs for the purpose of prediction has nothing to do with grammar.' Elsewhere (p. 125, No. 42) he even speaks of the 'synthetic character of mathematical propositions'. It is said there: 'It might perhaps be said that the synthetic character of mathematical propositions appears most obviously in the unpredictable occurrence of the prime numbers. But their being synthetic (in this sense) does not make them any the less *a priori* ... The distribution of prime numbers would be an ideal example of what could be called synthetic *a priori*, for one can say that it is at any rate not discoverable by the analysis of the concept of a prime number.' As can be seen, Wittgenstein returns here from the concept 'analytic' of the Vienna Circle to a concept-formation which is more in the Kantian sense.

A certain approach to the Kantian conception is embodied also in Wittgenstein's view that it is mathematics which first forms the character, 'creates the forms of what we call facts' (see p. 173, No. 15). In this sense Wittgenstein also strongly opposes the opinion that the propositions of mathematics have the function of empirical propositions. On the other hand he emphasizes on various occasions that the applicability of mathematics, in particular of arithmetic, rests on empirical conditions; on p. 14, No. 37, for example, he says: 'This is how our children learn sums, for we make them put down three beans and then another three beans and then count what is there. If the result were at one time, five, at another time seven ..., then the first thing we should do would be to declare beans to be unsuitable for teaching sums. But if the same thing happened with sticks, fingers, strokes and most other things, then that would be the end of doing sums. — "But wouldn't it then still be that $2 + 2 = 4$?" — This sentence would then have become unusable.'

Statements like the following, however, remain important for Wittgenstein's conception (p. 160, No. 2): 'He who knows a mathematical proposition is supposed still to know *nothing*.' (The words in the German text are:'*soll noch nichts wissen*'.) He repeats this twice at short intervals and adds: 'That is, the mathematical proposition is only to supply the scaffolding for a description.' In the manner of Wittgenstein we could here ask: 'Why is the person in question *supposed* to still know nothing?' What need is expressed by this 'supposed to'? It appears that only a preconceived philosophical view determines this requirement, the view, namely, that there can exist but one kind of factuality: that of concrete reality. This view conforms to a kind of nominalism as it figures also elsewhere in the discussions on the philosophy of mathematics. In order to justify such a nominalism Wittgenstein would have to go back further than he does in this book. At all events he cannot here appeal to our actual mental attitude. For indeed he attacks our tendency to regard arithmetic, for example, 'as the natural history of the domain of numbers' (see p. 117, No. 13 and p. 116, No. 11). However, he is not fully at one with himself on this point. He asks himself (p. 142, No. 16) whether 'mathematical alchemy' is characterized by the mere fact that mathematical propositions are regarded as statements about mathematical objects. 'In a certain sense it is not possible, therefore, to appeal to the meaning of signs in mathematics, because it is mathematics itself which first gives them their meaning. What is typical for the phenomenon about which I am speaking is that the *mysteriousness* about any mathematical concept is not *straight away* interpreted as a misconception, as a fallacy, but as something which is at all events not to be despised, which should perhaps even be respected. All that I can do is to show an easy escape from this obscurity and this glitter of concepts. It can be said, strangely enough, that there is so to speak a solid core in all these glistening concept-formations. And I should like to say that it is this which makes them into mathematical products.'

One may doubt whether Wittgenstein has succeeded here in showing 'an easy escape from this obscurity'; one may be more inclined to suspect that here the obscurity and the 'mysteriousness' actually have their origin in the philosophical concept-formation, i.e. in the philosophical language used by Wittgenstein.

The fundamental division between the sphere of mathematics and the sphere of facts appears in several passages in the book. In this connection Wittgenstein often speaks with a certitude which strangely contrasts with his readiness to doubt so much of what is generally accepted. The passage on p. 26, No. 80 is characteristic of this; he says here: 'But of course you cannot get to know any property of the material by imagining.' Again we read on p. 29, No. 98: 'I can calculate in the imagination, but not experiment.' From the point of view of common experience all this certainly does not go without saying. An engineer or technician has doubtless just as lively an image of materials as a mathematician has of geometrical curves, and the image which any one of us may have of a thick iron rod is no doubt such as to make it clear that the rod could not be bent by a light pressure of the hands. And in the case of technical inventing, a major rôle is certainly played by experimenting in the imagination. Wittgenstein apparently uses here without being aware of it a philosophical schema which distinguishes the *a priori* from the empirical. To what extent and in what sense this distinction, which is so important particularly in the Kantian philosophy, is justified will not be discussed here; but in any case its introduction, particularly at the present time, should not be taken too lightly. With regard to the *a priori*, Wittgenstein's viewpoint differs from the Kantian viewpoint particularly by the fact that it includes the principles of general mechanics in the sphere of the empirical. Thus he argues, for example (p. 114, No. 4): 'Why are the Newtonian laws not axioms of mathematics? Because we could quite well imagine things being otherwise ... To say of a proposition: "This could be imagined otherwise" ... ascribes the rôle of an empirical proposition to it.' The concept of 'being able to imagine otherwise', also used by Kant, has the inconvenience of ambiguity. The impossibility of imagining something may be understood in various senses. This difficulty occurs particularly in geometry. This will be discussed later.

The previously mentioned tendency of Wittgenstein to recognize only one kind of fact becomes evident not only with regard to mathematics, but also with respect to any phenomenology. Thus he discusses the proposition that white is lighter than black (p. 30, No. 105) and explains it by saying that black serves us as a paradigm of what is dark, and white as a paradigm of what is light, which makes the statement one without content. In his opinion statements about differences in brightness have content only when they refer to specific visible objects and, for the sake of clarity, differences in the brightness of colours should not be spoken about at all. This attitude obviously precludes a descriptive theory of colours.

Actually one would expect Wittgenstein to hold phenomenological views. This is suggested by the fact that he often likes to draw examples from the field of art for the purpose of comparison. It is only the philosophical program which prevents the development of an explicitly phenomenological viewpoint.

This case is an example of how Wittgenstein's method aims at eliminating a very great deal. He sees himself in the part of the free-thinker combating superstition. The latter's goal, however, is freedom of the mind; whereas it is this very mind which Wittgenstein in many ways restricts, through a mental asceticism for the benefit of an irrationality whose goal is quite undetermined.

This tendency, however, is by no means so extreme here in the later philosophy of Wittgenstein's as in the earlier form. One may already gather from the few passages quoted that Wittgenstein was probably on the way to giving mental contents more of their due.

A fact that may be connected with this is that, in contrast to the assertive form of philosophical statement throughout the *Tractatus,* a mainly aporetical attitude prevails in the present book. There lies here, it is true, a danger for philosophical pedagogics, especially as Wittgenstein's philosophy exerts a strong attraction on the younger minds. The old Greek observation that philosophical contemplation frequently begins in philosophical astonishment[4] today misleads many philosophers into holding the view that the cultivation of astonishment is in itself a philosophical achievement. One may certainly have one's doubts about the soundness of a method which requires young philosophers to be trained as it were in wondering. Wondering is heuristically fruitful only where it is the expression of an instinct of research. Naturally it cannot be demanded of any philosophy that it should make comprehensible all that is astonishing. Perhaps the various philosophical viewpoints may be characterized by what they accept as ultimate in that which is astonishing. In Wittgenstein's philosophy it is, as far as epistemological questions are concerned, sociological facts. A few quotations may serve to illustrate this (p. 13, No. 35): '... how does it come about that all men ... accept these figures as proofs of these propositions? Indeed, there is here a great — and interesting — agreement.' (p. 20, No. 63): '... it is a peculiar procedure: I *go through* the proof and then accept its result. — I mean: this is simply how we *do* it. This is the custom among us, or a fact of our natural history.' (p. 23, No. 74): 'When one talks about *essence* one is merely noting a convention. But here one would like to retort: "There is no greater difference than between a proposition about the depth of the essence and one about a mere convention." What, however, if I reply: "To the *depth* of the essence there corresponds the *deep* need for the convention."' (p. 122, No. 30): 'Do not look on the proof as a procedure that *compels* you, but as one that *guides* you ... But how does it come about that it so guides *each one* of us in such a way that we are influenced by it conformably? Now how does it come about that we agree in *counting*? "That is just how we are trained", one may say, "and the agreement produced in this way is carried further by the proof."'

II

So much then for the general characterization of the present observations by Wittgenstein. Their contents, however, is by no means exhausted in the general philosophical aspects that are here raised: various specific questions concerning the foundations of philosophy are discussed in detail. We shall deal in what follows with the principal viewpoints occurring here.

Let us begin with a question which concerns the problem previously touched on, that of the distinction between the *a priori* and the empirical: the question of geometrical axioms. Wittgenstein does not deal specifically with geometrical axioms as such. Instead, he raises generally the question as to how far the axioms of a mathematical system of axioms should be self-evident. He takes as his example the parallel axiom. Let us quote a few sentences from his discussion of the subject (p. 113, No. 2): 'What do we say when such an axiom is presented to us, for example, the parallel axiom? Has experience shown us that this is how it is? ... Experience plays a part, but not the one we should *immediately expect.* For we have not, of course, made experiments and found that actually only *one* straight line through the given point fails to cut the other straight line. And yet the proposition is evident. — Suppose I now say: "It is quite indifferent why it should be evident. It is sufficient that we accept it. All that is important is how we use it" ... When the wording of the parallel axiom, for example, is given ..., the way of using this proposition, and hence its sense, is still quite undetermined. And when we say that it is evident to us, then we have by doing so already chosen, without realizing it, a certain way of using the proposition. The proposition is not a mathematical axiom if we do not employ it precisely *for this purpose.* The fact, that is, that here we do not make experiments, but accept the self-evidence, is enough to decide its use. For we are not so naîve as to let the self-evidence count instead of the experiment. It is not the fact that it appears to us self-evidently true, but the fact that we let the self-evidence count, which makes it into a mathematical proposition.'

   In discussing these statements it must first be borne in mind that we have to distinguish two things: whether we recognize an axiom as geometrically valid, or whether we choose it as an axiom. The latter, of course, is not determined by the wording of the proposition. But here we are concerned with a rather technical question of deductive arrangement. However, what interests Wittgenstein here is surely the recognition of the proposition as geometrically valid. It is on this light that Wittgenstein's assertion ('that the recognition is not determined by the wording') must be considered, and it is in any case not immediately evident. He puts it so simply: 'We have not, of course, made experiments.' Admittedly, there has been no experimenting in connection with the formulation of the parallel axiom here considered, and this formulation does not lend itself to this purpose anyway. However, within the scope of the other geometrical axioms the parallel axiom is equivalent to one of the following statements of metrical geometry: 'In a triangle the sum of the angles is equal to two right angles. In a quadrilateral in which three angles are right angles the fourth angle is also a right angle. Six congruent equilateral triangles with a common vertex *P* (lying consecutively side by side) exactly fill up the neighborhood of point *P*.' Such propositions — in which, it will be noted, there is no mention of the infinite extension of a straight line — can certainly be tested by experiment. As is known, Gauss did in fact check experimentally the proposition about the sum of the angles of a triangle, making use, to be sure, of the assumption of the linear diffusion of light. This is, however, not the only possibility of such an experiment. Thus Hugo Dingler in particular has emphasized that for the concepts of the straight line, the plane and the right angle there exists a natural and, so to speak, compulsory kind of experimental realization. By means of such an experimental realization of geometrical concepts statements like in particular the second one above can be experimentally tested with great accuracy. Moreover in a less accurate way they are continually being implicitly checked by us in the normal practice of drawing figures. Our instinctive estimation of lengths and of the sizes of angles can also be considered as the result of manifold experiences, and propositions which are to serve as axioms of elementary geometry must at all events agree with that instinctive estimation.

It cannot be maintained, therefore, that our experience plays no part in the acceptance of propositions as geometrically valid. But Wittgenstein does not mean that either. This becomes clear from what follows immediately after the passage quoted (p. 114, Nos. 4 and 5): 'Does experience teach us that a straight line is possible between any two points? ... One could say: *Imagination* teaches us it. And this is where the truth lies; one has only to understand it aright. *Before* the proposition the concept is still pliable. But might not experience cause us to reject the axiom? Yes. And nevertheless it does not play the part of an empirical proposition ... Why are the Newtonian laws not axioms of mathematics? Because one could quite well imagine things being otherwise ... Something is an axiom, *not* because we recognize it as extremely probable, indeed as certain, but because we assign it a certain function, and one which conflicts with that of an empirical proposition ... The axiom, I would say, is another part of speech.' Further on (p. 124, No. 35) he says: 'What about, for example, the fundamental laws of mechanics? Whoever understands them must know on what experiences they are based. It is otherwise with the propositions of pure mathematics.'

In favour of these statements it must certainly be conceded that experience alone does not determine the theoretical recognition of a proposition. A more exact theoretical statement is always something which must be conceived beyond the facts of experience.

The view, however, that there exists in this respect such a fundamental difference between mathematical propositions and the principles of mechanics is scarcely justified. In particular the last quoted assertion that, in order to understand the basic laws of mechanics, the experience on which they are based must be known, can hardly be maintained. Of course, when mechanics is taught at the university, it is desirable that the empirical foundations should be made clear; this is, however, not for the purpose of the theoretical and practical manipulation of the laws, but for the epistemological consciousness and with an eye to the possibilities of eventually necessary modifications of the theory. Yet an engineer or productive technician in order to become skilled in mechanics and capable of handling its laws does not need to bother about how we came upon the laws. To these laws also applies what Wittgenstein so frequently emphasizes in reference to mathematical laws: that the facts of experience which are important for the empirical motivation of these propositions by no means make up the contents of that which is asserted in the laws. It is important for the manipulation of mechanical laws to become familiar with the concept-formations and to obtain some sort of evidence for these laws. This way of acquiring it is not only practically, but also theoretically significant: the theory is fully assimilated only by the process of rational shaping to which it is subsequently subjected. With regard to mechanics most philosophers and many of us mathematicians have little to say here, not having acquired mechanics in the said manner. — What distinguishes the case of geometry from that of mechanics is the (philosophically somewhat accidental) circumstance that the acquisition of the world of concepts and of the evidence is for the most part already completed in an (at least for us) unconscious stage of mental development.

Ernst Mach's opposition to a rational foundation of mechanics has its justification insofar as such a foundation endeavours to pass over the rôle of experience in arriving at the principles of mechanics. We must keep in mind that concept-formations and the principles of mechanics comprise as it were an extract of experience. On the other hand it would be unjustified to reject outright on the basis of this criticism the efforts towards a construction of mechanics that is as rational as possible.

What is specific about geometry is the phenomenological character of its laws, and hence the important rôle of intuition. Wittgenstein points only in passing to this aspect: '*Imagination* teaches us it. And this is where the truth lies; one has only to understand it aright' (p. 8). The term 'imagination' is very general, and what is said at the end of the second sentence is a qualification which shows that the author feels the theme of intuition to be a very ticklish one. In fact it is very difficult to characterize satisfactorily the epistemological rôle of intuition. The sharp separation of intuition and concept, as it occurs in the Kantian philosophy, does not appear on closer examination to be justified. In considering geometrical thinking in particular it is difficult to distinguish clearly the share of intuition from that of conceptuality, since we find here a formation of concepts guided so to speak by intuition, which in the sharpness of its intentions goes beyond what is in a proper sense intuitively evident, but which separated from intuition has not its proper content. It is strange that Wittgenstein assigns intuition no definite epistemological rôle although his thinking is dominated by the visual. A proof is for him always a picture. At one time he gives a mere figure as an example of a geometrical proof. It is also striking that he never talks about the intuitive evidence of topological facts, such as for instance the fact that the surface of a sphere divides the (remaining) space into an inner and an outer part in such a way that the curve joining up an inside point with an outside one always passes over one point on the surface of the sphere.

Questions relating to the foundations of geometry and its axioms still belong primarily to the field of inquiry of general epistemology. What is today called in the narrower sense mathematical foundational research is mainly directed towards the foundations of arithmetic. Here one tends to eliminate as far as possible what is specific about geometry by splitting it up into an arithmetical and a physical side. We shall leave the question open whether this procedure is justified; this question is not discussed by Wittgenstein. On the other hand he deals in great detail with the basic questions of arithmetic. Let us now take a closer look at his observations concerning this field of questions.

The viewpoint from which Wittgenstein regards arithmetic is not the usual one of the mathematician. Wittgenstein has concerned himself more with the theories on the foundations of arithmetic (in particular with the Russellian one) than with arithmetic itself. Particularly with regard to the theory of numbers, his examples seldom go beyond the numerical. An uninformed reader might well conclude that the theory of numbers consists almost entirely of numerical equations, which indeed are normally regarded not as propositions to be proved, but as simple statements. The treatment is more mathematical in the sections where he discusses questions of set theory, such as denumerability and non-denumerability, as well as the Dedekind cut theory.

Wittgenstein maintains everywhere a standpoint of strict finitism. In this respect he considers the various types of problem concerning infinity, such as exist for a finitist viewpoint, in particular the problem of the *tertium non datur* and that of impredicative definitions. The very forceful and vivid account he gives is well suited to conveying a clearer idea of the finitist's conception to those still unfamiliar with it. However, it contributes hardly anything essentially new to the argumentation; and those who consciously hold the view of classical mathematics will scarcely be convinced by it.

Let us discuss a few points in more details. Wittgenstein deals with the question whether in the infinite expansion of π a certain sequence of numbers ϕ, such as, say, '777', ever occurs. Adopting Brouwer's viewpoint he draws attention to the possibility that to this question there may not as yet be a definite answer. In this connection he says (p. 138, No. 9): 'However strange it sounds, the further expansion of an irrational number is a further development of mathematics.' This formulation is obviously ambiguous. If it merely means that the determination of a not yet calculated decimal place of an irrational number is a contribution to the development of mathematics, then every mathematician will agree with this. But since the assertion is held to be a 'strange sounding' one, certainly something else is meant, perhaps that the course of the development of mathematics at a given time is undecided and that this undecidedness can influence also the progress of the expansion of an irrational number given by definition, so that the decision as to what figure is to be put at the ten-thousandth decimal place of π would depend on the course of the history of thought. Such a view, however, is not appropriate even according to the conception of Wittgenstein himself, for he says (p. 138, No. 9): 'The question ... changes its status when it becomes decidable.' Now the digits in the decimal fraction expansion of π can be determined up to any chosen decimal place. Hence the view about the further development of mathematics does not contribute anything to the understanding of the situation in the case of the expansion of π. In this regard we can even say the following. Suppose we could maintain with certainty that the question of the occurrence of the sequence of numbers ϕ is undecidable, then this would imply that the figure ϕ never occurs in the expansion of π; for if it did occur, and if k were the decimal place which the last digit of ϕ has on the first occurrence in the decimal fraction expansion of π, then the question whether the figure ϕ occurs before the $(k + 1)$th place would be a decidable question and could be answered positively, and thus the initial question would be answerable. (This argument by the way does not require the principle of the *tertium non datur.*)

Further on Wittgenstein repeatedly reverts to the example of the decimal fraction expansion of π; in one place in particular (p. 185, No.34) we find an assertion which is characteristic of his view: 'Suppose that people go on and on calculating the expansion of π. An omniscient God knows, therefore, whether by the end of the world they will have reached a figure "777". But can his *omniscience* decide whether they *would* have reached this figure after the end of the world? It cannot do so ... For him, too, the mere rule of expansion cannot decide anything that it does not decide for us.'

That is certainly not convincing. If we conceive the idea of a divine omniscience at all, then we would certainly ascribe to it the attribute of being able to survey at *one* glance a totality of which every single element is in principle accessible to us. We must pay here particular heed to the double rôle of the recursive definition of the decimal fraction expansion: on the one hand as the definitory fixing of the decimal fraction, and on the other as a means for the 'effective' calculation of decimal places. If we here take 'effective' in the usual sense, then even a divine intelligence can *effectively* calculate nothing other than what we are able to effectively calculate (no more than it would be capable of carrying out the trisection of an angle with a ruler and compass, or of deriving Gödel's underivable proposition in the related formal system); however, it is not inconceivable that this divine intelligence should be able to survey in another (not humanly effective) manner all the possible calculation results of the application of a recursive definition.

In his criticism of the theory of Dedekind's cut, Wittgenstein's main argument is that the extensional approach is mixed up in this theory with the intensional approach. This criticism is applicable in the case of certain versions of the theory where the tendency is to create the impression of a stronger character of the procedure than is actually achieved. If one wants to introduce the cuts not as mere sets of numbers, but as defining arithmetical laws of such sets, then either one must utilize a quite vague concept of the 'law', thus gaining little; or, if one sets about clarifying the concept, one meets with the difficulty which Hermann Weyl termed the vicious circle in the foundation of analysis and which for some time back was sensed instinctively by various mathematicians, who thereupon advocated a restriction of the procedure of analysis. This criticism of impredicative concept-formation even today plays a considerable rôle in the discussions on the foundations of mathematics. However, difficulties are not encountered if the extensional standpoint is consistently retained, and Dedekind's conception can certainly be understood in this sense and was probably so understood by Dedekind himself. All that is required here is that we should recognize, besides the concept of number itself, also the concept of a set of natural numbers (and in consequence of this the concept of a set of fractions, too) as an intuitively significant concept not requiring reduction. This implies a certain renunciation in respect of the goal of arithmetizing analysis, and thus geometry, too. 'But' — one could here ask in the Wittgensteinian manner — 'must geometry be entirely arithmetized?' Scientists are often very dogmatic in their attempts at reductions. They are frequently inclined to treat such an attempt as completely successful even when it succeeds not in the manner intended but only in some measure and with a certain degree of approximation. Where such standpoints are encountered, considerations of the kind suggested by Wittgenstein's book can be very valuable.

Wittgenstein's detailed discussion of Dedekind's proof is not satisfactory. Some of his objections can be disposed of simply through a clearer account of Dedekind's line of thought.

In the discussion of denumerability and non-denumerability, the reader must bear in mind that Wittgenstein always understands by cardinal number a finite cardinal number, and by a series one of the order type of the natural numbers. The polemics against the theorem of the non-denumerability of the totality of real numbers is unsatisfactory insofar as the analogy between the concepts 'non-denumerable' and 'infinite' is not brought out clearly. Corresponding to the way in which 'infinity of a totality G' can be defined as the property whereby to a finite number of things out of G there can always be assigned a further one, the non-denumerability of a totality G is defined by the property that to every denumerable sub-totality there can be assigned an element of G not yet contained in the sub-totality. In this sense the non-denumerability of the totality of real numbers is demonstrated by the diagonal procedure, and there is nothing foisted in here, as would appear to be the case according to Wittgenstein's argument. The theorem of the non-denumerability of the totality of real numbers is attainable without comparison of the transfinite cardinal numbers. Besides — this is often disregarded — there exist for that theorem other proofs more geometrical than the one provided by the diagonal procedures. From the point of view of geometry we have here a rather gross fact.

It is also strange to find the author raising a question like this: 'How then do we make use of the proposition: "There is no largest [scil. finite] cardinal number."? ... First and foremost it is to be noticed that we put the question at all, which indicates that the answer is not obvious' (p. 57, No. 5). We might think that one need not spend long searching for the answer here. Our entire analysis with its applications in physics and technology rests on the infinity of the series of numbers. The theory of probability and statistics make continually implicit use of this infinity. Wittgenstein argues as though mathematics existed almost solely for the purposes of housekeeping.

The finitist and constructive attitude on the whole taken by Wittgenstein towards the problems of the foundations of mathematics conforms to the general tendency of his philosophizing. However, it can hardly be said that he finds a confirmation for his viewpoint in the situation of the foundational investigations. All that he shows is how this standpoint has to be applied when engaging in the questions in dispute. It is generally characteristic of the situation with regard to the foundational problems that the results obtained hitherto clearly favor neither the one nor the other of the main two opposing philosophical views — the finitist-constructive and the 'Platonic'-existential view. Either of the two views can advance arguments aginst the other. The existential conception, however, has the advantage of enabling us to appreciate the investigations directed towards the establishment of elementary constructive methods (just as in geometry the investigation of constructions with ruler and compass has significance even for a mathematician who admits other methods of construction), while for the strictly constructivist view a large part of classical mathematics simply does not exist.

To some extent independent of the partisanship in the mentioned opposition of viewpoints are those observations of Wittgenstein's which concern the rôle of formalization, the reduction of number theory to logic, and the question of consistency. His views here show more independence, and these considerations are therefore of greater interest.

With regard to the question of consistency he asserts in particular what has meanwhile also been stressed by various other investigators in the field of foundational research: that within the bounds of a formal system the contradiction should not be considered solely as a deterrent, and that a formal system as such can still be of interest even when it leads to a contradiction. It should be observed, however, that in the former systems of Frege and Russell the contradiction already arises within a few steps, almost directly from the basic structure of the system. Furthermore, much of what Wittgenstein says in this connection overshoots the mark by a long way. Particularly unsatisfactory is the frequently quoted example of the producibility of contradictions by admitting division by nought. (One need only consider the foundation of the rule of reduction in order to see that this is not applicable in the case of the factor nought.)

Wittgenstein recognizes at all events the importance of demonstrating consistency. Yet it is doubtful whether he is sufficiently well aware of the rôle played by the condition of consistency in the reasoning of proof-theory. Thus the discussion of Gödel's theorem of non-derivability in particular suffers from the defect that Gödel's quite explicit premiss of the consistency of the considered formal system is ignored. A fitting comparison, which is drawn by Wittgenstein in connection with the Gödel-ian proposition, is that between a proof of formal unprovability and a proof of the impossibility of a certain construction with ruler and compass. Such a proof, Wittgenstein says, contains an element of prediction. The remark which follows, however, is strange (p. 52, No. 14): 'A contradiction is unusable as such a prediction.' Such proofs of impossibility in fact always proceed by the deduction of a contradiction.

In his considerations on the theory of numbers Wittgenstein shows a noticeable reserve towards Frege's and Russell's foundation of number theory, such as was not to be found in the earlier stages of his philosophy. Thus he says on one occasion (p. 67, No. 4): '... the logical calculus is only — frills tacked on to the arithmetical calculus.' This thought had hardly been formulated previously as pregnantly as here. It might be appropriate to reflect on the sense in which the assertion holds good. There is no denying that the attempt at incorporating the arithmetical, and in particular, the numerical propositions into logistic has been successful. That is to say, it has proved possible to formulate these propositions in purely logical terms and to prove them within the domain of logistic on the basis of this formulation. Whether this result may be regarded as yielding a proper philosophical understanding of the arithmetical proposition is, however, open to question. When we consider the logistical proof of an equation such as 3 + 7 = 10, we observe that within the proof we have to carry out quite the same comparative verification which occurs in the usual counting. This necessity shows itself particularly clearly in the formalized form of logic; but it is also present when we interpret the content of the formula logically. The logical definition of three-numberedness (*Dreizahligkeit*), for example, is structurally so constituted that it to some extent contains within itself the element of three-numberedness. The property possessed by the predicate P (or by the class that forms the extension of P) of being three-numbered is indeed defined by the condition that there exist things x, y, z having the property P and differing each from the others, and that further everything having the property P is identical with x or y or z. Now the conclusion that for a three-numbered predicate P and a seven-numbered predicate Q, in the case that the predicates do not apply in common to one thing, the alternative P v Q is a ten-numbered predicate, requires for its foundation just the kind of comparison that is used in elementary arithmetic — only that now an additional logical apparatus (the 'frills') comes into operation. When this is clearly realized, it appears that the proposition of the logical theory of predicates is valid because 3 + 7 = 10, and not vice versa.

Thus in spite of the possibility of incorporating arithmetic into logistic, arithmetic constitutes the more abstract ('purer') schema; and this appears paradoxical only because of a traditional, but on closer examination unjustified view according to which logical generality is in every respect the highest generality.

Yet it might be good to look at yet another aspect of the matter. According to Frege a number (*Anzahl*) is to be defined as the property of a predicate. This view already presents difficulties for the normal use of the number concept; for in many contexts where a number occurs, the indication of a predicate of which it is the property proves to be highly forced. In particular it should be noted that numbers occur not only in statements: they also occur in directions and in demands or requests — such as when a housewife says to an errand-boy: 'Fetch me ten apples.'

The theoretical elaboration of this conception is not without complications either. A definite number does not generally belong as such to a predicate, but only with reference to a domain of things, a universe of discourse (apart from the many cases of extra-scientific predicates to which no definite number at all can be ascribed). Thus it would be more accurate to characterize a number as a relation between a predicate and a domain of individuals. In Frege's theory, it is true, this complication does not arise since he presupposes what might be called an absolute domain of individuals. But, as we know, it is precisely this starting point which leads to the contradiction noted by Russell. Apart from this, the Fregean conception of his predicate theory, in which the value distributions (extensions) of the predicate are treated as things quite on a par with ordinary individuals, already implies a clear deviation from our customary logic in the sense of a theoretical construction of a formal derivative frame. The idea of such a frame has retained its methodological importance, and the question as to the most favorable formation of it is still one of the main problems in foundational theory. However, with respect to such a frame one can speak of a 'logic' only in an extended sense; logic in its usual sense, stating merely the general rules for deductive reasoning, must be distinguished from the latter.

Wittgenstein's criticism of the incorporation of arithmetic into logic is, it is true, not advanced in the sense that he recognizes arithmetical theorems as stating facts *sui generis*. His tendency is rather to deny altogether that such theorems express facts. He even declares it to be the 'curse of the invasion of mathematics by mathematical logic that any proposition can now be represented in mathematical notation and we thus feel obliged to understand it, although this way of writing is really only the translation of vague, ordinary prose' (p. 155, No. 46). Indeed he recognizes calculating only as an acquired skill with practical utility. In particular, he seeks to explain away in a definitory manner what is factual about arithmetic. Thus he asks, for instance (p. 33, No. 112): 'What do I call "the multiplication 13×13"? Only the correct pattern of multiplication at the end of which comes 169? Or a "wrong multiplication" too?' Likewise, the question often arises as to what it is that we 'call calculating' (p. 97, No. 73). And on p. 92, No. 58 he argues: 'Suppose one were to say that by calculating we become acquainted with the properties of numbers. But do the properties of numbers *exist* outside of calculating?' The tendency is apparently to take the correct additions and multiplications as defining calculating and to characterize them as 'correct' in a trivial manner. But one cannot succeed in this way, i.e. one cannot express in this way the many facts of relatedness which appear in the numerical computations. Let us take, say, the associativity of addition. It is certainly possible to fix by definition the addition of the single figures. But then the strange fact remains that the addition $3 + (7 + 8)$ gives the same result as $(3 + 7) + 8$, and that the same holds whatever numbers replace 3, 7, 8. The number-theoretic expressions are, from the definitory point of view, so to speak, over-determined. It is indeed on this kind of over-determinateness that the many checks are based of which we may make use in calculating.

Occasionally Wittgenstein raises the question as to whether the result of a calculation carried out in the decimal system is also valid for the comparison of numbers carried out by means of the direct representation with sequences of strokes. The answer to this is to be found in the usual mathematical foundation of the method of calculating with decadic figures. Yet here Wittgenstein touches upon something fundamental: the proofs to be given for the justification of the decadic rules of calculation rest, if they are obtained in a finitist way, upon the assumption that every number we can form decadically is producible also in the direct stroke notation, and that the operations of concatenation, etc., as also of comparison, are always performable with such stroke sequences. From this it appears that the finitistic theory of numbers, too, is not in the full sense 'concrete', but utilizes idealizations.

The previously mentioned assertions in which Wittgenstein speaks of the synthetic character of mathematics are in a certain apparent contrast with the tendency to regard numerical calculating as being characterized merely by way of definition and to deny that arithmetical propositions have the character of facts. In this connection the following passage may be noted (p. 160, No. 3): 'How can you maintain that "... 625 ..." and "... 25 × 25 ..." say the same thing? — It is only through our arithmetic that they *become one.*'

What is meant here is about the same thing that Kant had in mind in the argument against the view that $7 + 5 = 12$ is a merely analytical proposition, and where he contends that the concept 12 'is by no means already conceived through my merely conceiving this union of 7 and 5', and then adds: 'That 7 *are to be* added to 5, I have, it is true, conceived in the concept of a sum $= 7 + 5$, but not that this sum is equal to the number 12' (*Critique of Pure Reason*, B 14ff.). The Kantian argument could be expressed in a modern form somewhat as follows. The concept '7 + 5' is an individual concept (in accordance with Carnap's terminology) expressible by the description $1_x (x = 7 + 5)$, and this concept is different from the concept '12'; the only reason for this not being so obvious is that we involuntarily carry out the addition of the small numbers 7 and 5 directly. We have here the case, so often discussed in the new logic following Frege, of two terms with a different 'sense' but the same '*Bedeutung*' (called 'denotation' by A. Church); in order to determine the synthetic or analytic character of a judgment one must, of course, always go by the sense, not the '*Bedeutung*'. The Kantian thesis that mathematics is of a synthetic character does not at all conflict with what the Russellian school maintains when it declares the propositions of arithmetic to be analytic. We have here two entirely different concepts of the analytic — a fact which in recent times has been pointed out in particular by E.W. Beth.[5]

A further intrinsic contrast is to be found in Wittgenstein's attitude towards logistic. On the one hand, he often tends to regard proofs as formalized proofs. Thus he says on p. 93, No. 64: 'Suppose I were to set someone the problem: "Find a proof of the proposition ..." — The solution would surely be to show me certain signs.' The distinctive and indispensable rôle of everyday language compared with that of a formalized language is not given prominence in his remarks. He often speaks of the 'language game' and by no means restricts the use of this expression to the artificial formal language, for which alone it is indeed appropriate. Our natural language has in no way the character of a game; it is peculiar to us, almost in the way our limbs are. Apparently Wittgenstein is still governed by the idea of a language of science comprehending the whole of scientific thought. In contrast with this are the highly critical remarks on usual mathematical logic. Apart from the one already mentioned concerning 'the curse of the invasion of mathematics by mathematical logic', the following in particular is worthy of notice (p. 156, No. 48): '"Mathematical logic" has completely distorted the thinking of mathematicians and philosophers by declaring a superficial interpretation of the forms of our everyday language to be an analysis of the structures of facts. In this, of course, it has only continued to build on the Aristotelian logic.'

We shall come closer to the idea which probably underlies this criticism if we bear in mind that logical calculus was intended by various of its founders as a realization of the Leibnizian conception of the *characteristica universalis.* As to Aristotle, Wittgenstein's criticism, if we look at it more closely, is not directed against him. For all that Aristotle wanted to do with his logic was to fix the usual forms of logical arguing and to test their legitimacy. The task of the *characteristica universalis,* however, was intended to be a much larger one: to establish a concept-world which would make possible an understanding of all connections existing in reality. For an undertaking aimed at this goal, however, it cannot be taken for granted that the grammatical structures of our language have to function as the basic framework of the theory; for the categories of this grammar have a character that is at least partially anthropomorphic. Yet nothing even approaching the same value has hitherto been devised in philosophy to replace our usual logic. What Hegel in particular put in place of the Aristotelian logic in his rejection of it is a mere comparison of universals by way of analogies and associations, without any clearly regulative procedure. This certainly cannot pass as any sort of approach to the fulfilment of the Leibnizian ideas.

From Wittgenstein, however, we can obtain no guidance on how conventional logic may be replaced by something philosophically more efficient. He probably considered an 'analysis of the structures of facts' to be a task wrongly set. Indeed he did not look for a procedure determined by some directive rules. The 'logical compulsion', the 'inexorability of logic', the 'hardness of the logical must' are always a stumbling block for him and ever again a cause of amazement. Perhaps he does not always realize that all these terms have the character of merely a popular comparison which in many respects is inappropriate. The strictness of the logical and the exact does not limit our freedom. Our very freedom enables us to achieve precision through thought in a perceptive world of indistinctness and inexactness. Wittgenstein speaks of the 'must of kinematics' being 'much harder than the causal must' (p. 37, No. 121). Is it not an aspect of freedom that we can conceive virtual motions subject merely to kinematic laws, as well as real, causally determined motions, and can compare the former with the latter?

Enlightened humanity has sought in rational definiteness its liberating refuge from the dominating influence of the merely authoritative. At the present time, however, this has for a large part been lost to consciousness, and to many people scientific validity that has to be acknowledged appears as an oppressing authority.

In Wittgenstein's case it is certainly not this aspect which evokes his critical attitude towards scientific objectivity. Nevertheless, his tendency is to understand the intersubjective unanimity in the field of mathematics as an heteronomous one. The agreement, he believes, is to be explained by the fact that we are in the first place 'trained' in common in elementary technique and that the agreement thus created is continued through the proofs (cf. quotation on p. 195). That this kind of explanation is inadequate might occur to anybody not attracted by the impression of originality of the aspect. The mere possibility of the technique of calculating with its manifold possibilities of decomposing a computation into simpler parts cannot be regarded merely as a consequence of agreement (cf. remark on pp. 17 and 18). Furthermore, when we think of the enormously rich concept-formations towered up on each other, as for instance in function theory — where one can say of the theorems obtained at any stage what Wittgenstein once said: 'We lean on them or rest on them' (p.124, No. 35) — we see that the conception mentioned does not in any way explain why these conceptual edifices are not continually collapsing. Considering Wittgenstein's viewpoint, it is, in fact, not surprising that he does not feel the contradiction to be something odd; but what does not appear from his account is that contradictions in mathematics are to be found only in quite peripheral extrapolations and nowhere else. In this sense one can say that the fact of mathematics does not become at all understandable through Wittgenstein's philosophy. And it is not his anthropological point of view which gives rise to the difficulty.

Where, however, does the initial conviction of Wittgenstein's arise that in the region of mathematics there is no proper knowledge about objects, but that everything here can only be techniques, standards and customary attitudes? He certainly reasons: 'There is nothing here at all to which knowing could refer.' That is bound up, as already mentioned, with the circumstance that he does not recognize any kind of phenomenology. What probably induces his opposition here are such phrases as the one which refers to the 'essence' of a color; here the word 'essence' evokes the idea of hidden properties of the color, whereas colors as such are nothing other than what is evident in their manifest properties and relations. But this does not prevent such properties and relations from being the content of objective statements; colors are not just a nothing. Even if we do not adopt the pretensions of the philosophy of Husserl with regard to 'intuition of the essence', that does not preclude the possibility of an objective phenomenology. That in the region of colors and sounds the phenomenological investigation is still in its beginnings is certainly bound up with the fact that it has no great importance for theoretical physics, since in physics we are induced, at an early stage, to eliminate colors and sounds as qualities. Mathematics, however, can be regarded as the theoretical phenomenology of structures. In fact, what contrasts phenomenologically with the qualitative is not the quantitative, as is taught by traditional philosophy, but the structural, i.e. the forms of being aside and after, and of being composite, etc., with all the concepts and laws that relate to them.

Such a conception of mathematics leaves the attitude towards the problems of the foundations of mathematics still largely undetermined. Yet, for anyone proceeding from the Wittgensteinian conception, it can open the way to a viewpoint that does greater justice to the peculiarity and the comprehensive significance of mathematics.

Notes

1. *Remarks on the Foundation of Mathematics*, by Ludwig Wittgenstein. Edited by G.H. von Wright, R. Rhees, G.E.M. Anscombe. Translated by G.E.M. Anscombe. Basil Blackwell, Oxford, 1956.
2. The book was originally published in German, with the English translation attached. All pages and numbers quoted refer to the German text.
3. David Pole, *The Later Philosophy of Wittgenstein*, University of London, The Athlone Press, 1958.
4. θαυμάζειν.
5. 'Over Kants Onderscheiding von synthetische en analytische Oordeelen,' *De Gids*, vol. 106, 1942. Also: The 'Foundations of Mathematics,' *Studies in Logic*, Amsterdam, 1959, pp. 41-7.

61

Wittgenstein's Philosophy of Mathematics*

Michael Wrigley

Wittgenstein's contributions to the philosophy of mathematics, in contrast to his work in so many other areas of philosophy, have often been dismissed as of little value. Georg Kreisel, for example, ends his review of the *Remarks on the Foundations of Mathematics* by saying that 'it seems to me to be a surprisingly insignificant product of a sparkling mind'.[1] I hold the opposite opinion, and my aim in this paper is to show that Wittgenstein's philosophy of mathematics has only been held in such low regard because it has been misunderstood, and that in fact it is no less original and important than the rest of his work.

Some writers have taken Wittgenstein's philosophy of mathematics to be an extreme form of constructivism, i.e. he is said to hold that the only valid mathematics is that which uses constructive proof methods. This type of philosophy of mathematics is familiar from the work of Brouwer and his followers, but Wittgenstein's constructivism is supposed to be of a much more restricted kind than Brouwer's intuitionism. Wittgenstein is, we are told, a strict finitist who holds that the only comprehensible and valid kind of proof in mathematics takes the form of intuitively clear manipulations of concrete objects. In his article on the *Remarks on the Foundations of Mathematics* Michael Dummett has attributed just such a position to Wittgenstein. According to Dummett 'Wittgenstein adopts a version of constructivism'[2] which 'is of a much more extreme kind than that of the intuitionists'.[3] Similarly Paul Bernays writes of 'the finitist and constructive attitude . . . taken by Wittgenstein towards the problems of the foundations of mathematics',[4] and he explicitly claims that Wittgenstein 'maintains everywhere a standpoint of strict finitism'.[5] But such an interpretation is completely at odds with Wittgenstein's general conception of philosophy. In the *Investigations* we read that 'philosophy may in no way interfere with the actual use of language; it can in the end only describe it. For it cannot give it a foundation either. It leaves everything as it is. *It also leaves mathematics as it is*' (*PI* §124) (my italics). But an extreme constructivist philosophy of mathematics involves drastic revisions of mathematics and by no means leaves it as it is. As Bernays points out, 'for the strictly constructivist view a large part of classical mathematics simply does not exist'.[6]

183

So it is clear that Dummett's and Bernays' interpretation of Wittgenstein cannot be correct.

A different interpretation of Wittgenstein, but one which none the less makes him into a kind of finitist, has been put forward by Kreisel and Kielkopf. Kreisel claims that 'Wittgenstein's views on mathematics are near those of strict finitism' but he adds the qualification that 'perhaps one should say he concentrates on the strictly finitistic aspects of mathematics ... [because] all the mathematics which [he] considers clear fits comfortably within the framework of strict finitism'.[7] Kielkopf concludes his examination of Wittgenstein's philosophy of mathematics by claiming that Wittgenstein is an 'open-ended strict finitist',[8] that is, he 'accepts strict finitism as an adequate philosophy of only as much mathematics as can be done by strict finitistic means. However, he resolves to understand the remainder of mathematics by deviating as little as possible from the strict finitistic philosophy.'[9] Kreisel and Kielkopf are, I think, putting forward much the same interpretation of Wittgenstein. Having grasped the point that for Wittgenstein philosophy is a descriptive activity they reconcile this with their claim that he is a finitist by claiming that he is, at any rate primarily, interested only in those very elementary areas of mathematics of which strict finitism is the correct description. However, even when thus modified the claim that Wittgenstein is a finitist does not square with his descriptive conception of philosophy. Even for those parts of mathematics which can be re-done in a finitistic way the new finitistic version is a different piece of mathematics from the original. We do not do *any* of our mathematics in a finitistic way at present, and so if Wittgenstein's aim is to describe mathematics *as it is now* he could not accept strict finitism as a correct description of *any* part of it. Nor is it true that Wittgenstein is primarily or solely interested in very elementary mathematics. Whilst Wittgenstein's mathematical examples are predominantly of an elementary kind, and this is particularly true of the *Remarks on the Foundations of Mathematics* — the text Kreisel, Kielkopf, Dummett and Bernays base their interpretations on — if we consider Wittgenstein's work on the philosophy of mathematics as a whole it becomes quite clear that his interest in mathematics is by no means limited to its relatively elementary areas. As we shall see later, there are good philosophical reasons why Wittgenstein does avoid very complicated examples, but they have nothing to do with finitism.

I want to devote the rest of this paper to the positive task of setting out some of the themes in Wittgenstein's philosophy of mathematics which seem to me to be the most fundamental. Naturally I have had to leave out many important topics which Wittgenstein considers at length, such as the problems concerning the applicability of mathematics, the infinite, the question of what constitutes a proof, etc., but nevertheless I think that the topics which I discuss do give a clear enough picture of Wittgenstein's philosophy of mathematics for its highly original character to emerge.

Since philosophy for Wittgenstein is essentially a descriptive activity the aim of the philosopher of mathematics is to understand mathematics *as it is*, and it is no business of his to criticise the way mathematicians go about their work. So it is no part of the philosopher's task to rewrite all or part of mathematics in new and supposedly better ways, as logicist, formalist and intuitionist philosophers of mathematics had thought it was. The philosopher should focus his attention on what mathematicians actually do and try to give a correct description of it. He should be careful not to be misled by the descriptions which mathematicians themselves give of what they are doing, for these may very well be philosophically quite confused. Augustine knew well enough how to use the word 'time' but could not answer the question 'what is time?' It is the same, Wittgenstein believes with mathematics. Mathematicians can discover mathematical facts but 'what a mathematician is inclined to say about the objectivity and reality of mathematical facts is not a philosophy of mathematics, but something for philosophical *treatment*' (*PI* §254). So if the philosopher wants to describe mathematics he must be careful to separate mathematics itself from the things which mathematicians and philosophers have said *about* mathematics. 'Time and again', Wittgenstein emphasises, 'I would like to say: what I check is the *account books* of mathematicians; their mental processes, joys, depressions, and instincts as they go about their business may be important in other connections, but they are no concern of mine' (*PG* p. 295).

Wittgenstein saw this distinction between mathematics itself, on the one hand, and what is said about mathematics, on the other, as of fundamental philosophical importance. He held that *all* the problems of traditional philosophy of mathematics which appeared to be problems *within* mathematics were in fact just confusions in what was said *about* mathematics which resulted from an incorrect description of mathematics. Like language, mathematics must be in order just as it is, and the belief that philosophical investigations of mathematics might have repercussions *within* mathematics and perhaps show that certain areas of mathematics were in some way invalid must be mistaken. Philosophical problems about mathematics, as about anything else, are, in Wittgenstein's view, simply a matter of not seeing things clearly. When we achieve a clear *Übersicht* of the subject matter under consideration the problems should disappear. In philosophy of mathematics a first step towards achieving this is to separate the mathematics from the comments, asides and explanations which accompany it — what Wittgenstein calls 'prose'. The proof of a theorem is mathematics, but a verbal explanation of its significance is 'prose'. As Wittgenstein explained to Waismann, 'It is very important to distinguish as strictly as possible the calculus and this kind of prose. Once people have become clear about this distinction all these questions, such as those about consistency, independence, etc., will be removed' (*WVC* p. 149). In this passage Wittgenstein contrasts the verbal 'prose' which accompanies mathematics with the 'calculi' which make up mathematics itself. Wittgenstein is using the term 'calculus' in a special sense, and in fact this concept of a calculus lies at the heart of Wittgenstein's account of mathematics. So I now want to discuss some aspects of this concept and show how Wittgenstein's views on some specific topics flow from it.

Frege had thought that either mathematics was simply about the properties of marks on paper or else those marks *stood for* something and what they stood for was the subject matter of mathematics. Since, for example, the sign '0' does not have the property that when added to the sign '1' it yields the sign '1', Frege argued that mathematical propositions must be about certain abstract entities. But Wittgenstein showed that there is a third alternative. For consider the question 'what is chess about?' Plainly it is not about the properties of the pieces used to play the game, but on the other hand the pieces do not *stand for* or *mean* anything in Frege's sense. Wittgenstein gives the same answer to the question 'what is mathematics about?' 'I have been asked ... whether I believe that mathematics is about strokes of ink on paper. To this I reply that it is so in just the sense in which chess is about wooden pieces' (*WWk* pp. 103-4) Wittgenstein is thus saying that mathematical formulae do not *stand for* or *mean* anything in themselves, but have significance only in so far as they are manipulated according to rules. A 'calculus' is just a particular procedure for manipulating mathematical formulae which is defined simply by its rules. In Wittgenstein's usage to 'calculate' means to operate within a calculus, so that any piece of mathematics, be it a piece of algebra, analysis or arithmetic, is just as much a piece of *calculation*. Wittgenstein's account of mathematics can now be stated very simply. 'Mathematics consists entirely of calculations' (*PG* p. 468), and so it is a mistake to think that in mathematics we are dealing with *propositions*; for mathematics has no subject matter and is not *about* anything. A mathematical 'proposition' is not a *proposition* at all, for it is just a piece in the symbolic game and has no *sense*. Mathematical 'propositions' thus cannot be true or false, and so 'proof' in mathematics is not proof at all in the logical sense. Even mathematical propositions which contain words have no sense and do not express genuine propositions. Here too we are just dealing with a formula in a calculus which is a mere piece in the game along with all the other signs. 'In mathematics', Wittgenstein tells us, 'everything is *algorithm* and nothing *meaning*; even when it doesn't look like that because we seem to be using *words* to talk *about* mathematical things. Even these words are used to construct an algorithm' (*PG* p. 468).

Traditional philosophers of mathematics have all failed to realise this, and as a result have puzzled over the status of mathematical propositions — are they truths of logic (Frege and Russell), synthetic *a priori* propositions about our forms of sensible intuition (Kant), or descriptions of mental constructions (Brouwer)? Wittgenstein shows that there are no mathematical propositions or truths, and so all the theories of traditional philosophy of mathematics which flow from the assumption that there are, are so many *Luftgebäude*. In set theory the idea that Cantor was proving propositions about the 'transfinite' generated storms of controversy. But both Cantor's supporters and his opponents were talking nonsense for, as Wittgenstein remarked in another context, 'the decisive move in the conjuring trick has been made, and it was the very one we thought quite innocent' (*PI* §308).

This view of mathematical 'propositions' leads to radical differences between Wittgenstein and all the traditional philosophies of mathematics. In particular it makes it quite clear that Wittgenstein could not have been a finitist of any sort, for even the finitist thinks that mathematics proves propositions *about* something.

A picture which many traditional philosophers of mathematics have endorsed sees certain parts of mathematics — set theory and the various branches of mathematical logic — as more fundamental than the rest. Consequently it has been thought that it is philosophically illuminating to study those parts of mathematics, the so called 'foundations of mathematics'. For example, an eminent contemporary logician and philosopher, Jaakko Hintikka, has said that 'it is not likely that any substantial progress can be made in the genuinely philosophical study of mathematics without using the concepts and results of [symbolic logic and foundational studies] to a much greater extent than has happened so far'.[10] Wittgenstein is completely opposed to such a view. Of course any philosophically valuable work in philosophy of mathematics requires a knowledge of more than elementary school mathematics, but Hintikka's suggestion that the so called 'foundations of mathematics' are peculiarly relevant to the philosopher is mistaken. Wittgenstein's position is that 'the *mathematical* problems of what is called foundations are no more the foundations of mathematics than a painted rock is the support of a painted tower' (*RFM* p. 378). The 'foundations of mathematics' are in no way more fundamental than any other part of mathematics. They have merely been made to *look* as if they are because of the terminology which has been incorporated into these calculi, and in this way they have acquired their aura of philosophical significance. But appearances are misleading — 'Certain parts of mathematics tend to be regarded as specially deep ... [They are] as any calculus ... If you think you're seeing into unknown depths — that comes from a wrong imagery' (*LFM* p. 254).[11] The idea behind the traditional conception is 'since the propositions of the rest of mathematics can be analysed into propositions about set theory and mathematical logic (as the efforts of the logicists showed) then the propositions of set theory and mathematical logic are those which support the rest of mathematics and on which the validity of other branches of mathematics depends'. But for Wittgenstein, since there are no mathematical *propositions*, the whole picture is a false one. Results in algebra, topology and analysis, etc., do not logically depend on propositions about 'foundations' because they are not *propositions* and do not logically depend on anything. If mathematics can be said to have foundations at all they are of quite a different kind from that usually supposed. Mathematics has its foundations in the activity of calculating and outside this neither has nor needs any other foundations. 'What we have to do is to describe the calculus — say of the cardinal numbers — that is, we must give its rules and by doing so we lay the foundations of arithmetic. Teach it to us and you have laid its foundations' (*PG* p. 297).

An immediate consequence of Wittgenstein's description of mathematics as consisting 'entirely of calculations' is that there can be no 'metamathematics'. Metamathematics is conceived of as expressing propositions *about* mathematics in a formal metalanguage, but since for Wittgenstein the calculi of mathematics do not express anything, a formal mathematical 'metalanguage' cannot express propositions about mathematics. The only language which can do this in the way metamathematics is supposed to is ordinary non-formalised language, but this is 'prose' and not mathematics. For Wittgenstein, so-called metamathematics is just more mathematics on all fours with the rest. It is no more *about* mathematics than chess is about draughts. If the calculi of 'metamathematics' appear to contain propositions about mathematics then this is just the misleading result of their containing words as well as other signs, but here as everywhere else in mathematics 'everything is algorithm and nothing meaning'. Wittgenstein used his favourite analogy to explain this point to Waismann: 'I can play with chessmen according to certain rules. But I can also invent a game in which I play with the rules of chess, and the rules of the game are, say, the rules of logic. *In that case I have yet another game and not a metagame.* What Hilbert does is mathematics and not metamathematics. It is another calculus just like any other' (*PR* p. 319). This radical attitude to metamathematics means that metamathematical results like Gödel's incompleteness theorem, decidability results, etc., have only as much philosophical significance as any other mathematical theorem, to wit, *none.*

Hilbert's whole motivation for inventing 'metamathematics' was to deal with the problem of consistency and, as we should expect, Wittgenstein's radical views about metamathematics go hand in hand with equally radical views about questions of consistency. Wittgenstein's way of dealing with the problem of consistency is to show us what an inconsistency in mathematics *really is* so that it becomes clear that the traditional ideas about inconsistency and the need for consistency proofs have arisen from an incorrect characterisation of what it is for a mathematical calculus to be inconsistent. The root of the trouble is the mistaken idea that in mathematics we are dealing with propositions. As Wittgenstein said to Waismann: 'the idea of inconsistency ... is contradiction, and this can only *arise in the true/false* game, i.e. when we are making assertions' (*PR* p. 321). Wittgenstein's basic thesis is of course that 'playing the true/false game' is just what we are *not* doing in mathematics. In mathematical calculi all we do is *calculate*, and we do not *prove* anything in the logical sense, and so the possibility of producing a logical contradiction does not arise. Since all we do is calculate all that can go wrong is that we find ourselves in a position where we cannot calculate further, and once this point has been grasped the need for a consistency proof vanishes, for it is seen that when an inconsistency arises in mathematics, the situation is precisely analogous to finding that the rules of a game conflict, and is as easily dealt with. 'If an inconsistency were to arise between the rules of the game of mathematics, it would be the easiest thing in the world to remedy. All we have to do is to make a new stipulation to cover the case where the rules conflict and the matter's resolved' (*PR* p. 319). The discovery of an inconsistency in a mathematical calculus is nothing more than a momentary hiatus in our calculating which is over once we have laid down a new rule to resolve the conflict. The philosophical need for consistency proofs vanishes because all it means to say that a calculus is consistent is that we *can* calculate in it and no proof is needed to tell us whether this is the case or not. Indeed no proof *could* tell us that, for no piece of mathematics could *prove* anything.

Formalist philosophers of mathematics think that the fact that we can go on calculating in a calculus is not sufficient to show that it is consistent, for might there not be hidden inconsistencies waiting to be discovered? But Wittgenstein would reply that it is nonsense to talk of 'hidden inconsistencies', for 'an inconsistency is only an inconsistency when it arises' (*PR* p. 319), a point he makes vividly with the following example: 'Suppose two rules of a game were to contradict one another. I have such a bad memory that I never notice this, but always forget one of the two rules or alternately follow one and then the other. Even in this case I would say that everything's in order. The rules are instructions how to play, and so long as I can play they must be alright. They only cease to be alright the moment I *notice* they are inconsistent, and the only sign for that is that I can't apply them any more!' (*PR* pp. 321-2).

In his paper on the *Remarks on the Foundations of Mathematics* Alan Ross Anderson singled out Wittgenstein's view on inconsistency for special criticism. According to Anderson in 'trying to alter our attitude towards contradictions Wittgenstein sometimes seems to be recommending that we stop playing the consistency-game altogether',[12] and he criticises Wittgenstein for describing the formalist attitude towards inconsistency as 'the superstitious fear and awe of mathematicians in the face of contradiction' (*RFM* p. 122). But once we see inconsistency for the harmless thing it is we see the pointlessness of Hilbert's programme of proving the certitude of all mathematical methods by giving consistency proofs. Taken to its proper conclusion Hilbert's view implies that there is no point in doing any further mathematics until the calculus in question has been proved consistent. But if Wittgenstein is right we can perfectly well describe such an attitude as 'superstitious fear and awe in the face of contradiction'. Wittgenstein is not of course suggesting that we just ignore inconsistencies when they arise and stop 'playing the consistency-game', as Anderson seems to suggest, but simply showing us that inconsistencies can only be dealt with when they arise and dealt with very easily at that.

It might appear that Wittgenstein's position implies that mathematicians ought to stop doing consistency proofs, for if they see what an inconsistency really is then the pressing need for such proofs vanishes. But Wittgenstein is not committed to such a view. He has nothing to say about what are called 'consistency proofs' in mathematics *qua* mathematics, but he wishes to point out that since they are not *proofs* of anything they do not prove anything about consistency. The search for relative consistency proofs is a major interest of set theorists. But Wittgenstein's position in no way affects the status of such proofs as perfectly respectable mathematics. They can be called 'consistency proofs' on the grounds that the word 'consistent' appears in the calculus, but Wittgenstein wishes to make it clear that the words 'consistent' and 'inconsistent' are just signs in the calculus like any others, and this does not mean that those calculi have anything to do with *consistency*. Just as everywhere else in mathematics here too 'everything is algorithm and nothing meaning'.

I now want to turn to another aspect of Wittgenstein's views on mathematics which brings out in a different way the distance between his approach and traditional philosophies of mathematics. Apart from sharing a conception of philosophy of mathematics as a critical and revisionary activity the logicists, formalists and intuitionists also shared a picture of mathematics as a single homogeneous and monolithic structure. In contrast to this Wittgenstein emphasises that the calculi which make up mathematics are extremely diverse and heterogeneous — what he calls the 'motley' of mathematics. Since philosophy is a descriptive activity it should do justice to this fact about mathematics. The philosopher 'feels changes in the style of a derivation which a contemporary mathematician passes over calmly with a blank face' (*PG* p. 381). These changes in style are in fact of great philosophical importance since they reveal where one calculus stops and another begins. It is one of the philosophically misleading effects of rewriting mathematics in an axiomatic way, as advocated by logicists and formalists alike, that it obliterates this all important 'motley'. The formalist and logicist ideal of presenting mathematics as a single all-embracing axiomatic system would 'veil the important forms of proof to the point of unrecognizability, as when a human form is wrapped up in a lot of cloth' (*RFM* p. 162) so that far from being a prerequisite of a clear philosophical view of mathematics it would be a major obstacle to it. Here, as with consistency proofs, we should stress that Wittgenstein is not impugning such axiomatic projects *qua* mathematics. His objections are aimed solely at the philosophical view which motivates this kind of project, namely the idea that such axiomatisation provides mathematics with secure foundations and reveals its fundamental structure. As we have seen, Wittgenstein regards this whole programme as nonsensical, but the mathematics produced in the attempt to carry it out is just as respectable as any other *qua* mathematics. It is only when such axiomatised mathematics is thought of as *replacing* non-axiomatised mathematics and as being a better version of the *same thing* is the all-important motley obscured. When it is recognised that axiomatisation just produces more new and different mathematics and just adds to the motley collection of calculi which make up mathematics then all is well. So, for example, Wittgenstein would regard axiomatic set theory and 'naive' set theory as just two different calculi, one no better or more rigorous than the other.

The traditional picture of mathematics is misleading in another way, for it leads to thinking of more complex calculi as extensions of simpler ones, e.g. the real numbers are thought of as an extension of the integers. This way of thinking is, in Wittgenstein's view, totally misguided. *Each* calculus, he stresses, is complete and self-contained with no gaps which need to be filled in by 'extensions' of the calculus, and this is true no matter how simple the calculus may be. Indeed, to talk of 'extending' a calculus is nonsense, for since a calculus is defined by its rules if we add a new rule then we have not extended the old calculus but invented a new one. Thinking of one calculus as an extension of another is like thinking of chess as an extension of draughts.

One of the most important consequences of the fact that each calculus is autonomous is that *all* calculi are, *qua* calculi, on an equal footing from a philosophical point of view. This is of great importance for the philosophy of mathematics for if our aim is to understand the concept of a calculus and the associated issues, then, from a philosophical point of view, one calculus is as good, i.e. as interesting as any other. 'None of them is more sublime than any other' (*PG* p. 334). It will therefore be just as philosophically illuminating to consider very simple calculi as to consider more complex ones. In fact there are good philosophical reasons why simpler calculi are considerably better suited to the philosopher's purposes, for the more complex a calculus is the greater the danger of committing what is in Wittgenstein's view the original sin of traditional philosophy of mathematics and confusing the calculus with the surrounding 'prose'. Also with more complex calculi there is more danger of getting involved in purely mathematical problems which are none of the philosopher's business. Wittgenstein thought that in 'foundations' these dangers were at their greatest, and the fact that they have been preoccupied with just these areas of mathematics is no doubt the main reason why traditional philosophers of mathematics have been led so far astray. In contrast to this Wittgenstein wants to focus our attention on the simplest calculi so that the genuinely *philosophical* problems can be seen the more clearly and the *Übersicht* which is needed to dissolve them can be more easily achieved. But this in no way implies that Wittgenstein is interested solely in such very simple calculi. As he put it, 'with my full philosophical rucksack I can only climb slowly up the mountain of mathematics'.

This brings us back to the topic with which I started, Wittgenstein's alleged finitism. It is easy to see that it is his concentration on only the most simple calculi which has been largely responsible for misleading people into thinking that Wittgenstein is a finitist. For example, the following passage from the *Blue Book* has been cited by Kielkopf[13] in support of his strict finitist interpretation of Wittgenstein. 'If I wished to find out what sort of thing arithmetic is, I should be very content indeed to have investigated a finite cardinal arithmetic. For (a) this would lead me on to all the more complicated cases, (b) a finite cardinal arithmetic is not incomplete, it has no gaps which are filled in by the rest of arithmetic' (p. 20). I think it is clear enough that what Wittgenstein is actually doing here is setting out the methodological principle explained above and this has nothing to do with what he himself referred to as 'the absurdities ... of what the finitists say' (*LFM* p. 111).

I have only scratched the surface of the wealth of material which Wittgenstein has left us on the philosophy of mathematics, but I hope it is clear from even such a brief and selective survey that Wittgenstein as a philosopher of mathematics has much to offer that is highly original and of great interest. When it is more fully studied his work on mathematics may well provide a much needed impetus for a genuinely *philosophical* philosophy of mathematics, in contrast to the disquisitions on the niceties of mathematical logic which often pass for philosophy of mathematics. At present, however, everything is still to be done to bring this about.[14]

Notes

*This is a revised version of a paper which originally appeared in *Philosophical Quarterly* (January 1977).

1. G. Kreisel, 'Wittgenstein's *Remarks on the Foundations of Mathematics*', *British Journal for the Philosophy of Science*, *9* (1958-9), p. 158.
2. Michael Dummett, 'Wittgenstein's Philosophy of Mathematics', *Truth and Other Enigmas* (Duckworth, London, 1978), p. 169.
3. Ibid., p. 180.
4. P. Bernays, 'Comments on Ludwig Wittgenstein's *Remarks on the Foundations of Mathematics*', *Philosophy of Mathematics: Selected Readings* (ed. Paul Benacerraf and Hilary Putnam) (Blackwell, Oxford, 1964), p. 522.
5. Ibid., p. 519.
6. Ibid., p. 522.
7. Kreisel, 'Wittgenstein's *Remarks on the Foundations of Mathematics*', pp. 147-8.
8. C.F. Kielkopf, *Strict Finitism: An Examination of Wittgenstein's 'Remarks on the Foundations of Mathematics'* (Martinus Nijhoff, The Hague, 1970), p. 186.
9. Ibid., p. 182.
10. J. Hintikka (ed.), *The Philosophy of Mathematics* (London, Oxford University Press, 1969), p. 1.
11. Cf. Wittgenstein's remarks about the 'charm' of Cantor's work (*LA* p. 28).
12. Alan Ross Anderson, 'Mathematics and the "Language Game"' in Benacerraf and Putnam (eds.), *Philosophy of Mathematics: Selected Readings*, p. 489.
13. Kielkopf, *Strict Finitism*, p. 177.
14. I have been much helped in writing this paper by Anthony Hodgetts, Roger Picken, Colin Radford, Michael Sissons and Philip Welch. My discussions with Hartley Slater were particularly helpful.

62

The Foundations of the Foundations of Mathematics

S.G. Shanker

Where do the origins of the foundations dispute lie? It has generally been assumed that the answer to this question is relatively straightforward, and that the impetus for the investigations into the foundations of mathematics can be traced back directly to the nineteenth-century revolution in analysis; or rather, that the movements in analysis and the birth of logicism were both part of the same search for mathematical rigour.[1] Certainly Frege perceived the matter in these terms, and at the beginning of *Foundations of Arithmetic* he deliberately sought to align his efforts with the mainstream of the investigations into the foundations of analysis:

> The concepts of function, of continuity, of limit and of infinity have been shown to stand in need of sharper definition. Negative and irrational numbers, which had long since been admitted into science, have had to submit to a closer scrutiny of their credentials.
>
> In all directions these same ideals can be seen at work — rigour of proof, precise delimitation of extent of validity, and as a means to this, sharp definition of concepts.
>
> Proceeding along these lines, we are bound eventually to come to the concept of Number and to the simplest propositions holding of positive whole numbers, which form the foundation of the whole of arithmetic.[2]

The central theme presented here would clearly seem to bear out Dummett's claim that Frege's primary motive in the construction of his *Begriffsschrift* was 'simply to attain the ideal of that rigour to which the whole of nineteenth-century mathematics had been striving'.[3] However, Philip Kitcher has recently disputed this assumption, arguing that this passage glosses over an extremely important difference between studies in the foundations of analysis and the examination of the foundations of arithmetic upon which Frege embarked.[4] The arguments which Kitcher raises are worth serious consideration, if only because they serve to highlight the nature of the philosophical problem underlying the foundations dispute.

Pointing to the example of Leibniz and his followers (e.g. the Bernouilli brothers), whose main concern was to *extend* rather than make the calculus more rigorous, Kitcher argues that whereas nineteenth-century mathematicians were seeking to clarify the concepts of analysis in order to expand their application, thus enabling analysis to resolve more diverse types of problems, Frege's purpose in the search for a 'sharp definition' of the concept of number was to place mathematical knowledge itself on a firm foothold of epistemological certainty:

[F]oundational work is not usually undertaken by mathematicians because of apriorist epistemological ideas, but because of mathematical needs... [T]he foundational work of the great nineteenth-century mathematicians... was not inspired by any exalted epistemological aims, but was, instead, an attempt to respond to the needs of mathematical research.[5]

In a detailed 'Case Study' of the development of analysis, Kitcher sets out to substantiate his claim with a close reading of the fundamentally *mathematical* objectives which motivated the great developments in analysis. In each example his purpose is to establish, as in the case of Cauchy, for example, that:

It is a gross caricature to suppose that Cauchy's work was motivated by a long-standing perception that mathematics had lapsed from high epistemological ideals and that it was accepted because it brought relief to a troubled mathematical community.[6]

Cauchy's foundational activities were prompted

not in response to an urgent problem of rigorization, but simply because his approach to *other* analytic problems in terms of the concept of limit permitted him to incorporate reconstructions of reasonings about infinitesimals which had previously been offered.[7]

Similarly, Weierstrass' foundational activities were spurred by 'his desire to extend the elliptic function theory of Abel and Jacobi'.[8]

Frege's concerns, however, were categorially different from these purely mathematical concerns, as is demonstrated in the following passage:

There is little cause for satisfaction with the state in which mathematics finds itself at present, if you have regard not to the outside, to the amount of it, but to the degree of perfection and clarity within. In this respect it leaves almost everything to be desired if you compare it with the ideal you may reasonably propose for this discipline, and when you consider that by its very nature it ought to be better fitted to approach its ideal than is any other discipline. If you ask what constitutes the value of mathematical knowledge, the answer must be: not so much what is known as how it is known, not so much its subject-matter as the degree to which it is intellectually perspicuous and affords insight into its logical interrelations. And it is just this which is lacking.[9]

Clearly we are meant to be concerned with the final two sentences in this passage, which provide the background for Kitcher's criticism. Kitcher is certainly quite right to draw attention to the importance of the epistemological framework of Frege's logicism. The only trouble with Kitcher's argument is that very much the same sort of sentiments as those which Frege expresses frequently occur in writings dealing specifically with the foundations of analysis.

As early as 1743 we find D'Alembert complaining that the chief problem in mathematics is that:

Up to the present ... more concern has been given to enlarging the building than to illuminating the entrance, to raising it higher than to giving proper strength to the foundations.[10]

As Kitcher himself admits, this was a refrain that was to become a standard introduction to foundational activities in analysis. Even Cauchy begins the *Cours d'Analyse*, as Kitcher acknowledges, with the declaration:

As for my methods, I have sought to give them all the rigor which is demanded in geometry, in such a way as never to run back to reasons drawn from what is usually given in algebra.[11]

There can be no denying that Kitcher has made out an extremely strong case for his distinction between mathematical and philosophical activities; but what are we to make of his argument that we must distinguish between two species of foundational activities in the light of this *prima facie* contradictory evidence? Kitcher himself tries to dismiss the problem as a matter of no importance:

Lagrange, like Cauchy, fulminates against the failure of rigor in contemporary analysis in his preface — and quickly allows himself virtually any algebraic technique that seems useful![12]

The answer to this, of course, is that it is precisely the preface in which we are interested! Or as Wittgenstein repeatedly expresses this point in his writings on the philosophy of mathematics, our interest as philosophers is precisely in the *prose*, the area where mathematicians are tempted to abandon the *terra firma* of their calculations and seek to *interpret* their results.

If there is a fault to be found in Kitcher's argument, therefore, it is clearly not in the demarcation which he draws between the technical work of Cauchy and Weierstrass and the philosophical work of Frege and Russell. Moreover, it is hardly surprising that the professional mathematician should be more concerned with refining and, as Kitcher suggests, expanding the application of the tools with which he works, whereas the philosopher of mathematics is searching for a completely different type of knowledge. But the problem with Kitcher's argument is that he is tempted to overstate his case, assuming that, because someone is involved in the mechanics of mathematics, his sole interest is technical. Indeed, as Wittgenstein struggles to demonstrate in his discussion of Skolem's proof, it is a mistake to assume that the working mathematician is specially guarded against allowing philosophical confusions to enter his mathematical work: even within the actual body of a mathematical proof.[13]

One manifestation of Kitcher's liability to overstatement is the extent to which he ignores the key role which Berkeley played, via his influence on the foundations of analysis, in the genesis of the foundaions of mathematics. Kitcher argues that the influence of *The Analyst* was largely limited to British mathematicians who were eager to defend Newton from any criticism which might have been used to bolster the Leibnizian attacks on Newton's work in analysis:

> After the acrimonious wrangling about priority between Newton and Leibniz, the mathematicians who succeeded Newton were inclined to contrast their own "rigorous" approach to the calculus with the algebraic approach of the Leibnizians. Newton was perceived as following "the true methods of the Ancients," while Leibniz's followers were criticized for their free use of algebraic manipulation of "empty symbols." Hence, when Berkeley challenged the rigor of the Newtonian calculus in 1734, his critique was taken very seriously.[14]

Passing over the question of whether this dispute was as one-sided as Kitcher suggests, what must obviously strike us here are the overtones of the debate which was later to erupt into the foundations crisis. Kitcher insists that it was because of this preoccupation with largely irrelevant philosophical questions that 'the British mathematical community fell further and further behind'.

> Berkeley's critique had unfortunate consequences. Colin Maclaurin, the most talented of Newton's successors, presented his major work on the calculus, the *Treatise on Fluxions,* in cumbersome geometrical style, explicitly responding to Berkeley's objections. In the course of his attempt at defense, Maclaurin was drawn into philosophical issues which are largely irrelevant to mathematical research, and, in an effort to make his mathematics conform to his philosophical presuppositions, he developed a style for the Newtonian calculus which widened the gap between British and Continental mathematics.[15]

On Kitcher's reading, if Berkeley's motives in his investigation into 'Whether the Object, Principles, and Inferences of the Modern Analysis Are More Distinctly Conceived, or More Evidently Deduced, than Religious Mysteries and Points of Faith' were, as Kline also suggests, to thwart 'the growing threat to religion of the mathematically inspired philosophy of mechanism and determinism',[16] then his strategy was expertly chosen; for by diverting the attention of mathematicians from the concrete world of pure mathematics into the nebulous void of philosophy, Berkeley's arguments effectively retarded the development of analysis in Britain. But was that Berkeley's motive?

Certainly Berkeley presents his argument as part of a general defence of religious faith, but there is an empiricist undertone to his argument which if anything is even more important than the actual criticisms which he raises. Berkeley asks

> whether the mathematicians of the present age act like men of science in taking so much more pains to apply their principles than to understand them ... Whether mathematicians who are so delicate in religious points, are strictly scrupulous in their own science? Whether they do not submit to authority, take things upon trust, and believe points inconceivable? Whether they have not their mysteries, and what is more, their repugnances and contradictions?[17]

Before we cast Berkeley in the role of religious obscurantist it is important to notice that there is never any question as far as he is concerned as to whether science deals with a body of truths; and more importantly, for our purposes, there is never any question whether mathematics deals with a body of truths. It is crucial that we recognise that Berkeley accepts the premise that mathematics aspires to be a science, and that the truths yielded by mathematics are categorially identical to the truths yielded by science, and hence demand precisely the same type of evidential support. The importance of this theme cannot be emphasised enough. As important as the sceptical element which Berkeley introduced into the philosophy of mathematics undoubtedly was, equally significant was the very premise which underlay his criticism, and which has haunted the philosophy of mathematics for the past two centuries. Certainly Wittgenstein felt that the principal confusion which he was compelled to attack time after time in the various topics which he considers is the assumption that there is no categorial distinction between mathematical and scientific propositions.

The problem that Berkeley raises is that, as a responsible scientist, it is incumbent on the mathematician to render perfectly precise the manner in which mathematical truths (viz. the inferences drawn from the calculus) have been established.

> I say that in every other science men prove their conclusions by their principles, and not their principles by their conclusions. But if in yours you should allow yourselves this unnatural way of proceeding, the consequence would be that you must take up with Induction, and bid adieu to Demonstration. And if you submit to this, your authority will no longer lead the way in points of Reason and Science.

> I have no controversy about your conclusions, but only about your logic and method.[18]

Clearly no mathematician *qua* self-respecting scientist could refuse the challenge laid down here.

What exactly is the nature of that challenge? On the one hand Berkeley is conceding that mathematics deals with a body of truths, but on the other hand he is objecting: no legitimate science would be content with the lack of rigour and the metaphysical evasions with which you derive these truths.

> That men who have been conversant only about clear points should with difficulty admit obscure ones might not seem altogether unaccountable. But he who can digest a second or third fluxion, a second or third difference, need not, methinks, be squeamish about any point in divinity.[19]

Most bitter of all, Berkeley suggests that mathematicians have arrived at the truth by a 'compensation of errors', where two errors cancel each other out, enabling mathematicians to arrive

> not at Science, yet at Truth, For Science it cannot be called, when you proceed blindfold, and arrive at the Truth not knowing how or by what means.[20]

Berkeley's criticisms found their mark; in the wave of empirical zeal sweeping England, few mathematicians were prepared to countenance Leibniz and Euler's comforting advice that mathematicians could turn a blind eye to the use of metaphysical assumptions in analysis with an easy conscience, provided that they arrived at the right results.[21] But this attitude was hardly confined to the British mathematicians. In 1784 the Berlin Academy offered a prize for the best solution of the 'problem of the infinite':

> The utility derived from mathematics, the esteem it is held in, and the honorable name of "exact science" *par excellence* justly given it, are all the due of the clarity of its principles, the rigor of its proofs, and the precision of its theorems.
>
> In order to ensure the perpetuation of these valuable advantages in this elegant part of knowledge, there is needed *a clear and precise theory of what is called Infinite in Mathematics.*[22]

This announcement provides us with what is perhaps the central theme to bear in mind in response to Kitcher's thesis. The real point is that, so long as the concept of the infinite had not been clarified, the foundations of analysis had not been completed. This is precisely the point that Hilbert stresses at the beginning of 'On the Infinite', where he warns that discussions on the foundations of analysis have not yet come to an end, despite Weierstrass' definitive work on the notions of minimum, function and derivative; for although Weierstrass was able to remove mention of infinitesimals (by reducing propositions about them to propositions about the relations between finite magnitudes), nevertheless Weierstrass was still forced to rely fundamentally on the notion of the infinite in regard to number sequences.[23] Thus, the foundations of analysis should be seen as both the source of subsequent activity in the foundations of mathematics, and in a crucial sense, dependent on these latter findings if it is to be ultimately successful in securing its own foundations. Moreover, not only is it the case that the foundations of analysis and mathematics are inextricably intertwined, but it also bears noting just how important Weierstrass' work in analysis was in the actual development of Hilbert's programme. For Hilbert tells us in 'On the Infinite' that what he was essentially trying to do in the construction of his consistency proof was to emulate Weierstrass' technique in replacing mention of infinitesimals with finitary processes.

This is not the place to become embroiled in a lengthy historical dispute about Kitcher's interpretation of the development of analysis.[24] Whatever the outcome of this debate, we can certainly concede to Kitcher that it is crucial that we recognise the categorial difference between pure mathematical analysis and the foundations of mathematics. But we cannot adopt this attitude to Kitcher's larger thesis that the use of the same term — foundationalism — in each case does not at all mean they are both engaged in the *same type of activity*. According to Kitcher, it is precisely because of the difference that is involved here, which Frege unsuccessfully tried to obfuscate, that *Grundlagen* received so little response from the mathematical community:

> On the account of the interests which motivated research into the foundations of analysis that I have offered above, we can easily understand why Frege's investigations into the concept of number were ignored... Instead of continuing a line of foundational research, Frege contended for a new program of rigor at a time when the chain of difficulties which had motivated the nineteenth-century tradition had, temporarily, come to an end... They failed to provoke a response because the unclarities to which Frege called attention ... did not stand in the way of mathematical research.[25]

But this is an uncharitable interpretation. One might equally well argue — as Frege himself did — that Frege's crime was to bring out into the open the full implications of the foundational problems which mathematicians were struggling to contain.

The basic problem with Kitcher's argument, however, is that it tends to obscure the difference between the historical distinction between pure mathematicians and philosophers of mathematics, and the philosophical distinction between pure mathematics and the philosophy of mathematics. This is precisely the point which Wittgenstein is driving at when he forces us to distinguish between mathematics and prose. One could argue that there are two strands running through the history of foundational activities in analysis: a prose tradition and a mathematical tradition. What Kitcher has done is to focus on the latter element, ignoring — as far as the continental mathematicians are concerned — the presence of the former. The difference between British and continental mathematicians on this point is surely one of degree, not of kind. But it is folly to deny the presence of both threads in the development of analysis on both sides of the Channel during the nineteenth century.

Kitcher weights the argument in his favour by concentrating on the nineteenth century's greatest pure mathematicians, yet not even they were totally immune from the philosophical doubts sweeping the mathematical community, as is betrayed by their excursions into prose in their prefaces. Moreover, it is misleading to call the technical development of analysis which Kitcher isolates the 'foundations of analysis'. Rather, the use of the term 'foundations' referred specifically to the themes that were being discussed in these important prefaces, but the two threads were so closely intertwined that it would have been virtually impossible to try to separate this element out from the technical work which was then immediately pursued. It might well be the case that there is a sharp contrast between what nineteenth-century mathematicians *said* they were doing and what they were actually doing. But what concerns us here is that when they spoke about the need for providing a foundation for analysis, they were thinking of the need to secure the evidence on which the truths of analysis were based. Thus, from its earliest — *philosophical* — use the term 'foundations' has been tied to the need to secure the grounds on which a piece of knowledge is based.

Perhaps the real importance of Kitcher's argument lies, not in the sharp contrast which he wishes us to draw, but rather, in the (increasingly) blurred lines between these disparate activities, and the pressing need to separate out these strands on a *conceptual* level. It is certainly essential that we keep both of these points in mind when we approach Wittgenstein's remarks on the foundations of mathematics: the nature of the *categorial* distinctions between pure activities in analysis and foundational activities, whether in analysis or in the use of fundamental mathematical concepts; and the extent to which this demarcation was obscured by working mathematicians and philosophers alike.

Thus, it is not the calculus which concerns us, it is the prose. But in a fundamental sense, our chief interest in the calculus just does lie in the prose: in the interpretation of what has been accomplished. And as soon as the mathematician or scientist attempts to perform this task, he has exposed himself to the scrutiny of philosophy. Of course, there is a sense in which we can use the term 'foundations' to refer solely to the calculus, but when we speak of the 'foundations crisis', we are specifically referring to the prose. Wittgenstein explicitly addressed this problem when he told his students in 1934:

> When one talks of the foundations of mathematics there are two different things one might mean. One might mean the kind of thing meant by saying that algebra is the foundations of calculus. In order to learn calculus one learns algebra. Mathematics in this sense is like a building, and in this sense a calculus such as *Principia Mathematica* is a bit of mathematics. The bottom layer is the one you begin with. One might also mean by foundations a means of shoring up something that is

problematic. If there were something problematic about mathematics as such, then foundation is less problematic, and giving one does not help. This is not to say that a calculus has no philosophical importance. The drudgery, the calculation, are unimportant, but the calculus may be useful philosophically in showing various things.[26]

Above all else, we must bear in mind Wittgenstein's frequent insistence that his sole concern is with the prose: an insistence based very much on Kitcher's distinction. The technical developments which Kitcher isolates are never, Wittgenstein repeatedly insists, part of his investigation. But running beneath the surface of the technical work in analysis was the ever-present awareness of a sting contained in Berkeley's argument: how can we be certain that mathematics is 'an exact science *par excellence* — that we really are dealing with a body of truths — until we have established the principles whereby we have drawn our conclusions?' Indeed, Berkeley had posed a problem which was to become the *idée fixe* of the foundations of mathematics when he asked:

Query 23: Whether inconsistencies can be truths?[27]

With the discovery of non-Euclidean geometries the somewhat unreflective faith in the truth of mathematics which characterises early writings in the foundations of analysis was seriously rocked: how can we be sure which system of geometry is true, or for that matter, whether any of them is true? Thus, buried within Berkeley's attack are the seeds of a startling sceptical worry. Which brings us back to the sentences we noted above in Frege's argument:

If you ask what constitutes the value of mathematical knowledge, the answer must be: not so much what is known as how it is known, not so much its subject-matter as the degree to which it is intellectually perspicuous and affords insight into its logical interrelations.

Here indeed are grounds to wonder whether, at least as far as mathematics is concerned, if we can discover the solution for one foundations problem we will have understood the principle for resolving the other. For in both areas of the foundations crisis mathematicians and philosophers alike were responding to the same form of worry. Indeed, one might even argue that the real seeds of the foundations dispute extend as far back as the philosophical revolution instituted by the Sophists, who attacked the pre-Socratic philosophers' tacit assumption that knowledge of reality, whether it is acquired by reason or through the senses, is unproblematically possible. When they questioned the justifiability of this premise, the Sophists laid the framework for a general scepticism which is as powerful today as at any time in the history of western philosophy. Epistemology has extended its tentacles into virtually every aspect of philosophical activity, and for two millennia philosophers have stoutly battled the spectre of scepticism.

Despite their preoccupation with the technical problems of analysis, not even pure mathematicians were immune from the doubts being voiced by the philosophers amongst — or within — them.

Notes

1. Cf. R. Bunn, 'Developments in the Foundations of Mathematics, 1870-1910', *From The Calculus to Set Theory 1630-1910* (ed. I. Grattan-Guinness), London, Duckworth, 1980, p. 220.
2. G. Frege, *The Foundations of Arithmetic* (trans. J.L. Austin), Oxford, Basil Blackwell, 1950, pp. 1, 2.
3. Michael Dummett, *Frege: Philosophy of Language*, London, Duckworth, 1981, pp. xxxiv, xxxv.
4. Cf. Philip Kitcher, *The Nature of Mathematical Knowledge*, New York, Oxford University Press, 1983, chapter 10.
5. Ibid., pp. 246, 268. Cf. also 'Frege's Epistemology', *Philosophical Review*, 88, 1979, pp. 238ff.
6. Kitcher, *The Nature of Mathematical Knowledge*, p. 248.
7. Ibid., p. 251.
8. Ibid., p. 257.
9. G. Frege, *Posthumous Writings* (trans. P. Long & R. White), Oxford, Basil Blackwell, 1979, p. 157.
10. Morris Kline, *Mathematics: The Loss of Certainty*, New York, Oxford University Press, 1980, p. 166.
11. Kitcher, *The Nature of Mathematical Knowledge*, p. 247.
12. Ibid., p. 248.
13. Cf. L. Wittgenstein, *Philosophical Grammar* (trans. A. Kenny), Oxford, Basil Blackwell, 1974, Part II, §VI.
14. Kitcher, *The Nature of Mathematical Knowledge*, p. 239.
15. Ibid., p. 240.
16. Kline, *Mathematics: The Loss of Certainty*, p. 145.
17. *The Analyst*, reprinted in *The Works of George Berkeley* (eds. A.A. Luce & T.E. Jessop), vol. IV, p. 102.
18. Ibid., p. 76.
19. Ibid., p. 68.
20. Ibid.
21. Cf. Kline, *Mathematics: The Loss of Certainty*, p. 152.
22. Ibid., p. 150.
23. Cf. 'On the Infinite', reprinted in *From Frege to Gödel* (ed. Jean van Heijenoort), Cambridge, Harvard University Press, 1967, pp. 763ff.
24. Cf. I. Grattan-Guinness' 'The Emergence of Mathematical Analysis and its Foundational Progress, 1780-1880' in *From the Calculus to Set Theory*.
25. Kitcher, *The Nature of Mathematical Knowledge*, pp. 268, 269.
26. *Wittgenstein's Lectures: Cambridge 1932-1935* (ed. A. Ambrose), Oxford, Basil Blackwell, 1979, pp. 121, 122.
27. Berkeley, *The Analyst*, p. 95.

63

Wittgenstein on Some Questions in Foundations of Mathematics

Alice Ambrose

'Philosophy is a battle against the bewitchment of our intelligence by means of language.'[1] This pronouncement in Wittgenstein's posthumously published book is an index to the philosophical outlook which prompted Wittgenstein to scrutinize with the greatest attentiveness the language in which philosophers have stated their problems. Each problem is according to him the product of an obsession — a linguistic obsession that is not recognized.[2] In consequence of this the philosopher envisages his task not as the elimination of the obsession, but rather as the solution of a scientific problem. It is as if he had to find out something new, as if he faced a question of fact about which we do not yet know enough.[3] 'The real discovery', Wittgenstein says, 'is the one that makes me capable of stopping doing philosophy when I want to. — The one that gives philosophy peace, so that it is no longer tormented by questions which bring *itself* in question.'[4] The sign that this discovery has been made is that we cease to seek a *solution* of a particular philosophical problem. These problems are not the kind that have a solution, in the usual sense of 'solution'. They should *dis*solve, '*completely* disappear',[5] once clarity about our use of language is achieved.

Rather than launch into an extended discourse on method I shall try here to exhibit Wittgenstein's procedure in dealing with certain philosophical problems, and I shall at the same time expound the substance of what he had to say about them. The problems I have chosen come from the foundations of mathematics. They were treated by Wittgenstein in lectures I attended in Cambridge in 1934-35 and in the 1939 lectures on foundations of mathematics of which I possess notes. Initially I shall set a question which Wittgenstein did not formulate in precisely my fashion; but my formulation provides a springboard for the exposition of his treatment of problems intimately connected with it.

I shall begin with a question which parallels Kant's question about pure mathematics: How is applied mathematics possible? How is it that *a priori* propositions have an application to matter of fact? The puzzle suggested by this question is, more specifically, the puzzle as to how an *a priori* proposition, e.g. 2 + 3 = 5, can both be true independently of matter of fact and be true of collections of two apples and three apples. If *a priori*, such that its truth-value is unaffected by any theoretically possible state of affairs, it can give no information about any actual state of affairs. How then can it be about apples? Puzzlement about this may very well have been one source of Mill's denial that '2 + 3 = 5' is anything more than an empirical generalization. If it cannot both be true regardless of fact and also imply a truth about apples or other observable objects — in particular about objects which do not coalesce or reproduce themselves in the course of being counted — one must discard one of the two seemingly incompatible accounts of it. Mill discarded the account of it as a necessity. And yet the arithmetic statement '2 + 3 = 5' seems obviously to possess all the properties ascribed to necessary truths: it can be known without recourse to experience; its opposite would be self-inconsistent; no state of affairs could possibly disconfirm it, nor would any be required to confirm it. How then can one account for the harmony between the two quite different areas of logic and of empirical fact? How is that that we can apply arithmetical calculations to physical objects, or trigonometric calculations to physical lines and angles? Is there a genuine mystery here or only a gratuitous puzzle?

The suggestion which my question makes, unlike that which Kant intended by his, is that there is a difficulty in conceiving any application of a proposition of logically incorrigible status to matters of fact — that application is impossible. The question thus has what Wittgenstein singled out as the earmark of every philosophical difficulty: the presence in its expression of the words 'cannot' or 'must', or their equivalents. These are the words which signalize a philosophical obsession. How, we ask, *can* the statement '2 + 3 = 5', whose truth is independent of experience, apply to apples, i.e. be such that the numerical equality it asserts not only tallies with, but seems to be empirically established by, a count of the members of the two sets of apples, and seems even to *predict* the empirical result of counting? As Russell said, 'We do not know who will be the inhabitants of London a hundred years hence; but we know that any two of them and any other two of them will make four of them. This apparent power of anticipating facts about things of which we have no experience is certainly surprising.'[6]

But the applicability of mathematics is not surprising to common sense. That arithmetic, geometry, and trigonometry have an application is a commonplace, and no philosopher in his ordinary pursuits questions whether mathematical propositions can apply to matters of fact any more than he questions whether motion is possible. But one cannot as a philosopher dismiss the question by an appeal to common sense. The common-sense answer to 'How can "2 + 3 = 5" imply a truth about collections of apples?', namely, 'It simply does', is true; but it is not the proper answer to the philosophical question. The proper answer should rid one of the puzzle. This, says Wittgenstein, is the business of philosophy: to rid one of puzzles which do not arise for common sense.[7] Doing philosophy according to him consists of three activities: first, seeing the common-sense answer to these problems; second, getting oneself so deeply into the problems that the common-sense answer seems unbearable;[8] and finally, getting oneself from that situation to the common-sense answer again. But the common-sense answer by itself is no solution; one must first allow oneself to be dragged into the mire and then get out of it.[9]

Were it proper to describe an arithmetic proposition as an empirical generalization having no exceptions, then its application to fact would present no puzzle. But tempting as it is to escape a difficulty in this way, I think it is clear that we should do violence to the current usage of the term 'empirical generalization' were we to take this way out. For an empirical generalization can be falsified, and it is clear that we will accept nothing as a counter-instance to '2 + 3 = 5'. Mill's theory re-classifies arithmetic propositions, and furthermore, in such a way as to leave us with no proper use of the word 'necessary'.[10] For if arithmetic propositions are not necessary, we are at a loss to describe what would be necessary, just as we should be at a loss to say what would be a religious belief if the description 'religious belief' were refused to 'There is a God'. Wittgenstein says that what he does under the name 'philosophy' 'may in no way interfere with the actual use of language'.[11] 'It is not our aim to refine or complete the system of rules for the use of our words in unheard-of ways.'[12] 'What *we* do is to bring words back from their metaphysical to their everyday usage.'[13]

Let us begin then with acceptance of two facts: (1) that it is proper to describe mathematical propositions as necessary, and (2) that applied mathematics is possible. Whatever the philosophical difficulties involved, these are the facts which common sense dictates that we begin and end with. But philosophical difficulties in which it is easy to become mired do exist. I shall try to expound these difficulties as Wittgenstein envisaged them, together with the attempts he made to clarify them and, by clarification, to dissolve them. These are all intimately connected with whatever problem may be felt about the possibility of applied mathematics, though Wittgenstein did not make this particular problem central in the cluster of related problems he investigated. All of them concern the connection of mathematical propositions with experience, and in my opinion it would not be a misrepresentation of Wittgenstein to say they all arise directly or indirectly from the misleading question, 'What are mathematical propositions *about*?'.

It has sometimes been held that '2 + 3 = 5' is a proposition about numbers, necessarily true in virtue of the nature of numbers, whereas '2 apples + 3 apples = 5 apples' is a proposition about apples, which is factually true in virtue of the nature of the apples our world provides — non-generating, non-coalescing apples. We can use arithmetic to count, and to predict the result of adding two apples to three, because, so it is claimed, it is a fact about apples that they do not either vanish or multiply when this operation is performed. The application of arithmetic thus depends on whether or not certain empirical conditions are satisfied. It will be true then to say 'If no apples disappear or multiply, 2 apples + 3 apples = 5 apples', but not unqualifiedly true that 2 apples + 3 apples = 5 apples. Now Wittgenstein says that whether this is a correct account of the proposition '2 apples + 3 apples = 5 apples' is to be determined by the *use* we make of it. It is not that the use is determined by whether the proposition states a contingent truth about apples or a necessary connection between concepts. If, unexpectedly, apples increase or diminish in number when addition is performed, and we accept this fact as constituting a falsification, then our statement is experiential. But if we excuse every case in which five apples fail to be present when three apples are added to two, i.e. if no such fact is accepted as disconfirming it, then our statement is necessary. One and the same sentence can be used in either of these two ways, and of course it is a fact that the latter way is by far the more usual.

If we examine this more usual use of '2 apples + 3 apples = 5 apples', i.e. to express a necessary proposition, we shall see its proper relation to the empirical fact that apples remain discrete when added. This fact is not an empirical condition of the truth of the proposition it is used to express; rather, that this proposition applies to apples is the criterion for their having remained discrete. And if in an imaginable case it did not apply, i.e. if the number of apples counted was not five, this would be the criterion, not for the equation's falsity, but for the number of apples not having remained constant during the process of their being counted. Similarly, that the equation '2 quarts + 3 quarts = 5 quarts' does not hold for the *physical* addition of two quarts of alcohol to three quarts of water indicates something about the mixture of these substances, but the behaviour of these substances when mixed implies nothing about the truth of '2 quarts + 3 quarts = 5 quarts'. Their behaviour does imply the falsity of the statement '2 quarts physically added to three quarts yield five quarts', but it is logically irrelevant to the statement which asserts the arithmetic addition of units — as our usual use of this statement shows.

One likely source of the temptation to disregard how such a statement functions (as necessary rather than empirical) is the compulsion to ask, and to answer, the question, 'What is the proposition about?' 'About apples', 'about discrete entities', etc., are the natural answers. Similarly, 'about numbers' is the natural answer to 'What is "2 + 3 = 5" about?'; and of course it cannot be denied that it is proper to distinguish this proposition from empirical propositions by characterizing it as being about numbers. But our question, according to Wittgenstein, is misleading, since we thereby treat '2 + 3 = 5' as analogous to empirical propositions, and only differing from them in being about non-empirical, abstract entities. Mathematics, according to this way of looking at it, becomes a sort of physics of mathematical entities, and mathematical research an expedition of discovery. This is the conception which Professor G.H. Hardy had. He writes: 'I have myself always thought of a mathematician as in the first instance an *observer*, a man who gazes at a distant range of mountains and notes down his observations. His job is simply to distinguish clearly and notify to others as many different peaks as he can....'[14]

Wittgenstein says that philosophy arises out of prejudices in favour of certain grammatical forms. We try always to work from one paradigm, which operates as a grammatical obsession.[15] 'What are mathematical propositions about?' is a question motivated by the obsessional emphasis on the analogy of these propositions to empirical ones. To rid one of this obsession it has some point to say, as Wittgenstein says in a number of places, that arithmetic propositions are not about numbers, nor are geometric propositions about geometrical figures. But this is also misleading, since, like Plato's answer to this question, it seems to give information in the way in which a scientific answer does. If we wish not to be misled we shall do well to direct our attention away from the question as to what they are about to the *use* we make of them. And by examining their use the connection between their necessity and their application will no longer appear puzzling.

Now what we do when we allow nothing to count against a proposition, when we enshrine it amongst the incorrigibles and refuse to surrender it in the face of any conceivable facts is to assign to the expression for the proposition a special rôle in our language. According to Wittgenstein we have decided on using the sentence in a certain way, namely, as a rule for the use of expressions, i.e. a rule for the application of certain words.[16] To elucidate, let us consider an example similar to one he used: Suppose I multiply 25 by 17 in order to find out the number of squares in a rectangle 25 squares long by 17 squares wide. If the number of squares is found upon counting not to be 425, the result got by multiplying according to the rules, and I thereupon say '25 × 17 = 425' is false, I use it to express a proposition testable by experience. But if I say it is correct regardless of what number of squares I find on counting, and use it as a criterion of the correctness of my count, I thereby make it independent of experience. And to do this is to resolve on a certain use, namely, that it shall function analogously to a rule for the use of numerical terms — for one thing, that 425 can be substituted for 25 × 17, for another, that the two statements, 'The number of roses I received is equal to the quotient 425/17' and 'The number of roses I received is two dozen', may not describe the same fact. Similarly, the statement that it is impossible to construct a heptagon with straight edge and compasses functions as a rule which prevents my saying with sense, 'I drew a heptagon on the board using only straight edge and compasses'.

Mathematical propositions are *preparations* for the use of language, says Wittgenstein, almost as definitions are.[17] Note that he does not say they *are* either definitions or statements about symbols; but they function as explicitly formulated linguistic rules in fact function. Euclid's proof that a line can be bisected by a certain method serves to provide a rule for the application of 'equal lengths', and arithmetic serves to give rules for the use of number words, whereas no non-verbal empirical proposition ever functions analogously to a rule governing the use of language. If, then, the function of mathematical propositions is to govern usage it is no more surprising that they have an application than that a knife should cut. The connection between them and their application is like that between a rule for the use of an expression and the occurrence of that expression in various verbal contexts.[18] For example, 'exactly one straight line can be drawn between any two points' functions prescriptively: in understanding it we know it makes sense to say that one physical straight line, but not to say that more than one, is drawn between two points. One tends to look upon the geometrical proposition as asserting a truth about ideal lines which somehow also holds of coarse drawn lines. But the application of a geometrical proposition in an experiential context is to show, not what is true or false, but what makes sense or nonsense.[19] It obscures an important difference between empirical generalizations and their purported instances and mathematical propositions and the things to which they apply to say that both kinds of propositions show what is true, or false. Necessary propositions about ellipses and circles show that 'I cut an elliptical cake in eight equal parts' does not make sense, whereas 'I cut a round cake in eight equal parts' does. The relation of the necessary propositions about circles to the physical circle is like that between a rule and its application, not between a generalization about ideal circles and a rough approximation.[20]

This account squares with the fact that mathematical propositions do not get confirmed or disconfirmed by experience: one does not confirm or disconfirm by seeing, feeling, etc., a proposition whose use is to show what makes sense rather than to assert what is in fact true, or false. Further, there are certain puzzles about the connection of mathematics with experience which this account helps clarify. One is that mathematical propositions when applied seem to make predictions whereas, being necessary, they cannot. Suppose we say that two crystals which separately weigh three grams each must together weigh six grams, or that six two-foot boards must fit into a space twelve feet wide. If these are predictions, then they can be false. It could happen that six two-foot boards cover more or less than twelve feet, and that the two crystals weigh more or less than six grams. But '$6 \times 2 = 12$' and '$3 + 3 = 6$' are not predictions. They function as criteria for judging when the boards do not fit or the scales read five, that something *must* have happened.[21] '$6 \times 2 = 12$' does not even assure us that, unless the boards change, six two-foot boards will fit into twelve feet, for the criterion of change is their not fitting. If we say they *must* fit, and cite '$6 \times 2 = 12$' as evidence while at the same time refusing to accept any other method of showing the width of the boards, then, says Wittgenstein,[22] we are not saying anything about measurement. The burden of what we are saying is that what is called two feet is what goes six times into twelve. Were we making an experiment to determine whether six such boards will fit the space, the result would not be fixed in advance, and prediction of the result would be appropriate. The difference between a mathematical calculation and an experiment is that in fixing the rules of the calculation one fixes the result.[23]

What Wittgenstein says about the nature of mathematical propositions also has a bearing on the further puzzle, namely, that we sometimes seem to discover a fact of experience which we then go on to prove must be so. It looks as if a matter of fact has an *a priori* demonstration. Pythagoras' theorem is a case in point. But the puzzle is gratuitous. According to Wittgenstein what happens is that an empirical proposition, which experience discovers, is converted into a proposition which no experience could make us give up. The proposition which is made independent of experience is suggested by experience. For example, the proposition, 'A pentagram is a pentagon plus five triangles', is certainly suggested by experience, but it functions as a rule because we allow no method of construction to invalidate it. To see a pentagram as this composite is an experience, but as Wittgenstein says, there is no comparable process of seeing that a rule holds.[24]

Now what may appear as a surprising harmony between mathematical propositions and their application is merely due to our assigning the functions of a rule to those propositions which conform to fact, other things being equal.[25] Because the specific gravity of iron is 7.86 it would be natural and might be useful to say 'No matter what experiment shows, the specific gravity of iron is 7.86'. By this token an empirical proposition would be given a status and function like that of a rule of language. But the matter of fact does not compel acceptance of this change of status. The kind of fact which persuades us to accept it is that it is useful; and that it has applications is a mark of its usefulness. Thus, if we had a world in which counting the members of two groups having 2 members and 3 members, respectively, *never* totalled up to 5, some other proposition than '2 + 3 = 5' would have been adopted as necessary. If circumstances made it practical to calculate differently than we do, e.g. because things multiplied or disappeared regularly upon being counted, we should adapt arithmetic calculation to the circumstances.[26] If we got different results every time we counted the squares of a rectangle 17 by 25, we should probably not say the calculation, 17 multiplied by 25, was a proof that 17 × 25 = 425. We might still call the calculation a piece of arithmetic just as 'it is not the case for all *a* and *b* that $a \times b = b \times a$' is a part of group theory. But we should either have different arithmetics, or we should have an arithmetic in which certain multiplications had different results. For example, as our world is now, there is no phenomenon for which '23 × 18 = 800' has any use. But if these numbers were constants relating to all natural phenomena, says Wittgenstein,[27] we could imagine an arithmetic in which this multiplication, among all others, had two results. To the objection that it is in the nature of 23 and 18 to give 414, he replies that in giving a rule of multiplication we do not give an infinity of applications of it. Behind the use of a rule is a habit of reacting in a certain way. Given the rules of multiplication we do in fact agree in getting the result 414; to do this is natural. And it is this fact which makes us say this result is correct. But we can imagine having always agreed in getting 800. And if this were in fact the case, would not 800 be the *correct* result? What would it be like to say that we always had made a mistake in thinking 23 × 18 = 800? Our agreement, not that such and such a result *is* the case, but *in getting* that result, is what determines what is called a correct calculation. Thus arithmetical propositions, though independent of experience, are in two ways dependent upon experience: in being suggested by experience, and in having their special function rest on common linguistic habits.[28]

In the remainder of this essay I should like to examine certain things which Wittgenstein appears to be saying concerning the connection between the necessity of mathematical propositions and their origin in and application to matter of fact. He seems to be saying that it is by an arrangement of ours that, for example, the arithmetic proposition 2 + 3 = 5 tallies with the empirical result of counting two groups of 2 and 3 things, respectively, and that if circumstances were different, so that counting the members of such groups never resulted in 5, we should adapt counting to the circumstances and accordingly have a different arithmetic. That is, if circumstances were different, we should have a different necessary proposition. A proposition can be 'suggested by experience and then made independent of experience'.[29] Thus an expression which is given a special place in our language by being used to denote a necessary proposition is somehow connected with fact. I should like to examine both the hypothesis and the consequent of the statement, 'If circumstances were different we should have a different necessary proposition'; for there is an unclarity about both.

How are we to understand the words 'circumstances such that the members of two groups of 2 and 3 things, resp., never total up to 5'? One possible interpretation of these words, though I advance it with hesitation and without intending to imply it was Wittgenstein's, is the following: that the juxtaposition of two groups of objects, each of which we correctly counted as having 2 and 3 members, respectively, should result in the creation or destruction of, say, one individual, so that subsequent counting of the combined sets showed more, or fewer, than 5 objects. It is of course perfectly conceivable that something like this should happen. Wittgenstein has said[30] that if, for example, things disappeared regularly in certain ways it might be practical to count differently, that one might adapt one's technique of counting to the circumstances. Our arithmetic might then include the statements '$2 + 3 = 4$', '$1 + 1 = 1$', etc. That is, we should adopt those as expressing necessary propositions, so that in the exceptional case when our final count was 5, or 2, we should say not that these propositions were false, but that the objects must have reproduced, just as now we say, when one object put in juxtaposition with another results in one, 'the objects must have coalesced', or 'one must have vanished'. That we should say this sort of thing is a sign that we are in the two comparable cases taking '$2 + 3 = 4$' and '$2 + 3 = 5$', respectively, to be necessary: we accept nothing as a falsification.

Throughout this paper it will be noted that I am interpreting Wittgenstein to be taking arithmetic to consist of what are commonly called necessary propositions, i.e. propositions that are both non-empirical and *true*. The problem is to explain the connection of such propositions with matter of fact, with their application. Professor G.E. Moore, relying on lectures of the period 1930-33, points out[31] that Wittgenstein characterized '$2 + 3 = 5$' and the like as 'rules of grammar', 'treating only of the symbolism', and as being neither true nor false. This Wittgenstein undeniably did; '$2 + 3 = 5$' was said to be a rule specifying a possible manner of speaking or writing (which one might adopt or not). But he also stated at various times that '$2 + 3 = 5$' is not a definition nor *about* the symbolism in the way '"$2 + 3$" is interchangeable with "5"' is about the symbolism, although it is used analogously to the way we use such a rule. For example, it prevents our saying such things as 'I augmented my savings of three hundred dollars by two hundred more but did not have a total of five hundred'. Moore thought he might be using such an expression as '$2 + 3 = 5$' in two different ways, to express a necessary proposition and to state a rule for using words or sentences, and even that when he used it in the first way it expressed something neither true nor false.[32] But it is obviously self-contradictory to describe necessary propositions as being neither true nor false; and one can find support in Wittgenstein's lectures (e.g. in his comparison of necessary and empirical propositions) for his supposing them to be *true*, though of course not true in the sense in which an empirical proposition is true. It may be no consistent account is to be had. I am going to assume that though he holds that such expressions as '2 + 3 = 5' are *used* to proscribe certain linguistic combinations,[33] he also holds that they do nonetheless express necessary truths, and hence that in a world of coalescing objects what is expressed by '2 + 3 = 4' might be a necessary truth.

Now in this hypothetical world is it proper to say we should have a different *arithmetic* — in particular, that *arithmetical* addition of 2 and 3 would yield a different result than 5? We can easily conceive of '2 + 3 = 4' expressing a necessary proposition (it is easy to conceive of the involved symbols being used differently), but if we use '2', '3', and '4' as we do now, surely the meaning of some other symbol or symbols must change. The natural assumption is that '+' can no longer mean arithmetic addition of two numbers, nor '=' arithmetic equality. '2 + 3' must denote not the arithmetic sum of two numbers, but the physical combination of two sets, and '=' must mean something like 'yields'. '2 + 3 = 4' would be a shorthand for '$(x). 2x + 3x = 4x$', interpreted as '2 things physically conjoined with 3 yield 4'. But it describes this world paradoxically to say its arithmetic is different from ours. '2 + 3 = 4' only appears shocking if taken to express an equality between a number and an arithmetic sum of numbers, as it does now. If '+' had a different usage in this hypothetical world, and if we also had our arithmetic for sums of numbers, the expressions '2 + 3 = 4' and '2 + 3 = 5' both could without inconsistency express necessities, although confusion might result. And if there were but one arithmetic, what we might call the arithmetic of invariant coalescence, it is misleading to say that we have made '4' and '2 + 3' interchangeable as though *in preference to* '5' and '2 + 3', since '2 + 3' has two entirely different uses when equated with '4' and with '5'. The sentence 'In different circumstances some other proposition would be necessary' suggests that were facts different we should arrange that the *addition* of 2 and 3 would necessarily yield a different result. This is unobjectionable if we reinterpret 'addition'. What Wittgenstein says is then little more than that in a different world we might have a different language. What is interesting about his statement is the claim that a difference in the language of arithmetic is influenced by the exigencies of making application of arithmetic to fact.

There is reason to suppose that what I have described as possibly illustrating a circumstance in which we might have a different arithmetic, and the account I have given of it, is not in fact what Wittgenstein had in mind. It will be worthwhile to consider an example which Professor Moore reports in Wittgenstein's 1930-33 lectures,[34] in order to note differences and to elaborate what Wittgenstein has said. In this example I think it is clear that '+' continues to be interpreted as arithmetic addition, however puzzling this may be; and this is the main respect in which it differs from the case I have discussed. I shall alter the numerals used in the lectures so as to make comparison easier. Wittgenstein supposes the following imaginable circumstances: (1) that one has the two experiences of counting first up to 2, then up to 3 in the case of two groups of apples, and (2) then a third and subsequent experience of (correctly) counting *all* the apples and finding only 4. This is imaginable because it is a mere matter of experience that one usually finds 5, inasmuch as apples do not vanish without cause. '2 + 3 = 5' makes no prophecy as to what experience one *will* have upon counting *all* the apples. But if one were to find 4 apples, the most natural comment to make would be that one must have vanished. By this comment Wittgenstein says we can only mean 'If we keep to the arithmetical rule "2 + 3 = 5" we have to say "one must have vanished"'. In analyzing this latter statement and what he takes to be its consequences Moore augments the circumstances (1) and (2) above by two further ones which he supposed Wittgenstein to have had in mind as the situation in which one made the comment 'one apple must have vanished': (3) that one knows, because one has kept watch, that nothing has happened to account in any normal way for there being only 4, (4) that one does *not* know, by counting done by oneself or by someone else, that one has counted out a total of 5, so that if one said there were 5 apples in all, this would be a deduction from the fact that one had counted out 2 + 3 of them. It is important to keep circumstance (3) in mind in appraising the consequences Moore draws from his analysis of Wittgenstein's claim that by 'one must have vanished' we can only mean 'If we keep to the rule "2 + 3 = 5" we must say "one must have vanished"'.

Suppose one says there are 5 in all. Moore claims that Wittgenstein's reason for explicating 'one must have vanished' as he did, is that 'there are 5', if asserted under circumstances (1) and (4), means something different from what it would mean had one discovered by counting, rather than deduced, that there are 5, namely, B: 'One keeps to the rule "2 + 3 = 5" if one asserts there are 5 apples and violates it if one asserts anything inconsistent with saying there are 5'.[35] And this is the only thing meant by 'there are 5' in circumstances (1) and (4). Now one can keep to the rule, i.e., speak correctly, without saying what is true: it can be correct but not true to say there are 5. Moore concludes that Wittgenstein's insistence on proposition B as the only thing that we mean by 'there are 5' is intended to prevent the mistake of supposing we mean 'If one sets out 2 + 3 apples then *necessarily* one sets out 5'. This proposition Moore takes Wittgenstein to suppose is false, which is to say he supposes it imaginable that one should count 2 + 3 apples and that a correct count of the total *at that very time* should show only 4. Further, Moore thinks that whether or not this interpretation of Wittgenstein is correct, it is quite certain that he held that '2 + 3 = 5' is never used in arithmetic to express a proposition from which it follows that if one counts out 2 + 3 apples one necessarily counts out 5.[36] In this case I should take it that neither '2 + 3 = 5' nor 'If one has 2 + 3 apples one has 5 apples' is a necessary proposition.

Wittgenstein has at various times certainly said things which support the account Moore has given, e.g. that '2 + 3 = 5' is 'purely arbitrary', which suggests that there is no necessity about 'If one counts out 2 + 3 apples the total is 5'. I am not now in a position to judge whether this account of what Wittgenstein held is in fact correct, although I heard the 1932-33 lectures in which there was some discussion of the example under consideration. Nor for that matter am I sure that I am correctly reporting what he said in the lectures I heard in 1934-35 and in later lectures to which I have access at second-hand. If Wittgenstein did commit himself to holding it to be imaginable that one should count out 2 + 3 apples and not at the same time have a total of 5, I think, with Moore, that he was surely mistaken. If he did, then 'If one counts out 2 + 3 apples one has a total of 5' would be an empirical proposition. But I wish to make plain that I have not supposed him to imply this and my criticism will not presuppose thinking he does.

For one thing, (a) when Wittgenstein said that '2 + 3 = 5' functions analogously to a rule of language, i.e., so that 'I counted out 2 + 3 apples but did not at that time have a total of 5' does not make sense, I took it that what does not make sense could not express an imaginable state of affairs. Further, the reason for its not expressing an imaginable state of affairs is that the truth of 'the total is not 5 apples' is inconsistent with the truth of 'I counted out 2 + 3'. That is, if I did count out 2 + 3 apples it necessarily is *true* that I counted 5. It is not merely that I must engage in this manner of speaking (and say there are 5) if I am to speak in accordance with a rule. This certainly seems to me to be correct, although I am not at all sure but that Wittgenstein held what Moore reports.

For another thing, (b) what makes convincing Moore's concluding that Wittgenstein held to be imaginable a logically inconceivable state of affairs is circumstance (3) of the example. (3) is to the effect that it is *known*, because one has kept watch, that nothing has happened to account in any normal way for there being only 4 apples, e.g. it is known that none has been removed, or has flown away. Only if Moore means that knowing this implies that *none has vanished* could it be inferred that one could set out 2 + 3 apples which total up to 4. But if we *know* that none has vanished, should we say, on counting 4, 'one must have vanished'? I doubt that Wittgenstein intended this circumstance to figure in the example he was considering; rather, it seems to me that he supposed not that one knew an apple had *not* vanished, but that one did *not* know that it had, although it in fact had, by some process quicker than sense-observation could detect. When Moore says he can imagine that one really has vanished, even under circumstance (3),[37] it appears that he also is holding not that one knows none has vanished but that one merely knows none has vanished *in any normal way*, though one has in fact done so. But then it could not be inferred from Wittgenstein's example that he held that one could set out 2 + 3 apples and have *at that time* 4. Rather, if one set out 2 + 3 apples and one vanished, one would have 4. And then we should have our present arithmetic — unless '2 apples + 3 apples = 4 apples' were interpreted as a statement about physical combination.

However, Wittgenstein made a comment on the example, according to my lecture notes of 1932-33, which might well have led Moore to suppose that

Wittgenstein is committed to holding it to be imaginable that one should set out 2 + 3 apples and have a total of 4. The comment was that in circumstances (1) and (2) we can *either* say 'one must have vanished' or we can '*change the rules*'.[38] That is, we can choose either to say 'I set out 5 apples' (and thereby speak in accordance with the present rule '2 + 3 = 5') or to adopt the rule '2 + 3 = 4' — and accordingly speak correctly in saying 'I set out 4'. Moore took it that since we can speak correctly without saying what is true, it could conceivably be false that one set out 5 apples when one set out 2 + 3. Wittgenstein's insistence that 'there are 5' only means 'If the rule "2 + 3 = 5" is adhered to one must say one put 5', Moore took to indicate that a proposition commonly held to be true was false, namely, 'If one sets out 2 + 3 apples *necessarily* one sets out 5'. And if this is false it would seem that one could set out 2 + 3 apples and not have a total of 5.

I have placed a different construction on what Wittgenstein said. Because he held that as language is used 'I set out 2 + 3 apples but did not have a total of 5' does not make sense, I am supposing (as Moore does not) that he held that '2 + 3 = 5' is used in arithmetic to express a proposition from which it follows that if one set out 2 + 3 apples one necessarily sets out 5, that is, that if '2 + 3 = 5' is a necessary proposition so is 'If I set out 2 + 3 apples I have a total of 5'. And the latter *is* necessary because '2 + 3 = 5' expresses a necessity, as we use language now. When Wittgenstein says that under circumstances (1) and (2) one can either say 'one must have vanished' or change the rules, I take him to be saying that either we can keep to our present arithmetic, whence 'If I set out 2 + 3 apples I have 5' would be necessary, or we can have a different arithmetic, whence, for example, 'If I set out 2 + 3 apples I have 4' would be necessary. Thus with present arithmetic 'I counted out 2 + 3 but did not have a total of 5' would express a self-contradiction, and *with a different arithmetic* it would be a redundancy expressing a possible state of affairs. But what is expressed would be contingent on which arithmetic we chose. Now it is rather different to think (as I believe Moore did) that Wittgenstein is committed to holding it to be possible that one should set out 2 + 3 apples and have only 4 and to think him committed to holding that it would be possible *if* our arithmetic were different. It must be admitted, however, that the one position seems no whit better than the other. The example seems rather clearly to use '2', '3', '4', '+', and '=' precisely as we do now: the numerals to stand for the numbers we correlate with a couple, a trio, and a quartet, '+' to mean addition (not physical conjunction, as in my first interpretation), and '=' to mean 'equals'. But if this is their use it is difficult to know what could possibly be meant by saying '2 + 3 = 4' is necessary, or by saying that if our arithmetic were different (e.g. if this proposition were necessary) then it would be necessary that if I set out 2 + 3 apples I should have a total of 4.

The unclarity about this matter makes it unclear what is meant by saying that depending on the circumstances different propositions would be necessary. I should like now to examine this claim together with the view Wittgenstein apparently held that it is a matter of choice whether or not '2 + 3 = 4' expresses something necessary (whether we have 'a different arithmetic'). According to Wittgenstein *we adopt* necessary propositions, and which ones we adopt is 'suggested by experience'. Present circumstances are such that we deduce 'I set out 5 apples' from 'I set out 2 + 3'; but we could choose to deduce 'I set out 4 apples' instead. The fact that the arithmetic in use tallies with the result of counting is presumably explained by our choice being suggested by experience. Facts do not compel the choice, but they suggest it. Other things being equal, we take as necessary the proposition conforming to fact.[39] For example, were we to say 'The specific gravity of iron is 7.86, no matter what experiment shows', we should thereby make independent of experience a proposition which experience suggests. Had we a different arithmetic presumably the difference would be explained by what is suggested by experience: in our example, by the experience of always finding 4 apples when one counts out a couple and a trio.

But now *what* is suggested by experience? That it would be useful to adopt *these propositions* as necessary? *These* propositions are first of all factual truths, empirical propositions. Hence *they* cannot be made independent of experience, i.e. *these* propositions cannot be necessary. One and the same proposition cannot depend for its truth or falsity on matter of fact and also have its truth-value quite independent of fact.

Suppose one maintains instead that because the proposition expressed by the sentence '2 + 3 = 4' is true as a matter of fact, this suggests making the *sentence* express something which no fact will falsify — something Wittgenstein possibly meant. The sentence, '2 + 3 = 4', which is first understood as expressing a generalization about sets of things in juxtaposition or about the number one arrives at by counting a couple and a trio, is made to express something to which the behaviour of sets of things or the experience one has upon counting the total group comprised of 2 + 3 objects is irrelevant. It is made to do this by being made to serve an entirely different purpose — to function as a rule for the use of the expressions '2 + 3' and '4'. What once served to express a generalization which a different world could confute comes to serve as a guide in the conduct of language, proscribing such statements as 'I put 3 apples into a bowl containing 2, but there were in all more than 4.' The proscription, of course, is not of a falsity but of a use of language — of the use of '2 + 3 but not 4' to characterize any set of objects. What experience 'suggests' is then the *choice* of language — because such a choice would be useful.

Does this description of the change in status of the sentence '2 + 3 = 4' explain the harmony between the arithmetic proposition and the fact that 4 is the result got by counting a couple and a trio? Does it explain the connection of the necessary proposition with its application? The difficulty I find is in specifying any connection between the sentence expressing a necessity and the empirical proposition originally expressed in the same words. When the truth of the proposition '2 + 3 = 4' was verified by experience, the expression '2 + 3 but not 4' at that stage had a use, whereas at the stage where the sentence is taken to express what is necessary this same expression is thereby denied a use. And this is to say that '2 + 3' has different uses, i.e. different meanings, at the two stages. '2 + 3' means something in the one case which is inconsistent with 'not 4', and in the other case not. If the sentence '2 + 3 = 4' has different meanings at the two stages, what connection is there between the sentence for the necessary proposition and the observed fact that when a couple and a trio are counted the result is found to be 4 — i.e. with the fact which verifies the empirical proposition which the sentence no longer expresses?

Notes

1. *Philosophical Investigations* (New York, Macmillan, 1953), p. 47.
2. Lectures, 1934-5.
3. Ibid.
4. *Philosophical Investigations*, p. 51.
5. Ibid.
6. *The Problems of Philosophy*, p. 132, 17th impression (Oxford University Press, 1943).
7. Lectures, 1934-5.
8. In this connection C.D. Broad's comment on common sense is worth remarking: 'Let it go out and hang itself' (*The Mind and Its Place in Nature*, p. 186).
9. Lectures, 1934-5.
10. See M. Lazerowitz, *The Structure of Metaphysics* (Routledge & Kegan Paul), pp. 258-59.
11. *Philosophical Investigations*, p. 49.
12. Ibid., p. 51.
13. Ibid., p. 48.
14. 'Mathematical Proof', *Mind*, Vol. XXXVIII (1929), p. 18.
15. Lectures, 1934-5.
16. Lectures, 1939.
17. Ibid.
18. Lectures, 1939.
19. Lectures, 1934-5.
20. Ibid.
21. Ibid.
22. Lectures, 1934-5.
23. Ibid., 1939.
24. Ibid., 1934-5.
25. Ibid.
26. Lectures, 1939.
27. Ibid., 1934-5.
28. Ibid.
29. Lectures, 1939, 1934-5.
30. Ibid., 1939.
31. 'Wittgenstein's Lectures in 1930-33', II, *Mind*, Vol. LXII (1954), no. 251, pp. 298-308.
32. Ibid., p. 302.
33. Note that such might be their use without their translating into rules 'treating of the symbolism'.
34. *Loc. cit.*, 302-4.
35. Ibid., p. 306.
36. *Loc. cit.*, 307-8.
37. *Loc. cit.*, 309.
38. Here is a clear case of Wittgenstein's characterization of '2 + 3 = 5', etc., as rules. I shall use his language in expounding what he said.
39. Lectures, 1934-5.

64

Wittgenstein and the Correlation of Logic and Arithmetic

Emily Grosholz

Wittgenstein's philosophy of mathematics has not received the attention it deserves. I believe that this is partly due to his failure to support and amplify his many profound insights into the constitution and growth of mathematical knowledge with evidence drawn from the history of mathematics. Wittgenstein wrote, after all, in a philosophical context where the historical dimensions of knowledge were generally slighted, and long before the importance of history of science to the analysis of scientific knowledge was fully recognized. His peculiarly atemporal notion of 'language game', for example, cannot do the conceptual work he requires of it, to explain how mathematical knowledge is justified, or why mathematics should be regarded as a motley, a collection of heterogeneous fields. In this essay, I will explain how certain kinds of historical evidence can clarify and deepen arguments found in *Remarks on the Foundations of Mathematics*[1] and *Wittgenstein's Lectures on the Foundations of Mathematics.*[2]

I

The combinatorial facts of arithmetic, like $7 + 5 = 12$, can be translated into sentences of Russell's system of logic, and will in fact be theorems of that system. Thus the translation of $7 + 5 = 12$ into logical notation can be furnished with a proof, its derivation from the axioms of Russell's system. Wittgenstein represents Russell as claiming that the correlated translation and associated proof justify the arithmetical rule $7 + 5 = 12$ and secure it from skeptical attack. For the axioms of logic are so clearly true, it is argued, that they are immune to skeptical questioning, and the rules of inference are guaranteed to transmit that immunity. Likewise, the correlation of the whole system of rules of arithmetic with the corresponding logical theorems serves to justify the whole of arithmetic and preserve it from the skeptic. (And similarly, it is assumed, for the other branches of mathematics, geometry, analysis and so forth.)

What worries Wittgenstein about Russell's project is his foundation-alism, his attempted homogenization of mathematics (assimilating all other branches to logic), and his platonism. The foundationalist narrowly construes the justification of mathematical knowledge as deducibility from true axioms; once an allegedly adequate set of axioms is given, all the truths of mathematics will be given along with it. On this account, genuine invention in mathematics is impossible. But what most interests Wittgenstein, and myself, in rational mathematical practice is the variety of strategies for justification (not all of which involve establishing relations of deducibility) and invention radical enough to extend mathematical systems in ways which, while natural and mathematically fertile, cannot be proved from what was accepted before. Such strategies, moreover, cannot be properly understood unless one recognizes the heterogeneity of mathe-matical domains, their partial autonomy and complex relations of interdependence.

Finally, Wittgenstein also attacks Russell's platonism, which he seems to equate with the assumption that all the truths of mathematics are somehow 'already given'. However, as I will argue, one can examine the issues of justification and invention without becoming embroiled in the classical debate between platonism and other theories about the ontological status of mathematical objects, which actually distracts from the issues without clarifying them. The best place to look for evidence in this examination is the history of mathematics.

II

One of Wittgenstein's favorite avenues of approach to the question of mathematical justification and invention is the topic of correlation. Given a certain initial correlation of two mathematical systems, what justifies our decision to extend it in a certain way? His insight is that in certain situ-ations the correlation is itself a novel element, which cannot be deduced from either of the initial correlates taken in isolation.

However, the examples which he chooses to illustrate this insight, and the use which he makes of them, are disappointingly sketchy. For example, he discusses at length the case of correlating natural numbers with the roots of a polynomial equation.

> If you have *only* the sign, it isn't clear offhand how you should count it:
>
> $$-\frac{a}{2} + \sqrt{\frac{a^2}{4} - c}$$
>
> Suppose we said, 'This has two parts'. Would this be absurd? Not at all. It would really be laying down a rule. If you say, 'These are really two parts, only looking alike; so are these; and thus there are four' — this is all right, but the application will be different. And whether one rule or the other should be adopted depends on consequences, practical consequences. (*Lectures*, p. 154)

A little further on, Wittgenstein remarks that the notion of 'root' might be translated into Russell's notation, but such a translation would not determine how roots are to be counted. 'But this does not mean that from Russell it *follows*.' What justifies the choice of how to count roots is surely not a deduction from the laws of logic.

But then, what does justify it? Wittgenstein says merely, 'practical consequences', and this is just where the introduction of historical illustration would be appropriate. In order to understand what justifies the decision to stipulate that a polynomial of degree n will have n roots, which entails recognizing negative and complex numbers as roots, one must analyze the development of algebraic geometry, to see how this decision reorganized and unified the field, and opened up certain lines of research within it. For example, Euler saw that it was necessary first to sort out the difficulties involved in multiple and imaginary roots before a result of Apollonius (for the case m = n = 2) could be generalized properly: that two algebraic curves, of degree m and n, will intersect in mn points.[3]

What justified the decision to count roots in a certain way was, at the very least, the successful solution of extant problems, the generation of new ones, and the development of new methods for ordering and realigning items and problems in algebraic geometry. My contention is that claims about mathematical items are justified with reference to the constellation of problems and methods in which those items are (always!) embedded. Such constellations are sometimes (in recent times, more frequently) accompanied by a partial axiomatization, but this collection of axioms and theorems should be regarded as derived from, and dependent upon, the problem-constellation. Henceforth in this essay I will refer to a grouping of problems, items, methods and problem-solving techniques which display the unity that we require of a science as a mathematical field.[4]

As Jean Cavaillès has argued so persuasively, the striking feature of mathematical fields is their tendency to grow beyond previously established boundaries. Solutions to given problems will often generate new problems, which will require ever more complex and profound methods for their solution. This open-endedness of mathematical fields is covered over by the artificial closure of axiomatization. Even those fragments of mathematics which seem adequately covered by formal theories (for example, the decidable theory of compact, two-dimensional manifolds) disguise important exclusions. What about manifolds of higher dimension? Or those characteristics of naively-conceived topological objects which are not captured by the notion of manifold or simplicial complex?[5] Or those topological problems which simply are not amenable to the methods of algebraic topology?

III

Another one of Wittgenstein's favorite examples involves the researches of Cantor on the transfinite. Wittgenstein observes that Russell assumes that any two classes, even infinite ones, which can be put in one-to-one correspondence have the same cardinality, without worrying about what justifies this assumption. Indeed, it rests upon Cantor's work, in which he extends the correlation of cardinal numbers and sets into the transfinite.

> You can interpret 'correlate' in such a way that you'll say, 'Yes, there are as many ...' But in what sense can you say you have *proved* this? You do a new thing and you *call* it 'correlating them one-one'; and you call an entirely new thing 'having the same number'. All right. But you have not found two classes which have the same number; you have only invented a new way of looking at the thing. (*Lectures*, p. 161)

What justifies the extension of the correlation between sets and cardinal numbers from the finite cases into the transfinite? Wittgenstein is certainly right that the claim that there are, for example, 'as many' natural numbers as even natural numbers cannot be proved solely by appeal to mathematical facts which were accepted prior to Cantor's extension. The extension itself establishes new facts. But the interest of the matter lies in the detail of Cantor's work. What relations precisely did he establish between the finite and the infinite cases? If some strict relation of deducibility does not account for the extension, then what relation might? Here again Wittgenstein disappoints, for he only makes rather vague reference to his notion of language game.

> Mathematical truth isn't established by their all agreeing that it's true — as if they were all witness to it. Because they all agree in what they do, we lay it down as a rule, and put it in the archives. One of the main reasons for adopting this as a standard is that it's the natural way to go — for all these people. (*Lectures*, p. 107)

A brief look at Cantor's work will indicate some of the answers to the questions which Wittgenstein raised but did not answer.[6] The extension of arithmetic into the transfinite which appears in *Grundlagen einer allgemeinen Mannigfaltigkeitslehre* was initially a response to problems in functional analysis, concerning whether certain functions could be uniquely represented by trigonometric series. Cantor generalized his results by proving first that the representation would continue to be unique when the function behaved badly on a finite number of points in its domain, and then, most significantly, on an infinite number of points. During these studies, Cantor's attention shifted from the functions themselves to sets of points in their domain of definition. He began to realize that the study of these sets posed problems related to the structural properties of the continuum and went on to investigate the differences between denumerably infinite sets like the rationals, and continuous sets like the reals. In his classification of these sets he developed a notation which he eventually came to regard as an extension of the system of (finite) natural numbers. The correlation of number and set, and the prior existence of well-known infinite point sets suggested the hypothesis, by degrees substantiated, of the existence of transfinite numbers.

In the *Grundlagen*, Cantor set forth procedures for generating and ordering transfinite numbers, as well as for defining analogues of the arithmetic operations and prime factorization appropriate to them. Though he was forced to modify some of the ordinary algebra of arithmetic to accommodate the peculiar properties of transfinite numbers, nonetheless the resulting structure had, he felt, the determinateness and coherence required of a number system.

Cantor's extension of the number system is justified, then, by certain relations in which it stands to other areas of mathematical research. On the one hand, it arose in a natural way from the study of functions, and indeed played an important role in further developments of that study, the theory of Lebesgue integration and measure theory. On the other hand, it was justified by the strong analogies it displayed with finite arithmetic, by the way it reproduced, on the transfinite level, certain important structural features and problems of number theory. These connections held it in place, so to speak, allowing the development of new techniques and problems in the domain of transfinite numbers, and allowing the transfer of results there back to the fields of number theory and analysis.

IV

I want to give an account of the motley of mathematics (*RFM*, II 48)

I should like to say: mathematics is a *motley* of techniques of proof. — And upon this is based its manifold applicability and its importance. (*RFM*, II 45)

Not only does Russell's project of translating all of mathematics into a collection of theorems of logic disguise the open-endedness of mathematical fields, but it also disguises their real heterogeneity. Russell, in trying to reduce other mathematical fields to logic, minimizes the difficulties of translation.

'It is only a different notation.' Where does it stop being — just a different notation? (*RFM*, II 47)

To minimize these difficulties is to play down the ways in which mathematical fields resist assimilation to each other. One discovers that this is a mistake by examining how correlations between fields are actually established historically. The task of correlation is often far from trivial, when the adequacy of the correlation itself cannot be proved from either of the correlated fields taken in isolation.

When do we say that one calculus 'corresponds' to another, is only an abbreviated form of the first? 'Well, when the results of the latter can be translated by means of suitable definitions into the results of the former.' But has it been said how one is to calculate with these definitions? What makes us accept this translation? (*RFM*, II 56)

However, Wittgenstein does not seem to see clearly how these two themes, the growth of mathematical fields, and the nontrivial nature of their correlation, are linked. I suspect this is because he concentrates so heavily on the correlation between Russellian logic and arithmetic (a topic to which I will return shortly), the point of which eludes him because he is primarily intent on criticizing it, and thus neglects other examples in the history of mathematics where the link is apparent.

It is characteristic of mathematical fields to give rise to problems for which on their own they cannot provide a solution. The point of many correlations, historically, was to connect the field which first generated such a problem with another, auxiliary field, in order to bring the resources of both fields to bear upon the unsolved problem. How this correlation is to be set up in the first place and, having been set up, how it is to be elaborated, must be determined by new principles (and often, indeed, by whole new theories) added to those governing the two original fields.

Descartes' correlation of algebra and geometry is a most interesting example of such a situation. Classical geometry gave rise to Pappus' problem, which the Greeks could neither fully generalize nor solve. This problem consists of the determination of loci whose points C satisfy the following condition: given 2n (or 2n + 1) fixed lines, let the product of the distances from C to n of the lines be equal to, or proportional to, the product of the distances from C to the other n (or n + 1) lines. The following figure illustrates the case for four fixed lines, where one wishes to determine the locus of point C such that CB × CF = CD × CH.

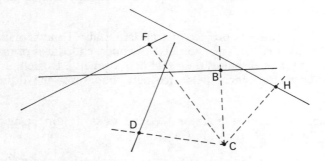

This problem, and its partially completed solution, form the centerpiece of Descartes' *Geometry*.

In the first pages of the *Geometry*, Descartes gives his 'calculus of lines', which correlates the five arithmetic operations, operating on numbers to produce numbers, with geometric constructions, operating on line segments to produce line segments. This correlation is initially an hypothesis, which conjectures that numbers will faithfully reproduce various characteristics of points on the geometric line, and algebraic equations characteristics of geometric diagrams. This correlation must initially be an hypothesis because it is a novel element in the context of problems which gave rise to it. It is transformed as algebra and geometry are transformed and extended under its guidance, to ever more precise and powerful formulations, such as 'there is an order-isomorphism between points of n-dimensional Euclidean space and n-tuples of real numbers', or 'there is a structure-preserving mapping (which turns out not to be an isomorphism) between polynomials and geometric loci'.

It is not, therefore, a simple task to answer the question, what justifies this correlation, first in its initial stages and then later on. This question bothered Wittgenstein, but he does not have enough to say in answer to it.

> A new proof gives the proposition a place in a new system; here there is often a translation of one kind of operation into a quite different kind. As when we translate equations into curves. And then we realize something about curves and, by means of that, about equations. But what right have we to be convinced by lines of thought which are apparently quite remote from the object of our thought?
> ... If you ask: 'What right have we?' the answer is: perhaps none. — What right have you to say that the development of this system will always run parallel with that one? (*RFM*, V 7)

Descartes' first way of justifying his correlation was to exhibit a (partial) solution of Pappus' problem. In Book I of the *Geometry*, Descartes shows how to reduce the problem of determining the geometric loci in the case of four fixed lines to solving a system of equations in two unknowns, relating all the lines involved to two specified lines. For three or four fixed lines, the equation of the locus will be a quadratic, for five or six lines, a cubic, and so forth. In Book II, he gives an exhaustive treatment of the loci constructed in the cases of three and four fixed lines, indicating that a similar procedure would work for the increasingly complex cases of $n > 4$ fixed lines. Significantly, this indication was a promissory note which Descartes himself could not have cashed in, since he lacked the specific techniques for working back and forth between graph and equation. These techniques were developed by two generations of his successors, and it was Newton who finally managed to give a relatively complete account of all the cubics.

Viewed diachronically, analytic geometry is a successor field to classical geometry. Descartes' solution to Pappus' problem was central to establishing the legitimacy of his correlation-hypothesis because it reproduced results already attained in the predecessor field, that is, it reduced to accepted solutions in established cases, and then went on to exhibit how these results could be extended in systematic fashion.[7] It generated a research program of further problems to be solved, involving a new hierarchy of plane algebraic curves, and gave useful, though incomplete, directives for attacking those problems.

In attempting to carry out Descartes' research program, mathematicians developed ever more powerful and refined methods for working between the algebraic equation and the geometric diagram. These techniques generated new problems which Descartes never foresaw, which became the core of the new interface fields of algebraic geometry and the infinitesimal calculus. The emergence of these fields gave fresh justification to Descartes' correlation-hypothesis, providing the theories to which we now appeal in deductively justifying various correspondences between the realms of number and geometry.

Here we can appreciate the real motley of mathematics. While algebra and geometry continued to generate their own problems independently and were in that sense autonomous, they were now linked by a correlation which was far from being a trivial change in notation. Rather, this link is a substantive one, embodied in the emergent interface fields of algebraic geometry and the infinitesimal calculus, whose theories provide the warrant for that link. Here also the growth of mathematical fields which correlation engenders is apparent.[8]

V

Wittgenstein's remarks on proof are especially interesting, and flawed, when regarded in light of the preceding example. Reacting against Russell's claim that all the truth of mathematics ought to be deducible from a set of logical axioms, he writes,

> The idea that a proof creates a new concept might also be roughly put as follows: a proof is not its foundations plus the rules of inference, but a new building — although it is an example of such and such a style. A proof is a *new* paradigm ...
> The proof creates a new concept ... by giving the proposition which is its result a new place. (*RFM*, II 41)

This observation can be read in two different ways, which Wittgenstein does not properly distinguish. Consider the case of Goldbach's theorem, to which Wittgenstein often refers as an example of a yet-unproved proposition of number theory. What can be said about its possible proof, which hasn't yet been discovered? Wittgenstein says that we have no right to claim that it already exists, folded up, so to speak, in the axioms of number theory.

> Prof. Hardy says, 'Goldbach's theorem is either true or false.' We simply say that the road hasn't been built yet ... The mathematical proposition says: the road goes there. Why we should build a certain road isn't because mathematics says that the road goes there. Because the road isn't built till mathematics says it goes there. (*Lectures*, p. 139)

Now on the one hand it may be that Goldbach's theorem can be proved from the axioms of number theory alone. In this (less interesting) case, there is a sense in which the theorem is not a radically new element, and the axiomatization does already include it, even before it has been articulated. Wittgenstein insists on the radical novelty of *any* proof, I think, because he is attacking what he perceives as Russell's platonism, as if the claim that a proposition is 'already there' before it is articulated entailed the assumption of a shadowy realm of mathematical ideas and some quasi-perceptual access to it. But the claim that a collection of axioms specifies and delimits a certain set of theorems is compatible with many different assumptions about the ontological status of mathematical items. Platonism is not the issue; the issue is the possibility of genuine novelty in mathematics, and how such additions are to be justified.

However, granted that a set of theorems is mechanically generable from certain axioms, those axioms 'plus the rules of inference' do not tell us which theorems are most important nor which proofs of those theorems will be most useful and illuminating. That is, the axiom set alone contains too much information, an overabundance which is ultimately obfuscating and less informative. The discrimination of more from less important consequences of the axioms, and chains of inference through the formal system, must be referred to the collection of solved (and unsolved!) *problems* which constitute the field, of which the formal theory is only a part. Thus the discovery of a particular pathway through a formal theory is new information in the context of the field as a whole.

On the other hand, if Goldbach's theorem turns out to be provable not from the axioms of number theory alone, but involves as well axioms from an auxiliary field (say, functional analysis or set theory) then Wittgenstein's claim that the proof is a new paradigm is true in a much stronger sense.

> One would like to say: the proof changes the grammar of our language, changes our concepts. It makes new connections, and it creates the concept of these connections. (It does not establish that they are there; they do not exist until it makes them.) (*RFM*, II 31)

We have seen that Descartes' proof of Pappus' problem inspired and served as a display-case for Descartes' correlation-hypothesis. Though the original problem was first enunciated within the axiomatized system of Euclidean geometry, its full solution (which Descartes could not yet give) invoked not only the axioms of a much extended geometry, but of algebra and new correlation principles linking geometry and algebra as well. Here the proof plays an important part in making 'new connections', though its creative function must be understood in the context of the fields which gave rise to it and those which it helped generate.

VI

To conclude this essay, I return to the correlation of arithmetic and logic. Wittgenstein's complaint in general is that he cannot see the point of it. The examples he considers are facts of arithmetic, like $7 + 5 = 12$, which may be translated into theorems of logic and furnished with a proof in Russell's system. But, as Wittgenstein rightly points out, these examples already had a solution within arithmetic, that is, the ordinary calculation of sums. The new proof in logical notation is redundant and moreover adds nothing to their certainty.[9] So viewed, Russell's translation does indeed seem pointless. Though Wittgenstein mentions in passing that this correlation of proofs might lead to some 'new insight' (*Lectures*, p. 133), he does not specify what this insight might be, nor does he pursue the matter.

But I would argue that the correlation of logic and arithmetic is useful, in the way that Descartes' joining of algebra and geometry was, though perhaps not so profound or fruitful. The examples which Wittgenstein chose to consider prevented him from seeing this, since the finding of sums, products, and so forth, are precisely the first problems which number theory is equipped to handle, and there is no point in bringing in logic as an auxiliary for their sake.

However, the correlation of logic and arithmetic has served to help solve problems arising in both number theory and logic. For example, Gödel made use of number theoretic results in the proof of his Incompleteness Theorem, imported by the translation of logical formulae into numbers by his technique of Gödel numbering.[10] Paris and Harrington, in their construction of an undecidable sentence of number theory which is more natural than Gödel's, similarly imported number-theoretic results into logic.[11]

In the other direction, the direction with which Wittgenstein is most concerned, the results of Ax and Kochen, solving certain outstanding number theoretic problems concerning Diophantine equations over Q_p (the p-adic completion of the rationals), provide a nice example of the importation of results from logic into number theory. In turn, these results can be transferred back to logic, for they provide a counterexample to Tarski's conjecture that the only decidable fields are the finite, algebraically closed, and real closed fields.[12]

In more general terms, it is also evident that this correlation, as in the case of algebra and geometry, has led to the extension of both original systems. For it has played an important role in the extension of arithmetic from the finite to the transfinite, and in the elaboration of recursion theory, which gives the study of logical formulae unprecedented precision and scope.

In a few of his reflections on correlation, Wittgenstein does allude to this kind of mathematical growth, and modifies his harsh judgment of the translation of arithmetic into logic.

> We might say: we interpret one in terms of the other — which means that we have a way of translating from one to the other. But this works both ways. If you say that Russell gives the point of arithmetic, you can also give the point of Russell by translating Russell into arithmetic. (*Lectures*, p. 266)

This insight requires only adequate illustration.

In this essay, I have tried to retrieve from Wittgenstein's philosophy of mathematics those features which seem to me deepest and most suggestive: his concern with the motley of mathematics, mathematical invention and the variety of ways in which mathematical knowledge is justified. To exhibit these concerns in the best light, I have supplied them with a context of examples from the history of mathematics, and an account of the correlation of mathematical fields based on those examples. Such historical considerations, I believe, provide a critical perspective on Wittgenstein's remarks on mathematics, which at the same time exhibit their intrinsic interest.

Notes

*I would like to thank Robert Fogelin, Carol Wood, Charles Larmore and Alec Fisher for reading various drafts of this paper and giving me many useful suggestions.

1. G.H. von Wright, R. Rhees, G.E.M. Anscombe, Eds. MIT Press, 1967. A posthumous collection of Wittgenstein's unpublished writings on mathematics; I will refer to it as *RFM*.

2. Cora Diamond, Ed. Cornell, 1976. A compilation of class notes taken during Wittgenstein's lectures at Cambridge in 1939; I will refer to it as *Lectures*.

3. For further detail, see *Cours de géométrie algébrique*, Jean Dieudonné, Presses Universitaires de France, 1974.

4. This terminology is borrowed from Nancy Maull, 'Unifying Science Without Reduction', in *Studies in the History and Philosophy of Science* 8 (1977), no. 2, pp. 144f.

5. For an interesting discussion of this exclusion, see the last sections of Imre Lakatos' 'Proofs and Refutations', *The British Journal for the Philosophy of Science*, Vol. 14 (1963), pp. 221-45 and 296-342.

6. For a more extensive account, see *George Cantor, His Mathematics and Philosophy of the Infinite*, by Joseph Dauben, Harvard, 1979.

7. For further discussion of the way in which successor fields are justified by this kind of reference back to predecessor fields, see T. Nickles' 'Two Concepts of Intertheoretic Reduction', *The Journal of Philosophy*, Vol. LXX, No. 7 (1973), pp. 181f.

8. For a more comprehensive discussion of this context, and the pattern of growth which it exhibits, see my 'Descartes' Unification of Algebra and Geometry' in *Descartes: Philosophy, Mathematics and Physics*, S. Gaukroger, Ed., Harvester, 1980.

9. Wearing a skeptic's hat and appealing to the unsurveyability of these logical proofs, Wittgenstein sometimes seems to argue that such proofs are in fact less certain than their arithmetical counterparts. But these arguments are both wrong and beside the point.

10. 'Über formal unentscheidbare Sätze der Principia Mathematica und verwandter Systeme' in *Monatshefte für Mathematik und Physik*, 38 (1931).

11. 'A Mathematical Incompleteness in Peano Arithmetic' in *Handbook of Mathematical Logic*, J. Barwise, Ed., North Holland, 1977, pp. 1133f.

12. 'Diophantine Problems over Local Fields, Part I' in *American Journal of Mathematics*, Vol. LXXXVII (1965), pp. 605f.

65

Wittgenstein and Intuitionism

Robert J. Fogelin

In this essay I shall discuss one important strain that runs through Ludwig Wittgenstein's *Remarks on the Foundations of Mathematics*:[1] his commitment to themes characteristic of the intuitionistic movement in mathematics. Chief among these are his attacks upon the unrestricted use of the Law of Excluded Middle,[2] his distrust of non-constructive proofs,[3] and his impatience with the idea that mathematics stands in need of a foundation.[4]

There is a well-known historical connection between Wittgenstein and the intuitionistic movement. Presumably a person with Wittgenstein's interests would have encountered this movement before 1928, but in any case we know that he heard Brouwer lecture in March of that year. In von Wright's cautious words, "It is rumoured to have been this which stirred him to take up philosophy again."[5] But I shall not here undertake the monumental task of tracing the connections between what Wittgenstein heard in 1928 and what he ultimately wrote in the 1940's. Instead, I shall content myself with exploring these themes as they reach maturity in the *Remarks on the Foundations of Mathematics*.

Broadly speaking, these intuitionistic motifs combine Ramsey's notions of the *normativity* of logic and mathematics with the intuitionists' implicit *modal* conception of mathematical propositions. This synthesis constitutes one of Wittgenstein's most important achievements, for it allows him to bring together a wide range of those commitments that give his later philosophy its characteristic physiognomy. Seeing this will illuminate more than his philosophy of mathematics.

I

Virtually everything that Wittgenstein says about mathematics forms part of a critique of Platonism (or Realism) in that field; most of the remainder is a criticism of unsuccessful attempts to avoid Platonism. There is something inherently compelling about the following reasoning:

228

"5 × 5 = 25" expresses a true proposition. Thus, there must exist a domain of objects that it is true of. Furthermore, it expresses a necessarily true proposition, hence these objects must be ideal, not empirical, objects.

Under the influence of this reasoning (which admits of a much stronger statement) we come to think of mathematics as the natural history of mathematical objects,[6] except that it is not really a natural history since the relevant objects are not natural objects and the method of investigation is not experimental.

Wittgenstein's critique of Platonism goes as deep as possible: he calls into question the root notion that mathematical judgments express assertoric propositions. We can notice some of the things he says on this matter:

> Of course, we teach children the multiplication tables in the form of little *sentences*, but is that essential? (I, 143.)

> We are used to saying "2 times 2 is 4," and the verb "is" makes this into a proposition, and apparently establishes a close kinskip with everything we call a "proposition." Where it is a matter only of a superficial relationship. (I, Appendix I, 4.)

If mathematical constructions are only superficially related to other things that we call propositions, what, in fact, are they like? On this score, Wittgenstein says two things that, at first glance, may seem unrelated. First of all, he says that mathematics is normative:

> The proposition proved by means of a proof serves as a rule — and so as a paradigm. For we *go by* the rule. (I, Appendix II, 4.)

> What I am saying comes to this, that mathematics is *normative*. But "norm" does not mean the same thing as "ideal." (V, 40.)

> Mathematics forms a network of norms. (V, 46.)

Paralleling these passages are others that speak about our *mode of acknowledging* a mathematical expression:

> One might, so to speak, preface axioms with a special assertion sign.

> We give an axiom a different kind of acknowledgment from any empirical proposition.... An axiom, I should like to say, is a different part of speech. (III, 5.)

On one occasion he brings these two strands together:

I am trying to say something like this: even if the proved proposition seems to point to a reality outside itself, still it is only the expression of acceptance of a new measure (of reality). (II, 28.)

Thus if we say straight out what we in fact acknowledge, mathematical expressions undergo the following transformation: "5 × 5 = 25" (acknowledged as a law) becomes "It is a law that 5 × 5 = 25." That Wittgenstein had something very like this in mind is brought out by the following striking passage:

The opposite of "there exists a law that p" is not "there exists a law that $-p$." But if one expresses the first by means of P, and the second by means of $-P$, one will get into difficulties. (IV, 13.)

We might put it this way: mathematical propositions are modal propositions with their modal aspects suppressed.

We can bring these reflections into sharper focus by sketching a modal logic for the operator "It is a rule that ..." In the style of Fitch,[7] we shall lay down natural deduction rules for the introduction and elimination of an R-operator. The introduction rule will employ the following subproof format:

The top 'R' flags the column to its right as a *rule subproof.* We shall call 'ϕ' the strict reiterate of "$R\phi$" and then insist that items may be introduced into a rule subproof only by strict reiteration. We then say:

"$R\phi$" is a direct consequence, by *rule introduction,* of any rule subproof that has no hypothesis and has "ϕ" as an item.

The elimination rule has the following form:

"$-R-\phi$" is a direct consequence of "$R\phi$" by rule elimination.

The system so constructed has obvious analogies with modal system D. The plausibility of this analogy should further emerge as we go along.

Our leading idea is this: *at work* the mathematician suppresses the modal character of his propositions, or, as we can now say using Fitch's perspicuous format, he operates within a rule subproof without attending to the logical surroundings. At the same time, an essential feature of mathematical practice is captured by the introduction rule we have adopted. Why, in particular, is it not simply perverse for the mathematician to exclude an empirical proposition from his derivation when the empirical proposition is quite beyond any sensible doubt? The Platonist answers this by saying that mathematics is not about empirical objects, but about a domain of objects of its own. The present approach offers a viable alternative to Platonism. Empirical propositions are excluded from the mathematician's proofs because his proofs are modal proofs (albeit, with their heads and tails missing).

We can now see why Wittgenstein challenges the application of the Law of Excluded Middle to mathematical expressions. In order to drive "$Pv-P$" (where "P" and "$-P$" are mathematical expressions in their normal guise), we would have to produce "Rp v $R-p$" as the last step of a completed proof, and this is not a theorem of the system we have created by taking Wittgenstein's suggestions seriously. The upshot of this is that the acceptance of "P v $-P$" as an instance of the Law of Excluded Middle is nothing more than a mistake due to the lack of perspicuity of our mathematical language.

> ... the understanding of a mathematical proposition is not guaranteed by its verbal form, as is the case with most non-mathematical propositions. (IV, 25.)

These purely formal results tally exactly with Wittgenstein's comments about the Law of Excluded Middle. The discussion turns upon the following question: Does the pattern ϕ (a particular arrangement of digits, e.g., "770," "777," and sometimes "7777") occur in the infinite expansion of π? Of course, we do not know the answer to this question.

> But what are you saying if you say that one thing is clear: either one will come on ϕ in the infinite sequence, or one will not?

> It seems to me that in saying this you are yourself setting up a rule or postulate. (IV, 9.)

The second passage is crucial for an understanding of Wittgenstein's position; why should adopting this principle amount to setting up a rule or postulate? Do we have any right to assume that the expansion rule either *prescribes* or *proscribes* the occurrence of such an arrangement within the expansion?

> What if someone were to reply to a question: "So far there is no such thing as an answer to this question?"

> So, e.g., the poet might reply when asked whether the hero of his poem has a sister or not — when, that is, he has not yet decided anything about it.

> I want to say: it *looks* as if a ground for the decision were already there: and it has yet to be invented. (IV, 9.)

Why should it even *look* as though "the ground for the decision were already there?" Essentially, this is an illusion generated by a faulty analogy with the finite case.

> "But surely all the members of the series up to the 1,000th, up to the 10^{10}th, and so on, are determined." This is correct if it is supposed to mean that it is not the case that, e.g., the so-and-so-many'th is *not* determined. But you can see that *that* gives you no information about whether a particular pattern is going to appear in the series (if it has not appeared so far). *And so we can see* that we are using a misleading *picture.* (IV, 11.)

For an expansion of finite length, we can simply generate it and see if the pattern occurs. If it does occur, then it is obviously prescribed by the expansion rule; if it does not occur, then it is proscribed in virtue of the fact that the rule of expansion permits *only* the one sequence that it in fact generates. But there is nothing corresponding to this in the infinite case; no sense attaches to the notion of running through the *whole* of an infinite sequence in order to assure ourselves that a given pattern does *not* arise. Nothing, then, rules out the possibility that the rule of expansion simply doesn't cover the case.

But isn't Wittgenstein just wrong about all this? Couldn't we perhaps produce a non-constructive proof showing that the sequence "777" occurs in the expansion of π even though it doesn't show where it occurs? Wittgenstein responds directly to this possibility.

> Well, proved in this way this "existential proposition" would, for certain purposes, not be a *rule.* But might it not serve, e.g., as a means of classifying expansion rules? It would perhaps be proved in an analogous way that "777" does not occur in π^2 but it does occur in $\pi \times e$, etc. The question would simply be: is it reasonable to say of the proof concerned: it proves the existence of "777" in this expansion? This is simply misleading. (V, 34.)

We have thus come to Wittgenstein's second "intuitionistic" theme: his distrust of non-constructive proofs.

Non-constructive proofs come in various forms, but the simplest paradigm is an indirect proof concerning existence. In its classical employment such indirect proofs take two forms: (1) we assume the denial of a proposition, derive a contradiction, and in virtue of this assert it; and (2) we assume a proposition, derive a contradiction, and in virtue of this assert its denial. Wittgenstein's commitments lead to a different treatment of these two proof patterns.

His challenge to the first pattern of proof follows immediately from what we have said about the Law of Excluded Middle. When the classical mathematician attempts to establish "P" by assuming "$-P$," he is *misapplying* the rule of indirect proof by assuming the *contrary* — not the *contradictory* — of the proposition to be established. Schematically, his proof looks like this:

$R-p$ Assumption
.
.
.
$q \& -q$
Rp Conclusion

In fact, it should have the following form:

$-Rp$ Assumption
.
.
.
$q \& -q$
Rp Conclusion

Formally, this replacement of the contradictory by the contrary amounts to accepting the following modal principles:

$-Rp \to R-p$

For other quite natural reasons, the classical mathematician tacitly accepts the entailment in the reverse direction, and as a result, takes over a reduction axiom that altogether destroys the modal character of mathematical propositions. After this move, how can he distinguish mathematical propositions from empirical propositions? For want of a modal distinction, a material distinction is invoked, i.e., mathematical propositions are assigned a special subject matter. Once more we are back to the Realist's conception of mathematics as the not quite natural history of not quite natural objects. This is one important way in which Platonism and the classical employment of an indirect proof are inextricably bound together.

Given a modal interpretation of mathematics, the second pattern for the indirect proof fares a bit better. We can establish something of the form "$-Rp$" by assuming "Rp" and deriving a contradiction from this assumption. Schematically, such a proof would have the following form:

Rp Assumption
.
.
.
$q \& -q$
$-Rp$ Conclusion

What does such a proof establish? Our overriding idea is that mathematical propositions are elliptical for expressions having the form "Rp," and, of course, the derived conclusion does not have this form. We have not established a mathematical proposition by this proof, but a meta-mathematical proposition to the effect that a given rule cannot be introduced without an attendant loss of consistency. This is precisely Wittgenstein's position:

> What an indirect proof says, however, is: "If you want *this* then you cannot assume that: for only the opposite of what you do not want to abandon would be compatible with *that.*" (IV, 28.)

Thus an indirect proof, even when employed properly, cannot be used to *extend* a system. Its only legitimate use is limiting; it shows that the introduction of a new rule would engender a loss of consistency.

How does all this square with Wittgenstein's repeated claim that he leaves mathematics just as it is and only changes our way of viewing it?[8] Hasn't he here, at least, called into question the very *validity* of a standard method of proof? I do not think that Wittgenstein speaks directly to this specific question, but from what he says about the Law of Excluded Middle, it should be clear what his response must be. Through the use of an indirect proof, the mathematician does establish something *about* a system: he shows that the introduction of "*Rp*" will lead to inconsistency. If in virtue of this he goes on to treat "*R−p*" (or "*−P*") as a theorem, he has, in effect, *laid down a new rule* or *made a new decision*. Looked at in this way, the method of indirect proof becomes an engine of creation and not, as the Platonists believe, a device for discovering new mathematical facts. Alternatively, we can say that the classical mathematician accepts a second order rule to the effect that anything is a rule if the introduction of the contrary rule leads to inconsistency. We can call this the principle of mathematical growth.

Wittgenstein's remarks about indirect proofs are connected with another important theme in his philosophy of mathematics. For him, a perspicuous direct proof traces a pathway within our conceptual system. The proof *creates* this pathway and *eo ipso* creates a new mathematical concept that exhibits *internal relationships* within the system.

> If the proof registers the procedure according to the rule, then by doing this it produces a new concept. With this is connected the fact that we can say that proof must show the existence of internal relations. For the internal relation is the operation producing one structure from another, seen as equivalent to the picture of the transition itself — so that now the transition according to this series of configurations is *eo ipso* a transition according to those rules for operating. (V, 51.)

In contrast, if what we have said in following Wittgenstein is correct, an indirect proof (as it is normally employed) is not like this at all; it does not exhibit the process of evolving one structure from another. In essence, the method of indirect proof is a rule for stipulating new rules under special constraints. With such a proof pattern the conceptual pathway is abruptly broken by this stipulation and thus we are not edified by seeing something new unfold out of the old.

Thus the formal side of Wittgenstein's theory, that mathematical expressions are suppressed modal propositions, ties into an important philosophical theme, that mathematics is a creative activity. A perspicuous direct proof presents an extension of mathematics from *within*; an indirect proof (in its classical employment) simply adds to the stock of theorems without enhancing our conceptual understanding. To see the full significance of this difference and to get further insight into the "deontic" aspect of Wittgenstein's modal picture of mathematics, we must now attend to his remarks concerning the *application* of mathematical propositions.

II

In a crucial passage Wittgenstein ties mathematical discourse to empirical discourse: "Concepts which occur in 'necessary' propositions must also occur and have a meaning in non-necessary ones" (IV, 41). And less abstractly:

> I want to say: it is essential to mathematics that its signs are also employed in *mufti* [*in Zivil*].

> It is the use outside mathematics, and so the meaning of the signs that make the sign game into mathematics. (IV, 2.)

The numeral '2' occurs in the empirical proposition "There are 2 horses on the elevator" and also in the necessary proposition "$2 + 2 = 4$"; Wittgenstein here insists that without significant occurrences in expressions of the first sort, the numeral '2' could not have significant occurrences in expressions of the second sort.

Wittgenstein's reflections on this point have a curious form: he repeatedly considers the possibility that calculating is an experimental procedure, i.e., in calculating we set out to discover what results from applying certain rules to, say, given numbers. This view, however unattractive it is in every other respect, is at least hard-headed:

> It looks like obscurantism to say that a calculation is not an experiment.... But only because people believe that one is asserting the existence of an intangible, i.e., a shadowy, object side by side with what we can all grasp. (II, 76.)

The experimental analysis of calculation blocks Platonism by treating mathematical propositions as statements *about* a human activity. But this will not do just because mathematical propositions are not statements about what people do.

> We say, not, "So *that's* how we go!," but "So *that's* how it goes!" (II, 69.)

The same thing can be seen by reflecting upon the difference between the result of an experiment and the result of a calculation. Getting the *right* result is part of doing a calculation correctly, but it cannot be part of doing an experiment correctly. "*There are no* causal connexions in a calculation, only the connexions of the pattern." (V, 15.) In an experiment we do something and then *await* the result; in a calculation we produce the result itself.

But if we abandon the experimental interpretation of calculation how do we avoid falling back into Platonism?

"To be practical, mathematics must tell us facts." But do these facts have to be mathematical facts? But why should not mathematics instead of "teaching us facts" create the forms of what we call facts? (V, 15.)

For arithmetic to equate two expressions is, one might say, a grammatical trick.

In this way arithmetic bars a particular kind of description and conducts description into other channels. (And it goes without saying that this is connected with facts of experience.) (V, 3.)

These passages contain the core of Wittgenstein's conception of how mathematical propositions find application: (1) the vocabulary of mathematics provides us with *modes of description*, and (2) the laws of mathematics supply us with *rules for the identity of descriptions*. I shall examine these points separately.

(1) A quotation from Wittgenstein should adequately illustrate the first point:

"It is interesting to know *how many* vibrations this note has." But it took arithmetic to teach you this question. It taught you to see this kind of fact.

Mathematics — I want to say — teaches you, not just the answer to a question, but a whole language-game with questions and answers. (V, 15.)

This does not commit Wittgenstein to the position that the note did *not* have so many vibrations before people learned to count. This is worth saying if only to block an overly Kantian interpretation of the text.

(2) The second idea, that the laws of arithmetic supply us with rules for the identity of descriptions, is more difficult to make articulate. As a start, we can consider the simple identity statement: "5 × 5 = 25." This expression can play a double role in our mathematical activities. For one thing, it is an item we learn as part of the multiplication table and is used, more or less mechanically, when working out complex products. Here it is much like a rule for decoding — given these signs, we write down others under the governance of a rule. If we attend to just this use of the

expression, we shall be led in the direction of a pure conventionalism, a position that Wittgenstein rejects as strongly as he rejects Platonism.

Beyond this, the expression relates two ways of describing a collection of things. The sense of the numeral "25" is grounded — or was originally grounded — in the practice of counting. The sense of the expression "5 × 5" is grounded in a more complex practice: roughly, through counting we put things into equi-numerous batches of a certain number and then count up the batches. The identity statement lays down the principle that where one mode of description is correct, so too is the other.

How do we *know* when two modes of description are so related? Suppose I try to convince someone that five times five equals twenty-five by having him count out five batches each containing five items and then have him count up the total. Is it obvious that he will come up with the expected result? To vary one of Wittgenstein's examples, suppose he counts out the batches this way:

```
×  ×  ×  ×  ×      1.
×  ×  ×  ×  ×      2.
×  ×  ×  ×  ×      3.
×  ×  ×  ×  ×      4.
×
5.
```

Has he done what we told him to do? *Of course he has*; what he did fits our description perfectly. Yet he has not done what we *wanted* him to do; he has yet to master the technique that underlies *our* use of this expression and since our use is part of the instituted practice, he has yet to grasp the role of the expression "5 × 5" in *mufti*.

Even after the student has mastered the appropriate techniques he can still come up with the wrong answer. To say that a person knows how to count does not mean that he cannot miscount. Miscounting is not a skill, knack, or achievement, but still, it presupposes skills, knacks, and achievements. Thus it is simply wrong to say that mathematical identity statements predict the result that a person will reach when he carries out a certain computation. Yet we do insist that they predict what he will get if he carries out these activities *correctly*. We now want to know how inserting the word "correctly" can make this difference. Wittgenstein's answer runs something like this: although our training in mathematics consists — at least in part — of checking results, the outcome of this activity is not a generalization about what turns up when people count things, group things, etc., but instead, we are led to view the result of our exercise as a paradigm for carrying out future computations. Once we elevate a specific result to the status of a paradigm, the language of correct and incorrect computation finds its place. For the upshot of our instruction is not the conclusion:

(a) *This time* the product of five times five is twenty-five,

nor even:

(b) *In general* the product of five times five is twenty-five,

but instead:

(c) *It is a rule* that the product of five times five is twenty-five.

We are thus back to the "modal picture" of mathematics discussed in the first part of the paper.

All this still seems somehow unsatisfactory, for pushing things back one step, we now want to know why one computation should be given the status of a paradigm and thus made the measure for others to follow. We make this move with reasons — indeed, with very good reasons — but if we entertain sceptical doubts concerning the understanding, these reasons simply evaporate. To return to our student, after he has mastered the requisite techniques, and, in fact, has arrived at the required result, he may still feel dissatisfied and protest that he does not see that the result *has to* come out in this way. In short, nothing *compels* the student to adopt the results of his exercises as paradigmatic. Here we have an echo of Hume's sceptical doubts concerning causality — and it is this side of Wittgenstein's position that many have emphasized. There is nothing that can put this move to a paradigm out of reach of every possible criticism. It is only from *within* mathematics, i.e., only under the guidance of assumed paradigms, that mathematical expressions appear internally connected. From the outside they appear both "separate and loose."

Thus expressions of the form "It is a rule that *p*" can be given either an *inner* or an *outer* acknowledgment. We can say (from the outside) that it is a rule for this primitive tribe that $7 \times 7 =$ many, but we can also say, (from the inside) that it is a rule (for us) that $7 \times 7 = 49$. Speaking from the inside involves what Wittgenstein has called entering into a form of life. Nothing necessitates the adoption of a form of life, for necessity (internal relatedness) emerges only *after* the adoption of a form of life.

The comparison between Hume and Wittgenstein goes deeper: Wittgenstein not only presents sceptical doubts, he also offers a sceptical solution to these doubts.[9] It is a fact about human beings that we sometimes raise things to the status of a paradigm as the result of a proof:

For it is a peculiar procedure: I *go through* the proof and then accept its result. — I mean: this is simply what we *do*. This is use and custom among us, or a fact of our natural history. (I, 63.)

Thus there is no wholly external way of justifying a proof: "It is not something behind the proof, but the proof that proves" (II, 42). And if the whole procedure of acceptance from proof is called into question, there is no way of meeting the challenge:

The danger here, I believe, is one of giving a justification of our procedure where there is no such thing as a justification and we ought simply to have said: *that's how we do it*. (II, 74.)

We can now double back upon a previous point and again ask why a perspicuous direct proof enjoys a privileged status for Wittgenstein. At first glance, the Humean motifs in Wittgenstein's writings may seem to undercut our previous reflections. If mathematical propositions are separate and loose, aren't the results of a direct proof every bit as external as the results of an indirect proof? From a spectator's standpoint, the answer to this question must be *Yes*, but for a person working under the guidance of paradigms, the difference remains striking. Our original paradigms grew from the soil of application, and a perspicuous direct proof conserves this applicability and thus leads us to adopt a new paradigm. In contrast, if an indirect proof involves a new decision or stipulation, it will not bestow upon its conclusion a linkage with previous paradigms and through them a linkage with application.

Finally, we can notice why Wittgenstein was impatient with the idea that mathematics stands in need of a foundation. His attitude here is simply one instance of his general critique of foundational studies. In the sense that philosophers have used the term, Wittgenstein came to think that *nothing* stands in need of a foundation.

> What does mathematics need a foundation for? It no more needs one, I believe, than propositions about material objects — or about sense impressions, need an *analysis*. What mathematical propositions do stand in need of is a clarification of their grammar, just as do these other propositions. (V, 13.)

Mathematics has its foundation in human practice and needs no other.

As far as work that goes under the heading of studies in the foundations of mathematics, he flatly denies that this *portion* of mathematics is the underpinning for the rest of the mathematical edifice.

> The *mathematical* problems of what is called foundations are no more the foundations of mathematics than the painted rock is the support of the painted tower. (V, 14.)

In back of this attitude is the doctrine that the proposed systems derive whatever sense they have from the system they are intended to support, and not the other way around. For example, in the decimal notation we have a "short" calculation and corresponding to it in the Russell notation we have an extraordinarily long calculation. Does the long calculation either justify or elucidate the "short" calculation? According to Wittgenstein, no![10]

In even a less charitable mood, Wittgenstein views foundational research as an exemplar of reasoning carried on with the connection to application totally ignored.

> The question, "What was it useful for?" was a quite essential question. For the calculus was not invented for some practical purpose, but in order "to give arithmetic a foundation." But who says that arithmetic is logic, etc. (II, 85.)

And problems within the foundations of mathematics can also arise through this severance from application. We start out with principles that are both intelligible and plausible through their connection with ordinary discourse, then later we get into trouble by extending the system in ways initially never dreamed of. We introduce a predicate such as "heterological" and then a contradiction is found, but how is the notion of a heterological predicate connected with the initial reasons for setting up the calculus?

> What Russell's "$-f(f)$" lacks above all is application, and hence meaning. (V, 8.)

Why not, following Wittgenstein's suggestion, just call the derived contradiction a *true* contradiction and note, perhaps with satisfaction, that it is part of our system (V, 21)?

The worry, of course, is that the presence of the contradiction will render the system useless. Here, belatedly, a recognition of the importance of application reappears. We are now set the task of *sealing off* the contradiction while at the same time preserving the features of the system that we want. If we cannot accomplish this, this merely shows that our system is not transparent to us; we do not know our way about.

> But how is it possible not to know one's way about in a calculus: isn't it there, open to view? (II, 80.)

Wittgenstein seems to suggest that this would not happen if we stayed in touch with application at every stage in the development of the system:

> I would like to say something like this: "Is it usefulness you are out for in your calculations? — In that case you do not get any contradiction. And if you aren't out for usefulness — then it doesn't matter if you get one." (II, 80.)

This suggestion is not far fetched. In effect, it amounts to the demand that every extension of a system be accompanied by a relative consistency proof within the domain of intended application. Anyway, these passages clarify Wittgenstein's supposedly *laissez-faire* attitude toward contradictions:

> "Then you are in favor of contradiction?" Not at all; any more than of soft rulers. (IV, 12.)

III

The sympathetic commentator on Wittgenstein can do one of two things: either say again what he has said in the hope that someone will listen, or reconstruct the position in a way that reveals its systematic coherence. Using the intuitionistic themes as a starting point, I have here attempted the second approach. This isn't a Wittgensteinian way of doing business, but perhaps this loss of purity will be repaid by a new appraisal of Wittgenstein's contribution to the philosophy of mathematics.

Notes

1. Ed. by G.H. von Wright, *et al.* (Oxford, Basil Blackwell, 1956).
2. E.g., IV, 9-13, 17-20.
3. E.g., IV, 26-7, 46.
4. E.g., II, 18, 46-8, 53, 85; IV, 24; V, 13.
5. See, G.H. von Wright's 'Biographical Sketch' in Norman Malcolm, *Ludwig Wittgenstein: A Memoir* (London, Oxford University Press, 1958), pp. 12-13.
6. This is one of Wittgenstein's favorite phrases. See, for example, I, Appendix II, 10 and III, 11-13.
7. Frederic B. Fitch, 'Natural Deduction Rules for Obligation,' *American Philosophical Quarterly*, vol. 3 (1966), pp. 27-38.
8. E.g., I, Appendix II, 18; II, 81-2; IV, 52; V, 16.
9. I am using the phrase 'sceptical solution' in precisely the way that Hume uses it in Sect. V of *An Enquiry Concerning Human Understanding.*
10. For this argument see especially II, 18.

66

The Constructivist Model in Wittgenstein's Philosophy of Mathematics

Pasquale Frascolla

1.

When one speaks of Wittgenstein's philosophy of mathematics, one usually stresses its constructivist and utterly anti-platonistic character. Now, the first problem I would like to tackle concerns precisely the meaning of the expression 'constructive procedure' within the context of Wittgenstein's analyses. Unquestionably the Austrian philosopher shares with Poincaré, Brouwer and Weyl the general assumption of the constructivist approach to mathematical infinity, i.e. the idea according to which to grasp an infinite set simply amounts to grasping the possibility of indefinitely iterating the process of generation of its elements. However, this conception of an infinite set as an open field of possibilities of construction, as a process *in fieri* never to be completed, doesn't suffice to pinpoint Wittgenstein's notion of a constructive procedure. In fact it undergoes such strong restrictions that the domain of mathematical methods it delimitates doesn't coincide, for example, with the domain of the constructive procedures admitted by Brouwer's intuitionism. The comparison with intuitionism brings to light the specific features of Wittgenstein's conception of infinity; an especially significant example is given by the model of the real number outlined by the Viennese philosopher and by his related criticism of the intuitionistic notion of an unlimited free choice sequence.

The theory of real numbers is an excellent test for any philosophy of mathematical infinity because it has to deal with objects that are infinite sets (sequences) of rational numbers. The task Wittgenstein sets himself in the sections of the *Philosophische Bemerkungen* and of the *Philosophische Grammatik* devoted to a discussion of the theory of real numbers, is to make clear what kind of law or prescription for the formation of convergent series of rationals can be legitimately considered a genuine generator of a real number.[1] In determining the requirements defining this class or kind of laws, he makes explicit the restrictions which characterise his notion of 'constructive procedure'. Wittgenstein imposes two basic conditions on the laws of generation, which jointly determine his model of the real number. In the first place the prescription must be of a recursive type, because only 'via the recursion each stage becomes arithmetically comprehensible',[2] and must provide an operational technique of expansion, an effective method of computation of the approximated rational values. The 'arithmetic heart' of the real number is this effective rule of construction of the infinite series of rationals, which satisfies Cauchy's criterion. The second condition is expressed in the requirement of the effective comparability with every rational number: the law must provide a decision procedure which allows one, given an arbitrary rational number, to decide if it is greater, less or equal to the real number in question.[3]

The identification of the law of construction of an infinite set with a recursive procedure which, furthermore, allows one to decide mechanically any question belonging to a certain relevant class, is, in my opinion, the distinguishing feature of Wittgenstein's constructivism. This identification occurs throughout the whole of Wittgenstein's reflections on the concept of infinity: from the representation scheme of the formal series of the *Tractatus Logico-Philosophicus*, consisting in the indication of the first term of the series and of the general form of the step from any arbitrary term to the next, to the latest remarks on the mathematical infinitary techniques, contained in the *Bemerkungen über die Grundlagen der Mathematik*. The delimitation of the constructive to the domain of the recursively generable is quite strict, as it is meant to be the only adequate analysis of the grammar of the infinite. So the idea mentioned earlier, that the irrational number is essentially a *figure-producing machine*, has the effect of excluding from the range of legitimate mathematical constructs all those structures that are not in accordance with the recursive model.

The lawless infinite decimals of the classical theory of the continuum are the first victims of the Wittgensteinian discriminations: they are disposed of as misleading products of the extensional point of view, i.e. of the 'wrong' point of view which links the infinity of the decimal expansion not to the technique of figure production, but to the image of a huge finite extension, 'of an unsurveyable series reaching into the distance'.[4] This attack on the classical theory of real numbers can, however, be considered fairly discounted, considering the anti-platonistic premises of the Austrian philosopher. Much more interesting is the fact that Wittgenstein's criticism also extends to the typically intuitionistic procedure of generating real numbers by means of unlimited sequences of free choices. This procedure, Wittgenstein says dryly, doesn't qualify as a mathematical method, but is something empirical (*'etwas Empirisches'*).[5] Here the concept of 'constructive procedure' undergoes the restriction of which we have spoken above. The notion of an unlimited sequence of free choices is clearly faithful to the general principle of constructivism, according to which an infinite structure is an open process, an unlimited possibility. But the requirement of a law uniquely determining each step of the sequence is here dropped, and this extension of the constructive beyond the domain of the effectively generable is rejected by Wittgenstein as illegitimate. If there is no effective rule governing the infinitely many possible operations on the symbolism, if there is no mechanical method for the continuation of the sequence (and this is what happens in the case of unlimited free choice sequences), one is no longer dealing with acceptable mathematical entities. About real numbers Wittgenstein says explicitly: 'The true nature of real numbers must be the induction. What I must look at in the real number, its sign, is the induction. The *so* of which we may say "and so on"'.[6]

2.

What is, then, the source of this limitation on recursive procedures that characterises Wittgenstein's conception of the constructive? To answer this question we must take into account the overall picture of mathematical activity worked out by the Viennese philosopher in the context of the methodological assumptions of his theory of language. We have already seen that irrational numbers are conceived by him as figure-producing machines; now it is this concept of 'machine' that can lead us right to the roots of the Wittgensteinian constructivist model. In one of his conversations with the members of the Vienna Circle — reported in Friedrich Waismann's famous collection of notes — Wittgenstein claims that mathematics is always a machine ('*eine maschine*'), a calculus, and that calculus is simply an abacus, a computing machine ('*eine Rechenmaschine*').[7] It is not a yearning for his experience as an elementary school teacher that induces him to say that the final aim of his anti-foundational criticism is to make us reconsider mathematics in the same light in which it appears to us in the elementary school, where people work with the abacus.[8] As a matter of fact, the way mathematics is done in the elementary school is for Wittgenstein the concrete model we must keep in mind to get an adequate idea of mathematics, of the role it plays within the context of the symbolic activities and of the human institutions, in short, of its grammar. Working with the abacus becomes the paradigm of doing mathematics; the analysis of the use of the abacus can be, therefore, the key for understanding Wittgenstein's picture of mathematics.

The computation of the value of an arithmetic function by means of the abacus amounts to a series of operations or actions on concrete objects (pebbles, beads, etc.). These operations consist of displacements of such objects, so as to produce new patterns which represent, by virtue of suitable conventions, the value of the arithmetic function for a given argument. The operations succeed each other in accordance with certain rules (rules for the computation), and the latter are finite instructions schematically defining *the behaviour, the actions*, necessary to the computation. One must note that the procedure according to which the value of an arithmetic function is computed by means of the abacus, is simply a concrete example of that sort of general, schematic procedures called 'algorithms'.[9] When Wittgenstein maintains that mathematics is an acting ('*handeln*'),[10] that 'the mathematical signs *are* like the beads of an abacus',[11] when he assumes the operating with the abacus as a paradigm of doing mathematics, he places just this concept of 'algorithm' at the centre of his view of mathematics.

The algorithms — operational procedures whose application is specified by a certain set of finite rules concerning the use of the signs — form that 'motley of techniques of proof', mentioned by Wittgenstein in the *Bemerkungen über die Grundlagen der Mathematik*.[12] He uses the term 'calculus' ('*Kalkül*') to denote these sign manipulation procedures, whose possibilities are fixed which schematically determine the admitted transformations. A calculus produces a system ('*ein System*'), that is a series whose members are generated through the application of the rules of the calculus.[13] Doing mathematics is conceived, in this frame, as a formal activity that is carried out within a certain system, i.e. as a way of handling the symbolism which presupposes as already given a set of operational rules (in Turing's words, 'the book of the rules'): 'In mathematics — Wittgenstein says — we cannot talk of systems in general, but only *within* systems ... A system is, so to speak, a world'.[14] Mathematical practice actually coincides with the application of the rules of a calculus, that is with the carrying out of instructions concerning the use of the signs and, therefore, with behaviour and actions in accordance with certain given operational schemes: 'We may only put a question in mathematics (or make a conjecture), where the answer runs: "I must work it out"'.[15] The stress on the algorithmic, purely computational aspect of the mathematical practice, is in full agreement with the general conception of linguistic behaviour developed by Wittgenstein, at least from the *Brown Book* on, in connection with the definition of the descriptive methods of philosophical analysis. It is well known that the linguistic games were conceived by him as patterns of behavioural responses in the presence of signs, regulated by operational models that the techniques of linguistic training turn into commonly accepted rules. As a consequence of this 'merciless' training, people tend to react to signs according to regular patterns, and the linguistic practice is reduced to the carrying out of moves fixed in a 'book of the rules' which is a social institution and is passed on to each member of the linguistic community. The description of these activities in terms of public and observable behaviour is the only one satisfying the conditions Wittgenstein imposes, at a methodological level, on philosophical analysis. In adopting his point of view, the symbolic rule-conforming behaviour appears to be instinctive, animal reactions, objective processes we cannot theoretically justify, 'the bedrock' on which the 'spade is turned'.[16]

In the system of co-ordinates established by the methodology of grammatical analysis, doing mathematics is inescapably reduced to the mere application of algorithms, to a behaviour of an automatic kind by means of which certain operational instructions concerning the symbolism are carried out. Calculation is the whole of mathematics for a man whose operations on signs are nothing else but automatic moves, the carrying out of symbolic procedures based on socially established and unanimously followed rules. In one of his Viennese conversations, Wittgenstein had said that mathematics is always a machine; but in the *Bemerkungen über die Grundlagen der Mathematik* he adds quite significantly: 'If calculating looks to us like the action of a machine, it is *the human being* doing the calculation that is the machine'.[17] This idea of the man doing mathematics as a computing machine is a more or less evocative image: if we keep in mind that a behavioural approach (that is, a definition in terms of regular behaviour in accordance with certain general schemes) is the starting point of the theory of automata, we can see that the expression 'automatic activity' is a fully adequate description of mathematical practice as conceived by Wittgenstein. This theoretical background is, in my opinion, the source of the central role the concept of an algorithm plays in his view of mathematics. But the following remark is now in order: the fact of regarding the man doing computations as a machine operating in accordance with certain rules, should not engender misunderstandings as to Wittgenstein's conception of the uniformity of symbolic behaviour. As is well known, this regularity is never seen by him as forced upon us by some linguistic construct enjoying a privileged status, or by some 'hidden' mental state. The regularity is a datum of human natural history, a social agreement in people's acting, which only makes it possible to speak of a man following a rule.

At this point we are able to suggest an answer to the question, raised at the beginning, concerning the source of Wittgenstein's restriction of the constructive to the domain of the recursive procedures. To speak of an infinite set means to speak of an open process, of a never completed structure; but this is not enough to fully characterise the set, because what is relevant is the possibility of an indefinite application of an effective law generating its elements the one from the other. The inductive rule, provided it satisfies the requirement of effectiveness, gives the operational scheme of the step from an arbitrary term of the series to the next one. This is the only way infinity can occur in those algorithmic methods whose application exhausts, for Wittgenstein, the mathematical practice. Thus the limitation of the constructive to the recursively generable sets finds itself with absolute coherence in the overall frame of mathematics outlined by the Austrian philosopher.

3.

This frame, however, raises some problems: I would like to examine here briefly two of the most relevant.

It is well known that Wittgenstein's explicit aim is to describe the use 'in mufti' of the mathematical signs, i.e. to analyse the ways in which this rule governed behaviour inscribes itself in the net of the habits and institutions of a human community. The use of calculi in everyday life, in connection with the ordinary practices of measuring, of weighing, etc., or in connection with the 'higher' computational activities of the physicist and the engineer, is the privileged subject of Wittgenstein's inquiry. But what about that different way of doing mathematics which we might designate with the expression 'creative production'? Wittgenstein provides an answer to such a question when he states that 'the mathematician creates *essence*',[18] that he makes up models, paradigms of sign manipulation which, under certain conditions, are assumed in the universe of the rules of the language. In the *Philosophische Bemerkungen* he talks, using a slightly different terminology, of the creative activity of the mathematician as the invention of 'new systems'. Not surprisingly, he thinks that a large part of the creative production of the mathematician consists in the invention of new systematic procedures, whose application leads to the solution of a certain class of problems. Now, even if we accept this thesis, the Wittgensteinian approach appears to be unsatisfactory to the extent to which it neglects as irrelevant to the analysis a substantial part of the mathematical activity which can be a proper subject of methodological research. According to Wittgenstein, on the one hand there is the automatic execution of operational instructions about the use of the symbolism, on the other hand there is a creative activity which reduces to no further analysable acts of vision. In such a way all the region lying between these two extremes, being made up of strategies of research, of choices among different possible models of intellectual conduct and of their justification, disappears from the horizon of the philosophical description.

We face now the last question, concerning the role played by the recursive constructivist model with respect to the possible alternative approaches to the mathematical concept of infinity. An example can help to illustrate the problem: in discussing the status of the axiom of choice within set theory, Wittgenstein maintains that to talk of the choice of an element from every set of an infinite collection of sets makes sense only if reference is made to a law of selection. To talk of an infinite selection which is arbitrary, that is not governed by such a law, is simply meaningless ('*unsinnig*').[19] The demarcation between the constructive and the platonistic is therefore presented as the demarcation between the meaningful and the meaningless. We face here a consequence of the claim that the ordinary linguistic practice provides an objective paradigm, legitimising the conceptual and methodological frames modelling the mathematical techniques. According to Wittgenstein the term 'infinite' gets its genuine meaning from the recursive procedure of calculation we mentioned before. Conceptual frameworks such as Cantor's, which endorse uses of the term 'infinite' unlike those assumed to be the unique depositories of its meaning, are regarded as grammatical misunderstandings, intellectual confusions. The peculiarities of Wittgenstein's approach to non-constructive mathematics follow from this premise. This approach is meant to separate the grain from the chaff, 'the pure calculus' from 'the prose', 'the gas' of the wrong ideas by which it is surrounded. Consider, for example, the analysis of Cantor's proof of the non-denumerability of the set of the real numbers, carried out in the *Bemerkungen über die Grundlagen der Mathematik*.[20] According to Wittgenstein there is, surrounding this proof, a 'glitter of the concepts' which has to be dissipated in order to extract the 'solid core'.[21] This glitter irradiates from the image of the ascent to an infinite power greater than the denumerable that this image suggests. Wittgenstein questions the starting hypothesis of Cantor's argument, that is the hypothesis that *all* the real numbers (or simply those lying in the interval 0-1 of the real line) have been ordered in a numerated succession. This hypothesis is, of course, out of the question within a classical frame; from Wittgenstein's constructivist point of view, instead, it is unacceptable and turns Cantor's proof into a 'puffed-up proof', a proof that 'proves more than its means allow it'.[22] The application of the method of the denumeration to the set of the reals, which would not give the expected result because of the excessive size of the set itself, is really the simulation of a procedure.[23] And in effect one is dealing with simulation if one presupposes, with Wittgenstein, that the reference to an infinite totality is but the reference to a law of construction of its elements: in the case of the set *R* no such a law is available. Having thus dismantled the scaffolding of Cantor's argument, there is still the problem of clarifying what the demonstration 'really' proves, of separating the 'pure calculus' from the 'misleading images' accompanying it. The 'pure calculus' is *the operational method* that allows us, given a denumerable sequence of real numbers, to construct a new number not belonging to the sequence. In other words, the calculus is a set of instructions concerning the symbolism that provide 'a method of upsetting any order'.[24] The 'solid core' of Cantor's proof is what can be translated into a precise operational language, into the kind of procedures that, as we have seen, constitute, in Wittgenstein's opinion, 'the rough ground' of mathematical activity. Then the 'genuine' mathematical content of Cantor's argument is nothing but the kind of mathematical procedure which is in agreement with the only model of infinity accepted as valid. This attitude prevents Wittgenstein from admitting as equally legitimate the various conceptual frameworks on which different styles, techniques and results of the mathematical practice are based.

Notes

1. Cf. L. Wittgenstein, *Philosophische Bemerkungen*, Frankfurt am Main, 1964 (English translation, Oxford, 1975 — *Philosophical Remarks*), sections 179-204; *Philosophische Grammatik*, Oxford, 1969, pp. 471-85.

2. L. Wittgenstein, *Philosophische Bemerkungen*, section 194.

3. Ibid., sections 195-6. An example of a law meeting the first requirement but not the second is the following: (G) Write as the n-th term of the expansion '0' if 2n is the sum of two prime numbers, '1' otherwise. The first requirement is obviously met; the second is not met because *at the moment* a mechanical procedure for deciding whether the number generated by (G) is greater than or equal to 0, is not available to us.

4. L. Wittgenstein, *Bemerkungen über die Grundlagen der Mathematik* with English translation, Oxford 1956, IV, section 10.

5. Cf. F. Waismann, *Wittgenstein und der Wiener Kreis*, Frankfurt am Main- Oxford, 1967, p. 83.

6. Wittgenstein, *Philosophische Bemerkungen*, section 189. (Wittgenstein's italics.)

7. Cf. Waismann, *Wittgenstein und der Wiener Kreis*, pp. 105-6.

8. Ibid., p. 105.

9. See H. Hermes, *Enumerability, Decidability, Computability*, Berlin-Heidelberg-New York, 1965, chapter 1.

10. Cf. Wittgenstein, *Bemerkungen über die Grundlagen der Mathematik*, III, 56.

11. Wittgenstein, *Philosophische Bemerkungen*, section 157. (Wittgenstein's italics.)

12. Cf. Wittgenstein, *Bemerkungen über die Grundlagen der Mathematik*, II, 46.

13. Cf. Wittgenstein, *Philosophische Bemerkungen*, section 154.

14. Ibid., section 152. (Wittgenstein's italics.)

15. Ibid., section 151.

16. L. Wittgenstein, *Philosophische Untersuchungen*, with English translation, Oxford 1953, I, section 217.

17. Wittgenstein, *Bemerkungen über die Grundlagen der Mathematik*, III, 20. (Wittgenstein's italics.)
18. Ibid., I, section 32. (Wittgenstein's italics.)
19. Cf. Wittgenstein, *Philosophische Bemerkungen*, section 146.
20. Cf. Wittgenstein, *Bemerkungen über die Grundlagen der Mathematik*, I, Appendix 2.
21. Ibid., IV, section 16.
22. Ibid., I, Appendix 2, section 3.
23. Ibid.
24. Ibid., I, Appendix 2, section 6.

67

Wittgenstein on Mathematical Proof

Alice Ambrose

In *Remarks on the Foundations of Mathematics*, and elsewhere, Wittgenstein made some general statements about mathematical proof which can only be described as paradoxical. What he says is directed to proofs for which there is no general method of solution such as there is for statements of the form $a \times b = c$ where a simple calculation is sufficient. His concern is with propositions for which one cannot in advance of proof describe any procedure which will demonstrate them. Examples are: 'For all natural numbers n, $2^{2^n} + 1$ is prime', 'There is no greatest prime', 'Every equation of nth degree has exactly n roots', 'Any even number is the sum of two primes'. In an earlier study,[1] 'Proof and the Theorem Proved', I singled out a group of propositions for which his account of proof seemed correct, and not paradoxical. Examples given were the propositions '$a^0 = 1$', 'a/o represents any number whatever', whose proofs provide justification for introducing or excluding an expression, namely 'a^0' and 'a/o', resp. But I did not succeed in making his account of deductions of connections between established concepts paradox-free. I should like to return to his account as applied to such demonstrations, with the aim of explaining what justification there is for it, and what his account comes to.

Consider the following statements from Wittgenstein which taken together summarise his views about proof:

'If you want to know *what* is proved, look at the proof.'[2]
'The result of a mathematical proof gets its meaning from the proof.'[3]
[Certain mathematical questions] 'give us a sort of hint as to what we are to do, but the proof provides them with content'.[4]
'Proofs that construct *propositions* make us forget that the *sense* of the result is not to be read off from this by itself, but from the proof.'[5]
'The problem of finding a mathematical decision of a theorem might with some justification be called the problem of giving mathematical sense to a formula.'[6]
'I should like to say: the proof shews me a new connexion, and hence also gives me a new concept.'[7]
'One would like to say: the proof changes the grammar of our language,

changes our concepts, makes new connexions ... (It does not establish that they are there; they do not exist until it makes them).'8

'The question — I want to say — changes its status, when it becomes decidable. For a connexion is made then, which formerly *was not there*.'9

These quotations speak for themselves. Their paradoxical consequences are the following:

1. Before proof of the proposition expressed by the sentence '*p*', '*p*' has a different sense than after proof of *p*, and correspondingly, the answer to a question concerning the truth-value of *p* does not answer the original question.

2. A proposition can have but one proof. To elaborate, if proof gives sense to the concluding sentence '*p*' of the proof-sequence of sentences, then prior to arriving at the sentence, either it had no meaning or it had a different meaning. If it had no meaning, then there was no proposition to be proved; and if the concluding sentence '*p*' came to have a different meaning from its original one, the original proposition has not been proved. The proved proposition is not an answer to any question about the truth-value of the initial proposition. In order for a question to be relevant to the *proved* proposition, Wittgenstein agrees that it would already have to have been answered.[10] For 'the proof provides it with content'.[11] If an interrogative expression does not ask a question about the demonstrated proposition, then what is demonstrated is not an answer to whatever question it did ask. Further, if the sense of the terminal sentence of a proof-sequence of sentences is to be 'read off from the proof', then 'each proof will demonstrate something which it alone can demonstrate',[12] so that one and the same proposition can have but one proof.

Now Wittgenstein was not unaware of the difficulties inherent in his claims, and even stated some of them himself. In lectures he asserted that 'to say it is the proof which gives sense to the question is absurd because it misuses the word "question"'.[13] And he asked himself in *Remarks on the Foundations* (p. 164), '... should I say that the same sense can only have *one* proof? Or that when a proof is found the sense alters?' Earlier in the *Remarks* (p. 92), he stated flatly that 'of course it would be nonsense to say that *one* proposition cannot have two proofs — for we do say just that'. His comments on these admissions are singularly unhelpful. To the person who says 'Then the proof of a proposition cannot ever be found, for, if it has been found, it is no longer the proof of *this* proposition', he replies that 'to say this is so far to say nothing at all' (p. 164), '... that these proofs prove the same proposition means, e.g., both demonstrate it as a suitable instrument for the same purpose ...' (p. 165).

It might be thought that the paradoxes under discussion here arise from Wittgenstein's use of what might be called the mixed mode of speech: the use of 'proposition' where 'sentence' should be used, or vice versa. To illustrate his ambiguous use of the words 'proposition' and 'question', his way of describing the role of proof of *p* in relation to the meaning of the sentence 'p' was that 'there seem to be propositions which have no sense until we know whether they are true or false',[14] and also, '... a question or proposition does not make sense until a proof, or method of proof, is given' (p. 199). But the difficulty is not removed when put as I have done: 'Proof of p gives "p" a meaning', where p is a proposition and 'p' a sentence. For this also translates into the paradox that the sentence 'p' *acquires* meaning when one establishes the truth-value of p: if 'p' has a meaning p_1 different from the meaning which it acquired on proof of p_2, then one has not proved what one set out to prove. The sentence 'p' acquires meaning via proof of a proposition which could not have been the goal of the proof. For one proves something different from what one supposed oneself to be proving. Presumably a person who tried to prove p_1 would always demonstrate a different proposition p_2 and would never succeed in doing what he set out to do.

Wittgenstein said both that 'one can frame a mathematical proposition in a grammatically correct way without understanding its meaning'[15] and that when a proof is found the sense *alters*. Far from being a correct description of a working mathematician who is trying to solve a problem, these claims appear to be in violation of usage. To say that a proof gives meaning to a statement under consideration and that in the beginning one cannot be said to understand it goes against the common usage of such words as 'conjecture' and 'suppose'. For it is undeniably proper usage to describe Fermat as having conjectured that the sentence 'for all n, $2^{2^n} + 1$ is prime' expressed something true; and this implies, in normal discourse, that the sentence had meaning and that it was understood. It must be admitted that very seldom does the word 'understand' occur in mathematicians' 'proof-talk'. Nor are sentences or other symbolism very often described by them as having or lacking meaning. But both terms, 'understand' and 'having meaning', are connected with terms such as 'conjecture' and 'suppose' which do occur in the course of what the mathematician does. Thus Wittgenstein's claims are by implication in violation of usage rather than correct descriptions.

Nevertheless, in this paper I wish to hold that there is justification for maintaining both that the meaning a sentence 'p' has when it is correctly followed by 'Q.E.D.' is different from the meaning it had before proof was given, and that one proposition can have but one proof. These claims were presented as true accounts of the relation of mathematical proofs to the meaning of sentences denoting the theorems they prove. I shall consider first the reasons which might be adduced for holding that they are true. They rest ultimately on a feature of mathematical propositions which empirical propositions do not have. A sentence denoting an empirical proposition expresses the same proposition no matter which truth-value the proposition has. The truth-value it has is determined by factors external to the proposition. That is, the sentence will express a true proposition if the facts make the proposition true; but the facts might be otherwise, in which case the truth-value of *that* proposition would be falsity. One and the same proposition can have either of two truth-values. By contrast, one and the same *a priori* proposition cannot have a different truth-value than the one it has. It would not be *that* proposition if it had a different truth-value. So a necessarily true *proposition* is never identical with a necessarily false one. This is to say that a sentence expressing a necessarily true proposition must express a different proposition from one that expresses a self-inconsistency.

Consider the sentence 'for all n, $2^{2^n} + 1$ is prime'. Before it was discovered by calculation that $2^{2^5} + 1$ was factorable, Fermat conjectured that this sentence expressed a truth. Evidently, as the discovery indicates, this came into question. Prior to the calculation both Fermat who made the conjecture and Euler who made the calculation did not know *which* proposition the sentence expressed, a necessarily true one or a necessarily false one. I think it might with justice be claimed that a person who did not know which proposition a sentence expresses did not understand by the sentence what he understood when he arrived at this knowledge. All he had in the beginning were, in Wittgenstein's words, 'signposts for mathematical investigation, stimuli to mathematical constructions'.[16] He knew the meanings of the individual words and the fact that their combination was grammatical. This much is required for initiating the proof. But it is surely minimal knowledge. It gives him only 'a sort of hint as to what he is to do'.[17] What he understood was not only less than but different from what he understood when he came to know which proposition — in this case a necessarily false one — was expressed by it.

Precisely how a sentence acquires an additional meaning with proof may be seen by considering the question asked about the roots of the equation $x^2 + 2x + 1 = 0$, and its answer $(-1, -1)$. Initially, the interrogative, 'What are the roots?', meant as much and no more than one's explanation of it indicated, namely, 'What values of the variable will satisfy the equation, i.e., reduce both of its members to the same term?' By trying out values of the variable, -1 is seen to satisfy it. After the invention of a general formula for solving equations of the form $ax^2 + bx + c = 0$, 'roots' meant

$$x_1 = \frac{-b + \sqrt{b^2 - 4ac}}{2a}, \ x_2 = \frac{-b - \sqrt{b^2 - 4ac}}{2a}.$$

With this formula at hand the sentence 'There are two roots of $x^2 + 2x + 1 = 0$' has an augmented meaning: it records the result of a new method which connects coefficients with roots. As Wittgenstein remarked, 'I should like to say: the proof shews me a new connexion, and hence also gives me a new concept; the connexion did not exist until it was made.'[18] 'The question — I want to say — changes its status, when it becomes decidable. For a connexion is made then, which formerly *was not there*,' (ibid., p. 138). And the answer, in this case $(-1, -1)$, 'has more in it than the question. Normally it is not like this.'[19]

What Wittgenstein's account serves to point out, and stress, is the difference between showing an empirical proposition to be true, and demonstrating a mathematical proposition. That we understand something different before and after proof singles out a difference which does not obtain when an empirical proposition is verified or falsified. Prior to the discovery of a general method of solving quadratics, one could not have described the solution. In the case of an empirical proposition the method, or methods, of showing it to be true, or false, can be described in advance; and the same proposition will be expressed by the empirical sentence regardless of which truth-value it is shown to have and even if it is not shown to have either.

It is to be noted that only about language do questions about meaning and understanding arise. Sentences, not propositions, have literal meaning (a proposition *is* the meaning of an indicative sentence), and sentences, not propositions, are understood. How then does Wittgenstein's examination of proof of mathematical *propositions* come to involve questions about sentences occurring in the statement of proof — questions about their meaning and our understanding of them? The answer Wittgenstein gave is that mathematical propositions are 'instruments of language'.[20] 'The proposition proved by means of a proof serves as a rule', '. . . it shews us what it makes SENSE to say'.[21] 'Let us remember that in mathematics we are convinced of *grammatical* propositions, so the . . . result of being convinced is that we *accept a rule*' (ibid.) — a rule about the use of words. For example, the proof that it is impossible to trisect an angle by straight edge and compasses convinces us to exclude the expression 'trisection of an angle by straight edge and compasses' from describing any operation. It will not make sense to say 'I effected the trisection of an angle using only straight edge and compasses'. That is, correlated with every proof which is accepted is the acceptance of a rule for the use of language. As Wittgenstein wrote: 'I go through the proof and say: . . . I must fix the use of my language in *this* way' (ibid., p. 78). By contrast, when one confirms or establishes an empirical hypothesis, such as 'Iron has a specific gravity of 7.86', nothing is shown about the use of words. That the words have a use is presupposed by the empirical tests. What is shown by the tests is whether what the words assert corresponds to the facts.[22] With regard to the use of words, the lack of parallelism between sentences which express *a priori* true propositions and sentences which assert empirical facts shows up in the following. The fact that 'There is no greatest prime' expresses a true *a priori* proposition is equivalent to the fact that 'The phrase "greatest prime" has no use to describe a number' expresses a true verbal proposition. That is, to know that this sentence expresses an *a priori* truth, all that is required is that we know a fact about the use of the phrase 'greatest prime'. On the other hand, the fact that 'there are no dinosaurs' expresses a true empirical proposition is *not* equivalent to any fact to the effect that 'The word "dinosaurs" has no use' expresses a true verbal proposition.[23] There is no such fact. Indeed, that the word 'dinosaurs' has a use is already presupposed by the fact that 'There are no dinosaurs' expresses an empirical proposition. What we have to know in order to know that it expresses a *truth* is something in addition to knowing that 'dinosaur' has a use, something extra-verbal, namely, that there is in fact no creature falling under the concept *dinosaur*.

We are now in a position to explain the paradox that the meaning a sentence has when it occurs at the end of a proof-sequence is different from the meaning it had when it first came under consideration. On learning that 'There is no greatest prime' expresses a true proposition we learn a fact about the use of the phrase 'greatest prime', that is, about its meaning. After proof of *There is no greatest prime* we accept the exclusion of 'greatest prime' from descriptive use. It is interesting that *reductio ad absurdum* proofs, of which the proof of an infinity of primes is an example, sometimes conclude with 'But this is absurd'. The absurdity is logical, and as a correlate, the expression 'greatest prime' is an absurdity of language. In the context of a mathematical demonstration 'This is absurd' makes an oblique reference to a fact of language, namely, that a certain expression has no use. In the example at hand, what one knows after proof that one did not know before is that 'greatest prime' has a self-contradictory meaning. The phrase 'greatest prime' could not have been understood from the beginning to have this meaning, else the proof would have been unnecessary. With proof, the use of this phrase becomes fixed. It is to be expected that when it is demonstrated whether or not every even number is the sum of two primes the demonstration will make entirely new conceptual connections, as was done in constructing the formula for solving quadratics. And with new conceptual connections there is a new piece of language. Wittgenstein wrote: 'The proof creates a new concept by creating or being a new sign.'[24] 'Could we say: "mathematics creates new *expressions*, not new propositions"?' (ibid., p. 78).

The proof that $x^2 + 2x + 1 = 0$ has two roots is a typical example of a proof which assigns a meaning to a sentence which in the first place only gives 'signposts for mathematical investigation'. So it may be useful to pause with this example. On discovery of a general method for solving quadratics, 'root' came to mean 'values of the form

$$\frac{-b \pm \sqrt{b^2 - 4ac}}{2a},$$

and hence the sentence '$x + 2x + 1 = 0$ has two roots' acquired a different meaning. As Wittgenstein put it, '... the proposition "this equation has n roots" hasn't *the same* meaning if I've proved it by enumerating the constructed roots as if I've proved it in a different way. If I find a formula for the roots of an equation I've constructed a new calculus.'[25] The new calculus is a new piece of language which the proof connects with the concluding 'therefore'. What appears to be a discovery of truth is the creation of an extension of language in which symbolism is given a use, that is to say, a meaning. In an earlier paper I showed that often so-called proofs, such as the proof of $a^0 = 1$, were better described as giving a reason for introducing a new symbol, in that case 'a^0'. In this paper I have interpreted Wittgenstein as holding that all proofs which do not make use of an established technique (as do proofs of propositions of the form $a \times b = c$) are justifications for, or involve creations of, new pieces of language. So the difference between proofs which introduce a new symbol and proofs which involve a new combination of symbols is not as great as might at first appear.

If to give a proof is to give a justification for accepting a new use of language, a use consistent with and in addition to the former use, then we apparently have an explanation of the paradox of proving a proposition which is other than the one we set out to prove. But a further consequence of the claim that 'the result of a mathematical proof gets its meaning from the proof' is a paradox which has yet to be explained. Wittgenstein's recognition of the consequence is reflected in his asking himself '... should I say that the same sense can only have *one* proof?'[26] 'Is it correct to say that every proof demonstrates something to us which it alone can demonstrate?' (ibid., p. 93). The answer seems to be 'Yes'; and yet he is forced to admit that 'Of course it would be nonsense to say that *one* proposition cannot have two proofs — for we do say just that' (ibid., p. 92). The paradox lies in the stalemate between the answer and the admission.

The clue to an explanation lies in two claims of Wittgenstein, first, that '*we* fix whether there is to be only one proof of a certain proposition, or two proofs, or many proofs',[27] and second, the fact 'that we allow several patterns to be called proofs of the same proposition is due to the application of the symbols in question' (ibid., pp. 38-9). For two proofs to prove the same, 'It is not enough', he says, 'that [they] meet in the same propositional sign'.[28] 'Two proofs prove the same when what they convince me of is the same — and when is what they convince me of the same?' (ibid., p. 92). When they 'lead [me] to apply this proposition in such-and-such a way — determine [me] to accept this as sense, that not.... The result of our being convinced is that we *accept a rule*' (ibid., p. 77), a rule about the use of an expression. One might suppose that this acceptance is compelled. For it appears that when one goes through a proof and says 'I must fix the use of my language in *this* way', one is compelled 'to accept this as sense, that not'. Wittgenstein denies that when two proofs 'meet in the same propositional sign' they determine that the propositional sign rules the same use for the same expression. One proof does not demonstrate that another proof gives the concluding sentence the same applicability (ibid., p. 92). 'Why', asks Wittgenstein, 'do I always speak of being compelled by a rule; why not of the fact that I can *choose* to follow it?' (ibid., p. 193). The suggestion is that what lies ahead of the concluding sentence of two proof-sequences, its application, we can choose. And we usually choose the same thing. It is a fact that people who go through two demonstrations to infer a proposition which is expressed by the same sentence, use that sentence to legislate the *same* use of language. When this is the case they say that the two proofs convince them of the truth of the *same* proposition.

To illustrate, when it is established that $x^2 + 2x + 1 = 0$ has two roots, first by trying out values of the variable and then by use of the formula, instead of describing the two proofs as proofs of two different propositions, it is usual to say that one and the same proposition is proved in two ways. Further, we say that the one proof must give the same result as the other. *Because* people 'agree in *getting*'[29] the result -1 (because there is a consensus of action[30]), says Wittgenstein, we lay it down as a rule.[31] And this is different from agreeing that it is true. 'To say of the many methods which might be shown you as leading to the same result that they *must* lead to the same result, looks like a prophecy; but really it is a resolution we have made.'[32] In a proof one 'wins through to a decision'.[33] Admittedly, 'when two proofs meet it looks as if one had two independent proofs leading to the same result, and not as if one had made them do so'.[34]

It might well be maintained that trying out values of the variable to determine the roots of the equation $x^2 + 2x + 1 = 0$, together with observing that the equation is a square, $(x + 1)^2$, shows but one root, whereas calculating the roots by the formula shows two, since we get -1 twice over. N.J. Lennes in discussing this kind of equation stated that 'there is only one root' but that 'it is said to have two *coincident roots*'.[35] Here is an example of accepted legislation of a result. The various different proofs of the general theorem, *Every equation of nth degree has n roots*, are said to prove the same thing in that they are accepted as legislating what we are to say about the number of roots. The application, within mathematics, is to count n as the number of roots of an equation of nth degree, though, as Wittgenstein points out, we should not count one and the same chair in this way.[36] Proof, he says, 'very often teaches us the most useful form of expression' (ibid., p. 63). It is useful to be able to classify $x^2 + 2x + 1 = 0$ and $x^2 + 3x + 2 = 0$ as having the same number of roots. The effect of accepting the various proofs of the general theorem is to rule out the *same* expression, '*the* root of a quadratic equation'. And its having the same application regardless of what proves it is one reason for saying that the same proposition is proved by a number of proofs.

I wish to conclude with a brief comment on Wittgenstein's account of proof. Though his language suggests that he supposes himself to be giving a true description of the relation between proofs and the meaning of sentences denoting the theorems they prove, it may be that he is not doing this. He justifies his claim that with a different proof a different proposition results by calling attention to the connection between mathematical propositions and rules for the use of words which sets them off so radically from empirical propositions. The addition of a new piece of language effected by a new proof is taken to justify saying that the new proof has not proved the same proposition as did other proofs. It appears to me that under the guise of giving a correct description of the results of different proofs Wittgenstein is citing reasons for altering the use of the phrase 'the *same* proposition'. In general, the reasons stress the difference between establishing an empirical proposition and proving a mathematical proposition. To say that with a different proof we understand something different, that the same sentence does not express the same proposition, is to *stress* this difference. It may be that what Wittgenstein says of the philosopher, that 'all he wants is a new notation',[37] applies to his own thesis. What he says argues for precluding the use of 'the same proposition', 'understands the same' from descriptions of what a proof effects and what we know after proof. He is able to mitigate the resultant paradox by reinstating the use of 'same proposition' as a description of proved theorems which, regardless of the proofs, are accepted as legislating the same use of words.

Notes

1. *Essays in Analysis*, pp. 13-25.
2. *Philosophical Grammar*, p. 369.
3. *Wittgenstein's Lectures, Cambridge, 1932-1935* (ed. by A. Ambrose), p. 212.
4. Ibid., p. 198.
5. *Remarks on the Foundations of Mathematics*, p. 76.
6. Ibid., p. 153.
7. Ibid., p. 154.
8. Ibid., p. 78.
9. Ibid., p. 138.
10. *Wittgenstein's Lectures, Cambridge, 1932-1935*, p. 197.
11. Ibid., p. 198.
12. *Remarks on the Foundations of Mathematics*, p. 93.
13. *Wittgenstein's Lectures, Cambridge, 1932-1935*, p. 200.
14. *Wittgenstein's Lectures, Cambridge, 1932-1935*, p. 197.
15. *Remarks on the Foundations of Mathematics*, p. 146.
16. *Philosophical Grammar*, p. 371.
17. *Wittgenstein's Lectures, Cambridge, 1932-1935*, p. 198.
18. *Remarks on the Foundations of Mathematics*, p. 154.
19. *Wittgenstein's Lectures, Cambridge, 1932-1935*, p. 197.
20. *Remarks on the Foundations of Mathematics*, p. 78.
21. Ibid., p. 77.
22. See *Philosophical Grammar*, pp. 370-71.
23. This contrast was first brought out by M. Lazerowitz. See his *The Structure of Metaphysics*, pp. 267-71.
24. *Remarks on the Foundations of Mathematics*, p. 82.
25. *Philosophical Grammar*, p. 373.
26. *Remarks on the Foundations of Mathematics*, p. 164.
27. *Wittgenstein's Lectures, Cambridge, 1939* (ed. by Cora Diamond), p. 39.
28. *Remarks on the Foundations of Mathematics*, p. 93.
29. *Wittgenstein's Lectures, Cambridge, 1939*, p. 107.
30. Ibid., p. 184.
31. Ibid., p. 107.
32. *Wittgenstein's Lectures, Cambridge, 1932-1935*, p. 189.
33. *Remarks on the Foundations of Mathematics*, p. 77.
34. *Wittgenstein's Lectures, Cambridge, 1932-1935*, p. 188.
35. *College Algebra*, p. 57.
36. *Wittgenstein's Lectures, Cambridge, 1939*, pp. 152-53.
37. *The Blue Book*, p. 57.

68

Wittgenstein and the Character of Mathematical Propositions

Donald W. Harward

I intend to discuss an issue which may be of some interest to both mathematicians and philosophers. The topic is Wittgenstein's account of the nature of mathematical propositions.[1]

Two impressions or themes will recur in my argument. First I shall claim that with regard to the nature of a mathematical proposition there is a strong continuity in Wittgenstein's position from the *Tractatus* to his later philosophy of mathematics.[2] This continuity is due to Wittgenstein's doctrine of showing. Secondly, because the very nature of a mathematical proposition is tied to the uses to which we put it, the proper analysis of a mathematical proposition turns out to have much to do with ordinary sensible uses of descriptive language (cf. *RFM*, p. 133).

There have been a number of characterizations of Wittgenstein's position which are wholly mistaken. In a most popular article, M. Dummett leads us to believe that Wittgenstein was a conventionalist.[3] Moreover Wittgenstein's conventionalism is false, Dummett says, because conventionalism cannot explain regularity in mathematical proofs and the *non*-stipulative justification of mathematical propositions. Chihara modifies Dummett's interpretation by claiming that Wittgenstein was not a simple conventionalist but a 'complex' one.[4] And Shwayder in a publication out in January 1970 suggests that to claim Wittgenstein was a conventionalist of any sort is erroneous. Indeed, Shwayder continues, if anything, Wittgenstein was more of a Platonist — or what Shwayder terms a 'trans-Platonistic conceptualist' — in our jargon, an intuitionist.[5]

In addition to the misleading character of labels, these characterizations are far from adequate. Wittgenstein was neither conventionalist nor intuitionist, formalist nor logicist, Platonist nor naturalist. There is something quite right about many of these positions and their analysis of mathematics; but there is something very wrong with each of them and Wittgenstein is generous in his criticism.

Mathematics, thought Wittgenstein, is not the necessary description of mathematical objects, for we are not obliged to populate the universe with ontological constructs to account for the significance of a mathematical proposition. Platonism, therefore, in mathematics is at least unnecessary.

The conventionalist seems to be clearly mistaken in thinking that the rules of mathematics can be constructed arbitrarily. '2 + 2 = 4' does not mean that 'here and now, 2 + 2 = 4' or 'in general contexts 2 + 2 = 4'. On either of these readings he would be misconstruing what the mathematician is most interested in: the necessity of mathematical propositions. The form of a mathematical proposition *shows* itself as necessary (i.e., tautological) and this showing is not dependent on contextual variables. Wittgenstein's argument rests on an appeal to what we do and must mean by any mathematical proposition — and not on what mathematical problems could be solved if what we meant by a particular mathematical proposition was relevant to some arbitrarily designed context. The naturalistic (psychologistic, or empiristic) efforts are also wrong. Again, Wittgenstein is insistent on the character of mathematical necessity. We cannot replace necessities of mathematics with contingencies of thought or nature, for the proposition shows its tautological form independently of showing itself as the form of someone's thought. What can be thought can be said sensibly, so the form of sensible thought is quite different from the form of a mathematical proposition. For Wittgenstein, a mathematical proposition is not sensible.

The traditional theories of the *nature* of mathematics are also soundly attacked by Wittgenstein in both the early and later material. Formalism is right in insisting on the necessity of mathematics, and it is right in seeing the non-sensible character of a mathematical proposition, but it grandly misses the role of mathematical propositions and concepts. It fails to appreciate *why* mathematics cannot say anything (sensible) for it fails to see that the function of mathematical propositions is to show the relation of mathematics to the ordinary, sensible, uses of language.

Intuitionism is right in stressing the immediacy of understanding a mathematical concept or proposition but quite mistaken in holding that there is a subject matter, even though it be invented, to which mathematical propositions refer. That is, the intuitionist is mistaken in thinking that mathematical propositions are about anything. Mathematical propositions do not have significance for Wittgenstein, they do not say something, they are not about anything; their proper analysis lies elsewhere.

Logicism is also mistaken. Russell, Frege and others cannot be right in grounding mathematics in logic. They are mistaken in claiming that mathematical propositions are about abstract entities (for the reasons we structured above); and they are wrong in thinking that mathematical propositions are *about* all or some general objects or relations. Like the formalist, the logicist fails to appreciate the role of mathematical concepts and propositions. Wittgenstein then, takes a new, different look at mathematics. Mathematical propositions are not about anything, they have no descriptive content! The reason is to be found in the *Tractatus doctrines* of showing and saying. What is sensible, what can be pictured, what has descriptive content can be thought and said in language. What is not sensible, what does not have descriptive content cannot be said but may show some formal features. This is just what is the case with mathematical and logical propositions. They show certain formal features (e.g., their necessary character and their function to arrange and order what is sayable or sensible). Any thesis which opts for mathematical propositions being about something (be it abstract entities or created abstractions, or natural phenomena) is fundamentally mistaken. We cannot say what shows itself in language. What shows cannot be said for there is no other language, argued Wittgenstein, in which the saying can be performed. The formal features which show are the formal features of the only possible (truth functional) language. The *Tractatus*, then, is responsible for the following emphases in Wittgenstein's position:

a) Mathematical propositions are not descriptive for they are not sensible.

b) Mathematical propositions show their necessity, they are obvious tautologies.

c) A mathematical proposition functions to make explicit (to show) what is essential in our forms of thought and language.

d) Against Frege and Russell (as logicists), Wittgenstein argues in the *Tractatus* that they fail to indicate what the relation might be between the language of mathematical propositions and the referents they demand. Both Frege and Russell took propositions of mathematics to be general propositions about abstractions or about what we ought to take as true. On the contrary, Wittgenstein argues that the relation between mathematical propositions and what they supposedly describe cannot be said; the relation cannot be said because *nothing* is said by tautologies, they are not about anything but they do show their tautological character.

Wittgenstein did not alter these emphases in his later writings although it is well known that he certainly changed his position on a great many other issues.

In both *Remarks on the Foundations of Mathematics* and an unpublished manuscript on the philosophy of mathematics circulated in this country after 1949, Wittgenstein extends the position we have sketched above. Mathematical propositions cannot be descriptive! They are not statements about anything; they are, however, often prescriptive. They can, as Wittgenstein suggests, be considered as 'norms', as 'rules' for the use of our ordinary, sensible, thinking and talking. Mathematical propositions do not have their own subject matter; like laws of logic, they show what we do with language, not by expressing anything but by governing, as rules, the use of language in some way of life. To this extent, the conventionalist is correct; there is no real distinction between pure and applied mathematics. Where the conventionalist erred is in thinking that because the rules were applicable in different ways of life or contexts that the necessity of a mathematical proposition would be dependent on that context.

'I should like to say: mathematics is a motley of techniques ... and upon this is based its manifold applicability and its importance' (*RFM* 48e).

'The mathematical must is another expression of the fact that mathematics forms concepts. And concepts help us to comprehend things. They correspond to a particular way of dealing with situations. Mathematics forms a network of norms' (*RFM* 194e).

'Notice the difference between asking is there a reality corresponding to 30 × 30 = 900, taken alone and saying this of it as a proposition in a system. Taken by itself we shouldn't know what to do with it — it's useless. But there is all kinds of use for it as a part of a calculus. If we had a different calculus, 30 × 30 = 900 wouldn't have any meaning.

Mathematical and logical propositions are *preparations* for the use of language, almost like definitions are. It's all a put-up job. It can all be done on a blackboard. We just look at the signs, and never go outside the blackboard.

The correspondence of mathematical propositions to reality is like the correspondence of "negation" to reality, rather than like the correspondence of "It rains" to reality. It's like the correspondence of a word to its use. In mathematics the signs don't have a meaning — the meaning is given to them by the calculus. "0" and "300" are given a meaning, like "This is a chair" gives a meaning to a "chair". If I wanted to show the reality corresponding to 30 × 30 = 900 I do it by showing all the connections in which this transformation occurs. Mathematics and logic are part of the apparatus of language, not of the applications of language. The calculus *prepares* 900 for the work it has to do.

When asked what propositions are about numbers, almost everyone says "mathematical propositions" and in a way it is silly to dispute this — except for the fact that it always leads to a muddle.

If one says "which propositions of Euclid are about triangles?" I have no objection to saying the propositions on page 30 are about triangles, those on 40 are about circles, etc. I don't say it's wrong to say that mathematical propositions are about numbers. I am only pointing out the way into which it is likely to lead. I'm pointing out a source of confusion. "Being about" means two entirely different things, and it may lead to an enormous confusion.

This brings an entirely different sense of how a reality corresponds to mathematics. We will look for the reality in an entirely different place. When we consider propositions about 0 we are not dealing with a realm of entities in the most important sense of "about" — we are giving rules for the use of 0. And if we want to see what realm these propositions are about we must see in what sentences we use it'.[6]

Mathematical propositions function to provide rules for our sensible talk in ordinary contexts. 'Mathematical propositions can be put in the Paris Archives'.[7] There is no way, on Wittgenstein's grounds, to justify mathematics as an autonomous body of propositions about mathematical objects or even about marks on the page. On this matter Wittgenstein's position was unchanged from the *Tractatus* through his 1949 manuscript. Mathematical propositions are prescriptions or forms of rules, and what they provide are frameworks in which a variety, a 'motley', of application can be made (*RFM* 84e).

Notes

1. I discuss an issue which may be of some interest to both mathematicians and philosophers. The topic is Wittgenstein's account of the nature of mathematical propositions.

Two impressions or themes recur in my argument. First I claim that with regard to the nature of a mathematical proposition there is a strong continuity in Wittgenstein's position from the *Tractatus* to his later philosophy of mathematics. This continuity is due to Wittgenstein's doctrine of showing. Secondly, because the very nature of a mathematical proposition is tied to the uses to which we put it, the proper analysis of a mathematical proposition turns out to have much to do with ordinary sensible uses of descriptive language.

2. In the *Tractatus* Wittgenstein gave a completely rigorous account of the nature of language — an account which provided us with a clear means of appreciating both the logic of the language and the relationship which may be seen to hold between language, thought and reality. Within the scope of that work Wittgenstein claimed that he had provided for the fundamental analysis, once and for all times, of every possible significant assertion and logical form in which it could be said.

Even the limits for the non-significant were set in the *Tractatus*. Some assertions which do not have sense, which don't say anything or can't be used to say anything about the way things are, do show themselves to have some function. Their function is to order and arrange significant assertions. Mathematical and logical propositions fall into this class of not significant but useful remarks.

There is also in the *Tractatus* a third set, viz. those remarks which are neither sensible nor senseless-though-useless. For instance the remarks of speculative metaphysics, theistic assertions, claims about values, etc.; these are to be found in this third category of the wholly non-sensical.

3. M. Dummett, 'Wittgenstein's Philosophy of Mathematics', *Philosophical Review*, 68 (1959), 324-48, pp. 121-37 above.

4. C.S. Chihara, 'Mathematical Discovery and Concept Formation', *Philosophical Review*, 72 (1963), 17-34, pp. 264-76 below.

5. D.S. Shwayder, 'Wittgenstein on Mathematics', *Studies in the Philosophy of Wittgenstein*, Humanities Press, 1969.

6. L. Wittgenstein, *Unpublished manuscript*, pp. 108-9.

7. Ibid., p. 28.

69

Mathematical Discovery and Concept Formation

Charles S. Chihara

It has recently been claimed that in the philosophy of mathematics, Platonists, who hold among other things that the mathematician is primarily a discoverer of truths which are in some sense independent of us, stand opposed to constructivists who claim that the activity of the mathematician is essentially one of creating rather than finding.[1] Now, is the mathematician a discoverer or a creator? Compare:

> The discovery of the proof that π is transcendental did not create any logical relations but showed us what the relation always has been.[2]

> [A proof] makes new connexions, and it creates the concept of these connexions. (It does not establish that they are there; they do not exist until it makes them).[3]

Here, we certainly seem to have completely opposed views of mathematics, and in this paper I shall examine the nature of this opposition. I shall consider the question: Is the mathematician a discoverer or a creator? not with a view to answering it, but in order to bring out some of the considerations that have led various philosophers to take one side or the other; to point out mistakes and confusions that have muddied up the issue, and to indicate a few regions that require clarification before any sound answer can be given.

I

When Wittgenstein claimed that the mathematician creates rather than discovers, he was writing in opposition to the view of many realists who held that the mathematician is essentially one whose business is to apprehend and describe "internal relations" between certain things called "universals," "concepts," or "ideas." In recent years, traditional realists have been charged with committing such outrageous logical fallacies that it

264

might appear no sensible philosopher could have held such a position. For example, in his article "Properties and Classes" Anthony Quinton presents us with the following argument:

"We are able to classify these things together because we apprehend the universal of which they are instances" looks fairly substantial, until you ask what else can be meant by the apprehension of universals beyond the ability to classify. I am not objecting to the intermediary theories interpreted in this way just because they are repetitious. ... But this repetition is both unilluminating and misleading; it casts no light and a good deal of darkness. It is unilluminating because the use of a re-applicable word is something more concrete and definite than the apprehension of a universal and it is misleading in its suggestion that these are quite different things, and in particular that there is some other way of finding out about universals than that of inspecting concrete activities of classification.[4]

I do not know what traditional philosophers Quinton has in mind, but it does seem clear that few, if any, identified the "apprehension of a universal" with "having the ability to classify in a certain way." Most traditional realists would claim that apprehending a universal is something one does — having an ability is not. Again, when one apprehends a universal, one must in some sense be aware of the universal, whereas one can have an ability though one is not aware of anything. The early Russell, it should be recalled, claimed, in his well-known article, "Knowledge by Acquaintance and Knowledge by Description," that we have direct acquaintance with universals and defined acquaintance in the following way: "I say that I am *acquainted* with an object when I have a direct cognitive relation to that object, i.e. when I am directly aware of the object itself."[5]

Of course, many realists did think that our apprehension of a universal, in some sense, explained our ability to classify, but I think many realists thought this apprehension explained much more. Some realists have held it explained how we discover certain necessary relations between universals. For example, Russell writes in *The Problems of Philosophy*:

The statement "two and two are four" deals exclusively with universals, and therefore may be known by anybody who is acquainted with the universals concerned and can perceive the relation between them which the statement asserts. It must be taken as a fact, discovered by reflecting upon our knowledge, that we can have the power of sometimes perceiving such relations between universals.[6]

Quinton might argue that the realist is merely using the misleading expression "perceiving such a relation between universals" to mean simply "coming to know one classifies in such a way that whenever one can say there are two and two things that have a certain property, one can also say there are four things that have a certain property; and conversely, when one can say there are four things that have a certain property, one can also say there are two and two things that have the property." I do not think, however, this is what the realist means. Coming to know that such a relation obtains is not the same as perceiving or apprehending the relation, according to some realists; for one might come to maintain that a certain relation holds between universals not on the basis of an apprehension of the relation but on the basis of induction.

As Russell puts it,

> Our general proposition may be arrived at in the first instance by induction, and the connexion of universals may be only subsequently perceived. For example, it is known that if we draw perpendiculars to the sides of a triangle from the opposite angles, all three perpendiculars meet in a point. It would be quite possible to be first led to this proposition by actually drawing perpendiculars in many cases, and finding that they always met in a point; this experience might lead us to look for the general proof and find it. Such cases are common in the experience of every mathematician.[7]

Now someone might fail to perceive this connection of universals but be certain on the basis of examining particular instances that the connection holds. He might even claim to know, saying, "I know that this is true but I can't see why" — his not seeing why is perhaps what Russell would call "his not perceiving the connexion." One could, of course, argue that such a person would not really know that the connection holds, but I shall not go into that here. It would seem at any rate, that he does have true belief and that he does have grounds for his belief. Thus, we might speak of two reasons for holding that a certain relation holds between universals: (1) the direct apprehension of the relation, and (2) induction. There are also other reasons. One might do so on the basis of being informed of the fact by some authoritative source or by a reliable person who is in a position to know. For instance, a mathematician, say an analyst, might use a theorem of algebra in one of his proofs even though he had never actually gone through the proof of the theorem, and, if asked if he knew whether or not the algebraic statement is a true one, he might very well, and with some justification reply, "Oh yes — it's a well-known theorem of algebra."

It would seem then that the realist has grounds for denying Quinton's implication that there is no other way of "finding out about universals ... [except by] inspecting concrete activities of classification." Indeed, none of the three ways noted above could be described as "inspecting concrete activities of classification."

This claim of Quinton is similar to a claim made by Norman Malcolm in an early article entitled, "Are Necessary Propositions Really Verbal?"[8] Malcolm, in attempting to dispel the metaphysical mystery from the discovery of necessary truths, argued that "the question as to whether one proposition entails another is a question as to how certain words are used."[9] And to find out how words are being used requires no intellectual vision or intuition; for, as Malcolm puts it, "we find out necessary truths in the same way we find out the empirical truth that if you suddenly jab a man with a pin he will jump ... it is by observing how people use expressions in certain circumstances that we learn necessary truths."[10]

Malcolm's view, however, suffers from a serious defect — it makes a complete mystery of mathematical discovery; for if the discovery of necessary truths is simply a matter of observing people use expressions, mathematics should be, it would seem, an empirical science. There then should be a way of finding out whether or not Fermat's "last theorem" is true by observing the way people use symbols. That this absurdity is not implied by Malcolm's thesis certainly needs to be shown. Furthermore, what in the world is the mathematician doing when he sits locked in his room proving theorems that have hitherto been unknown? According to Malcolm's analysis, he cannot be discovering necessary truths. Yet to deny that the mathematician is making discoveries is paradoxical and surely requires justification. But aside from these difficulties, is it as a matter of fact true that we always discover necessary truths by simply observing the way people react in certain situations? This is surely not a point for argument — we need simply recall that there are countless occasions on which we discover necessary truths without observing the way people use symbols.

Both Malcolm and Quinton, then, seem to overlook the obvious and common phenomenon of seeing conceptual connections — something that realists are not likely to overlook. Thus, the well-known mathematician, G.H. Hardy, unblushingly suggests that "mathematical reality lies outside us, that our function is to discover or to *observe* it, and that the theorems which we prove and which we describe grandiloquently as our 'creation,' are simply our notes of our observations."[11] Realists on the whole, I think, have been struck by certain similarities between our knowledge of the physical world and our "knowledge of universals." I know certain things about J.F. Kennedy secondhand, so to speak, from newspaper accounts, magazine articles, and the like. Other facts about Kennedy, I know firsthand from actually seeing and hearing him. Analogously a realist might claim that I know certain things about the number π secondhand from reading about it in books on mathematics; other things, firsthand from actually seeing that π must have certain mathematical properties and relations to other numbers. And just as one can make conjectures about the physical world, form hypotheses on the basis of observations and experiments, test and confirm them, so in the case of mathematics, one can make conjectures about mathematical relations, form hypotheses on the basis of the results obtained by a number of operations or computations, test the hypotheses, and finally prove some of the hypotheses to be true.[12]

For many realists, then, the essential difference between mathematics and the natural sciences is to be found in the peculiar "sphere of reality" which is the object of mathematical explorations.[13] It is not my purpose in this paper, however, to discuss or defend the details of this aspect of realism. I do wish to point out that traditional realists, in attempting to explain our knowledge of necessary truths and to clarify the nature of proof and mathematical discovery, have taken into account certain facts about the activity of mathematicians that are frequently overlooked by philosophers overzealously attempting to sweep away metaphysical explanations.

II

But is not this talk about "mathematical reality" obscure, misleading and, in some ways, an obstacle to obtaining a clear understanding of the nature of mathematics? Wittgenstein, reacting against such a platonic view, wrote, "The mathematician creates *essence*" (*RFM*, I, 32). To see what is behind Wittgenstein's claim, imagine that we are trying to teach a young person named John the meaning of such words as "circle," "triangle" and "square." We show John many cardboard cutouts, telling him that these objects are all circular, those are triangular, and these are square. Perhaps we also draw a number of figures for him telling him which ones are circular, and so on. Let us suppose that after a while John catches on. He learns to distinguish figures as being circles, triangles, or squares. If you ask him to pick out those figures on the blackboard that are circles, he is able to do so. He also learns to characterize particular figures as being circles, squares, or triangles.

Russell would have claimed, I think, that John must have apprehended the relevant universals. He seems to have thought it obvious that if one understands the meaning of a term one must be acquainted with something for which the term stands. Of course, John does not fully understand the meaning of these shape-terms, since he has not yet learned to refer to these shapes and talk about the shapes; he is able to pick out squares, but he has not yet learned to talk about the property of being square. He has not learned to characterize the property or discuss its relation to other properties. Russell might have claimed that John only dimly apprehended the universal. I shall not criticize this view.

Suppose that a little later John is taught various referring uses of these shape expressions. I do not mean he merely learns to refer to particular figures by means of these shape expressions ("That square is larger than this one"). I mean he also learns to refer to the shape *qua* shape ("Being square differs from being rectangular in that squares must have sides all of which are equal in length"). To use the language of the realist, he learns to refer to the *universal*. At this point, there is little temptation to explain John's newly acquired skills in terms of a clearer intellectual apprehension of the shape universals. Someone might suggest that John has apprehended instead a bit more of the "workings of language," but this does not seem especially apt nor will it do as an explanation. Of course, it is not clear in what respect the acquiring of an intellectual ability requires explanation. But this is another matter.

Imagine now that we show John various connections between squares, angles, sides, and triangles. We show him, for example, that the angles formed by the sides of a square are all equal, not only to each other, but to any angle of any square. He is also brought to see that a diagonal joining opposite vertices of any square must divide the figure into two congruent isosceles triangles. Russell, in "Knowledge by Acquaintance and Knowledge by Description," stated that he did not know how we could know such facts unless we were acquainted with the relevant universals.[14]

But what did take place in John's mind when he perceived these "internal" relations? Or is that important? What I am interested in is what this perceiving amounts to.[15] Perhaps we should ask: In virtue of what do we say John has perceived these "internal" relations? Surely not merely his saying that he sees.

Let us start with the first example. John claims to see that the angles of a square must all be equal. But suppose we show him a figure which at first glance seems to be square but whose angles when measured turn out to be clearly unequal in magnitude, and John does not see that this fact has any relevance to the claim that the figure is a square. I think this would be grounds for thinking John had not really seen the connection between squares and angles.

What I am driving at is this: what is called "apprehending an internal relation" or "seeing a conceptual connection" seems to affect, in one way or another, the way one applies the relevant terms. One might be tempted to say that seeing that the angles of a square must all be equal involves, as Wittgenstein would have put it, "accepting a new criterion" for the application of the term "square," and with this "acceptance," a combination of words would become for John senseless. For if John "accepts" the equal angle criterion for determining squareness, then it would not make sense to him to describe a figure as being a square with angles that are not equal in magnitude. Perhaps one can see now a bit of what lies behind Wittgenstein's statements:

The mathematical proposition is to show us what it makes SENSE to say.

The proof constructs a proposition.... When we say that the construction must *convince* us of the proposition, that means that it must lead us to apply this in such-and-such a way. That it must determine us to accept this as sense, that not [*RFM*, II, 28].

Assuming that John sees the connection between squares and their angles, we might wonder if John has the same concept of square after this apprehension. It is easy to see that John might now refuse to characterize certain figures as being square which he previously would have so characterized, and this, taken with the consideration above, might lead one, as I think it led Wittgenstein, to claim that seeing a conceptual connection of this sort involves altering one's concepts.[16] One must keep it in mind, however, that John might insist that he means now by "square" the very same thing he meant before being shown this "internal" relation. John might claim that he means the same thing though he now knows a bit more about the nature of squares. In spite of this, according to Wittgenstein, what we have here is a case of concept formation, which brings out an essential role of an informal proof.

Let us start at the beginning with the educating process of John. At first John has, one might say, a primitive concept of square. He is able to do such things as pick out square figures simply by the "look" of the figures, though he has not yet learned to do so by measuring the magnitude of angles and sides. We now show him that squares must have equal angles by showing him, for example, the way various figures which he calls non-square differ from those that he calls square. As a result, he applies the term "square," so Wittgenstein would have put it, in a new way, which shows that he has formed a new concept of square.

The thesis that the role of mathematical proofs is to be understood in terms of the application of mathematical propositions and concept formation explains to some extent Wittgenstein's wanting to say:

> It is essential to mathematics that its signs should also be used in civil life.
>
> It is their use outside mathematics, in other words the *meaning* of the signs, that makes the sign-game mathematics.
>
> Just as it is not a logical conclusion if I change one configuration into another (say one arrangement of chairs into another) unless these configurations have some use in language *besides* the making of these transformations.[17]

And this thesis perhaps lies behind Wittgenstein's extreme claim regarding a proved mathematical proposition that "you do not understand the proposition so long as you have not found the application."[18]

Now consider John again. He sees that one of the diagonals of a square divides the square into two congruent isosceles triangles. How is there concept formation in this case? In the light of Wittgenstein's thesis, one might suggest the following considerations. John has a piece of paper which appears to be square. He folds the square along a diagonal by bringing opposite vertices together, but the triangles formed are clearly not congruent. This would show him that the piece of paper was not square. John would be "utilizing a new criterion" for determining squareness which he had "adopted" as a result of being shown the proof.

Suppose that prior to seeing the proof above, John had been trying to construct a square with diagonals dividing the figures into triangles that are not congruent. Of course, after seeing the proof, he would see that there are no squares of this sort, but his seeing this, Wittgenstein argued, is in an important respect different from his seeing, say, that there are no unicorns. For though realists like Hardy and the early Russell would have emphasized the similarities by describing John as exploring the mathematical realm in an attempt to find a certain geometric construction, Wittgenstein continually emphasized the differences and, indeed, felt that such "exploration-discovery" talk obscured the differences. According to Wittgenstein, the discovery that there is no geometric construction of a certain sort involves concept formation, unlike the discovery that there are no unicorns.[19] And in this connection Wittgenstein is reported by Moore to have said:

"Looking for" a trisection by rule and compasses is not like "looking for" a unicorn, since "There are unicorns" has sense, although in fact there are no unicorns, whereas "There are animals which show on their foreheads a construction by rule and compasses of the trisection of an angle" is just nonsense like "There are animals with three horns, but also with only one horn" ... by proving that it is impossible to trisect an angle by rule and compasses "we change a man's idea of trisection of an angle" but ... we should say that what has been proved impossible is the very thing he had been trying to do, because "we are willingly led in this case to identify two different things."[20]

But what two different things do we identify? According to Wittgenstein, as a result of seeing the proof, the person forms a new concept, and we identify the new concept with the one he had prior to seeing the proof, though "the old concept is still there in the background" (*RFM*, III, 30).

III

Wittgenstein's construction view of mathematics is perhaps least persuasive when one considers simple calculating examples. One can, of course, *discover* that there is a 9 in the decimal expansion of π by simply calculating. Indeed, one can discover an indefinite number of "mathematical truths" by simply calculating more and more places of the expansion; and the platonic picture of all the digits in the decimal expansion spread out, so to speak, in "mathematical space" comes readily to mind. But for Wittgenstein, "we learn an endless technique ... what is in question here is not some gigantic extension" (*RFM*, IV, 19), and in exercising my mastery of the technique by calculating, I form new concepts.

Part of the difficulty one finds in trying to understand Wittgenstein's constructivism is generated by his murky use of the term "concept" which for some reason he does not bother to define. Unlike his use of the term "criterion," it has been given little attention despite the intimate connection between *criterion* and *concept*, and despite the prominent role *concept* plays in Wittgenstein's philosophy of mathematics.[21] It is, of course, paradoxical to claim that the proving of a new theorem of mathematics results in new concepts being formed, but perhaps we should consider how Wittgenstein is using the term "concept" ("*Begriff*") in those passages where he discusses proof and concept formation. Unfortunately this is not very clear from the fragmentary notes which comprise the *Remarks on the Foundations of Mathematics*. He does tell us, bringing to mind his early *Tractatus* view, that "'concept' is something like a picture with which one compares objects" (*RFM*, V, 50). And since the picture analogy seems to have dominated so much of Wittgenstein's thinking on the subject, I shall put the analogy to work in an attempt to clarify a little Wittgenstein's peculiar constructivistic doctrine as it is applied to the case of the expansion of irrational numbers.

In the *Brown Book*, Wittgenstein describes a "language game" involving the use of a table consisting of pictures of objects (a chair, a cup, etc.) with written signs opposite each picture, the table being used in the following way: one person writes one of the signs, and the other, after locating the sign in the table, fetches the object represented in the picture opposite the sign in the table.[22] This language game can be extended, I imagine, so that the tables would be used for actions analogous to, say, referring to objects or describing things. Interestingly enough, Wittgenstein classifies the pictures of this language game among the "instruments of language" and calls "instruments" which are similar in function to the pictures, as for example color samples in a color chart, "patterns" (*BB*, p. 84). This explanation of what he means by "pattern," he admits, is vague. Still, one can understand the transition he makes from these simple pictures and color-chart examples to the claim that in the sentence "He said 'Go to Hell,'" "Go to Hell" is a pattern also (*BB*, p. 84). And from examples of this sort, it is only a short step to "numeral-patterns" like "3.14159265."

Thus, one can see why Wittgenstein might claim that by actually calculating the expansion of π, one can produce new "patterns" — new "instruments of language" — which can be used as objects of comparison to determine, say, whether someone else is correctly expanding π. And notice for Wittgenstein, "the concept of infinite decimals in mathematical propositions are not concepts of series, but of the unlimited technique of expansion of series" (*RFM*, IV, 19). These "patterns," then, that are constructed and accepted as correct patterns, provide us, according to Wittgenstein, with criteria for recognizing correct expansions.

Let us say that when π was first defined for me, I was given only a rule for calculating the decimal expansion. At that point, I had no "numeral-pattern" to use as a standard of comparison for recognizing correct expansions. Later, by calculating the first four places of the expansion, I produced a "numeral-pattern" which I accepted as correct. Since this provides me with a new criterion for recognizing correct expansion, I would have, on Wittgenstein's view, a new concept of π. However, there is no reason why I must have calculated the "numeral-pattern" in order for this sort of concept formation to occur. A pattern produced by a calculating machine would do just as well. In fact, sequences of numerals produced by machines, copied and printed in mathematical tables are, as I interpret Wittgenstein, concept-forming "patterns" which we frequently do use.[23] Furthermore, there is no reason why one would have to carry such "patterns" around as long as one is able to memorize them.[24] Thus, in discussing calculations, Wittgenstein writes:

You *find* a new physiognomy. Now you can e.g. memorize or copy it.
   A *new* form has been found, constructed. But it is used to give a new concept together with the old one [*RFM*, III, 47].

Logicians frequently define a *proof in a formal system* to be a finite sequence of well-formed formulas each of which is one of the axioms or derived according to one of the transformation rules of the system from one or more of the well-formed formulas which precede it in the sequence, calling a proof of this sort the proof *of* the last well-formed formula in the sequence.[25] If we look at proofs in this way,[26] there is a striking similarity between producing such proofs and calculating the expansion of irrational numbers, and this sheds light, I think, on Wittgenstein's comment: "When I said that a proof introduces a new concept, I meant something like: the proof puts a new paradigm among the paradigms of the language" (*RFM*, II, 31).

Wittgenstein's use of the term "rule" is notoriously eccentric, and it is rather surprising to find him claiming that it is in accordance with *ordinary usage* that he applies the term "rule" to the tables of his "language games," ostensive definitions, and similar "instruments" (*BB*, p. 91). (Is Wittgenstein really an "ordinary language philosopher"?) In view of this, however, it should not surprise us that he would call such things as "numeral-patterns" rules also, which gives us an indication of what lies behind his paradoxical claims that, "when I calculate the expansion further, I am deriving new rules which the series obeys" (*RFM*, IV, 11). And in view of the considerations above, perhaps one can get some rough idea of what led Wittgenstein to say, "However queer it sounds, the further expansion of an irrational number is a further expansion of mathematics" (*RFM*, IV, 9).

There is a great deal that is obscure in Wittgenstein's constructivistic talk, however, and some of the obscurity is due to Wittgenstein's imprecise and confusing use of such crucial terms as "concept," "criterion," and "use." Even Wittgenstein has to admit, at one point, that the meaning of the term "concept" is "by far too vague" (*RFM*, V, 38). And the vagueness here is not simply a matter of the existence of a vague boundary — there seems to be a great deal in Wittgenstein's use of the term that is unspecified and indeterminate. One wonders, for example, when it would be correct to say, "John and Mary have the *same* concept of square." When John and Mary know precisely the same theorems about squares? In that case, it would be a rather remarkable coincidence if two mathematicians, picked at random, happen to have the same concept of square. And does the fact that two persons have different concepts of π imply that they mean different things by "π"? If this is so, Wittgenstein's doctrine would have the strange consequence that two persons mean different things by "π" simply because one has calculated the decimal expansion to more places than the other.

I do not think that Wittgenstein's thoughts on the subject at this time were especially precise or clear. Very probably, *he* was not satisfied with much of his work in this area, and it is significant that he included so little of this work in his *Philosophical Investigations*.

IV

Michael Dummett contends that to adopt the picture of our creating mathematics as we go along "involves thinking with Wittgenstein that we are *free* in mathematics at every point; no step we take has been forced on us by a necessity external to us, but has been freely chosen."[27] Now what has being free or not free to do with the construction notion of mathematics? Indeed, what does it even mean to say that we are or are not free in mathematics or that some step in a proof has been forced on us? For Wittgenstein did not deny that, in some sense, we are compelled to accept the results of certain proofs.[28]

Suppose, to use Dummett's own example,[29] that we humans are like calculating machines when it comes to doing such things as calculating the decimal expansion of π — we are, so to speak, "compelled" by some mechanism to get certain results. Would this preclude concept formation and the construction model of mathematics? I do not think it is obviously so at all. Wittgenstein himself, it should be noted, considered this analogy, remarking, "If calculating looks to us like the action of a machine, it is *the human being* doing the calculation that is the machine" (*RFM*, III, 20), and, as we have already seen, there are indications that Wittgenstein allowed that calculating machines play a part in concept formation.

When one calculates and gets a certain result, it might appear that one is, in some sense, *compelled* to get the result one gets. Yet Wittgenstein frequently writes as if one were not compelled — at least not "logically compelled" — to get the result one does get. But what is "logical compulsion"? Wittgenstein's discussions on the topic are, for the most part, in terms of metaphors, analogies, and models, again making it difficult to get a precise idea of Wittgenstein's own position. But since I have discussed this aspect of Wittgenstein's philosophy of mathematics elsewhere,[30] I shall pass over it, though a great deal more needs to be said on the topic.

V

Does accepting Wittgenstein's construction view of mathematics commit one to a rejection of the realist's discovery view? This is not clearly so. Even if one grants the soundness of Wittgenstein's construction doctrine, additional consideration, I think, would have to be brought to bear on the problem to refute the realist's view. Could not a realist allow, without inconsistency, that in calculating decimal expansions one constructs "patterns" which serve as new "instruments of language"? And could not a realist hold that one's "concepts" (in Wittgenstein's sense, whatever that is) may undergo a change as a result of being shown a proof without giving up the notion of a "mathematical reality" awaiting exploration? These questions are difficult to answer, for one thing, because the realist's "mathematical reality" doctrine is so vague and obscure. But then there is a great deal that is obscure on both sides of the issue, for what Wittgenstein says about concepts and mathematical discovery is hardly a model of clarity. And although both sides are able to generate a certain amount of sympathy for their positions by emphasizing particular aspects of "mathematical discovery," the opposition between the sides is much too vague and uncertain for me to make any clear-cut and confident judgment about the matter. I suggest, however, that both sides have exaggerated certain features of our activities at the expense of overlooking other important features, yielding incomplete and distorted philosophical accounts.

Notes

1. Michael Dummett, 'Wittgenstein's Philosophy of Mathematics,' *Philosophical Review*, LXVIII (1959), pp. 324-5.
2. Morris Cohen, *Reason and Nature*, (Glencoe, Ill., 1953), p. 193.
3. Ludwig Wittgenstein, *Remarks on the Foundations of Mathematics* (New York, 1956), II, 31. Cited here as *RFM*.
4. *Proceedings of the Aristotelian Society*, LVIII (1957-1958), 39-40.
5. Bertrand Russell, *Mysticism and Logic* (New York, 1918), p. 202.
6. Oxford, 1912, p. 105.
7. Ibid., p. 107.
8. *Mind*, XLIX (1940), 189-203.
9. Ibid., p. 193.
10. Ibid., p. 192.
11. *A Mathematician's Apology* (Cambridge, 1941), pp. 63-4.
12. Consider the following example from G. Polya's *Mathematics and Plausible Reasoning* (Princeton, 1954), I, pp. 108-9. The quotient

$$\frac{1^2 + 2^2 + \ldots + n^2}{1 + 2 + \ldots + n}$$

takes on the following values for $n = 1, 2, 3, 4, 5, 6$: 3/3, 5/3, 7/3, 9/3, 11/3, 13/3. Upon examining these values, one might plausibly conjecture that

$$\frac{1^2 + 2^2 + \ldots + n^2}{1 + 2 + \ldots + n} = \frac{2n + 1}{3},$$

and one might then verify that the formula is true for $n = 7, 8, 9, 10$, etc. Indeed, as a result of testing the formula for a large number of cases, one might become convinced that the formula is true for all natural numbers, though of course, one would still lack the proof and, in this sense, not know why the formula is true. Later, one might find a proof using mathematical induction. Polya, in his book, masterfully brings out many striking similarities between the way mathematicians and the way natural scientists discover truths.
13. Cf. Russell's claim that 'mathematics takes us ... from what is human, into the region of absolute necessity, to which not only the actual world, but every possible world, must conform; and even here it builds a habitation, or rather finds a habitation eternally standing, where our ideals are fully satisfied and our best hopes are not thwarted' (*Mysticism and Logic*, p. 65). Cf. also E.W. Beth's talk about 'spheres of reality' in *The Foundation of Mathematics* (Amsterdam, 1959), pp. 644-5.
14. *Mysticism and Logic*, p. 206.
15. Cf. Wittgenstein's comment: 'The proof convinces us of something — though what interests us is, not the mental state of conviction, but the applications attaching to this conviction' (*RFM*, II, 25).
16. 'The proof changes the grammar of our language, changes our concepts' (*RFM*, II, 31).
17. *RFM*, IV, 2. I use R. Rhees's translation, in 'Wittgenstein's Builders,' *Proceedings of the Aristotelian Society*, IX (1959-60), 179. Cf. Frege's statement: 'It is applicability alone which elevates arithmetic from a game to the rank of a science. So applicability necessarily belongs to it' (*Translations from the Philosophical Writings of Gottlob Frege*, ed. by P.T. Geach and Max Black [Oxford, 1952] p. 187). In 'Wittgenstein's Builders,' Rhees makes the interesting comment on Wittgenstein's wondering whether there might be a society in which there was no pure mathematics but only applied mathematics: 'Could we still say that they calculated and had proofs[?] ... These proofs would have nothing to do with "concept

formation," as the proofs of pure mathematics do.... But just for this reason their whole position or rôle as proofs would become obscure. "What puzzles me," Wittgenstein said, "is how these proofs are *kept*" (pp. 178-9).

18. *RFM*, IV, 25. But the concept of applying mathematical propositions, especially when one is dealing with highly abstract mathematical systems, is hardly clear and precise; and this gave Wittgenstein trouble.

19. Cf. 'What I always do seems to be — to emphasize a distinction between the determination of a sense and the employment of a sense' (*RFM*, II, 37).

20. G.E. Moore, 'Wittgenstein's Lectures in 1930-33,' *Philosophical Papers* (London, 1959), pp. 304-5. Moore also indicates the kind of view Wittgenstein held at this time concerning arithmetic and concept formation. In this regard, Wittgenstein says of a proof that 200 and 200 added together yield 400: 'It defines a new concept: "the counting of 200 and 200 objects together." Or, as we could also say: "A new criterion for nothing's having been lost or added"' (*RFM*, II, 24). We see the stresses and strains on Wittgenstein's thesis as he tries to account for the 'motley' of mathematics.

21. For discussion of what Wittgenstein means (or may have meant) by 'criterion,' see Norman Malcolm, 'Wittgenstein's *Philosophical Investigations*,' *Philosophical Review*, LXIII (1954), pp. 530-559; also Rogers Albritton, 'On Wittgenstein's Use of the Term "Criterion,"' *Journal of Philosophy*, LVI (1959), 845-7, see Volume Two, pp. 183-93.

22. Ludwig Wittgenstein, *The Blue and Brown Books* (Oxford, 1958), p. 82. Cited here as *BB*.

23. Wittgenstein implies, however, that he does not think it is necessary that such machine-calculated results form concepts: people might have adopted a quite different attitude toward machines, not trusting them for calculation purposes (*RFM*, II, 81).

24. It should be recalled that in the *Brown Book* Wittgenstein considers various cases in which persons compare objects with patterns 'from memory' (*BB*, p. 85).

25. Cf. A. Church, *Introduction to Mathematical Logic* (Princeton, 1956), I, 49.

26. Cf. 'A proof — I might say — is a *single* pattern, at one end of which are written certain sentences and at the other end a sentence (which we call the "proved proposition")' (*RFM*, I, 28).

27. Michael Dummett, 'Truth,' *Proceedings of the Aristotelian Society*, LIX (1958-59), 162.

28. Cf. 'And although ... proof is something that must be capable of being reproduced *in toto* automatically, still every such production must contain the force of proof, which compels acceptance of the result' (*RFM*, II, 55).

29. Dummett, 'Wittgenstein's Philosophy of Mathematics,' p. 331.

30. C.S. Chihara, 'Wittgenstein and Logical Compulsion,' *Analysis*, XXI (1961), pp. 136-40. See also in this regard, Dummett, 'Truth'; also the symposium in which J.F. Bennett and O.P. Wood discuss 'On Being Forced to a Conclusion,' *Proceedings of the Aristotelian Society*, Sup. Vol. XXXV (1961), 15-44. I do not think, however, that the position in this symposium criticized by Bennett should be identified with Wittgenstein's. In this regard, too, Joseph L. Cowan recently has given a radical interpretation of Wittgenstein's philosophy of logic in suggesting that Wittgenstein claimed 'that (in a sense) *there is no such thing as a rule*. There is no such thing as (or state or condition of) understanding a rule, or knowing a rule, or meaning of a rule. There is no such thing as behavior guided by, or even according to, a rule' ('Wittgenstein's Philosophy of Logic,' *Philosophical Review*, LXX [1961], 364). Cowan does not cite passages which really support this remarkable interpretation, and I am at a loss to explain how he came to it. But regardless of whether or not Wittgenstein held such a position (and I doubt that he did), I do not understand how Cowan can think sufficient grounds for accepting such a paradoxical metaphysical position have been provided by the considerations that he brings to bear on the question in his article.

70

Beyond Knowledge: Paradigms in Wittgenstein's Later Philosophy

C.G. Luckhardt

Although paradigms are often mentioned in connection with Wittgenstein's later philosophy,[1] no sustained attempt has yet been made to investigate Wittgenstein's conception of paradigms, or the precise role they play in his philosophy. In this paper I shall undertake such an investigation.

Paradigms are mentioned in almost all of the later Wittgenstein's published works, but it is in the *Remarks on the Foundations of Mathematics* and *On Certainty* that they are most fully discussed. Since their role in the former work bears an important relation to their role in the latter, I shall begin with a discussion of them in the *Remarks*. I shall show that paradigms as there conceived have three different identifying characteristics which they share with many empirical propositions. Understanding these empirical propositions as paradigms, I shall show in section II, is the key to understanding what Wittgenstein meant when he said that the propositions G.E. Moore claimed to know in "A Defence of Common Sense" have a "peculiar logical role in the system of our empirical propositions."[2] In section III I present and answer an objection to Wittgenstein's view of this role. Since this role is an important part of the epistemology implicit in *On Certainty*, I conclude by showing how Wittgenstein's view offers an alternative to one of the most fundamental but questionable assumptions of traditional epistemology.

I

One of the principal concerns of the *Remarks on the Foundations of Mathematics* is to elucidate the nature of mathematical proofs — what they are, what they are not, and how they function. At times "proof" is used synonymously with "model" and "picture" (*RFM* I-36, II-22, 24, 33, 39, V-6), all of which are to be distinguished from "experiment." Whereas an experiment has an "outcome," which is either right or wrong, a proof has a "result," which is taken as furnishing a model for experiments. The proof,

Wittgenstein says, "serve(s) as the picture of an experiment" (I-36). It serves as "our model for what it is like if nothing gets added and nothing taken away when we count correctly" (II-39). As such, proofs furnish "new paradigms" (II-31, 41), which are conceived by Wittgenstein as standards. They show "what *ought* to come out" (II-55). In his unpublished *Math Notes* Norman Malcolm quotes Wittgenstein as suggesting in a lecture that as standards, mathematical paradigms might be deposited in the Archive of Measurement, as the standard metric measures were at one time deposited in the archives at Paris: "Why can't we put a general rule of multiplication in the Archives? We have a meter rod in the archives ... We could put the multiplication table in the archives" (*MN* 23, see also *RFM* I-164, II-29, II-36). In this same lecture Wittgenstein is also quoted as advising that we make it a rule to ask "whether mathematical propositions are not paradigms or objects of comparison" (*MN* 14), and he compares the setting up of mathematical paradigms to the setting up of standards for writing capital letters:

> It is as if somebody said to me, "How do you write a capital F?" I write one. Then he declares: "From now on this is *the* capital F;" or "All capital F's shall be described in terms of this one, as more or less deviations from it." (*MN* 23)

Similarly, in the well-known paragraph in the *Investigations* in which he discusses the standard meter in Paris, and refers to the possibility of setting up samples of color, such as sepia, as paradigms, Wittgenstein is clearly thinking of paradigms as objects of comparison. He refers, for example, to a paradigm in our language-game as being "something with which comparison is made" (*PI* I-50). It is this characteristic of furnishing standards of comparison that I shall treat as one of the essential characteristics of paradigms.

Since paradigms furnish standards of comparison, Wittgenstein regards them as quite primitive and fundamental in any language-game in which they are used. Indeed, many of the metaphors he uses pictorially drive home this point: paradigms serve as "roads" along which traffic can travel, they are as "buildings," are "hardened" rather than fluid, are "measures" or "yardsticks," are "bedrock" or are "fossilized," are elements in one's "frame of reference," and act as "foundations," "foundation walls," or "hinges," (*RFM* I-66, I-162, II-41, *OC* 96, *RFM* II-21, 24, *OC* 492, *PI* I-217, *OC* 248, 657, *M* 92, *OC* 401, 411, 414, 614, 248, 341, 343, 655).

This primitive nature of paradigms furnishes another way of characterizing them. Since paradigms provide standards of comparison, agreement in paradigms is necessary for engaging in any practice which employs them. "In demonstration," Wittgenstein says, "we *get agreement* with someone. If we do not, then our roads part before it comes to traffic by means of this language" (*RFM* I-66). "If anyone *doesn't* acknowledge (a demonstration as a demonstration), then he has parted company with us even before it comes to talk" (*RFM* I-61). Or again:

We say that a proof is a picture. But this picture stands in need of ratification (*Approbation*), and that we give it when we work over it.

True enough: but if it got ratification from one person, but not from another, and they could not *come to any understanding* — would what we had here be calculation?

So it is not the ratification by itself that makes it calculation but the agreement of ratifications. ...

The agreement of ratifications is the pre-condition of our language-game, it is not affirmed in it. (*RFM*, V-6; also *PI* I-242)

The requirement for the agreement of ratifications may seem at first sight trivial, or perhaps even tautological. But taken together with another claim Wittgenstein makes, this requirement generates an important claim which is easily overlooked. It is tempting to think that agreement in paradigms is an easy thing to come by, since in order to secure it we need only to determine "what the facts are." This temptation is particularly strong when the agreements required are agreements of mathematical paradigms; for it is in mathematics, perhaps, that there is the strongest temptation to think that our paradigms are "inexorable" (*RFM* I-62), that they are not a matter of our choosing, but rather that our (correct) choosing is determined by something external to the language-game. Wittgenstein strongly resists this temptation and insists that we mislead ourselves when we yield to it. The temptation is to think "But I can only infer what actually does follow." Wittgenstein interprets this remark as liable to mislead. For by "what actually does follow" is meant, "What the logical machine really does produce. The logical machine — that would be an all-pervading ethereal mechanism. — We must give warning against this picture" (*RFM* I-119). The picture it presents is one of compulsion. We feel compelled to accept the proof of $12 \times 12 = 144$; we do not feel that we choose to accept it (*RFM* V-45). This feeling, that "the picture forces itself on us" (*RFM* I-14), is entirely wrong, Wittgenstein claims, for the "mathematician is an inventor, not a discoverer" (*RFM* I-167),[3] who "creates essence" (*RFM* I-32). It is we as mathematicians, who "deposit what belongs to the essence among the paradigms of language" (*RFM* I-32). Since it is we who deposit them it is also we who accept them. But the fact that they are deposited seems to imply that we *must* accept them. To this feeling Wittgenstein responds, "Why do you say you have to? Because at the end of the proof you say e.g.: 'Yes, I have to accept this conclusion.' But this is after all only the expression of your unconditional acceptance" (*RFM* I-33; also *PI* I-231). The proof of paradigm's compulsion consists solely in our "refusing any other path" (*RFM* I-34). It is we who refuse, and are therefore compelled, but only by our own decision, and not by any "very abstract, very general, and very rigid," "reality" (*RFM* I-8).

Now since agreement in paradigms is necessary, and since there is no "reality" which we could use to secure this agreement, it follows that those who do not have the same paradigms as we do are simply not measuring as we are. It does not follow, contrary to the temptation to believe so, that they are wrong. The feeling which presses itself on us is that one is mistaken if he accepts a rule of multiplication according to which $18 \times 15 \neq 270$ (*RFM* V-31), or if he believes that $-p$ could entail p (*RFM* V-23). Wittgenstein urges, however, that since there is no "reality" against which to judge rules such as these, adopting them could not be wrong, but at most unusual. He imagines, for example, a people who pile their timber in heaps of arbitrary, varying height and then sell it at prices proportionate to the area covered by the piles, disregarding their height (*RFM* I-148). He asks how one might convince these people that you do not really buy more wood when you buy a pile of greater area. One might try, he suggests, to rearrange one of their "small" piles into a "large" one. But if they agreed that the new pile *was* larger, and therefore ought to cost more than the "smaller" one, "that would be the end of the matter. We should presumably say in this case: they simply do not mean the same by 'a lot of wood' and 'a little wood' as we do; and they have a quite different system of payment from us" (*RFM* I-149). Failure to agree on paradigms is simply that, and nothing more.

I have mentioned two characteristics which paradigms possess, and which can be used to identify them. There is, however, a third identifying characteristic of paradigms which is perhaps the most important. Wittgenstein mentions this characteristic several times in his works. A particularly clear statement of it occurs in the *Investigations*:

> There is *one* thing of which one can say neither that it is one metre long, nor that it is not one metre long, and that is the standard metre in Paris. — But this is, of course, not to ascribe any extraordinary property to it, but only to mark its peculiar role in the language-game of measuring with a metre-rule. (*PI* I-50; see also *RFM* V-5)

The paradigm meter, Wittgenstein says in this same passage, is "not something that is represented, but is a means of representation." He asserts this distinction emphatically when he says:

> We do not judge the pictures, we judge by means of pictures.
> We do not investigate them, we use them to investigate something else.
> The picture of an arrangement is not an arrangement; the picture of a separation is not a separation; the picture of something's fitting not a case of fitting. And yet these pictures are of the greatest significance. *That is what it is like*, if an arrangement is made; if a separation; and so on. (*RFM* III-14)

Now since "the establishment of a method of measurement is antecedent to the correctness or incorrectness of a statement of length" (*RFM* I-155), paradigms are themselves neither true nor false, and hence in a sense are "beyond" or "above" truth and falsity, right and wrong, correctness or incorrectness. Just as the standard meter cannot be said to be a meter long, so too is it false to say that it is *not* a meter long. For just as saying it is a meter long implies that one has measured it according to some standard for meter length (which is ex hypothesi impossible, since *it* is the standard), so also saying that it is not a meter long implies that one has used some meter standard to measure it, according to which it was greater or less than a meter long. But since this latter is ex hypothesi impossible for the same reason as the former, the standard meter plays a role quite different from those things that are measured according to it. It is "above" or "beyond" the predication made possible by virtue of its being regarded as a standard.[4]

Wittgenstein remarks on this characteristic of paradigms several times, in works as early as *Philosophical Grammar*:

> The rules of grammar are arbitrary in the same sense as the choice of a unit of measurement. But that means no more than that the choice is independent of the length of the objects to be measured and that the choice of one unit is not 'true' and of another 'false' in the way that a statement of length is true or false. Of course that is only a remark on the grammar of the word "unit of length." (*PG* I-133)

> What is unshakably certain about what is proved?
> To accept a proposition as unshakably certain — I want to say — means to use it as a grammatical rule: this removes uncertainty from it. (*RFM* II-34)

> ... (T)he rules of inference are involved in the determination of the meaning of the signs. In this sense rule of inference cannot be right or wrong. (*RFM* V-23)

> What is proved by a mathematical proof is set up as an internal relation and withdrawn from doubt. (*RFM* V-5)

> There *can* be no mistake of calculation in '12 × 12 = 144'. Why? This proposition has assumed a place among the rules, (*RFM* II-73; also *OC* 34)

These last quotations are echoed in one of the paragraphs of *On Certainty*: "If the proposition 12 × 12 = 144 is exempt from doubt, then so too must non-mathematical propositions be" (*OC* 653). In the next section I shall discuss the passage from mathematical paradigms to empirical paradigms.

II

So far I have characterized paradigms as having three notable characteristics: (1) they are standards by which particular cases are judged, (2) agreement in them is necessary for engaging in any practice which employs them, and (3) they can never be said to be (or not to be) what particular cases judged according to them can be said to be (or not to be). I have already quoted from a paragraph in the *Investigations* in which Wittgenstein makes all of these points concerning paradigms. One of his examples of a paradigm in that paragraph is that of a meter-stick. This example is used again in *On Certainty*, only now metaphorically, for it is now certain beliefs that are yardsticks.

> ... What if it *seemed* to turn out that what until now has seemed immune to doubt was a false assumption? Would I react as I do when a belief has proved to be false? Or would it seem to knock from under my feet the ground on which I stand in making any judgements at all? ...
>   Would I simply say "I should never have thought it!" — or would I (have to) refuse to revise my judgment — because such a 'revision' would amount to annihilation of all yardsticks? (*OC* 492)

The suggestion here is, I think, that certain beliefs function as yardsticks against which the correctness of other beliefs is measured. If this is so (and I shall try to show that Wittgenstein thought it was), then such beliefs may be regarded as paradigmatic, provided that they also possess the other two characteristics which I have said Wittgenstein viewed paradigms as having.

The results of calling certain ordinary beliefs into question are pointed out in two other passages in *On Certainty*:

> If the water over the gas (literally — "flame") freezes, of course I shall be as astonished as can be, but I shall assume some other factor I don't know of, and perhaps leave the matter to the physicists to judge. But what could make me doubt whether this person here is N.N., whom I have known for years? Here a doubt would seem to drag everything with it and plunge it into chaos. (*OC* 613)
> ... The fact that I use the word "hand" and all the other words in my sentence without a second thought, indeed that I should stand before the abyss if I wanted so much as to try doubting their meanings — shews that absence of doubt belongs to the essence of the language-game, that the question "How do I know ..." drags out the language-game, or else does away with it. (*OC* 370)

These beliefs, without which we would be "plunged into chaos" are beliefs such as "The earth has existed for many years past" (*OC* 411), "My name is L.W." (*OC* 570, 571, 577, 579), "Cats do not grow on trees" (*OC* 282), and "I had a father and a mother" (*OC* 282; also *OC* 327). Wittgenstein sees such beliefs as propositions "exempt from doubt" which act as "hinges" (*OC* 341, 655) on which questions, disputes, and doubts can turn. Since the very practice of doubting, and hence also the practice of knowing occurs within a system (*OC* 247; also 102, 105), it is necessary that we agree on our paradigms before we begin to doubt. Agreement is a condition for the possibility of a language-game (*OC* 617), and hence without it different language-games are being played. In this respect it is clear that certain empirical propositions resemble some of the propositions of mathematics in a second way.

This parallel between some empirical propositions and some mathematical ones is suggested quite strongly in the passage from *On Certainty* quoted at the end of section I, but it is also brought out clearly in other places. For example, in the *Remarks* mathematics had been said to be normative (*RFM* V-40), and to form a "network of norms" (*RFM* V-46). These statements have their empirical counterpart in *On Certainty*:

> It is clear that our empirical propositions do not all have the same status, since one can lay down such a proposition and turn it from an empirical proposition into a norm of description. (*OC* 167; also 98, 321)

Or again, the similarity between mathematical and empirical propositions is suggested in the following statements:

> I cannot be making a mistake about 12 × 12 = 144. And now one cannot contrast *mathematical* certainty with the relative uncertainty of empirical propositions. (*OC* 651)
>
> ... (T)here is a close resemblance between some experiential statements and mathematical ones — namely, future experience won't provide reasons for rejecting them. (*M* 91)
>
> I want to say: If one doesn't marvel at the fact that the propositions of arithmetic (e.g. the multiplication tables) are 'absolutely certain,' then why should one be astonished that the proposition "This is my hand" is so equally? (*OC* 448)

I have stated that the second respect in which this similarity between certain mathematical and certain empirical propositions obtains is that agreement in paradigms is necessary for engaging in the practice made possible by the paradigms. This requirement in agreement is thus the requirement that we accept certain rules (*OC* 98, 309) which make it possible for us to judge the truth and falsity of other empirical propositions. But, as with mathematical paradigms, to speak of empirical paradigms as providing rules is to imply that although the paradigms can be applied to *other* propositions, they cannot be applied to themselves, and hence to imply that they cannot be judged true or false.

This point can be put another way. Doubting, Wittgenstein says, requires that some things not be doubted (*OC* 354), in order that there be "foundations" on which doubt can rest (*OC* 248, 401, 403, 411, 414, 614); empirical propositions, in order to be known, require standards so that we can assign "values" to particular propositions based on these standards (*OC* 410). Presumably such values are values like "known" or "dubitable," "true" and "false." But if the acceptance of paradigm propositions is what makes predication in terms of truth or falsity possible, then paradigm propositions are not true or false, and therefore not either known or not known. "If the true is what is grounded, then the ground is not *true*, nor yet false" (*OC* 205), Wittgenstein says, and suggests that what "lies beyond being justified or unjustified" is "as something animal" (*OC* 359). It is something we accept, assume, believe, or about which we are satisfied (*OC* 299), but as with mathematical paradigms, it is not something which is true or false, doubted or certain, known or not known.

We may, then, speak of paradigm empirical propositions (as opposed to paradigm mathematical propositions, or proofs) which, for Wittgenstein, furnish "norms" or "standards" for judging other empirical propositions. He regards agreement in such paradigms as being necessary for using them to judge many empirical propositions, although the paradigms cannot themselves be said to be doubted or known to be true or false.

It is precisely this last point which Wittgenstein accuses G.E. Moore of having failed to realize. Indeed, his failure to do so, according to Wittgenstein, is precisely what renders suspect his entire methodology in "A Defence of Common Sense." "Moore's mistake lies in this — countering the assertion that one cannot know that, by saying that I do know it" (*OC* 521). Moore was mistaken, Wittgenstein suggests, because he did not either know or fail to know the propositions he claimed to know. Although he might truly have said that he knew many other propositions (e.g., that "in such-and-such a part of England there is a village called so-and-so" (*OC* 462)), the propositions he enumerated "have a peculiar role in the system of our empirical propositions" (*OC* 136), which role precludes their being known. Insofar as they are paradigm propositions they are "beyond" knowledge. Not to realize this leads one to misuse the the word "know" (*OC* 6), for it is like trying to say of the standard meter that it *is* a meter long. For paradigms, as we have seen, cannot be used to judge themselves, and thus cannot be true or false, known or dubitable, etc., since they form a background or "frame of reference" (*M* 92) against which such predication as "is true," "is false," "is known," etc., can occur. They are what make possible the use of these predicates; hence, they cannot have the predicates applied to themselves.

In short, one might say that Wittgenstein's fundamental criticism of Moore's method was that he was wrong in believing that he could refute the skeptic by elucidating a series of propositions that were indubitable, known, and certain. In doing this Moore misused the word "know," since the way these propositions usually function is as paradigms for propositions which we can be said to know or not to know. *Qua* paradigms they do not themselves enter (directly) into the "known-is not known" language-game. Doubt ends somewhere, and where it ends is not in propositions of which we are certain, or which we know, but in propositions A) which we do not doubt, because B) they do not enter directly into the language-game of doubting and knowing, but rather C) function as yardsticks or standards according to which such language-games are played.

III

I have sketched the outlines of what Wittgenstein saw as the "peculiar logical role" of paradigm empirical propositions. It is now time to turn to an objection that is certain to be brought against this view. Dealing with it will help to fill in some of what his view entails, and will thus serve as preparation for a discussion in section IV of the importance of Wittgenstein's view in both epistemology and ethics.

The objection can be expressed as follows: despite what Wittgenstein says, we very often *do* say that we know, and are certain, of those very propositions about which, on the analysis I have given, we *cannot* be certain and which we cannot know, *viz.*, what I have called "paradigmatic propositions." Hence if my analysis is correct then we must be mistaken when we say that we know that cats do not grow on trees, or that we are certain we had a father and a mother, etc.

Wittgenstein was cognizant of this objection. In some sections of *On Certainty* he seems to respond to it by openly acknowledging that we do know the propositions he has said we do not know, and hence to contradict himself. But many other paragraphs suggest that Wittgenstein thought an answer could be given to the objection. This answer is that despite the fact that such propositions as Moore listed may and usually do function as paradigms, it is also possible to imagine circumstances in which such propositions might not function as paradigms. In all such cases there would be nothing philosophically problematic about them.

> Then why don't I simply say with Moore "I *know* that I am in England"? Saying this is meaningful *in particular circumstances*, which I can imagine. But when I utter the sentence outside these circumstances, as an example to shew that I can know truths of this kind with certainty, then it at once strikes me as fishy. (*OC* 432)
>
> But now it is also correct to use "I know" in the contexts which Moore mentioned, at least *in particular circumstances*. . . .
>
> For each one of these sentences I can imagine circumstances that turn it into a move in one of our language-games, and by that it loses everything that is philosophically astonishing. (*OC* 622)

When used in certain particular circumstances, therefore, paradigm propositions make perfectly good sense. But it is important to see that in these circumstances they are not being used as paradigms. And hence the objection is an *ignoratio*. Wittgenstein does not require that paradigm propositions always function as paradigms. "(T)he same proposition," he says, "may get treated at one time as something to test by experience, at another as a rule of testing" (*OC* 98). Just as the meter-stick *could* be regarded simply as an object to be measured, provided that one had some way to measure it, so could "I know that I am conscious" be used as a straightforward assertion in some circumstances, provided there was an appropriate framework within which it was uttered. Furthermore, that we treat a *class* of propositions as paradigms does not entail that one or another cannot be extracted from the class, to be used in particular circumstances as a straightforward empirical proposition: "What I hold fast to is not *one* proposition but a nest of propositions" (*OC* 225).

In addition to this response which Wittgenstein himself makes to the above objection, it is important to emphasize that, for Wittgenstein, saying that paradigm propositions are not objects of knowledge does not entail saying that they are propositions which we do not know. For to say this would be tantamount to admitting that they *can* participate in the "is known-is not known" language-game. And that is precisely the thesis he means to deny. Just as it is not true of every physical object that it either is or is not a meter long (since the standard meter lies outside of such predication), so it is not true of every empirical proposition that it is either known or not known, certain or dubitable, etc. In both cases the assertion makes no sense. When I am seated at the bedside of a sick person it makes no sense to say either that I know that a sick man is lying here, or that I do not know it (*OC* 10). So from the fact that Moore's assertion that he knows that there is a hand in front of him is mistaken, it does not follow that he does *not* know that there is a hand in front of him. Similarly, to say that "Cats don't grow on trees" is not a proposition that is known does not imply that it is a proposition that we do not know. Rather it lies "beyond" both knowing and not knowing, in the sense that neither epistemic term is applicable to it.

IV

No doubt other objections than the one raised above can be brought against Wittgenstein's view, and no doubt this view is not the whole of *On Certainty*. It will be necessary to waive a discussion of these issues here, however, in favor of noting the profound implications such a view has for both epistemology and ethics. For if Wittgenstein is correct, then one of the central presuppositions of traditional epistemology is undermined, and one of the central difficulties of cognitivism in ethics is avoided.

Following Aristotle, many epistemologists have been concerned to identify certain propositions as belonging to what they have termed a class of "basic knowledge." Aristotle himself had argued that the "grounds" for knowing must themselves be known, and known better, than what is based on those grounds.[5] Accordingly, Aristotle and his followers believed that it was necessary to locate a series of primitive, indubitable, and basic propositions which are themselves known to be true, on which empirical knowledge could ultimately be grounded. The motivation behind this search for propositions that are basic and are known has apparently been the feeling that if the "grounds" for what is known are not themselves known, then skepticism must result. Houses built on sand can never stand — rocky foundations at least as firm as the houses to be built on them are necessary.

There are several problems with this line of reasoning, however. The first is that, metaphors aside, it is more of an assumption than an argument. Aristotle, for example, does not present any *argument* which might show that the grounds for knowledge must be known. He simply assumes that it must be so. Indeed, one will look hard in the history of philosophy to find even an attempt to justify this assumption.

But there is more wrong with this assumption than its being just an assumption. It is in fact self-stultifying, and any argument that arises out of it will necessarily be circular. For if the grounds of what we know, which are used to explain how we come to know, must themselves be known, it must be explained how we can know them. But this is precisely what was to be explained, *viz.*, how we can know. Since this is so, it follows that any analysis of knowledge which depends on basic knowledge must ultimately presuppose what it was designed to show.

Furthermore, even disregarding this circularity, it seems that if the grounds for knowledge are to be known, they must be known either primitively, i.e., without the backing of more basic propositions, or nonprimitively. If they are known primitively, then it must be shown why the propositions of nonbasic knowledge cannot also be known primitively. For unless this can be shown, the need for basic knowledge will be obviated. But if the grounds for knowledge are known nonprimitively, then an infinite regress seems imminent, and the skepticism which the knowledge of such grounds was thought to prevent seems inevitable.

If I am correct, however, Wittgenstein's contention that the grounds for our knowledge are not themselves known to be true offers a way out of these problems. Accepted, countenanced, lived with, and assumed, these grounds are not themselves known (or doubted). The propositions contained in the background against which talk about knowing takes place simply do not have to be known in order for propositions based on them to be known, any more than it is required of the standard meter that it be a meter long in order for objects measured according to it to be a meter long. Standards are never predicable of themselves, and so the search for grounds for knowledge which are themselves known is not only unnecessary, but futile. Our language-game of knowing simply does not work the way it is assumed it must.

Furthermore, insofar as this assumption of traditional epistemology is undermined, arguments in other fields which depend on the same assumption will also be shaken. A prime example of its use occurs in ethics. One of the principal reasons in favor of non-cognitivism has been the alleged failure of cognitivists to "justify" their ultimate moral principles, i.e., to show how the truth-values of these principles can be determined. Since this is notoriously difficult to do (what *evidence* can one give to show that the useless infliction of suffering upon another human is wrong?), many philosophers have concluded that cognitivism in ethics is impossible. But this conclusion is based on the assumption that it is necessary to know the truth of ultimate ethical principles in order to know the propositions based on them. If, following Wittgenstein, this is *not* necessary, then the cognitivists' search for a justification for ultimate moral principles is unnecessary, if not simply self-contradictory. If our knowledge of ordinary empirical propositions does not entail our knowledge of background propositions against which they are assessed, then it is not clear why we are required to "know" ultimate ethical principles in order to know propositions based on them.[6]

Notes

1. See, for example, Allan Janik and Stephen Toulmin, *Wittgenstein's Vienna* (New York: Simon and Schuster, 1973), p. 176; Stephen Toulmin, *Human Understanding* (Princeton: Princeton U.P., 1972), Vol. I, pp. 106-7; P.M.S. Hacker, *Insight and Illusion* (Oxford: Clarendon Press, 1972), pp. 154-6; and Ernst Konrad Specht, *The Foundations of Wittgenstein's Late Philosophy*, tr. D.E. Walford (New York: Barnes and Noble, 1969), pp. 160-1.

2. Ludwig Wittgenstein, *On Certainty*, ed. G.E.M. Anscombe and G.H. von Wright, tr. Denis Paul and G.E.M. Anscombe (New York: Harper and Row, 1969), 136. Hereafter I shall cite this work in the text as *OC*, followed by section number. Other works cited in this way are: Wittgenstein, *Remarks on the Foundations of Mathematics*, ed. G.H. von Wright, R. Rhees, G.E.M. Anscombe, tr. G.E.M. Anscombe (Cambridge, Mass.: The M.I.T. Press, 1967), *RFM* (part and section number); Wittgenstein, *Philosophical Investigations*, tr. G.E.M. Anscombe (New York: The Macmillan Co., 1958), *PI* (part and section number); Wittgenstein, *Philosophical Grammar*, ed. R. Rhees, tr. Anthony Kenny (Oxford: Basil Blackwell, 1974) *PG* (part and section number); Norman Malcolm, *Math Notes* (San Francisco: no publisher, 1954), *MN* (page number); Norman Malcolm, *Ludwig Wittgenstein: A Memoir* (London: Oxford U. Press, 1962), *M* (page number).

3. See also *MN* 7: 'One talks of mathematical discoveries. But I will try to show that what is called a "mathematical discovery" ought better to be called a "mathematical invention."'

4. For an elaboration and a defense of Wittgenstein's argument concerning the standard meter, see my paper, 'Wittgenstein: *Investigations* 50,' *The Southern Journal of Philosophy*, XV (1977), pp. 81-90.

5. Aristotle, *Posterior Analytics*, Bk. I, Chapters 2 and 3. For a similar view in Plato, see the *Republic*, 533c.

6. For their helpful advice and criticisms of an earlier version of this paper I am indebted to Professors Norman Malcolm, Robert Arrington, and John Beversluis. Acknowledgment and thanks are also given to the National Endowment for the Humanities for its sponsorship of the 1974 Summer Seminar for College Teachers program, during which an earlier draft was written.

71

Wittgenstein and Logical Necessity

Barry Stroud

Michael Dummett has described Wittgenstein's account of logical necessity as a "full-blooded conventionalism."[1] On this view, the source of the necessity of any necessary statement is "our having expressly decided to treat that very statement as unassailable" (p. 329). Even faced with a rigorous mathematical proof:

> at each step we are free to choose to accept or reject the proof; there is nothing in our formulation of the axioms and of the rules of inference, and nothing in our minds when we accepted these before the proof was given, which of itself shows whether we shall accept the proof or not; and hence there is nothing which *forces* us to accept the proof. If we accept the proof, we confer necessity on the theorem proved; we "put it in the archives" and will count nothing as telling against it. In doing this we are making a new decision, and not merely making explicit a decision we had already made implicitly [p. 330].

This implies that it is possible for someone to accept the axioms and the rules of inference and yet to reject the proof, without having failed to understand those axioms or rules. But, Dummett objects:

> We want to say that we do not know what it would be like for someone who, by ordinary criteria, already understood the concepts employed, to reject this proof.... The examples given in Wittgenstein's book are — amazingly for him — thin and unconvincing. I think that this is a fairly sure sign that there is something wrong with Wittgenstein's account [p. 333].

Dummett is obviously on strong ground here — it seems impossible to understand this alleged possibility — but I think Wittgenstein would agree. His examples are not designed to show that we do understand this. What is important for the problem of logical necessity is to explain what makes the denial of a necessary truth "impossible" or "unintelligible." It is not enough to say that it is "logically impossible," since an explanation of logical necessity is just what is in question. Dummett appears to agree with this (pp. 328-9). In the rest of this paper, I shall try to say what, according to Wittgenstein, is responsible for the unintelligibility in such cases.

In defending the claim that he is not committed to saying that everybody could infer in any way at all, Wittgenstein points out that it is essential to inferring, calculating, counting, and so forth, that not just any result is allowed as correct. If everybody continues the series as he likes, or infers just any way at all, then "we shan't call it 'continuing the series' and also presumably not 'inference' " (*RFM*, 1, 116). General agreement among people as to the correct results of inferences or calculations and general agreement in the results that one gets oneself at different times are both necessary in order for there to be inferring or calculating at all (*RFM*, II, 66, 73). The same holds for counting, continuing a series, and so on. These are all activities in which the possibility of different results at different times and places is not left open. It is just here that a calculation differs from an experiment, where people at different times and places can get different results.

These remarks suggest that the source of necessity in inferring or calculating is simply that any activity in which just any results were allowed would not be *called* "inferring," "calculating," and so forth. In case of drawing logical conclusions:

> The steps which are not brought in question are logical inferences. But the reason why they are not brought in question is not that they "certainly correspond to the truth" — or something of the sort — no, it is just this that is called "thinking," "speaking," "inferring," "arguing" [*RFM*, I, 155].

This looks like the standard claim that all necessity finds its source in definitions or in the meanings of words. In inferring, one must write down "q" after "$p \supset q$" and "p" because to do otherwise is to cease to infer correctly, and correct inference is just "defined" by the laws of logic. That is what we call correct inference. This would presumably mean that, since it is possible for something else to be meant by "correct inference," it would also be possible for something else to be the conclusion. Despite suggestions of this "standard conventionalism" in Wittgenstein, I agree with Dummett that he does not hold such a view, although it is not always easy to see how what he says differs from it.

The main target of Wittgenstein's writings on necessity is the Platonism of Frege and the early Russell. In this respect he and the logical positivists are alike. According to Platonism it would be impossible for someone, when given the order "Add 2," to write down all the same numerals as we do up to "1000" and then to go on "1004, 1008, ...," and still be able to justify his going on in that way. It would be impossible because it is simply wrong, in continuing the series "+2," to write down "1004" right after "1000"; that is not, in fact, the next member of the series. So the pupil must either have misunderstood the instructions or have made a mistake.

Anyone who puts anything other than "1002" is wrong and should be declared an idiot or an incorrigible if he persists in his perversity. As Frege puts it: "here we have a hitherto unknown kind of insanity."[2]

The conventionalist's opposition to Platonism consists primarily in showing that our present ways of inferring, counting, calculating, and so forth, are not the only possible ones. But the standard conventionalist would also reject the alleged possibility on the grounds that the description of such a state of affairs is contradictory. If the person has understood the instructions, if he has just written down "1000,"and if he is to continue following the instructions, then he *must* write down "1002." Of course, he is free not to continue the series at all, or to claim that he has been following instructions like "Add 2 up to 1000, 4 up to 2000," and so forth, but it is logically impossible (involves a contradiction) for him to have understood the instructions correctly and to write down "1004" right after "1000." His claiming that "1004" is the correct step is a sufficient condition of his having abandoned the ordinary sense attached to the order "Add 2." That it is correct to write "1002" is already contained in the meaning of those instructions, and once one has agreed to follow them, then because they mean what they do there are certain steps which one logically must take.

The crucial notion in this conventionalistic theory is that of understanding the meaning of a word or a rule, and this is something to which Wittgenstein devotes a great deal of attention. Part of his interest in it is in the sense, if any, in which someone's having understood the instructions somehow logically guarantees that he will write down "1002" right after "1000." If this is logically guaranteed, then it would seem that his going on "1004, 1008, ..." could be due only to misunderstanding or to a mistake; in any event, he could not have understood correctly. But what is it to understand correctly? What determines which move is the correct one at a given point? The answer would appear to be that the way the order was meant, or what was meant by the person giving the order, determines which steps are correct. But again, Wittgenstein asks, what shows which way the order was meant? It is not the case that the teacher very quickly thought of each particular step which he wanted the pupil to take, and even if he did, that would not show that "meaning 1002, 1004, ..." meant "thinking of 1002, 1004, ..." (*PI*, 692). Rather, what the order means will be shown in the ways we use it, in what we do in following it, in the ways we are taught to use it, and so on (*RFM*, I, 2).

If someone who had learned to continue various series just as we do began to differ from us when he went beyond any point he had reached in his training, would it follow that he simply had not understood the instructions? If he continued to do this, must we say that he is unintelligent, perhaps idiotic? Wittgenstein tries as follows to suggest negative answers to these questions:

If my reply is: "Oh yes of course, *that* is how I was applying it!" or: "Oh! That's how I ought to have applied it —!"; then I am playing your game. But if I simply reply: "Different? — But this surely *isn't*

different!" — what will you do? That is: somebody may reply like a
rational person and yet not be playing our game [*RFM*, I, 115].

He tries to show that not all cases of deviating from what we expect or from
what we all do in continuing the series can be put down to simple misunderstanding, stupidity, or deliberate perversity on the part of the pupil. It
is almost certain in any particular case we come across that some
discoverable mistake has occurred, and that the pupil will come to recognize this. But *must* he do so? Is there no possibility other than those
mentioned above? The example is intended to suggest that there is. But the
important, and difficult, problem is to say exactly what this alleged
possibility comes to. Although Frege said it would be a new kind of
insanity, "he never said what this 'insanity' would really be like" (*RFM*, I,
151). To see what it would be like is to understand on what our being compelled in inferring, calculating, counting, and so forth, rests.
  The person who continues the series "1004, 1008, ..." is described as
"finding it natural" to go on in that way; it "strikes him as the same" as he
has done earlier. In trying to get such a person to continue the series as we
do it would no longer be useful for us to go through the training and give
him the old explanations over again. And providing him with a rule
precisely formulated in mathematical terms would not avoid the difficulties,
since it is just the possibility of his understanding such a rule that is in
question.

> In such a case we might say, perhaps: It comes natural to this person to
> understand our order with our explanations as *we* should understand the
> order: "Add 2 up to 1000, 4 up to 2000, 6 up to 3000, and so on."

> Such a case would present similarities with one in which a person
> naturally reacted to the gesture of pointing with the hand by looking in
> the direction of the line from finger-tip to wrist, not from wrist to finger-
> tip [*PI*, 185].

For Wittgenstein, it will not be enough to object that, if we are patient
and careful, surely we could eventually get the pupil to see that he is to
make the same move after "1000" as before — that he is not to change the
size of the steps. He is convinced that he is making the same move, and
"who says what 'change' and 'remaining the same' mean here" (*RFM*, I,
113)? One is inclined to reply, I think, that nobody *says* what is the same
and what is different; it is just a fact that the pupil is wrong in supposing
that going on "1004, 1008, ..." is doing the same as he was in writing
down "2, 4, 6, ..." But is there some discoverable fact of which we are
aware, and which he is missing? What sort of fact is it, and how could he be
brought to acknowledge it? Trying to explain to him that he has not gone
on in the same way would be like trying to teach someone how to carry out
the order "Go this way" when I point in a particular direction. If that
person naturally reacted to the gesture of pointing by looking in the
direction of the line from fingertip to wrist, it would not be enough to say

to him, "If I point this way (pointing with my right hand) I mean that you should go *this* way (pointing with my left hand in the same direction)." Isn't every explanation of how someone should follow an arrow in the position of another arrow (*BB*, p. 97)?

Or, to choose another example, suppose we come across some people who find it natural to sell wood, not by cubic measure or board feet as we do, but at a price proportionate to the area covered by the pile of wood, and they pay no attention to the height of the pile.

> How could I show them that — as I should say — you don't really buy more wood if you buy a pile covering a bigger area? — I should, for instance, take a pile which was small by their ideas and, by laying the logs around, change it into a "big" one. This *might* convince them — but perhaps they would say: "Yes, now it's a *lot* of wood and costs more" — and that would be the end of the matter [*RFM*, I, 149].

This case is analogous to that of trying to get the deviant pupil to see that the next step after "1000" is really "1002."[3] But can we describe what these people do as "selling wood the wrong way"? Is it a way whose "incorrectness" we could point out to them? And surely it is not logically impossible for there to be such people: the example does not contain a hidden contradiction.

The natural reply to this example is that it shows only that such people mean by "a lot of wood" and "a little wood" something different from what we mean by it, and similarly, as Dummett suggests, anyone who agrees with us in accepting all the steps in a proof but who then refuses to accept what we all accept as the conclusion must be blind to the meaning that has already been given to the words in the premises or in previous proofs. It seems as if he could not remain faithful to the meanings of those words and still reject the conclusion. Dummett concludes from this that he is simply *deciding* to accept some particular statement as necessary in complete isolation from everything else he has accepted. This is why Wittgenstein is called a "full-blooded"conventionalist. The strange people Wittgenstein describes differ from us only in having "adopted different conventions." But does it follow from the case which Wittgenstein tries to construct that the deviant pupil simply chooses to write "1004" and that his choice makes that the correct step? Can the people in Wittgenstein's examples properly be said to differ from us only in having adopted different conventions? I think the answer is "No." One thing implied by saying that we have adopted, or are following, a convention is that there are alternatives which we could adopt in its place. But in the case of writing "1002" right after "1000" there appear to be no alternatives open to us. It seems impossible to understand how we could "adopt the convention" that writing "998, 1000, 1004, ..." is going on in the same way, or taking steps of the same size. Surely if writing "998, 1000, 1002, ..." is not taking steps of the same size, then nothing is.

I have been trying to suggest so far that for Wittgenstein such "alternatives" are not inconceivable or unimaginable because they involve or lead to a logical contradiction. Just as there is no logical contradiction involved in the supposition that people might sell wood, and defend their doing so, in the way described earlier, so there is no logical contradiction involved in supposing that someone might agree with us in all uses of words or in all steps of a proof up to the present, and that he should now accept something different from what we all accept as the conclusion, without being simply idiotic or deliberately perverse. Wittgenstein's examples are designed to show this; it is part of the attack on Platonism. But as long as such alternatives are inconceivable in whatever sense, it looks as if Dummett is right in pointing out that "we do not know what it would be like for someone who, by ordinary criteria, already understood the concepts employed, to reject the proof." And if we do not know what this would be like, how can we find at all plausible Wittgenstein's purported examples of someone who "replies like a rational person" and yet is not "playing our game"? So it appears that, as Dummett says, Wittgenstein's examples are "thin and unconvincing," as they presumably must be if they are supposed to be examples of something that is unimaginable or inconceivable.

This seems to present the interpreter of Wittgenstein with a choice between two alternatives. Either Wittgenstein has not succeeded in giving any clear or intelligible examples of people whose ways of calculating, and so forth, are radically different from ours, and therefore he has not begun to support his anti-Platonistic account of logical necessity; or else he has succeeded in giving intelligible, perhaps convincing, examples which commit him to a "full-blooded conventionalism." And if the latter is the case, then Dummett's successful attack on radical conventionalism will be equally successful against Wittgenstein. But this choice is not an exhaustive one. There can be plausible examples to show the possibility of ways of counting, inferring, calculating, and so forth, different from ours, but which do not imply that our doing these things as we do is solely a result of our abiding by, or having adopted, certain more or less arbitrary conventions to which there are clear and intelligible alternatives. Nor do such examples imply that "at each step we are free to accept or reject the proof" or that "a statement's being necessarily true is solely a result of our having decided to treat that very statement as unassailable." But at one point Wittgenstein says:

So much is clear: when someone says: "If you follow the rule, it *must* be like this," he has not any *clear* concept of what experience would correspond to the opposite.

Or again: he has not any clear concept of what it would be like for it to be otherwise. And this is very important [*RFM*, III, 29].

If this is true, how can he hope to be successful in giving examples of what it would be like for it to be otherwise, while still maintaining that there is logical necessity in such cases? How can he have it both ways? The solution to this dilemma is to be found in the explanation of why we do not have any clear concept of the opposite in the case of logical necessity, and why Wittgenstein speaks of our not having a *clear* concept here. How could we have any concept at all?

Wittgenstein gives many examples of people whose ways of inferring, counting, calculating, and so forth, are different in significant ways from ours. As well as the wood-sellers mentioned earlier, there might be others who sell wood at a price equal to the labor of felling the timber, measured by the age and strength of the woodsman. Or perhaps each buyer pays the same however much he takes (*RFM*, I, 147). Also, there might be people who measured with soft rubber rulers, or with rulers which expanded to an extraordinary extent when slightly heated (*RFM*, I, 5). Or suppose that people in their calculations sometimes divided by "(n-n)" and yet were not bothered by the results. They would be like people who did not prepare lists of names systematically (for example, alphabetically), and so in some lists some names would appear more than once, but they accept this without worrying (*RFM*, V, 8). Or there might be people who count, but when they want to know numbers for various practical purposes ask certain other people who, having had the practical problem explained to them, shut their eyes and let the appropriate number come to them (*RFM*, V, 14). There are many more such examples, merely mentioned or briefly discussed, throughout Wittgenstein's *Remarks*.[4] They are all intended to be analogous in various ways to the "possibility" that someone might go on "1004" right after "1000" in continuing the series "+2."

When first presented with these examples it seems that we can understand them, and that we can come to know what such people would be like. We do not happen to do things in these strange ways, but, it seems, we could. If these examples represent clear alternatives, then why doesn't it follow that our calculating, counting, measuring, and so forth, as we do is purely a matter of convention? If this is not a matter of convention, how can these examples be perfectly intelligible to us? In suggesting answers to these questions I will have begun to show how Wittgenstein can escape between the horns of the above dilemma.

When we look more closely at the examples, are they really as intelligible as they seemed at first? For instance, consider the people who sell wood at a price proportionate to the area covered by the pile of wood and who defend their doing so in the way described earlier. Surely they would have to believe that a one-by-six-inch board all of a sudden increased in size or quantity when it was turned from resting on its one-inch edge to resting on its six-inch side. And what would the relation between quantity and weight possibly be for such people? A man could buy as much wood as he could possibly lift, only to find, upon dropping it, that he had just lifted more wood than he could possibly lift. Or is there more wood, but the same weight? Or perhaps these people do not understand the expressions "more" and "less" at all. They must, if they can say, "Now it's a lot of wood, and costs more." And do these people think of themselves as shrinking when they shift from standing on both feet to standing on one? Also, it would be possible for a house that is twice as large as another built on exactly the same plan to contain much less wood.

How much wood is bought need have no connection with how much wood is needed for building the house. And so on. Problems involved in understanding what it would be like to sell wood in this way can be multiplied indefinitely.

If so, then so far we do not really know what it would be like for us to sell wood, and to try to justify our doing so, in the way Wittgenstein has described. And we have already noted the difficulties in trying to understand the example of continuing the series "+2." I think the initial intelligibility and strength of Wittgenstein's examples derive from their being severely isolated or restricted. We think we can understand and accept them as representing genuine alternatives only because the wider-reaching consequences of counting, calculating, and so forth, in these deviant ways are not brought out explicitly. When we try to trace out the implications of behaving like that consistently and quite generally, our understanding of the alleged possibilities diminishes. I suspect that this would happen with most, if not all, of Wittgenstein's examples, but I do not need to prove this in general, since if my interpretation is right these examples will fulfill their intended role whether or not this point holds.

The reason for this progressive decrease in intelligibility, I think, is that the attempt to get a clearer understanding of what it would be like to be one of these people and to live in their world inevitably leads us to abandon more and more of our own familiar world and the ways of thinking about it upon which our understanding rests. The more successful we are in projecting ourselves into such a world, the less we will have left in terms of which we can find it intelligible. In trying to understand these alleged possibilities, we constantly come across more and more difficulties, more and more questions which must be answered before we can understand them. But this is not to say that we do not understand them because they are "meaningless" or "contradictory," or because what they purport to represent is "logically impossible."

Wittgenstein's examples are intended to oppose Platonism by showing that calculating, counting, inferring, and so forth, might have been done differently. But this implies no more than that the inhabitants of the earth might have engaged in those practices in accordance with rules which are different from those we actually follow. It is in that sense a contingent fact that calculating, inferring, and so forth, are carried out in the ways that they are — just as it is a contingent fact that there is such a thing as calculating or inferring at all. But we can understand and acknowledge the contingency of this fact, and hence the possibility of different ways of calculating, and so forth, without understanding what those different ways might have been. If so, then it does not follow that those rules by which calculating, and so forth, might have been carried out constitute a set of genuine alternatives open to us among which we could choose, or even among which we could have chosen. The only sense that has been given to the claim that "somebody may reply like a rational person and yet not be playing our game" is that there might have been different sorts of beings from us, that the inhabitants of the earth might have come to think and behave in ways different from their actual ones. But this does not imply that we are free to put whatever we like after "1000" when given the instructions "Add 2," or that our deciding to put "1002" is what makes that the correct step. Consequently, Wittgenstein's examples do not commit him to a "radical conventionalism" in Dummett's sense. In trying to explain more fully why he is not committed to this I will return to the sense in which he can be called a "conventionalist."

In several places Wittgenstein describes what he is doing in some such way as this:

> What we are supplying are really remarks on the natural history of man: not curiosities however, but rather observations on facts which no-one has doubted, and which have only gone unremarked because they are always before our eyes [*RFM*, I, 141].

What facts does he have in mind here, and what role do they play in his account of logical necessity? The reason for calling them "facts of our natural history" is to emphasize both what I have called their contingency — that is, that they might not have obtained — and the fact that they are somehow "constitutive" of mankind — that is, that their obtaining is what is responsible for human nature's being what it is.

Part of human behavior consists of calculating sums, distances, quantities, of making inferences, drawing conclusions, and so forth. It is a fact that we engage in such practices: "mathematics is after all an anthropological phenomenon" (*RFM*, V, 26). There are various facts which make it possible for calculating to occur at all. For example, our memories are generally good enough for us not to take numbers twice in counting up to 12, and not to leave any out (*RFM*, V, 2); in correlating two groups of five strokes we practically always can do so without remainder (*RFM*, I, 64); somebody who has learned to calculate never goes on getting different results, in a given multiplication, from what is in the arithmetic books (*RFM*, I, 112); and so on. The inhabitants of the earth might have lacked these and other simple abilities, and if so there would be no such thing as calculating at all. In that way the possibility of calculating depends on such contingent facts. These are examples of what Wittgenstein calls the "physical," "psychological," and "physiological" facts which make activities such as calculating possible (*RFM*, V, I, 15).

A contingent fact which is responsible for our calculating as we actually do is the fact that we take "1002, 1004, ..." to be going on in the same way as putting down "996, 998, 1000, ..." It is a fact that we naturally go on in this way, but people might not have done so. Since they might naturally have followed the rule in a different way, our rules alone do not logically guarantee that they will not be taken or understood in deviant ways. A rule itself does not make "strange" ways of following it impossible, since a rule is not something which stands apart from our understanding of it, and which mysteriously contains within it all of its future applications. How we naturally understand and follow the rule determines which applications of it are correct, and the way a rule is followed will depend in part on what we take to be "going on in the same way ... The use of the word 'rule' and the use of the word 'same' are interwoven" (*PI*, 225). It is because people might not share our natural reactions, or might not be in accord with us in their "judgments of sameness" that their understanding the instructions does not rule out their taking a different step from ours at some point while still finding what they have done to be in accord with the rule. So understanding the rule in the way we do depends on such things as finding it natural to go on to "1002" right after "1000." That we take just the step we do here is a contingent fact, but it is not the result of a decision; it is not a convention to which there are alternatives among which we could choose. And that we share any such "judgments" at all (whatever they might be) is also a contingent fact, but without this agreement there would be no understanding of any rules at all.

> If language is to be a means of communication there must be agreement not only in definitions but also (queer as this may sound) in judgments. This seems to abolish logic, but does not do so [*PI*, 242].

Those described as "not playing our game" are the people who are not in accord with us in the "judgments" on which the possibility of language and communication rests. Wittgenstein's examples of the possibility of people like this serve to bring out the contingency of the fact that, as things are, we are in accord in these "judgments." Anyone who did not go on as we do need not be simply continuing a different series (for example, "Add 2 up to 1000, 4 up to 2000," and so forth), and in that way be "playing a game" different from the one we happen to be playing; nor need he have misunderstood the instructions in a way that can be pointed out to him by more careful explanations. But someone like this would not be fully intelligible to us. Our relation to him would be like our relation to people who naturally reacted to the gesture of pointing by looking in the direction of the line from fingertip to wrist, or who sold wood in the way described earlier. It is not simply that they happen to have chosen to do things one way, and we happen to have chosen to do them differently, but that they would be different sorts of beings from us, beings which we could not understand and with which we could not enter into meaningful communication. They would ultimately be unfathomable to us (compare, for example, *RFM*, I, 34, 61, 66, 152). In order to have a "clear concept" of what it would be like to think and behave as they do we would have to be able to abandon many, if not all, of those "judgments" on which our being able to think or conceive of anything at all rests.

What I have been saying will explain what would otherwise be a puzzling distinction which Wittgenstein makes in a well-known passage:

> I am not saying: if such-and-such facts of nature were different people would have different concepts (in the sense of a hypothesis). But: if anyone believes that certain concepts are absolutely the correct ones, and that having different ones would mean not realizing something that we realize — then let him imagine certain very general facts of nature to

be different from what we are used to, and the formation of concepts different from the usual ones will become intelligible to him [*PI*, 230].

The point of Wittgenstein's examples of people who do not "play our game" is only to show that our having the concepts and practices we have is dependent upon certain facts which might not have obtained. They show only that "the formation of concepts different from the usual ones" is intelligible to us; but it does not follow from this that those concepts themselves are intelligible to us. And since the intelligibility of alternative concepts and practices is required by the thesis of radical conventionalism which Dummett ascribes to Wittgenstein, I think that thesis is not borne out by Wittgenstein's examples.

The "shared judgments" (for example, of sameness) upon which our being able to communicate rests, and which are responsible for our calculating, inferring, and so forth, as we do are not properly seen, then, as the results of free decisions in the manner of the logical positivists. They might have been different and, if they had been, then calculating, inferring, and so forth, would have been done differently. But this does not make them conventions in the positivists' sense. In defending the claim that we had made the correct move after "1000" in following the rule "Add 2" we could ultimately get back to something like our "shared judgment" that putting down "1002" is doing the same as we were doing earlier. There is nothing further we could appeal to. These "judgments" represent the limits of our knowledge, and thus they have a role similar to the explicit conventions of the positivists.

From what has been said so far it might still look as if our "sharing judgments" is nothing more than our all agreeing that certain propositions are true or unassailable. But the "agreement" of which Wittgenstein speaks here is not the unanimous acceptance of a particular truth or set of truths.

"So you are saying that human agreement decides what is true and what is false?" — It is what human beings *say* that is true and false; and they agree in the *language* they use. That is not agreement in opinions but in form of life [*PI*, 241].

This "agreement" is the universal accord of human beings in behaving in certain ways — those "natural reactions" which we all share, or those human practices the engaging in which makes a creature human. Those are the "facts of our natural history" which he is appealing to. The correctness of steps in calculating is not ultimately established on the basis of their agreeing with or being entailed by certain truths which we have accepted without foundation, or which are "self-evident":

The limits of empiricism are not assumptions unguaranteed, or intuitively known to be correct: they are ways in which we make comparisons and in which we act [*RFM*, V, 18].

This distinguishes Wittgenstein both from the Platonist and from the standard conventionalist. I shall comment on only one other aspect of this difference.

I have said that it is a "fact of our natural history" in Wittgenstein's sense that we agree in finding certain steps in following a rule "doing the same." In some cases we all naturally go on in the same way from the steps which have already been taken. This is what makes it possible for us to follow any rules at all.

> And does this mean e.g. that the definition of "same" would be this: same is what all or most human beings with one voice take for the same? — Of course not.

> For of course I don't make use of the agreement of human beings to affirm identity. What criterion do you use, then? None at all [*RFM*, V, 33].

But if there is no criterion for the truth of assertions of identity, how can we know they are true? Without a proof to the contrary, might not all human beings, for all their agreement, be wrong in supposing that writing "1002" is going on in the same way as writing "1000" after "998"? Wittgenstein replies that "to use a word without a justification does not mean to use it wrongfully" (*RFM*, V, 33). And in this case, at this stage, there is no "justification" of the sort the empiricist seeks. But why not?

The correctness of particular calculations, inferences, and so forth, is decided by appeal to the rules, but can't we also ask whether those rules themselves are correct, whether our techniques of calculation, inference, and so forth, are the correct ones?

> The danger here, I believe, is one of giving a justification of our procedure when there is no such thing as a justification and we ought simply to have said: *that's how we do it* [*RFM*, II, 74].

The ultimate appeal in seeking a "foundation" for our procedures of calculating, inferring, and so forth, can only be to "ways in which we make comparisons and in which we act." That is all that an account of the "foundation" or "source" of logical necessity can achieve. This perhaps helps to explain the point of passages like this:

> What has to be accepted, the given, is — so one could say — *forms of life* [*PI*, 226].

Because these procedures cannot be given a "justification" it does not follow that they are shaky or unreliable, or that we are courting trouble if we decide to engage in them. We do not decide to accept or reject them at all, any more than we decide to be human beings as opposed to trees. To ask whether our human practices or forms of life themselves are "correct" or "justified" is to ask whether we are "correct" or "justified" in being the sorts of things we are.

At the end of his paper Dummett recommends interposing between the Platonist and constructivist pictures of thought and reality an intermediate picture

> of objects springing into being in response to our probing. We do not *make* the objects but must accept them as we find them (this corresponds to the proof imposing itself on us); but they were not already there for our statements to be true or false of before we carried out the investigations which brought them into being [p. 348].

As far as I understand this, it seems to be just the picture to be derived from Wittgenstein if my interpretation is in general correct. Logical necessity, he says, is not like rails that stretch to infinity and compel us always to go in one and only one way; but neither is it the case that we are not compelled at all. Rather, there are the rails we have already traveled, and we can extend them beyond the present point only by depending on those that already exist. In order for the rails to be navigable they must be extended in smooth and natural ways; how they are to be continued is to that extent determined by the route of those rails which are already there. I have been primarily concerned to explain the sense in which we are "responsible" for the ways in which the rails are extended, without destroying anything that could properly be called their objectivity.

Notes

1. Michael Dummett, 'Wittgenstein's Philosophy of Mathematics,' *Philosophical Review*, LXVIII (1959), 324. Page numbers alone in parentheses in the text always refer to this article. References to Wittgenstein's writings always contain an abbreviation of the title of the book in question. '*PI*' will refer to Wittgenstein's *Philosophical Investigations* (New York, 1953), and unless otherwise indicated, parenthetical references will be to the numbered sections of Pt. I. '*RFM*' will refer to *Remarks on the Foundations of Mathematics* (Oxford, 1956).

2. G. Frege, *Grundgesetze der Arithmetik* (Jena, 1903), p. xvi.

3. There are some important features of the two cases as presented which are not analogous. We are imagining a single pupil who makes a single deviant move after having done exactly as we had expected up till now, whereas the example of the wood-sellers is presented from the outset as one in which we come across a whole, flourishing society. Consequently, what appears to be a sudden and inexplicable change, or an individual aberration, in the former case is not present in the latter. Furthermore, and crucially, the society of wood-sellers is not our own, but the strange pupil has apparently sprung up right in our midst. I think that these and other disanalogies can be avoided by presenting both cases in the same way from the beginning, although Wittgenstein never does this. (Some of the difficulties which these differences appear to create for the later stages of my argument were pointed out to me by Professor Stanley Cavell.)

4. E.g. *RFM*, I, 136, 139, 152, 168; II, 76, 78, 81, 84; III, 15, 17; IV, 5; V, 6, 12, 27, 29, 36, 42, 43, 44.

Wittgenstein, *Aposteriori* Necessity and Logic for Entailment

Charles F. Kielkopf

Wittgenstein's answer to his question in *Remarks on the Foundations of Mathematics* (Wittgenstein [1956] = *RFM*), offers an insight similar to S. Kripke's in Kripke [1972] that there are *aposteriori* necessary truths. Wittgenstein asked: "But then what does the peculiar inexorability of mathematics consist in?" In his answer he reminded us that there are necessary truths which we can classify as *aposteriori* although he did not classify them in such terms. In *RFM*, Wittgenstein suggested that the inexorability of many mathematical truths can be regarded as stemming from necessary connections which we accept as a result of inspecting connections between observable aspects of observable patterns. My *Strict Finitism* [1970], especially Chapters II and III, presents Wittgenstein's analysis of mathematical necessity in terms of such *aposteriori* necessities. Here, though, I shall investigate the problem of providing a logic for these *aposteriori* necessities when they are regarded as first degree material entailments.

I investigate the problem in the following way. In Part I, I give examples of establishing *aposteriori* necessary truths while calling attention to some of their features. Part I may be of interest by itself. In Part II, I explain how these *aposteriori* necessities can be regarded as first degree entailments because we create a meaning connection between predicates when we establish, i.e., prove, an *aposteriori* necessary truth. These *aposteriori* necessary truths are labelled 'first degree material entailments,' i.e., fd. material entailments. Occasionally I call them essential truths. In Part III, I characterize the task of developing a logic for fd. material entailments. In order to search for the logic, if any, of fd. material entailments, I try to provide a logical form for these *aposteriori* necessary truths. A special *de re* modal operator is introduced but immediately translated by use of van Fraassen's quantifier $(/x)$ of his [1967] and [1969]. The quantifier $(/x)$ can be read as: For all possible objects. In Part IV, I identify fd. material entailments with certain quantification forms using $(/x)$. In Part V, I consider whether some restriction of a consequence relation in van Fraassen's quantification theory can give a plausible logic for fd. material entailments. No satisfactory logic is found. So, for Part VI the fundamental question of whether or not we want such a logic arises. Maybe we ought to establish each *aposteriori* necessity by recourse to experience and hence independently of other *aposteriori* necessities. I close by suggesting that Wittgenstein would not want such a logic either.

I

The following from *RFM* III-39 provided the clue to Wittgenstein's analysis of mathematical necessity.

> The propositions 'a = a ', 'p ⊃ p', "The word 'Bismarck' has 8 letters", "There is no such thing as reddish-green", are all obvious and are propositions about essence: What have they in common? They are evidently each of a different kind and differently used. The last but one is most like an empirical proposition. And it can understandably be called a synthetic *apriori* proposition.

> It can be said: unless you put the series of numbers and the series of letters side by side, you cannot know how many letters the word has.

I take the kind of necessity we find in "The word 'Bismarck' has 8 letters" as Wittgenstein's paradigm of mathematical necessity. To be sure, Wittgenstein suggested calling it synthetic *apriori*. However, in addition to Wittgenstein's own reference to experience, the following synopsis will remind us of the crucial role of experience in establishing the necessity of such truths. Hence, we realize that in these cases we are well-advised to follow Kripke's bold departure from ordinary philosophical usage and talk of *aposteriori* necessity.

We establish the necessity of "The number of letters in 'Bismarck' is 8" by first producing a typical 'Bismarck'. We next portray counting its letters by picturing its letters as being in one-to-one correspondence with a paradigm for applying the term 8. A series of slanted lines such as: / / / / / / / /, is a paradigm for applying '8'. Our portrayal of counting the letters of a typical 'Bismarck' gives us the following kind of picture.

```
B  i  s  m  a  r  c  k
↕  ↕  ↕  ↕  ↕  ↕  ↕  ↕
/  /  /  /  /  /  /  /
1  2  3  4  5  6  7  8
```

This picture of how an experiment, to determine how many letters a Bismarck-configuration has, would almost always come out shows us that this particular Bismarck-configuration would not be the figure which it is if it had more or less letters than 8. (In *RFM* 1-36, Wittgenstein wrote: "the proof does not serve as an experiment; but it does serve as the picture of an experiment," while in *RFM* V-15 he wrote: "the calculation is the picture of an experiment as it practically always turns out.") We conclude, in addition to our conclusion about the particular Bismarck-configuration pictured, that not only must this Bismarck-configuration have 8 letters to be the structure which it is but also that any 'Bismarck' must have 8 letters to be the structure which it is. Here it is important to emphasize that we have made a move from 'is' to 'must' by concluding that Bismarck-configurations *must* have 8 letters from seeing what it *is* like for a typical Bismarck-configuration to have 8 letters.

Similarly, we move from a portrayal of a particular OVER being reversed to give a REVO, as below, to a conclusion that the reverse of an OVER is a REVO.

over   revo

Let us call bringing ourselves to a conclusion that a certain kind of structure must have a property P by inspecting a picture of a typical structure of this kind having P 'pictorial proving.' Because in pictorial proving we judge that a structure would not be what it is if it lacked a certain property, we can call pictorially proved truths essential truths. Chapter II of my [1970] as well as my [1966], go into some more detail on what goes on in pictorial proving.

Let us briefly consider why these so-called essential truths are not analytic, why they are not true by convention, and how they depend upon sociological, physical, and pyschological factors. Part II begins by considering what we use them to assert.

If they were analytic they would be so by definition of some of the crucial terms, since they do not explicitly have universally valid forms. But there are no definitions of 'Bismarck' or OVER which specify that the first has 8 letters and that the reversal of the second is REVO. Certainly there may be definitions or rules which tell us how to produce Bismarck-configurations, OVERs, countings, and reversals. But these rules do not specify what the count or reversal will give. We need to produce some instance in accordance with the rule to see what comes out of the pro-duction. Of course, we could stipulate definitions of 'Bismarck-configuration' and OVER which specify that the first has 8 letters and that the second reverses to REVO. However, we would first have to determine that the count of letters in 'Bismarck' is 8 and that the reverse of OVER is REVO to insure that our stipulation, if you want to call it 'stipulation', is correct.

Similarly, it is not by convention that Bismarck-configurations have 8 letters and that OVERS reverse to REVOS. Because experience of clear situations has led us to realize that Bismarck-configurations must have 8 letters and that a reversal of an OVER must produce a REVO, we cannot stipulate otherwise. Of course, definitions and conventions guide us in calling certain figures 'Bismarcks' and OVERS and in calling certain operations counting or reversing. So, sociological factors do influence what we can pictorially prove. For instance, we could not read-off what must be true from a very messy or from a very complex diagram. Due to the role of physical factors, I am not sure that pictorial proving will establish the kind of *aposteriori* necessities which Kripke cites in his [1972]; I doubt that we could get a picture of heat being molecular motion and read-off from the picture that heat would not be what it is unless it were as pictured. However, I do not want to specify prior to proof which non-analytic propositions can or cannot be pictorially proved. This inability to characterize what can or cannot be pictorially proved is a major source of our inability to have a logic for essential truths.

Pyschological factors are tremendously influential in pictorial proving. What we do, or do not, prove pictorially depends upon what we cannot think and what we can think. We can think of OVERS being several different colors while we cannot think of their reverses being anything except REVOS. Wittgenstein's remark in *RFM* 1-45 can be applied to our inability to think of OVER being reversible to anything except REVO: "A demon has cast a spell around this position and excluded it from our space." I submit that *RFM*, and especially *RFM* III-3, can be interpreted as reminding us that intuiting that P must be true or our inability to think that P is false are *causes* of our concluding that P must be true. But these causes are not facts which we can legitimately cite in concluding P. We look at the picture to prove P and prove P to others by presenting them with the picture plus some heuristic comments. The picture is the proof; so it would be irrelevant to cite biographical details about what we or others can or cannot think. Wittgenstein reminded us in *RFM* II-42 that it is not something behind the proof, such as psychological states, which prove but that it is the proof that proves.

II

So what we pictorially prove does not serve to announce that we are in a certain psychological state or that our thinking is subject to certain limitations. What do we accomplish as a result of pictorially proving a proposition? In other words, what are we doing when we make the move to what *must* be on the basis of what *is* in a vivid picture? In *RFM* III-29 Wittgenstein asked and suggested an answer to such a question.

What is the transition that I make from "It will be like this" to 'It *must* be like this"? I form a different concept. One involving something that was not there before.

I interpret this and similar passages as showing us that in pictorial proofs we not only create essences of structures, as Wittgenstein reminded us in *RFM* I-32, but that we also create implicatory links between concepts or

meaning connections between predicates. As he suggested in *RFM* II-31:
"I want to say that the *must* corresponds to a track which I lay down in
language." For instance, we have changed our concept of Bismarck-
configuration so that it now includes having 8 letters and we have "laid
down the track in our language" between 'being an OVER' and 'having a
REVO as its reverse.' We can dispense with talk of concepts and linguistic
tracks by saying that we have established the following.

1) Being a 'Bismarck' entails having 8 letters.
2) Being an OVER entails having a REVO as a reverse.

In the above two entailment claims 'entails' represents a material entailment in the sense that we have to pay attention to the material or specific
subject matter to determine whether the entailment holds. These entailments do not hold on the basis of the forms of the antecedent and
consequent as does P&Q entails Q. The terms used in the antecedent and
consequent do not make these to be formal entailments. Even if we did not
use the pictorial names such as 'Bismarck' or 'Bismarck-configuration' but
talked merely of B-structures we would still have: Being a B-structure
entails having 8 letters. Without pictorial names we would not be able to
read-off the truth of the entailment from its statement; and hence not be
tempted to think that formal considerations told us of its truth. Note that
even with the pictorial names we need to go through a rapid bit of pictorial
proving to accept the entailment. With the pictorial name we use the name
as the basis for a pictorial proof which we complete in our head. So with
pictorial names we still pay attention to the material discussed, viz.,
Bismarck-configurations or OVERS. It cannot be over-emphasized that
what is here called material entailment has nothing to do with so-called
material implication. If there are any material implications, it is notorious
that they can be said to be true without any close attention to the subject
matter being discussed. A material implication can be said to be true simply
if we know the antecedent to be false or the consequent to be true.

III

The difference from material implication and the more important
difference between formal and material entailment will come clearer by
sketching out what it is to have a logic for formal first degree sentential
entailments. In addition, knowing what it is like to have a logic for first
degree formal entailments gives us a better idea of what we are looking for
when we ask whether there is a logic for fd. material entailments. A formal
sentential first degree entailment claim, i.e., an fde. claim, is of the form
$(A \rightarrow B)$ where A and B are formulas of some standard sentential logic
using sentential variables, some operators from &, v, $\supset$, $\sim$ as primitive,
and with other operators defined in standard ways in terms of the primitive
ones. Thus $(p \lor q) \rightarrow (p \& q)$ and $p \rightarrow (p \lor q)$ are fdes. while $(p \rightarrow q) \rightarrow (\sim q \rightarrow \sim p)$ is not an fde. because of the occurrence of $\rightarrow$ in a place other than

that of the main connective. Typically an fde. $(A \rightarrow B)$ is said to be true if $(A \rightarrow B)$ is a standard tautology and meets some other conditions. In the limiting case we have the so-called system of classical fdes. in which $(A \rightarrow B)$ is true if and only if, i.e., iff $(A \supset B)$ is a standard two-value tautology. Other examples are: $(A \rightarrow B)$ holds iff it is a tautological entailment in the sense of Anderson and Belnap, an analytic implication in the sense of Parry, or a first degree entailment in the sense of Geach, von Wright, and Smiley. These notions of formal sentential entailment are now all presented in Anderson's and Belnap's [1975] and Kielkopf's [1978]. We are not, though, so much interested in which formal considerations tell us that an entailment holds as we are interested in formal considerations which show that we have one entailment given certain others. For instance, if $\vdash$ represents deducibility we want to know if we have inference rules such as: $(A \rightarrow B), (B \rightarrow C) \vdash (A \rightarrow C), (A \rightarrow B), (A \rightarrow C) \vdash (A \rightarrow (B\&C))$, and $(A \rightarrow B) \vdash (\sim B \rightarrow \sim A)$. A set of such rules we call a *logic* for first degree entailments. A logic for classical fdes. is provided by the simple rule: $(A \rightarrow B) \vdash (C \rightarrow D)$ iff $(A \supset B) \vdash (C \supset D)$ holds in standard sentential logic. In our sense of 'logic' the rules, both primitive and derived, for the system E_{fde} on p.158 of Anderson and Belnap give a logic for the tautological entailments. Admittedly the notion of logic used here is a bit narrow because only inference rules, and not axioms or theorems, are included in the extension of 'logic'. Some logics for fdes. do include axiom schemas such as $(A \rightarrow (A \vee B))$. But in our search for a logic for material fd. entailments we are not concerned with formal considerations which simply give entailments. For the kind of entailments with which we are concerned we have the material considerations of pictorial proofs to give us entailments as premises for inferences. Hence, we are concerned only with inference rules, if any.

Let us simplify the search for a logic even further by restricting our attention to assertions of material entailments between properties expressible as one-place predicates. Let us use a Lambda operator to symbolize properties. Thus $\lambda x\, Fx$ symbolizes being an F or the property of F. In what follows, regardless of what other complexity may be hidden in an expression λxFx there will be no mention of any entailment between properities hidden therein. Thus because no entailment claim is in a λxFx we may talk of first degree entailments. We symbolize a typical such entailment as: $(\lambda xFxc \rightarrow \lambda xGx)$. For instance, if λxFx symbolizes being an OVER and λxGx symbolizes having a REVO as a reverse, entailment claim (2) is expressible as a $(\lambda xFx \rightarrow \lambda xGx)$. So, we want to find out whether we have inference rules such as: $(\lambda xFx \rightarrow \lambda xGx) \vdash ((\lambda xFx \,\& \, \lambda xHx) \rightarrow \lambda xGx)$.

To try to get a logic for fd. material entailments we should try to express them in a form in which it is fairly easy to judge whether such-and-such an inference holds. A search for the logical form of a kind of sentence is a search for a way of expressing them so that we can work out, syntactically or semantically, a logic for them. I find use of the Lambda notation helpful for stating rules but unhelpful for justifying claims about inferences. A typical way of dealing with $(\lambda xFx \rightarrow \lambda xGx)$ would be to re-express it as:

*((x)(Fx ⊃ Gx)), where *( ) is some device for converting ⊃ to the stricter
→. Since we have talked of essential truths and since we have techniques
for working with modal operators it is tempting to try to develop a modal
operator as the *( ) for essential truths. We may try to introduce an
operator $\boxed{e/F}$, — it is essential to F, to give: $\boxed{e/F}$ ((x)(Fx ⊃ Gx)), which
would be read as: It is essential to F that all F's are G's. Use of this new
operator may enable us to say what we want; but very brief consideration
of the likely complexity in developing rules for the use of this property
relative and noniterable operator in relation with quantifiers leads me to
welcome B.C. van Fraassen's introduction of a slightly new quantifier for
expressing meaning relations between predicates.

IV

In his [1967] and [1969], van Fraassen develops formal semantics for a
first order predicate language with = and a symbol E!x whose intended
interpretation is: x exists. The primitive quantifier is (/x) whose intended
interpretation is: for all possible x. The standard universal quantifier can be
defined in context as follows: (x)Ax = $_{df}$(/x)(E!x ⊃ Ax). We need not go
into details of the formal semantics; I shall only sketch some of the
significant features of his formal semantics. If we have a set of predicate
signs in this formal language let us call it a *formalism* until we have interpreted the predicate signs different from E!x. When all the predicate signs
different from E!x are interpreted we will say that we have a *language*. To
interpret a formalism we start with a domain of objects H which includes
both the objects we call actual and those which we call possible. Predicates
of a formalism are interpreted in the usual way by being given extensions
which are subsets of H and powers of H. Of course, since H will have
possible as well as actual objects, possible objects may be in the extension
of predicates. We also select a subset of H as the actual objects. In effect,
the actual objects are the extension of E!x. Truth of formulas is defined in
the usual way just as if H were a domain of only actual objects. Once truth
is defined we get two notions of validity and two consequence relations.

Given an interpretation of the predicates a formula A is *valid* if A is true
for all choices of the actual objects, i.e., for all interpretations of E!x in H.
An induction readily establishes that for formulas with no occurrence of
E!x, a formula A is true iff A is valid. For formulas with no occurrence of
E!x, 'true' means 'true of the actual and the possible'. A formula A is
universally valid if A is true for all interpretations of predicates in H.
Taking (/x) as our primitive quantifier, van Fraassen assures us that A is
universally valid iff A is a theorem of standard predicate logic with =, and
E!x is treated simply as another predicate. Remember that once we fix the
interpretations of all the predicates except E!x we have a language L. So,
we can define a language relative consequence relation: Γ⊩$_L$A, where Γ
is a set of formulas, as holding if A is true if all of the Γ are true. We can
define an unrestricted consequence relation: Γ⊩A, as holding if A is true
whenever all of the Γ are true regardless of how we interpret the predicates

in any non-empty H. We have $\Gamma \Vdash A$ iff. $\Gamma \vdash_c A$, where $\vdash_c$ is the provability relation of classical predicate logic.

We now follow van Fraassen's suggestion on p.179 of [1967] and identify our $\boxed{e/F}$ ((x)(Fx $\supset$ Gx)) with a valid (/x)(Fx $\supset$ Gx) which is not also universally valid. (Note that this identification gives a nice explication of the fact that the *de re* $\boxed{e/F}$ cannot be iterated.) Also we will not consider (/x)(Fx $\supset$ Gx) forms with either = or E!x in them since the essential truths with which we are concerned will not be about existence. We don't picture existence on a diagram. And we already have a logic for =. Van Fraassen makes a plausible case that claims of a meaning connection can be expressed as a claim about all possible objects. It does seem as if a claim that being a 'Bismarck' entails having 8 letters does assert that if anything, actual or possible, were a 'Bismarck' it would have 8 letters.

V

Now our search for a logic is narrowed down to whether or not we can accept one of van Fraassen's consequence relations, or some modified version of it, as giving the inference relation between fd. material entailments. We do not want the weak language relative consequence relation. If both (/x)(Fx $\supset$ Gx) and (/x)(Hx $\supset$ Ix) are valid, then (/x)(Fx $\supset$ Gx) $\Vdash_L$ (/x)(Hx $\supset$ Ix), regardless of any relevance between the formulas. So, if we moved from $A \Vdash_L B$ to $A \vdash B$, where $\vdash$ is the deducibility relation between fd. material entailments, any two fd. material entailments would yield one another. But the fd. material entailments about 'Bismarck' and OVER do not yield one another.

So, we consider the unrestricted consequence relation. We immediately encounter problems because we do not allow universally valid forms to represent fd. material entailments. We can get (/x)(Fx $\supset$ (Fx v Gx)) from (/x)(Fx $\supset$ Gx) because (/x)(Fx $\supset$ Gx) $\vdash$ (/x)(Fx $\supset$ (Fx v Gx)) holds. But /x)(Fx $\supset$ (Fx v Gx)) is not an fd. material entailment representative because it is universally valid. We are justified in rejecting formal logical truths as expressing meaning connections which are established by pictorial proofs. The formal validity makes the recourse to pictures pointless. Unfortunately, then, fd. material entailments are not closed under logical consequence. So, we reject the unrestricted consequence relation and try the following modification.

(/x)(Fx $\supset$ Gx) (/x)(Hx $\supset$ Ix) iff (/x)(Fx $\supset$ Gx) $\vdash$ (/x)(Hx $\supset$ Ix), but it is not the case that $\vdash$ (/x)(Hx $\supset$ Ix).

If there is going to be any logic of fd. material entailments, some modifications of this proposal, which is reminiscent of Strawson's [1948] will be it. I say "some modifications" because we may still have to restrict the complexity of the predicates. Do we get reasonable rules with this proposal? Consider (/x)(Fx $\supset$ (Gx&(Ix v ~ Ix))). Could we move from this to: $(/x)(Fx \supset (Ix \vee \sim Ix))$? Clearly we cannot because $(/x)(Fx \supset (Ix \vee \sim Ix))$ is universally valid. So, it seems that the very reasonable $(A \rightarrow (B \& C)) \vdash (A \rightarrow C)$ will not be a principle of the logic of fd. material entailments. However, we may want to go back to try to make a case that no essential truth will have the form: $\lambda xFx \rightarrow (\lambda xGx \& \lambda xIx)$, or at least neither Gx nor Ix will be a universally valid form. But I have little confidence that we can specify prior to proof what we can prove pictorially except that we cannot prove formally valid truths pictorially. Similarly, the fact that the highly plausible: $(A \vee B) \rightarrow C \vdash (A \rightarrow C)$ fails may make us even more unhappy with the Strawsonian type proposal. To see that Simplification of Disjunctive Antecedents fails consider: $(/x)(((Fx \& \sim Fx) \vee Gx) \supset Hx)$.

VI

The need for tampering with a straightforward consequence relation suggests that there is not any inference rule or rules for fd. material entailments. Once this suggestion arises, we immediately realize that some of the sociological, physical, or psychological conditions for proving an $\lambda xHx \rightarrow \lambda xIx$ could fail despite the fact that some logic gave $\lambda xHx \rightarrow \lambda xIx$ as a consequence of a $\lambda xFx \rightarrow \lambda xGx$ which had already been proved. I fear that this last point is a sufficient reason for abandoning hope that we will ever get a logic for fd. material entailments.

In closing, let us return to Wittgenstein to ask two questions. Should he have wanted a logic for essential truths? Would he have wanted a logic for essential truths? For the reasons just given I think that the answer to the first question is no. The exegetical question can also be answered negatively. I think that Wittgenstein held in *RFM* that we should not think that logic takes care of itself by giving us many more logical truths once we start with a few. (I think that rejection of *Tractatus* 5.473 which claims that logic takes care of itself is a significant feature of the later Wittgenstein.) Wittgenstein thought that we should be working to develop our mathematics and conceptual connections; we should not mechanically grind out results we do not understand and we should not think that the results are already there and that the job of inference is only to make us aware of them. Consider pictorial proving as a mathematical technique and read *RFM* IV-24.

> The harmful thing about logical technique is that it makes us forget the special mathematical technique. Whereas logical technique is only an auxiliary technique in mathematics.

Finally regard seeing how a result must hold as seeing it vividly pictured and read *RFM* IV-46.

> The curse of the invasion of mathematics by mathematical logic is that now any proposition can be represented in mathematical symbolism and this makes us feel obliged to understand it.

So, we could symbolize a proposition and have a logic which tells us that it is a consequence of an essential truth. We may then force ourselves to accept it as an essential truth although we do not see from any proof that it must be true.

References

Anderson, A.R. & Belnap Jr. N.D. [1975] *Entailment: The Logic of Relevance and Necessity*, Princeton 1975.

Kielkopf, C.F. [966] 'Deduction and Intuitive Induction' *Journal of Philosophy and Phenomenological Research* 26 (1966) 379-90.

_____ [1970] *Strict Finitism: An Examination of Ludwig Wittgenstein's Remarks on the Foundations of Mathematics*, Mouton & Co., The Hague.

_____ [1978] *Formal Sentential Entailment*, U. Press Am. Washington D.C.

Kripke, S. [1972] 'Naming and Necessity' *Semantics of Natural Language* eds. G. Harman and D. Davidson, D. Reidel, Dordrecht, pp. 253-355.

Strawson, P.F. [1948] 'Necessary Propositions and Entailment Statements' *Mind* 57 (1948), pp. 184-200.

van Fraassen, B.C. [1967] 'Meaning Relations among Predicates' *Nous 1* (1967) 161-79.

_____ [1969] 'Meaning Relations and Modalities' *Nous 3* (1969) 155-67.

Wittgenstein, L. [1956] *Remarks on the Foundations of Mathematics*, eds G.H. von Wright, R. Rhees, G.E.M. Anscombe, Transl. G.E.M. Anscombe, Macmillan 1956

73

Wittgenstein's Solution of the Paradoxes and the Conception of the Scholastic Logician, Petrus de Allyaco

Anton Dumitriu

I Introduction

We have very few facts about Wittgenstein's life, and these are practically only those given by Malcolm and by von Wright. They inform us that Wittgenstein was not a scholar, that he was a spontaneous genius (I should say, an explosive one), and that his work is less an original organization of others' ideas or of his own than a collection of intellectual intuitions. This assertion is confirmed by the fact that neither the *Tractatus Logico-Philosophicus* nor the *Philosophical Investigations* are systematically expounded as theories, but are only lapidary and aphoristical notations of intellectual fulgurations.

The origins of his inspiration are thus hard to identify and, outside Frege's and Russell's works (which, according to his own acknowledgement, influenced him greatly), there can be only speculation. As for the logic of the Middle Ages, we cannot say whether and to what extent Wittgenstein knew it. We do know, however, that he mentions Occam's motto in the *Tractatus* twice. At 3.328 he says, "*Wird ein Zeichen nicht gebraucht, so ist es bedeutungslos. Das ist der Sinn der Devise Occams*" (or, in our translation, the first English translation having deviated from the original meaning: "If a sign is *not used* then it is meaningless. That is the meaning of Occam's motto"). And at 5.47321 we find that "*Occams Devise ist natürlich keine willkürliche, oder durch ihren praktischen Erfolg gerecht-fertigte, Regel: Sie besagt, dass unnötige Zeicheneinheiten nichts bedeuten*" ("Occam's motto is, of course, not an arbitrary rule, nor one justified by its practical success: it says that *unnecessary* sign elements mean nothing"). Note that in the first English translation from the *Tractatus* the expression "Occam's razor" appears, but in German it is only "*Occams Devise.*"

Can we infer from these two propositions that Occam's philosophy was familiar to Wittgenstein, or, even more, that he was acquainted with the

312

whole logic of the Middle Ages? We cannot make such an affirmation, all the more so since Occam's motto has become in philosophy a sort of aphorism that Wittgenstein could have known without reading Occam's books. This economical law, which had been expressed by others too, was stated by Occam in his treatise on the *Sentences*: "*Nunquam ponendo est pluralitas sine necessitate*" (One never must use more without necessity). Or, in another form, in the famous treatise *Summa totiua logicae*, "*Frustra fit per plura, quod potest fieri per pauciora*" (It is useless to make with more what can be made with less).

Now it is obvious that we can conclude nothing with respect to the knowledge Wittgenstein could have had about Occam's logic. But there is a great scholastic logician, Petrus de Allyaco, whose conception of the problem of paradoxes is almost identical to Wittgenstein's. Is this only a mere coincidence? Wittgenstein himself refuses to give the sources of his thought. He writes in the preface of the *Tractatus*, "How far my efforts agree with those of other philosophers I will not decide. Indeed what I have here written makes no claim to novelty on points of detail, and therefore I give no sources, because it is indifferent to me whether what I have thought has already been thought before me by another." This statement and its obvious sincerity makes it difficult to discover any connection of inspiration with that of the scholastic logician.

This paper has a threefold aim: (1) To show that Wittgeinstein gives a logical solution to the logico-mathematical paradoxes, which we think has not been taken into consideration only because of its brevity. (2) To prove that this solution does not reject the theory of types but interprets it in the simplest way. (3) To show that Wittgenstein's solution is the solution given to the paradoxes called *Insolubilia* by the famous scholastic logician, Petrus de Allyaco (Pierre d'Ailly). We must still add that those who have dealt with the exegesis of Wittgenstein's philosophy have overlooked this problem as well as his solution. Only one author — Max Black (*A Companion to Wittgenstein's* Tractatus) — has paid attention to the problem, but only in connection with the theory of types. George Pitcher (*The Philosophy of Wittgenstein*) does not cite at all the problem of Wittgenstein's paradoxes nor the solution advanced by him.

II Theory of Symbolism

Even from the "Preface" of the *Tractatus*, Wittgenstein indicates the aim of his work, which is "to draw a limit to the expression of thoughts," for the problems of philosophy are formulated erroneously and the method of formulating them rests on the misunderstanding of the logic of our language. Later, Wittgenstein writes:

3.323 In the language of everday life it very often happens that the same word signifies in two different ways — and therefore belongs to two different symbols — or that two words, which signify in different ways, are apparently applied in the same way in the proposition....

3.324 Thus there easily arise the most fundamental confusions (of which the whole of philosophy is full).
3.325 In order to avoid these errors, we must employ a symbolism which excludes them, by not applying the same sign in different symbols and by not applying signs in the same way which signify in different ways. A language of signs, therefore, which obeys the rules of *logical* grammar — of logical syntax.

(The logical symbolsim of Frege and Russell is such a language, which, however, does not exclude all errors.)

We are thus in the presence of a general theory of sophisms. Wittgenstein explains the appearance of the errors of logic by the confusion between the different symbols and their different meanings. Here Wittgenstein draws a subtle distinction between sign and symbol. A sign may be a symbol but it may be simply only a sign. A sign becomes a symbol only when it has a significant use (3.326). "The sign determines a logical form only together with its logical syntactic application" (3.327). In other words, and to sum up Wittgenstein's thought, we can build up a logical grammar of signs, without taking into consideration their symbolic meanings, for these signs must be void of content. Or in Wittgenstein's terms, "In logical syntax the meaning of a sign ought never to play a role; it must admit of being established without mention being thereby made of the *meaning* of a sign; it ought to presuppose *only* the description of the expressions" (3.33). This is Wittgenstein's conception of symbolism and logical syntax. It seems incontestable. A formal logic must indeed neglect any content otherwise it is not a formal one. And this is the condition Wittgenstein requires of any logical system of signs.

These ideas of Wittgenstein seem to have their origin in Aristotle's *De Sophisticis Elenchis* (165 a 7; 169 a). Here is what Aristotle says:

> One of the reasons, the most natural and usual cause of sophisms, concerns the use of words. In a discussion there is no possibility of bringing in the things themselves; but we must use, in their places, the words that symbolize them. So we think that what is valid for words is valid also for things.... The number of words is finite, as well as the number of ideas, while the numbers of things is infinite. That is why the same idea and the same word must indicate several things.... Those who do not know the power of signification of words make paralogisms.

Aristotle further adds that "It is very difficult indeed to distinguish what kind of things are signified by the same word and what kind of things are signified by different words. He who can make this difference is very close to the truth."

III Rejection of the Theory of Types?

The most noticeable attempt to solve the logico-mathematical paradoxes is Bertrand Russell's "theory of types," as its author called it. According to this theory, no class can be formed if it contains members that cannot be defined but with the aid of the class whose members they are (vicious circle principle). Or, in other words, a class is a logical entity which presupposes a propositional function $\varphi(x)$, being noted $\hat{x}(\varphi x)$. In this case, the expression $\varphi[\hat{x}(\varphi x)]$ is meaningless because the argument of a function cannot be the class determined by the function itself. Such expressions are inadmissible by virtue of the vicious circle principle. In this way Russell was obliged to classify the concepts by their types: objects, properties of objects, properties of properties, etc. Such a division of the concepts leads rapidly to the conclusion that it is not possible to apply a property of a certain type to itself, but only to logical concepts of an immediately inferior type.

But Wittgenstein thinks that Russell's theory is erroneous — *in this form*. What are Wittgenstein's reasons for denying Russell's form of this theory? They are clearly summed up in propositions 3.331, 3.332, 3.333, and we shall divide them into two arguments:

1. "Russell's error is shown by the fact that in drawing up the rules of the signs he has to speak about the meaning of these signs." Here Wittgenstein emphasizes the actual impossibility of a formal sign to speak of its content. Indeed, if the problem is to constitute a syntax of signs void of any content, their possible meanings cannot be hinted at since otherwise their formal nature would be altered.

After having explained the nature of Russell's error, Wittgenstein gives another argument of a different kind — the second objection to the theory of types.

2. "No proposition can say anything about itself, because the propositional sign cannot be contained in itself (that is the whole 'Theory of types')."

"A function cannot be its own argument, because the functional sign already contains the prototype of its own argument and it cannot contain itself."

This rejection of self-reference is the central point of Wittgenstein's conception of the problem of the paradoxes. But it is in close connection with the first ideas from the *Tractatus*. The *Tractatus* actually begins by establishing the notion of picture of the facts, the picture presenting the facts in logical space and being a model of reality (2.1, 2.11, 3.12). However, the picture is also a fact, but this time we have a logical fact. A picture is a connection of elements and this connection is a structure. The possibility of this structure is called the representational form of the picture. The picture can represent every reality whose form it has (2.1711). But — and here is the most important remark of Wittgenstein concerning the paradoxes — he adds:

2.172 The picture, however, cannot represent its form of representation; it shows it forth.

2.173 The picture represents its object from without (its standpoint is its form of representation). . . .

2.174 But the picture cannot place itself outside of its form of representation.

We can now grasp Wittgenstein's thought: (1) To ground his theory of types, Bertrand Russell was obliged to speak about the things the symbols represent, and this is an error because he did not remain on the pure ground of the logical syntax. (2) What is valid in the theory of types is that "No proposition can say anything about itself, because the propositional sign cannot be contained in itself ..." (3.332).

From this conception it follows that Wittgenstein does not reject the theory of types, but only its interpretation. Proposition 3.332 shows Wittgenstein's essential idea: He rejects the proposition which has self-reference and grounds his attitude on the assertion that no propositional sign can be contained in itself. This is the logical foundation of the theory of types and he himself adds that "*das ist die ganze* 'Theory of types'." Therefore there can be no question of rejecting the theory of types, but only of reducing it to its logical formal basis — what is expressed by Wittgenstein in the above propositions.

IV Max Black's Criticism

Max Black criticized Wittgenstein's position towards the theory of types, but his criticism is not irreproachable, as we shall immediately see. In *A Companion to Wittgenstein's* Tractatus Black brings forward the following objections against Wittgenstein's rejection of the theory of types.

[1] But Wittgenstein's reason for dismissing the theory — that its formulation requires Russell to speak about the meanings of signs (3.331) — will not survive examination. The principle to which Wittgenstein is implicitly appealing, that reference to meaning must be absent from logical syntax (3.33), requires more defence than he supplies; but in any case, he quite overlooked the possibility of a purely syntactical version of the theory of types (for which see, for instance, Church's 'Formulation'). (p. 145)

[2] W.'s reason for excluding self-references is not immediately convincing: it is not clear why the propositional sign must 'include itself' in order to be the expression of a proposition about its own meaning. If I can talk about a man without using a name, why should I be unable to talk about a proposition's meaning by using some description which is part of the propositional sign? (p. 147)

Then Black quotes Wittgenstein: "A proposition cannot occur in itself. This is the fundamental truth of the theory of types (*Notes on Logic*, 106(2) ..." (p. 147).

Let us examine these statements, beginning with the above quotation from Wittgenstein. This proposition confirms once more our interpretation, i.e., that Wittgenstein does not reject the theory of types but only its formulation by Russell in terms of a hierarchy of logical entities. Concerning the fact that Wittgenstein did not know the purely syntactical "Formulation" of his theory, as it is given by Church, we must state explicitly that Wittgenstein refused to admit a metalanguage (whose parts are the logical syntax and semantics). Gilles Granger clearly showed this in his article "Wittgenstein et la métalangue" (*Revue Internationale de Philosophe* [1969], 88-9). Wittgenstein says in the *Philosophische Bemerkungen* (1.6) that to express the proprieties of the language we must go out of the language, and this is impossible: "*Ich kann nicht mit der Sprache aus der Sprache heraus.*" Professor Granger translates it so: "*Le langage ne peut exprimer ses propres propriétés.*" Consequently, one cannot oppose Church's syntactical "Formulation" of the theory of types to Wittgenstein because such a "Formulation" is impossible in principle, in his conception, and therefore illusive. Finally, the reason for excluding the self-reference appears evident — if we do not omit anything in the series of logical ideas from the *Tractatus*.

We have already quoted propositions 2.171 and 2.172, which state from the beginning that between "Object" and "*Bild*" there is a relationship between what is represented and what represents and therefore the representation of something cannot be its own representaton, because, in this case, one of the terms of this relation does not exist. This problem (of the "representation") is very ancient and it can be found in Plato, in Aristotle, and especially in the Stoics, but we can find it in the Middle Ages just in the form Wittgenstein gave it, as we shall see.

In short, and to speak Wittgenstein's language, we shall say that to express something there must be something expressible and a system of signs that expresses it. The two poles in this problem are the expressed thing and its expression. But then the expression cannot be its own expression, by definition. Therefore a sign cannot be its own sign, and a symbol cannot be its own symbol, because the idea of signs or symbols requires by definition two different terms.

Max Black's statement that "Wittgenstein's reason for excluding self-references is not immediately convincing" does not consider the problem in its own generality. Wittgenstein's argument is based on the contemporary conception of formal logic. Formal logic is the science of forms void of any content. That is why Wittgenstein says that when drawing up the rules of the signs we must not speak about the meaning of these signs. Self-reference is rejected by Wittgenstein by virtue of a more general principle, which is the principle of modern mathematical logic — no sign can speak about anything, therefore it cannot speak about itself. If we do admit the self-reference we infringe the very conception of modern formal logic: "the meaning of a sign ought never to play a role" (3.33).

The distinction between sign and its meaning which were not to be mistaken, was already made by the Stoics. They divided dialectics into two great chapters: Science "of what expresses" (σημαῖυου, *verbum*) and science "of what is expressed" (σημαιυόμευου, *significatio*). Wittgenstein's conception does not confuse between *verbum* and *significatio*.

V Wittgenstein's Conception of the Paradoxes

We shall occupy ourselves with the proper solution of the paradoxes given by Wittgenstein. Until now this solution has not even been considered as a solution. Above all we notice that in the problems of this kind, that is to say of logico-mathematical paradoxes, the attitudes adopted can be classified as either the philosophical solutions or the purely logical solutions. We shall call a *philosophical* solution of a paradox any solution which tries to explain the contradiction by a new principle, by a new axiom, that does not belong to the logical system in which it has appeared. Such solutions were given in the past by the philosophers of Elea to their famous paradoxes; analogous philosophical solutions were given by the Sceptics to the sophisms; and also Kant philosophically explained the antinomies of pure reason. There is no need to prove the philosophical character of the actual logico-mathematical attitude, for it has been acknowledged by the most representative authors. Bertrand Russell acknowledges that "In this sense and by the fact that it treats of problems not yet solved, the mathematical logic has a philosophical character" (*Introduction to Mathematical Philosophy*). And in *The Present State of Investigations on the Foundations of Mathematics* (Warsaw, 1955) A. Mostowski states: "These problems are of philosophical nature and we can hardly expect to solve them within the limits of mathematics alone and by applying only mathematical methods."

Concerning the purely *logical* solution of the sophisms or paradoxes, Aristotle's attitude in the past was that a paradox is a sophism and is only an error of logic. All the logicians after Aristotle adopted this position, and all through the Middle Ages the scholastic logicians never did give up the discovery of errors of the countless sophisms they studied. Among the logicians and mathematicians of our times whose attitude remained unchanged towards the logico-mathematical paradoxes we shall mention Richard and Poincaré, and subsequently Perelman and Barzin. We can cite here also the mathematician Behmann, whose solution of the paradoxes, based on Pascal's condition of the definition, is a logical solution.

Wittgenstein completes this long series of logicians with his Aristotelian position. Indeed, he shows in the *Tractatus* that no contradiction can be real. We have recalled that Wittgenstein starts with the idea of the picture of the facts. Let us take up the thread of his ideas.

2.18 What every picture, of whatever form, must have in common with reality in order to be able to represent it at all — rightly or falsely — is the logical form, that is, the form of reality.

2.181 If the form of representation is the logical form, then the picture is called a logical picture.

2.19 The logical picture can depict the world.

2.2 The picture has the logical form of representation in common with what it pictures.

2.201 The picture depicts reality by representing a possibility of the existence and non-existence of atomic facts.

3 The logical picture of the facts is the thought.

3.001 "An atomic fact is thinkable" means: we can imagine it.

3.02 The thought contains the possibility of the state of affairs which it thinks.

What is thinkable is also possible.

3.03 We cannot think anything unlogical, for otherwise we should have to think unlogically.

3.032 To present in language anything which "contradicts logic" is as impossible as in geometry to present by its coordinates a figure which contradicts the laws of space; or to give the coordinates of a point which does not exist.

3.0321 We could present spatially an atomic fact which contradicted the laws of physics, but not one which contradicted the laws of geometry.

Herewith, the position of Wittgenstein towards the problem of the paradoxes is completely clarified; it is impossible to express a contradiction in the logical space. Thus the author of the *Tractatus* finds his place in the line of the classic logicians, which begins with Aristotle and ends with him. The contradictions are only errors of logic and as we have already said they are due to a confusion of signs or of symbols. "In order to avoid these errors, we must employ a symbolism which excludes them, by not applying the same sign in different symbols and by not applying signs in the same way which signify in different ways" (3.325). That is Wittgenstein's general conception of the sophism or paradoxes.

VI Wittgenstein's Solution

Let us now sum up these considerations, which could have been completed with the aphorisms 4.1272, 5.251, and 5.252.

1. Wittgenstein holds the classical position on the problem of the paradoxes, and according to it any contradiction is, and cannot be but, an error of logic.

2. The picture contains the form of the reality, but does not speak about this form; it only reflects it.

3. No sign can be its own sign; no symbol can be its own symbol. Thus no proposition can say anything about itself, because the propositional sign cannot be contained in itself. A function cannot be its own argument, because the functonal sign already contains the prototype of its own argument and it cannot contain itself (3.333).

With these ideas Wittgenstein solves the paradoxes. Their brevity and aphoristical expression prevented their receiving their due acknowledgement. Consequently, nobody has considered till now that Wittgenstein's solution is really a solution.

Here is his solution as it appears in the text:

3.333 If, for example, we suppose that the function F (fx) could be its own argument, then there would be a proposition "F(F(fx))," and in this the outer function F and the inner function F must have different meanings; for the inner has the form φ(fx), the outer form ψ(φ(fx)). Common to both functions is only the letter "F," which by itself signifies nothing.

This is at once clear, if instead of "F(F(u))" we write (∃φ): F(φu). φu = Fu."

Herewith Russell's paradox vanishes.

Let us now explain this solution which probably because of its brevity, as we mentioned, was not taken into consideration as a solution. We see that, for Wittgenstein, if a function could be its own argument, then the expression "F(F(fx))" could be formed, but in this case both letters "F" which appear in it would each signify something different, and therefore nothing. In order to avoid the errors we have quoted above, Wittgenstein applies here the general principle that the same symbol cannot at the same time represent different things. Moreover, Wittgenstein asserts that the letter F by itself represents nothing.

H. Behmann noted the problem of the letter "F" in the functions which became their own argument, and he concluded that F was not defined. In his paper "Zu den Widersprüchen der Logik und Mengenlehre" (*Jahresbericht der deutschen mat. Ver.*, Band 40 [1931]), Behmann pointed out that in the definition F (φ) = ~ φ(φ), which causes the paradox, F is only an abbreviation and as such it is not necessary and therefore it can easily be eliminated by replacing it with the sign which was employed for its definition. This is just Pascal's condition of the definition. But, if we try to eliminate F in the above expression, we obtain ~F(F), and if we go further we get ~~F(F), and so on. In other words, and according to Behmann, the abbreviatory sign F has been incorrectly used, for it cannot be eliminated; there are not the signs which define it and therefore F is not defined.

Though Behmann is quite close to Wittgenstein's solution, the author of the *Tractatus* did not use this argument. Instead, he based his argument on another condition of the definition without stating it explicitly: "A definition must not be built *idem per idem*, it must not be tautological; one cannot define the definite by the definite — *definiendum per definiendum*." A more developed form of the false definition *idem per idem* is the *circulus in definiendo* or *diallela*: a thing defined by another, but each of them is defined by elements belonging to the other. For instance: "The representations are complexes of sensations" and "The sensations are elements of the representations." We consider that Wittgenstein uses implicitly that condition of the definition when he is saying that a function cannot be its own argument, otherwise the sign remains by itself and therefore it is not defined. The distinction between the sign F and the sign f, in the expression F(fx), shows that the sign F is defined in its place (as a proposition function) by the sign f, and when we build the expression F(F(fx)), F is defined as a function by means of F itself, and therefore this definition degenerates into an *idem per idem* definition.

Let us now summarize this discussion: Wittgenstein states the condition of principle that no sign can be its own sign, no symbol its own symbol, no proposition can speak anything about itself, no propositional function can be its own argument. From the point of view of the conditions of the definition, which prevent the *idem per idem* definition, Wittgenstein's affirmations mean that if a sign is not used, it is senseless; when used it receives a sense and this sense is defined by means of other signs. In order to avoid a definition *idem per idem* the sign cannot be its own sign (it cannot define it itself); the propositional sign cannot speak about itself, otherwise it could define itself. Lastly, the propositional function cannot be its own argument since then the sign of propositional function would define itself as a sign of propositional function, and that would be a definition *idem per idem*.

This is Wittgenstein's solution, which he apparently conceived in its formal basis; this solution makes useless Russell's theory of types (in its form) though it contains, as Wittgenstein acknowledges, just this condition, that no sign can contain itself ("*das ist die ganze* 'Theory of types'").

VII Recapitulation

Wittgenstein solves the problem of the paradoxes by two principles, which constitute in reality two aspects of the same solution.

1. *Rule of different signs*: We must not apply the same sign in different symbols or different signs for the same symbol. We have seen the logical justification of this rule. But this rule is sufficient to exclude paradoxes. Indeed, as is well known, the expressions leading to contradictions generally assume either the form

$\alpha \varepsilon \alpha$ = "α is an element of the set α"
$\sim\alpha \varepsilon \alpha$ = "α is not an element of the set α"

or the form

$\phi(\phi)$ = "ϕ has the predicate ϕ."
$\sim \phi(\phi)$ = "ϕ has not the predicate ϕ".

Wittgenstein's rule excludes the possibility of forming such expressions. The sign α is placed as a matter of fact for a set and also for an element of it, that is, for two different things which have different logical functions. Similarly, the sign ϕ in the expressions $\phi (\phi)$ or $\sim \phi (\phi)$ is placed for the argument and for its predicate too, that is, for two different logical ideas; and thus, according to Wittgenstein's rule, these expressions are not admissible.

2. *Rule of no self-reference.* By excluding self-reference, Wittgenstein rules out the possibility that a sign appear in a formal system by defining itself its logical function or its logical value. We have seen that this rule has a perfectly logical justification and that if we do not take it into account we obtain erroneous definitions — *idem per idem* — which lead to contra-

dictions. Indeed, the expression ϕ (ϕ), which tends to denote a propositional function, is defined with the aid of the argument ϕ, that is, with the sign placed for the function.

Russell defines the propositional function in the following manner: "Let øx be a statement containing a variable x and such that it becomes a proposition when x is given any fixed determined meaning. Then øx is called a propositional function" (*Principia Mathematica* [1910], I, 15). The symbol x is the argument of the propositional function. In itself a propositional function does not represent anything, it is only a variable. The propositional function is $\phi(x)$, where the argument is x. To make evident the variable function, taken as an isolated entity, Russell writes: øx̂. In a function there are consequently two variables at least: the argument and the function.

Let us consider now the particular propositional function $\phi(\phi)$. The function in itself is $\phi\hat{\phi}$. Consequently, the variable $\phi\hat{\phi}$ is defined as an expression containing one indetermined constituent ϕ. In other words, the variable $\phi\hat{\phi}$ is defined by means of the variable ϕ, that is, by a definition *idem per idem*. Consequently, the expressions $\phi(\phi)$ and ~$\phi(\phi)$, or α ε α and ~ α ε α, cannot be built up, the variables they represent being defined (or constructed) by erroneous definitions *idem per idem*. That is, in our opinion, the logical foundation of the rule of no self-reference.

VIII Wittgenstein and Petrus de Allyaco

We now will point to an astonishing fact which we do not venture to explain. The solution given by Wittgenstein to the logico-mathematical paradoxes had already been given in the Middle Ages by Petrus de Allyaco (Pierre d'Ailly [1350-1425]). This famous scholastic logician had dealt especially with the problem of paradoxes already known at that time, and generally called *Insolubilia*, whose core was the paradox of the liar with all its different readings. Among Petrus' books we find a special treatise on the *Insolubilia*, which had been published together with two other works under the heading *Destructiones modorum significandi. Conceptus et insolubilia secundum viam nominalium magistri Petri de Allyaco.* The title itself tells us that Petrus was an Occamist, that is, a nominalist.

Here is how Petrus begins his treatise on the *Insolubilia*: "Numerous are those who have had different opinions on the so-called insolubilia. Seeking a way to get out of the difficulty and to refute it [*viam evadendi et evacuendi difficultatem*], I have not been able to find a way by which to arrive at a satisfactory demonstration for my mind [*meae menti*]. Therefore I shall try a probable explanation by which must appear the root of the difficulty [*radix difficultatis*] and a radical solution of the problem." According to Petrus' opinion, there are two kinds of difficulties in this problem: A *general* difficulty, concerning the truth and the falsehood of propositions. A second difficulty, of a *special* nature, concerning the propositions of a certain type, which have reflections about themselves, *propositiones habentes reflexionem supra se.* Petrus accepts Occam's

division of the propositions into three categories: (1) *Propositio mentalis*;
(2) *Propositio vocalis*; and (3) *Propositio scripta* (this division has its origin
in Aristotle's *Analytics*). "The two last categories of propositions are subordinated directly and immediately to the mental proposition," according
to Petrus, "but they are not subordinated one to another as some are
maintaining." The mental proposition (*proprie dicta*) is a true or false discourse in a natural way (*naturaliter*), but it is not true or false because it
would signify the truth or the falsehood from outside. In other words, the
truth or the falsehood of a mental proposition is to be found in the mental
essence of the judgement, that is to say in the mental apprehension of an
objective state of affairs. And here appears the interesting idea of Petrus:
only the *propositio mentalis*, which is above the linguistic differences, has
an essential sense giving it the possibility of being true or false.

Now which is the proposition *habens reflexionem supra se* and by what
does it distinguish itself from the *propositio mentalis*? Here is his opinion:
"The vocal or written propositions represent something; the representation
of something can be made in two ways: objectively or formally [*obiective et
formaliter*]. For instance, the picture of the king represents the king
objectively [*obiective*], but the mental concept of the king represents the
king formally. No created thing can be its own and distinct formal
knowledge. No vocal or written proposition can represent itself or something other formally" (... *Nulla res creata potest esse propria et distincta
cognitio formalis sui ipsius. Nulla pro-positio vocalis vel scripta potest significare se ipsam vel aliquid aliud formaliter*).

But we have found in Wittgenstein's *Tractatus* the following propositions: "The picture, however, cannot represent its form of representation;
it shows it forth" (2.172). "The picture cannot place itself outside of its
form of representation" (2.174).

In short, Petrus de Allyaco makes this natural distinction: the mental
proposition can be true or false, according to whether it represents a real
state of affairs or not, but cannot state anything about itself; it cannot consequently declare itself true or false. Or, as the author himself says: *Nulla
propositio mentalis proprie dicta potest significare se ipsam esse verram ...
nec potest habere reflexionem supra se*. However we can pronounce or
write any proposition which ascribes a truth to a mental proposition, as for
instance, *Aliqua propositio mentalis est falsa*.

Petrus thinks he has solved the problem of *Insolubilia* only by taking
into account this distinction, for he is convinced he has found the propositions which falsify themselves (*falsificari se ipsas*). According to Petrus,
all this *insolubilitas* does not alter the mental judgement, but it can appear
in improper mental propositions and especially in the vocal or written
propositions. The solution of *Insolubilia* consists thus in remarking that "in
consequence of a parallelization made between the oral or written proposition and the corresponding mental proposition, the so-called *insolubile*
seems sometimes true and sometimes false and herewith it is only
apparent" (C. Prantl: *Geschichte der Logik im Abendlande*, IV, 114). The
confusion between mental propositions and oral or written ones is the
cause of the *insolubilia*.

IX Conclusions

If we now draw a comparison between the solution given by Wittgenstein to the logico-mathematical paradoxes, and that of other contemporary logicians, we must make a remark: If Wittgenstein, just as Petrus de Allyaco, wants to show where the logical knot of the problem is, that is, where the error of logic lies, and thus give an explanation of the paradox, contemporary logicians, on the other hand, in the presence of these contradictions, are establishing the conventions to be made in order to avoid them. Logicians do not want elucidation of the logical difficulty; they are no longer looking for the truth of the logical rules but only wish to have practical rules to avoid the difficulty. Here is for instance, Hans Reichenbach's opinion on these rules: "The question has been asked whether it is necessary to introduce these rules. One thing seems to be clear: the only reason we can give for such rules is that they exclude contradiction. There is no question of whether the theory of types or the theory of levels of language is true" (*Elements of Symbolic Logic* [New York, 1948]).

It is now clear how Wittgenstein's solution was more logical, for he wanted to explain logically the contradiction, and by this flash of light cast upon the knot of the problem, cause the contradiction to vanish. Indeed, we understand very well when we read: "No created thing can represent itself distinctly formally" (*Nulla res creata potest distincte representare se ipsam formaliter*). That is a logical question and not a prohibitive convention. The logical character of such a solution was understood only by a logician, Ludwig Wittgenstein, who — without any hint that he knew the scholastic logicians — expressed exactly and almost verbatim the ideas of Petrus de Allyaco. Of course, the brevity of Wittgenstein's solution makes its understanding difficult, and here Max Black's objection is right: "Wittgenstein's summary disposal of the paradoxes that provoked the theory of types is as unsatisfying as its brevity would lead one to expect" (*A Companion to Wittgenstein's* Tractatus, p. 146). We tried to explain the real sense of "the rejection of the theory of types" in Wittgenstein's *Tractatus*.

Concerning Wittgenstein's and Petrus de Allyaco's shared views along this line, there is no fully justified basis for asserting that the author of the *Tractatus* had any knowledge of the scholastic logician's treatise on the *Insolubilia*. Here we may apply in its deepest meaning the French saying, "*Les beaux esprits se rencontrent.*"

74

Wittgenstein's Analysis of the Paradoxes in his Lectures on the Foundations of Mathematics

Charles S. Chihara

Ludwig Wittgenstein is still regarded in many circles as the greatest philosopher of the Twentieth Century.[1] Hence, the publication of his 1939 lectures on the foundations of mathematics[2] will undoubtedly be hailed by many as an important event, which makes a major contribution to the philosophical literature. From the point of view of Wittgensteinian scholarship, there can be little doubt that this publication is valuable, for the text was prepared by the editor from the copious notes of the lectures taken by four students and provides us with a detailed account of what Wittgenstein said and how he responded to questions and comments.

These lectures have been described by Malcolm[3] and also by D.A.T. Gasking and A.C. Jackson;[4] and it is enlightening to find out just what Wittgenstein said that so impressed these philosophers.[5] Thus, Gasking and Jackson wrote in their article that nearly "every single thing said [by Wittgenstein in his lectures] was easy to follow and was usually not the sort of thing anyone would wish to dispute" (p. 51). Having read these notes, I find it hard to understand how anyone who attended these lectures, as Gasking did, could have made that statement. (Wittgenstein is still regarded by many as a "common-sense philosopher," but even a superficial study of these lectures should dispel that conceit.)

This publication is useful not so much because of the views expressed in them — students of *PG* and *RFM*[6] will not be surprised by much of what Wittgenstein says — but because Wittgenstein's ideas on the foundations of mathematics are presented within the framework of a series of lectures, where there are interchanges with those in attendance and where Wittgenstein could make use of the reactions of his class to determine when to explain more fully obscure or difficult points.

I found especially interesting the interaction between Wittgenstein and the eponymous logician, Alan Turing, who seems to have been the only person attending the lectures willing or able[7] to challenge him on any significant point. At times, Wittgenstein must have been hard pressed by the logician's challenges. In Lecture VI, for example, we find Wittgenstein trying to convince his class that a mathematical proof of the impossibility of constructing a heptagon by ruler and compass merely explains the use of the word 'analogous'. Turing is skeptical and suggests that when one asserts the impossibility of such a construction, one is not trying to convey information about one's use of the word 'analogous.' Wittgenstein replies:

> You might say, "No, I'm not trying to convey this information. Mathematicians don't even use the word 'analogous'." — But does one not prove that there is no analogue in the case of the heptagon?

> A proof goes in fact step by step by means of analogy — by help of a paradigm [p. 62].

Later in the lecture, he attempts to clarify his position by asserting that such impossibility proofs, in effect, give *new meanings* to the word 'analogous.' The doctrine that mathematical proofs change the meanings of words — a view that I have discussed in some detail elsewhere[8] — is an essential part of Wittgenstein's ideas on mathematical proofs as expounded in *PG* and *RFM*. What is remarkable about the position taken in this lecture is this: Wittgenstein was not claiming then that as a result of seeing the proof, a person is made to change his use of such words as 'heptagon' and 'can construct:' it is the use of the word 'analogous' that supposedly is changed! Thus, of the case in which the mathematician proves that a heptacaidecagon is constructable and the heptagon is not, Wittgenstein says:

> We could say "he has been led to change his use of the word 'analogous'." And that is quite true.

> At first when he says "analogous" he explains, "Look, this is the construction of the pentagon, and this is the construction of the hexagon; I want to do so-and-so." But afterwards he would say, "This is the analogue in the case of the heptacaidecagon to the construction of the pentagon." He explains to use a new way of using "analogous" [pp. 63-4].

Not surprisingly, Turing is skeptical: he responds that the mathematician who proves these theorems surely doesn't invent what 'analogous' is to mean since we already know what the word means. Wittgenstein then says:

> Yes, certainly it's not a question merely of inventing what it is to mean. For if that were the problem, we could settle it much easier by making "analogous" mean "cushion".

> The point is indeed to give a new meaning to the word 'analogous'. But it is not merely that; for one is responsible to certain things. The new meanings must be such that we who have had a certain training will find it useful in certain ways [p. 66].

Shortly thereafter, Wittgenstein asks Turing if he understands what is being claimed. Turing's answer is sensible, direct, and, I would assume, honest. "I understand" he says, "but I don't agree that it is simply a question of giving new meanings to words." Wittgenstein has been quoted as saying about his lectures, "I shan't say anything that you won't all immediately agree with, and if you do dispute something I'll drop it and go on to something else."[9] Here, Turing was disputing a view that Wittgenstein had been attempting, with considerable force, to put across — a view that is central to Wittgenstein's ideas on the nature of mathematics. How would Wittgenstein respond to this challenge? Would he drop this position and go on to something else? Wittgenstein's recorded response is:

> Turing doesn't object to anything I say. He agrees with every word. He objects to the idea he thinks underlies it. He thinks we're undermining mathematics, introducing Bolshevism into mathematics[10] [p. 67].

At the time of these lectures, Turing was a respected logician, who had already published his important papers on computable functions.[11] That Wittgenstein would reply to him in this cavalier manner suggests to me that he had essentially run out of ideas on the point at issue.

I should now like to focus my discussion of these lectures on the semantical and set-theoretical paradoxes that Russell called "vicious circle paradoxes," since Wittgenstein's views on this topic have been sadly neglected. The topic is important, because much of the fruitful research on the foundations of mathematics in the first half of this century was stimulated or motivated by the goal of understanding or, at least, avoiding such paradoxes; and it is hard to imagine what form logic and set theory would have today had the paradoxes not been discovered and *taken seriously.*

Those familiar with *PG* or *RFM* will not be surprised at the drift of Wittgenstein's lectures on these paradoxes. Wittgenstein pooh-poohs the concerns that the early logicists and formalists expressed about hidden contradictions in logical systems. He asks his class to suppose that Russell's logic is used to draw conclusions. Would such a use be vitiated by the fact that a contradiction can be produced somewhere in the system? "And how would it be vitiated?" he asks (p. 209). Later, he gives the example of mathematicians who use what we would consider an inconsistent system of mathematics but who are unaware of the "hidden contradiction" in their system. Then after asking, "But what should we call the hidden contradiction?" Wittgenstein comments, "Is it hidden as long as it hasn't been noticed? Then as long as it is hidden, I say that it's as good as gold. And when it comes out in the open it can do no harm" (p. 219).

Now on the face of it, the views Wittgenstein puts forward here are absurd. So one would expect some rather strong reasons for accepting them. But if one is looking for rigorous argumentation to support this position, one will be disappointed. Wittgenstein's reasons for thinking that a system of logic or mathematics is "as good as gold" so long as the contradiction is hidden are brought out by examples. Thus, on p. 221, we find him developing the following examples. Imagine that a prison is built with the aim of keeping all the prisoners apart. The rooms and corridors are so designed that each prisoner can walk along certain corridors and into certain rooms, but no two prisoners can ever meet. It turns out, however, that whenever two corridors meet at right angles, it never occurs to the prisoners to turn right and they always go straight ahead. But were a prisoner to turn right at some of these intersections, he would be able to get into the room of another prisoner. Since this possibility does not strike any of the prisoners, the prison "functions as good as gold" (p. 221).

Another example clarifies the previous point and also illustrates Wittgenstein's reason for believing that the inconsistency of the system "can do no harm" when it is uncovered. He asks us to imagine a country with an inconsistent set of statutes. One statute requires the vice-president to sit next to the president on feast days, and another requires him to always sit between two ladies. This inconsistency is unnoticed for some time, because the vice-president is ill on feast days. But on one feast, he is not ill. What are we to do?

I may say, "We must get rid of this contradiction." All right, but does that vitiate what we did before? Not at all.

Or suppose that we always acted according to the first rule: he is always put next to the president, and we never notice the other rule. That is all right; the contradiction does not do any harm.

When a contradiction appears, then there is time to eliminate it. We may even put a ring around the second rule and say, "This is obsolete" [p. 210].

It can be seen that Wittgenstein's main idea is this: It is silly for the foundationalists to be worried about hidden inconsistencies in our mathematical and logical system, since so long as no contradiction has been found, the system is perfectly all right; and if an inconsistency is uncovered, "it can do no harm" since it is a simple matter to alter the rules so as to prevent us from drawing any unwanted conclusions. Thus, in reply to the statement "From a contradiction everything would follow" Wittgenstein says:

Well then, don't draw any conclusions from a contradiction; make that a rule. You might put it: There is always time to deal with a contradiction when we get it. When we get to it, shouldn't we simply say, "This is no use — and we won't draw any conclusions from it?" [p. 209].

Lest it be thought that Wittgenstein put forward these amazing views without a period of careful deliberation and assessment, it should be mentioned that he had written much the same thing many years earlier in *PG*, as the following quotation shows:

Something tells me that a contradiction in the axioms of a system can't really do any harm until it is revealed. We think of a hidden contradiction as like a hidden illness which does harm even though (and perhaps precisely because) it doesn't show itself in an obvious way. But two rules in a game which in a particular instance contradict each other are perfectly in order until the case turns up, and it's only then that it becomes necessary to make a decision between them by a further rule [p. 303].

Applying these ideas specifically to the contradiction Russell discovered in Frege's system, Wittgenstein suggests that there is no real problem for the Fregean since he can simply add to the rules one that says, "Don't draw any conclusions from any self-contradiction, i.e. from a sentence of the form '*P & -P*'." As he puts it:

You might get *p. p̄* by means of Frege's system. If you can draw any conclusion you like from it [i.e. from *p. p̄*], then that, as far as I can see, is all the trouble you can get into. And I would say, "Well then, just don't draw any conclusions from a contradiction" [p. 220].

In the usual formal axiomatic systems, any previously proved theorem may be inserted at any point in a derivation of the system: so if ϕ & $-\phi$ were proved, one could then derive any sentence one wanted from the axioms. And this, Wittgenstein suggests in the above quotation, is all the trouble one can get into from the contradiction. He then suggests that we can preclude getting this unwanted result by simply not inferring anything from a contradiction. As he said in the quotation I gave earlier: "make that a rule."

Turing replies: "But that would not be enough. For if one made that rule, one could get round it and get any conclusion which one liked without actually going through the contradiction" (p. 220). The point Turing is making is an elementary one, for what Russell showed was that there is a sentence ø of Frege's logical theory such that:

(1) ϕ is derivable from $\sum$ (the axioms of the system);

and

(2) $-\phi$ is derivable from $\sum$;

and hence

(3) ϕ & $-\phi$ is derivable from $\sum$.

But one cannot prevent the derivation of unwanted conclusions from the axioms by simply barring inferences from self-contradictory sentences, since by the rules of the propositional calculus we can get:

(4) $-\phi \rightarrow \psi$ is derivable from $\sum$ (from (1));

So

(5) ψ is derivable from $\sum$ (from (2) and (4)).

Thus, for any sentence ψ, we would be able to derive ψ from $\sum$, and without inferring anything from the conjunction ϕ & $-\phi$.

Furthermore, even expanding the set of sentences from which no inferences are to be drawn to include both ϕ and $-\phi$, in addition to ϕ & $-\phi$, will not preclude obtaining unwanted conclusions. Once one understands Russell's paradox, it is easy to construct indefinitely many paradox-producing sentences (and it is not necessary to derive an explicitly self-contradictory sentence with them in order to generate bizarre results). One can also construct sentences that, so far as one can tell at the time, are *likely* to be paradox/producing — others that are *quite possibly* paradox-producing.

Turing's point was a simple one, intelligible, one would think, to anyone with an understanding of elementary logic; yet there are reasons for thinking that Wittgenstein failed to grasp it. In the first place, Wittgenstein made no attempt to answer it. Turing's criticism comes at the very end of a lecture, and Wittgenstein begins the next lecture with the words: "We were in a mess at the end of last time and we shall probably get into the same mess again today" (p. 220). But he doesn't explain what the mess was or even try to show that Turing was mistaken in any way. He then goes on to express views in the lecture that can be criticized in the way Turing objected to Wittgenstein earlier.[12] He says, for example:

> We have seen that if we didn't recognize a contradiction, or *if we allowed a contradiction but*, for example, *did not draw any further conclusion from it*, we could not then say we must come into conflict with any facts [p. 230, italics mine].

In another place, he returns to a discussion of Frege's logical system, saying:

> Why should you say even when the contradiction is discovered, "Now everything is wrong"? Not even the contradiction itself is wrong, or a false mathematical proposition. The only point would be: how to avoid *going through* the contradiction unawares [p. 227].

Turing tries again to get Wittgenstein to see his previous point, by returning to the prison example. He asks Wittgenstein to suppose that there is a circus off one of the main corridors of the prison. When the prisoners find that they can turn right, they get into this circus. But, according to Turing, getting into the circus is only a "symptom" of the real difficulty: it is the turning right that is the real problem. "And one cannot get rid of the trouble simply by barring the circus" he says.

At this point, Wittgenstein decides to counterattack not the main point of whether one could eliminate the trouble by "barring the circus," but Turing's development of the prison example, suggesting that the case is not appropriately analogous to that of Frege's logic: he wished to counteract the suggestion that Russell's paradox showed that one could prove anything in Frege's system, saying "It isn't actually that people went through doors into places from which they could go any damn where. It isn't true that this happened with Frege's logic" (p. 228). And shortly after, he goes on to say:

He [Frege] was led by the normal rules of logic: the rules of such words as "and", "not", "implies", and so on. He was led also by our normal use of words. As we never ask whether "Fox" is a fox or "predicate" is a predicate, the question didn't arise and he never got into trouble . . . . .

So it is not quite right to say "Frege might have proved anything else." And this is shown by the fact that Russell, almost immediately on finding the contradiction, found a remedy in the theory of types; "We would never say 'Fox' is a fox; so eliminate that" [p. 229].

Notice that Wittgenstein is here suggesting that Russell was able to generate his contradictions in Frege's system by asking such questions as 'Is 'fox' a fox?' (he is more explicit on p. 222 where he describes Russell's paradox as arising from asking of the predicate "predicate that does not apply to itself" whether it applies to itself); and that Russell was able to fix up the system "almost immediately" by eliminating such questions. There is also a third idea, only hinted at here, that Russell generated his paradox by asking a perverse, unnatural, question. This idea is more clearly set out in another place where he says:

Take Russell's contradiction: There are concepts which we call predicates — "Man", "chair", and "wolf" are predicates, but "Jack" and "John" are not. Some predicates apply to themselves and others don't. For instance "chair" is not a chair, "wolf" is not a wolf, but "predicate" is a predicate.

You might say this is bosh. And in a sense it is. No one says " 'Wolf' isn't a wolf." We don't know what it means. Is "Wolf" a name? — in that case Wolf *may* be a wolf. If someone asked, "Is 'wolf' a wolf?", we simply would not know what to answer [p. 222].

It is important to notice that quotation marks are here being used in two distinct ways: (1) they are used to indicate that the *word* inside the quotation marks is being referred to; (2) they are used to indicate that the *concept* expressed (or denoted by) the word inside the quotation marks is being referred to. But this second use of quotation marks may not have been due to Wittgenstein at all.[13] Probably, the above quotation is the result of a purely oral presentation, where an utterance of 'Wolf is a wolf' would be indistinguishable from one of 'Wolf' is a wolf,' unless the utterer signaled the quotation marks in some way or other. And it is quite possible that Wittgenstein was, himself, confused by the above fact. Thus, if the word 'Wolf' is a name, say, of John's pet wolf, then Wolf is a wolf. But it does not follow from this that the *concept* 'wolf' is a wolf or that the *word* 'wolf' is a wolf. To suggest otherwise (as evidently Wittgenstein did) is to invite even more confusion than was already present in the class at that point in the lecture (see p. 223).

Now is it true that Russell "almost immediately" found a way of fixing up Frege's system *via* his theory of types? Well, if *Principia Mathematica* is supposed to be a fixed up version of Frege's system, then we can see that it took Russell many years of very intensive work, in collaboration with Whitehead, to come up with his "remedy."[14] Furthermore, it is grossly inaccurate to assert that one gets Russell's extremely complicated ramified theory of types from Frege's system by merely banning such questions as 'Is 'fox' a fox?' (Indeed, had such a trivial "remedy" as Wittgenstein suggests been available, is it likely that Frege, himself, would have failed to find it?)[15] For one thing, it is not true that the contradiction Russell produced in Frege's system was generated by asking such questions as 'Is 'wolf' a wolf?' In his famous letter to Frege,[16] Russell did sketch derivations of two contradictions, the first of which was formulated in terms of a predicate β that is to apply to all predicates that do not apply to themselves; and he did think a contradiction would result from asking if β applies to itself. As essentially the same paradox is described by Russell in his *Principles*,[17] Wittgenstein may have been led to think that the contradiction Russell constructed in Frege's system was due to asking of a predicate whether it applies to itself. But as Frege pointed out in his reply to Russell, a predicate for him is, as a rule, a first-level function of a certain sort (a first-level concept) which cannot meaningfully take itself as an argument.[18] In Frege's system, it makes no sense to say of any first-level concept that it falls under a first-level concept. So one cannot generate a contradiction in the first way suggested by Russell. As Frege's rules already preclude asking such questions as 'Does β apply to β?' or 'Does β fall under β?' one could not fix up Frege's system by banning such questions. Wittgenstein was quite confused in thinking otherwise.

It is well known that Frege's system is a sort of type theory: concepts, for example, are stratified into types in such a way that a concept is always of a higher level than that of its possible arguments.[19] Russell was able to generate his paradox in Frege's system because all extensions of concepts are regarded as "objects" and as such belong to one and the same type. If one wishes to regard Russell's theory of types as a sort of "remedy" for the paradoxes, then one essential part of the remedy is this: in Russell's system, classes or extensions of concepts are regarded as "logical fictions": strictly speaking, there are no classes in the ontology of *Principia Mathematica,* and all talk of classes is translated into talk about propositional functions. And although this basic idea is simple enough, carrying out the details of the idea is no simple task. So Wittgenstein's conception of Russell's solution to the paradoxes is both superficial and erroneous.

Let us now reconsider Wittgenstein's view that an inconsistent logical or mathematical system is "as good as gold" so long as the inconsistency is not noticed. Imagine that the scientists of some nation make use of a formal first-order language — for concreteness, let us say that the language is Mates' $\mathcal{L}$[20] — and imagine that they formulate some of their scientific theories and even their experimental data in $\mathcal{L}$ whenever possible. Suppose now that their logicians develop the following logical system of inference rules:

P: Any sentence may be entered on a line, with the line number taken as the only premise-number.[21]

T: Any sentence may be entered on a line if it is a tautological consequence of a set of sentences that appear on earlier lines; as premise-numbers of the new line take all premise numbers of those earlier lines.

C; The sentence $(\phi \to \psi)$ may be entered on a line if ψ appears on an earlier line; as premise-numbers of the new line take all those of the earlier line, with the exception (if desired) of any that is the premise number of a line on which ϕ appears.

US: The sentence $\phi\alpha/\beta$ may be entered on a line if $(\alpha)\phi$ appears on an earlier line; as premise-numbers of the new line take those of the earlier line.

UG: The sentence $(\alpha)\phi$ may be entered on a line if $\phi\alpha/\beta$ appears on an earlier line and β occurs neither in ϕ nor in any premise of that earlier line; as premise-numbers of the new line take those of the earlier line.

E: The sentence $(\exists\alpha)\phi$ may be entered on a line if $-(\alpha)-\phi$ appears on an earlier line, or vice versa; as premise-numbers of the new line take those of the earlier line.

This system is inconsistent, that is, '$P \& -P$' is derivable from the empty set of premises and hence is a theorem of this logic. But these rules are so close to Mates' sound rules[22] that one could easily carry out indefinitely many derivations, *getting correct results* (that is, deriving sentences that are indeed consequences of their premises) without ever deriving a contradiction from the empty set of premises. So we can easily imagine that the scientists of our example fail to notice the inconsistency of their rules.

Now is this inconsistent system of logic "as good as gold"? Is it as good as any of the sound systems we in fact use? Surely not. A sound system will carry one from truths to truths; the above will not. And the fact that the inconsistency is not noticed will not make it right, any more than not noticing that a person has cancer will make him well. Indeed, it is not hard to see how, by relying on such a system in reasoning about, say, the number of steel beams of such and such tested strength needed in a bridge to support a load of N tons, a disaster could result. Here, we could imagine the engineers working with such a large number of premises and carrying out such an intricate chain of inferences that a computer is used to check their work. If we imagine that they carry out their inferences rather mechanically, following set routines in accordance with general rules of strategy (as many students in logic courses do), it is not hard to see how they could start with true premises and end with false conclusions without noticing anything wrong with their logical system (especially when a computer is checking all their work).

The above example is relevant to another strange view advanced by Wittgenstein. In response to Turing's assertion that one could not be confident about applying a system of logic or mathematics until one assured oneself that there was no hidden contradiction in it, because a bridge might collapse or some such thing, Wittgenstein says:

> Now it does not sound quite right to say that a bridge might fall down because of a contradiction. We have an idea of the sort of mistake which would lead to a bridge falling.
> (a) We've got hold of a wrong natural law — a wrong coefficient.
> (b) There has been a mistake in calculation — someone has multiplied wrongly.
> The first case obviously has nothing to do with having a contradiction; and the second is not quite clear [p. 211].

Later, Wittgenstein returns to the same point, saying: "I'd say things can go wrong in only two ways: either the bridge breaks down or you have made a mistake in your calculation — for example, you multiplied wrongly. But you seem to think that there may be a third thing wrong: the calculus is wrong" (p. 218). And in another place, we find him considering the question "Why are people afraid of contradictions?"

> Turing says, "Because something may go wrong with the applications." But nothing need go wrong. And if something does go wrong — if the bridge breaks down — then your mistake was of the kind of using a wrong natural law (p. 217).

Suppose that the bridge the engineers design in our example subsequently collapses. Surely, we could distinguish at least three different possible explanations for the disaster: (1) the empirical theories and data the engineers relied upon were inaccurate or incorrect; (2) they made mistakes in calculation or didn't follow their rules of derivation correctly; (3) the logical system they used was unsound and led them to make invalid inferences (that is, they followed the rules of derivation correctly, but their calculus was wrong). In the above passages, Wittgenstein seems to be denying this third possibility. But as our example brings out, the collapse of the bridge need not be due to a faulty empirical theory or bad data. In fact, as I have described the situation, if the engineers were to recheck their data and retest their empirical theories, they would find everything in order. Hopefully, there would be some nonWittgensteinian logicians around to discover the unsoundness of their logical system.

Not surprisingly, Wittgenstein's attitude towards such semantical paradoxes as The Liar is closely related to his view of contradictions in logical and mathematical systems. In one place, he expresses the belief that it is "queer" that The Liar should have puzzled anyone; and he goes on to say:

> Now suppose a man says "I am lying" and I say "Therefore you are not, therefore you are, therefore you are not ..." What is wrong? Nothing. Except that it is of no use; it is just a useless language-game, and why should anybody be excited? [p. 207].

To Turing, who suggests that people are puzzled by The Liar because one usually takes the derivation of a self-contradictory sentence from apparently true propositions as a sign that one has done something wrong, Wittgenstein replies: "Yes — and more: nothing has been done wrong" (p. 207).

But is it true that nothing has been done wrong? Suppose we examine a slightly more rigorous version of The Liar. On page 65 of the June 1969 issue of *Scientific American,* one will find exactly one sentence ϕ printed in red and ϕ says: "The sentence printed in red on page 54 of the June 1969 issue of *Scientific American* is false." By one form of the law of excluded middle, either ϕ is true or ϕ is false. Assume the former. Then, since ϕ is the very sentence said to be false, we can conclude that ϕ is false. But if ϕ is false, it follows that the sentence in red on page 65 of the June 1969 issue of *Scientific American* is not false; hence ϕ is both true and false. But how can that be? Surely, we have done something wrong: we have either accepted a false premise or used an unsound rule of inference. What is so puzzling about The Liar is the fact that the argument is so simple and tight. Putting one's finger on the wrong move is extremely difficult, as practically everyone who has thought deeply about the paradox will agree. After all, The Liar has remained a paradox without a generally accepted solution for approximately two thousand years, despite strenuous attempts at solving it by some of the very best minds in logic and philosophy. Wittgenstein's hasty dismissal of this ancient and venerable problem is, in my opinion, neither well-reasoned nor insightful.[23]

The rationality of Wittgenstein's attitude toward the paradox can be judged more easily, I believe, by returning to the example of the scientists who use an inconsistent logical system. Suppose that one day someone produces a derivation '*P* & -*P*' from a tautology. As in the case of the paradoxes, traditional logicians would see the derivation of a contradiction from a tautology as a symptom that something is wrong with the system — as showing, in fact, that the rules cannot be sound as they had assumed. They would then investigate the rules in an attempt to find out what specifically is wrong. On the other hand, as we have seen from his analysis of The Liar, Wittgenstein thinks this traditional attitude is misguided. He says in an earlier lecture:

> One might say, "Finding a contradiction in a system, like finding a germ in an otherwise healthy body, shows that the whole system or body is diseased." — Not at all. The contradiction does not even falsify anything. Let it lie. Do not go there [p. 138].

Later, he reiterates his position that "it is vitally important to see that a contradiction is not a germ which shows a general illness" (p. 211). Which of these positions, the logician's or Wittgenstein's, is the more rational, I leave to the reader's judgment.

Cora Diamond should be thanked for both doing such a good job of editing (this version is incomparably better than one I read many years ago) and also making these lectures available. It is to be hoped that other lectures of Wittgenstein's that have been circulated, such as his lectures on philosophical psychology, will also be published. As more and more of Wittgenstein's thoughts are made readily available to all philosophers and not just a privileged few, we can expect more realistic appraisals of his contributions to philosophy to emerge than have been given thus far.[24]

Notes

1. This, at any rate, is an impression I got from attending the recent Wittgenstein conference in London, Ontario.

2. *Wittgenstein's Lectures on the Foundations of Mathematics: Cambridge, 1939*, edited by Cora Diamond from the notes of R.G. Bosanquet, Norman Malcolm, Rush Rhees, and Yorick Smythies, Cornell University Press (Ithaca, 1976). In this paper, all page numbers inside parentheses, unless otherwise indicated, are references to the above work. As a rule, single quotation marks are used to indicate that what is being referred to is the expression appearing within the quotes. However, at one point in this paper, I follow the lead of Cora Diamond in using quotation marks to 'mention' concepts. Double quotation marks are used as "scare quotes" and for quotation. The reader should note that my use of quotation marks does not coincide with Cora Diamond's (see note 13). Conventions governing the use of variables and logical constants are those of Benson Mates, *Elementary Logic*, 2nd ed. (New York, 1972). See especially p. 26.

3. Norman Malcolm, *Ludwig Wittgenstein: A Memoir* (London, 1958).

4. 'Wittgenstein as Teacher', in K.T. Fann (ed.) *Ludwig Wittgenstein: The Man and His Philosophy* (New York, 1967) 49-55.

5. One gets the impression from Malcolm's memoir (*op. cit.*, pp. 23-4) that it was not so much what Wittgenstein said that so impressed him as how he said it (cf. *infra.*, n. 7). Also, there seems to be some disagreement about whether Wittgenstein prepared his lectures. Malcolm thinks not (*op. cit.*, p. 24), whereas Gasking and Jackson write: 'Each lecture was obviously carefully prepared — its general strategy planned and numerous examples thought up' (*op. cit.*, p. 52).

6. Here, as elsewhere in this paper, I abbreviate references to Wittgenstein's *Philosophical Grammar* (Oxford, 1974) to '*PG*' and his *Remarks on the Foundations of Mathematics* (New York, 1956) to '*RFM*'.

7. Cf. 'I think that I understood almost nothing of the lectures, until I re-studied my notes approximately ten years later.' Malcolm, *op. cit.*, p. 23.

8. Charles S. Chihara, 'Mathematical Discovery and Concept Formation,' *Philosophical Review* 72 (1963) 17-34, pp. 264-76 above. Cf. also C.S. Chihara and J.A. Fodor, 'Operationalism and Ordinary Language: A Critique of Wittgenstein'. *American Philosophical Quarterly* 2 (1965) 281-95. The latter article puts forward an interpretation of Wittgenstein's philosophy of language (according to which he accepted a sort of operationalistic theory of meaning) that receives new support from these lectures. For example, Wittgenstein says on p. 256: 'It may seem queer that Euclidean geometry talks of "length" and "equality of length" and yet not of any method of comparing lengths. Especially since "this length is equal to that" changes its meaning when the method of comparison is changed .... But we could say that Euclidean geometry gives *rules* for the application of the words "length" and "equal length", etc. Not *all* the rules, because of these depend on how the lengths are measured and compared.'

9. Gasking and Jackson, *op. cit.*, p. 51.

10. It might be suggested that Wittgenstein was quite right to say that Turing agrees with every word. After all, had not Wittgenstein also said that it is not *merely* a question of giving new meanings to words? Had he not maintained that the new meanings must be such that we find it useful in certain ways? But had Wittgenstein responded to Turing's remark by pointing this out, would not Turing have responded with the words, 'I don't agree that it is simply a question of giving new meanings to words in such a way that we find it useful in certain ways'? It is possible that Wittgenstein's comment about Bolshevism stems from a statement of P.F. Ramsey's in 'The Foundations of Mathematics,' in his *The Foundations of Mathematics and Other Logical Essays*, edited by R.B. Braithwaite (London, 1931), in which he speaks of preserving mathematics 'from the Bolshevik menace of Brouwer and Weyl' (p. 56).

11. For a discussion of Turing's work on computable functions, see Stephen Kleene, *Introduction to Metamathematics* (Princeton, 1950), Chapter 13.

12. It should be noted that even in *RFM*, we find Wittgenstein thinking along similar lines. For example, of the Russellian antinomy in Ferge's system, he says: 'And suppose the contradiction had been discovered but we were not excited about it, and had settled e.g. that no conclusions were to be drawn from it. (As no one does draw conclusions from the 'Liar'.) Would this have been an obvious mistake?' (p. 170).

13. Indeed the conventions for the use of quotation marks Cora Diamond seems to be following in this work are by no means obvious. She claims in the preface that she is just following the conventions of *RFM*. But what are they? Given the nature of these lectures, an explicit statement of these conventions is surely called for. I recently received a letter from Professor Diamond informing me that she had planned to include in her preface a description of the conventions she was following, but that she changed her mind when she realized that such a discussion would require a considerable amount of space. Evidently, her main deviation from standard conventions results from an attempt to use single quotation marks as "idea quotes." Unfortunately, I am not in a position to explain what "idea quotes" are.

14. For a detailed discussion of Russell's solution to the paradoxes and his Theory of Types, see my *Ontology and the Vicious-Circle Principle* (Ithaca, 1973), Chapter 1.

15. To see how Frege explored possible remedies to Russell's paradox, the reader should study the appendix to Frege's *The Basic Laws of Arithmetic*, translated and edited by Montgomery Furth (Berkeley, 1964).

16. In Jean van Heijenoort (ed.) *From Frege to Gödel: A Source Book in Mathematical Logic 1879-1931* (Cambridge, Massachusetts, 1967) 124-5.

17. *The Principles of Mathematics* 2nd ed. (London, 1937), Chapter 10.

18. Jean van Heijenoort, *op. cit.*, p. 128.

19. For more details, see Chihara, *op. cit.*, Chapter 1, §7.

20. This is the formal first-order language of Mates, *op. cit.*

21. Such terms as 'premise number', 'line number', etc. are defined in Mateds, *op. cit.*

22. Ibid., pp. 112-13. Mates' system is, of course, a natural deduction system (as is the inconsistent system presented in the above example), unlike the logical systems Wittgenstein explicitly discusses in the lectures in connection with 'hidden contradictions.' But clearly the main point of the above example does not depend on the fact that the inconsistent predicate logic is a natural deduction system.

23. It is ironic that Russell's work on the paradoxes, of which Wittgenstein is so critical, has turned out to be very fruitful, generating much significant research in logic and mathematics. Indeed, I believe that Russell's idea (borrowed from Poincaré) that the paradoxes are due to viciously circular definitions is essentially on the right track, at least, in the case of the semantical paradoxes. See in this regard, my 'A Diagnosis of the Liar and Other Semantical Vicious-Circle Paradoxes', forthcoming in G. Roberts (ed.), *Bertrand Russell: The Memorial Volumes*, Volume 1.

24. Thanks are due to Barry Stroud, David Shwayder and Hans Sluga for their comments on an earlier version of this paper. The latter two suggested ways in which the view I attribute to Wittgenstein regarding 'hidden contradictions' might be defended or at least made more plausible. I certainly agree with them that much more than I have indicated in this paper can be said to make Wittgenstein's position appear more reasonable, especially by connecting it with his constructivistic views of mathematics. However, lack of space prevents me from going into this more deeply. Besides, as I am convinced that Wittgenstein's position is wrong-headed, it would be best to leave Wittgenstein's defense to others more sympathetic to the view.

75

Wittgenstein on Contradiction

Robert L. Arrington

In his *Remarks on the Foundations of Mathematics* Wittgenstein tells us that it is his aim "to alter the *attitude* to contradiction."[1] We should lose the superstitious fear of contradiction and cease to think of it as *the* bogy. He writes:

> There is *one* mistake to avoid: one thinks that a contradiction *must* be senseless: that is to say, if e.g., we use the signs 'p', '~', '.' *consistently*, then 'p and not-p' cannot say anything (*RFM*, V, 14).

When Wittgenstein poses the question of whether the law of non-contradiction is a fundamental law governing all conceivable language-games, his answer appears to be negative. Although a language-game may lose its sense through a contradiction, this need not necessarily be the case (*RFM*, II, 80).

Wittgenstein imagines several possible situations in which a contradiction would have a definite function and sense. Consider the following three cases:

> Why should not a calculation made for a practical purpose, with a contradictory result, tell me "Do as you please, I, the calculation, do not decide the matter" (*RFM*, III, 56)?

> The contradiction might be considered as a hint from the gods that I am to act and *not* consider (*RFM*, III, 56).

> Let us suppose that a contradiction in an order ... produces astonishment and indecision — and now we say: that is just the purpose of contradiction in this language-game (*RFM*, III, 57).

Whether these be actual or merely possible uses of a contradiction is a matter of no consequence. Wittgenstein's point is that a contradiction may be given a use and hence acquire a sense. Our use, or lack of a use, of the

338

expression 'p and not-p' is no sure indicator of the necessity of erecting a "super-fence" around contradiction.

These suggestions concerning contradiction seem to constitute a special case of Wittgenstein's more general thesis in the *Remarks* and, to some extent, the *Philosophical Investigations*[2] that logical rules, although made necessary by human convention, are suggested by contingent facts of experience. If these facts and/or our purposes were different, we might engage in entirely different language-games. For example, the language-game into which we fit the concept of pain is dependent upon there being certain natural responses to pain, certain activities which by their generality come to be incorporated into our criterion of pain. Or again, the fact that objects generally do not coalesce or divide in our world is at the heart of our arithmetic language-game in which $2 + 2 = 4$. Insofar as all of these general facts are contingent — the world could have been different — our language practices are also contingent, one among other possible sets, each with its own rules of logic. By taking into account both the experiential origin of what he calls "grammar" *and* the role of convention, Wittgenstein attempts to steer a course between the Scylla of Platonism, which would turn grammar into a set of time-independent necessary facts, and the Charybdis of positivism, which so divorces logic from experience as to make the application of logic unintelligible. As with other rules of grammar, the law of non-contradiction need not be true in all possible worlds. When experience in its general aspects changes, so does convention.

Wittgenstein is also concerned in the *Remarks* to diagnose those language-games in which a contradiction is indeed undesirable. Speaking of contradiction as a "sickness" or "disorder," he tells us that it is "for practical, not theoretical purposes, that the disorder is avoided" (*RFM*, II, 83). If a calculus contains a contradiction, this should be taken to mean that we do not know our way about in the calculus; we are unable to *do* anything with it. Hence he writes:

Is it usefulness you are out for in your calculus? — In that case you do not get any contradiction. And if you aren't out for usefulness — then it doesn't matter if you do get one (*RFM*, II, 81).

This diagnosis applies only to those games or calculi whose purposes or applications are frustrated by the presence of contradiction. For instance, he tells us that we may calculate with Frege's calculus, contradiction and all, because these calculations "do not serve the usual purposes of logical calculations" (*RFM*, II, 80). If we wish to translate Frege's logic into a system in which contradictions do not exist, we seek to avoid these contradictions because our new purposes make them undesirable. The order introduced by the law of non-contradiction is sought because we fare ill without it.

This practical justification of non-contradiction is the outcome of Wittgenstein's peculiar method, the method which he repeatedly refers to in the *Remarks* as one of anthropological description.

We shall see contradiction in a quite different light if we look at its occurrence and its consequences as it were anthropologically — and when we look at it with a mathematician's exasperation. This is to say, we shall look at it differently, if we try merely to *describe* how the contradiction influences language-games, and if we look at it from the point of view of the mathematical law-giver (*RFM*, II, 88).

Such a method amounts to what Wittgenstein referred to in the *Investigations* as the adducing of external facts about language (*PI*, I, 120). Or, again, it seems to be the point behind his claim in the *Remarks* that it is his task "not to attack Russell's logic from within, but from without" (*RFM*, V, 17). Otherwise, he tells us, he would be doing mathematics, rather than describing the position or office of this logic. We are to treat mathematics as an "anthropological phenomenon' (*RFM*, V, 26), one fact in the "natural history of man" (*RFM*, I, 141), pointing out very general features of experience on which the possibility of this fact depends. If, as Wittgenstein argues by way of an example, "the technique of calculation is part of the technique of house-building" (*RFM*, 1, 142), the aims and frustrations of construction will have a role in the elucidation of mathematics.

Both the claim that there may be language-games in which contradictions have sense and the diagnosis of those games in which contradictions are excluded run counter to Wittgenstein's early treatment of the topic in the *Tractatus*.[3] So much seems fairly obvious. The relationship of these notions to the thought of the *Investigations* is more complicated. There are two pertinent passages in the latter work which require initial comment. In section 125 the problem of the civil status of a contradiction is posed. Wittgenstein implies that finding ourselves in a contradiction amounts to being entangled in our own rules. "The fundamental fact here is that we lay down rules, a technique, for a game, and then when we follow the rules, things do not turn out as we had assumed" (*PI*, I, 125). An example of my own will show that this interpretation coincides to some degree with that of the *Remarks*. We talk of temporal duration and measure time in terms of hours, minutes, seconds, and so on. As we are accustomed to ask how long an event lasted, we might innocently inquire, "How long is the present?" When no answer is acceptable — the present being neither a minute nor a second long — we become confused and claim that the present is a durationless point. But then time becomes a series of durationless points, and as the series is likewise without duration, time cannot be measured. Our rules led us to think that the present could be measured. It cannot, and this fact reflects on the validity of temporal measurement altogether. We boldly declare that the concept of time is self-contradictory: time is unreal.

The *Investigations* offers us a therapy with which we may remove this theoretical catatonia. Our inability to "go on" and measure time is a result of a confusion which can be removed by calling to mind our use of the terms 'present,' 'past,' and 'future' and seeing that these are governed by other rules which make it senseless to ask for a measurement of the present in the first place. Here, then, the diagnosis overlaps that of the *Remarks*. A contradiction is a sign of our inability to use words as we wish. We are frustrated in the accomplishment of our purposes. But here it is suggested that it is not our language which is to blame, but rather our muddled insight into that language.

The other passage in the *Investigations* which I mentioned above tells us something different:

> When a sentence is called senseless, it is not as it were its sense that is senseless. But a combination of words is being excluded from the language, withdrawn from circulation (*PI*, I, 500).

If we apply this comment to the case of contradiction, we might take Wittgenstein as saying that the law of non-contradiction is a rule to which we appeal when we draw the boundary of what can be said in our language. To utter a contradiction is not so much to be entangled in our rules as to *violate* a syntactical rule.

If we look closely at Wittgenstein's analysis of following a rule, however, we will see that this latter interpretation coincides with the treatment of contradiction and logical necessity in the *Remarks*. To follow a rule is not to be guided, like a streetcar, down a set of rails extending indefinitely; nor is it to have a sudden vision of all the possible applications of the rule, including the particular application in question. To follow a rule is not to be guided by a picture in the mind, for a picture can be applied in many different ways. The same may be said for the symbolic formulation of the rule: no matter how precise the formulation, there are various ways to interpret this symbolism. Following a rule *is*, in the first place, to make judgments which are in accord with that *natural* consensus of judgment on which, Wittgenstein tells us, logic is based. In the second place, it is to engage in a practice which has been given conventional authority. The symbolic formula or the picture could have been applied differently, so it is a contingent matter of fact that a particular application is, naturally and conventionally, considered valid. The final justification of any practice, including the practice of applying the law of non-contradiction, is simply "This is what we do." We could have done otherwise, and hence our practice of not applying a predicate and its negation to the same object is not a super-practice which must have universal authority.

There is still another overlap between the teaching of the *Investigations* and the treatment of contradiction we are considering. Look again at the examples given at the beginning of this paper of possible functions of a contradiction. The expression 'p and not-p' might be given the use of saying that a person is to do as he pleases, or of advising him that his practical concern is not a subject amenable to rational analysis or is a matter too urgent to wait on the counsel of reason. Or a contradiction might be used, not to *say* anything at all, but rather to induce astonishment and perplexity. Here we have Wittgenstein's method at work: look for the uses of an expression; do not assume that an expression has one and only one use, or that it has no use at all. So with contradiction, rather than claim *a priori* that 'p and not-p' is always senseless, let us consider the multiplicity of uses we give it. And if we cannot find a use, let us remember that we can always create one.

There seems to me to be another crucial aspect of the *Investigations*, however, the spirit of which is violated by the treatment of contradiction in the *Remarks*. This leads me to speak of a fundamental ambiguity in the later Wittgenstein's philosophy, an ambiguity in his conception of the proper method of philosophical inquiry. On the one hand, there is in the *Remarks* and the *Investigations* the method of anthropological description and its issue, the concept of language-games. On the other hand, there is the set of methodological requirements laid down in the following passages of the *Investigations*:

> Philosophy may in no way interfere with the actual use of language; it can in the end only describe it.
> For it cannot give it any foundation either.
> It leaves everything as it is (*PI*, I, 124).
> Grammar does not tell us how language must be constructed in order to fulfill its purpose, in order to have such-and-such an effect on human beings. It only describes and in no way explains the use of signs (*PI*, I, 496).

If we abide by these requirements, I propose to show that we must reject the suggestions that a contradiction may have sense, that it is necessarily valid only within a practice or language-game which is itself contingent, and that it is justified in those games in which it has authority by virtue of its practical utility. The conflict between the two methodologies becomes apparent in the case of contradiction.

I wish to argue that Wittgenstein's analysis of contradiction does not leave language as it is. Furthermore, I propose that the method of anthropological description — and the diagnosis of contradiction achieved by means of this method — involves the explanation of language and construes grammar as an indicator of purposive activity. That is to say; I am claiming that Wittgenstein is himself guilty in this instance of possessing what Pears has called the Protean desire to transcend language,[4] the desire to explain the contradictions for the possibility of language. Rather than placing himself within our language and conducting philosophical inquiry by exhibiting, *showing* the statements and distinctions which this language allows — including the meta-statements it allows — he has, through his explanatory devices, changed our language. Or, phrased differently, he has said of our language that which cannot sensibly be said.

Let me begin my criticism by taking note of the fact that the examples of useful, significant contradictions given in the *Remarks* by no means live up to their reputation. If 'p and not-p' is to be used to enjoin unthinking action or to induce astonishment, it is only because it is senseless. Its senselessness is the foundation of its practical instrumentality. Rather than say that it acquires through these uses secondary meanings or pragmatic meaning, it would be clearer to appeal to Austin and say that these uses constitute perlocutionary acts which have no logical bearing on meaning.[5] This could lead us to assert with some inductive probability that a contradiction in fact says nothing and that our law of non-contradiction is indeed a rule guiding all of our language-games. There is no rule of natural-conventional practice in accordance with which 'p and not-p' becomes a meaningful expression.

Proceeding on the assumption that this is correct, I next wish to show that we cannot say in our language that the law of non-contradiction is a rule of a contingent practice and that it might not have authority in another practice. When I assert the law of non-contradiction I may be taken as formulating a rule which legislates against a certain form of expression. In saying that this rule is necessarily true, we are not uttering nonsense, as some have claimed, for Wittgenstein himself has taught us that 'true' does not apply to propositions or descriptions because the concept *fits* the concept of a proposition and no other (*PI*, I, 136). Now I ask: what is entailed by my assertion 'not both p and not-p'? To my mind this assertion entails 'it is necessary that not both p and not-p'. It has been denied both that a necessary statement implies its own necessity and that a statement to the effect that a tautology *is* a tautology is itself a necessary statement.[6] I wish to challenge both of these claims. If I am successful, then the assertion of 'not both p and not-p' commits one to the necessary assertion 'it is necessary that not both p and not-p.' And if this is so, one cannot assert the law of non-contradiction and in *the same language or any other language* assert that the necessity of this rule is relative to a contingent practice. Insofar as the assertion that the rule is only contingently necessary is a vital part of Wittgenstein's analysis of it, I will have shown the inadequacy of this analysis.

First, then, the demonstration that a necessary statement entails the statement that it is necessary. Rather than begin with the case of the law of non-contradiction, let me take the standard example of a necessary statement: "All bachelors are unmarried." I am claiming that this statement, which I call A, entails the further statement B, "It is necessary that all bachelors are unmarried." I mean by 'entails' that there would be an inconsistency in my asserting the conjunction of A and the denial of B, when this inconsistency is not present in either conjunct taken separately. To demonstrate that A entails B, let us ask what is being claimed when I assert that all bachelors are unmarried. It is not enough to say that this means that there are no bachelors who are married, for such an analysis would be compatible with A being a contingent statement. Rather, we must say that A means "It is impossible for there to be a bachelor who is married." Given this analysis of our necessary statement, we are in a position to see that it entails its own necessity. If it did not, it would be consistent to assert the following conjunction: "It is impossible for there to be a bachelor who is married, and it is not necessary that all bachelors be unmarried." Insofar as this may be rephrased to read "It is impossible for there to be a bachelor who is married and it is possible for there to be a bachelor who is married," it is clearly inconsistent. As Ambrose has pointed out, the explicitly modal statement is redundant: knowing its truth involves nothing beyond what is required in knowing the truth of the inexplicitly necessary proposition.[7] Knowing the truth of both is simply a matter of understanding the meaning of what is said.

We may now proceed to show that the explicitly modal statement B is itself necessary. This is demonstrated by the fact that it is entailed by the necessary statement A, for a necessary proposition cannot entail a contingent proposition. Another related demonstration is the following: If the explicitly modal proposition were not necessary, then it would be contingent or impossible; if it is contingent, it may be false. To assert it as contingent would be to allow for its falsification, but to do this would be to allow that "All bachelors are unmarried" may be false. This, however, is inconsistent with the assertion of A as a necessary truth.[8]

Could not the same arguments be used to show that the law of non-contradiction also entails its own necessity and that the statement of its necessity is itself necessary? It might be claimed that the arguments above assume the law of non-contradiction and cannot therefore be used to justify it. This rejoinder, however, would miss the point. It is not the *truth* of the law of non-contradiction that stands in need of justification; what requires defense is my claim that this necessary truth is not only contingently necessary. My arguments above assume only the truth of the law. I have claimed that our language practices incorporate this law as a necessary rule. The question is can we, remaining within these practices, sensibly assert that this rule might not have prevailed, that this necessary truth might not have been necessarily true. Assuming our practices, we assume the truth of this law, and this truth makes logically inconsistent and senseless the assertion "'It is necessary that not both p and not-p' is a contingent statement."

I emphasized above that it makes no sense to say in our language or in any *other* language that the rule of non-contradiction is only conditionally valid. The existence of multi-valued logics in which the law of the excluded middle and perhaps the law of non-contradiction are not proper parts may tempt us to claim the contingency of our ordinary logic, just as the existence of divergent moral codes leads us to assert the hypothetical nature of our own. Such a temptation rests on a confusion. Kneale has argued convincingly that alternative logics are not truly alternatives.[9] They do not mean the same thing by a 'truth value' as we do but are talking rather of something like the concept of certainty. Pap and other critics of logical conventionalism have contended that the conventionalists confuse symbolism and meaning.[10] From the obvious fact that the symbols 'and' and 'not' are arbitrarily assigned their meanings, it does not follow that what we express by means of these symbols is arbitrary. These points bear a relation to my criticism of Wittgenstein's anthropological method.

When Wittgenstein points out that a symbolic formula such as 'p and not-p' may have different applications, or, in some games but not others, no application, it does not follow that those games in which it has an application condone contradiction while those games in which it has no application do not. A difference in application constitutes for Wittgenstein a difference in meaning. Hence when 'p and not-p' has an application its meaning is different from what it 'means' to us, namely a set of symbols without meaning. If by 'contradiction' we mean an arrangement of symbols which is excluded from the realm of sense, then our alternative practice is not admitting what we mean by contradiction.

The emphasis on the application of a symbol is closely correlated with Wittgenstein's concept of use. There is an ambiguity involved in this concept, however, as well as one in the related concept, description of use. To look for the use can and 'often does mean no more than to look for the actual employment of a word, seeking out its applications and the context of responses and questions which surround this employment. But once we talk of the employment of a word, the anthropological concept of human activity raises its head. We engage in actions with ends in view, with intentions and motives. And so we begin to think of using a word as a purposive act, an act which can be explained in terms of those purposes and the environmental conditions which make possible their realization. To describe the use of language is then to characterize langauge in terms of the concept of purposive action. And that is to explain it and give it a foundation.

The latter understanding of describing the use is to be contrasted with the following: to describe the use is to show or exhibit the use by actually participating in the language-game in question, making the moves of that game, rather than making some comment on the moves. Much in the spirit of the *Tractatus*, the logic of our language shows itself and cannot be said. It is this view of use and description of use which is, to my mind, closer to the requirements of Wittgenstein's demand that we leave everything as it is, giving no foundation to or explanation of language. I have tried in this paper to exhibit some aspects of the logical form of our talk about contradiction and to show that this talk is not amenable to the anthropological analysis given it by Wittgenstein.

Notes

1. Wittgenstein, L.: *Remarks on the Foundations of Mathematics*, ed. by G.H. von Wright, R. Rhees, and G.E.M. Anscombe; trans. by G.E.M. Anscombe (Oxford: Basil Blackwell, 1964), II, 82; hereafter referred to as *RFM*.

2. Wittgenstein, L.: *Philosophical Investigations*, trans. by G.E.M. Anscombe (New York: The Macmillan Company, 1953); hereafter referred to as *PI*.

3. Wittgenstein, L.: *Tractatus Logico-Philosophicus*, trans. by D.F. Pears and B.F. McGuinness (London: Routledge and Kegan Paul, 1961).

4. Pears, D.F.: 'Universals,' in *Logic and Language*, second series, ed. by A.G.N. Flew (Garden City: Anchor Books, 1965), p. 281.

5. Austin, J.L.: *How To Do Things With Words*, ed. by J.O. Urmson (Oxford: Oxford University Press, 1962), Lectures VIII, IX, and X.

6. For the former claim, see C. Lewy 'Entailment and Necessary Propositions,' in *Philosophical Analysis*, ed. by M. Black (Englewood Cliffs: Prentice-Hall, Inc., 1963), pp. 183-97; for the latter claim, see P.F. Strawson, 'Necessary Propositions and Entailment-Statements,' *Mind*, LVII (1948), p. 184.

7. Ambrose, A.: 'On Entailment and Logical Necessity,' *Proceedings of the Aristotelian Society*, LVI (1956), p. 254.

8. *Cf*, C. Lewy, *op. cit.*, p. 186.

9. Kneale, W. and Kneale, M.: *The Development of Logic* (Oxford: Oxford University Press, 1962), pp. 572-4.

10. See, e.g., A. Pap, *Semantics and Necessary Truth* (New Haven: Yale University Press, 1958), Chapters V and VII.

76

Wittgenstein on Inconsistency*

Michael Wrigley

1.

Professor Charles S. Chihara has criticized the views on the subject of inconsistency which Wittgenstein put forward in his recently published 1939 lectures.[1] Chihara notes that these views are not peculiar to the 1939 lectures, and in fact they are to be found in all Wittgenstein's later writings on mathematics (e.g. *WWK* pp. 173ff., *PR* p. 189, *PG* pp. 303ff., *RFM* pp. 202ff.). So these ideas about inconsistency appear not to be just a momentary aberration on Wittgenstein's part. One would therefore expect that he had some good reasons for holding them. But Chihara justly complains that the kind of strong argumentation one would hope for is not forthcoming in these lectures. Instead Wittgenstein's usual procedure is to try to defend his views by producing series of rather unconvincing examples.

This unpromising state of affairs nothwithstanding, I want to try to show that what Wittgenstein says about inconsistency does have a rationale and that the criticisms Chihara levels against Wittgenstein can be met. Chihara throws out the suggestion that a defence of Wittgenstein's views might be possible if we bear in mind the constructivist tenor of his later writings on mathematics.[2] But this suggestion is quite incorrect. The key to understanding Wittgenstein's views on inconsistency, and indeed the whole of his later philosophy of mathematics, is to realize that it is underpinned and unified by a global or 'radical' conventionalist theory of necessity and is no species of constructivism.[3]

2.

What then are Wittgenstein's views on inconsistency? Of the views he puts forward among the most startling are: (1) 'hidden', i.e. as yet undiscovered, inconsistencies in a mathematical system are unimportant. 'As long as it's hidden I say that [an inconsistency] is as good as gold' (*LFM* p. 219). (2) When the inconsistency is actually derived and ceases to be hidden all that is necessary is to make an *ad hoc* stipulation to prevent deriving it again. (3) It is not even mandatory to do this much, for 'When [an inconsistency] comes out into the open it can do no harm' (*LFM* p. 219).

The first claim, that hidden inconsistencies are unimportant, may seem more plausible if we see it as directed against a Hilbert-type formalist, or at least someone who shared Hilbert's views on the importance of consistency proofs. Hilbert's attitude was that since the set-theoretic paradoxes had appeared in a branch of mathematics apparently meeting the highest standards of rigour we are no longer entitled to think that any other equally rigorous branch of mathematics may not equally suddenly and equally unexpectedly spring a contradiction on us. Accordingly we must try to find consistency proofs for as much of mathematics as possible. Only in this way can we make mathematical practice safe. As Hilbert himself put it, 'The goal of my theory is to establish once and for all the certitude of mathematical methods'.[4]

But if we take this attitude seriously then we ought to forswear completely working in any area of mathematics for which we lack a consistency proof. In the face of this attitude Wittgenstein's *laissez faire* approach might well seem relatively sensible. Wittgenstein's more extreme pronouncements against the very idea of *discovering* contradictions are on this interpretation simply to be taken as deliberate exaggerations aimed at shaking us out of the Hilbertian attitude. *If* we do suddenly come upon a contradiction in some well established branch of mathematics we shall deal with it *then*, but for the meantime do not worry about the possibility. This attitude is probably that of most working mathematicians, at least outside the foundations of mathematics, and we do after all have good inductive evidence that we shall *not* find such contradictions. This attitude has received support from Gödel's results; we now realize that there are limitations to what we can expect in the way of consistency proofs.

3.

Perhaps the foregoing was one component of Wittgenstein's views on inconsistency. But it is to be hoped that this is not all that underlies them, because there is an obvious objection to Wittgenstein's second claim which the views just sketched provide no way of meeting. Assuming that the above is correct as far as it goes the question arises of whether it is sufficient to say with Wittgenstein:

> If an inconsistency were to arise between the rules of the game of mathematics, it would be the easiest thing in the world to remedy. All we have to do is to make a new stipulation to cover the case where the rules conflict and the matter's resolved (*PR* p. 319).

Granted that we do not go around haunted by the imminent danger of an inconsistency in the system, what are we to do when the evil day finally drawns and a contradiction *is* derived? Hilbert's view is no doubt excessive, and to this extent most working mathematicians are with Wittgenstein, but they would certainly *not* agree with the way in which Wittgenstein suggests we deal with contradictions which are no longer hidden. Surely more is required than a mere *ad hoc* stipulation. In his lectures Wittgenstein had said:

> You might get *p*. ~ *p* by means of Frege's system. If you can draw any conclusion you like from [the contradiction], then that, as far as I can see, is all the trouble you can get into. And I would say, 'Well, then, just don't draw any conclusion from a contradiction' (*LFM* p. 220).

But this surely will not do. As Turing said to Wittgenstein in reply to this remark:

> But that would not be good enough. For if one made that rule, one could get round it and get any conclusion which one liked without actually going through the contradiction (*LFM* p. 220).

For an inconsistent system is precisely one in which *every* well-formed formula is derivable, and there is no need to infer anything from any particular explicitly derived contradiction in order to do this. But how does Wittgenstein deal with the objection? Instead of making a direct reply to Turing he describes a rather thin series of examples (*LFM* pp. 211ff., 220ff.). This behaviour seems to confirm some people's worst suspicions about the later Wittgenstein's loss of intellectual muscle. Turing's objection is simple and powerful yet Wittgenstein's reaction does seem to suggest on a superficial reading that he had no reply to it or had not even understood it.

4.

Wittgenstein's position has rather more depth than it might so far appear to have. Wittgenstein's views on inconsistency are neither a mere piece of philosophical therapy nor a bizarre piece of silliness totally unconnected with the rest of his work. Although both in his lectures and in what he wrote for his private use Wittgenstein expounds his views in an unsystematic way there is none the less a considerable amount of underlying system in them.[5] And this is just as much true of his philosophy of mathematics as the rest of his work. The central thesis of his philosophy of mathematics is a radical conventionalist account of necessity. Once this fact is appreciated it becomes clear both why Wittgenstein said what he did about inconsistency and how the objections made by Turing and Chihara can be met.

The more usual form of conventionalism, associated with Logical Positivism, held that certain basic necessary truths owed their necessity purely to our having an explicit convention to that effect, and that all other necessary truths were consequences of these basic conventions.[6] This theory of necessity is immediately attractive because it removes the epistemological mystery from necessary truth. Its crucial flaw, however, is its inability to explain this notion of consequence. The fact that such-and-such basic conventions have such-and-such consequences is a necessary truth but it cannot be a basic convention. What then is the source of its necessity?[7] Wittgenstein takes the only possible course to preserve conventionalism from this objection when he claims that *all* necessary truths, including statements of logical consequence, are conventional. This account of necessity is not without its critics,[8] but two things are clear. Firstly, that Wittgenstein held such a view. I have argued elsewhere that many aspects of Wittgenstein's later philosophy of mathematics are most plausibly seen as aspects of his radical conventionalism.[9] But perhaps the clearest manifestations of this theory of necessity are his repudiation of the idea that internal connections can exist unacknowledged — 'We cannot make any discoveries in syntax' (*PR* p. 182) — his claim that proofs *create* conceptual connections — 'The proof changes the grammar of our language, changes our concepts. It makes new connections ... it does not establish that they were there; they do not exist until it makes them' (*RFM* p. 166) — and his claim that 'The truths of logic ... are determined by a consensus of *action*' (*LFM* pp. 183-4).[10]

Secondly, it is clear how his radical conventionalism bears on Wittgenstein's views on inconsistency. For a radical conventionalist all necessary truths are conventions and it is obviously nonsense to talk of *discovering* conventions, for conventions are precisely things which we *set up*. No convention exists until it has been laid down. This means it is nonsense to speak of 'hidden' contradictions, for this assumes that it is determinate that a given formula, viz. a contradiction, follows from the axioms *before* we have derived it. But for a radical conventionalist it is only by actually deriving it that we set up the convention which determines that the contradiction so follows. Hence in a very literal sense 'A contradiction is only a contradiction when it arises' (*PR* p. 321), because before the contradiction is derived the system is not inconsistent. We can now see why Wittgenstein polemicizes so much against the idea of a 'hidden' contradiction, for his account of necessity implies that this idea is incoherent. We do not discover that a contradiction is a consequence of a system, we stipulate that it is. The rationale for Wittgenstein's claim that all we need do to deal with a contradiction once it is derived is to make an *ad hoc* stipulation is also clear. The orthodox view is that a contradiction shows that there is something deeply wrong with the system, and that a searching analysis is required to expose and correct the defect which is responsible for it. Wittgenstein repudiates this idea because the derivation of one contradiction cannot by itself show that there is some deep fault in the system — i.e. that other contradictions are in the offing — because that would amount to one contradiction showing that others would be derived, but whether they will be derived or not is as yet undetermined. This is why Wittgenstein says 'It is vitally important to see that a contradiction is not a germ which shows a general sickness' (*LFM* p. 211). It is also clear how Wittgenstein should reply to Turing's objection, for this too relies on the idea that the derivation of one contradiction implies that other formulae, viz. all the well-formed formulae of the system, are derivable too. But Wittgenstein will reject this, since it is not yet determinate whether any well-formed formula so follows which has not actually been derived.[11]

It may be replied that even if Wittgenstein's views on inconsistency can be defended by invoking his radical conventionalism, this does not advance his cause very much, for the latter view is no more plausible than the former. Radical conventionalism is certainly a somewhat startling position, and it does not have much immediate plausibility. But the same can be said of plenty of widely held philosophical positions (Quine's rejection of necessity, and his indeterminacy of translation thesis, for example). So it will not do just to boggle at radical conventionalism and ignore the argumentative support which can be produced for this position. Wittgenstein's arguments are to be found in his extensive discussions in *Remarks on the Foundations of Mathematics* and the *Investigations* of rule-following. There is no topic that Wittgenstein discusses in greater or more persuasive detail.

It is true that, especially in his 1939 lectures, Wittgenstein rather confuses the issue and masks the presence of his underlying radical conventionalism and his rejection of the idea of discovering logical consequences by frequently talking as though 'hidden' contradictions *do* exist undiscovered (e.g. *LFM* pp. 210, 216, 221 and 225). But in the first place it would just be cumbersome to avoid all talk of 'discovery'. None the less one might have expected Wittgenstein in at least a few places to draw attention to his rejection of the idea that we *discover* contradictions. I think this extreme reticence can be explained, if not justified, by bearing in mind Wittgenstein's very unusual conception of the correct way of practising philosophy, as I shall explain in Section 6.

5.

We have seen how Wittgenstein's first two theses about inconsistency can be defended. But what of the third? What Wittgenstein claims is that even if we have actually derived a contradiction in a system we are not obliged to do *anything* about it, not even make an *ad hoc* stipulation. Once again the obvious objection to this proposal was put to Wittgenstein by Turing and is taken up by Chihara. Turing's point is simply that if we leave an explicit inconsistency in our system then this will be likely to have disastrous practical consequences if we apply the system, e.g. in building bridges. As Turing says 'The real harm [in an inconsistent system] will not come in unless there is an application, in which case a bridge may fall down or something of that sort' (*LFM* p. 211).

The idea is presumably that with an inconsistent system such disasters will occur very much more frequently than they do with our consistent systems. For of course our bridges occasionally collapse even though our mathematics has no explicit inconsistency. So it is not immediately clear how Turing's point can claim to reveal some inherent defect in an inconsistent mathematical system. The difference between our arithmetic, say, and a deviant inconsistent arithmetic in respect of the frequency of constructional disasters resulting from their application is only one of degree. And how can this show that there is some essential defect in the inconsistent system in contrast to our own? Our confidence in our own arithmetic in this respect is after all only inductive, and is it not conceivable that the properties of building materials might alter drastically so that *our* mathematics led to very much more frequent empirical disasters, say if the properties of materials took to fluctuating wildly? None of this is to deny that the use of a deviant arithmetic *would* almost certainly lead to very frequent disasters, but it is as yet unclear how this is supposed to show that there is an *a priori* defect in an inconsistent mathematical system.

But what is wrong with an inconsistent system is of course that, as Chihara says, 'A sound system will carry one from truths to truths; [an inconsistent one] will not'.[12] Or at more length:

> Suppose that the bridge the engineers design ... collapses. Surely we could distinguish at least three different possible explanations for the disaster: (1) The empirical theories and data the engineers relied upon were inaccurate or incorrect; (2) They made mistakes in their calculation or didn't follow their rules of derivation correctly; (3) The logical system they used was unsound and led them to make invalid inferences (that is, they followed the rules of inference correctly, but their calculus was wrong) ... Wittgenstein seems to be denying this third possibility.[13]

Now it is quite correct that Wittgenstein does deny this third possibility (cf. *LFM* pp. 217-20). But it remains to see why. It turns out that, as with the other aspects of what he says about inconsistency, the motivation for this claim too is to be found in Wittgenstein's radical conventionalism.

A conventionalist account of necessity involves denying that necessary 'truths' are genuine *truths*. This aspect of conventionalism never became explicit in expositions of the half-baked conventionalism advocated by the Logical Positivists. The reason is clear enough, for otherwise the problem arises of how non-conventional non-basic necessary truths can follow from basic conventions which are not *truths* at all. But it clearly *is* inappropriate to think of conventions governing the use of words as *truths*. A more appropriate way to think of them is as rules or stipulations which have a normative rather than descriptive role. The whole idea of a convention is of something which we *set up* and which owes its existence purely to our decision to do this. So a convention is not something which states a fact about the world. Rather necessary 'truths' are rules which determine our framework for describing the world. They do not themselves describe any thing. They are not truths but are 'antecedent to truth', as Wittgenstein puts it:

> There is not any question at all ... of some correspondence between what is said and reality [in logic]; rather logic is *antecedent* to any such correspondence; in the same sense, that is, as that in which the establish-

ment of a method of measurement is *antecedent* to the correctness or incorrectness of a statement of length (*RFM* p. 96).

It is now clear what the reply to Chihara's objection should be. The objection is that a mathematical system which is inconsistent will not be truth-preserving among contingent propositions, it will not allow only valid inferences between the facts. But this is only possible if we can describe 'the facts' independently of which necessary truths we have and go on to inquire whether our necessary truths allow the right inferences among the possible facts. But the antecedence doctrine which radical conventionalism implies can allow no such possibility, for our framework of necessary truths itself determines what are the possible facts. Since they are rules which lay down the possible uses of words, if we find ourselves in apparent conflict with them then we *must* say that we have misdescribed the facts. So we can have no access to the facts independently of which necessary truths we have, and we cannot convict our necessary truths of failing to do justice to the facts in the way Chihara suggests. Certainly if we used a deviant inconsistent arithmetic we would very likely find ourselves faced with collapsing bridges rather often, but Wittgenstein's antecedence doctrine rules out the possibility of blaming this on some *a priori* defect in our mathematics. What we would do in this situation would be what we now do when such a disaster occurs — we say that we *must* have made an error in our calculations or we must have been using a faulty empirical theory. If necessary truths are to have a normative role then we *must* explain away apparent conflict with them in this way. Of course there is no guarantee that we shall be able to find a mistake, but that goes whichever mathematics we use.

All this can seem unnecessarily implausible if we do not realize that in ruling out *a priori* justification and criticism of our mathematics Wittgenstein is not ruling out all possible kinds of justification and criticism. It is after all no accident that we have the arithmetic we do. And if we came across a tribe who used a deviant arithmetic we might well be able to get them to abandon it in favour of ours by showing them that ours was superior in point of safety, convenience, etc. That such *a posteriori* pragmatic ways of justifying and criticizing mathematical systems exist Wittgenstein does not for a moment deny (cf. *LFM* pp. 47, 83, 257-8). But although an alternative arithmetic may be highly inconvenient it is not *wrong*. 'Inventing a technique: 12, 14, 13, ... would be immensely impractical, inconvenient — but not wrong' (*LFM* p. 83). There are no rights and wrongs in the realm of pure convention.

6.

There must be an obvious question-mark over all this. If such a defence of his views on inconsistency was available to Wittgenstein why did he not make it in reply to Turing? I suggested earlier that Wittgenstein does not spell out his claim that the idea of a 'hidden' contradiction is incoherent because that would conflict with his conception of the correct philosophical method. I think much the same is true of his lack of explicit defence of what he says about inconsistency.

Wittgenstein's conception of the nature and practice of philosophy was highly idiosyncratic. He held that philosophy ought to avoid any kind of explanation — 'We must do away with explanation and description must take its place ... philosophy neither explains nor deduces anything' (*PI* §126). Connected with this is the claim that philosophy should avoid any kind of generality. The craving for generality is identified as a prime source of philosophical confusion (*BB* p. 17). So philosophy must be purely descriptive and eschew generality. But Wittgenstein places even more severe restrictions on the correct philosophical method, for not only must the philosopher avoid all generality and merely describe, but what he says by way of description must be completely uncontroversial. 'If one tried to advance *theses* in philosophy it would never be possible to debate them, because everyone would agree to them' (*PI* §127; cf. §599). This much is by way of restrictions which Wittgenstein imposes on philosophical method, but he also has positive ideas about the cause and treatment of philosophical puzzlement which shape his conception of the correct philosophical method. In Wittgenstein's view philosophical misunderstandings stem from our putting an incorrect interpretation on our grammar and enshrining these misunderstandings in various distorted and misleading ways of speaking. 'Philosophy is a battle against the bewitchment of our intelligence by language' (*PI* §109). The philosopher's task, like the psychoanalyst's, is to enable us to see through what we are doing for ourselves. For this reason Wittgenstein is extremely reluctant to impose what he thinks are the solutions to particular philosophical problems on his audience. When Lewy said in reply to a question of Wittgenstein's 'I know what you *want* me to say' Wittgenstein answered 'I have no right to want you to say anything except just one thing "Let's see"' (*LFM* p. 55).

So here we have the explanation of Wittgenstein's extreme avoidance of connected argument and debate in these 1939 lectures. And it is for this reason too that Wittgenstein is willing to talk of 'discovering' contradictions rather than calling into question such ways of speaking on every possible occasion. He is simply trying to put into practice his conception of the correct philosophical method. For Wittgenstein to have trotted out his radical conventionalist theory of necessity in reply to Turing's objections would have infringed all his methodological principles. It would have been to go beyond pure description and advance a general, explanatory theory and it would, to say the least, hardly have been something 'everyone would agree to'. It would also have involved Wittgenstein in imposing his views on his audience in a way he wished to avoid. So in dealing with Turing the way he does Wittgenstein is simply keeping the promise he made in his first lecture — 'I won't say anything which anyone can dispute. Or if he does dispute it, I will let that point drop and pass on to say something else' (*LFM* p. 22). My point is that, despite appearances, Wittgenstein's behaviour when faced with Turing's objection is not an indication that he has run out of ideas or has failed to grasp Turing's point. On the contrary, it is a conscious attempt to put into practice his views on philosophical methodology. Equally the fact that he does not explicitly formulate them in response to his audience's objections is no objection to the defences I have sketched as Wittgensteinian exegesis.

Relating his lecturing style to his conception of philosophical methodology also allows us to explain what Wittgenstein *does* do, viz. describe strings of examples, for this is just another aspect of the correct philosophical method. Wittgenstein wants to bring people to realize for themselves what philosophical knots they are tied in and this he conceives of as an essentially slow, gradual process. 'In philosophizing we may not *terminate* a disease of thought. It must run its natural course, and *slow* cure is all important' (*Z* §382). Hence the importance of the strings of examples. Each of these is supposed to illuminate one aspect of the puzzle under consideration at the stage in the therapy so far reached and so gradually dissolve it (cf. *PI* §§122, 127, 133 and *RFM* p. 376).

It is of course quite another matter whether Wittgenstein's conception of philosophy and philosophical method is defensible, and whether he could ever hope to achieve what he wanted by the method he advocates. (He does not seem to have been very successful in his 1939 lectures.) Clearly the avoidance of generality, explanation and argument has little to recommend it on purely practical grounds, and Wittgenstein nowhere attempts to *defend* this conception of philosophical method. Indeed his self-imposed restrictions would seem to preclude any such defence since it would presumably have to take the form of argument. So Wittgenstein's conception of philosophical method seems to be self-stultifying. No doubt Wittgenstein had reasons for feeling obliged to try to expound his views in this way, but it is quite unclear what those reasons are.

Fortunately this conception of philosophy and philosophical method seems to have a pretty tenuous connection with the rest of Wittgenstein's work, so I think that the rest of us need not have any qualms about defending Wittgenstein's views in a way which he would not have approved of. All the more so since his conception of philosophical method seems actually to be in conflict with other more important strands in his work. Despite his avowed rejection of generality Wittgenstein's work contains plenty of general and highly controversial philosophical theories. The radical conventionalist account of necessity and the criterial account of our knowledge of other minds are two particularly clear examples. Furthermore, in putting forward both these theories Wittgenstein also produces palpable arguments. So, except when lecturing, even Wittgenstein himself does not seem to have taken his ideas on philosophical method very seriously.[14]

7.

Wittgenstein's ideas on inconsistency can withstand Chihara thus far. I want to conclude by considering a further objection Chihara makes, which, while being admittedly much less powerful and of a somewhat different character, is worth discussing because it raises some important general points about Wittgenstein's philosophy of mathematics. Chihara's objection is that if mathematicians in the first half of the century had become convinced of a Wittgensteinian view of inconsistency mathematical logic would almost certainly not have developed as vigorously and fruitfully as it has. For there would not have been the same interest in avoiding inconsistencies in the first place, since they can easily be dealt with when and if they turn up. So isn't a Wittgensteinian view of these matters undesirable on pragmatic grounds?

Now of course even if this is correct it does nothing to show that Wittgenstein's views are *wrong*. Yet Chihara seems to have a point, since Wittgenstein himself conceives of his work as having just this kind of effect:

> What will distinguish the mathematicians of the future from those of today will really be a greater sensitivity, and *that* will — as it were — prune mathematics; since people will then be more intent on absolute clarity than on the discovery of new games.
>
> Philosophical clarity will have the same effect on the growth of mathematics as sunlight has on the growth of potato shoots. (In a dark cellar they grow yards long) (*PG* p. 381).

On the face of it it might well seem as though Wittgenstein's ideas will have even more impact on mathematics than this, in that they look like having actually revisionary consequences by leading us to give up certain established branches of mathematics. Consistency proofs are one clear example, for if we accept Wittgenstein's critique of the idea of a 'hidden' contradiction and the rest of it then not only shall we not look for new consistency proofs but we shall no longer regard ones we already have as of any importance. Another clear example of the revisionary potential of Wittgenstein's ideas appears to be set theory. Here Wittgenstein says that 'In set theory one is doing a branch of mathematics of whose application one forms an entirely false idea' (*RFM* p. 260) and this seems to echo intuitionist criticisms of the mathematics of the transfinite. Of course Wittgenstein claims that 'Philosophy ... leaves mathematics as it is' (*PI* §124) and wishes at all costs to avoid 'meddling with the mathematicians' (*LFM* pp. 13, 223). Indeed he explicitly states that set theory is not open to philosophical criticism, saying that 'It is odd to believe that this kind of mathematics is imperilled by any kind of philosophical ... investigation' (*PG* pp. 467-8). But these claims begin to seem a little disingenuous when set alongside passages like these:

> [Hilbert] said 'No one is going to turn us out of the paradise which Cantor has created'. I would say 'I wouldn't dream of trying to drive anyone out of this paradise'. I would try to do something quite different: I would try to show that this is not a paradise — so that you leave of your own accord — I would say 'You're welcome to this; just look about you' (*LFM* p. 103).

And

> [I don't] mean that certain mathematical propositions are *wrong*, but that we think their interest lies in something in which it does not lie. I am *not* saying that transfinite propositions are *false*, but that the wrong picture goes with them. And when you see this the result may be that you lose your interest (*LFM* p. 141).

But this second passage reveals what the nature of Wittgenstein's critique of set theory is. Unlike the intuitionists he is not claiming that set theory is totally incoherent. It is rather that it is associated with misleading imagery. In general Wittgenstein thinks that 'Mathematics is dressed up in false interpretations' (*PG* p. 385) and that much mathematics owes its interest to this misleading but attractive imagery. Because his aim is to dispel this imagery Wittgenstein conceives of his work as likely to have an inhibiting effect on the growth of mathematics. But if this is what lies behind Wittgenstein's quasi-revisionism then I think we can question whether his ideas will have the kind of effect he expects. The general point he seems to be making is that only if there is suitably 'charming' imagery associated with it will mathematicians have any interest in a branch of the subject. Thus he says things like 'If you can show there are numbers bigger than infinity, your head whirls. This may be the chief reason this was invented' (*LFM* p. 16). (Cf. *LFM* pp. 140-1, 150, 235-54, and *LA* p. 28.)

Now it may be that imagery of this sort has some heuristic role to play,[15] but it is quite false to suggest that it is only because of such associated imagery that any branch of mathematics has any interest. At least when discussing set theory Wittgenstein appears almost entirely to overlook the extent to which a branch of mathematics can have purely technical interest regardless of what images go with it, if any. To take an extreme case, Kreisel points out in discussing Hilbert's programme that what Hilbert found so paradisial about Cantor's set theory was the 'abundance of transfinite machinery', i.e. the possibility of using transfinite techniques to obtain results in more mundane areas of mathematics.[16] *This* interest will obviously remain when any imagery associated with the transfinite is removed. Indeed Hilbert himself seemed to regard set theory purely as consisting of 'ideal' elements devoid of significance in themselves.

My point is that in the case of set theory the grounds Wittgenstein has for thinking that his philosophical views about mathematics will tend to lead people to lose interest in the subject do not seem to be very good ones. In general the imagery Wittgenstein draws attention to contributes nothing to the real interest of mathematics. So Wittgenstein's project of stripping mathematics of the false interpretations in which it is dressed will have no tendency to stunt the future growth of mathematics nor any revisionary potential by making us lose interest in established areas. It is surprising that Wittgenstein does not see this point in general because in some contexts he seems to appreciate it well enough. For example when he is talking about the exotic imagery sometimes associated with imaginary numbers he says:

It is a harmless misunderstanding because the interest of mathematicians and physicists has nothing to do with the 'imaginary' character of the numbers. What they are chiefly interested in is a particular technique or calculus (*LFM* p. 15).

So far, then, even though Wittgenstein himself seems to accept it, Chihara's point has no force. A Wittgensteinian philosophical perspective need have no effect of any kind on mathematical practice.[17] But I think it might be objected to this that although Chihara's point can be met in most cases, with the particular case of consistency proofs things are surely different. Here adopting a Wittgensteinian perspective really does amount to depriving the search for consistency proofs of all point, and so compelling us to abandon this type of mathematics. For surely a consistency proof can only have a point if contradictions *can* exist undiscovered. The purpose of such a proof is to show that there are no undiscovered contradictions in a system. But if Wittgenstein is right we know that there are none without going to the trouble of finding a consistency proof. However to think this would be a mistake. Although Wittgenstein does reject the idea of hidden contradictions and so the idea that we *discover* that a system is consistent he can still allow that consistency proofs have a perfectly good role to play. For whilst Wittgenstein rejects the idea of a contradiction lying undiscovered in a system this does not mean that no contradiction will be derived in the future. On Wittgenstein's radical conventionalist account of necessity, until we lay own the relevant stipulation by actually deriving it, it is quite *open* — logically — whether any particular formula is derivable from the axioms. A consistency proof should be regarded not as effecting a discovery but as making a new stipulation which blocks this possibility of deriving a contradiction. Viewed thus consistency proofs very much retain their interest and there is every reason to construct them. In fact they have precisely as much importance as we always thought they had. Even here Wittgenstein's views fail to have the inhibiting effect which Chihara suggests they will have and Wittgenstein's views are quite in harmony with his principle of not 'meddling with the mathematicians'.[18]

Notes

*This is a revised version of a paper which originally appeared in *Philosophy* (October 1980).

1. Charles S. Chihara, 'Wittgenstein's Analysis of the Paradoxes in his 1939 Lectures on the Foundations of Mathematics', *Philosophical Review*, July 1977.

2. Ibid., p. 381n.

3. This claim is not uncontroversial. I have defended it in my paper 'Wittgenstein's Alleged Mathematical Constructivism' (forthcoming).

4. Hilbert, 'On the Infinite', *Philosophy of Mathematics: Selected Readings* (eds. Paul Benacerraf and Hilary Putnam) (Oxford, Blackwell, 1964), p. 135.

5. As is noted by P.M.S. Hacker, Wittgenstein is not unique in this (*Insight and Illusion: Wittgenstein on Philosophy and the Metaphysics of Experience* (Clarendon Press, Oxford, 1972), p. 140). Hacker cites Nietzsche as another philosopher whose unsystematic style of exposition disguises the considerable degree of underlying system to his thought.

6. Cf., for example, A.J. Ayer, *Language, Truth and Logic* (Harmondsworth, Penguin,

1971), ch. 4 for a classic account of this theory of necessity.

7. Cf. Michael Dummett's 'Wittgenstein's Philosophy of Mathematics' (*Truth and Other Enigmas* (London, Duckworth, 1978), ch. 11 pp. 121-37 above) for further discussion of this objection. An attempt to salvage moderate conventionalism has been made by Jonathan Bennett in his 'Being Forced to a Conclusion', *Proceedings of the Aristotelian Society*, supp. vol. (1961). It has been convincingly argued by Crispin Wright that the attempt fails (ch. 18 of his *Wittgenstein on the Foundations of Mathematics* (London, Duckworth, 1980)).

8. Notably Dummett: his 'Wittgenstein's Philosophy of Mathematics' contains an incisive presentation of the objections which underlie the intuitive resistance to this position. Wright in *Wittgenstein on the Foundations of Mathematics* (*passim*) makes a persuasive case that it is far from clear that these objections are fatal to radical conventionalism.

9. Michael Wrigley, 'Wittgenstein's Philosophy of Mathematics', *Philosophical Quarterly*, 27, 106 (1979); reprinted in this volume.

10. Despite such persuasive evidence the claim that Wittgenstein was a radical conventionalist has not been universally accepted. The most widely accepted alternative reading of Wittgenstein is that put forward by Stroud in his 'Wittgenstein and Logical Necessity' (*Philosophical Review*, 1965 pp. 289-301 above). The crucial problem with Stroud's more anodyne reading of Wittgenstein is its inability to do justice to Wittgenstein's stress on the essential role of *decision* in proof. Cf. Wright, *Wittgenstein on the Foundations of Mathematics*, pp. 379ff where this point is pursued.

11. *Logically* determinate that is. It may for all we know be causally determinate what we shall derive, but until we actually do so we have yet to set up the conventions which will decide whether it is the logically correct thing to derive.

12. Chihara, 'Wittgenstein's Analysis', pp. 377-8.

13. Ibid., pp. 378-9.

14. Cf. Hacker, *Insight and Illusion*, ch. 5 for an illuminating discussion of Wittgenstein's later conception of philosophy, and in particular of the tension between it and other aspects of his work.

15. Cf. Hardy's talk about 'what Littlewood and I call *gas*, rhetorical flourishes designed to affect psychology, pictures on the board in the lecture, devices to stimulate the imagination of pupils', 'Mathematical Proof', *Mind*, 1929 (cited by Cora Diamond, *LFM* p. 13).

16. Kreisel writes, 'We note in passing an interesting aspect of Hilbert's idea of a *paradise*: a characteristic of Cantor's set theory ... is the abundance of transfinite elements which Hilbert regarded ... as "ideal" elements to be used as gadgets to make life smoother', 'Hilbert's Programme', *Philosophy of Mathematics: Selected Readings* (ed. Paul Benacerraf and Hilary Putnam (Blackwell, Oxford, 1964), p. 159).

17. I say Wittgenstein's views *need* not have any such effect because the question of how a practising mathematician might react to them is ultimately an empirical one. For example, someone who became convinced of a radical conventionalist view of mathematics might give up mathematics because the depth which he thought the subject had now seemed to him to be illusory. Instead of discovering facts about a timeless Platonic realm of abstract objects all mathematics did was to set up human conventions. (Cf. Russell's description of the disillusionment with mathematics which he felt when he abandoned his earlier extreme Platonism for a kind of conventionalism, *My Philosophical Development*, New York, Simon and Schuster, 1959, pp. 211ff.) However, there is certainly no reason why the mathematician must react in this way. Strongly anti-Platonist views have been held by extremely creative mathematicians. Both Hilbert and von Neumann were formalists, and Hahn accepted an explicitly conventionalist view of mathematics. According to Philip J. Davis and Reuben Hersh (*The Mathematical Experience*, Harmondsworth, Penguin, 1983, pp. 321ff) the view most widespread in the mathematical community is a kind of incoherent combination of Platonism and formalism. So it seems that an interest in mathematical problems is capable of being sustained by all kinds of pictures and imagery, of varying degrees of coherence. Clearly, then, there is no reason why someone who accepted Wittgenstein's view of mathematics would be *compelled* to lose interest in mathematics. He might, but equally well he might not. In this Wittgenstein's views contrast with, e.g. intuitionism. So Wittgenstein's claim that he leaves mathematics as it is is quite justified.

18. I am grateful to Gordon Baker and Crispin Wright for valuable comments on an earlier draft of this paper.

77

Critical Study: Wright's *Wittgenstein*

Cora Diamond

Crispin Wright. *Wittgenstein on the Foundations of Mathematics*. London: Duckworth, 1980. pp. xix+481.

Professor Wright's book was advertised in the United States by Harvard University Press as

> A sympathetic and welcome attempt to elucidate Wittgenstein's views on the philosophy of mathematics in terms of his later philosophy of language. Conspicuously free of mathematical technicality, like its subject, Wright's effort is both illuminating and persuasive.

"A sympathetic and welcome attempt": certainly welcome, and in intention sympathetic. To understand Wittgenstein's views of mathematics, we must, Wright thinks, know what can be said in their defence. Much of what can be said for them is that you must accept them if you are convinced by Wittgenstein's arguments about language and understanding. Hence Wright concerns himself with explaining and defending *those* arguments, and showing their force against alternative views of mathematics. Wittgenstein's philosophy of mathematics is taken to be initially repugnant to common sense, but much of the repugnance can, Wright thinks, be overcome. Many of the difficulties which defenders of such views run into can be resolved satisfactorily, while exploration of others shows the sort of work that remains to be done by anyone taking no matter what view about mathematics. While Wright believes that there are serious objections to Wittgenstein's views, he tries to convince us that they should be taken far more seriously than commentators like Georg Kreisel, Alan Ross Anderson and Charles Chihara have suggested.

"Conspicuously free of mathematical technicality." Yes, but no joy for the reader anyway, who has to get through very lumpy prose ("Both views will regard our acceptance of the necessity of a statement as signposted by an abrogation of the ordinary practical standards of defeasibility for a generalisation postulating the availability of a satisfactory, conflict-dissolving explanation for any situation in which things are *prima facie* other than as the statement in question requires"[1]), and must struggle with arguments of Byzantine complexity in which objections, possible replies and conceivable rejoinders go on so long that what was at stake (often not deserving of such elaboration) disappears from view.

"... illuminating and persuasive". Wright wants to persuade us of so many things that one cannot say yes or no to 'persuasive'. He should convince anyone who goes through the book carefully that Wittgenstein's philosophy of mathematics is far stronger than its denigrators suggest or than one might gather from a brief summary. And the book is as persuasive about the inseparability of the philosophy of mathematics from the philosophy of language. On other points it is less persuasive; this hangs together with its being less illuminating than one might wish. For that there are several reasons: (1) the book stays too close to the lectures on which it was based; (2) there is too little attention to the *Tractatus*; (3) while the book is critical of Michael Dummett's views, it stays too close to his conception of the nature of philosophical questions and of how they can be answered; (4) there is inadequate understanding of Wittgenstein's conception of grammar and its relation to philosophical method. I shall say more about each of these. Taken together, the last three add up to a major flaw: Wright's Wittgenstein is too far from Wittgenstein.

I

The book has three parts, corresponding to three sets of lectures, given in 1974, 1975 and 1977. Wright had intended to make of these a book with a single integrated point of view, but decided against that; he says that the three parts remain "close in content and organisation to the original lectures". The whole is thus, as he says, a "document of ideas in progress" (p. viii). In trying to understand or explain Wittgenstein, one needs to find a good route into the material: otherwise there appear to be problems which are actually nothing but the reflection of one's having taken things in the wrong order. By keeping to his lectures, Wright does make things harder. Take, e.g., Part II of the book, concerned with Wittgenstein's view that philosophy of mathematics should not be *revisionary*. What does that mean? Wright introduces the notion at the beginning of Part II: a philosophical view is revisionary of mathematics in his sense if it could lead one to question generally accepted assumptions or methods of pure mathematics. Wright immediately turns to the question how Wittgenstein's idea that philosophy should not be revisionary can be reconciled with other views of his, without raising the question whether Wittgenstein's "anti-revisionary" remarks (e.g., about not interfering with the mathematicians) are anti-revisionary in *Wright's* sense. Again, the question is not raised whether the doctrines which might seem incompatible with the anti-revisionary remarks can properly be understood independently of the anti-revisionism (whatever exactly it is) and then examined for compatibility with it. Much of this is clarified in the sixth and seventh chapters of the sequence, but the reader is left wondering how many of the problems discussed in the first five chapters of the section could have been avoided had the material been re-ordered. It is — usually — self-indulgent to offer readers a document of the progress of one's ideas. In this case, the book could have been greatly improved by reorganisation and cutting, which would have made the central lines of argument emerge much more clearly.

II

Wright's book has a great cast of characters whose views are compared with Wittgenstein's, criticised in the light of his and used to explain and criticise his: we have the intuitionist, the strict finitist, various anti-realists, the platonist and quasi-platonist, the radical and modified conventionalists; Dummett, Davidson and Quine appear, as do John Stuart Mill, Jonathan Bennett, A.J. Ayer and A.C. Ewing. The author of the *Tractatus* is conspicuously absent: he makes two brief appearances in footnotes. It is puzzling that he gets so little attention when so much is given to so many other views of mathematics, logic and language. Various things go wrong because of his absence and others not so well as they might. Here are three examples:

(a) The essential thing in conventionalism, as characterised (several times) by Wright, is the denial that "necessary statements state a priori *facts* whose acknowledgement constitutes our recognition of necessity, and failure to acknowledge which is a kind of worldly ignorance" (p. 365). With conventionalism so characterised, the *Tractatus* counts as conventionalist. Wright recognises that in the *Tractatus* necessary statements are not significantly true, but perhaps the recognition was simply an afterthought. At any rate, unless he counts the *Tractatus* as conventionalist, he needs an alternative account of conventionalism.

(b) Wright devotes a chapter to the relation between Davidson's programme and Wittgenstein's views, focusing on the question whether the validity of principles of inference can be explained in terms of a theory of meaning. The *Tractatus* is not mentioned — although it bears directly on the question: what kind of explanation — if explanation is possible at all, in any sense — of principles of inference can be given? If one wants to know what Wittgenstein would have questioned in Davidson's programme, one might investigate how it would be criticised from the *Tractatus* point of view — which he never entirely repudiated. Wright regards it as something of a scandal that Davidsonians never discuss how "their programme complements, supersedes, advances or undermines the ideas of the most original philosophical thinker of the twentieth century" (p. 279), and tries to show that the undermining may go the other way. Indeed, but how much of that undermining was well under way in 1919?

(c) Wright often touches on Wittgenstein's later view of internal relations. But that view can hardly be got clear without consideration of the

Tractatus and of the respects in which the views in it were modified later and those in which they were not. Wright's discussion of following a rule — perhaps the most important single theme of the book — suffers from his neglect of these matters, running into difficulties that might have been avoided by attention to the *Tractatus* (and to such passages as *Philosophical Remarks* III, which help one trace the path from the *Tractatus* views to the later discussions of following a rule, intention and expectation). What goes wrong in Wright's account is that he misdescribes the significance of "agreement in judgement". To explain this, I shall summarise and examine part of Wright's "rehearsal and elaboration" of Wittgenstein on following rules. Here is the summary:

Prior to our verdicts, it is not determined — not objectively — what counts as, e.g., *red* in as yet unconsidered cases. If I call some previously unexamined thing red, I can be said to recognise what application of 'red' continues the familiar pattern of use; but the word 'recognise' is appropriate only because there is the possibility of my agreeing or disagreeing with the communal verdict on the case, and thus the possibility of significantly judging my response correct or incorrect. If there is no communal verdict on that case, I nevertheless have standard inductive grounds for supposing that there *would be* agreement with my judgement, and may thus justifiably claim to have *recognised* what it is to continue in the same way. 'Correct' and 'incorrect', which thus have significant application to the responses of individuals (because there is "the authority of securable communal assent on the matter") have no real content applied to the communal verdict itself (because there is no comparably available standard). (See pp. 216-20.) — That account of Wittgenstein's view is directly connected with Wright's claim that the rule-following considerations rest on an anti-realist argument. I shall return to that matter, but shall first explain — differently — the role "agreement in judgement" has for Wittgenstein, making use of three points: to say that someone has applied a word consistently with past practice is to describe what he did *via* an internal relation with past practice; one major difference between Wittgenstein's earlier and later work concerns *where to look for* internal relations; one major similarity is that when a description is given *via* internal relations, the relations in question are not hypothetical.

Instead of considering what it is for me, in my verdict on some hitherto unconsidered thing, to use 'red' as it has been used, let us consider what it is for me to have given a verdict — at all — on the colour of something, or to have described something, or even to have spoken English. No such description needs to be justified in terms of what a solicitable communal verdict on my activity *would be*. It is not, e.g., a well-grounded hypothesis that I was speaking English. What makes something I do a giving of a verdict or a description is largely a matter of its place and mine in a life of, among other things, description-giving, verdict-making. One feature of that life (one of the things giving it its characteristic physiognomy) is "agreement in judgement" on many matters, including the kind of agreement there is (and the extent of it, its limits) in the application of colour terms. In certain circumstances, of which an important one is one's having learned to participate in linguistic activities with the feature of agreement, one's saying certain words may be the giving of a description.

Suppose that I come back from the garden and tell you that the tomatoes are still green. What is it for me to have used the words in accordance with our past practice? The words 'in accordance with' mark a connection, an internal relation, which on Wright's account is still to be made, still only hypothetical: for the communal verdict is, when I tell you about the tomatoes, something we could only hypothesise about. On Wittgenstein's view, though, a claim that someone has adhered to a past practice needs the *general* background of shared responses (the "peaceful agreement" which is "the characteristic surrounding of the use of the word 'same'"[2]) but does not need justification in terms of an actual or hypothetical communal verdict on the particular case.

But — it may be said — the background of peaceful agreement, and the fact that someone has learned English, do not alone mean that he *has* adhered to past practice. Indeed; but if you want to know what it is to have done so, ask how you would put someone in a position to judge. You would teach him English — including those modes of criticism and evaluation which are part of speaking the language. Although it is possible to question whether someone has used a word in accordance with a practice, such questions are settled without giving to "securable communal assent" the determinative role Wright thinks it must have.

> If when a language is first learnt, speech, as it were, is connected up to action ... then the question arises, can these connections possibly break down? If they can't, then I have to accept any action as the right one; on the other hand if they can, what criterion have I for their having broken down? For what means have I for *comparing* the original arrangement with the subsequent action?[3]

Wright thinks that Wittgenstein's answer is that an individual's action can be compared with the original arrangement only because what is involved in the original arrangement is settled by what the community agrees is involved in it, for any application of the rule. And my action can be compared with *that*. But what makes comparison with the original arrangement possible is not that *there is* something, the communal verdict on what that arrangement involved in *this* case, with which my action can be compared, but that *we do* something, criticise ("You can't be sticking to your own definitions; look. ...") without running into unsettlable disputes; in that context, a judgement can be a comparison with what was originally arranged, and I may be justly criticised for departing from it.

I have gone over this partly because of its connection with the matter of anti-realism. Wright takes Wittgenstein's views about following rules to rest on "the fundamental anti-realist thesis that we have understanding only of concepts of which we can distinctly manifest our understanding" (p. 221). That thesis enables one to reject as empty the idea that the communal verdict (on what is in accord with past practice) is correct or incorrect in virtue of its relation to an objective standard. If *that* is empty, then the communal verdict alone can provide a standard against which an individual's response may be compared; and we can thus explain (what otherwise is inexplicable) why a "community of assent" is a necessary part of the background against which an individual's response may be judged correct or incorrect. — But the anti-realist underpinnings are necessary only if "agreement in judgement" plays the role for Wittgenstein that Wright thinks it does. But an account of that role should cohere with a story about how Wittgenstein's earlier views changed; Wright's does not.

Wright asks in passing (p. 400) which doctrines from the *Tractatus* survive to explain the continuity throughout Wittgenstein's life of his view of necessary statements as not significantly true. If Wright was trying to find these strands in Wittgenstein's thought which make intelligible and perhaps defensible his view of necessity, why was that question asked only to be dropped? The point applies not only to continuities in Wittgenstein's view of necessity but to the other important continuities in his views of logic and mathematics and of the possibility of philosophical discoveries about their nature.

III

In the Preface, Wright says of Dummett's ideas about Realism that they "have enormously influenced my approach to these questions and constitute, indeed, almost as much as Wittgenstein's own ideas the subject matter of this book" (p. ix). — The presence of Dummett's ideas in the book is no weakness; the effect of Dummett's approach on Wright's is, because it is not made clear how very different that approach is from Wittgenstein's.

Dummett has introduced us to the Realist and anti-Realist, who turn up in any number of philosophical disputes. The Realist in them is characterised by his insistence that the meaning of the statements in dispute is explained by an explanation of their truth-conditions; understanding such a statement is knowing what must hold for it to be true, and need not include knowing how we should establish whether it is. We can indeed understand such a statement independently of whether its truth or falsity can be established. Dummett's anti-Realist will insist that the general form of explanation of meaning is explanation not of truth-conditions but of assertability-conditions. We are trained in the use of statements of the sort in dispute by being taught to assert them in certain conditions; this training does not fix what it is for such statements to be true or false independently of the obtaining of conditions which we could take to establish their truth. Hence the anti-Realist may dispute the principle of bivalence or that of excluded middle or both for statements of the disputed class.

To make clear the problem created by using Dummett's approach in discussing Wittgenstein, I shall look further at a particular dispute important for both Wright and Dummett, that concerning statements about the past. Here the Realist holds that such statements are true or false independently of there being memories or evidence that would enable us to assert or deny them, and the anti-Realist denies that. Let me use a picture to make the dispute clear.

The box on the left represents a past state of affairs — say, using Dummett's example, it is Dummett's being in his college room at 2:45 on February 12, 1969. The vertical line separates the person considering some present traces of that past state of affairs from it itself. The past state of affairs is not itself accessible to him; the line between him and it is as it were the wall behind which the past lies. All he has accessible to him is whatever evidence of that state of affairs there now remains (represented by the dotted box). We could add to the picture a representation of later stages, in which different, or no, traces of the original state of affairs are accessible to an investigator.

The Realist takes the picture as showing what it is to grasp the meaning of 'Dummet *was* in his college room at 2:45 on February 12, 1969'. One has to grasp what it is for Dummett to be in his college room; one thus grasps what has to lie on the far side of the line for the sentence stating that Dummett was in his room to be true. We can only *go by* what is on the other side of the line, but even if there is nothing on that side, the truth-conditions of the past tense sentence are clear and are either met or not.

The anti-Realist rejects the picture as incorporating an illegitimate point of view above or outside of time. It misleads us about the possibility of explaining the meaning of past tense statements, misleads us into thinking that we have some grasp of what it would be for such a statement to be true independently of any situation which would any longer enable us to assert it. How, he asks, in the nature of the case, could we have come to understand what that is? We could hardly have been shown circumstances in which a past tense sentence could be seen to be true, entirely independently of there being anything which made it any longer possible to tell that it was.[4]

While this is hardly the whole dispute, the central issue is clear: *viz.,* whether we *can have a conception* of what it would be for a statement about the past to be true independently of any situation which would justify its being asserted, now or in the future. A feature of much of Wright's book is that it is similarly concerned with arguments about whether we *can have certain conceptions,* and Wittgenstein is read as implying that we *cannot.* Wright claims, e.g. that we "cannot give content" to the idea that meanings "can be determinate in such a way as to settle that some statements are incapable of conflict with contingent fact, irrespective of whether we ever appreciate as much" (p. 389). This claim is used in explaining what we grasp from Wittgenstein's discussions of following a rule. Again, on p. 340, we are told that we must drop the picture of objective constraints, imposed by our prior understanding of concepts, which make it the case that an untried calculation has a unique proper outcome. We must drop it because there are no investigation-independent facts about how our concepts must be applied if we are to be faithful to them; as a result there is no sense in the idea that rules of inference "already determine certain connections which proof and calculation can draw to our attention, but whose status does not depend on that event". That argument is said to be explicit in Wittgenstein's discussion of "the mathematical machine" in *Remarks on the Foundations of Mathematics*, III (Wright refers to II) §§47-8.

The Realist takes it that we logically cannot be in the position which we ideally (so it seems) should want to be in to explain the truth-conditions of sentences about the past. That is, the past fact that I should ideally like to point to for you in explaining some past tense sentence is necessarily *not* here for me to point to. So if you ask me to explain what would make that sentence true, this may appear like asking me whom I meant in a case in which I have to answer: unfortunately he has gone and will never come back, so I cannot put you into the *best* position to grasp who it is, i.e. by *showing* him to you; all I can do is a sad second best, giving you a description or a picture.

My last paragraph is based on Wittgenstein's discussion in the *Blue Book* (pp. 37-8) of the relation between a wish and the wished-for fact (which is — unfortunately — not here for me to point to in explaining my wish to you). In another discussion of similar cases (beginning at *Philosophical Investigations*, §§425-6) he draws attention to a symptom of confusion: its seeming to us that in *our* use of some expression we go by indirection, we make detours: "we see the straight highway before us, but of course we cannot use it, because it is permanently closed". Applying this to the dispute about the past: the "straight highway" that is permanently closed (the closure marked by the line in the picture) would give access to the *past event itself.* As we know, Wittgenstein believes that in such cases we are confused by a picture; and this may seem to put him with Dummett's anti-Realist. But the important thing to get clear is how Wittgenstein differs from the anti-Realist, despite the inclination he had towards such a view. (In discussing whether it is the foot or the sense datum of it which is real, he said: "I have never experienced the temptation to realism. I have never said "What exists is the foot", but I have been strongly tempted to idealism."[5] That temptation to a kind of anti-Realist view is visible in many places in his work, but usually with criticism of it, as, e.g., in the discussion of "logical machinery" in his 1939 lectures.[6])

The trouble with the anti-Realist is that he thinks that he can see — well enough — what it would be for the Realist's picture to be correct, and differs in that he thinks we *cannot have* a conception representable in that way. Against Realist and anti-Realist, Wittgenstein's point is that the picture does not at all make clear what is involved in having such a conception. The case of talk of the past is like others which Wittgenstein discusses in many places. We learn the use of certain sentences; we then learn to use others constructed from these: for example, we teach someone who knows how to use '*p*' the phrases 'A wishes that *p*' or 'A expects that *p*' or 'It is not the case that *p*'. Wittgenstein once described such sentences as composed of '*p*' with an "index"; we can then ask what the relation is between the use of '*p*' and that of '*p*' with the index. For '*p*' and '*p*'-with-index are *used* in utterly dissimilar circumstances; what role then does the understanding of '*p*' itself play in our understanding of the new sentence?[7]

In the case of talk of the past, we may note such things as:

(a) One can show someone *what* it is that one said *was* so (when one said that Dummett *was* in his college room) by showing him something that *is* so (Dummett now in his college room), just as one can show someone what one wants him *not* to do by doing just that.

(b) If someone has not yet learned to talk of the past, we can teach him to say that *p was* so only if (in general) he is already capable of using '*p*' or is learning to do so. While there are cases in which this is not so, in general if he were taught to assert '*p* was the case' in those circumstances in which we do, and was hesitant or doubtful just when we were, but had not been taught to use '*p*' or similar sentences, then whatever capacity he acquired it would not be the capacity we exercise when we say that *p* was the case. To learn to talk about the past is to learn a new way of using things we have already learned or are learning. Just as expectation can only be expressed in a language that can express the present state of affairs,[8] what can be said about the past in a language depends on what can be said about the present.

Just as expectation of a future state of affairs is represented by a sentence constructed in a characteristic way from a present tense sentence ('It is raining', 'A expects that it will rain'), a past state of affairs is represented by a sentence constructed in a characteristic way from a present tense sentence ('It is raining', 'It rained'). What is thus shown in the structure of the new sentence is a relation between its truth-conditions and those of the old. The concept of expectation is so made that what is describable as a present state of affairs (expecting ...) can be "fulfilled" by a future state of affairs, and will be fulfilled or not (cf. *Investigations*, §§438, 445, 461); the concept of the past is so made that a present tense sentence transformed in certain ways is made true ("satisfied") by what may have been the case, and will in any case be made true or not by what was the case (in the same grammatical sense as that in which order, wish or expectation are fulfilled *or not* by what turns out; again see *Investigations*, §461). It is perfectly true that these features of the grammar of expectation and of the past do not show us at all how to *apply* the concepts with these features; we are as yet told nothing about when we can say that someone expects that *p*, or what is evidence for Dummett's having been in that room in 1969. But an adequate description of the use of these concepts will not be a matter merely of giving the criteria used in applying them and indicating when they are defeasible; simply to have learned when to say '*p* was so' and when to doubt it will not in general be to have learned when to say that *p* was so. One's learning must embody connections between the practice of using '*p*' and that of using '*p* was so' or one will not have learned to speak of the past.

To return to the misleading picture. The Realist's picture is, if understood properly, perfectly all right. The two elements on the left — the representation of some state of affairs and the vertical line marking it off as "in the past" — correspond to elements of a past tense sentence, constructed from a present tense sentence with an "index". The vertical line in the picture serves as index. A representation of a state of affairs, together with the past index, has a use different from that of the sentence without the index. It is used on the basis of present criteria; and that is represented on the right hand side of the picture.

The picture shows that the truth-conditions of the past tense sentence are "in the past". It is what Wittgenstein calls a "pictorial representation of our grammar" (*Investigations*, §295). This means in part that the picture may be wrongly taken to show more than that, to show how concepts with that grammar would "ideally" be used.

In the disputes between Realist and anti-Realist, we should see Wittgenstein as critical of both. (Cf. *Investigations*, §402.) Failure to grasp how he differs from the anti-Realist in particular will leave us without an understanding of his approach to many issues. Further, whenever we find ourselves thinking that there cannot be a conception of a certain character, we are slipping into just the sort of position that the anti-Realist takes up against the Realist about the past.

IV

Wright does not see the force of Wittgenstein's notion of grammar nor its relation to his philosophical method. Let me take objectivity, a central notion of the book, as illustration. Wright's idea is that we have certain ordinary beliefs about objectivity which are called into question by Wittgenstein. For example, we normally believe that the truth or falsity of ordinary decidable statements is an objective matter. Thus, e.g., we believe that an object whose shape we have not yet observed has got a determinate shape irrespective of whether we actually ever do inspect it. That is a belief in what Wright calls the "investigation-independence" of decidable statements; he argues that it requires there to be objective patterns in our use of concepts. That is, the belief that a thing has an objectively determinate shape depends on the belief that "there are facts about how we will, or would, assess its shape if we did so correctly, in accordance with the meaning of the expressions in our vocabulary of shapes". That itself is a belief that the pattern of our use of expressions for shapes "extends of itself to cases we have yet to confront" (p. 216) — and we do, he thinks, ordinarily suppose that our use of language conforms to such objective patterns. These ideas of ours about objectivity Wright thinks are called into question by Wittgenstein, in particular by his arguments about following rules.

Wright denies that it need be possible to formulate these ideas about objectivity clearly or coherently in order to attack them; a philosopher may reject a notion precisely because he believes that no coherent account of it can be given. What sort of understanding of it must he have if he is going to reject it? In the case of investigation-independence, Wright says that "the Wittgensteinian" opposing that idea may "contend that we have a sufficient grasp of the essential spirit of this conception to evaluate its shortcomings, and that our possession of that degree of grasp is quite consistent with an irremediable unclarity concerning what a belief in the investigation-independence of a particular class of statements really consists in" (p. 206). Some such claim as that ascribed to "the Wittgensteinian" is, it seems, one Wright must make *in propria persona* and ascribe to Wittgenstein as well at many other points in the book, where he discusses whether an idea or notion should be rejected for philosophical reasons. Thus, e.g., in summarising the bearing of Wittgenstein's discussion of rule-following on the objectivity of necessary truths, Wright gives as one point in the argument this: "We cannot give sense to the idea that our communal speech habits pursue objective tracks which we laid it down as our intention to follow" (p. 390). But what does it mean to say that we cannot give sense to some idea? We should take Wright as claiming, *in propria persona* here, that we have sufficient grasp of the essential spirit of the idea to evaluate its shortcomings. For Wright does not want to say that we cannot give sense to the *sentence* 'Our communal speech habits pursue objective tracks'. Throughout the book he takes it that such sentences may be merely "embroidery" on the facts of our continued agreement in use. There is, however, on his view a distinct and objectionable sense we can grasp clearly enough to criticise.

Wittgenstein's remarks that philosophy leaves everything as it is appear puzzling — as Wright recognises — if his arguments go against widely held ideas. But we can tell whether that *is* how to take the arguments only if we see how he saw the "ideas" Wright thinks they undermine. I shall look at three cases.

(a) Wright thinks that we have a notion of the length of an object as an objective property which we can determine by accurate measurement. This conception imposes on us the principle that "accurate measurement of an object gives different readings on different occasions if and only if the object has changed" (p. 106). — What is wrong here is that grammar is being represented as an idea about the relation between measurements and reality. To say 'Length is an objective property' would on Wittgenstein's view be to characterise the grammar of length; part of this grammar is that we say that an object has changed its length if, from what we take to be accurate measurements of an object's length, we get divergent results.

(b) Wright thinks that most people accept the "investigation-independence" of statements about shape, and that it is undermined by Wittgenstein's arguments. There are (this is what those arguments establish) no investigation-independent facts of the shapes of as yet unexamined things. — But that is not Wittgenstein's view; for him the question 'Are there or aren't there such facts?' would itself be confused: it makes it seem that there is something which we do not know and which philosophy can find out; it makes grammar look like facts. For 'Things have determinate shapes independent of our investigations' and 'Nothing has a determinate shape until it is examined' are grammatical statements. The latter gives part of a different grammar of 'shape' from ours, one in which it would be nonsense to speak of the shape of an unexamined object.

(c) Wright discusses whether philosophical considerations should lead us "to think of ourselves as bringing necessity *into being* when we judge a statement to have that status" (p. 391). But 'We bring necessity into being when we judge a statement to have that status' would be a characterisation of the grammar of necessity. It says that '*p* became necessary last Tuesday' makes sense; that is to say, it is a characterisation of the grammar of a language we do not speak. In our language there is no question 'When did the necessity of *p* come into being?'; and that grammatical point can also be put (more misleadingly) by saying that if *p* is necessary it was always necessary. The idea that we might critically evaluate the view that what is necessary was necessary independently of our judging it to be so rests on mistaking grammar for facts.

A philosopher may say 'We bring necessity into being when we judge a statement to have that status' in a philosophical enquiry into the character of necessity. But what needs to be said about it then is like what Wittgenstein says (*Investigations*, §339) about 'Thinking is not an incorporeal process'. That is not the right way to reject 'Thinking is an incorporeal process'. The latter makes a grammatical distinction (between 'thinking' and, e.g., 'eating') in a way "that makes the difference ... look *too slight*". If we say that "thinking is not an incorporeal process" we are still in the unclarity shown in 'Thinking is an incorporeal process'.

Wright thinks that philosophical insight (e.g., getting straight whether necessity is brought into being by our judgements) might properly lead us to want to "straighten out" our grammar if it is misleading. But Wright and Wittgenstein have different notions of what it is for grammar to be misleading. For Wright, there is a getting straight whether necessity *is* brought into being by our judgements, and the misleadingness of our grammar would lie in its suggesting the wrong answer; for Wittgenstein, the misleadingness of our grammar lies in part of its suggestion of question and answer. No "straightenings out" of grammar will remove the tendency to take grammar as fact; Wright's idea of attempting to "straighten out" grammar itself suggests a possible comparison between what grammar suggests and what philosophy shows us is so.

Wright touches on the problems here when, towards the end of the book, he sketches an argument showing that philosophical reasoning does not lead to *discoveries* (in at least some cases in which we might have thought it did). But this is merely noted in passing (p. 441), not developed or connected with his earlier and inconclusive discussions of the nature and limits of philosophical enquiry.

I have not tried to explain or defend Wittgenstein's use of the notion of grammar, but to show its bearing on Wright's presentation of the philosophical issues he is discussing and the views of Wittgenstein's he is expounding. In particular I have not tried to show *why* the things Wright takes as ideas or notions subject to philosophical evaluation would not be regarded by Wittgenstein in that way, nor why Wittgenstein would think that we are cheating ourselves if we believe we have a "sufficient grasp of the essential spirit" of a notion — despite its incoherence — to judge its shortcomings.

Wittgenstein's later philosophy of logic and mathematics is continuous with that of the *Tractatus,* is distorted if seen in anti-Realist terms, and does not involve the denials of objectivity Wright sees. So much for what I take to be major weaknesses of the book. I turn now to two of its strong points, illuminating in different ways of the real Wittgenstein.

V

The best thing in the book is the discussion of E.J. Craig's attempt (in "The Problem of Necessary Truth"[9]) to show the inadequacy of conventionalist accounts of necessity. The conventionalism Craig attacks would not, Wright argues, be held by an astute conventionalist. Craig's conventionalist thinks it possible for it to seem (and to continue to seem) to all well-placed observers as if a count had been properly carried out in all respects, despite conflict between its results and our arithmetic (as in Dummett's case: the count first of 5 boys and 7 girls and then of 13 children altogether in an apparently unchanged group). This conventionalist thinks that we make arithmetical statements like '5 + 7 = 12' necessarily true (make it a convention that results like the Dummett one indicate a miscount) in the face of such possibilities. But a more astute conventionalist can claim that part of the convention that such-and-such results indicate a miscount is the convention that when we get such results *there is* independent perceptual evidence for the occurrence of some particular miscount, which we should uncover if we were able to investigate properly. But, as Wright shows, even the astute conventionalist is in for trouble from Craig's argument.

Such a conventionalist can regard our arithmetic as preferable to an alternative (say, in which 7 + 5 = 13) on practical grounds: given the usual behaviour of the things we count, we get into less trouble with our arithmetic than we should with another. But Craig shows that it is not a contingent matter: if a situation appears to support a deviant arithmetic and to conflict with ours, it *cannot* continue to do so if we carry out checks of a sort which he describes in detail. It is possible to go on holding an alternative arithmetic in the face of the absence of support from such perceptual checks (and to go on maintaining that *there is* independent evidence supporting the alternative arithmetic in the face of failure to find such evidence). But Craig's demonstration that alternative arithmetics necessarily run into a certain kind of trouble gives support to the idea that our arithmetic is superior to alternatives not merely on practical grounds, but because things *cannot* be as another arithmetic requires them to be. Whenever they appear so, Craig shows us *how* to find out that they really are not.

In the most important part of his discussion, Wright makes clear that Craig has not produced what he thinks he has. He thinks he has produced an argument about what in the nature of things *underlies* our arithmetic (its relation to the perceptual criteria for counting properly); Wright claims against this that what Craig has given is the most fundamental sort of proof-strategy for elementary arithmetical statements. We are indeed,

Wright points out, led by reasoning of the sort Craig gives to the conclusion that it is *unimaginable* that a situation should persistently appear to conform to an arithmetic in which, e.g., $1 + 1 = 3$. Any convincing proof of elementary arithmetical statements

> *must* seem to show something about the potentialities of the perceptual criteria for counting correctly, etc.; if no such proof could be given, their status really would be comparable to that of any (consequences of) explicit conventions. But it is not. The intuitively natural response to a query about one of them is not, for example: "That is simply what we *mean* by '5', '+', ...", but: "How could things possibly be *otherwise*?" (p. 438)

Thus what Craig provides is argument of precisely the kind that gives its characteristic physiognomy to our acceptance of elementary arithmetical statements. A conventionalist has no need to reject the claim that our arithmetic can be supported by such demonstrations — any more than he need deny the existence of mathematical proof.

Wright's discussion puts Craig's argument another way up, as it were; turns it in a direction we did not see that it could be turned. Even on a second reading, the surprise, the drama here, remain intact. Without specifically appealing to Wittgenstein at any point in the crucial section, Wright provides one of the most elegant illustrations of what Wittgenstein tries to get us to do in philosophy.

Wright's treatment of Craig's argument should be connected with two remarks of Wittgenstein's:

> When the proposition seems not to be right in application, the proof must surely show me why and how it *must* be right; that is, *how* I must reconcile it with experience.[10]

Wright brings out that Craig's discussion shows us exactly how to do this in the case of elementary arithmetical propositions; that is, he shows us how Craig's proof-technique fits exactly what Wittgenstein thinks a proof should accomplish.

In discussing what it is to describe the function of language and of rules, Wittgenstein writes:

> The difficult thing here is not, to dig down to the ground; no, it is to recognize the ground that lies before us as the ground.
> For the ground keeps on giving us the illusory image of a greater depth, and when we seek to reach this, we keep on finding ourselves on the old level. (ibid., §31)

Craig tries to reach the level *below* that of our mathematical practice — the level of necessary relations between arithmetic and perceptual criteria for counting correctly; Wright shows that Craig gives a full, detailed and illuminating description of the *old* level, of mathematical practice itself: in particular the practice of giving certain sorts of convincing demonstrations that lead (on Wittgenstein's view) to the fixing of our concepts. Craig reminds us how utterly convincing such demonstrations are.

Immediately after those last remarks, Wittgenstein has "Our disease is one of wanting to explain". In this splendid section of the book, Wright does not try to explain why we cannot explain; he shows that Craig's attempt to give a certain sort of explanation is not what Craig thinks. The explanations of which the rest of the book is full try to take us to the underlying level even when they say that things are *not* there that we need for our (Realist) attempts at explanation, or that there is no point of view from which we could tell anything about such a level. Wright keeps gesturing at it to tell us what we cannot do. And he does not do so in showing what is right and what is wrong with Craig's paper.

VI

Wright raises important questions for anyone seeking to understand Wittgenstein's philosophy of mathematics. Here are two of them.

(a) Wittgenstein holds that we could infer, calculate and measure in ways very different from the actual ones — just as we could have a different unit of length. The last part of the claim is important; the first part is not specifically characteristic of Wittgenstein but is accepted by, e.g., Frege (people could infer in ways which conflicted with ours; they would be not only mad but *wrong*). Dummett had complained that Wittgenstein's examples are thin and unconvincing; and Barry Stroud had attempted to show that the thinness of the examples does not indicate a weakness in Wittgenstein's approach. Wright makes it clear why there really is a problem here.

Consider the case of measurement and Wittgenstein's example: the people who do something with elastic rulers that he refers to as measuring. But the criteria for an activity's being *measuring* are not that it *looks* like our measuring; for it to be measuring, its function in these people's lives must be analogous to that of measuring in ours. Wright's point is now this:

> Measurement with soft rulers will be useless if the results are applied for the kinds of purposes for which we measure; but if they are not, it is seriously unclear what good grounds there could be for saying that these people who, talking apparent English, solemnly lay floppy rulers alongside things and seem to record readings are doing anything that may informatively be described as "measuring". (p. 71)

Wright argues that Wittgenstein's examples, if looked into and developed, will "destabilise": it will appear *either* that the activity described has an application so unlike that of measuring (inferring, calculating) as to make it unreasonable to describe it as such; *or* the application, the purposes, of the activity will be like enough to ours to make it clear that these people are using procedures inferior to ours: if it is really measurement that they are using these soft rulers for, they would be well advised to change over to more rigid ones. One unit of measurement may be superior to another in certain circumstances and inferior to it in others; but if Wright is correct that is now how it is with the choice of rigid rather than soft rulers. If your purposes allow the description of what you are doing as *measurement*, you must be better off with rigid ones.

This is surely a problem that needs raising. A useful approach might be to examine the range of purposes and applications which enable us to identify a people as measuring something, say, but in a different way, to see whether Wright's claim that such cases will destabilise in one of the two directions is sound. That it may not be is suggested by the case of measuring time. What people do is identifiable as reckoning time if the reckoning is used, e.g., to co-ordinate activities and to keep track of their history and relationships. Time has been reckoned by "soft rulers" — in the middle ages.

> Reckoning ordinarily ... twelve hours of day and twelve of night, whatever the season, people of the highest education become used to seeing each of these fractions, taken one by one, grow and diminish incessantly according to the annual revolution of the sun.[11]

Is this clearly inferior to the use of a more uniform measure? A more uniform measure (the burning of candles of uniform length) was known but was not generally used because it was not wanted; people were generally indifferent about what would be marked by less "elastic" measures. Given *their* purposes, "elastic" measurement is not inferior.

In this case and others (the Nuer system of time reckoning described by Evans-Pritchard is a good example[12]), we can see people who reckon differently from the way we do, whose purposes are close enough to ours for there to be no problem in describing them as reckoning time but far enough away for it to be most unclear whether they should achieve *their* purposes any better by going over to our methods. I do not know how far attention to such cases can help resolve the issue Wright raises; but he has done a service by raising it.

(b) When Wittgenstein discusses necessity and related subjects, he often points out that a sentence which has been used so that it is experimentally verifiable may be given a *new* use, as a rule. It is thus made "aloof" from experience, withdrawn from doubt; it is now non-temporal, a standard or norm by which we can describe what happens. With the aid of such notions, Wittgenstein tries to characterise the sorts of use distinctive of necessary statements. Wright emphasises that Wittgenstein does not intend the contrast between rules of description and descriptive propositions as a sharp one: he quotes *Remarks on the Foundations of Mathematics*, V §5, where Wittgenstein first says of the contrast that it shades off in all directions and then adds that "*that* in turn is not to say that the contrast is not of the greatest importance".

The problem Wright raises concerns this contrast. He points out that a deeply held conviction of the truth of some statement may be reflected in the way apparently conflicting evidence is treated. The hypothesis that all such evidence can — somehow — be explained away may be held to, even when all ordinary standards for rejecting it have been met. The willingness to treat apparently conflicting evidence this way is itself a "measure of the depth, or stubbornness, of a conviction" (p. 412). If we want to draw a contrast, even one that is not sharp, between descriptive propositions and rules of description, how should we distinguish between that "aloofness" from experience characteristic of rules of description and that "aloofness" showing the depth of the conviction that some descriptive proposition is true?

Wittgenstein does not discuss this problem in his writings on mathematics, though, as Wright mentions, there are remarks touching on it in *On Certainty*. The questions Wright raises are of great importance, bearing not just on the nature of mathematics but in general on what it is for some characteristic of the use of an expression to belong to its grammar. Obscurity about the matter affects the question too how Wittgenstein's philosophical methods are to be applied; it leaves unclear the force of 'This is what we do', said of our treating some kinds of claim as indefeasible, some kinds of doubt as not to be raised.

The strong points of the book are what leave one disappointed with the rest of it, and with the book as a whole. The last third of it is the best: more assured, more consistently interesting and less cluttered. It is indeed a very valuable book for anyone concerned with the main problems of philosophy — but how many 'buts' one wants to add!

The book is badly produced; there is much sloppiness that is Wright's fault and some that is a copy editor's. Most of the quotations are inaccurate. Where Wright has improved a translation, that is clear enough; what I am complaining of is distinct and is simply carelessness: words are rearranged, added or removed without any indication; punctuation is altered any which way, sentences chopped up or stuck together; italics are added or removed, usually without any indication; sense is changed (e.g., by adding 'it seems', putting 'reality' into scare quotes, changing 'amend' to 'emend'); ordinary brackets are for no reason changed to square ones — and so on. Incorrect references are given, e.g., on pp. 27, 238, 341 and 375. Spelling is inconsistent and so is hyphenation. Letters fail to come out, spacing becomes irregular, pagination jumps into italic and back to roman, and an odd little black rectangle turns up in a formula. There are misprints on pp. 7, 52, 64, 70, 80, 102, 118, 146, 151, 164, 172, 174, 183, 195, 205, 215, 220, 221, 228, 243, 244, 247, 256, 258, 270, 272, 275, 289, 298, 299, 301, 316, 318, 330, 337, 343, 344, 345, 347, 349, 350, 351, 353, 355, 357 (2), 359 (2), 361 (4), 363, 364, 375, 376, 384, 385, 388, 396, 400, 401, 402, 404, 405, 408, 411, 417, 423, 477. There are many unclassifiable errors: things which might have been misprints or mis-spellings, misprints or grammatical errors, misprints or inaccuracies of quotation or of reference. The overall impression left is that no one cared to get things right. On the other hand, the index (prepared by Michael Wrigley) is one of the best I have seen, and the analytical table of contents is very helpful.

Notes

1. Pp. 411-12. All page references are to *Wittgenstein on the Foundations of Mathematics* unless otherwise specified.

2. Ludwig Wittgenstein, *Remarks on the Foundations of Mathematics* (third edition: Oxford, 1978), VI §21. References not specifying the third edition of this book are to the second (Oxford, 1967)

3. Wittgenstein, *Philosophical Remarks* (Oxford, 1975), §23.

4. See Michael Dummett, 'The Reality of the Past', in *Truth and Other Enigmas* (London, 1978), 358-74, especially pp. 362 and 369.

5. Margaret Macdonald, unpublished notes on Wittgenstein's Lectures on 'Personal Experience', 1935-36, lecture of 19 February 1936.

6. *Wittgenstein's Lectures on the Foundations of Mathematics, Cambridge 1939*, ed. Cora Diamond (Ithaca, 1976), pp. 194-9.

7. See *Wittgenstein's Lectures, Cambridge 1932-1935*, ed. Alice Ambrose (Totowa, N.J., 1979), p. 113.

8. *Wittgenstein's Lectures, Cambridge 1930-1932*, ed. Desmond Lee (Totowa, N.J., 1980), p. 6.

9. In *Meaning, Reference, and Necessity*, ed. Simon Blackburn (Cambridge, 1975), 1-31.

10. *Remarks on the Foundations of Mathematics* (third edition), VI §3.

11. Marc Bloch, *Feudal Society*, vol. I (London, 1965), pp. 73-4.

12. E.E. Evans-Pritchard, *The Nuer* (New York and Oxford, 1974), ch. III.

78

Wittgenstein and Mannheim on the Sociology of Mathematics*

David Bloor

One of the central problems of the sociology of knowledge is the status of logic and mathematics. These branches of knowledge are so impersonal and objective that a sociological analysis scarcely seems applicable. Time and again, in his *Ideology and Utopia* Karl Mannheim's determined advocacy of the sociology of knowledge stops short at this point.[1] He could not see how to think sociologically about how twice two equals four. The argument in this paper is that Wittgenstein's *Remarks on the Foundations of Mathematics*[2] shows how sociology can penetrate to the very basis of these topics. Wittgenstein solves Mannheim's problem.[3]

I

The aim of the sociology of knowledge is to explain how people's beliefs are brought about by the influences at work on them. This programme can be broken down into four requirements. The first is that the sociology of knowledge must locate causes of belief, that is, general laws relating beliefs to conditions which are necessary and sufficient to determine them. The second requirement is that no exception must be made for those beliefs held by the investigator who pursues the programme. Special pleading must be avoided and causes located for those beliefs subscribed to, as well as for those which are rejected. The programme must be impartial with respect to truth and falsity. The next requirement is a corollary of this. The sociology of knowledge must explain its own emergence and conclusions: it must be reflexive. The fourth and final requirement is a refinement of the demand for impartiality. Not only must true and false beliefs be explained, but the same sort of causes must generate both classes of belief. This may be called the symmetry requirement. From now on these four requirements, of causality, impartiality, reflexivity and symmetry, will be referred to as the strong programme of the sociology of knowledge.[4]

Certain features of the strong programme call for immediate comment.

A complete study of the influences that bring about belief needs an account of the object on which the causes work. A model of man's biological nature is required to supplement the sociology of knowledge. Conversely the sociologist must not ignore the sensory input with which people must cope. What is seen, heard and touched makes up part of the total causal picture along with the human capacity for processing or failing to process such information. But typically the sociologist contributes a further question, though one which cannot be disconnected from these issues. This question is: How do beliefs relate to the institutionalized ways of behaving in a society? As the first step towards answering it he will document any respects in which different positions in the social structure may correlate with different beliefs.

Mannheim's conception of the sociology of knowledge is a close approximation to the strong programme. First, he wanted to locate causes of belief,[5] or what he called 'existential determiners' of knowledge.[6] Second, he advocated a form of the sociology of knowledge which went beyond the mere unmasking of ideology and which did not imply the falsity of what was explained.[7] Third, he was well aware that the sociology of knowledge must account for itself.[8] It will be seen later that it was with respect to the all-important symmetry principle, demanding the same types of cause for both true and false beliefs, that he faltered.

II

In this section it will be argued that adherence to a certain theory about the nature of mathematics prevents the strong programme from being applied to logical and computational skills.[9] The theory in question sees mathematics as being, in Mannheim's words, a realm of 'truth as such'. Mathematics and logic are seen as being about a body of truths which exist in their own right independently of whether anyone believes them or knows about them. On this view even if there were no human beings mathematical truths would still be true. Valid inferences would still be valid, but they would remain undrawn. To see mathematics in this way is to think of it as analogous to the world of material objects. Mathematical truths are like material objects in the sense that they are set over against the knowing subject who moves (in thought) amongst and through them. The mathematician discovers mathematical truths as he traces a path through a pre-existing realm: they are not invented. This theory has sometimes been called 'Platonism', sometimes 'Realism'; in what follows it will be called 'Realism'.

Wittgenstein characterizes this view as follows:

> Here what is before our minds in a vague way is that this reality is something very abstract, very general, and very rigid. Logic is a kind of ultra-physics, the description of the 'logical structure' of the world. ...[10]

Realism is the theory explicitly held by the mathematician G.H. Hardy. In his *A Mathematician's Apology*,[11] he says:

> I believe that mathematical reality lies outside us, that our function is to discover or *observe* it, and that the theorems which we prove, and which we describe grandiloquently as our 'creations', are simply our notes of our observations.

> 317 is a prime, not because we think so, or because our minds are shaped in one way rather than another, but *because it is so,* because mathematical reality is built that way.

What effect does it have on an account of knowledge or belief to build into it the picture of mathematics as an independent realm of truth as such? What epistemology conforms to this ontology? A commitment to Realism is a commitment to a certain cluster of metaphors and analogies. The analogy with material objects has already been mentioned. Hardy's remarks showed that this suggests that knowing a mathematical truth is rather like seeing an object, that is, a form of perceiving or intuition. The causes of knowledge, of someone's seeing certain truths, are those that put them into the position to be able to make the appropriate form of intuitive contact. Another metaphor which helps to give Realism a meaning is that of mathematics as a 'world' or 'realm'. To think of mathematical truths as having an independent existence is to think of them as a structured and bounded territory, with an inside and an outside. This suggests that knowledge consists in gaining access or entry to this realm, of crossing a boundary from the outside to the inside.

Both of these ways of looking at mathematics have an important, common structural feature. They imply that an account of mathematical belief or knowledge will have two parts to it. One part concerns the initial gaining of access to the realm of truth as such, or the initial moving into position before the objective truth. The other part will concern all the subsequent movement and activity within mathematics, or the subsequent acts of intuitive contact.

An example will show what effect this bifurcation has in practice. Consider the question of why a mathematician does or says a certain thing in the course of his professional activity. The type of answer that immediately suggests itself is that the proposition or action follows logically as a consequence of the line of reasoning being pursued. It might be said that mathematics or logic itself furnishes the explanation: the behaviour is structured by the pre-existing logic of the connections that the mathematician is exploring. If the further problem is then raised of why the person in question became a mathematician or took up a certain speciality, then the answer will be of a different sort. It will no longer make reference to mathematical or logical principles but to job prospects, the influence of teachers and so on. These two different sorts of explanatory principle correspond to the division mentioned above. One sort refers to the process whereby the mathematical realm is approached and entered, that is, how someone gets into the position to do mathematics. The other sort explains the ongoing activity of mathematics: what goes on within the realm of logic. It is clear that characteristically sociological explanations belong to the stage during which someone is becoming a mathematician. The process of selection and education, the influences which promote or inhibit access to mathematical skill are open to sociological analysis. But equally, on this model, the sociologist must be silent about what goes on within mathematics.

A simple refinement to this view can enhance its appeal. If a mathematician makes a mistake or has some characteristic form of incompetence then, again, the sociologist has an explanatory job to do. The cause of the mistake can perhaps be located in a defect of training or education. This is perfectly compatible with the two-fold character of explanation which is suggested by the Realist theory. To make an error is to deviate from the straight and narrow path of logic. So the refinement conforms to the idea that the sociologist's concern is with factors *outside* mathematics proper.

It would be desirable to establish decisively that, on the above model, the sort of explanation appropriate to behaviour within mathematics really is radically different from the sociological one appropriate outside. To sharpen the issue consider a simple case. Suppose that it is asked why someone concluded that twice two equals four? The sort of answer whose status is in question would be of the form: the conclusion was drawn because twice two does indeed equal four. The explanation of the belief is that it is true. G.H. Hardy would perhaps say that he believed it because he had observed it to be so. Here again the answer has the same structure: it is the truth of a proposition, or the way that mathematical reality is the cause of belief.

It can be seen at once that the word 'cause' here cannot plausibly mean 'necessary and sufficient conditions', which is how the word is used in the strong programme of sociological explanation. If it were to mean this then truth would be a necessary and sufficient condition for belief: and there would be neither error nor ignorance.

There is, however, another sense of the word 'cause' which fits with what has gone before and which would be consistent with the idea that a proposition is believed because it is true. This is the teleological, purposive or goal-directed sense that is sometimes given to the word. Suppose it were assumed that man has a natural tendency to perceive the truth when presented with it, that there is a natural movement, as it were, towards the truth. In this case only beliefs that are false would require explanation. Beliefs that are true are natural and require no comment, for their truth is all the explanation that is required. It might be said, on this view, that truth is the cause of true beliefs, whilst a variety of other factors cause the deviations into ignorance or error. This teleological picture has neatly built into it the asymmetry that belongs to the account of knowledge associated with the Realist theory. It is plausible to conjecture that a Realist theory of mathematics requires a teleological conception of knowledge, because only a teleological theory, or something very like it, has the requisite structure.

An example from Mannheim's work will show how the Realist picture of

382   *The Sociology of Mathematics*

mathematics (and its attendant asymmetries) exerts its influence in a disguised way. Mannheim suggests certain techniques that sociologists can use to locate social processes as they enter into the production of knowledge and belief. He suggests that wherever a body of belief deviates from the line of development suggested by its own inner or 'immanent' logic, there social processes have been at work. He says:

> The existential determination of thought may be regarded as a demonstrated fact in those realms of thought in which we can show ... that the process of knowing does not actually develop historically in accordance with immanent laws, that it does not follow only from the 'nature' of things' or from 'pure logical possibilities', and that it is not driven by an 'inner dialectic'. On the contrary, the emergence and the crystallization of actual thought is influenced in many decisive points by extra-theoretical factors of the most diverse sort.[12]

On this view social causes are equated with 'extra-theoretical' factors. But where does this leave behaviour conducted in accordance with the inner logic of a theory? Clearly it is excluded from sociological explanation precisely because it functions as the base-line for locating those things that do require explanation. It is as if Mannheim said to himself, 'When people do what is logical and proceed correctly, nothing more needs to be said'. But to see certain sorts of behaviour as unproblematic is to see them as natural. In this case what is natural is proceeding correctly, that is, via or towards the truth. So this is another way of formulating the teleological viewpoint.

Although Mannheim had a keen sense of the dangers to sociology of belief in a realm of truth-as-such[13] he failed to avoid those asymmetries which are its hallmark.[14]

The strong programme of the sociology of knowledge will be blocked as long as Realism holds sway as a theory of mathematics. To accept Realism as a theory of mathematics will result in the intrusion of a radically different picture of human nature and knowledge into the very centre of the programme. It entails a sudden switch from fully causal to teleological concepts as the sociologist moves across the scheme of human activity from say, ethical and political belief, to mathematical skills.[15]

III

If the strong programme of the sociology of knowledge is going to be pursued some response must be found to the Realist theory of mathematics, and its associated asymmetries. Is it possible, perhaps, to dismiss teleology as unscientific? If this step can be taken then the road is clear for a programme which treats both knowledge and ignorance, truth and error in a symmetrical fashion. But it is surely not in order to dismiss teleology as if it were foolish. The point can be made in two ways, metaphysically and pragmatically. First, the teleological picture might, for all anyone knows, be true. Second, no one knows what the requirements of science might be in the future. A teleological theory may be just what is needed in some circumstances to permit research to go forward. So without being dogmatic teleology cannot be dismissed.

Can *a priori* objections be made against Realism? If it could be shown that this view is untenable then, again, the way is open for the strong sociological programme. Wittgenstein offers what might be taken to be a forceful refutation of Realism, and this will now be examined.

Wittgenstein's argument appeals to one of his most characteristic examples of a mathematical calculation: the production of a number sequence like 2, 4, 6, 8 ... The production and continuation of a number sequence serves for Wittgenstein as a representative example of a mathematical or logical inference. Although it is extremely simple it captures all the essential features of the process. It is rule governed but open ended; a meeting point of constraint and creative production. If Realism fails to account for this example, then it fails totally. Conversely if another account can cope with number sequences then it is set fair to general success.

Superficially the Realist theory fits neatly with some of the facts which surround the number sequence problem. On being asked to continue the sequence, 2, 4, 6, 8 in the same way, by adding two each time, the feeling imposes itself that there is only one right way of going on. Deviation would involve failure to continue in the same way, a failure to apply the rule of the sequence as it was meant. For Realism the correct continuation of the sequence, the true embodiment of the rule and its intended mode of application, exists already. To obey the rule is to trace out what is already faintly there, existing 'in advance' as Wittgenstein puts it.

Wittgenstein argues that the Realist conception of rule following signally fails to provide answers to the problems that it was designed to solve. These problems are: How can we make the *same* steps again and again; what makes 'the same' the same; what guarantees the identical character of the steps at the different stages of the rule's application? Indeed, Wittgenstein believes that there can be no guarantees of the sort that Realism requires and believes itself to have furnished. In a typically compressed passage the argument is stated like this:

> And if I know it *in advance*, what use is this knowledge to me later on? I mean: how do I know what to do with this earlier knowledge when the step actually has to be taken? ... 'But do you mean to say that the expression '+2' leaves you in doubt what you are to do *e.g.* after 2004?' — No; I answer '2006' without hesitation. But just for that reason it is superfluous to suppose that this was determined earlier on. My having no doubt in face of the question does *not* mean that it has been answered in advance.[16]

This argument can be broken down into a number of steps. The Realist position assumes that there exists some logical or arithmetical archetype which corresponds to the true continuation of the number sequence. This archetype is of no use to the world of men unless it can be brought into contact with human actors — in this case those who are trying to follow the rule consistently. But, if it could be brought into contact how would it help? Well, if men could get access to the archetype (the true number sequence) they could use it to guide their behaviour. Don't they then know the steps of the sequence in advance? But now, says Wittgenstein, the original problem repeats itself. For how does the human actor, following the supposed archetype, know that it really is the correct embodiment of the rule that he wants? To know that the archetype is correct requires exactly the knowledge that was considered problematic in the first place, *viz.* knowledge of how the rule goes. It emerges that this argument is quite general. It works for any archetype, this-worldly or other-worldly. The trouble with Realism does not lie in the puzzling nature of its ontology but in the circular character of its epistemology. It presupposes precisely what it sets out to explain.

Despite the obvious power of this argument it does not refute Realism. Examination of the argument reveals that Wittgenstein is taking for granted that teleological or goal-directed assumptions are not conjoined with Realism. He is assuming that the only sort of contact between the archetype and the actor is that the actor has to select an archetype in order to follow or copy it. Under these assumptions the argument works because the process of selection presupposes the very skill in question. If teleological assumptions are introduced then the circularity vanishes. For now the mere existence of the archetype provides the conditions under which rule following naturally takes place. On teleological assumptions, instead of the actor having to select the archetype by appeal to question begging knowledge there is a natural movement towards the truth. The trouble with Wittgenstein's argument is that it only tackles half the issue. If Realism is to be refuted then arguments must be directed against the full unity of Realism and teleology.

It might be objected that to appeal to teleology to protect Realism is to beg important questions and to cloak real problems by a verbal manoeuvre. It is an indication of the depth of this feeling that Wittgenstein tacitly excluded teleological possibilities from his argument. But it has already been argued that teleology cannot be dismissed out of hand. Something has to be taken as natural and the starting point of any investigation will, from *some* point of view, beg *some* questions. There is, of course, a tradition of finding purposive arguments intellectually unsatisfying. To belong to this tradition is to be oriented favourably towards the thorough-going causality of the strong programme of sociological explanation.

Wittgenstein's argument is still important even if it does not refute Realism. It establishes that Realism cannot stand alone: it is incompatible with a view of man and knowledge that is causal rather than teleological. Realism is not shown to be false, but inconsistent with a thoroughly causal perspective. This point has already been established but Wittgenstein's argument provides a new route to the conclusion.

If the combined picture of mathematical Realism and teleology has not been refuted where does this leave the strong programme of the sociology of knowledge? The position is surely that if the programme cannot be victorious by refuting its opponents then, at least, it must not go to the other extreme and lose by default. It must articulate its own theory of the nature of mathematics and fill the gap in the programme which has been occupied, inconsistently, by Realism. This is as it should be. Both the strong sociological programme and the picture based on Realism and teleology are pieces of metaphysics. They are highly general orientations, suggesting lines of theory construction but not open to empirical testing. With schemes of such generality the idea of convincingly eliminating one or the other is utopian. At this stage the idea should be to develop them to the point where they yield practical ideas for research. In the case of the strong programme this can be done with the help of Wittgenstein's *Remarks*. It provides precisely the theory of mathematics required.

IV

The point of this section is to show that the approach that Wittgenstein takes to mathematics is non-Realist, carries no teleological assumptions and deploys characteristically sociological concepts. It will not be possible to do justice to all the facets of this theory, but enough should be said to show the promise of the approach. To stress the sociological character of Wittgenstein's theory may help to correct some of the misreadings to which his work in this area has been subject.

First the general orientation. Much of the *Remarks* focuses on elementary arithmetic. Its concept of 'the foundations of mathematics' is the robust one of the teacher who speaks of elementary schooling as laying the foundations for later learning. So from the beginning Wittgenstein takes a social rather than a logical definition of his subject matter. He is not concerned to construct axiom-systems. They would not answer his purpose, which is to explain why mathematical arguments are compelling, and to illuminate the character of logical steps in reasoning.[17] The purely formal manipulation of symbols presupposes the very activity of following rules of inference which is at issue. Elementary arithmetic by contrast brings to mind the context in which patterns of inference are laid down in each generation as part of the process of cultural transmission. These fundamental activities of counting and calculating are often mischaracterized. If they do not reflect absolute necessities does this not make them matters of individual choice? It will emerge that Wittgenstein avoids this dilemma by stressing social processes.

In order to see Wittgenstein's sociological approach in action consider again the test case of following the rule of a number sequence. Wittgenstein addresses himself to two questions: First, what is it that determines the application of a rule in any given instance, what makes *this* a correct application of the rule? Second, what makes a number of applications of a rule *consistent* applications of it?

It would seem that the answer to the first question is that it is the meaning of the formula which determines its application. But the question must be pressed: how does what a formula means bring about its application? It sounds as if there are two things here, a meaning and an application, the one mysteriously influencing the other. Wittgenstein avoids any such mystery by his well-known doctrine of the unity of meaning and use. What a formula means *is* the way it is generally applied:

> The way the formula is meant determines which steps are to be taken. What is the criterion for the way the formula is meant? Presumably the way we always use it, the way we are taught to use it.[18]

Wittgenstein has here taken the basic arithmetical process of using a formula and shown the necessity of embedding it in standardized social practice. The crucial terms are sociological: 'the way we always use it,' 'the way we are taught to use it'. This means that, from this perspective, every instance of the use of a formula is the culmination of the process of socialization. Every communication involving a formula stands witness to the existence of a custom, a particular social practice. To see an arithmetical formula in use is to have before one an indicator and an expression of a complex underlying social process. On this theory the application of a formula *is* a social process.

The second question concerned consistency of application. Wittgenstein's theory of consistency begins with the fact that people are trained to behave in certain ways. When they are placed in new circumstances they then continue in a fashion that they, and other actors, feel constitutes a natural, matter of course, extension of their training. There is no *external* guarantee that this natural continuation is the same or consistent with previous practice: rather, this is what counts as the same for that group. Wittgenstein offers a behavioural theory of consistency. Whereas the teleological theory assumed that behaviour was naturally oriented towards truth, Wittgenstein's theory simply accepts as basic that behaviour which is naturally emitted without any assumptions about its character or direction. He does not assume that natural extensions of previous behaviour are consistent, he defines 'consistent' in terms of what is found natural.

This theory has the virtue of corresponding with the intuitive feeling that what is to count as the same is just obvious. It also prompts some worries. If there is no standard outside the practice of a group to which appeal can be made, doesn't this imply that social practices can never be deemed incorrect? Fortunately the theory does not have this conclusion. Social practices can be readily criticized: by appeal to another set of social practices. The possibility of criticism resides in diversity. Far from entailing that errors can never be perceived or denounced, this is a theory about the nature of the standards used in such cases. Exactly the same worry may be formulated about the possibility of scientifically studying the taken for granted, natural, practices of a group. Are they not too basic to be studied on this view? There is some evidence that Wittgenstein himself may have thought this (cf. III — 24) but the same answer applies here as above. One set of taken-for-granted procedures can be utilized to study another set.

Wittgenstein says:

Isn't it like this: so long as one thinks it can't be otherwise, one draws logical conclusions. ... The steps which are not brought in question are logical inferences.[19]

The danger here ... is one of giving a justification of our procedure where there is no such thing as a justification and we ought simply to have said: *that's how we do it.*[20]

What are the factors which determine the standard practices of a group? It might seem that by appealing to what happens as a matter of course, and to what happens naturally, that this theory grounds mathematics in biology rather than sociology. Undoubtedly this account assumes a certain background of physical and psychological facts.[21] Without the physiological community of man the underlying coherence of judgments, on which the theory depends, would not be possible. But man's innate repertoire of behaviour is consistent with wide variation on the cultural level. So the question is whether mathematical rule following is to be located amongst the instincts or the institutions? For Wittgenstein the innate sociability of man was a necessary but not a sufficient condition for the use of socially structured concepts:

If we agree, then we have only set our watches, but not yet measured any time.[22]

As evidence for the idea that mathematical notions are cultural products, consider the historical case of the concept zero. Our present concept is not the one that all cultures have used. The Babylonians, for example, used a place-value notation but had a different, though related, concept. Their nearest equivalent to zero operated in the way that ours does when we use it to distinguish, say, 204 from 24. They had nothing corresponding to our use when we distinguish, say, 240 from 24. As Neugebauer[23] puts it, 'context alone decides the absolute value' in Babylonian mathematics.[24]

Before it can be safely concluded that the two concepts are really different an interesting objection has to be overcome. It might be said that the Babylonian calculators surely had to *think* of a zero when they made distinctions like that between 24 and 240. Surely they had the same idea or thought in their heads: it was just that they did not express it fully in their notation. In reply it can be said that this objection is like arguing that nobody can really think just 'She is beautiful' where the context makes the reference clear. It would be like insisting that the real structure and content of the thought must always be 'Miss M, at time T and place P, is beautiful', where the preamble frees the thought from its context. If the Babylonians used a zero which left some aspects of a calculation context dependent, then, thus far, their concept of zero differs from ours.

If it is granted that there are real differences in these two notions of zero, then the example shows that the concept is neither a dictate of logic nor of our instincts. Rather, the structure of the concept depends on the prevailing modes of calculation into which it enters. These in their turn, on the present perspective, would be structured by the forms of social interaction of which they are a part. For example: research in other fields suggests that permissible degrees of context dependence in a communication and required amounts of explicitness do not vary randomly.[25] They are a function of what can or cannot be taken for granted amongst the actors engaging in communication, or in this case, utilizing the calculation. All of this is a way of saying that the concept of zero is (or is part of) a social institution. If zero is an institution then on grounds of simplicity it may be supposed that the rest of the number concepts brought into contact with it are of a like nature.

In close conformity with this example the terms in which Wittgenstein conducts his analysis are the concepts of training and drill,[26] custom and use,[27] institution and norm,[28] convention and consensus,[29] and the behaviour that we can be brought to produce as a matter of course.[30]

What are the repercussions of this very sociological approach? What happens to the belief that to be committed to a premise is to be compelled to draw conclusions in one way rather than another? Wittgenstein considers the charge that he has reduced logical to psychological compulsion but argues:

am I acquainted with both kinds of compulsion, then?![31]

Logic compels by the sanctions of our fellow men:

Nevertheless the laws of inference can be said to compel us; in the same sense, that is to say, as other laws in human society.[32]

Wittgenstein does not deny that logic compels. What he offers is an explanation of the content of that compulsion. He *does* deny that in any absolute sense of 'must' we must draw the conclusions that we do, for he says:

No, it is not true that it *must* — but it *does* follow: we *perform* this transition.[33]

Similarly the inexorable character of mathematics is explained in terms of training in counting and calculating. The importance of the institution explains why we learn to count as we do:

with endless practice, with merciless exactitude; that is why it is inexorably insisted that we shall all say 'two' after 'one', 'three' after 'two' and so on.[34]

It is *we* who are inexorable.[35] Those who calculate are right to feel that they are dealing with something external to them, but they are often possessed by a misleading picture.[36] The feeling that there is some truth to which a calculation corresponds is not rejected by Wittgenstein, though he relocates that truth in utility and the enduring character of social practice:

'But is this counting only a *use*, then; isn't there also some truth corresponding to this sequence?' The *truth* is that counting has proved to pay.[37]

Referring to a case of logical inference he says:

And of course there is such a thing as right and wrong ... but what is the reality that 'right' accords with here? Presumably a *convention*, or a *use*, and perhaps our practical requirements.[38]

Perhaps the most significant conclusion is that mathematics can now be seen as invention rather than discovery.[39] There is a sense in which mathematics comes into existence when and as it is done.[40] To stop this conclusion from sounding paradoxical, the sociological character of Wittgenstein's theory has to be remembered. Mathematics is an institution, and institutions, though human products, are not subject to individual whim. There is a sense in which institutions exist in their own right over and above the specific acts of the people who play roles within them. This is because institutions involve ways of behaving which have become settled and routinized. Certain ways of behaving have become ingrained in the dispositions of a group of actors and expectations have crystallized. But of course, dispositions can hold sway and expectations exist even when particular actions conforming to them are not being performed. Likewise the concept of 'norm' refers to something relatively permanent and distinct from the episodic actions which conform to it or violate it. Thus when Wittgenstein says:

Mathematics forms a network of norms,[41]

he is proposing a non-Realist theory of the objectivity of mathematics. He is offering a sociological account of that objectivity, not calling it into question.

Institutions and norms are more than dispositions and expectations. They are also the focus of attitudes and bring forth potent images.[42] Wittgenstein takes account of this when he says:

Our children are not only given practice in calculation but are also trained to adopt a particular attitude towards a mistake in calculating.[43]

(See also III, 35 and V, 46.) The attitude is typified by the feeling that the calculation goes its own way, though the calculator may lapse.[44] The theories of mathematics that Wittgenstein is opposing mistake this attitude for the whole of the reality that they are trying to explain. For institutions such as the law or the monarchy this confusion (discussed in I, 118 and V, 3) would be a case of mistaking an ideology for the reality that it seeks to legitimate. Perhaps the same should be said here too.

The conclusion so far is that Wittgenstein has presented and developed a very simple but potentially very profound idea. Mathematics and logic are collections of norms. The ontological status of logic and mathematics is the same as that of an institution. They are social in nature. An immediate consequence of this idea is that the activities of calculation and inference are amenable to the same processes of investigation, and are illuminated by the same theories, as any other body of norms. They must be inculcated, justified and elaborated in the same way as the norms of any other institution. They will change by the same means, and are sustained in the same ways, as any other social process. Stated like this the theory sounds simplicity itself. From the point of view of an implicit Realism, such as gripped Mannheim, it is hardly a conceivable thought.

V

The argument of the previous section has shown that it is possible to retrieve a consistent sociological orientation towards mathematics from Wittgenstein's *Remarks*. This fact holds despite what use others may make of that work and despite what the intentions of the writer might have been.[45] But in that book there is no more than the sketch of a theory. It is, as yet, unconnected with any detailed factual inquiries and it is incomplete in itself. For example: sometimes Wittgenstein treats Realism as a pathological form of self-consciousness to which mathematicians are prone. At other times he presents it as being, or arising from, a natural response to our training; compare, say, V, 45 with I, 14 and 22. He fails to raise the question of why this reification takes place, what function it has or what its historical course has been.

Despite the programmatic nature of Wittgenstein's *Remarks* the value of having a solution to Mannheim's problem is considerable. Wittgenstein shows how a behavioural theory can begin to come to terms with those features of logic and mathematics which have always seemed most resistant to anything but a Realist or Platonist interpretation. The great insight of the *Remarks* is that it treats the grip that logic has upon us as a fact to be explained rather than the revelation of a truth to be justified. In doing so it has the consequence that the sociologist is no longer excluded *a priori* from dealing with mathematical activity itself. He is no longer constrained to deal with everything *but* mathematics, with error or confusion but never accepted knowledge. A sociology of knowledge rather than a sociology of error is possible.

It might be feared that if the sociologist comes to grips, Wittgenstein fashion, with accepted mathematical knowledge, then he will be committed to denying the autonomy of mathematics. Will 'external history' rather than 'internal history' be the order of the day? The answer is 'no'. The extent to which one segment of social life is separated from others is itself a social variable. The sociologist must take it as he finds it. Where there is a relatively autonomous tradition of activity this does not make what goes on within it any the less a social process. The ideas and practices which govern an autonomous range of activity, 'theoretical factors' as Mannheim called them, *are* social factors. On Wittgenstein's theory they are norms like any others. To behave in accordance with the logical consequences of a set of governing ideas is itself a piece of behaviour that needs explaining. That is why Wittgenstein focused on the nature of rule following. To refer to a piece of behaviour as a case of rule following is perfectly in order. But, as Wittgenstein saw, it is only the beginning, not the end, of an explanation. What is more, it is open to different interpretations depending on whether the assumptions in terms of which it is understood are causal or teleological. An account has to be given of what it is to follow a rule. It has been seen that Wittgenstein gave such an account and that it was in principle a sociological one.[46]

Notes

*The first draft of this paper was read at a Science Studies Wednesday seminar in Edinburgh in October 1971. I should like to acknowledge the great value of the discussions that I have had, on that occasion and later, with my colleague Barry Barnes.

1. K. Mannheim, *Ideology and Utopia* (London: Routledge and Kegan Paul, 1936), 39, 244, 263, 268.

2. L. Wittgenstein, *Remarks on the Foundations of Mathematics* (Oxford: Blackwell, 1956).

3. All the quotations from Wittgenstein come from the *Remarks* and will be identified by their part and section number in that order. All quotations or references to Mannheim are from *Ideology and Utopia*.

4. This paper is concerned only with the programme of the sociology of knowledge. It does not depend on any of the alleged findings which are still a source of controversy, for example, the role of the intellectuals.

Some misconceptions about this programme need to be removed. In his *Concepts and Society* (London: Routledge and Kegan Paul, 1972) I.C. Jarvie refers to the 'premise of the sociology of knowledge, that people believe what serves their interests ...' (189). He says that he understands the sociology of knowledge to assert that 'fundamentally, what [people] believe will be things that serve their personal or class interests' (132). If Jarvie means that sociologists are logically committed to relating beliefs to interests rather than to any other feature of social life then he presents no arguments to establish this: and surely none could be produced. Presumably Jarvie believes that sociologists *in fact* believe that interests determine belief. In this he is simply wrong. A wide range of determining factors have been considered plausible. R.K. Merton, *Social Theory and Social Structure* (enlarged edition, New York: The Free Press, 1968), 514, offers a whole list in his authoritative textbook, though he does not see this lack of consensus as a source of satisfaction. Mannheim, for his part, explicitly stated that interest was not an adequate basis for explanation in the sociology of knowledge (49, 51, 52). Over and above this he was careful to leave the exact character of the existential determination of thought an open question to be filled in later by empirical investigation (239). Furthermore he believed that the units with which different beliefs were to be correlated were not simply classes but generations, status groups, occupational groups etc. (248).

Another misconception is Jarvie's reiteration of Popper's charge that the sociology of knowledge 'looks upon science or knowledge as a process in the mind or 'consciousness' of the individual scientist, or perhaps as the product of such a process' (K.R. Popper, *The Open Society and Its Enemies*, II [London: Routledge and Kegan Paul, 1945], 217). As Jarvie puts it, 'Science does not consist in a mind (or consciousness) directly perceiving the true or the real' (133). This charge is not documented by either author. Whoever is guilty of this approach it is not a characteristic of Mannheim. Thus: 'Men living in groups ... do not confront the objects of the world from the abstract levels of a contemplating mind as such, nor do they do so exclusively as solitary beings' (3, see also the entire 3rd section of Ch. 1). These points should be borne in mind when assessing Jarvie's dismissal of 'Mannheim's vulgarisms' (137 and 135).

5. Mannheim claims at one point (239) that he does not strive to locate a 'mechanical

cause-effect sequence'. How can this be squared with the assertions that his programme is causal? The answer is that Mannheim is here disassociating himself from a crude technological determinism rather than the search for causes as such. Instead of assuming that windmills produce societies with feudal lords and steam mills industrial capitalists, the question becomes one of taking into account the impact of innovations on an already existing situation. The result will vary according to the background or initial conditions.

6. *Op. cit.* note 5, 240 (quoted below).

7. *Op. cit.* note 5, 71.

8. *Op. cit.* note 5, 69.

9. This is the only objection to the strong programme that will be considered in the body of the paper. It deserves special treatment because it constitutes a problem even for those who are committed to the ideals underlying the strong thesis. Many people dismiss these ideals almost out of hand, as they dismiss Mannheim. The most frequently used argument is that the sociology of knowledge leads to a self-defeating relativism. For just two examples see A. von Schelting's early review in *American Sociological Review*, I (1936), 666-73, and Popper *op. cit.* note 4. A lonely exception is C. Wright Mills in *Power, Politics and People*, I.L. Horowitz (ed.) (New York, 1963).

Mannheim denies that he is a relativist on the grounds that none of his doctrines undermine the idea that there are agreed criteria for rightness and wrongness in a discussion (*e.g.* 254) nor that there exists 'the possibility of arriving at decisions in factual disputes' (269). The existence of such criteria and the facts of actual agreement are part of the data that the sociologist takes for granted and tries to explain. Of course, he, too, has to use agreed standards and procedures in order to carry out investigations and construct theories. But what is logically objectionable about a never ending sequence of questions which *can* be raised? That the investigator can be investigated does not produce the chaos of relativism as Mannheim understands the word: it does not mean that anybody is free to say what they like. There are standards and there is coherence. Nor does it mean that no sociological investigation is ever finished — as if the sociologist could not reasonably announce a finding until he had been investigated *ad infinitum.* It only means that sociology, like any other science is never finished. In fact the same possibilities of regress are present in the structure of Popper's epistemology (K.R. Popper, *The Logic of Scientific Discovery* (London: Hutchinson, 1959). As he says very clearly, the regress is not vicious because the ground of scientific work consists in accepting some things as a matter of convention which can in principle always themselves be subject to further scientific scrutiny (Ch. v). The sociology of knowledge simply takes Popper at his word.

The sociology of knowledge is also at one with a Popperian epistemology over the role of the sensory input, mentioned above. Popper's theory of the empirical base (Ch. v) gives experience a purely causal function. Experience is not an infallible or direct apprehension of the truth. It is neither a decisive nor a probable justification for a belief, it is a motivator and a prompter. This causal role is exactly what the strong programme needs, because in explaining beliefs a sociologist will frequently make conjectures about the current or past sensory causes impinging on his subjects (and he will himself use sensory cues in doing this). A person's belief that there is a table in front of him will often be causally related, among other things, to the objects he can see or touch. This simple fact about causes should be kept separate from slippery locutions with which it may be confused, *e.g.* 'He believes there is a table in front of him because it is true there is a table in front of him'. Material objects can be causes but this formulation can be read as attributing causal efficacy to truth. The point of avoiding this sort of talk will emerge later in the paper.

10. I, 8.

11. G.H. Hardy, *A Mathematician's Apology* (First edition 1940), (Cambridge: University Press, 1967), 123-4, 130.

12. *Op. cit.* note 1, 239-40.

13. *Op. cit.* note 1, 267-8.

14. The clearest case of a sociologist who holds to the doctrine of Realism would appear to be Max Scheler, who postulated a realm of timeless essences. He sharply separated the question of the validity and content of knowledge from those factors which bring about belief in some sample or selection of truths. Only the process of selection is the business of sociology. As Scheler puts it: 'in a definite fashion and order, existential factors open and close the

sluice-gates to the flood of ideas' (quoted in Merton *op. cit.*, note 4, 534, from whom this account of Scheler is taken). The sluice-gate metaphor with its division of the content and occasion of knowledge has the same two-fold structure as those previously discussed.

15. In practice the effect that Realism and teleology will have is to reduce the strong programme of the sociology of knowledge to the weaker programme of what might be called the sociology of error.

One difference between the two programmes can be illustrated as follows: In his *A History of Mathematics*, 2nd edn. (New York: Macmillan, 1919), Cajori says, 'The calculation with the zero was the portion of Arabic mathematics earliest adopted by the Christians ... The new notation was accepted readily by the enlightened masses, but, at first, rejected by the learned circles. The merchants of Italy used it as early as the thirteenth century, while the monks in the monasteries adhered to the old forms' (121). For the sociology of error the problem would be: why did the monks resist the change? The acceptance of the merchants would be taken for granted as natural because the innovation was an advance towards a more rational and powerful form of mathematics (witness our present superiority over the older techniques). By contrast for the strong sociology of knowledge the two groups would be treated with complete parity.

The fact that Cajori makes evaluations, calling the merchants enlightened, is not harmful in itself, for the values are clearly visible. But such evaluations may predispose a researcher towards the weaker rather than the stronger programme of sociological explanation, because evaluations are essentially ways of adopting an asymmetrical stance. This link suggests that the Weberian demand for a value-free science can be seen as an expression of the symmetry postulate. The virtue of the symmetry formulation is that it derives solely from the search for maximum attainable generality, given currently accepted scientific standards. These standards are themselves almost certainly linked with the ideal of finding causal rather than teleological explanations and could themselves change if accepted scientific procedures change. However this interconnection of ideals and practices does not make it any the less desirable to have an explicit formulation of them.

16. I, 3.

17. I, 17-23.

18. I, 2.

19. I, 155.

20. II, 74.

21. V, 1, 15.

22. V, 2.

23. O. Neugebauer, *The Exact Sciences in Antiquity* (New Jersey: Princeton University Press, 1952).

24. *Op. cit.* note 1, 20.

25. B. Bernstein, *Class, Codes and Control*, I (London: Routledge and Kegan Paul, 1971), argues that the role structure of certain working-class and middle-class families brings about the different degrees of elaboration observed in their 'codes' of communication. The strongly taken-for-granted division of roles in the former permits a large tacit element in many of the communications. The highly individualized structure of the latter requires that much more of the communication is articulated and made explicit. In a related fashion the extreme forms of compression and abbreviation of inner speech or verbal thought is associated by Vygotsky with the fact that its function frees it from the necessary explicitness required of social speech (L.S. Vygotsky, *Thought and Language*, ed. and trans. by E. Hanfmann and G. Vakar [Cambridge, Mass.: The M.I.T. Press, 1962]).

26. I, 22, 36.

27. I, 9, 63.

28. II, 36; V, 46.

29. I, 74; II, 67.

30. I, 155; II, 74.

31. I, 118.

32. I, 116.

33. I, 12.

34. I, 4.

35. I, 119; V, 46.

36. V, 4.
37. I, 4.
38. I, 9.
39. I, 167; IV, 9.
40. II, 31; IV, 9.
41. V, 46.
42. I. 14.
43. V, 40.
44. III, 48; V, 4.
45. The final papers of a recent collection devoted to Wittgenstein's work (G. Pitcher, [ed.], *Wittgenstein: a Collection of Critical Essays* [London: Macmillan, 1968]) reveal the difficulty that some readers have in retrieving the sociological approach which is so prominent in the *Remarks*. For example Dummett repeatedly presents Wittgenstein's arguments as if they dealt with the psychology of individuals making personal choices, deciding to calculate in this way or that, or refusing to accept some conclusion. Wittgenstein, says Dummett, 'appears to hold that it is up to us to decide to regard any statement we happen to pick up as holding necessarily' (433, see also 435, 437). The first of Chihara's two papers is also devoid of any mention of the normative and institutional conceptions that Wittgenstein deploys. No wonder these papers report a failure to discern any coherent approach in the *Remarks*. The basic conceptions around which Wittgenstein's ideas are organized have simply been filtered out. Stroud's paper, which is both searching and well documented, similarly filters out the sociological concepts. In coming to terms with Wittgenstein's emphasis on the contingency of our ways of reasoning Stroud places all the emphasis on what it is necessary for me to do in virtue of the constraints of his physiological make up. Wittgenstein does indeed mention these factors. They are necessary conditions for social behaviour, but there are no reasons to think that our biological nature determines a unique way of reasoning and calculating. Stroud tries to support his approach by arguing that we do not really understand Wittgenstein's examples of societies which reason differently to us. When we begin to fill out the picture, our understanding fails. The implied cause of failure is that we have run up against the limitations of our biologically determined ways of thinking. But this is not good evidence because there would equally be limitations on our ability to grasp the implications of different customs even in societies where it was clear that their mode of reasoning was just like ours. Unlike Stroud, Wittgenstein always runs the biological and the social in harness as when he says: 'I mean, this is simply what we *do*. This is use and custom amongst us, or a fact of our natural history' (I, 63).
46. A useful discussion of Wittgenstein's conception of rule following is given by P. Winch, *The Idea of a Social Science* (London: Routledge and Kegan Paul, 195). Whereas Winch thinks that much sociology is misbegotten philosophy, the argument of this paper has been that much philosophy is misbegotten sociology. There is an irony about Winch's position which seems to have passed unnoticed. He believes that a proper philosophical understanding will illuminate our understanding of society. The example of philosophical clarity that he appeals to, which is Wittgenstein's analysis of rule following, in fact illustrates the opposite. It shows that a proper grasp of social and institutional processes is necessary for philosophical clarity. Rather than philosophy illuminating the social sciences Winch unwittingly shows that the social sciences are required to illuminate philosophical problems.

79

The Appel-Haken Solution of the Four-Colour Problem

S.G. Shanker

The Appel-Haken solution of the four-colour problem presents what, *prima facie* at least, might seem to be a doubly embarrassing result for Wittgenstein's arguments about the nature of mathematical proof (viz. that proofs are grammatical constructions which establish the rules for applying mathematical concepts and hence must be surveyable). For not only do Appel and Haken claim to have solved the four-colour problem with a proof which employs a humanly unsurveyable computer program to establish its key lemma — thereby blurring the sharp demarcation which Wittgenstein wished to draw between *proof* and *experiment* — but their proof also seems to strike a blow at Wittgenstein's argument that we cannot make sense of the notion of an *undecidable* problem. This is far from being a matter whose sole interest is limited to questions pertaining to the exegesis of Wittgenstein's writings on the philosophy of mathematics, however, for the heated debate which the Appel-Haken solution has initiated rests on what Thomas Tymoczko calls 'The new four-colour problem': viz. 'whether the Appel-Haken four-colour theorem is really a theorem'. That is, whether the Appel-Haken 'proof' is really a proof, and if so, what consequences this has for our understanding of the concept of proof.

It is a question which has received considerable attention lately, and the general consensus rapidly emerging is that the growing role of computer proofs in pure mathematics is forcing us to reconsider and 'liberalise' our concept of proof. The problem, so it is argued, is that there clearly seem to be theoretically decidable questions whose proofs would be so long that no human — indeed, perhaps no computer as well — could ever write them down; and that these provide us with obvious counter-examples to Wittgenstein's insistence on the 'surveyability' of mathematical proofs. (cf. 'Approaching the *Investigations*', Volume Two). Thus the charge has been levelled that, despite his emphasis on the importance of recognising 'proof' as a family-resemblance concept, Wittgenstein remained sadly blind to the possibility of extending the concept of proof in such a way as to allow for the possibility of a computer's establishing proofs which demand humanly impossible powers such as occurred in the Appel-Haken solution of the four-colour problem.

The key to the argument with which Wittgenstein would have responded to the Appel-Haken solution lies in his insistence that the barrier separating proof from experiment is *conceptual,* thereby preventing us from trying to shrink the parameters of this distinction by describing the difference between them as a matter of the *degree* of infallibility which each possesses. Saaty and Kainen argue in *The Four Colour Problem* that 'On a formal level, one may regard all mathematical proofs as thought experiments which contain a nonzero possibility of error. Well-known cases in the literature illustrate how such an error may be missed for years (sometimes because of the small number of times the experiment is repeated). Presumably, some are never found.'[1] We can clearly see here that the logical distinction between proof and experiment has already been transgressed. For rather than recognising that the concept of error is *a priori* precluded from applying to the concept of proof-construction, the problem has now become one of assessing the accuracy of the methods which have been employed to establish a given proof. But the concept of proof is not something which rests on fluid boundaries to the point that it can incorporate experimental operations, or indeed, accommodate highly probable experiments as members of the same conceptual family. To be a proof *just is* to exclude the possibility of error. Thus, when Michael Rabin, for example, asks us to allow computers some predetermined margin of error, he is not asking us to relax the stringency which we demand from proofs, but rather, to abandon completely our concept of proof as a grammatical construction in which the possibility of error is logically excluded.[2] From the premise that putative proofs might unbeknownst to us contain errors, the much stronger conclusion has been drawn that there is no logical reason why we should not extend our concept of proof in such a way that the possibility of error is formally introduced. But far more is involved here than the minor technical modification which the advocates of this argument suppose.

To assume that the concept of proof can be readjusted in order to allow for the presence of probabilistic proofs is similar to Quine's suggestion that linguistic conventions can be regarded as high-level empirical generalisations. In each case we are confronted with a conceptual violation masquerading as a technical reformulation. Thus, Tymoczko's description of the Appel-Haken solution as resulting in a 'new four-colour problem' is potentially misleading, in so far as it rests on the same confusion which Wittgenstein examined throughout his later writings in the philosophy of mathematics: a confusion which arises from the failure to clarify the nature of the conceptual distinctions between proof and experiment and between mathematical certainty and empirical probability. The central theme in Wittgenstein's discussions of mathematical propositions is that 'What is proved by a mathematical proof is set up as an internal relation and withdrawn from doubt.' (RFM VII §6) It is a point which bears quite strongly on the question of the nature of the Appel-Haken solution of the four-colour problem.

Tymoczko feels that the Appel-Haken 'four-colour theorem' forces us to revise our understanding of what constitutes a theorem, and *a fortiori*, 'forces us to modify our concept of proof', since 'the 4CT [is] the first mathematical proposition to be known a *posteriori*'.[3] That is, following Kripke's argument in *Naming and Necessity*, that it offers a clear example of an analytic *a posteriori* truth. (Although Tymoczko qualifies his support for Kripke's argument by maintaining that the 'four-colour theorem' is an example of an analytic *a posteriori* truth which could not even in principle be known *a priori*.[4]) Instead of presenting a surveyable proof of the 'four-colour theorem', the Appel-Haken solution provides us with what Tymoczko describes as 'mathematically convincing grounds for the 4CT ... where a key lemma is justified by an appeal to certain computer runs ... [which] help establish the 4CT ... on grounds that are in part empirical.'[5] Thus Tymoczko concludes that 'The reliability of the 4CT ... is not of the same degree as that guaranteed by traditional proofs, for this reliability rests on the assessment of a complex set of empirical factors ... The 4CT is a substantial piece of pure mathematics which can be known by mathematicians only *a posteriori*. Our knowledge must be qualified by the uncertainty of our instruments, computer and program.'[6] But in stating this conclusion Tymoczko has clearly slipped from regarding the problem as conceptual into treating it as empirical. The demarcation that is involved here has nothing to do with a matter of *degree*, but rather, has to do with *kind*: with the logical distinctions between the *a priori* and the *a posteriori*, between *convention* and *hypothesis*, and between *proof* and *experiment*. Such, I believe, is the outline of the response which Wittgenstein would want to make in response to the Appel-Haken solution of the four-colour problem.

The traditional version of the 'four-colour conjecture' presents a problem which has struck many as strikingly similar to such enigmas as Goldbach's conjecture and Fermat's last theorem. The problem asks whether *every* map can be four-coloured: a question which on the face of it does not seem all that different from asking whether every even number is the sum of two odd primes, or whether for any integer greater than 2, $x^n + y^n = z^n$. But whereas the source of the difficulty with e.g. Goldbach's conjecture lies in the fact that the concept of a *prime* is defined in terms of multiplication while the problem itself involves addition, the most conspicuous feature of the original 'four-colour conjecture' is the extent to which the concept of a *map* was vaguely defined.

After more than a century of failure mathematicians were beginning to despair of ever finding a solution to the four-colour problem.[7] To be sure, a limited amount of progress had been made; for example, by the time of Appel and Haken's solution, mathematicians had succeeded in raising the 'Birkhoff number' — the number of countries that a five-chromatic map must contain — to 96 (i.e. showing that every map with fewer than 96 countries is four-colourable). But this sort of progress is comparable to

Schnirelmann's proof that every positive integer can be represented as the sum of not more than 300,000 primes.[8] Indeed, we might even draw a parallel between this progress and Vinogradoff's non-constructive proof that every 'sufficiently large' even number can be written in the form $p + q$, where p is prime and q has at most two prime factors. (What Vinogradoff actually proved is that the assumption that infinitely many integers cannot be decomposed into at most four prime numbers results in a contradiction.)[9]

As work on the four-colour problem progressed in this century the conviction grew that, if the problem was to prove solvable, it would only be on the basis of proving by *reductio ad absurdum* that the concept of a 'minimal five-chromatic map' is impossible. Thus, the problem seemed to devolve on the question of whether a fairly large set of 'unavoidable configurations' could be proved to be 'reducible' (*infra*). Hence it seemed that the possibility of solving the four-colour problem rested on the size, if it could be found, of a reducible unavoidable set; had the set which Appel and Haken had to work with been much larger, then the resolution of the problem would have been 'medically impossible' (barring the future development of much more powerful computers). Thus, although the Appel-Haken solution demonstrated that the original 'four-colour conjecture' was only *undecided,* it thereby seemed to indicate the manner in which it could easily have turned out to be *undecidable.*

This latter criticism can be summarily dealt with. The success of the Appel-Haken solution, if such it should prove to be (and bear in mind that this is a question which does not concern Wittgenstein's argument; what we are investigating here is not the validity, but rather the *logical status* of the Appel-Haken solution), would not have forced Wittgenstein into the expediency of arguing that if it is indeed the case that the four-colour problem has been solved, then it must have been the case that the original 'four-colour conjecture' was merely *undecided* rather than *undecidable.* Such a retort would obviously be highly unsatisfactory, and we would certainly be entitled to demand an elucidation of where exactly the difference lies. We would quite rightly feel that, if the 'four-colour conjecture' is more similar to say Fermat's theorem [that if p is any prime which does not divide the integer a, then $a^{p-1} \equiv 1 \pmod{p}$] than it is to 'Fermat's last theorem', then this is a distinction which we should be able to draw merely by examining the formulation of the question, rather than having to wait for a successful solution. But, for several different reasons, this attack is misguided.

First, Wittgenstein would have rejected the very premise that it makes sense to speak of the 'four-colour conjecture' as having meaning before a proof had been constructed in which this otherwise ill-formed expression is decidable. Hence, the original 'four-colour conjecture' was *neither* undecided nor undecidable, for in the absence of a proof it was not, strictly speaking, a proposition, and only a meaningful proposition is capable of being decidable. What mathematicians were actually working with was a senseless expression which, because of the meanings associated with the sub-sentential expressions in their proper language games, exercised in this novel combination a heuristic influence which encouraged mathematicians to construct a new grammatical structure for this expression. (This skeleton outline is not intended as an actual genetic account, but rather, as an elucidation of the status of the various expressions and arguments that were developed.) Moreover, the concept of 'undecidability' applies to those ill-formed 'questions' which are logically incapable of being answered, because they rest on irreconcilable grammatical conflicts which render them unintelligible. In other words, we cannot make sense of the concept of an *undecidable question*: to be intelligible just is to be decidable, and it is nonsensical to suppose that e.g. a species of infinitary questions exists which we can understand but which are physically impossible for us to answer because of finitary limitations.

Thus, what we might say is that, if it is interpreted as asking a question about the infinite set of integers, then 'Fermat's last theorem' is indeed *undecidable*, assuming that we take this to mean that it is a priori unintelligible; but that does not rule out the possibility of a genuine (constructive) solution of Fermat's last theorem, interpreted in terms of the nature of the rules governing the construction of the integers. The point is that, until such a system has been constructed, it is profoundly misleading to speak of Fermat's last *theorem* or of Goldbach's *conjecture*. Wittgenstein's critique of these problems was directly concerned with the philosophical confusion prevalent at the time which assumed that 'Fermat's last theorem' and 'Goldbach's conjecture' were *undecidable* because the set of integers is infinite. In order for the 'four-colour conjecture' to be undecidable — irrevocably unintelligible — in this sense, it would have to assume that the set of countries contained in a map — and a fortiori the set of unavoidable configurations — is infinite (a confusion which is generally but not invariably avoided). Wittgenstein's response to the four-colour problem would surely have been that, provided that it is interpreted in terms of developing the rules governing the construction of the (infinite) series of planar maps, there is certainly no a priori reason to deny the possibility of constructing a solution for Guthrie's 'problem' (by creating a meaning for his 'question'); but then, neither is there any basis for suggesting that the problem was at any time *undecidable*. What this issue really turns on is the (nonsensical) syntax of the (unintelligible) concept of *undecidability* rather than the actual mathematical nature of the four-colour problem; and, of course, the explanation of the meaning of a mathematical proposition as determined by the totality of rules governing its use in a proof-system.

We must be clear from the start, therefore, precisely where Wittgenstein would have felt committed to respond to the Appel-Haken solution. It is not, according to Wittgenstein, the responsibility of the philosopher to decide which proofs are mathematically sound; rather, the philosopher's task is (in general terms) to clarify the significance (or otherwise) of a mathematical construction. The Appel-Haken solution raises two separate — although not completely independent — issues, however, only one of which violates Wittgenstein's strictures. Before we consider how Wittgenstein would have responded to the Appel-Haken 'reducibility lemma', we should first consider how he would have reacted to the very format of the Appel-Haken 'proof'; for the strategy of their argument is classically non-constructive in the precise sense which the Kroneckerians attacked. The basic premise of the Appel-Haken solution, which they inherited from the original Kempe attempt to prove the 'four-colour conjecture', is that rather than proving directly that *every* map can be four-coloured, we need only show that there is no map which must be drawn with five colours. The Kempe/Appel-Haken proof is thus an orthodox *reductio ad absurdum* which proceeds by assuming that there is at least one map which requires five colours. The burden of the proof is to establish that it is impossible to construct a minimal normal five-chromatic map (to demonstrate that the assertion that a minimal normal five-chromatic map exists leads to a contradiction). From this the conclusion is drawn that therefore four colours are always enough to colour a planar map. Such a method in no way results, however, in an effective method for actually four-colouring a map.

There are no serious grounds to suppose that Wittgenstein would have been hostile to the basic framework of this 'proof'. On the contrary, Wittgenstein stressed throughout his writings on the philosophy of mathematics that the use of indirect proofs is perfectly respectable (or at any rate, he registered his commitment to a principle of neutrality on this issue; for as far as he was concerned, this was strictly an internal mathematical affair). Wittgenstein repeatedly emphasised that his interest in constructivism did not rest on a dogmatic foundation (e.g. based on finitism); rather, it was a consequence of the account which he developed of the meaning and understanding of mathematical expressions in terms of rule-governed operations. Moreover, as we shall see below, the objections which he would have raised — indeed, which in a prescient way he did raise — against the unsurveyability of a computer proof such as that of the 'reducibility lemma' in the Appel-Haken argument, rest on the conclusions which he drew from his rule-governed conception of constructivism, and the light which is thereby shed on the grammatical nature of mathematical propositions and proofs.

The strategy of the Kempe argument, which Appel and Haken attempt to rescue from Kempe's failed proof for countries with five neighbours, is quite straightforward in outline. We begin by assuming that a minimal normal five-chromatic map exists. A map is said to be 'normal' if no country completely surrounds another country; if no more than three countries meet at one point; if no country has zero or one neighbour; and if no country is unconnected. A 'minimal' normal five-chromatic map is the map with the least number of countries requiring *more* than four colours. The argument already provides us, therefore, with an illustration of the manner in which, as Wittgenstein argued, a proof 'changes' — i.e. creates/ constructs — the meaning of the expressions stated in the conjecture (in this case, 'country' and 'map'), so that the ultimate *meaning* of these expressions may not coincide with the sense of the words as used in their original *Satzsysteme*. For example, according to the definition we are constructing, we would now have to disqualify the map of the United States as a genuine map on several independent grounds, let alone in terms of the changes that are wrought by Heesch's shift to the triangulation of a map in a planar dual in order to pursue the resolution of the problem with the techniques developed in graph theory.[10]

Kempe then proved that in every normal map there is at least *one* country with either two, three, four or five neighbours; i.e. that there is no normal map where *every* country has six or more neighbours. (De Morgan had already proved that it is impossible to construct five mutually-adjacent countries.) This is an essential step in the proof: the introduction of the concept of an *unavoidable* set of 'configurations', such that every normal map contains at least one member of the set. It might seem from the manner in which this step of the argument is expressed that it slips danger-ously into a platonist idiom, but in fact there is nothing here to which Wittgenstein need have objected, provided that we interpret this step as stating that we have defined the concept of a *normal map* in such a way that every normal map is 'unavoidable'. That is, the concept *normal map* is developed in very much the same way as, say, the concept *prime number*, and this feature is merely the consequence of the rules governing the con-struction of the infinite series of normal maps.

The next step in Kempe's argument was to show that, for any normal map M which contains (by definition) a configuration which is a member of this 'unavoidable set' U, we can derive another map M′ which contains fewer countries than M, such that, if M′ is four-colourable, then so too is the unavoidable map M. Where such a construction is possible we say that that configuration is reducible. (A 'reducible' configuration is one which cannot be part of a minimal normal five-chromatic map, for if it was, then there would by definition be another five-chromatic map with fewer countries. We say that a vertex is reducible if, by removing any vertex of degree *k* from a graph, the four-colourability of the resulting sub-graph implies the four-colourability of the original graph. A configuration is said to be reducible if the four-colourability of a planar graph containing it is deducible from the four-colourability of the sub-graph which results when that configuration is *reducible*. (A 'reducible' configuration is one which way so that, from a four-colouring of our reduced map, we can reconstruct a four-colouring of the original map.

No matter what the size of our original map, if we keep reducing often enough we will come to a reduced map with four or fewer countries, from which we then work backwards to reconstruct the four-colouring of the original map.[11] So the strategy of the proof is to show, at each step of the reduction, that we can four-colour the previous map provided that we can four-colour the existing reduced map. This process guarantees that we must eventually come to a map which we are certain can be four-coloured, from whence we then work backwards to our original map. Whereupon we are forced to conclude that M is four-colourable, contradicting our original assumption. Hence no minimal normal five-chromatic map exists, from which Kempe/Appel-Haken conclude that every normal map is four-colourable.

Thus, the upshot of the original Kempe proof is that it will suffice to prove the 'four-colour conjecture' if we can only construct an avoidable set of configurations that is reducible. Kempe's proof broke down because he could only prove that four of his five unavoidable vertices were reducible; his proof of the case of countries with five neighbours was soon destroyed by Heawood, who proved that, in general, vertices of degree 5 are not reducible. (There are certain configurations which are exceptions to this rule; e.g. Birkhoff's theorem that a five-degree vertex with three consecutive five-neighbours is reducible.) In order to follow through with the original inspiration of Kempe's argument, Appel and Haken were forced to alter the nature and size of Kempe's unavoidable set dramatically, and to shift from trying to prove that vertices of degree 5 were reducible to proving that *configurations* — clusters of vertices — are reducible. Obviously, the problem of finding a set of reducible configurations sufficiently rich enough that every planar graph contains one member of the set is vastly more complicated than Kempe's original project. The strategy of their proof thus remains faithful to Kempe's original strategy in one sense, in so far as it undertakes to construct an unavoidable set of configurations that are reducible; but by embarking on a route which must of necessity rely extensively on the use of computers, they completely altered the spirit underlying Kempe's original failed 'proof'.

Appel and Haken appear to have developed an extraordinary 'feel' for which set would prove so reducible, but their method remains none the less based on a somewhat random approach, a procedure in which they increasingly followed rather than directed the development of their heuristic computer program.[12] Whenever an unavoidable set of configurations could not be proved to be reducible (not by any means to be equated with a proof that it was not reducible), they developed a highly effective method of modifying it, and would then test the new set for reducibility. However, the larger the configuration the more difficult it becomes to prove reducibility. The 'ring size' of a configuration — the number of countries that form a ring around the configuration — provides a direct indication of the complexity involved in proving that the configuration is reducible. Working with formidably large ring sizes, Appel and Haken were not simply forced to rely on a sophisticated computer program to run through large unavoidable sets of configurations to test for reducibility, but were extremely fortunate that the computer program itself revealed to them how to keep the ring size down to a level where a computer could at least work through the configurations in a reasonable length of time. (As it was, their ultimate discovery of an unavoidable set of 1,500 reducible configurations took approximately 1,200 hours of computer time.)

The key to this achievement lay in the development of their successful 'discharging algorithm' (basically a rule for redistributing the 'charge' of vertices in a planar triangulation). That is, they devised an effective procedure for constructing a set of so-called 'obstructing configurations' (configurations which 'obstruct' the discharging of positive charges). Since the 'sum charge' of a planar graph is always positive, these 'obstructing' configurations are unavoidable. Hence the discharging algorithm enabled them to enumerate an unavoidable set U, and to modify this set continually by modifying the algorithm. (This part of the solution — that every planar graph must contain a configuration which is a member of U — is surveyable.)

The next step in their solution was firmly based on experimental methods. Heesch had described three 'reduction obstacles': embedded configurations which are regularly present in configurations which are irreducible. To prove that none of these 'reduction obstacles' is present in a configuration does not at all serve as a proof that the configuration is reducible, but it does make it probable that such a configuration could be proved to be reducible. Without this step the sheer size of the set of configurations that the computer would have had to examine would have required an impossible amount of computer time for the solution. Appel and Haken have seized upon this step as an example of the manner in which future mathematical investigations will have to rely heavily on computer-assisted operations. But, although this step clearly played a central role in the genesis of their solution, it obviously plays no role in the actual 'proof' which they claim to have discovered. The obvious parallel which one might draw here is to Archimedes' 'method of exhaustion'. Certainly, the discovery of the palimpsest containing the *Method* cleared up the mystery of how Archimedes was able to make so many exciting discoveries in the calculation of volumes and centres of gravity, but it did not in the least affect the logical status of the proofs which Archimedes would then subsequently construct. It is part of their general confusion that Appel and Haken should think that this empirical method should play any role in the presentation of their mathematical proof.

The experimental use of the computer in the development of the 'reducibility lemma' was thus two-fold. First the computer was used to develop a highly probable approach to determine which configurations might prove to be reducible. (The point of the 'reduction obstacles' is quite simply that no configuration which contains one of these configurations has as yet been proved to be reducible.) The next and final stage of the proof was to test these likely candidates for reducibility. In essence, the (D-) reducibility program which Appel and Haken employed tests the configuration to see whether every four-colouring of the ring around that configuration can be extended to a four-colouring of the configuration, and if not, whether it can be modified by one or more interchanges in the 'Kempe chain' of colours (the two-coloured paths leading from one country to another) and then extended, or finally, whether by the identification of distinct vertices it can be extended. Obviously the number of possible four-colourings of a circuit is proportionate to the size of the ring (a circuit with 13 vertices, for example, has 66,430 different four-colourings). But the process of generating these different four-colourings, they argue, is *purely mechanical,* and thus the problem really comes down to having a powerful enough computer to go through all the permutations in a reasonable length of time.

We must not confuse such a *mechanical operation,* however, with the concept of a recursive proof or a recursive calculation. Wittgenstein was certainly quite prepared to countenance the latter, but in doing so he deliberately contrasted such a method with the type of 'arithmetical experiment' that results in the 'reducibility lemma'. In *Philosophical Remarks*, for example, Wittgenstein asked: 'Is an arithmetical experiment still possible when a recursive definition has been set up? I believe, obviously not; because via the recursion each stage becomes arithmetically comprehensible.' (*PR* §194) We must consider this last point carefully when addressing the grammatical status of the 'reducibility lemma'. For the problem with the 'reducibility lemma' — *qua* mathematical construction — lies precisely in its unsurveyability, which in turn is merely a manifestation of the unintelligibility of describing this part of Appel-Haken's argument as a 'lemma' (as opposed to an empirical hypothesis). The logical distinction we must clarify here, therefore, is simply that between proof and experiment:

> In this context we keep coming up against something that could be called an 'arithmetical experiment'. Admittedly the data determine the result, but I can't see *in what way* they determine it. (cf. e.g. the occurrences of 7 in π.) The primes likewise come out from the method for looking for them, as the results of an experiment. To be sure, I can convince myself that 7 is prime, but I can't see the connection between it and the condition it satisfies. — I have only found the number, not generated it. (*PR* §190)

Likewise, the Koch computer program can convince us that U is reducible, but we can't *see* the connection between this result and the criteria for reducibility because we cannot *generate* this result as a consequence of applying the rules for reducibility. And this is precisely the source of the logical obstacles to describing the so-called 'reducibility lemma' as a *mathematical* construction.

In *Philosophical Remarks* Wittgenstein argued that a colour octahedron must be surveyable in the sense that we can *see* the logical articulations forged by the grammatical construction. Likewise, a proof must be surveyable in the sense that we can *see* the law of the series forged by the proof *qua* grammatical construction: 'I must be able to write down a part of the series, in such a way that you can *recognize* the law. That is to say, no *description* is to occur in what is written down, everything must be represented.' (*PR* §190) But this is precisely the criterion which the Appel-Haken solution fails to meet: what we are given just is a description of the operations which the computer has performed, rather than a 'manifestation of the law'. Hence, it commits the same fallacy which Wittgenstein warned against when he argued that 'A number as the result of an arithmetical experiment, and so the experiment as the *description* of a number, is an absurdity. The experiment would be the description, not the *representation* of a number.' (*PR* §196)

The point is that I cannot understand a mathematical construction as a *lemma* unless I understand the proof underlying it. ('This boils down to saying: If I hear a proposition of, say, number theory, but don't know how to prove it, then I don't understand the proposition either.' (*PR* §155)) But to *understand* the proof is to grasp the rules governing the construction:

> Suppose I wanted to construct a regular pentagon but didn't know how, and were now to make experiments at random, finally coming upon the right construction by accident: Haven't we here an actual case of a knot which is untied by trial and error? No, since if I don't understand this construction, as far as I'm concerned it doesn't even begin to be the construction of a pentagon.
>
> Of course I can write down the solution of a quadratic equation by accident, but I can't understand it by accident. (*PR* §157)

The 'reducibility lemma', however, is based on just such a random experiment, which came upon the right construction by accident. We can see the set, but we cannot generate it: 'I look for it, but I don't generate it. I can certainly see a law in the rule which tells me how to find the primes, but not in the numbers that result. And so it is unlike the case $+ 1/1!, - 1/3!, + 1/5!$, etc., where I can see a law *in the numbers*.' (*PR* §190)

It is worth remarking, *à propos* of this latter remark, that this disposes of Dummett's objection that:

> It is a matter of some difficulty to consider just what our mathematics would look like if we adopted [Wittgenstein's] 'anthropologistic' standpoint. Would the Peano axioms survive unaltered? 'Every number has a successor' would mean, in this mathematics, that if a number is accessible (that is, if we have a notation in which it can be surveyably represented) then its successor is accessible, and this at first seems reasonable. On the other hand, it seems to lead to the conclusion that *every* number is accessible, and it is clear that, whatever notation we have, there will be numbers for which there will not be a surveyable symbol in that notation.[13]

But Wittgenstein intended his argument to be anything but 'anthropologistic'. It is only because he misperceives the direction of Wittgenstein's sustained attack on the Frege-Russell attempt to *justify* our use of mathematical expressions that Dummett was led into this conclusion. On the contrary, Wittgenstein's fundamental concern was to rid us of our misguided preoccupation with the problem of such 'justification' (for what can we say on this topic, apart from that my justification for applying a rule in this manner is that this is the way it is applied), and shift our attention instead to the much more serious question of clarifying the nature of mathematical necessity and the logical status of mathematical expressions. The problem Wittgenstein was concerned with here was not, 'how can I be certain that the pupil knows the rule'; rather, he must circumvent this bogus sceptical worry and clarify what we describe as 'knowing how to apply the rule correctly'.

The point which Dummett has confused in this passage is the distinction which Wittgenstein was trying to draw between saying that the series of numbers must be surveyable and that the law generating the construction of the series must be surveyable. 'When we teach someone how to take his first step,' Wittgenstein explained, 'we thereby enable him to go any distance.' (*PR* §165) Clearly Dummett's objection is simply a variation of what Wittgenstein described as the *Satzsysteme* confusion of infinite processes with finite totalities: i.e. how could we 'survey' an infinite expansion? Moreover, what does it mean to suggest that our law for constructing e.g. the infinite series of integers generates numbers that will simply be too long for us to write down in our notation? As if, given that the series runs on to infinity, we must eventually come to a digit with more zeros than man can physically reproduce. But Wittgenstein dealt with just such a criticism when he argued:

> Our normal mode of expression carries the seeds of confusion right into its foundations, because it uses the word "series" both in the sense of "extension", and in the sense of "law". The relationship of the two can be illustrated by a machine for making coiled springs, in which a wire is pushed through a *helically* shaped passage to make as many coils as are desired. What is called an infinite helix need not be anything like a finite piece of wire, or something that that approaches the longer it becomes; it is the law of the helix, as it is embodied in the short passage. Hence the expression "infinite helix" or "infinite series" is misleading. (*PG* p. 430)

Obviously, if it is a point of our actually working with integers that are far too long for us to write out in standard Hindu-Arabic notation, we will need to devise some other form of notation, just as it is easier to work with 10 and 11 than with stroke notation.[14] The point of Wittgenstein's argument is not that we can *see* that $10 + 11 = 21$ whereas we cannot *see* the same thing in stroke-notation; rather, the point is that the truth of the proposition in either notation rests on the rules governing addition. The real question we are concerned with here is not: how can I be certain that an 'unrealistic' number such as Knuth's $10\uparrow\uparrow\uparrow\uparrow3$ is an integer; but rather, what renders such a figure an integer (cf. note 14). We must distance ourselves, therefore, from the attempts to force Wittgenstein's comments on surveyability into a sceptical framework, and recognise instead that what he was actually concerned with here is the relation of a number to the law which generates the series in which it occurs. Far from being concerned with the psychological question, how do we recognise that such and such a digit is an integer, the real question we are concerned with is, what are the rules which license us to describe such a figure as an integer? Hence it is the law governing the expansion of the series, not the actual expansion of the series, that must be surveyable. The latter interpretation is simply another example of the confusion generated by treating infinite series as finite totalities.

As far as Haken is concerned, on the other hand, the only problem posed by his and Appel's solution concerns the techniques that are permissible in *mechanical calculation*, and he has thus formally announced that he cannot see any conceptual problems in the approach they have adopted, which constitutes, he believes, a technical innovation in mathematical procedures which will have far-reaching methodological consequences. 'Anyone, anywhere along the line,' he argues, 'can fill in the details and check them. The fact that the computer can run through more details in a few hours than a human could ever hope to do in a lifetime does not change the basic concept of the mathematical proof. What has changed is not the theory but the practice of mathematics.'[15] The resistance with which some mathematicians have greeted their results thus strikes Appel and Haken merely as evidence of a reactionary attitude fostered by an antediluvian mathematical training:

> Most mathematicians who were educated prior to the development of fast computers tend not to think of the computer as a routine tool to be used in conjunction with other older and more theoretical tools in advancing mathematical knowledge. Thus they intuitively feel that if an argument contains parts that are not verifiable by hand calculations it is on rather insecure ground. There is a tendency to feel that verification of computer results by independent computer programs is not as certain to be correct as independent hand checking of the proof of theorems proved in the standard way.
>
> This point of view is reasonable for those theorems whose proofs are of moderate length and highly theoretical. When proofs are long and highly computational, it may be argued that even when hand checking is possible, the probability of human error is considerably higher than that of machine error; moreoever, if the computations are sufficiently routine, the validity of programs themselves is easier to verify than the correctness of hand computations.[16]

The fallacy contained in this argument is so subtle that it is no surprise that, despite their obvious apprehension, many have been bludgeoned into silence. The point is that it is not a question of the *certainty of the verification*, but rather, as Wittgenstein insisted, of the *method of verification*, that lies at the heart of the objection to calling the Appel-Haken argument a mathematical proof.

Ian Stewart complains in *Concepts of Modern Mathematics* that the problem with the Appel-Haken solution is that:

> it doesn't give a satisfactory explanation *why* the theorem is true. This is partly because the proof is so long that it is hard to grasp (including the computer calculations, impossible!), but mostly because it is so apparently structureless. The answer appears as a kind of monstrous coincidence. Why is there an unavoidable set of reducible configurations? The best answer at the present time is: there just is. The proof: here it is, see for yourself. The mathematician's search for hidden structure, his pattern-binding urge, is frustrated.[17]

In one sense Stewart's objection is somewhat misleading, for in an important way we *do* understand why U is reducible. Certainly Appel and Haken will be prompt to point out that some such account as the above just does constitute an explanation of why there is an unavoidable set of configurations. The real point of this issue is not that Appel and Haken failed to solve the four colour-problem, but rather, that their solution is empirical, not mathematical. Thus, it is not my intention to detract in any way from the success of Appel and Haken's accomplishment, but solely to clarify the precise nature of this achievement. For the central point remains that how the actual reducible set was discovered may not affect the validity of the argument which is then used to demonstrate the existence of this set. The crucial barrier preventing us from understanding their solution as a *mathematical proof*, however, just is that we understand the description, not the construction of this set. And it is at this point that the criticism which Stewart wishes to make finds its target: that we are not offered a (constructive) proof for the existence of this unavoidable reducible set of configurations, but are merely left with the experimental procedure that was used to discover it. The point is that the manner in which we know that U is reducible is empirical, not mathematical, a clarification which is established by the manner in which we understand/verify the 'reducibility lemma'. It is because we understand this 'lemma' as the end result of a highly probable mechanical experiment, therefore, that the Appel-Haken solution of the four-colour problem is empirical rather than mathematical.

Saaty and Kainen conclude that:

> The crux of the Appel-Haken proof of the four-colour theorem is a subtle and elegant probabilistic argument which establishes an a priori certainty that there must exist some discharging procedure producing an unavoidable set all of whose configurations are reducible. That is, they showed that the computer-assisted reducibility proof was overwhelmingly likely to succeed, and they appear to have been right.[18]

It is fascinating to see the ease with which Saaty and Kainen shift back and forth in this passage between the *a priori* and the *a posteriori*. The explanation for this laxity is clear: it is because they think that the *a posteriori* is related to the *a priori* on a scale of relative certainty, with absolute certainty finally reached at the level of the *a priori*, that they slip so effortlessly from the one concept to the other. Thus, they fail to distinguish between the two *kinds* of certainty involved in mathematical as opposed to empirical contexts: i.e. normative as opposed to inductive certainty. The confusion involved in this passage is similar to the misconception which interprets the limit which an infinite series approaches as the actual infinite. Just as the focus of Wittgenstein's critique of Cantor's interpretation of the transfinite cardinals lies in Cantor's attempt to define his constructions in terms of the 'larger than' relation that governs finite totalities (cf. 'Introduction: The Portals of Discovery' in this volume), so too the problem with the Saaty and Kainen argument is that they too try to describe the relation between probability and certainty in terms of a 'greater than' relation. But mathematical propositions are not *more* certain than empirical hypotheses; they are certain in a completely different way: namely, that the certainty of the former rests, not on inductive probability, but rather, on the logical *exclusion* of doubt.

The concept of probability tending towards the limit of (inductive) certainty is very much an empirical concept, but the concept of the *a priori* certain — the logical necessity which is the consequence of grammatical conventions — is separated from empirical probability by the unbridgeable gulf separating *conventions* from *empirical propositions*. That is, *a priori* truths are certain in a *completely different way* than highly probable empirical propositions. Indeed, the very concept of truth that is involved in each of these systems is different (we do not, for example, say that it is true that the bishop can only move diagonally in the same way that it is true that the bishop needs a new chasuble), and the fact that the concept of the truth of empirical propositions is so firmly tied to empirical verification renders it potentially misleading to speak of the *truth* of (*a priori*) conventions without drawing attention to this fundamental grammatical divergence.[19]

If we tighten up their argument, we see that what Saaty and Kainen really mean is that the Appel-Haken solution established a highly probable *a posteriori* truth because they showed that the computer program is overwhelmingly likely to succeed. (The greater the probability that an arbitrary colouration of a ring is extendable, the greater the probability that the bounded configuration is reducible. When the former reaches a probability greater than or equal to .30, the probability of the latter very nearly reaches 1.) The reason why Appel and Haken did not succeed in constructing a mathematical solution of the 'four-colour conjecture', therefore, has nothing whatsoever to do with the rigour or reliability of their findings. To be sure, it is because the 'algorithm' which the computer mechanically 'calculates' is not humanly surveyable (i.e. the algorithm which we use the program to calculate; cf. 'Introduction: The Nature of Philosophy', Volume Four) that we must deny that their argument constitutes a mathematical proof (a point which turns on the logical grammar of the concepts calculation, proof and mechanical symbol-manipulation); or that the *algorithm* is unsurveyable full-stop. Quite simply, the problem with the Appel-Haken 'four-colour theorem' is that it cannot be understood as the result of applying grammatical conventions. The point of focusing on *surveyability* is precisely that, by clarifying the manner in which we verify their 'proof', we clarify the logical status of their solution.

The fact that this argument forces us to interpret the Appel-Haken solution as what Wittgenstein calls an 'arithmetical experiment' — as an empirical solution of what in their hands has become an empirical problem — does not thereby force us to conclude that Guthrie's original 'four-colour conjecture' was an (empirical) hypothesis rather than a (mathematical) 'conjecture'. Indeed, the fundamental point which lies at the heart of this argument bears out Wittgenstein's concern that we must not interpret such 'conjectures' as well-formed (i.e. meaningful) mathematical questions prior to the construction of a grammatical structure (proof) in which they are decidable. The point is that the 'four-colour conjecture', as it occurs at the beginning of the Appel-Haken solution, is used to state an hypothesis, and that this is *because* of the empirical nature of their solution.

The force of this argument turns on the fact that it does make sense to express one's doubts about the reliability of the Appel-Haken solution precisely because it rests on a computer-experiment; whereas it makes no sense to doubt the reliability of a mathematical proof *qua* grammatical construction. Inevitably the defenders of the Appel-Haken 'proof' will argue that the 'calculations' performed by a computer may be much more reliable than the calculations performed by mathematicians (witness the history of Kempe's proof for degree-5 vertices). But here they confuse the reliability of the calculations which the mathematician has performed — the question of whether we can be certain that a rule has been applied correctly — with the question of what constitutes the correct application of a rule. We are not concerned with the question: 'how can we be certain that a 400-page proof is correct'; but rather, 'in what does a 400-page proof's being correct consist'. We are concerned here with *how* we would establish that an argument is correct, not *whether* a particular proof is correct. Hence the point which Wittgenstein was trying to make is not that an argument can only be described as a mathematical proof when we have demonstrated beyond all shadow of a doubt that it is correct, but rather, that in accepting an argument as a 'proof' we are treating it as the construction of a mathematical system which is logically immune from the possibility of doubt.[20]

Thus, the point that Wittgenstein was concerned with has nothing to do with the relative probability of alternative mathematical techiques, but rather is an elucidation of the logical grammar of the concept of *proof*. The infallibility of a mathematical proof lies simply in the fact that we have elected to treat it as a grammatical construction; hence the concept of probability is categorially alien to the infallibility of a proof. The reason why the criterion of *surveyability* is so important is not, therefore, that it is designed to guard against the possibility of falsification — to be 'put on the archieves' is to be *ruled* unfalsifiable — but rather, because you cannot have a grammatical construction with hidden rules.

Such a criticism does not in any way seek to cast doubt on the validity of the Appel-Haken solution. All it strives to establish is that the basic nature of their solution is experimental, and hence, that it makes no sense to speak, as Tymoczko supposes, of Appel and Haken 'proving' the 'four-colour theorem', let alone of their 'proof' forcing us to modify our understanding of the concepts of *proof* and *theorem*. Nor does this argument entail that the 'four-colour problem' that mathematicians had worked on prior to the Appel-Haken solution was really empirical rather than mathematical; not because, as Kripke suggested in *Naming and Necessity*, the same proposition could be proved mathematically, but rather, because it makes no sense to speak of the logical status of an expression before it has been located in a grammatical structure. The crux of the response which Wittgenstein would make to the Appel-Haken solution, therefore, is that we must examine the significance of the techniques which they employed in light of the logical grammar of the principal mathematical concepts involved. The result is not a piece of mathematical legislation or revisionism, but rather, of philosophical clarification.

Notes

1. T.L. Saaty and P. Kainen, *The Four Colour Problem: Assaults and Conquest*, New York, McGraw-Hill, 1977, pp. 97, 98.

2. To be more precise, Rabin's 'proof' establishes that the probability of a number's *not* being prime can be virtually insignificant. Cf. 'Probabilistic Algorithms', reprinted in J.F. Traub (ed.), *Algorithms and Complexity: New Directions and Recent Results*, New York, Academic Press, 1976.

3. Thomas Tymoczko, 'The Four-colour Problem and Its Philosophical Significance', *Journal of Philosophy*, LXXVI, 2 (February 1979), p. 58.

4. Ibid, p. 77.

5. Ibid., pp. 62, 63.

6. Ibid., pp. 74, 77-8.

7. Cf. Kenneth Appel and Wolfgang Haken, 'The Four Colour Problem' in L.A. Steen (ed.), *Mathematics Today*, New York, Springer-Verlag, 1978, p. 162.

8. Cf. Ernst Sonheimer and Alan Rogerson, *Numbers and Infinity*, Cambridge, Cambridge University Press, 1981, p. 18.

9. Cf. Richard Courant and Herbert Robbins, *What is Mathematics*, New York, Oxford University Press, 1978, pp. 30f.

10. Heesch projected a normal map into a dual (planar) graph, with each vertex in the graph representing a country, and the straight lines connecting the vertices representing borders, thus dividing the plane into polygonal 'faces'. Heesch established that when the map is normal these faces will all be triangles, in which case the resulting graph is called a 'triangulation of the plane'. We can now describe the number of 'neighbours' which a 'country' has in the planar graph as the 'degree' of the 'vertex': i.e. the number of lines meeting at the vertex, which represents the number of neighbours that the dual country in the original map has. The 'ring size' is defined as the boundary circuit of the configuration: the path of edges that starts and ends at the same vertex without crossing itself.

11. Saaty and Kainen, *The Four Colour Problem: Assaults and Conquest*, p. 23.

12. Cf. Appel and Haken's own account, 'The Four Colour Problem', p. 175.

13. 'Wittgenstein's Philosophy of Mathematics' in *Truth and Other Enigmas*, London, Duckworth, 1978, p. 182.

14. It is instructive to consider some of the confusion which surrounds this issue. In 'Mathematics and Computer Science: Coping with Finiteness', Donald E. Knuth warns that, 'Although we have certainly narrowed the gap between three and infinity, recent results indicate that we will never actually be able to go very far in practice.' (*Science*, vol. 194, no. 4271, p. 1235.) To illustrate this thesis, he constructs a new notation to represent enormous (what Knuth wants to call 'unrealistic') numbers. e.g.

$$10\uparrow\uparrow 10 = 10^{10^{10^{10^{10^{10^{10^{10^{10^{10}}}}}}}}}$$

The point of this exercise is ultimately to show us that, using this notation we can see that numbers exist which are simply too long to have ever been written down: 'unsurveyable' in the crude physical sense with which Wittgenstein has been lumbered. 'At any rate,' Knuth concludes, 'it seems to me that the magnitude of this number $10\uparrow\uparrow\uparrow\uparrow 3$ is so large as to be beyond human comprehension. On the other hand, it is very small as finite numbers go.' (Ibid., p. 1236.) But of course, the point is that the number is not beyond human comprehension: in the new notation which Knuth has just constructed! For, of course, the point is that the number just is meaningful, according to the rules which he has laid down for the generation of his series (viz. $x\uparrow\uparrow n = x\uparrow(x\uparrow(\ldots\uparrow x)\ldots)$), where the powers are taken n times). And this rule for the construction of the series is certainly surveyable; hence our ability to understand that $10\uparrow\uparrow\uparrow\uparrow 3$ is a number.

15. Quoted in Philip J. Davis and Reuben Hersh, *The Mathematical Experience*, Boston, The Harvester Press, 1981, p. 385.

16. Appel and Haken, 'The Four Colour Problem', pp. 178, 179.

17. *Concepts of Modern Mathematics*, Harmondsworth, Penguin Books, 1981, p. 304.
18. Saaty and Kainen, *The Four Colour Problem: Assaults and Conquest*, p. 83.
19. It is conspicuous that Wittgenstein insists near the beginning of *Remarks on the Foundations of Mathematics*:

"But doesn't it follow with logical necessity that you get two when you add one to one, and three when you add one to two? and isn't this inexorability the same as that of logical inference?" — Yes! it is the same. — "But isn't there a truth corresponding to logical inference? Isn't it *true* that this follows from that?" — The proposition: "It is true that this follows from that" means simply: this follows from that. And how do we use this proposition? — What would happen if we made a different inference — *how* should we get into conflict with truth? (I §5)

We must be careful that we do not allow the popular suggestion that Wittgenstein was interested in a 'redundancy theory of truth' to interfere with our perception of the fact that what Wittgenstein is specifically concerned with in this oft-quoted passage is the special manner in which the concept of *truth* applies to conventions.
20. Cf. *On Certainty* §§38, 39, 113.